Helping Children Cope

With Disasters and

Terrorism

Helping Children Cope With Disasters and Terrorism

Edited by

Annette M. La Greca, Wendy K. Silverman,

Eric M. Vernberg, and Michael C. Roberts

American Psychological Association • Washington, DC

Published by
American Psychological Association
750 First Street, NE
Washington, DC 20002
www.apa.org

To order
APA Order Department
P.O. Box 92984
Washington, DC 20090-2984
Tel: (800) 374-2721, Direct: (202) 336-5510
Fax: (202) 336-5502, TDD/TTY: (202) 336-6123
On-line: www.apa.org/books/
E-mail: order@apa.org

In the U.K., Europe, Africa, and the Middle East, copies may be ordered from
American Psychological Association
3 Henrietta Street
Covent Garden, London
WC2E 8LU England

Typeset in Goudy by AlphaWebTech, Mechanicsville, MD

Printer: United Book Press, Inc., Baltimore, MD
Cover Designer: Naylor Design, Washington, DC
Technical/Production Editor: Jennifer L. Macomber

The opinions and statements published are the responsibility of the authors, and such opinions and statements do not necessarily represent the policies of the American Psychological Association.

Library of Congress Cataloging-in-Publication Data

Helping children cope with disasters and terrorism / edited by Annette M. La Greca . . . [et al.].
    p. cm.
  Includes bibliographical references and index.
  ISBN 1-55798-914-1 (alk. paper)
   1. Psychic trauma in children. 2. Disasters—Psychological aspects. 3. Terrorism—Psychological aspects. I. La Greca, Annette M. (Annette Marie)
RJ506.P66 H45 2002
618.92'8521—dc21   2002020537

British Library Cataloguing-in-Publication Data
A CIP record is available from the British Library.

Printed in the United States of America
First Edition

To the children and families who have been witnesses
to or victims of disasters and terrorism.

CONTENTS

CONTRIBUTORS

Andrew Baum, PhD, Behavioral Medicine and Oncology, University of Pittsburgh, Pittsburgh, PA

Jorge V. Boero, MA, Disaster Mental Health Institute, University of South Dakota, Vermillion

Derek Bolton, PhD, CPsychol, FBPsS, Senior Lecturer in Psychology, University of London Institute of Psychiatry, De Crespigny Park, London

Virginia DeRoma, PhD, Department of Psychology, The Citadel, Charleston, SC

Teri L. Elliott, PhD, Disaster Mental Health Institute, University of South Dakota, Vermillion

Mary C. Grace, MEd, MS, Department of Psychiatry, University of Cincinnati Medical School, Cincinnati, OH

Bonnie L. Green, PhD, Department of Psychiatry, Georgetown University Medical School, Washington, DC

Robin H. Gurwitch, PhD, Department of Pediatrics, University of Oklahoma Health Sciences Center, Oklahoma City

Gerard A. Jacobs, PhD, Disaster Mental Health Institute, University of South Dakota, Vermillion

Russell T. Jones, PhD, Department of Psychology, Virginia Polytechnic Institute, Blacksburg

Avigdor Klingman, PhD, Department of Education, University of Haifa, Mount Carmel, Haifa, Israel

Mindy Korol, PhD, Department of Psychology, Mount St. Mary's College, Emmitsburg, MD

Teresa L. Kramer, PhD, Department of Psychiatry, University of Arkansas for Medical Sciences, Little Rock

Janis B. Kupersmidt, PhD, Department of Psychology, University of North Carolina, Chapel Hill

Annette M. La Greca, PhD, Department of Psychology, University of Miami, Coral Gables, FL

Brett M. McDermott, MBB FRANZCP, Department of Pediatrics, Princess Margaret Hospital for Children, Perth, Australia

Christine Mello, PsyD, Valley Central School District, New Paltz, NY

Kathleen Nader, DSW, Cedar Park, TX

Thomas H. Ollendick, PhD, Department of Psychology, Virginia Polytechnic Institute, Blacksburg

Lyle J. Palmer, PhD, Department of Pediatrics, University of Western Australia, Perth

Betty Pfefferbaum, MD, JD, Department of Psychiatry and Behavioral Sciences, University of Oklahoma Health Sciences Center, College of Medicine, Oklahoma City

Mitchell J. Prinstein, PhD, Department of Psychology, Yale University, New Haven, CT

Randal P. Quevillon, PhD, Disaster Mental Health Institute, University of South Dakota, Vermillion

Aline E. Rabalais, MA, Department of Psychology, Eberly College of Arts and Sciences, West Virginia University, Morgantown

Gilbert Reyes, PhD, Disaster Mental Health Institute, University of South Dakota, Vermillion

Michael C. Roberts, PhD, ABPP, Clinical Child Psychology Program, University of Kansas, Lawrence

Kenneth J. Ruggiero, PhD, Department of Pyschology, Eberly College of Arts and Sciences, West Virginia University, Morgantown

Conway Saylor, PhD, Department of Psychology, The Citadel, Charleston, SC

Joseph R. Scotti, PhD, Department of Psychology, West Virginia University, Morgantown

Ariana Shahinfar, PhD, Department of Psychology, La Salle University, Philadelphia, PA

Wendy K. Silverman, PhD, Department of Psychology, Child and Family Psychosocial Research Center, Florida International University, Miami

Karen A. Sitterle, PhD, Department of Psychiatry, Division of Clinical Psychology, University of Texas Southwestern Medical Center, Dallas

Elizabeth Todd-Bazemore, PhD, Disaster Mental Health Institute, University of South Dakota, Vermillion

Orlee Udwin, PhD, CPsychol, FBPsS, Consultant Clinical Child Psychologist, South London and Maudsley (NHS) Trust, London

Eric M. Vernberg, PhD, Clinical Child Psychology Program, University of Kansas, Lawrence

Mary Ellen Voegler-Lee, PhD, Department of Psychology, University of North Carolina, Chapel Hill

Minhnoi C. Wroble, PhD, Behavioral Medicine and Oncology, University of Pittsburgh, Pittsburgh, PA

Bruce H. Young, LCSW, National Center for Post-Traumatic Stress Disorder, Department of Veterans Affairs, VA Palo Alto Health Care System, Menlo Park, CA

William Yule, Dip Psychol, PhD, CPsychol, FBPsS, University of London Institute of Psychiatry, De Crespigny Park, London

PREFACE

In recognition of the need to focus greater scientific attention on the mental health needs of children and adolescents following disasters, the Section on Clinical Child Psychology (now the Society on Clinical Child and Adolescent Psychology, American Psychological Association [APA] Division 53) organized the Task Force on Children and Disasters (see Vogel & Vernberg, 1993, and Vernberg & Vogel, 1993, for task force reports[1]) and supported the development of one of the first texts on this topic (Saylor, 1993[2]). All four editors of this volume were involved in some key aspect of this special task force.

Soon after, in 1995, the APA adopted a resolution, "Children's Psychological Needs Following Disasters," which is now an APA policy (DeLeon, 1995[3]). The policy was initiated and developed by the APA's Committee on Children, Youth, and Families under the direction of an earlier committee chair, Carolyn Swift. Two of the editors of this volume (Michael C. Roberts and Annette M. La Greca) and a chapter contributor (Russell T. Jones) actively participated in the initiative. The policy recognized the need for building a greater research base for understanding children's needs and identifying effective, affordable intervention strategies, including preventive interventions. In addition, the policy recognized that children's needs and interventions might vary as a function of the characteristics of particular disasters.

This volume is, in part, an outgrowth of the APA policy statement. The editors of this volume, as well as several of the contributing authors,

---

[1] J. M. Vogel and E. M. Vernberg, "Children's Psychological Responses to Disaster," *Journal of Clinical Child Psychology* 22 (1993), 464–484; E. M. Vernberg and J. M. Vogel, "Interventions With Children After Disasters," *Journal of Clinical Child Psychology* 22 (1993), 485–498.

[2] C. F. Saylor, ed., *Children and Disasters* (New York: Plenum Press, 1993).

[3] P. H. DeLeon, "Proceedings of the American Psychological Association, Incorporated, for the Year 1994," *American Psychologist* 50 (1995), 633–682.

served as members of the APA Working Group on Children and Disasters (1996–1997), which was established with the financial support of the APA Board of Directors and the Board for the Advancement of Psychology in the Public Interest to explore ways of implementing the policy on children's psychological needs following disasters. This volume was viewed by the Working Group on Children and Disasters as one potentially useful implementation strategy and was readily supported and endorsed by the APA Committee on Children, Youth, and Families.

ACKNOWLEDGMENTS

This book was the product of many individual efforts. In particular, we wish once again to thank the chapter authors for their valuable contributions and to express our appreciation for their graciousness in accepting our suggestions for revisions. We also wish to recognize the various members of the APA Committee on Children, Youth, and Families, who provided encouragement, enthusiasm, and support for pursuing this volume. We particularly recognize Carolyn Swift, whose drive, dedication, and caring brought about the original APA resolution, and the unfailing and always supportive efforts of Mary Campbell, who serves as APA staff for Children, Youth, and Families; without her help, faith, and energy, this book would not have materialized. Thanks also go to our APA editor Susan Reynolds, who was patient and understanding about the various trials and tribulations of putting together an edited volume.

On a personal note, Annette M. La Greca would like to thank her students at the University of Miami (UM) for their willingness and eagerness to assist her with various endeavors, including this book. Ami Kuttler, Karen Bearman, Hannah Moore, and Lissette Perez were instrumental in reviewing chapters and helping to fine-tune some of the text. Annette is also grateful for the efforts of Ellen Lee and Elizabeth Reyes, administrative assistants at UM, who helped with some of the clerical aspects involved in assembling a volume of this size and scope. Finally, Annette would also like to thank her husband, Mat Dillon, for his unlimited support, caring, and wonderful sense of humor through all the ups and downs of this project.

Wendy K. Silverman would like to thank her students at Florida International University for their assistance with her various projects, including this volume. As always, she is grateful to her children, Daniel and Rachel, and her husband, Effie—they have taught her the true meaning of support, an essential element for working with children and families following disasters.

Eric M. Vernberg thanks the many colleagues who readily shared information and offered support for this project as well as the original task force (especially Juliet Vogel), which shaped his work in disaster mental health. He is indebted to the children, families, and schools that have allowed us to combine intervention and research during periods of turmoil and distress and hopes this volume will show the value of their collaboration. He, too, is thankful for the support and understanding of his family—his son, Stefan, and his wife, Dee.

Michael C. Roberts and Eric M. Vernberg thank Tammie Zordel for her organizational assistance as secretary of the University of Kansas Clinical Child Psychology Program. Michael also recognizes the feedback of program graduate students as well as the reasonably good-humored tolerance of his daughters, Erica and Alicia, and his wife, Karen, for the disorder in the basement office while he worked on this book.

Finally, the editors would like to give a big thank you to the "heroes" of the communities who help victims in the aftermath of disasters—the teachers, principals, firefighters, police officers, paramedics, clergy, neighbors, counselors, and the children themselves who have provided assistance to their peers, their parents, and their pets. To all those unnamed heroes and the many others who have faced some of the most terrifying moments of their lives in helping individuals and communities in the aftermath of disasters, we give our biggest and most important thanks. We hope that this book can help even further in improving the ways in which we all can help and support children and families following disasters.

Helping Children Cope

With Disasters and

Terrorism

INTRODUCTION

ANNETTE M. LA GRECA, WENDY K. SILVERMAN,
ERIC M. VERNBERG, AND MICHAEL C. ROBERTS

School shootings. Devastating earthquakes. Severe floods. Deadly motor vehicle crashes. Terrorist attacks. Many communities and individuals endure these and other extraordinary experiences so horrifying in their effects that we call them *disasters*. Furthermore, the events of September 11, 2001 highlighted the realities of *terrorism* for most Americans and underscored the importance of understanding how children and adolescents react to disasters and terrorism. The publication of this volume is especially timely given that the tragedies of September 2001 and subsequent events are still too recent to have yielded an empirical perspective on their impact on children, adolescents, and families. This volume reviews the current state of knowledge regarding children's reactions to disaster and terrorism, and provides the background and conceptualization needed for framing mental health interventions and future research efforts.

When disaster strikes, many people in the "helping professions," including psychologists, psychiatrists, social workers, mental health counselors, and nurses, move out of their offices to work in communities with the people affected by the event. Until recently, work with disaster victims had been dominated by practical considerations in times of crisis and had received relatively little attention in textbooks, coursework, and clinical train-

3

ing programs. The unpredictable nature of disasters and the crisis-oriented process of disaster relief, coupled with the cumbersome barriers to research (e.g., lack of funding and delays in assembling and deploying research teams), have limited efforts to establish an empirical literature on the ways in which individuals and communities cope with extraordinary stressors. The paucity of scientific evidence to guide practice in the area of disaster recovery has been perhaps most apparent in relation to children and adolescents.

In recent years, tremendous concern has developed regarding the ways in which disasters affect children and adolescents. It is true that victims, including youth, usually organize, adapt, and rebound in a manner that seems quite remarkable in light of some of the terrible situations that they either witness or face (Salzer & Bickman, 1999). Yet, a significant proportion of children show reactions following exposure to disasters that can substantially interfere with or impair their daily living and can cause significant distress to them and their families. Particularly for youth, the costs of disasters extend far beyond the amount spent to rebuild homes or replace possessions. Disasters take their toll in personal growth and development.

It is commonly—and erroneously—assumed that children are resilient and that their reactions to disasters are fleeting; as a result, their psychological and emotional needs may be neglected following disasters, particularly when parents or other significant adults in their lives are having trouble coping with the event themselves. Parents, teachers, and other adults may not realize the extent of children's distress and may underestimate their resulting problems. In addition, children and adolescents are hampered in the help-seeking process by their developmental status, lack of experience and knowledge about how to seek help and, possibly, their lack of awareness of their own distress.

This volume has two purposes. The first is to provide a systematic review of children's and adolescents' reactions to specific disasters and the factors that contribute to those reactions. The second is to review the current state of interventions that have been developed to address children's and adolescents' mental health needs following disasters. The treatment literature is in an early stage of development. As a result, the interventions covered in this book represent those that have preliminary, but promising, empirical support or have been derived from empirical research on factors that contribute to the development and maintenance of children's postdisaster stress reactions. We hope that this volume will increase understanding about children and disasters and stimulate additional research that will result in even more effective interventions for children and adolescents who have been exposed to disasters.

To accomplish the volume's goals, we have brought together an impressive and experienced group of scientist–practitioners who have intervened with children, adolescents, and families following specific types of disasters. The contributors are leaders in their fields, and it was an honor for us to have the opportunity to work with them. We are grateful for their contributions and believe that each chapter represents an invaluable source of information.

This volume is organized into five parts. Part I deals with broad conceptual and practical issues. It sets the stage for an approach that recognizes the importance of both individual and contextual factors in understanding the effects of disasters on children, and it highlights key issues in how to assess and intervene with youth following disasters. In chapter 1, Wendy Silverman and Annette La Greca define disasters, provide statistics about their scope and magnitude, and describe children's and adolescents' typical reactions. In addition, the authors present a conceptual framework for organizing and understanding factors that influence the development and maintenance of disaster-related reactions.

In chapter 2, Conway Saylor and Virginia DeRoma focus on the conceptual and practical issues affecting the assessment of postdisaster reactions in children and adolescents, including conducting assessments over time, and considering the specific purpose of the assessment (e.g., screening, diagnosis, treatment, forensic). The authors list a number of widely used assessment instruments and offer recommendations for improving the quality of future assessment methods (e.g., develop standardized batteries; enhance the cultural sensitivity of measures).

Eric Vernberg reviews the current state of empirically informed interventions for children and adolescents in chapter 3. The author uses a chronological system to describe interventions offered predisasters (i.e., preparation activities), while disasters are in progress, and during the short- and long-term aftermath. Preparatory and early interventions focus primarily on crisis management and enhancing coping skills; in contrast, children and adolescents with persistent and long-term difficulties are likely to need formal treatments for trauma symptoms and bereavement.

In the final chapter of Part I, Aline Rabalais, Kenneth Ruggiero, and Joseph Scotti note the lack of attention to issues of cultural diversity in disaster-related research, and review the limited studies available. The authors provide interesting and important ideas for incorporating diversity-related concepts (e.g., acculturation stress, cultural beliefs and customs, kin networks, etc.) into future research efforts with diverse populations.

Part II focuses on natural disasters. The chapters in this section describe the mounting empirical evidence of the relation between the level of traumatic exposure during natural disasters (e.g., life threat, injury, death, and property destruction) and trauma-related symptomatology. Although symptoms generally diminish with time, a subset of children and adolescents experience substantial disaster-related symptoms months or even years later. Intervention results remain preliminary, but important groundwork is being laid to enable researchers to articulate evidence-based treatments and conduct rigorous evaluation studies.

Annette La Greca and Mitchell Prinstein focus chapter 5 on hurricanes and earthquakes, although they touch briefly on the limited literature on other natural disasters, such as tornadoes, lightning strikes, and volcanoes. They present evidence indicating that many children and adolescents living in heavily damaged areas experience significant disaster-related symptomatology for months after the initial disaster and describe initial versions of manualized intervention materials.

The next two chapters describe wildfires and floods, natural disasters that typically play out over a period of days or months. Chapter 6, by Brett McDermott and Lyle Palmer, gives an excellent overview of how wilderness area and wildfires affect children and adolescents. The authors' work in this area is notable for providing a model for school-based screenings for children and adolescents who are experiencing extreme reactions. The chapter concludes by describing the use of an evidence-based "guided workbook" designed to address troublesome aspects of the wildfire experience.

Floods, as Gerard Jacobs, Jorge Boero, Randal Quevillon, Elizabeth Todd-Bazemore, Teri Elliott, and Gilbert Reyes describe in chapter 7, are a recurring problem in many regions. The authors describe their work with Project Recovery in South Dakota in the years following the devastating Midwest floods of 1993. The approach developed in Project Recovery is important for its attention to cultural factors in its work with a diverse population that included European Americans, Native Americans, and Latinos.

Russell Jones and Thomas Ollendick focus on residential fires in chapter 8. Considering how frequently residential fires occur, surprisingly little research has been conducted on children's reactions to this form of disaster or on psychosocial interventions following fires. The authors provide an overview of existing research and describe early results from their ongoing efforts to rigorously assess both the impact of residential fires and the effectiveness of specific intervention strategies for children and adolescents.

In Parts I and II, the authors focus on disasters and events that are considered natural. Parts III and IV, however, attend to trauma that results from the actions of humans, whether deliberate or through human neglect and lack of oversight. The chapters in Part III examine aspects of human-caused and technological disasters, such as toxic waste spills, nuclear accidents, dam breaks and flooding, transportation disasters (such as ship sinkings or train collisions), and motor vehicle crashes. As the chapters indicate, the role of human negligence in exacerbating or moderating the psychological impact of the traumatic events is not well understood.

In chapter 9, Minhnoi Wroble and Andrew Baum address the psychological consequences for children exposed to technological catastrophes. The authors examine the technology failures at the Three Mile Island (Pennsylvania) nuclear reactor, the Chernobyl (Ukraine) nuclear power plant, and three hazardous waste disposal sites in which children were exposed to toxic chemicals. Wroble and Baum conclude that children who experience disasters of this type do not demonstrate a serious adverse effect on psychological functioning, although some symptoms are manifested. They note that long-term psychological effects may result from the chronic physical threat of toxic exposure.

Chapter 10, by William Yule, Orlee Udwin, and Derek Bolton, focuses on events in which children experience threats to life and injury resulting from transit disasters. The authors review research on children involved in bus crashes and ship sinkings in several different countries and describe issues involved in intervention and treatment efforts. In chapter 11, Mindy Korol, Teresa Kramer, Mary Grace, and Bonnie Green discuss the results of a long-term study of survivors of a dam collapse that produced death and injury and led to physical relocation for the survivors. Age of the children at the time of the dam collapse, family environment, and parental responses to the disaster were among the variables found to influence long-term outcomes.

Joseph Scotti, Kenneth Ruggiero, and Aline Rabalais focus on car crashes in chapter 12. Despite the massive numbers of car crashes each year, research on child survivors has been rather sparse. The authors present case examples of such children and outline a paradigmatic model of PTSD related to the motor vehicle collisions in which death or injury occurred.

Part IV focuses on societal violence. Incidents of violence contain many elements that are thought to contribute to traumatization—notably, the threat to one's life or bodily integrity (see chapter 1)—and thus share many characteristics of natural disasters. The potential of violence-related disasters for causing severe, persistent stress reactions is high.

As Kathleen Nader and Christine Mello discuss in chapter 13, issues of trust and betrayal become paramount following shootings and hostage takings. In the wake of such incidents, children and adolescents may not know whom to trust or how to evaluate who is dangerous, and their belief that adults can and will protect them may be challenged. The authors describe issues involving school preparation as well as other measures that may help protect youth from physical and psychological harm when violence occurs in school settings.

Until recently, most Americans had not experienced acts of terrorism, nor did they believe such activities would ever happen in the United States. The bombing of the Alfred P. Murrah Federal Building in Oklahoma City in 1995 changed those perceptions and the attacks on the Pentagon and World Trade Center on September 11, 2001 profoundly affected the people of the United States. As Robin Gurwitch, Karen Sitterle, Bruce Young, and Betty Pfefferbaum describe in chapter 14, the bombing of the Murrah Building led to some of the first investigations of the effects of terrorism on U.S. children. Gurwitch and colleagues examine the prevalence of PTSD symptoms among children and adolescents following the bombing and point out how subsequent events related to the bombing (namely, the constant media attention to the bombing and the later criminal proceedings) took their toll on the victims and families who lost loved ones. Their findings highlight that the crisis-intervention model of handling disasters is insufficient, and the authors call for ongoing involvement by mental health professionals who have expertise in working with traumatized individuals and communities.

In chapter 15, Avigdor Klingman focuses on children under the "stress of war." Unlike most disasters, wars are usually preceded by an extended warning period and may last for months or years. Although Klingman reports that only a minority of children go on to develop chronic PTSD after war, he also reports that growing up in a war-affected community appears to promote aggressive behavior in some children. He advocates that communitywide interventions take precedence over individual therapeutic interventions and sees the extended warning periods that typically precede wars as an important time for initiating school-based preventive interventions.

In chapter 16, Janis Kupersmidt, Ariana Shahinfar, and Mary Ellen Voegler-Lee conclude Part IV by focusing on community violence. They summarize the relation between exposure to community violence and children's academic, social, cognitive, and psychological functioning. Because youth who have been a witness to or a victim of community violence experience high levels of distress, the authors highlight the need for effective interventions that can be used in the aftermath of children's exposure to crime and violence and underscore the value of intervening at the individual, family, community (i.e., school, neighborhood), and societal levels.

The book concludes with chapter 17, which provides an integrative summary of current knowledge and critical directions for future research.

The target audience for this book includes mental health professionals in school, clinical child, counseling, and pediatric psychology settings as well as professors, instructors, and graduate students in psychology programs that prepare psychologists to work with children and families. The book also may be useful to psychologists who are part of the American Psychological Association's Disaster Response Network or the American Red Cross, who often assist children and families in the aftermath of a disaster. In addition, the book may appeal to mental health professionals interested in applying theory and empirical findings related to the effects of disasters on children and youth to their clinical practice roles.

REFERENCE

Salzer, M. S., & Bickman, L. (1999). The short- and long-term psychological impact of disasters: Implications for mental health interventions and policy. In R. Gist & B. Lubin (Eds.), *Response to disaster: Psychological, community, and ecological approaches* (pp. 63–82). Philadelphia: Brunner/Mazel.

I

CONCEPTS AND KEY ISSUES

1

CHILDREN EXPERIENCING DISASTERS: DEFINITIONS, REACTIONS, AND PREDICTORS OF OUTCOMES

WENDY K. SILVERMAN AND ANNETTE M. LA GRECA

In the wake of devastating natural disasters (e.g., hurricanes, earthquakes, floods, and brushfires), human-made disasters (e.g., airplane crashes, ferry sinkings, toxic waste accidents), and recent acts of violence (e.g., school shootings, bombings, and terrorist activities), tremendous concern has developed among individuals who interact or work with children (e.g., parents, teachers, mental health professionals) regarding the impact of disasters on youth. It is true that victims, including youth, usually do organize, adapt, and rebound in a manner that seems quite remarkable in light of the horrific and gruesome experiences that they either witnessed or experienced (Salzer & Bickman, 1999). Nevertheless, significant proportions of children do show reactions following exposure to disasters that can lead to substantial levels of interference or impairment in their daily lives and that causes significant distress for them and their families.

This chapter provides an overview of the types of disasters that will be covered in the book, the primary reactions children display as a consequence of their exposure to disasters, and a general framework for considering the factors that influence the development and maintenance of children's postdisaster reactions. Specifically, the following section defines what disasters are and provides some statistics about their scope and magnitude. The chapter then discusses the main reactions that have been documented in children following disasters and presents a model that helps organize and understand children's reactions to disasters. The model incorporates characteristics of the disaster, child, and postdisaster recovery environment. The subsequent chapters in this initial section of the book provide a context for understanding how to assess children affected by disasters (chapter 2), how to intervene with those youth (chapter 3), and what special considerations may be important for culturally diverse populations (chapter 4).

DISASTERS: DEFINITIONS

Disasters are usually defined as overwhelming events that involve the destruction of property, include injury or loss of life, affect large communities, and are shared by many children and families (American Academy of Pediatrics, Work Group on Disasters [AAPWGD], 1995). In addition, disasters are viewed as being out of the realm of "normal" human experience; as such, they are viewed as traumatic, meaning that they can lead to or result in stress reactions, regardless of a person's prior functioning (AAPWGD, 1995; American Psychiatric Association [APA], 1980). The disaster literature commonly distinguishes between natural and human-made disasters. Natural disasters are caused by forces of nature, whereas human-made disasters are caused by human error, human involvement, or malfunctioning technology.

For the most part, the chapters in this volume cover events that fit the above definition of disasters and reflect the events that receive considerable attention in the media. The book includes three chapters on events that generally have been overlooked in the disaster literature—motor vehicle accidents, residential fires, and community violence—none of which technically fit the above definition because they do not involve entire communities. Nevertheless, those events are included because they affect large numbers of children on a daily basis and because children who experience those events display many of the same reactions as children exposed to large, community-wide disasters.

Impact of Disasters: Human and Financial Costs

Although statistics are not available on the number of children and adolescents affected by disasters, recent statistics from the International Federation of Red Cross and Red Crescent Societies (IFRC; 1998) indicate that a staggering number of people are affected by disasters worldwide. For example, in 1997 alone, 5.9 million people in Africa, 1.7 million in the United States and the Americas, 24.5 million in Asia, 0.5 million in Europe, and 0.8

million in Oceania (including Australia and New Zealand), were affected by disasters, for a total of more than 33.4 million! The statistics include many children and families. Moreover, the statistics are likely to underestimate the true numbers affected because they do not include people who died or were made homeless as a result of a disaster and do not take into account the diverse reporting mechanisms and standards used in different countries. In terms of deaths, an estimated 8,000 deaths occurred annually as a result of natural and human-made disasters in the United States (AAPWGD, 1995; Pynoos & Nader, 1990).

The effects of disasters extend well beyond the number of people who are killed. "Numbers killed make the headlines, but numbers affected give a far better indication of the long-term consequences of disaster" (IFRC, 1998, p. 143). This statement is true because people who are affected by disasters may need emergency support to rebuild their homes and lives, and the costs associated with rebuilding homes and communities can be staggering. The IFRC (1998) estimated disaster damage costs over a 10-year period from 1987 to 1996 to be $137 billion for natural disasters and $13 billion for human-made disasters (accidents, technological accidents, and fire). Destructive natural disasters, such as the Northridge earthquake in California (1994) or Hurricane Andrew in South Florida (1992), were each estimated to incur losses of $30 billion.

Why Consider Children and Adolescents in Disasters?

The statistics in the preceding section document that many children and families are affected annually by disasters. With children, in particular, "costs" extend far beyond the money spent rebuilding homes and replacing possessions. Disasters also take a toll in terms of children's personal growth and development. Some of the nonfinancial but potentially devastating costs of disasters for children include missed school and reduced academic functioning; missed social opportunities; and increased exposure to life stressors, such as family illness, divorce, family violence, and substance use.

Furthermore, although children are affected by disasters in far-reaching ways, they often are overlooked in the aftermath of a disaster. Adults, for example, may not realize the extent to which children are distressed and may underestimate their problems (see chapter 10). Parents and other adults (e.g., teachers) may assume that children are resilient and that their reactions to disasters are transitory and fleeting, even though that may not be the case.

The psychological and emotional needs of children and adolescents may be further neglected following disasters when parents or other significant adults in children's lives are affected by the disaster and have problems coping with the event. Typically, parents or teachers serve as primary sources of support for children and initiate help when children are having problems. When the adults in children's lives are distracted or affected by a disaster, however, they may overlook children's needs or may not be available to help children cope with disasters and the aftermath.

Following disasters, children are further disadvantaged in the help-seeking process by their own developmental status and lack of experience and knowledge about how to seek help. To some extent, the help-seeking process can be viewed as one that progresses from (a) being aware of one's distress; (b) interpreting or understanding one's problems; (c) considering possible coping strategies; and (d) enacting a coping strategy or alternative (Yates, Axsom, & Tiedman, 1999). Children are at a distinct disadvantage in the help-seeking process in that their skills in each help-seeking area are likely to be less well developed than adults. For example, children may be less aware of their own distress than adults. With the exception of coping, the various facets of the help-seeking process have been insufficiently studied in children and would be important to consider further in research.

CHILDREN'S REACTIONS TO DISASTERS

Children's and adolescents' reactions to disasters may vary (Vogel & Vernberg, 1993), but the most frequently studied reactions are those associated with posttraumatic stress disorder (PTSD) and related symptoms. In addition, some research has focused on depression, anxiety, academic problems, and other developmental issues (e.g., sleep and separation issues); this chapter briefly reviews that literature.

In describing children's reactions to disasters, it is critical to consider the timing of the postdisaster assessment. Specifically, the time periods around disasters can be divided into phases (Valent, 2000) that may be associated with different types of reactions:

- *Preimpact:* the period before the disaster;
- *Impact:* when the event occurs;
- *Recoil:* immediately after the event;
- *Postimpact:* days to weeks after the event; and
- *Recovery and reconstruction:* months or years after the event.

Figure 1.1 depicts the five disaster phases and highlights the idea that different trajectories of reactions may be evident following a disaster (Staab, Fullerton, & Ursano, 1999). Unfortunately, virtually nothing is known about why some children might show different trajectories of responses and how those patterns might vary with specific disaster characteristics. Furthermore, the figure suggests that time distinctions among the trajectories have to do with the degree or severity of responses. Qualitative differences also might exist, although direct research on this issue is sparse.

Most studies that have examined children's reactions following disasters have focused on the recovery-and-reconstruction period (months to years

Severity of Reaction

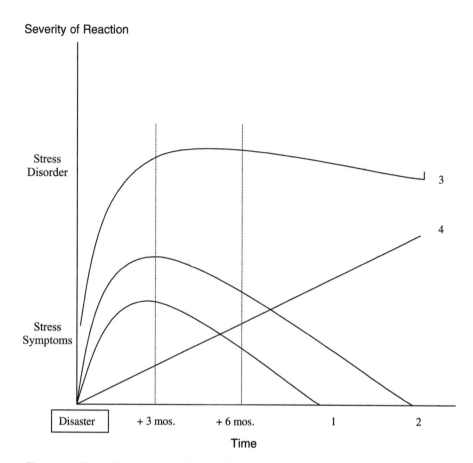

Figure 1.1. Potential trajectories for children's disaster reactions. Line 1 represents acute stress symptoms that resolve with time. Line 2 depicts Acute Stress Disorder (ASD) that also resolves over time. Line 3 represents ASD that progresses to PTSD. Line 4 shows delayed onset of posttraumatic stress disorder. From *Response to Disaster* (p. 122), by R. Gist and B. Lubin (Eds.). Copyright 1999. Adapted with permission of Routledge, Inc., part of The Taylor & Francis Group.

after the event) and, to a lesser extent, on the postimpact period (days to weeks after the event; see Vogel & Vernberg, 1993). As a result, the types of reactions studied generally have been ones that can be observed weeks to months after a disaster. This situation is not surprising, given that it is difficult to plan and implement research in the immediate aftermath of disasters, many of which occur without warning. It is extremely difficult, if not impossible, to assess children during the preimpact and impact phases of disaster.

Recoil Phase

Little is known about children's and adolescents' immediate reactions to disasters, but authors have described people's immediate reactions to other types of trauma as "psychic shock"—that is, shock, disbelief, and being stunned

(Valent, 2000). People have described the feeling as a "blow to the face," "being knocked out," a feeling of being overwhelmed, or a sense of unreality of the world and oneself (Valent, 2000). In an exploratory study of children's immediate reactions to Hurricane Andrew (Coffman, 1994), children described a "sense of strangeness" and felt that "life was weird" right after the hurricane.

Concurrent with the psychological symptoms of shock, a set of physiological symptoms of stress may be evident, referred to by Selye (1946) as the "general adaptation syndrome." Those symptoms include increased levels of cortisone, enlargement of the adrenal cortex (i.e., increased secretion of adrenaline), and suppression of immune functioning. Although biological reactions are important and, in fact, may set the stage for or interact with psychological reactions, this aspect of children's reactions has not been well studied.

Vernberg and Varela (2001) observed that trauma may induce alterations in physiological reactivity in adults, which could lead to long-term overreactions to trauma-related stimuli (e.g., Keane et al., 1998). In fact, studies of adult survivors of childhood sexual abuse (e.g., Orr et al., 1998) reveal long-term differences in physiological reactivity between those who develop chronic PTSD and those who do not (Vernberg & Varela, 2001).

Systematic efforts to document and understand the biological processes associated with children's reactions to disasters are much needed. Future studies might benefit from adapting concepts that have been formulated in understanding biological reactions to other types of trauma, such as severe child abuse and other forms of violence (e.g., Charney, Deutch, Krystal, Southwick, & Davis, 1993; Keane et al., 1998).

Postimpact Phase

Few studies have examined children's reactions to disasters during the first few days or weeks immediately following a disaster. When severe reactions occur, the most likely clinical diagnoses to emerge in the short-term period following a disaster are adjustment disorder and acute stress disorder, as described in the *Diagnostic and Statistical Manual of Mental Disorders, 4th Edition* (*DSM–IV*; American Psychiatric Association, 1994). Although the disorders are described in the following paragraphs, it is not clear how they manifest themselves in children following disasters. As noted, the lack of research in this area is largely a result of the practical constraints of conducting research in the immediate aftermath of a major disaster. Further research is needed to understand how the disorders manifest themselves in children following disasters.

According to the *DSM–IV* (1994), the main feature of adjustment disorder is the development of emotional or behavioral symptoms in response to an identifiable stressor. The symptoms must occur within 3 months of the stressor and be "clinically significant" (e.g., more distress than one might expect or signs of impairment in academic or social functioning). If the disturbance lasts less than 6 months, it is considered to be acute; if it lasts more than 6 months, it is considered to be chronic. Adjustment disorders are further differentiated by the characteristics of the predominant symptoms, such as depressed mood, anxiety, and conduct disturbance.

Acute stress disorder (ASD) was introduced as a new anxiety disorder in the *DSM–IV* (1994). As with PTSD (described in the following section), a diagnosis of ASD requires that the person be exposed to a traumatic event that causes or is capable of causing death, injury, or threat to the physical integrity of oneself or another person. In addition, a child's reaction to the traumatic event must include intense fear, helplessness, or horror—or even disorganized or agitated behavior. Many of the symptoms of ASD are similar to those of PTSD, with two key exceptions. First, ASD places greater emphasis on dissociative symptoms (e.g., a sense of numbing or detachment, reduced awareness of one's surroundings, and dissociative amnesia), which are not a prominent feature of PTSD. Second, ASD has an immediate onset and shorter duration than PTSD: In ASD the disturbance lasts for a minimum of 2 days and a maximum of 4 weeks, and it must be evident within 4 weeks of the event (American Psychiatric Association, 1994).

Given that ASD is a newly conceptualized disorder and that most studies have examined children's disaster reactions more than a month after the traumatic event, it is not surprising that ASD has not yet been studied systematically in children and youth following disasters. Future efforts to evaluate children's early reactions to disasters would do well to include symptoms and features of ASD. Also important for future research are studies that track the trajectories of children's responses to determine whether ASD eventually leads to PTSD in some children (as presumed) and to determine what factors cause some children to develop more persistent PTSD reactions than other children.

Recovery and Reconstruction

Most studies have focused on children's and adolescents' reactions during the weeks to months (or even years) following a disaster event (Vogel & Vernberg, 1993). In fact, this focus is typical of the literature reviewed throughout this text. Moreover, within the recovery-and-reconstruction period, the most widely studied reaction to disasters has been that of PTSD or related symptoms.

PTSD

The diagnostic category of PTSD was introduced in the *Diagnostic and Statistical Manual of Mental Disorders, 3rd Edition* (DSM–III; American Psychiatric Association, 1980) and was initially considered to be an adult disorder. The growing awareness that children and adolescents also experience symptoms of PTSD is reflected in the *DSM–IV* (1994).

In the *DSM–IV* (1994), PTSD refers to a set of symptoms that develop following exposure to an unusually severe stressor or event. As with ASD, the event should be one that (a) causes or is capable of causing death, injury, or threat to physical integrity and (b) results in intense fear and helplessness and disorganized or agitated behavior. In addition, specific criteria for three additional symptom clusters must be met: reexperiencing, avoidance or numbing, and hyperarousal.

The most commonly reported symptom of PTSD is reexperiencing, which includes recurrent or intrusive thoughts or dreams about the event and intense distress at cues or reminders of the event. With young children, reexperiencing is thought to be reflected in repetitive play with traumatic themes or by a reenactment of the traumatic events in play, drawings, or verbalizations (American Academy of Child and Adolescent Psychiatry, 1998; Drell, Siegel, & Gaensbauer, 1993). Systematic developmental research focusing on this particular symptom's manifestation is scant, however.

Symptoms of avoidance or numbing include avoiding thoughts, feelings, or conversations about the traumatic event; avoiding reminders of the event; having a diminished interest in normal activities; and feeling detached or removed from others. Children may report a lessened interest in their usual activities (e.g., athletics, reading, playing with friends, video games) or may feel distant from family and friends. Symptoms of avoidance and numbing are the least commonly reported aspects of PTSD in children and thus may represent a useful diagnostic indicator of the presence of the full disorder (Lonigan, Anthony, & Shannon, 1998).

Finally, symptoms of hyperarousal include difficulty sleeping or concentrating, irritability, angry outbursts, hypervigilance, and an exaggerated startle response. Startle reactions may be especially prominent after exposure to gunfire, shootings, or terrorist activities (see chapters 13 and 14). Symptoms of hyperarousal must be newly occurring since the traumatic event.

According to the *DSM–IV* (1994), for a diagnosis, PTSD symptoms must be evident for at least 1 month and be accompanied by significant impairment in the child's functioning (e.g., problems in school, social, or family relations). If the duration of symptoms is less than 3 months, PTSD is considered to be acute; if the duration is greater than 3 months, it is considered to be chronic. If the onset of symptoms is at least 6 months after the traumatic event, it is considered to be delayed onset.

Evidence suggests that most children who develop PTSD or its symptoms following disasters do so in the first weeks or months following the event. For example, Yule (see chapter 10) describes children's reactions following the 1998 Jupiter disaster—a cruise ship carrying approximately 400 British school children, that sank in the Eastern Mediterranean after being struck by a container ship. Most survivors who developed PTSD did so the first few weeks after the disaster; only 10% of the children experienced delayed onset, but they all displayed subclinical levels of PTSD before that point.

As can be seen throughout this book, most research has emphasized evaluating youngsters' PTSD symptoms following disasters. With perhaps the exception of toxic waste spills (chapter 9), studies have found that many children and adolescents report high levels of PTSD symptoms following all types of disasters (e.g., see chapters 5–8 and 10–14). Few studies have tried to establish whether children and adolescents meet all the criteria for a PTSD diagnosis or examined whether youngsters' functioning was impaired as a result of the PTSD symptoms.

A review of the material in this volume also makes it clear that little attention has been devoted to the assessment of disaster reactions other than PTSD or of conditions that may be comorbid with PTSD, even though such information may be of critical importance for treatment (e.g., see chapters 3 and 5). The section that follows highlights several disaster reactions that may be comorbid with, or occur independently of PTSD in youth following disasters.

Other Postdisaster Reactions

Traumatized children and adolescents often display depressive disorders or anxiety disorders, in addition to PTSD (Vernberg & Varela, 2001). In fact, rates of comorbidity are extremely high among youth diagnosed with PTSD (American Academy of Child and Adolescent Psychiatry, 1998). This finding also may be the case for children exposed to disaster. For example, following the devastating Armenian earthquake in 1988, many children in the most heavily affected areas met criteria for both PTSD and a depressive disorder, and a sizable number also met criteria for separation anxiety disorder (SAD; Goenjian et al., 1995; chapter 5, this volume). Of particular interest in that study was the late emergence of depression (months after the earthquake) relative to the onset of PTSD and SAD as well as the finding that depression was highest among youth who displayed chronic PTSD.

Disasters that involve loss of loved ones, such as earthquakes, bombings, shootings, or transportation disasters, may be especially likely to lead to depressive reactions in children (see chapters 10, 13, 14; see also Goenjian et al., 1995; Kinzie, Sack, Angell, Manson, & Rath, 1986; Singer, Anglin, Song, & Lunghofer, 1995). In such cases, depression may be a secondary disorder arising from bereavement (Vernberg & Varela, 2001) and unresolved PTSD. Consistent with this observation, Gurwitch (chapter 14) notes that PTSD can complicate the grieving process and interfere both with children's efforts to deal with personal loss and with their ability to adapt to subsequent life changes. To date, however, few studies of children's disaster reactions have differentiated between symptoms of PTSD and symptoms of grief and bereavement.

With respect to anxiety, evidence suggests that children's anxiety levels may be elevated following disasters, regardless of whether PTSD symptoms are present. Significant anxiety symptoms have been reported in children and adolescents following such diverse disasters as earthquakes (e.g., Goenjian et al., 1995; see chapter 5), hurricanes (e.g., La Greca, Silverman, & Wasserstein, 1998; Lonigan, Shannon, Taylor, Finch, & Sallee, 1994; see chapter 5), and transportation disasters (see chapter 10). Following other types of trauma, anxiety disorders appear to be the most common diagnoses that are comorbid with PTSD (American Academy of Child and Adolescent Psychiatry, 1998).

Increased concerns about safety and security are related to anxiety levels and also have been reported as common disaster reactions (e.g., see chapters 10 and 14). Young children may express those concerns as fear of separation from parents or loved ones. For example, Gurwitch (chapter 14) described high levels of separation fears (e.g., clinging to parents) among young children following the bombing of the Alfred P. Murrah Federal Building in Oklahoma City. In some cases, separation fears may be sufficient to meet criteria for a diagnosis of SAD, as was the case among youth affected by the Armenian earthquake (Goenjian et al., 1995).

Increased fears following a traumatic event or disaster also have been documented in some children and adolescents (see chapters 5, 10, 13, and 14). Often, those fears are directly related to the kind of trauma that was experienced. For example, fear of water, thunder, and rainstorms have been reported among children following hurricanes (Vogel & Vernberg, 1993). Security concerns, fears of reoccurrence (without warning), and exaggerated startle responses to loud noises also may be evident in the aftermath of sniper shootings, bombings, and other "unpredictable" acts of violence (Pynoos & Nader, 1988; see chapters 13–15).

Traumatic events have been viewed as a potential pathway to the development of phobias and other anxiety-based disorders in youth (see Silverman & Ginsburg, 1995). Evidence also indicates that exposure to disasters can increase anxiety levels in otherwise "normal" youth. For example, in a community sample of children, those who reported high levels of exposure to a natural disaster displayed significant increases in their anxiety levels several months postdisaster, compared with their predisaster levels of functioning (La Greca et al., 1998; see chapter 5).

Although symptoms of depression, anxiety, and related concerns appear to be fairly common following disasters and may even be sufficient to warrant a clinical diagnosis, other areas of children's functioning also may be affected. In particular, some attention has been directed to understanding the impact of disasters on children's academic functioning. Some limited evidence suggests that problems with academic achievement may result from children's exposure to disasters (e.g., Shannon, Lonigan, Finch, & Taylor, 1994; Vincent, La Greca, Silverman, Wasserstein, & Prinstein, 1994; Yule,

1994; see also chapters 5 and 10). Considering that disasters can seriously disrupt children's everyday routines and may precipitate problems with sleep and concentration, it is not surprising that children's academic functioning can be compromised by a disaster.

In summary, PTSD, other anxiety disorders (e.g., SAD), and depressive disorders constitute the most common types of clinical problems documented in children and adolescents following disasters, and they may be comorbid conditions. Even at subclinical levels, it is common for children and adolescents to report symptoms of anxiety, fears and security concerns, and depressive symptoms in addition to PTSD symptoms. What is less clear from existing research is the extent to which those symptoms interfere with children's day-to-day functioning and thus may be pathological or, alternatively, whether the symptoms might be considered to be normal reactions to abnormal events. It does appear that the longer the clinical symptoms persist at high levels, the greater the likelihood that problems will not dissipate over time. For example, in a rare longitudinal study, Vincent (1997) found that among children who reported moderate to severe symptoms of PTSD 10 months after Hurricane Andrew, 40% met criteria for PTSD nearly 4 years later, compared with only 5% of the children who reported mild PTSD symptoms 10 months postdisaster.

One additional caveat regarding children's disaster reactions is warranted. Because children's predisaster levels of functioning are usually unknown (see section on child characteristics), it is often difficult to determine whether certain symptoms or problems actually preceded the disaster or constitute reactions to trauma. Studies of natural disasters, however, suggest that predisaster levels of anxiety predict postdisaster symptoms of anxiety and PTSD following a hurricane (e.g., La Greca et al., 1998) and that predisaster levels of depression predict levels of depression and stress symptoms following an earthquake (Nolen-Hoeksema & Morrow, 1991).

In conclusion, given the potential effects of disasters on children and adolescents and the likelihood of comorbid symptoms or conditions, it is desirable to obtain a comprehensive assessment of children's functioning following disasters. In most clinical or research settings, it will be useful to evaluate children's functioning broadly, rather than limit the evaluation to symptoms of PTSD.

UNDERSTANDING FACTORS THAT CONTRIBUTE TO CHILDREN'S AND ADOLESCENTS' DISASTER REACTIONS

As highlighted in the preceding section, when disasters hit, a sizable proportion of children react. For large numbers of children, the reactions can be severe and distressing. Despite the progress in documenting children's reactions to disasters, little is known about the factors that predict or contribute to their reactions. Both treatment providers and researchers need to know why, and by what processes, some children develop generally mild reactions, some have moderate reactions, and others develop full-blown and debilitating symptoms of PTSD, and even the disorder itself, following disaster exposure. At this point, most of the research has examined correlates of and risk factors for children's disaster reactions.

For the next generation of studies, it will be important to adopt a developmental psychopathology perspective that focuses on the interplay between adaptive and maladaptive reactions and diverse domains of functioning (Cicchetti & Cohen, 1995). This perspective considers the transactional nature of children's disaster reactions and allows for the likelihood that disasters can lead to multiple types of reactions and that any given reaction (e.g., PTSD) can result from a disaster as well as from other origins. Within the developmental psychopathology literature, the former concept is referred to as *equifinality*, and the latter as *multifinality* (Cicchetti & Cohen, 1995). A developmental psychopathology perspective may lead to improved understanding of how variables may interrelate in complex ways to influence reactions in youth across child and adolescent development. Such a perspective would allow the field to move on to more theory-driven, clinical–developmental research, which would serve to advance understanding about how children's reactions develop and about how to most effectively intervene.

Most of the research on children and disasters is in an early, but necessary, stage. That is, although researchers have made initial efforts to develop a conceptual framework for understanding and investigating children's reactions (see chapters 5, 8, and 12), most of their work has focused on studying variables associated with children's reactions at a given point in time (i.e., correlates) and variables that precede children's reactions (i.e., risk factors). Considerably less is known about risk factors that reflect stable characteristics or traits but are not causally related to reactions (i.e., markers) or risk factors that directly or indirectly influence children's reactions (i.e., causal risk factors). Moreover, research in this area has not yet gone beyond simple "main effects" models to consider complex interactions (e.g., moderators) and understand the actual mechanisms or mediational processes involved in the development of children's disaster reactions. With these caveats in mind, the following sections review key factors that have been investigated in an effort to understand children's reactions to disasters.

CORRELATES OF AND RISK FACTORS FOR CHILDREN'S POSTDISASTER REACTIONS

The chapters in this book demonstrate that researchers generally have focused on a circumscribed set of variables in their efforts to understand and predict children's reactions. The reactions most often studied are those associated with PTSD, described previously. The variables linked with the development of PTSD symptoms largely fall within one of the following categories:

- Aspects of traumatic exposure (e.g., life threat, loss, or disruption);
- Preexisting characteristics of the child (e.g., demographic characteristics and predisaster functioning);
- Characteristics of the postdisaster recovery environment (e.g., availability of social support and occurrence of major life events or stressors); and
- The child's psychological resources (e.g., coping skills and self-efficacy).

Those variables are largely contained within a conceptual model that was initially developed by Korol (1990) and Green et al. (1991) and later modified (La Greca, Silverman, Vernberg, & Prinstein, 1996; Vernberg, La Greca, Silverman, & Prinstein, 1996).

Some of the categories in the model (and the variables contained within them) are best viewed as risk factors that might be useful for identifying the children and adolescents who are most likely to develop PTSD reactions following a disaster. The same categories and variables, however, might not be particularly useful for developing disaster-related interventions. For example, some preexisting child characteristics (e.g., age, gender, and ethnicity) are not modifiable and therefore could not be altered in an intervention; however, those characteristics could be used to identify "high-risk" populations. In contrast, some aspects of the recovery environment (e.g., social support, parental reactions) and elements of children's psychological resources (e.g., coping skills) are modifiable and could be targeted in treatment and preventive interventions. It seems important for future researchers to carefully delineate the relative influence of child characteristics and variables for the purposes of prediction and intervention. Doing so would include identifying characteristics and variables that are common to prediction and intervention and those that are specific to prediction and intervention. Moreover, as noted earlier, it is likely that these characteristics and variables contribute to children's reactions in complex ways. To date, however, potential interactions among the different variables have not been studied.

Aspects of Traumatic Exposure

Several aspects of traumatic exposure have been demonstrated as important for the emergence of children's disaster reactions. One particularly important aspect, viewed by some as essential to the emergence of PTSD symptoms (Green et al., 1991), is the presence or perception of life threat. As many of the chapters in this book (e.g., chapters 5–7, and 10–14) and other literature (e.g., La Greca et al., 1996, 1998; Lonigan, Shannon, Finch, Daugherty, & Taylor, 1991) indicate, the more children perceive their lives or the lives of loved ones to be threatened, the higher are their reports of PTSD symptoms. This finding helps explain why children who have been exposed to or who are witnesses of extreme acts of violence, such as sniper shootings or bombings, report considerable PTSD symptoms (see section IV of the book), and it helps explain why catastrophic and destructive natural or personal disasters (e.g., hurricanes, earthquakes, brushfires, residential fires, and motor vehicle accidents; see chapters 5–8 and 12) can similarly lead to PTSD symptoms. That is, such events elicit the perception of life threat in many children, even though no one may have actually been injured or hurt in that event. Similarly, not perceiving that one's own life or the lives of loved ones are threatened could help explain why most children do not report PTSD symptoms after some disasters. For example, Baum and colleagues (chapter 9) found that few children reported PTSD symptoms following the 1979 Three Mile Island disaster, the worst commercial nuclear accident to occur in the United States, in which hundreds of thousands of gallons of radioactive water spilt, releasing radioactive steam into the atmosphere. Few children reported PTSD symptoms following this accident because the children did not perceive their lives or those of their loved ones to be threatened.

Perhaps even more strongly linked to the development of PTSD symptoms in children are disasters that specifically lead to the death of a loved one (e.g., a parent, friend, or classmate), especially a violent death, as with shootings (see chapters 13–16). Stress reactions arising from such events appear to be further complicated by feelings of grief and guilt, which may interact and heighten the stress reactions. For example, children who lose a parent in a terrorist attack not only have to deal with the complicated task of processing the personal loss but also must reconcile why they survived and the loved one did not. For many children, this task may lead to impairing and interfering thoughts or ruminations regarding whether they could have done more (or less) to prevent the death from occurring in the first place.

Loss of possessions and disruption of everyday life, including displacement from home, school, and community, also have been found to contribute to PTSD symptoms in children following disasters (e.g., La Greca et al., 1996; Vernberg et al., 1996). This outcome has perhaps been most studied following catastrophic and destructive disasters, including hurricanes and earthquakes (see chapter 5) and residential fires (see chapter 8). Following hurricanes, for example, children are faced with a cascading series of life stressors that are set into motion by the disaster, including loss of home and personal property, a change of schools, shifts in parental employment and family finances, friends moving away, altered leisure activities, and so on. The stressors may last for weeks, months, and even years following the disaster, seriously challenging children's and families' adaptation and coping.

Despite the likely importance of this cumulative or cascading stress notion for understanding children's postdisaster reactions over time, few studies have directly and systematically investigated the specific number and types of ongoing stressors that children encounter in the aftermath of disasters and their specific short- and long-term effects on children's disaster reactions.

Another important aspect of traumatic exposure that has been demonstrated as important for the emergence of children's disaster reactions is children's proximity to the event (e.g., Pynoos & Nader, 1988; see chapters 5, 13, and 14). Specifically, evidence suggests that the more physically close children are to the disaster event, the more intense or severe are their reactions.

Duration and intensity of life-threatening events are additional aspects of traumatic exposure associated with symptom severity in children (see chapter 13; see also Vernberg & Verela, 2001), although those effects have been relatively less studied than the others mentioned above. For example, the prolonged nature of certain disaster events (such as floods), in which no immediate relief is in sight, appears to be what is so distressing to children (see chapter 7).

As described in some of the chapters in this volume, children's reactions are further influenced by whether children have been exposed to single or multiple incidents; greater distress occurs following multiple exposures. For example, youngsters who have multiple exposures to traumatic events have been found to be at higher risk for the development of PTSD symptoms following disasters (e.g., Robin, Chester, Rasmussen, Jaranson, & Goldman, 1997). As discussed in chapter 13, however, the relation between exposure incidents (i.e., single versus multiple) and PTSD is not simple. For example, although multiple exposure may place children at higher risk, children who have been exposed to multiple traumatic events and resolve them competently may actually have less distress and display greater competency when faced with another traumatic event or disaster than children who have had only a single incident exposure.

Preexisting Characteristics of the Child

Certain aspects of children's functioning prior to a disaster may put them at risk for greater postdisaster reactions. The most widely studied predisaster child characteristics are those that do not change as a result of a disaster—namely, sociodemographic variables, such as age, gender, and ethnicity. Few studies have examined other characteristics (e.g., psychological or academic functioning), in part because it is difficult to obtain accurate predisaster information on such characteristics; investigators generally need to rely on retrospective reporting of predisaster adjustment.

Although age has perhaps received the most research, it is difficult to generalize about children's vulnerability to stress reactions at different ages.

For the most part, findings on age-related differences have been inconsistent and few investigations have had sufficiently large samples of youth of different age groups to adequately evaluate potential developmental differences. Systematic and adequate investigations of developmental differences are further hampered by the fact that although diverse manifestations of PTSD are likely to exist at different ages (American Academy of Child and Adolescent Psychiatry, 1998), at present, no normative data on children's disaster reactions by age are available. Consequently, the need to further test and refine assessment instruments, such as the Pediatric Emotional Distress Scale (Saylor, Swenson, Reynolds, & Taylor, 1999; see chapter 2), takes on even greater importance; such instruments may prove useful in gathering developmental norms.

With regard to gender, some studies indicate that girls report more PTSD symptoms than boys following disasters, although the evidence on this point is mixed as well (see chapters 5 and 11). Moreover, even when differences emerge, their magnitude is relatively modest and their clinical meaningfulness is uncertain (Vernberg et al., 1996). It also is likely that boys' and girls' postdisaster reactions depend on the type of disaster and stress reactions that are studied. Following exposure to crime and violence, for example, boys display more aggressive behaviors (e.g., fighting) than girls do (see chapter 16; see also Garbarino & Kostelny, 1996). Further investigation of the patterns of interactions that emerge as a function of gender, type of disaster, and type of stress reaction is needed.

Children's ethnicity, race, and cultural background have been relatively understudied by researchers of children's reactions to disasters (see chapter 4). Although findings from community studies following natural disasters generally show that minority youth report higher levels of PTSD symptoms and have a more difficult time recovering from such events than nonminority youth (e.g., La Greca et al., 1996, 1998; Lonigan et al., 1994; see chapters 4, 5, and 8), the reasons for the observed ethnic differences are unclear. Perhaps children's ethnicity and race interact with socioeconomic status such that following a destructive, natural disaster, families from minority backgrounds possess fewer financial resources or have inadequate insurance to deal efficiently with the rebuilding and recovery process. That difficulty, in turn, could prolong the period of life disruption and loss of personal possessions that typically ensues after destructive natural disasters. Another possibility is that children from minority backgrounds have higher levels of predisaster exposure to trauma, which might "sensitize" them to the effects of disasters. For example, Berton and Stabb (1996) found that minority males were exposed to more violent crime in their neighborhood than other adolescents were and that exposure to community violence also predicted PTSD symptoms among those urban adolescents.

The role of sociodemographic characteristics and their associated factors in predicting youngsters' responses to traumatic events is not well understood and could be examined more closely. Sociodemographic variables, however, may be viewed best as markers for other variables that may play a more direct and causal role in the development of children's stress reactions. Rabalais and colleagues (chapter 4), for example, suggest that race and ethnicity may be markers for other variables, such as acculturation stress, stress from prejudices and discrimination, and cultural beliefs and religion. The latter variables are likely to have an important influence on children's disaster reactions, although they have not been studied.

Aside from sociodemographic factors, findings suggest that prior psychosocial functioning predicts stress reactions in children and adolescents as well (Earls, Smith, Reich, & Jung, 1988). Here, too, the available evidence is scant. As noted previously, the dearth of evidence can be attributed to the difficulty of obtaining accurate information on children's predisaster psychological functioning. Consequently, most of the work (e.g., Asarnow et al., 1999 and La Greca et al., 1998, are exceptions) has relied on retrospective reports of disaster victims or sources close to the victims (e.g., parents and teachers).

In general, findings suggest that preexisting anxiety is a significant risk factor for the development of PTSD symptoms (e.g., Asarnow et al., 1999; La Greca et al., 1998; Lonigan et al., 1994; see chapter 5). That is, anxious children may be vulnerable to developing PTSD reactions, even if their degree of exposure to a disaster is relatively low (see La Greca et al., 1998). Such findings are interesting in light of both the current conceptualization of PTSD (American Psychiatric Association, 1994), which suggests that trauma must be present for PTSD to emerge, and the work summarized earlier regarding the importance of exposure to the disaster.

Other research findings point to predisaster depression levels and ruminative coping styles as potential risk factors for stress reactions. For example, following the 1989 Loma Prieta earthquake that occurred on the Loma Prieta section of the San Andreas Fault in the San Francisco Bay area, measuring 7.1 on the Richter Scale, killing 62 people, injuring 3,757, and leaving 12,000 homeless, Nolen-Hoeksema and Morrow (1991) evaluated 137 students 2 weeks before and then 10 days and 7 weeks after the disaster. Youth who before the earthquake had elevated levels of depression and stress symptoms and a ruminative style of coping with symptoms had more depression and stress symptoms at both follow-up periods.

Finally, some evidence suggests that children with preexisting academic difficulties and attention problems may exhibit greater postdisaster problems than children without such difficulties (Vogel & Vernberg, 1993). For example, child survivors of a ferry sinking who had higher academic achievement exhibited fewer PTSD symptoms than those with lower academic achievement (see Yule, 1994; chapter 10). Other work has identified low achievement and high levels of attention problems as risk factors for PTSD symptoms during the first 3 months postdisaster (La Greca et al., 1998).

Aspects of the Recovery Environment

After the initial impact of a disaster, various aspects of the recovery environment may magnify or attenuate youngsters' subsequent reactions. The presence of parental psychopathology or of parental distress following the disaster, and the occurrence of additional life events or stressors have been among the most studied aspects of the recovery environment.

Given the numerous stressors that accompany a disaster, social support from a variety of sources should help minimize youngsters' postdisaster distress. Social support has been conceptualized and measured in a variety of ways, but most commonly as children's reports of perceived social support from significant others, such as parents, friends, and teachers. Children's perceived social support from significant others has been found to mitigate the impact of natural disasters on children and adolescents (La Greca et al., 1996; Vernberg et al., 1996; see chapter 5) and to predict fewer PTSD symptoms in reaction to crime and violence in high school students (see chapter 16). Such findings suggest that enhancing children's social support following disasters may be an important mental health goal.

Victims of natural disasters, in particular, report receiving substantial amounts of help and social support (see Kaniasty & Norris, 1999), although careful analysis of help and social support following disasters has documented a "pattern of neglect," in which lesser amounts of aid are provided to certain groups of people (Kilijanek & Drabek, 1979). Kaniasty and Norris (1995), for example, described a pattern of neglect in which less educated and Black adult victims received less help than did equally affected victims who were more educated or White. How such patterns affect children's disaster recovery remains a relatively understudied area.

Another aspect of the recovery environment that might affect children's functioning is the parents' psychosocial functioning, including their levels of psychopathology and their own reactions to the disaster. For example, Green et al. (1991) found that parental psychopathology predicted higher levels of PTSD symptoms in children and adolescent following the Buffalo Creek dam collapse (see chapter 11). In the case of a nuclear waste disaster, the psychological health of the parents was found to be a strong predictor of children's disaster reactions (Korol, Green, & Gleser, 1999; see chapters 7, 8, 10, and 11). Also, mothers' distress in the aftermath of Hurricane Hugo was associated with the persistence of their children's postdisaster emotional and behavioral difficulties (Swenson et al., 1996).

Other research has supported a linkage between children's symptoms of PTSD and parents' trauma-related symptoms (Foy, Madvig, Pynoos, & Camilleri, 1996). Because parents serve as the same informant for themselves and their children in many studies, Yule (chapter 10) cautions that it is important to consider what influence the informant has on the obtained results. Generally speaking, research is needed to further clarify the way in which parents' psychopathology or their own PTSD reactions may lead to either underestimation or overestimation of children's reactions. In all likelihood, parents who are having adjustment difficulties are less able to provide needed support and comfort to their children following disasters, which may adversely affect children's adjustment. Conversely, if children feel that adults are in control, it may prevent the children's symptoms from escalating (see chapter 13).

Major life events (e.g., death or hospitalization of a family member, parental divorce or separation) in the months following a disaster appear to significantly impede children's postdisaster recovery and are linked with greater persistence of PTSD symptoms in children over time (La Greca et al., 1996). As noted above, children who encounter major life events following a disaster, in addition to the typical cascading series of disaster-related life stressors, appear to represent a high-risk group for severe and persistent posttraumatic stress reactions; as a result, such youth bear close monitoring.

The psychological resources of the child, which are part and parcel of the concept of resilience (i.e., the idea that some children function well despite undergoing extraordinary adverse circumstances; see Garmezy, 1993), also have been linked to children's postdisaster reactions and recovery (Vernberg, 1999). Here, too, research is scarce. Nevertheless, the characteristics that have been discussed in the literature as potentially important include at least average intelligence, good communication skills, strong beliefs of self-efficacy, an internal locus of control, and adequate ways of coping (Vernberg, 1999).

Of the preceding factors, coping has received the most attention. Several community studies have found that children and adolescents with negative coping strategies for dealing with stress (e.g., anger, blaming others) show higher levels of PTSD symptoms than children and adolescents with positive coping strategies in response to natural disasters (La Greca et al., 1996; Vernberg et al., 1996; see chapter 5) and community violence (Berman, Kurtines, Silverman, & Serafini, 1996; see chapter 16). Moreover, children with negative coping strategies evidence greater persistence in their PTSD symptoms over time (La Greca et al., 1996). Because of these findings, efforts to encourage problem-solving and adaptive coping skills may be useful for interventions with children following traumatic events (see chapters 3 and 5).

CONCLUSIONS

Recent research on children's and adolescents' reactions to disasters is beginning to move away from simple descriptions of postdisaster reactions and is instead focusing on factors that predict which youngsters will have severe and persistent postdisaster reactions and why. The characteristics and variables contained within the conceptual model outlined in this chapter may be a useful initial framework for organizing such findings and represent an important first step toward theory building in this area. Moreover, as will be apparent in several of the subsequent chapters, this initial framework is a useful starting point for identifying children and adolescents who are at risk for psychological difficulties following disasters. Mental health professionals' ability to quickly, efficiently, and accurately identify high-risk children and youth following a disaster will be critical for successful prevention and intervention efforts.

REFERENCES

American Academy of Child and Adolescent Psychiatry. (1998). AACAP official action: Practice parameters for the assessment and treatment of children and adolescents with posttraumatic stress disorder. *Journal of the American Academy of Child and Adolescent Psychiatry, 37*(Suppl.), 4S-26S.

American Academy of Pediatrics, Work Group on Disasters. (1995). *Psychosocial issues for children and families in disasters: A guide for the primary care physician.* Retrieved March 7, 2001, from http://www.mentalhealth.org/publications/allpubs/SMA95-3022/default.asp.

American Psychiatric Association. (1980). *Diagnostic and statistical manual of mental disorders* (3rd ed.). Washington, DC: Author.

American Psychiatric Association. (1994). *Diagnostic and statistical manual of mental disorders* (4th ed.). Washington, DC: Author.

Asarnow, J., Glynn, S., Pynoos, R. S., Nahum, J., Guthrie, D., Cantwell, D. P., & Franklin, B. (1999). When the earth stops shaking: Earthquake sequelae among children diagnosed for pre-earthquake psychopathology. *Journal of the American Academy of Child and Adolescent Psychiatry, 38,* 1016–1023.

Berman, S. L., Kurtines, W. M., Silverman, W. K., & Serafini, L. T. (1996). The impact of exposure to crime and violence on urban youth. *American Journal of Orthopsychiatry, 66,* 329–336.

Berton, M. W., & Stabb, S. D. (1996). Exposure to violence and post-traumatic stress disorder in urban adolescents. *Adolescence, 31,* 489–498.

Charney, D. S., Deutch, A. Y., Krystal, J. H., Southwick, S. M., & Davis, M. (1993). Psychobiologic mechanisms of posttraumatic stress disorder. *Archives of General Psychiatry, 50,* 294–305.

Cicchetti, D., & Cohen, D. J. (1995). Perspectives on developmental psychopathology. In D. Cicchetti & D. J. Cohen (Eds.), *Development and psychopathology: Vol. 1. Theory and methods* (pp. 3–22). New York: Wiley.

Coffman, S. (1994). Children describe life after Hurricane Andrew. *Pediatric Nursing, 20,* 363–368.

Drell, M. J., Siegel, C. H., & Gaensbauer, T. J. (1993). Posttraumatic stress disorder. In C. H. Zeanah (Ed.), *Handbook of infant mental health* (pp. 291–304). New York: Guilford Press.

Earls, F., Smith, E., Reich, W., & Jung, K. G. (1988). Investigating the psychopathological consequence of disaster in children: A pilot study incorporating a structured diagnostic interview. *Journal of the American Academy of Child and Adolescent Psychiatry, 27*, 90–95.

Foy, D. W., Madvig, B. T., Pynoos, R. S., & Camilleri, A. J. (1996). Etiologic factors in the development of posttraumatic stress disorder in children and adolescents. *Journal of School Psychology, 34*, 133–145.

Garbarino, J., & Kostelny, K. (1996). The effects of political violence on Palestinian children's behavior problems: A risk accumulation model. *Child Development, 67*, 33–45.

Garmezy, N. (1993). Developmental psychopathology: Some historical and current perspectives. In D. Magnusson & P. Caesar (Eds.), *Longitudinal research on individual development* (pp. 95–126). Cambridge, UK: University Press.

Goenjian, A. K., Pynoos, R. S., Steinberg, A. M., Najarian, L. M., Asarnow, J. R., Karayan, I., Ghurabi, M., & Fairbanks, L. A. (1995). Psychiatric comorbidity in children after the 1988 earthquake in Armenia. *Journal of the American Academy of Child and Adolescent Psychiatry, 34*, 1174–1184.

Green, B. L., Korol, M. S., Grace, M. C., Vary, M. G., Leonard, A. C., Gleser, G. C., & Smitson-Cohen, S. (1991). Children and disaster: Gender and parental effects on PTSD symptoms. *Journal of the American Academy of Child and Adolescent Psychiatry, 30*, 945–951.

International Federation of Red Cross and Red Crescent Societies. (1998). *World disasters report*. New York: Oxford University Press.

Kaniasty, K., & Norris, F. (1995). In search of altruistic community: Patterns of social support mobilization following Hurricane Hugo. *American Journal of Community Psychology, 23*, 447–477.

Kaniasty, K., & Norris, F. (1999). The experience of disaster: Individuals and communities sharing trauma. In R. Gist & B. Lubin (Eds.), *Response to disaster: Psychosocial, community, and ecological approaches* (pp. 25–61). Philadelphia, PA: Brunner/Mazel.

Keane, T. M., Kolb, L. C., Kaloupek, D. G., Orr, S. P., Blanchard, E. B., Thomas, R. G., Hsieh, F. Y., & Lavori, P. W. (1998). Utility of psychophysiological measurement in the diagnosis of posttraumatic stress disorder: Results from a Department of Veteran Affairs cooperative study. *Journal of Consulting and Clinical Psychology, 66*, 914–923.

Kilijanek, T., & Drabek, T. E. (1979). Assessing long-term impacts of a natural disaster: A focus on the elderly. *The Gerontologist, 19*, 555–566.

Kinzie, J. D., Sack, W. H., Angell, R. H., Manson, S., & Rath, B. (1986). The psychiatric effects of massive trauma on Cambodian children, I: The children. *Journal of the American Academy of Child and Adolescent Psychiatry, 25*, 370–376.

Korol, M. S. (1990). *Children's psychological responses to a nuclear waste disaster in Fernald, Ohio*. Unpublished doctoral dissertation, University of Cincinnati.

Korol, M. S., Green, B. L., & Gleser, G. C. (1999). Children's response to a nuclear waste disaster: PTSD symptoms and outcome prediction. *Journal of the American Academy of Child and Adolescent Psychiatry, 38*, 368–375.

La Greca, A. M., Silverman, W. K., Vernberg, E. M., & Prinstein, M. J. (1996). Symptoms of posttraumatic stress after Hurricane Andrew: A prospective study. *Journal of Consulting and Clinical Psychology, 64*, 712–723.

La Greca, A. M., Silverman, W. K., & Wasserstein, S. B. (1998). Children's predisaster functioning as a predictor of posttraumatic stress following Hurricane Andrew. *Journal of Consulting and Clinical Psychology, 66*, 883–892.

Lonigan, C. J., Anthony, J. L., & Shannon, M. P. (1998). Diagnostic efficacy of posttraumatic symptoms in children exposed to disaster. *Journal of Clinical Child Psychology, 27*, 255–267.

Lonigan, C. J., Shannon, M. P., Finch, A. J., Daugherty, T. K., & Taylor, C. M. (1991). Children's reactions to a natural disaster: Symptom severity and degree of exposure. *Behaviour Research and Therapy, 13*, 135–154.

Lonigan, C. J., Shannon, M. P., Taylor, C. M., Finch, A. J., & Sallee, F. R. (1994). Children exposed to disaster: II. Risk factors for the development of post-traumatic symptomatology. *Journal of the American Academy of Child and Adolescent Psychiatry, 33*, 94–105.

Nolen-Hoeksema, S., & Morrow, J. (1991). A prospective study of depression and posttraumatic stress symptoms after a natural disaster: The 1989 Loma Prieta Earthquake. *Journal of Personality and Social Psychology, 61*, 115–121.

Orr, S. P., Lasko, N. B., Metzger, L. J., Berry, N. J., Ahern, C. E., & Pitman, R. K. (1998). Physiological assessment of women with posttraumatic stress disorder resulting from childhood sexual abuse. *Journal of Consulting and Clinical Psychology, 66*, 906–913.

Pynoos, R. S., & Nader, K. (1988). Psychological first aid and treatment approach to children exposed to community violence: Research implications. *Journal of Traumatic Stress, 1*, 445–473.

Pynoos, R. S., & Nader, K. (1990). Mental health disturbances in children exposed to disaster: Preventive intervention strategies. In S. Goldston, J. Yaker, C. Heinicke, & R. S. Pynoos (Eds.), *Preventing mental health disturbances in children* (pp. 211–234). Washington, DC: American Psychiatric Association.

Robin, R. W., Chester, B., Rasmussen, J. K., Jaranson, J. M., & Goldman, D. (1997). Prevalence and characteristics of trauma and posttraumatic stress disorder in a southwestern American Indian community. *American Journal of Psychiatry, 154*, 1582–1588.

Salzer, M. S., & Bickman, L. (1999). The short- and long-term psychological impact of disasters: Implications for mental health interventions and policy. In R. Gist & B. Lubin (Eds.), *Response to disaster: Psychosocial, community, and ecological approaches* (pp. 63–82). Philadelphia: Brunner/Mazel.

Saylor, C. F., Swenson, C. C., Reynolds, S. S., & Taylor, M. (1999). The Pediatric Emotional Distress Scale: A brief screening measure for young children exposed to traumatic events. *Journal of Clinical Child Psychology, 28*, 70–81.

Selye, H. (1946). The general adaptation syndrome and the diseases of adaptation. *Journal of Clinical Endocrinology, 6*, 117–196.

Shannon, M. P., Lonigan, C. J., Finch, A. J., & Taylor, C. M. (1994). Children exposed to disaster: I. Epidemiology of post-traumatic symptoms and symptom profiles. *Journal of the American Academy of Child and Adolescent Psychiatry, 33,* 80–93.

Silverman, W. K., & Ginsburg, G. S. (1995). Specific phobia and generalized anxiety disorder. In J. S. March (Ed.), *Anxiety disorders in children and adolescents* (pp. 276–300). NY: Guilford Press.

Singer, M. I., Anglin, T., Song, L., & Lunghofer, L. (1995). Adolescents' exposure to violence and associated symptoms of psychological trauma. *Journal of the American Medical Association, 273,* 477–482.

Staab, J. P., Fullerton, C. S., & Ursano, R. J. (1999). A critical look at PTSD: Constructs, concepts, epidemiology, and implications. In R. Gist & B. Lubin (Eds.), *Response to disaster: Psychosocial, community, and ecological approaches* (pp. 101–132). Philadelphia: Brunner/Mazel.

Swenson, C. C., Saylor, C. F., Powell, M. P., Stokes, S. J., Foster, K. Y., & Belter, R. W. (1996). Impact of a natural disaster on preschool children: Adjustment 14 months after a hurricane. *American Journal of Orthopsychiatry, 66,* 122–130.

Valent, P. (2000). Disaster syndrome. In G. Fink (Ed.), *Encyclopedia of stress* (Vol. 1, pp. 706–709). San Diego, CA: Academic Press.

Vernberg, E. M. (1999). Children's responses to disaster: Family and systems approaches. In R. Gist & B. Lubin (Eds.), *Response to disaster: Psychosocial, community, and ecological approaches* (pp. 193–210). Philadelphia: Brunner/Mazel.

Vernberg, E. M., La Greca, A. M., Silverman, W. K., & Prinstein, M. J. (1996). Predictors of children's post-disaster functioning following Hurricane Andrew. *Journal of Abnormal Psychology, 105,* 237–248.

Vernberg, E. M., & Varela, R. E. (2001). Posttraumatic stress disorder: A developmental perspective. In M. W. Vasey & M. R. Dadds (Eds.), *The developmental psychopathology of anxiety* (pp. 386–406). New York: Oxford University Press.

Vincent, N. R. (1997). *A follow-up to Hurricane Andrew: Children's reactions 42 months post-disaster.* Unpublished doctoral dissertation, University of Miami.

Vincent, N. R., La Greca, A. M., Silverman, W. K., Wasserstein, S. B., & Prinstein, M. J. (1994). *Predicting children's responses to natural disasters: Role of academic achievement.* Paper presented at the annual meeting of the American Psychological Association, Los Angeles, August.

Vogel, J. M., & Vernberg, E. M. (1993). Children's psychological responses to disaster. *Journal of Clinical Child Psychology, 22,* 464–484.

Yates, S., Axsom, D., & Tiedman, K. (1999). The help-seeking process for distress after disasters. In R. Grist, & B. Lubin (Eds.), *Response to disaster: Psychosocial, community, and ecological approaches* (pp. 133–155). Philadelphia, PA: Brunner-Mazel.

Yule, W. (1994). Posttraumatic stress disorder. In T. H. Ollendick, N. J. King, & W. Yule (Eds.), *International handbook of phobic and anxiety disorders in children and adolescents* (pp. 223–240). New York: Plenum Press.

2

ASSESSMENT OF CHILDREN AND ADOLESCENTS EXPOSED TO DISASTER

CONWAY SAYLOR AND VIRGINIA DEROMA

The past decade has seen tremendous progress in the understanding, identification, evaluation, and treatment of youngsters recovering from disasters. In spite of enhanced efforts to train mental health personnel for postdisaster assessment and intervention in the "predisaster" stage (i.e., before a disaster occurs; Saylor, Belter, & Stokes, 1997; Vernberg & Vogel, 1993), many of the professionals who find themselves working with disaster victims do so because natural or human-made disasters strike literally close to home, thrusting them into the role of "instant experts" (Rozensky, Sloan, Schwartz, & Kowalski, 1993). Although some of the assessment methods for screening and evaluating children and adolescents in traditional mental health settings have been used with children exposed to disaster, recent disaster literature suggests that different approaches, which target specific dimensions of stress (including the properties of the stressor itself as well as the child's and family's perceptions of it), coping, and behavioral and emotional reactions, may be more useful in the postdisaster environment.

Many good summaries have been written of the clinical and research progress to date in the area of children and disasters (e.g., Saylor, 1993; Vernberg & Vogel, 1993; Vogel & Vernberg, 1993). Authors also have done a thorough job of introducing basic principles of good assessment, such as the use of data from multiple sources and the selection of instruments with good reliability, validity, and relevant normative data (e.g., Finch & Daugherty, 1993). This chapter provides an update on the conceptual and practical issues that have emerged in the past decade in the area of assessment and puts forth recommendations about the development of improved assessment methods.

PURPOSE OF ASSESSMENT

The first step in the selection of proper assessment methods is to consider thoroughly the immediate and long-term goals of assessment. Is the role of the evaluator strictly clinical, or might the data be used for research purposes? The disaster literature certainly benefits each time it is ethically feasible for clinicians to collect and disseminate useful descriptions of their observations and experiences in a disaster environment. Special attention should be paid to the psychometric properties of instruments selected when descriptions of the children and families affected by a disaster may later be reported in the research literature. Reliable and valid measures, of course, as well as those that might allow cross-cultural, cross-study, or cross-disaster comparisons might be especially valuable.

The second consideration is the need for longitudinal follow up. Compelling evidence indicates that the response to disaster may be long term (e.g., Swenson, Powell, Foster, & Saylor, 1991; Terr, 1990) and may evolve in stages (Vogel & Vernberg, 1993). In selecting assessment instruments, it is important to attend to the development, test–retest reliability, and previous uses of the instrument, so that an empirical context is available for the interpretation of change (or lack thereof) in the scores of respondents over time.

Third, is the task of the evaluator one of intensive individual evaluation or screening? Neither the clinician nor the stressed families whose children are to be assessed have the resources to tolerate long assessment protocols until a clear need is demonstrated. In schools (Nader & Pynoos, 1993), pediatric practices (American Academy of Pediatrics, 1995), and community interventions (Scott, 1994) for children exposed to disaster, it may be desirable to use brief screening instruments, such as the Pediatric Emotional Distress Scale (PEDS; Saylor, Swenson, Reynolds, & Taylor, 1999) or the Reaction Index (Frederick, 1985). Shannon, Lonigan, Finch, and Taylor (1994) used a brief screening protocol to screen thousands of children and adolescents in the public school system of a hurricane-exposed county. Children who showed high risk for posttraumatic stress disorder (PTSD) were subsequently interviewed by a trained psychiatrist using an in-depth diagnostic interview. This model not only efficiently identified those most needing clinical support but also allowed for a fruitful database that subsequently contributed greatly to our knowledge of "normative" reactions in a culturally diverse sample.

Fourth, is the planned assessment likely to be used for forensic purposes? It is increasingly important for evaluators to clarify and contract explicitly with families about the planned and ethically possible uses of the assessment data. In technology-related and human-made disasters, in which someone may be to blame or may be held liable for the disaster, it is increasingly likely that future litigation will be initiated. Assessment of emotional damage for civil liability requires special expertise, including knowledge of relevant case law, state statutes, and limits of confidentiality. Even if no litigation is pending, it is possible that victims eventually may be compensated proportionately to their suffering. Our own recent research on the validity of parental report of child development in the context of social security income evaluations suggests that the prospect of potential financial gains associated with a certain outcome can drastically alter the validity of reporting (Coker, Saylor, Saylor, & King, 2000; King, Saylor, Saylor, Coker, & Lassiter, 2000).

Fifth, is the purpose of the assessment to diagnose PTSD or to look for other, subclinical levels of behaviors in children that may be problematic for families? Saylor et al. (1997) noted that both symptoms of PTSD and subclinical levels of other behaviors have been reported by those working with children after a disaster. The clinician's approach to assessment must be tightly focused and rigorous if the object is PTSD diagnosis. If other behavior clusters are being assessed or if subclinical symptoms of PTSD are being measured and reported, it is crucial to be precise in reporting one's data (whether in individual assessment reports or research reports of broad samples) so that elevations on a measure that screens for PTSD symptoms are not construed to be evidence of a disorder not yet properly diagnosed. One of the difficulties in reading and applying some of the earlier literature in disasters is a lack of precision about the constructs assessed and the meaning of elevated scores.

EXPANDING THE FOCUS OF ASSESSMENT: STRESS, COPING, AND PTSD SYMPTOMS

In the past decade, three areas have consistently emerged as crucial components of children's responses to disaster. The first and most obvious has always been the child's behavior and emotion. The latter is indicated by self-report and play, and the former is reported by teachers, parents and, in some cases, the young people themselves. The body of literature on children and disasters indicates that the public and private manifestations of PTSD symptoms most often are the target of assessment (e.g., Green, Korol, & Gleser, 1999; Jurgens, Houlihan, & Schwartz, 1996; Najarian, Goenjian, Pelcovitz, Mandel, & Najarian, 1996; Shannon et al., 1994; Shaw, 1997). Recently, documentation of the role of stress and coping has led to an increase in direct assessment of the two areas. This chapter focuses on assessment of stress and coping in postdisaster evaluation of children. The next sections present conceptual and practical developments in the assessment of stress, coping, and PTSD symptoms.

Severity of Stressors

The stress properties of a natural disaster can range from loss of daily routine to displacement and loss of home and life. In an attempt to typify the stress experienced across disasters, Azarian and Skriptchenko-Gregorian (1998) classified stressors common to the experience of disaster into four categories: psychophysiological, informational, emotional, and social. Although assessment of the universality of disaster stressors aids conceptualization, Saylor et al. (1997) noted that disasters have different stressor characteristics and vary on important qualitative dimensions (e.g., rapidity of onset and controllability). Recognizing this pattern, researchers developed scales that move beyond communal assessment of stressor severity that is based on threat or loss imposed by the disaster to assess respondents' context-specific relationship with or experience of stressor severity. This approach has spawned the development of instruments that assess demands in the context of earthquakes (e.g., the Earthquake Impact Survey; Carr et al., 1995), fires (e.g., the Fire Questionnaire; Jones, Ribbe, & Cunningham, 1994), and hurricanes (Anthony, Lonigan, & Hecht, 1999; Cheever & Hardin, 1999; La Greca, Silverman, Vernberg, & Prinstein, 1996; Shaw, 1997). As shown in Table 2.1, most measures reviewed are based on parent ratings of disaster stressors, and few are designed for child or adolescent report.

Coping

It is essential for potential interventionists to identify and understand children's efforts to self-protect. Until the past decade, assessment of self-protection through coping was conceptually centered mainly on Folkman and Lazarus' (1985) identified patterns of coping. Recently cited assessments of styles of coping used to master disaster stressors reflect a primary reliance on Kidcope (Spirito, Stark, & Williams, 1988) and examine coping in a single time frame. Given that patterns of coping are inherently related to developmental level (Compas & Epping, 1993), distinguishing between different subtypes of coping in disasters seems particularly important for child populations, given that stress associated with the disaster may provoke developmental setbacks for youth. In light of the association between specific coping strategies and particular disorders (e.g., wishful thinking and self-blame tend to be associated with affective disorders; Spurrell & McFarlane, 1993),

TABLE 2.1
Measures Used in Child Disaster Research

Instrument	Age Cited	Method	No. Items	Recent Citations
Exposure Instruments				
Earthquake Impact Survey	Parent	Self-report	NR	Carr et al. (1995)
Rating of Damage	Parent	Interview	1	Chemtob, Tomas, Law, & Cremniter (1997)
Perceived Disruption During Rebuilding Inventory	Parent	Interview	16	Burnett et al. (1997)
Stress Response Questionnaire	Parent	Self-report	4	Faupel & Styles (1993)
Stress Scale	Parent	Self-report	27	Norris & Uhl (1993)
Hurricane Exposure Instrument	Child 6–11 years	Self-report	17	Shaw (1997)
Trauma Severity Scale	Child 13–48 months	Observation	NR	Azarian, Miller, & Skriptchenko-Gregorian (1996)
Hurricane Related Traumatic Experiences	Child 9–15 years	Self-report	26	La Greca, Silverman, Vernberg, & Prinstein (1996); Vernberg, La Greca, Silverman, & Prinstein (1996)
Child Fernald Mental Experience Questionnaire	Child 7–15 years	Self-report	13	Green, Korol, & Gleser (1999)
Fire Questionnaire—Child	Child 7–18 years	Self-report Observation	NR	Jones, Ribbe, & Cunningham (1994)
Total Exposure to Hurricane Hugo Scale	Child 13–18 years	NR	5	Hardin, Weinrich, Weinrich, Hardin, & Garrison (1994)
Personal Loss Scale	Child 13 years	Interview	1	Milgram & Toubiana (1996)
Measure of Disaster Stress	Parent	Interview Observation	1	Kaniasty & Norris (1993)
Hurricane Exposure Measure	Child 9–19 years	Self-report Observation	NR	Anthony, Lonigan, & Hecht (1999)
A Lifestyle Disruption Measure	Child 13–17 years	Self-report	5	Cheever & Hardin (1999)

Table Continues

TABLE 2.1
(Continued)

Instrument	Age Cited	Method	No. Items	Recent Citations
Hurricane Related Experiences Questionnaire	Parents	Self-report	NR	Swenson et al. (1996)
Coping Instruments				
Interview: What is it Like to be a Parent? About the Future Scale	Parent Child 12–18 years	Interview Self-report	1 16	Coffman (1996) Jurgens, Houlihan, & Schwartz (1996)
Child Fernald Mental Experience	Child 7–15 years	Interview	12	Green, Korol, & Gleser (1999)
Structured Interview to Assess Types of Thinking About Disasters	Child 8–9 years; 15–16 years	Interview	298	Terr et al. (1997)
Life Orientation Scale (Optimism)	Child 15–17 years	Self-report	6	Zeidner (1993)
Perceived Benefit Scales	Adults	Self-report	40	McMillen, Smith, & Fisher (1997)
Evaluation of Cognitive Heuristics	Child 15–20 years	Self-report	60	Greening, Dollinger, & Pitz (1996)
Earthquake-Related Cognitions Questionnaire	Child 13–18 years	Self-report	5	Rustemli & Karanci (1996)
Kidcope	Child 8–18 years	Self-report	10–15	Jeney-Gamon, Daugherty, Finch, Belter, & Foster (1993)
Coping Resources Inventory–Hebrew version	Child 15–17 years	Self-report	60	Zeidner (1993)
Modified version of COPE scale	Child 15–17 years	Self-report	28	Zeidner (1993)
Social Support Scale–Modified Version	Child 13–18 years	Self-report	15	Hardin, Weinrich, Weinrich, Hardin, & Garrison (1994)

Instrument	Sample	Method	n	Citation
Confronting Behavior and Support Persons Questionnaire	Child 13 years	Self-report	11	Milgram & Toubiana (1996)
Social Support Scale for Children and Adolescents	Child 8–18 years	Self-report	24	La Greca et al. (1996) Vernberg, La Greca, Silverman, & Prinstein (1996)
Children's Coping Assistance Checklist	Child 9–15 years	Self-report	27	Prinstein, La Greca, Vernberg, & Silverman (1996)
Coppel's Index of Social Support	Child 13–17 years	Self-report	10	Cheever & Hardin (1999)
Posttraumatic Stress Instruments				
Posttraumatic Stress Disorder Research Inventory	Child 6–11 years	Interview	15	Shaw (1997)
Pynoos PTSD Reaction Index	Child 7–13 years	Interview	20	Shaw, Applegate, & Schorr (1996)
Pediatric Emotional Distress Scale	Child 3–12 years	Parent report	17–21	Stokes, Saylor, Swenson, & Daugherty (1995)
Clinician Administered PTSD Scale—Child/Adolescent Version	Child 8–18 years	Interview	NR	No citations found in the disaster literature
Story Telling Through Art	Child 4–11 years	Projective	NR	Roje (1996)
Anticipatory Stress Index	Child 16–18 years	Interview	30	Kiser et al. (1993)
Children's PTSD Inventory	Child 12–18 years	Interview	NR	Jurgens, Houlihan, & Schwartz (1996)
Parent PTSD Reaction Index	Child 7–15 years	Self-report	20	Green, Korol, & Gleser (1999)

Table Continues

TABLE 2.1
(Continued)

Instrument	Age Cited	Method	No. Items	Recent Citations
Frederick Reaction Index	Child under 12 years	Self-report	20	La Greca, Silverman, & Wasserstein (1998)
				Wasserstein & La Greca (1998)
Modified Version of Frederick Reaction Index	Child 9–19 years	Self-report	20	Lonigan, Anthony, & Shannon (1998)
Acute Stress Reactions Scale	Child 13 years	Self-report	13	Milgram & Toubiana (1996)
PTSD Section of the DICA-R	Child 11–13 years	Interview	NR	Najarian, Goenjian, Pelcovitz, Mandel, & Najarian (1996)
A PTSD Index	Child 6–11 years	NR	NR	Breton, Valla, & Lambert (1993)

Note. NR = not reported.

knowledge of a child's predominant coping styles might also cue a broad assessment to screen for symptoms of the associated disorder. Assessment of coping strategies also allows clinicians an opportunity to involve a child in determining how coping behavior functions and to invite the child to modify coping behaviors or develop a wider repertoire of coping responses.

Stress appraisal is a critical assessment target for children, given that different stages of development can significantly affect the meaning that a child attaches to stress. Cited measures of appraisal related to thoughts of a secure future include assessment of beliefs and worries about future disasters (Earthquake-Related Cognitions Questionnaire; Rustemli & Karanci, 1996), optimism (Optimism Life Orientation Test; Zeidner, 1993), and future orientation (About the Future Scale; Jurgens et al., 1996). Data from those measures can provide valuable information on covert verbalization antecedents that precipitate arousal, distress, or negative affect, which in turn lead to emotion-focused coping efforts. Assessment of types of thinking, as noted in Terr's use of structured interviews (e.g., Terr et al., 1997), also affords clinicians the opportunity to examine and intervene with judgments when overgeneralization or self-blame are detected.

Interaction with others (i.e., social support) is a critical process in developing coping skills of children, who are learning how to understand, interpret, and react to stress beyond one's control. Children who witness and survive disasters need to talk about their experiences and to have access to others who are emotionally and behaviorally supportive. The importance of social support is acknowledged in the research that presents measures of social support with this population. Recently developed social support measures capture specific types of support important to a child, including a sense of belonging (Modified Version of Coppel's Social Support Scale; Cheever & Hardin, 1999); activities participated in (Confronting Behavior and Support Persons Questionnaire; Milgram & Toubiana, 1996); and perceived support from school contacts, a potentially significant arena of interpersonal daily contact. A summary of recently cited measures of coping appraisal, strategy, and assistance (i.e., social support) is provided in Table 2.1.

Posttraumatic Stress Symptoms

How a traumatic event is interpreted and how the victim is supported are acknowledged as etiological influences of posttraumatic reactions, which typically have been assessed through documenting the frequency and severity of PTSD diagnostic symptoms. The measures selected for use in recent studies (summarized in Table 2.1) reflect an increasing focus on child self-report of PTSD, with less emphasis on parent-completed measures. This trend may have begun as a result of data indicating parents' tendency to underestimate PTSD symptomatology for children (McNally, 1998; Saylor et al., 1997). The task of assessing the extent to which reactions to the trauma might be overwhelming (i.e., hyperarousal) may be hampered by a child's skillful avoidance of recalling the traumatic event when a direct approach to assessment is used. Indirect methods of assessment of a child's representation of trauma through play, art, and verbalizations (i.e., storytelling through art assessment; Roje, 1996) have been successfully used as projective mediums of assessment.

MULTIMETHOD AND MULTISOURCE ASSESSMENT

In assessment, development of hypotheses about diagnosis and treatment targets is enhanced with consideration of data from multiple sources. Earls, Smith, Reich, and Jung (1988) examined the effects of disaster on children through parallel interviewing with three independent sources (child, teacher, and parent); their research presents a monomethod approach with a rich source of informants. Although each independent source used in assessment might provide an individual view of the youth's functioning in different settings, the people likely to provide any information on a youth are often survivors themselves attempting to deal with the emotional tolls of the trauma. Therefore, clinicians are sometimes governed by the ethical or practical limits of taxing the minimal number of sources through assessment.

The self-report of a child exposed to disaster is the most objective, direct source of information on symptoms of a private nature, such as coping efforts and PTSD symptoms (e.g., reexperiencing and arousal) following disaster (Finch & Daugherty, 1993). This reliance on the child as a priority source of assessment is reinforced by data indicating that indirect informants often underestimate the severity of youth disturbances (Azarian & Skriptchenko-Gregorian, 1998). When limitations in insight, objectivity, affect expression, comprehension, or language skills are present, however, clinicians may elect to rely on secondary sources. In this event, the secondary source of choice should not automatically default to a parent but instead should be identified on the basis of the opportunity and capacity to observe the youth in the setting most likely to evoke memories of or reactions to the trauma (Mash & Terdal, 1997).

Selection of assessment methods (e.g., interview, rating scales, nomination scales, behavioral observation, projective tests) is necessarily based on purpose, practicality, and population size. Finch and Daugherty (1993) have forwarded a cost–benefit analysis framework as a basis for method selection in assessment of disaster-exposed child populations. Although some studies have explored the use of a battery of methods, the motive for including more than one method has not been clear. Because information is being gathered for the purpose of making decisions, the identification of appropriate methods should be determined foremost by the decision-making purposes of the assessment (Mash & Terdal, 1997). For example, information needed for purposes of screening might best be gathered through rating scales, which can be administered quickly and with minimal clinician demand. If problems are detected in screening, a structured interview's sensitivity and specificity are well-suited for diagnostic purposes and ideographic treatment planning. Problems detected during the interview might be followed up using direct observation for baseline and postintervention assessment, which places the greatest resource demand on clinician and client.

Researchers who have structured multimethod disaster assessment studies to include interviews typically have used small sample sizes to afford themselves the opportunity for evaluation by a trained assessor. Both Najarian et al. (1996) and Jones et al. (1994), for example, used sample sizes of 25 or fewer youth when using structured interviews with questionnaires to assess the impact of disaster. Jurgens et al. (1996) also relied on a smaller sample size when using an ambitious multimethod (rating scales, interview), multi-source (teacher, parent, child) approach. Only a few studies using a multimethod approach have used large sample sizes. Korol, Green, and Gleser (1999) used a multimethod, multisource approach to examine the effects of a nuclear waste disaster on a sample of 120 children. The many studies that limit assessment to single method to evaluate sample sizes of more than 500 children (Milgram & Toubiana, 1996; Prinstein, La Greca, Vernberg, & Silverman, 1996; Shannon et al., 1994; Sullivan, Saylor, & Foster, 1991) do contribute to the much-needed development of normative and psychometric data.

FUTURE DIRECTIONS

The field of disaster assessment has been strengthened considerably by the development of instruments to define disaster-specific stressors and reactions. Unfortunately, the unpredictable nature of the stressor and the populations affected by it have presented obstacles in designing studies with pretest–posttest data, victim comparison groups, and replication (Baum et al., 1993). As challenging as it might be, professionals who are responsible for large numbers of children in schools, community mental health care systems, day care or Head Start programs, or pediatric practices would leave their children and family in a much better position for postdisaster screening and intervention if they would routinely screen for baseline rates of key behaviors at least annually, in the predisaster phase. The absence of predisaster comparison data is a major obstacle in interpreting assessment results after a disaster.

At a national and, perhaps, even international level, consensus on a model of assessment and specific assessment instruments will be needed to permit comparisons of findings across studies. Use of standardized assessment instruments also will provide a basis for evaluation of the soundness of psychometrics for measures on which those findings are built. Models such as those of La Greca, Silverman, and Wasserstein (1998), which propose the integration of the exposure, coping, and PTSD concepts highlighted in this chapter, may provide a framework for launching the collaborative efforts of instrument consensus. The unprecedented spirit of collaboration among investigators in disaster research suggests that professionals in this field are well-poised to accomplish this task.

Rapid and economical access to assessment instruments is a third crucial issue in assessment. Computer technology of the 21st century has advanced the accessibility and dissemination of postdisaster assessment instrumentation. Many of the measures featured in this chapter can be accessed through e-mail to the author or through Web sites that allow the reader to download measures without cost. The National Center for PTSD features a Web site, *Pilots Database Authority List* (http://www.ncptsd.org/treatment/ assessment/instruments_pilots.html), which highlights more than 350 of the measures designed for use with child and adult trauma populations. Development of a centralized bank of assessment measures for disaster-specific instruments would certainly advance the next phase of collaborative assessment endeavors. To accompany this central repository of assessment measures, authors might consider embedding tracking systems that structure follow ups on use of the measure or response modules in the Web sites that invite consumer communication of findings. Contact information for authors or publishers of instruments reviewed in this paper is presented in Table 2.2.

Many of the measures featured in the PTSD section of this chapter (e.g., Frederick's PTSD Reaction Index; Saigh's Children's PTSD inventory; Saigh et al., 2000) have been revised so that symptoms are consistent with criteria of the *Diagnostic and Statistical Manual of Mental Disorders, Fourth Edition* (DSM–IV; American Psychiatric Association, 1994). Few studies, however, have consistently incorporated the DSM–IV's concept of functional impairment into assessment. Research documenting how clinical symptom presentation affects important everyday experiences, such as academic (La Greca et al., 1998; Shannon et al., 1994) and peer functioning, should be explored further.

In the spirit of this decade of adaptation, revisions also should focus on piloting measures to clarify the age appropriateness of instructional sets and rating stimuli. Saigh's research investigating the development of stimuli that aid in children's comprehension (e.g., rewording of items), as in the development of the Children's PTSD Inventory, has been noted as precedent-setting (McNally, 1998).

Finally, most studies of large-scale disasters have used English-speaking, nondiagnosed participants. When disaster strikes a school or community, little is known about how to properly assess the needs of children in special education and the children whose primary language or culture may be different from those of the children in previously cited research. Adaptation

TABLE 2.2
List of Contacts for Disaster-Related Measures

Instrument	Contact	Address
Exposure Instruments		
A Stress Response Questionnaire	Charles Faupe	lfaupece@mail.auburn.edu
Perceived Disruption During Rebuilding Inventory	Kent Burnett	Kburnett@miami.edu
Hurricane Related Experiences Questionnaire	Cynthia Swenson	swensonc@musc.edu
A Stress Scale	Fran H. Norris	Fnorris@gsu.edu
An Exposure Experiences Questionnaire	Christopher Lonigan	Lonigan@psy.FSU.edu
Fernald Mental Experiences Questionnaire— Child	Bonnie Green	Bgreen01@georgetown.edu
Fire Questionnaire— Child Form	Russell T. Jones	R.T.Jones@vt.edu
Hurricane Related Experiences Questionnaire	Eric Vernburg	Vernberg@Ukans.edu
A Measure of Disaster Stress	Nuray Kaniasty	Kaniasty@Grove.IUP.edu
Personal Loss Scale	Norman Milgram	Fax: 011-972-3640-6722
Coping Instruments		
Structured Interview to Assess Thinking About Disaster	Lenore Terr	Jmusgrov@slip.net
About the Future Scale	P. A. Saigh	Psaigh@GC.CUNY.edu
Optimism Life Orientation Test–Revised	Charles Carver	ccarver@miami.edu
The Perceived Benefits Scale	Curtic McMillen	Cmcmille@gwbssw.wvustl.edu
Evaluation of Cognitive Heuristics	L. Greening	Legreeni@gp.as.ua.edu
Earthquake Related Cognitions Questionnaire	A. Nuray Karranci	Karanci@metu.edu.tr
Modified Version of COPE Scale	Charles Carver	ccarver@miami.edu
Kidcope	Anthony Spirito	Anthony_Spirito@Brown.edu
Coping Resources Inventory		www.cpp-db.com
Coppel's Index of Social Support	Coppel	Dbcphd@aol.com

Table Continues

TABLE 2.2
(*Continued*)

Instrument	Contact	Address
Social Support Scale for Children and Adolescents	Susan Harter	Sharter@nova.psy.Den.edu
Modified Children's Coping Assistance Checklist	Mitchell Prinstein	Mitchell.Prinstein@yale.edu
Confronting Behavior and Support Persons Questionnaire	Norman Milgram	Fax: 011-972-3640-6722
Posttraumatic Stress Disorder (PTSD) Instruments		
Posttraumatic Stress Disorder	R. Pynoos	Rpynoos@mednet.UCLA.edu
Pynoos PTSD Reaction Index	R. Pynoos	Rpynoos@mednet.UCLA.edu
Children's PTSD Inventory	P. A. Saigh	Psaigh@GC.CUNY.edu
Clinician Administered PTSD Scale—Child and Adolescent Versions		www.ncptsd.org
Pediatric Emotional Distress Scale	Conway Saylor	Saylorc@citadel.edu
Parent PTSD Reaction Index	C. Frederick	Cfrede2301@aol.com
Modified Version of Frederick Reaction Index	C. Lonigan	Lonigan@psy.FSU.edu
Acute Stress Reactions Scale	Norman Milgram	Fax: 011-972-3640-6722
When Bad Things Happen	K. Fletcher	Kenneth.fletcher@banyan.ummed.edu

of promising instruments also should extend to accommodate assessment of children with special developmental and health care needs, whose limitations may complicate the identification of coping efforts and expression of trauma symptoms as typically measured. Mental health professionals also must continue to pioneer translation of measures for evaluation of non-English speaking children to encourage cross-cultural research with standardized measures of coping and PTSD. By way of example, our own development of the PEDS has recently focused on examination of the measure with children who have behavioral and developmental problems (McNair, Saylor, Macias, Spratt, & Kessler, 2000) and with children who are from various Spanish-speaking cultures. Collaboration among researchers who have direct access to special populations, especially those affected by disaster, will be crucial if psychological assessment is to be useful in the future for all children and adolescents.

CONCLUSIONS

The field of assessment of children and adolescents has progressed rapidly from a gross process of administering traditional mental health instruments to a focused, collaborative, and purposeful process of examining stress, coping, and behavioral reactions among this unique clinical population. Collaboration among mental health professionals before and after disasters will be crucial if instrumentation for use following disasters is ever to be raised to a level of standardization and applicability to all populations who might be exposed to disaster.

REFERENCES

American Academy of Pediatrics. (1995). *Psychosocial issues for children and families in disaster: A guide for the primary care physician.* Elk Village, IL: American Academy of Pediatrics Press.

American Psychiatric Association. (1994). *Diagnostic and statistical manual of mental disorders* (4th ed.). Washington, DC: Author.

Anthony, J. L., Lonigan, C. J., & Hecht, S. A. (1999). Dimensionality of posttraumatic stress disorder symptoms in children exposed to disaster: Results from confirmatory factor analysis. *Journal of Abnormal Psychology, 108,* 326–336.

Azarian. A., Miller, T. W., & Skriptchenko-Gregorian, V. (1996). Baseline assessment of children traumatized by the Armenian earthquake. *Child Psychiatry and Human Development, 27,* 29–41.

Azarian, A., & Skriptchenko-Gregorian, V. (1998). Traumatization and stress in child and adolescent victims of natural disaster. In T. W. Miller (Ed.), *Children of trauma* (pp. 77–118). Madison, CT: International Universities Press.

Baum, A., Solomon, S. D., Ursano, R. J., Bickman, L., Blanchard, E., Green, B. L., Keane, T. M., Laufer, R., Norris, F., Reid, J., Smith, E. M., & Steinglass, P. (1993). Emergency/disaster studies. In J. P. Wilson & B. Raphael (Eds.), *International handbook of traumatic stress syndromes* (pp. 201–212). New York: Plenum Press.

Breton, J. J., Valla, J. P., & Lambert, J. (1993). Industrial disaster and mental health of children and their parents. *Journal of the American Academy of Child and Adolescent Psychiatry, 32,* 438–445.

Burnett, K., Ironson, G., Benight, C., Wynings, C., Greenwood, D., Carver, C. S., Cruess, D., Baum, A., & Schneiderman, N. (1997). Measurement of perceived disruption during rebuilding following Hurricane Andrew. *Journal of Traumatic Stress, 10,* 673–681.

Carr, V. J., Lewin, T. J., Webster, R. A., Hazell, P. L., Kenardy, J. A., & Carter, G. L. (1995). Psychosocial sequelae of the 1989 Newcastle earthquake: I. Community disaster experiences and psychological morbidity 6 months post-disaster. *Psychological Medicine, 25,* 539–555.

Cheever, K. H., & Hardin, S. B. (1999). Effects of traumatic events, social support, and self-efficacy on adolescents' self-health assessment. *Western Journal of Nursing Research, 21,* 673–684.

Chemtob, C. M., Tomas, S., Law, W., & Cremniter, D. (1997). Postdisaster psychosocial intervention: A field study of the impact of debriefing on psychological distress. *American Journal of Psychiatry, 154,* 415–417.

Coffman, S. (1996). Parents' struggles to rebuild family life after Hurricane Andrew. *Issues in Mental Health Nursing, 17,* 353–367.

Coker, W., Saylor, C., Saylor, B., & King, B. (2000, March). *Parent report on the CDI: Questionable for SSI evaluations with preschoolers.* Paper presented at the Southeastern Psychological Association Meeting, New Orleans, LA.

Compas, B. E., & Epping, J. E. (1993). Stress and coping in children and families. In C. F. Saylor (Ed.), *Children and disasters* (pp. 11–28). New York: Plenum Press.

Earls, F., Smith, E., Reich, W., & Jung, K. G. (1988). Investigating psychopathological consequences of a disaster in children: A pilot study incorporating a structured diagnostic interview. *Journal of American Academy of Child and Adolescent Psychiatry, 27,* 90–95.

Faupel, C. E., & Styles, S. P. (1993). Disaster education, household preparedness, and stress responses following Hurricane Hugo. *Environment and Behavior, 25,* 229–249.

Finch, A. J., & Daugherty, T. K. (1993). Issues in the assessment of posttraumatic stress disorder in children. In C. F. Saylor (Ed.), *Children and disasters* (pp. 45–66). New York: Plenum Press.

Folkman, S., & Lazarus, K. S. (1985). If it changes it must be a process: A study of emotion and coping during three stages of a college examination. *Journal of Personality and Social Psychology, 48,* 150–170.

Frederick, C. J. (1985). Children traumatized by catastrophic situations. In S. Eth & R. S. Pynoos (Eds.), *Post-traumatic stress disorders in children* (pp. 73–99). Washington, DC: American Psychiatric Press.

Green, B. L., Korol, M., & Gleser, G. C. (1999). Children's responses to a nuclear waste disaster: PTSD symptoms and outcome prediction. *Journal of the American Academy of Child and Adolescent Psychiatry, 38,* 368–375.

Greening, L., Dollinger, S. J., & Pitz, G. (1996). Adolescents' perceived risk and personal experience with natural disasters: An evaluation of cognitive heuristics. *Acta Psychologia, 91,* 27–38.

Hardin, S. B., Weinrich, M., Weinrich, S., Hardin, T. L., & Garrison, C. (1994). Psychological distress of adolescents exposed to Hurricane Hugo. *Journal of Traumatic Stress, 7,* 427–440.

Jeney-Gamon, P., Daugherty, T. K., Finch, A. J., Belter, R. W., & Foster, K. Y. (1993). Children's coping styles and report of depressive symptoms following a natural disaster. *Journal of Genetic Psychology, 154,* 259–267.

Jones, R. T., Ribbe, D. P., & Cunningham, P. (1994). Psychosocial correlates of fire disaster among children and adolescents. *Journal of Traumatic Stress, 7,* 117–122.

Jurgens, J. J., Houlihan, D., & Schwartz, C. (1996). Behavioral manifestations of adolescent school relocation and trauma. *Child & Family Behavior Therapy, 18,* 1–8.

Kaniasty, K., & Norris, F. N. (1993). A test of social support deterioration model in the context of natural disaster. *Journal of Personality and Social Psychology, 64,* 395–408.

Kiser, L., Heston, J., Hickerson, S., Millsap, P., Nunn, W., & Pruitt, D. (1993). Anticipatory stress in children and adolescents. *American Journal of Psychiatry, 150,* 87–92.

King, B., Saylor, C., Saylor, B., Coker, W., & Lassiter, K. (2000). Parent report on the CDI: Valid for SSI evaluations with infants? Paper presented at the annual convention of the American Psychological Association, Washington, DC.

Korol, M., Green, B., & Gleser, G. C. (1999). Children's responses to a nuclear waste disaster: PTSD symptoms and outcome prediction. *Journal of the American Academy of Child and Adolescent Psychiatry, 38,* 368–375.

La Greca, A. M., Silverman, W. K., Vernberg, E. M., & Prinstein, M. J. (1996). Symptoms of posttraumatic stress in children after hurricane Andrew: A prospective study. *Journal of Consulting and Clinical Psychology, 64,* 712–723.

La Greca, A. M., Silverman, W. K., & Wasserstein, S. B. (1998). Children's predisaster functioning as a predictor of posttraumatic stress following Hurricane Andrew. *Journal of Consulting and Clinical Psychology, 66,* 883–892.

Lonigan, C. J., Anthony, J. L., & Shannon, M. P. (1998). Diagnostic efficacy of posttraumatic stress symptoms in children exposed to disaster. *Journal of Clinical Child Psychology, 27,* 255–267.

Mash, E. J., & Terdal, L. G. (1997). *Assessment of childhood disorders* (3rd ed.). New York: Guilford Press.

McMillen, J. C., Smith, E. M., & Fisher, R. H. (1997). Perceived benefit and mental health after three types of disaster. *Journal of Consulting and Clinical Psychology, 65,* 733–739.

McNair, A., Saylor, C., Macias, M., Spratt, E., & Kessler, M. (2000). Using the Pediatric Emotional Distress Scale for children with disabilities. Paper presented at the annual meeting of the Southeastern Psychological Association, New Orleans, LA.

McNally, R. J. (1998). Measures of children's reactions to stressful life events. In T. W. Miller (Ed.), *Children of trauma: Stressful life events and their effect on children* (pp. 29–42). Madison, CT: International Universities Press.

Milgram, N. N., & Toubiana, Y. H. (1996). Children's selective coping after a bus disaster: Confronting behavior and perceived support. *Journal of Traumatic Stress, 9,* 687–702.

Nader, K., & Pynoos, R. S. (1993). School disaster: Planning and initial interventions. *Journal of Social Behavior and Personality, 8,* 299–320.

Najarian, L. M., Goenjian, A. K., Pelcovitz, D., Mandel, F., & Najarian, B. (1996). Relocation after a disaster: Posttraumatic stress disorder in Armenia after the earthquake. *Journal of the American Academy of Child and Adolescent Psychiatry*, *35*, 374–383.

Norris, F. H., & Uhl, G. A. (1993). Chronic stress as a mediator of acute stress: The case of Hurricane Hugo. *Journal of Applied Social Psychology*, *23*, 1263–1284.

Prinstein, M. J., La Greca, A. M., Vernberg, E. M., & Silverman, W. K. (1996). Children's coping assistance: How parents, teachers, and friends help children cope after a natural disaster. *Journal of Clinical Child Psychology*, *25*, 463–475.

Roje, J. (1996). LA '94 earthquake in the eyes of children: Art therapy with elementary school children who were victims of disaster. *Art Therapy*, *12*, 237–243.

Rosser, R., Dewer, S., & Thompson, J. (1991). Psychological aftermath of the Kings Cross fire. *Journal of the Royal Society of Medicine*, *84*, 4–8.

Rozensky, R. H., Sloan, I. H., Schwartz, E. D., & Kowalski, J. M. (1993). Psychological response of children to shootings and hostage situations. In C. F. Saylor (Ed.), *Children and disasters* (pp. 123–135). New York: Plenum Press

Rustemli, A., & Karanci, A. N. (1996). Distress reactions and earthquake-related cognitions of parents and their adolescent children in a victimized population. *Journal of Social Behavior and Personality*, *11*, 767–780.

Saigh, P. A., Yaskik, A. E., Oberfield, R. A., Green, B. L., Halamandaris, P. V., & Rubenstein, H. (2000). The children's PTSD Inventory: Development and reliability. *Journal of Traumatic Stress*, *13(3)*, 369–380.

Saylor, C. F. (Ed.). (1993). *Children and disasters*. New York: Plenum Press.

Saylor, C. F., Belter, R., & Stokes, S. J. (1997). Children and families coping with disaster. In S. A. Wolchik & I. N. Sandler (Eds.), *Handbook of children's coping* (pp. 361–383). New York: Plenum Press.

Saylor, C. F., Swenson, C. C., Reynolds, S. S., & Taylor, M. (1999). The Pediatric Emotional Distress Scale: A brief screening measure for young children exposed to traumatic events. *Journal of Clinical Child Psychology*, *28*, 70–81.

Scott, R. (1994). Dealing with the aftermath of a crisis, trauma, and disaster: An overview of intervention strategies for children. *Children, Youth, and Family Quarterly*, *17(3)*, 6–9.

Shannon, M. P., Lonigan, C. J., Finch, A. J., & Taylor, C. M. (1994). Epidemiology of post-traumatic symptoms and symptom profiles. *Journal of the American Academy of Child and Adolescent Psychiatry*, *33*, 80–93.

Shaw, J. A. (1997). Children of the storm: A study of school children and Hurricane Andrew. In C. S. Fullerton & R. J. Ursano (Eds.), *Posttraumatic stress disorder* (pp. 123–143). Washington DC: American Psychiatric Press.

Shaw, J. A., Applegate, B., & Schorr, C. (1996). Twenty-one-month follow up study of school-age children exposed to Hurricane Andrew. *Journal of the American Academy of Child and Adolescent Psychiatry*, *35*, 359–364.

Spirito, A., Stark, L. J., & Williams, C. (1988). Development of a brief coping checklist for use with pediatric populations. *Journal of Pediatric Psychology*, *13*, 555–574.

Spurrell, M. T., & McFarlane, A. C. (1993). Post-traumatic stress disorder and coping after a natural disaster. *Social Psychiatry and Psychiatric Epidemiology*, *28*, 194–200.

Stokes, S. J., Saylor, C. F., Swenson, C. C., & Daugherty, T. K. (1995). A comparison of children's behaviors following three types of stressors. *Child Psychiatry and Human Development, 26,* 113–123.

Sullivan, M. A., Saylor, C. F., & Foster, K. Y. (1991). Post-hurricane adjustment of preschoolers and their families. *Advanced Behavior and Research Therapy, 13,* 163–171.

Swenson, C. C., Powell, M. P., Foster, K. Y., & Saylor, C. F. (1991, August). Long-term reactions of young children to natural disasters. Paper presented at the annual meeting of the American Psychological Association, San Francisco.

Swenson, C. C., Saylor, C. F., Powell, M. P., Stokes, S. J., Foster, K. Y., & Belter, R. W. (1996). Impact of a natural disaster on preschool children: Adjustment 14 months after a hurricane. *American Journal of Orthopsychiatry, 66,* 122–130.

Terr, L. C. (1990). *Too scared to cry.* New York: Harper & Row.

Terr, L. C., Bloch, D. A., Beat, A., Michel, B. A., Shi, H., Reinhardt, J. A., & Metayer, S. (1997). Children's thinking in the wake of the Challenger. *American Journal of Psychiatry, 154,* 744–751.

Vernberg, E. M., La Greca, A. M., Silverman, W. K., & Prinstein, M. J. (1996). Prediction of posttraumatic stress symptoms in children after Hurricane Andrew. *Journal of Abnormal Psychology, 105,* 237–248.

Vernberg, E. M., & Vogel, J. (1993). Task Force Report Part 2: Interventions with children after disasters. *Journal of Clinical Child Psychology, 22,* 464–484.

Vogel, J., & Vernberg, E. M. (1993). Task Force Report Part 1: Psychological needs of children in the aftermath of disasters: Children's psychological response to disaster. *Journal of Clinical Child Psychology, 22,* 464–484.

Wasserstein, S. B., & La Greca, A. M. (1998). Hurricane Andrew: Parent conflict as a moderator of children's adjustment. *Hispanic Journal of Behavioral Sciences, 20,* 212–224.

Zeidner, M. (1993). Coping with disaster: The case of Israeli adolescents under threat of missile attack. *Journal of Youth and Adolescence, 22,* 89–108.

3

INTERVENTION APPROACHES FOLLOWING DISASTERS

ERIC M. VERNBERG

Interventions addressing mental health needs of children and adolescents following disaster have become increasingly common as evidence has accumulated for the adverse effects of disasters on a range of psychological and behavioral indicators. Systematic evaluations of postdisaster interventions remain relatively rare, although increasingly strong research evidence guides those efforts. It seems clear that disasters, as defined in this volume, vary widely with regard to the type of traumatic exposure and psychological tasks presented by that exposure. Within a specific type of disaster (e.g., hurricane or terrorism), numerous individual, family, and contextual factors influence the impact of disasters on mental health outcomes (see chapter 1).

It is important to consider how efforts to help therapeutic interventions match the challenges posed by specific disaster events and take into consideration the many factors influencing the course of disaster-related psychological effects. Many children and adolescents experience natural but time-limited distress following harrowing disaster-related events, but others with similar levels of traumatic exposure develop long-lasting difficulties, including posttraumatic stress disorder (PTSD) symptoms, mood disturbances, and behavioral problems. As exposure becomes more extreme, as indexed by additional elements of traumatic exposure (Green, 1990), prolonged, intense, or repeated exposure; and life-changing events, such as bereavement and serious injuries, the likelihood of long-term repercussions requiring professional intervention increases. Adversity in the postdisaster recovery environment, such as economic hardship, family and community disruptions, and low access to social support, also increases the probability of deleterious mental health repercussions (Vernberg & Varela, 2001). Developmental issues, such as social cognitive factors, biological maturity, and self-regulatory capabilities, influence both reactions to trauma and the capacity to benefit from various intervention strategies (Pynoos, Steinberg, Ornitz, & Goenjian, 1997; Vernberg & Johnston, 2001). Cultural features are another important consideration in developing and delivering disaster-related intervention, because core beliefs related to emotional expression, healing, and mental health service utilization affect children and their families (see chapters 4 and 7).

The form and content of disaster interventions change over time. Phases of disaster exposure and recovery are difficult to categorize in absolute terms because of the great variability in duration, intensity, injury or loss of life, and scope of community devastation among the many forms of disastrous events. Several typologies for phases of recovery appear in the literature, and some categorize phases in terms of common psychological responses (e.g., honeymoon phase and disillusionment phase; National Institute of Mental Health [NIMH], 1990). Stage models that are based on psychological responses to disasters are subject to similar difficulties as models for responses to other negative life events (e.g., Kubler-Ross, 1969): Not everyone goes through all stages in the same order, and many people may not experience certain stages at all. Typologies defining disaster phases in chronological relation to the onset and cessation of disaster exposure avoid problems inherent in psychological stage models, but they become problematic when describing disasters that unfold over a long period of time (e.g., civil wars or certain hostage situations) or cause so much death, destruction, and ongoing upheaval that exposure to traumatic events remains high for many months (e.g., earthquakes, major hurricanes, and floods).

Recognizing those difficulties, this chapter uses a chronological system by first describing interventions that are offered while disasters are in progress (i.e., the *impact phase*) and in the immediate aftermath (i.e., the *recoil phase*; Valent, 2000; see also chapter 1), including initial assessment and reactions to loss, injury, and damage. *Preimpact-phase*, or disaster-preparation, interventions also are considered in this initial section, because preparatory actions set the stage for the impact and recoil phases. Interventions for the three phases focus primarily on prompting safety and coping skills and providing crisis management. Interventions appropriate for the first few weeks after the initial phases of disasters (i.e., the *postimpact*, or *short-term adaptation, phase*) focus on immediate physical and psychological needs. Brief, present-focused interventions, such as instrumental aid, information giving, and trauma interviews or debriefings, feature prominently in this phase. Difficulties persisting months or even years after the impact phase has ended are addressed in the *recovery and reconstruction phase*. Formal treatment for trauma-related symptoms, such as those comprising PTSD and mood disorders, become more prominent, along with interventions intended to lessen disaster-related adversity.

Postdisaster intervention approaches vary in terms of selectivity, intensity, and cost, and this overview further organizes intervention strategies for various disaster phases on this basis (Table 3.1). Low-cost protocols applied to the entire population address risk factors that affect large numbers of children: *Universal interventions* are intended to promote positive coping; provide a forum for addressing commonly occurring worries, concerns, and emotions; and strengthen the family, school, or community's ability to promote healthy postdisaster recovery environments for children and adolescents (e.g., La Greca, Vernberg, Silverman, Vogel, & Prinstein, 1994). Intensive, *selected interventions* are offered for children who show marked signs of disaster-related distress, such as moderate to severe levels of PTSD symptoms that interfere with academic performance or social behavior, but who otherwise do not have extensive comorbid disturbances (e.g., March, Amaya-Jackson, Murray, & Schulte, 1998; Storm, McDermott, & Finlayson, 1994; see chapter 6). The most intensive strategies are reserved for children and adolescents who have moderate to severe posttraumatic distress and multiple risk factors for poor mental health outcomes, such as high life adversity, exposure to catastrophic levels of trauma, or multiple comorbid conditions; those *indicated interventions* typically involve intensive interventions with the child, family, school, and community over an extended period of time.

INTERVENTIONS IN THE PREIMPACT, IMPACT, AND RECOIL PHASES

The degree of exposure to objective and subjective elements of trauma during disasters is clearly related to the emergence of disaster-related symptomatology. Preimpact-, impact-, and recoil-phase interventions attempt to limit children's exposure to trauma and to decrease negative psychological reactions to traumatic exposure that does occur. Interventions in these phases also may identify children, adolescents, or parents with acute reactions (e.g., extreme dissociation, acute suicidality, or homicidal rage) who need immediate protection or care. Interventions during and shortly after disasters may attempt to activate coping or behavior sequences thought to offer a measure of protection against the feelings of terror and helplessness associated with the later development of traumatic stress reactions.

TABLE 3.1
Universal, Selected, and Indicated Intervention Approaches for Children and Adolescents for Different Phases of Disaster
Level of Selectivity, Intensity, and Cost

Disaster Phase	Universal	Selected	Indicated
Preimpact, Impact, and Recoil	• Preparedness training. • Ongoing communications regarding safety, coping. • Factual information regarding disaster events.	• Psychological first aid, including support activation, debriefing, defusing, and crisis-reduction counseling.	• Full range of emergency interventions for acutely impaired individuals, with preference for least restrictive options and continued role performance.
Postimpact	• Efforts to promote continuity by helping to restore familiar roles and routines and providing context for exploring the meaning of disaster events. • Dissemination of accurate disaster-related information promptly and fully. • Written information on postdisaster psychological needs of children, adolescents, and families.	• Assessment and brief interventions for acute stress reactions among children and adolescents. • Psychological first aid.	• Intensive treatments for children at extremely high risk of developing chronic PTSD or other trauma-related disorder (identified on the basis of the nature of the trauma, life circumstances, adaptive functioning), addressing individual, family and contextual factors influencing symptom course.
Recovery and Reconstruction	• Education and information regarding children's mental health needs and resources for assistance. • Manualized school-based curricula pertaining to disaster, including psychoeducation, coping strategies, and continuity. • Rituals and memorials.	• Identify and treat children and adolescents with persistent trauma-related symptoms using time-limited, disaster-focused protocols. • Community outreach to severely affected families.	• Comprehensive, integrated interventions addressing multiple needs for children in families evidencing parental distress, social support depletion, financial strains, and continued exposure to trauma.

Universal Interventions

Attention to the mental health ramifications of media messages and communication networks during these crisis periods appears to be increasing, although research on the effects of various communication strategies on children is just beginning. Collaboration between research-oriented child mental health experts and media and telecommunication outlets may have considerable benefit for shaping the messages and services offered during and immediately after disasters.

Mass media and telecommunication resources, including broadcast, Internet, telephone, and print communications, can serve to promote safety, reduce uncertainty and fear, and prompt positive coping while disasters are occurring. Klingman (see chapter 15) describes media, Internet, and telephone systems activated during attacks on Israel to give behavioral guidance, anxiety-reduction suggestions, and information intended to promote physical safety. Much of this information had been provided to the general population in preparatory activities, and presenting the same messages during the impact and recoil phases appeared to prompt use of the strategies during the actual crisis period. This type of proactive media network requires considerable planning and preparation prior to the occurrence of a disaster, but it offers the tremendous potential benefit of providing well-conceived psychological strategies in addition to physical safety guidance during both disaster-preparation drills and crisis periods.

The impact and recoil phases of many disasters described in this volume occurred over a period of several hours, days, or even weeks. Unfortunately, there is no shortage of "instant experts" during and immediately after disasters, and distinguishing evidence-based advice from opinion can be difficult. The growing role of mental health services in disaster planning and response (e.g., the American Psychological Association Disaster Response Network) offers hope for the increasing use of empirically supported messages and services. At the same time, wide and repeated exposure in the media to graphic depictions of death and destruction during disasters appears to prompt more than transitory traumatic stress reactions in children, giving evidence of potential harm from certain media practices (see chapter 14).

Many issues related to preparations for disaster remain to be addressed from a scientific perspective. Preparation is a good thing if a disaster strikes, but it remains difficult to know much effort should be devoted to disaster drills or how preparatory activities may affect children and adolescents. In areas prone to certain types of recurrent disasters (e.g., tornadoes, floods, and fires), extensive preparation is readily justified; less clear is the cost–benefit balance for relatively unlikely disasters. For example, the recent spate of school shootings has led some schools to hold drills for "lockdowns" and to provide instruction in taking shelter or other techniques for avoiding attention during attacks (see chapter 13). Do preparations of that kind make children feel more secure and result in fewer injuries, or do they contribute to a climate in which such attacks are seen as likely? For all the publicity and understandable fear from the attacks, the likelihood of being involved in a lethal attack at school remains small.

Selected Interventions

Psychological first aid addresses the confusion, disorganization, and emotional numbness often experienced during and immediately after acute traumatic exposure. Interventions focus on the here and now, enhancing current functioning, and providing sufficient environmental support to prevent further injury. Psychological first aid is typically delivered individually or in small groups, and it may be delivered by a team with a division of duties or objectives, especially in instances involving death or severe injury. Following the bombing of the Alfred P. Murrah Federal Building in Oklahoma City, for example, families suffering a death were assigned a mental health professional to provide emotional and instrumental support while waiting to learn their loved one's fate, but they were officially notified of deaths in a meeting with a medical examiner, a representative of the clergy, and another mental health professional (American Psychological Association, 1997).

As outlined in American Red Cross training materials (American Red Cross, 1991), the following activities are appropriate for psychological first aid:

- Providing direct, instrumental assistance for problem solving and practical needs;
- Offering assistance in evaluating information and developing a plan for the immediate future;
- Activating social support systems, including family and community networks; and
- Providing factual information about the disaster and typical reactions of adults and children who have experienced similar circumstances.

Debriefing or *defusing* sessions with survivors of disasters offer a format to review the major elements of a traumatic experience soon after exposure. The goals of those sessions include emotional release, activation of social support and reduction of isolation, and provision of information on typical stress reactions and stress-management techniques. The sessions also provide an opportunity to screen for severe posttraumatic impairment, which may require further evaluation and treatment (American Red Cross, 1991). The effectiveness of debriefing for children and adolescents as a means of preventing future distress or reducing initial negative reactions to trauma remains to be demonstrated (see chapters 5 and 14). Concerns also have been raised about the widespread use of formal debriefing protocols (e.g., Critical Incident Stress Debriefing; Mitchell & Everly, 1993) with adults following trauma exposure, both because of scant scientific evidence for benefits from the procedures and potential iatrogenic effects related to "overhelping" or interference in normal coping responses (Gist & Woodall, 1999; Lohr, Montgomery, Lilienfeld, & Tolin, 1999).

Crisis reduction counseling is a brief intervention carried out with an individual or family to facilitate problem solving and decision making. This form of counseling focuses on assessing psychological states, normalizing thoughts and feelings, identifying and prioritizing current problems, and identifying sources of social support (American Red Cross, 1991). As with other forms of psychological first aid, discussion is strictly limited to the disaster and process of recovery.

Indicated Interventions

Intensive evaluations and interventions are indicated for people who experience such extreme emotional distress or psychological disturbance as to pose a threat to themselves or others (American Red Cross, 1991). For children and adolescents, severely impaired functioning of parents may represent a serious concern. Access to medications for serious health or mental disorders may be disrupted by disasters, with potentially dangerous repercussions. American Red Cross training materials indicate that the following conditions, among others, heighten concern:

- The presence of a preexisting serious mental disorder that is exacerbated by a disaster;
- Extremely impaired functioning, as evidenced by dissociative episodes, thought disturbances, extreme overarousal or mood lability, or inability to care for personal needs;
- Acute risk of harm to self or others, including suicidality, homicidal ideation, extreme substance abuse, or inappropriate anger or abuse of others; and
- Evidence of a life-threatening health condition (e.g., diabetes or heart problem) for which treatment has been disrupted.

When one or more of those conditions is met, the full range of emergency intervention options available may be considered. It is generally preferable to use the least restrictive option necessary to prevent acute threat of harm to self or others to allow the person to continue or resume functioning in important life roles as soon as possible (Vernberg & Vogel, 1993; see also chapter 15). This approach may be especially important if the acutely impaired person is a parent, because promoting continuity in that role is important for parents and children.

INTERVENTIONS IN THE POSTIMPACT PHASE

In most instances, the impact and recoil phases of disasters give way to a period in which the scope of damage and loss is recognized and relief efforts are mobilized in earnest. Temporary arrangements for food and shelter are made, and needs assessment becomes a focus for emergency management teams (NIMH, 1990). Normal roles and routines remain disrupted for many children and adolescents, and questions abound about what happened, for what reasons, and with what implications. Adults who suffer substantial resource loss often are distressed and preoccupied with their own reactions to disaster events (Freedy, Saladin, Kilpatrick, Resnick, & Saunders, 1994), and they may struggle as parents to cope with their children's psychological needs (Norris & Uhl, 1993). Child and adolescent mental health interventions during this phase often focus on crisis management and support for the family as a group, with attention to helping parents function as well as possible and providing structure and meaningful activities for youngsters (see chapter 15).

Universal Interventions

The resumption of familiar roles and routines as much and as soon as possible following disasters appears to be a useful strategy for reducing the intensity and duration of debilitating posttraumatic reactions (McFarlane, 1987; Prinstein, La Greca, Vernberg, & Silverman, 1996; Vernberg & Vogel, 1993). So important is this strategy that Omer and Alon (1994) proposed the *continuity principle* as a primary organizing scheme for decision making in the wake of trauma and disaster (see chapter 15). By this principle, disaster management and treatment should focus on preserving and restoring continuities at the individual, family, organization, and community levels. Continuity is conceptualized in three related domains: *functional* continuity, or the ability to cope and function despite disturbances; *historical* continuity, or feelings of coherence and sameness of self, family, and community over time; and *interpersonal* continuity, or the sense that relationships of significance in the past will continue to be important in the present and future.

The continuity principle argues for providing accurate information promptly and fully, trusting the coping capacity of the population, and providing guidelines for autonomous functioning by individuals and communities (Omer & Alon, 1994). In the context of children and adolescents, it is important to reopen schools and other institutions as rapidly as possible and involve children and adolescents in tasks that use their energies and abilities in meaningful ways. This is not to suggest that it is helpful to ignore or minimize the impact of disasters; instead, the goal is to provide a context for performing competently at an age-appropriate level, explore the meaning of disaster events, and construct a view of the disaster experience that allows trauma to be acknowledged without being an overwhelming, defining influence of self-perceptions and interpersonal relationships.

A number of sources provide "fact sheets" or other written information on the psychological needs of children and adolescents during the postimpact phase. Such child-focused materials range from general information on trauma reactions (e.g., Lazarus, 1996; Monahon, 1993) to reactions to specific categories of disasters (e.g., American Red Cross, 1992; Federal Emergency Management Agency [FEMA], 1989; National Organization for Victim Assistance, 1991; see chapters 5–7 for disaster-specific resources). Newspapers, television broadcasts, and other media also offer advice and information of this nature. Distribution of the materials may be quite idiosyncratic, as may be the source of information. To date, little research has been conducted on the usefulness of postimpact-phase distribution of information related to children's psychological reactions. Common sense, as well as the continuity principle, argues that well-conceived, factually accurate information should be made available as widely as possible. At the same time, it would be helpful to evaluate the scientific basis of information disseminated following disasters and to study how parents, teachers, and children interpret and use that information.

In the United States, disaster mental health has emerged as an area of specialized training and certifications and the capacity to deploy mental health professionals for children and adolescents soon after disasters has increased. Following recent school shootings at Santana High School in southern California, for example, 200 mental health counselors (one for each classroom) were present when the school reopened 2 days after the shooting; they offered interventions ranging from school assemblies to individual counseling (Krueger, 2001). The school also received a $51,700 grant from the U.S. Department of Education to provide counseling for students and staff members for 45 days after the shootings (Spielvogel, 2001). A next step in developing an empirically guided disaster response for the postimpact phase is to evaluate the utility of those interventions. On the one hand, current rapid-response interventions may reduce distress or prevent the emergence of long-term difficulties. On the other hand, some interventions could prove to be problematic in that they expose peers to troubling images, provoke inappropriate self-disclosure, or encourage diminished behavioral control. In addition, creating the belief that formal intervention from professionals is a necessary component for psychological health following a disaster may carry some risks.

Selected Interventions

Children known to have experienced substantial traumatic exposure may benefit from brief individual or small-group interventions. Assessment and treatment for acute stress reactions among children and adolescents may be offered during this period. Models for screening acute reactions have been described (e.g., Eth, 1992; Klingman, 1987), and systematic brief interventions developed with adults have been used with children and adolescents (e.g., debriefing). As noted earlier, evidence on the benefits and possible risks of psychological interventions soon after trauma exposure remains limited, and acute stress reactions decline over time in many instances.

Indicated Interventions

Research increasingly documents individual, family, and contextual factors related to spontaneous or naturally occurring symptom resolution, on the one hand, and chronic trauma-related symptoms, on the other (chapter 1). To summarize briefly, chronic PTSD or other trauma-related disorders are more likely to occur under the following conditions:

- Traumatic exposure is extensive and terrifying.
- The trauma includes death or serious injury to a loved one.
- The child manifests high levels of symptomatology soon after exposure.
- The child has preexisting difficulties with emotion regulation or anxiety.
- Family functioning in the postdisaster period is markedly compromised in terms of social support and protective functions.
- Dislocation, adversity, and disruption of familiar roles and routines continues for many months (Vernberg & Varela, 2001; see also chapters 5, 13, and 14).

When all of those risk factors are present (or seem likely to develop) and acute stress symptoms are evident, psychosocial interventions may be warranted soon after traumatic exposure. Ideally, interventions for children and adolescents who meet the criteria for intensive treatments should address individual, family, and contextual factors influencing symptom course (Vernberg & Johnston, 2001).

In addition to multiple-risk scenarios, children or adolescents who experience prolonged, extreme episodes of life-threatening acts of terror, such as the kidnapping and interment of a busload of school children in Chowchilla, California, have been shown to produce longstanding symptoms of PTSD in most survivors (Terr, 1983). It is reasonable to believe that initiating intervention during the postimpact phase would be helpful with youngsters whose trauma exposure reaches catastrophic levels. The child trauma interview described by Pynoos and Eth (1986), in which the child is helped to express his or her understanding of the traumatic episode, offers one option for beginning intervention soon after trauma. In addition to perhaps facilitating the development of a long-term helping relationship, early interventions may offer an opportunity to explore and shape trauma reactions and coping responses before denial, minimization, or other barriers to intervention coalesce.

INTERVENTIONS IN THE RECOVERY-AND-RECONSTRUCTION PHASE

The need for present-focused, crisis-oriented interventions of the impact and postimpact phases eventually wanes as environmental conditions stabilize. Media attention diminishes, and relief efforts by emergency management agencies such as the American Red Cross and FEMA are scaled back or withdrawn. Schools, businesses, and government services regain a measure of normalcy. In developed countries, recovery and reconstruction progress rapidly for much of the community, leaving a subset of individuals and families immersed in disaster-related struggles that have become private, rather than communitywide, issues (Kaniasty & Norris, 1999). This phenomenon is one reason why the recovery and reconstruction phase has sometimes been referred to as the "disillusionment phase" (NIMH, 1990).

For children and adolescents, the psychological and behavioral effects of traumatic exposure often become less intense and obvious, and adults tend to refer to the natural resiliency of youth and avoid disaster-related topics (chapter 7). When asked directly, however, trauma-exposed children and adolescents often report significant trauma-related symptoms months after a disaster has occurred (chapter 2). Most children and adolescents with high exposure to trauma during and after catastrophic disasters, such as the Armenian earthquake of 1989 or war displacement and extended confinement in refugee camps, show trauma-related mental health disturbances months or years later (Goenjian et al., 1995; Hubbard, Realmuto, Northwood, & Masten, 1995; Kinzie, Sack, Angell, Manson, & Rath, 1986; Pynoos et al., 1993). Less extreme exposure produces few persistent psychological effects, yet many youngsters show some symptoms, and a subset report clinically significant symptoms (e.g., La Greca, Silverman, Vernberg, & Prinstein, 1996; Vernberg, La Greca, Silverman, & Prinstein, 1996).

Universal Interventions

Education and information regarding children's mental health needs and resources for assistance continue to be important forms of intervention in the recovery and reconstruction phase. Many adults underestimate the impact of disasters on children's mental life and behavior, especially as time passes following the impact phase of the disaster (chapter 7). Children themselves often do not overtly voice worries and concerns, and they may avoid talking about troubling disaster-related thoughts and feelings in an attempt to evade distress (Vernberg & Johnston, 2001). Parents, teachers, and other caregivers also may be uncertain about whether, when, and how to address disaster-related material months after the impact phase.

Increased concern for children's mental health needs after disasters and improved capacity for storing, cataloging, and transferring information have led to greater availability of factual information on children's varied reactions to disaster as well as recommendations and resources for action. For example, as part of Project Recovery for the Midwest floods of 1993, Jacobs and colleagues gathered and distributed thousands of copies of videotapes and booklets on child and adolescent coping with disasters for many months after the disaster, and they devoted great effort to identifying and publicizing sources of financial, health, and mental health assistance (chapter 7).

Schools provide a potentially valuable setting for communicating continuity and allowing exploration of disaster-related thoughts and feelings, and the past decade has seen the initial development of manualized material to be used broadly in schools following specific types of disasters (e.g., La Greca et al., 1994). Manualized curricula, however, remain scarce, as does careful evaluation of the effectiveness of these materials. Staff from Project Recovery, for example, were faced with the task of helping teachers develop curricula that would give children an opportunity to process issues related to the flood because well-defined curricula tailored to floods were not available.

Selected Interventions

Identifying children and adolescents who have persistent trauma-related symptoms is an important component of selected intervention in the recovery and reconstruction phase. Screenings in school settings offer one option, and several models have been described (e.g., March et al., 1998; McDermott & Palmer, 1999). The processes typically begin with self-reports of symptoms or trauma exposure, which are followed by interviews with children and adolescents who indicate elevated levels of symptomatology or exposure.

Some evidence indicates that relatively brief group or individual cognitive–behavioral interventions produce notable symptom reduction for children or adolescents who continue to have significantly elevated symptoms of PTSD months after experiencing single-incident stressors (March et al., 1998). The March et al. study, however, excluded children with multiple trauma exposures, comorbid disorders, and serious family dysfunction in these focused, time-limited interventions. Time-limited, manualized, cognitive–behavioral interventions appropriate for the recovery and reconstruction phase typically share a common set of features, including education and information giving, exposure to trauma-related stimuli, the teaching of coping skills, and cognitive restructuring (Cohen, Mannarino, Berliner, & Deblinger, 2000; Vernberg & Johnston, 2001).

At least one manualized, brief, time-limited intervention for symptomatic children has been developed and evaluated in a controlled study (Goenjian et al., 1997; see chapter 5). This intervention includes exposure and cognitive restructuring (i.e., reconstructing and reprocessing the traumatic event and identifying traumatic reminders); it is similar to cognitive–behavioral approaches and is based on a psychodynamic formulation of trauma and grief. It addresses coping skills by helping participants tolerate traumatic reminders and discussion of trauma and by teaching proactive measures to cope with disaster-related changes and losses. Bereavement is also addressed in this intervention—the population treated in the study (i.e., survivors of the 1988 Armenian earthquake) experienced the loss of many loved ones. Finally, continuity issues are addressed by identifying missed developmental opportunities and promoting normal developmental tasks.

Using parents to work through disaster-related material with their children offers a low-cost, innovative strategy for delivering interventions in the recovery and reconstruction phase (see chapter 6). Although the effectiveness of this approach for speeding the resolution of PTSD symptoms remains to be documented, most parents found the content and format appealing when this approach was used with children affected by bushfires in Australia (see chapter 6).

Indicated Interventions

Children and families who have endured extreme disaster-related trauma and adversity often could benefit from instrumental help, support, and mental health interventions long into the recovery-and-reconstruction phase. Depletion of social support affects even previously well-functioning families when postdisaster disruptions persist for many months (Kaniasty & Norris, 1999). In many instances, parents are exposed to the same or similar traumas as their children, and they bear continued or increased responsibilities at home and work. Increases in numerous forms of symptomatology, including depression, anxiety, anger, and suicidality, have been documented among adults who experience prolonged disruptions in work, family, and community settings following traumatic exposure (Green, 1991). Parental distress reverberates through the family system in numerous ways and contributes to poor recovery from disasters among children (Vernberg, 1999).

Family economic resources are likely to play a role in the course of children's psychological recovery in several important ways and ought to be taken into account in providing indicated interventions in the recovery and reconstruction phase (Kaniasty & Norris, 1999). Rebuilding and repairing disaster-related damage typically occurs more rapidly for families with good property insurance coverage and other financial assets. Poor families are less likely to have adequate personal property insurance; are more likely to work in service jobs, which are often disrupted following widespread disasters; and generally have few options for housing and child care. The lack of mental health insurance, or underinsurance, for low-income families also decreases access to mental health services that could help children and families cope with traumatic exposure.

Numerous stresses and daily hassles associated with poverty contribute to parental distress and continued exposure to frightening events and make recovery from acute, severely traumatic events more difficult. Recent research documents extreme variability in exposure to community violence, often related to socioeconomic status (Jenkins & Bell, 1997), and indicates high levels of psychological distress among parents living in impoverished areas with high levels of social toxins, such as street violence, pervasive substance abuse, and unemployment (e.g., Osofsky, Wewers, Hann, & Fick, 1993). Disaster research in developing countries further illustrates how financial resources affect the likelihood of exposure to trauma and the course of recovery: Psychiatric morbidity following disasters in developing countries is much higher than in developed countries, and the level of exposure to trauma is much higher for similar types of disasters (Goenjian et al., 1995).

Given the multiple factors related to prolonged disaster-related distress in children, effective intervention strategies must be broad and comprehensive. Individual treatment approaches in isolation are clearly insufficient for children in families evidencing parental distress, social support depletion, financial strains, and continued exposure to trauma. Unfortunately, resources for comprehensive interventions often are lacking, and preexisting community- or school-based systems of care seldom are able to offer sustained, long-term help following disasters. Emergency assistance from other areas may be discontinued before the needs of the most vulnerable and deeply affected children and families are met.

CONCLUSIONS

Increased attention is being paid to the mental health ramifications of disasters for children and adolescents in both applied work and research. In research, the course of recovery from trauma of various types is increasingly well understood, as are some of the long-term repercussions of traumatic exposure. Models for interventions, especially for youngsters who remain symptomatic several months after exposure to a single disaster, are increasingly manualized and are gradually being used in controlled studies. Noteworthy, too, are initial attempts to develop manualized approaches to interventions intended for widespread use with a broad population of children living in areas affected by disasters.

In applied areas, much effort has been devoted to developing comprehensive and coordinated mental health interventions for the impact through the postimpact phases. Crisis-management and emergency-response activities increasingly focus on children's perceived psychological needs immediately after disasters. Little has been done thus far to evaluate the effects of those interventions. Clearly, knowledgeable and experienced professionals have devoted great energy to developing systematic mental health responses focused on children and adolescents in the aftermath of disasters. An important next step is to overcome the many barriers to empirical examination of the effects of efforts. Given the evidence of long-term effects of disasters among a subset of children and adolescents, it also seems wise to allocate increased resources for helping chronically symptomatic youngsters and their families long after the initial disaster event has ended. Screenings of community samples of children, such as those conducted in preparation for the intervention trial by March and colleagues (1998), have found numerous children and adolescents with clinically significant trauma-related psychological symptoms, and most of the youth identified as symptomatic had not received prior treatment. The crisis phases of disasters deservedly garner a great deal of attention and efforts at help, but substantial need continues for some youth far into the recovery-and-reconstruction phase.

Finally, despite advances in research and practice, systematic efforts to incorporate cultural issues into child- and family-oriented disaster interventions remain limited. Basic principles for attending to those issues have been proposed (see chapters 4 and 7), but it appears to remain the exception, rather than the rule, for culturally sensitive systems of care to be implemented in areas affected by disasters. Similarly, developmental features influencing trauma-related interventions have been proposed, but much remains to be done to evaluate those interventions with children who vary in age and developmental status.

REFERENCES

American Psychological Association. (1997). *Final report: American Psychological Association task force on the mental health response to the Oklahoma City bombing.* Washington, DC: Author.

American Red Cross. (1991). *Disaster services regulations and procedures.* (ARC Document 3050M). Washington, DC: Author.

American Red Cross. (1992). *Helping children cope with disaster* (ARC Publication No. 4499). Washington, DC: Author.

Cohen, J. A., Mannarino, A. P., Berliner, L., & Deblinger, E. (2000). Trauma-focused cognitive behavioral therapy for children and adolescents: An empirical update. *Journal of Interpersonal Violence, 15,* 1202–1223.

Eth, S. (1992). Clinical response to traumatized children. In L. S. Austin (Ed.), *Responding to disaster: A guide for mental health professionals* (pp. 101–123). Washington, DC: American Psychiatric Press.

Federal Emergency Management Agency. (1989). *Coping with children's reactions to hurricanes and other disasters* (FEMA Document 1989 0-941-901). Washington, DC: U.S. Government Printing Office.

Freedy, J. R., Saladin, M. E., Kilpatrick, D. G., Resnick, H. S., & Saunders, B. E. (1994). Understanding acute psychological distress following natural disaster. *Journal of Traumatic Stress, 7,* 257–273.

Gist, R., & Woodall, S. J. (1999). There are no simple solutions to complex problems: The rise and fall of critical incident stress debriefing as a response to occupational stress in the fire service. In R. Gist & B. Lubin (Eds.), *Response to disaster: Psychosocial, ecological, and community approaches* (pp. 211–235). New York: Taylor and Francis.

Goenjian, A. K., Karayan, I., Pynoos, R. S., Minassian, D., Najarian, L. M., Steinberg, A. M., & Fairbanks, L. A. (1997). Outcome of psychotherapy among early adolescents after trauma. *American Journal of Psychiatry, 154,* 536–542.

Goenjian, A. K., Pynoos, R. S., Steinberg, A. M., Najarian, L. M., Asarnow, J. R., Karayan, I., Ghurabi, M., & Fairbanks, L. A. (1995). Psychiatric comorbidity in children after the 1988 earthquake in Armenia. *Journal of the American Academy of Child and Adolescent Psychiatry, 34,* 1174–1184.

Green, B. L. (1990). Defining trauma: Terminology and generic stressor dimensions. *Journal of Applied Social Psychology, 20,* 1632–1642.

Green, B. L. (1991). *Mental health and disaster: A research review.* Rockville, MD: Center for Mental Health Services.

Hubbard, J., Realmuto, G. M., Northwood, A. K., & Masten, A. S. (1995). Comorbidity of psychiatric diagnoses with posttraumatic stress disorder in survivors of childhood trauma. *Journal of the American Academy of Child and Adolescent Psychiatry, 34,* 1167–1173.

Jenkins, E. S., & Bell, C. C. (1997). Exposure and response to community violence among children and adolescents. In J. D. Osofsky (Ed.), *Children in a violent society* (pp. 9–31). New York: Guilford Press.

Kaniasty, K., & Norris, F. H. (1999). The experience of disaster: Individuals and communities sharing trauma. In R. Gist & B. Lubin (Eds.), *Response to disaster: Psychosocial, community, and ecological approaches* (pp. 25–61). Philadelphia: Brunner/Mazel.

Kinzie, J. D., Sack, W. H., Angell, R. H., Manson, S., & Rath, B. (1986). The psychiatric effects of massive trauma on Cambodian children: 1. The children. *Journal of the American Academy of Child and Adolescent Psychiatry, 25,* 370–376.

Klingman, A. (1987). A school-based emergency crisis intervention in a mass school disaster. *Professional Psychology: Research and Practice, 18,* 604–612.

Krueger, A. (2001, March 8). Students grapple with returning to scarred school. *San Diego Union-Tribune.* Retrieved April 17, 2001, from http://www.uniontribune.com

Kubler-Ross, E. (1969). *On death and dying.* New York: McMillan.

La Greca, A. M., Silverman, W. K., Vernberg, E. M., & Prinstein, M. J. (1996). Symptoms of posttraumatic stress in children following Hurricane Andrew: A prospective study. *Journal of Consulting and Clinical Psychology, 64,* 712–723.

La Greca, A. M., Vernberg, E. M., Silverman, W. K., Vogel, A. L., & Prinstein, M. J. (1994). *Helping children prepare for and cope with natural disasters: A manual for professionals working with elementary school children.* Miami, FL: Author.

Lazarus. P. J. (1996). *Trauma and children: A parent handout for helping children heal* [Brochure]. Washington, DC: National Association of School Psychologists.

Lohr, J. M., Montgomery, R. W., Lilienfeld, S. O., & Tolin, D. F. (1999). Pseudoscience and the commercial promotion of trauma treatments. In R. Gist & B. Lubin (Eds.), *Response to disaster: Psychosocial, community, and ecological approaches* (pp. 291–326). Philadelphia: Brunner/Mazel.

March, J. S., Amaya-Jackson, L., Murray, M. C., & Schulte, A. (1998). Cognitive-behavioral psychotherapy for children and adolescents with posttraumatic stress disorder after a single-incident stressor. *Journal of the American Academy of Child and Adolescent Psychiatry, 37,* 585–593.

McDermott, B. M., & Palmer, L. J. (1999). Post-disaster service provision following proactive identification of children with emotional distress and depression. *Australian and New Zealand Journal of Psychiatry, 33,* 855–863.

McFarlane, A. C. (1987). Posttraumatic functioning in a longitudinal study of children following a natural disaster. *Journal of the American Academy of Child and Adolescent Psychiatry, 26,* 764–769.

Mitchell, J. T., & Everly, G. S., Jr. (1993). *Critical incident stress debriefing: An operations manual for the prevention of traumatic stress among emergency services and disaster workers.* Ellicott City, MD: Chevron Press.

Monahon, C. (1993). *Children and trauma: A parent's guide to helping children heal.* New York: Lexington Books.

National Institute of Mental Health. (1990). *Training manual for human service workers in major disasters* (DHHS Publication No. ADM 90-538). Washington, DC: U.S. Government Printing Office.

National Organization for Victim Assistance. (1991). *Hurricane! Issues unique to hurricane disasters.* Washington, DC: Author.

Norris, F. H., & Uhl, G. (1993). Chronic stress as a mediator of acute stress: The case of Hurricane Hugo. *Journal of Applied Social Psychology, 23,* 1263–1284.

Omer, H., & Alon, N. (1994). The continuity principle: A unified approach to disaster and trauma. *American Journal of Community Psychology, 22,* 273–287.

Osofsky, J. D., Wewers, S., Hann, D. M., & Fick, A. C. (1993). Chronic community violence: What is happening to our children? *Psychiatry, 56,* 7–21.

Prinstein, M. J., La Greca, A. M., Vernberg, E. M., & Silverman, W. K. (1996). Children's coping assistance: How parents, teachers, and friends help children cope after a natural disaster. *Journal of Clinical Child Psychology, 25,* 463–475.

Pynoos, R. S., & Eth, S. (1986).Witness to violence: the child interview. *Journal of the American Academy of Child and Adolescent Psychiatry, 25,* 306–319.

Pynoos, R. S., Goenjian, A., Tashjian, M., Karakashian, M., Manjikian, R., Manoukian, G., Steinberg, A., & Fairbanks, L. A. (1993). Post-traumatic stress reactions in children after the 1988 Armenian earthquake. *British Journal of Psychiatry, 163,* 239–247.

Pynoos, R. S., Steinberg, A. M., Ornitz, E. M., & Goenjian, A. K. (1997). Issues in the developmental neurobiology of traumatic stress. *Annals of New York Academy of Sciences, 821*, 176–193.

Spielvogel, J. (2001, April 13). Shootings at area schools spur federal assistance. *San Diego Union-Tribune*. Retrieved April 17, 2001, from http://www.uniontribune.com

Storm, V., McDermott, B. M., Finlayson, D. (1994). *The bushfire and me: A story of what happened to me and my family*. Sydney, Australia: New South Wales Department of Health.

Terr, L. C. (1983). Chowchilla revisited: The effects of psychic trauma four years after a school-bus kidnapping. *American Journal of Psychiatry, 140*, 1543–1550.

Valent, P. (2000). Disaster syndrome. In G. Fink (Ed.), *Encyclopedia of stress* (Vol. 1, pp. 706–709). San Diego, CA: Academic Press.

Vernberg, E. M. (1999). Children's responses to disasters: Family and systems approaches. In R. Gist & B. Lubin (Eds.), *Response to disaster: Psychosocial, community, and ecological approaches* (pp. 193–209). Philadelphia: Brunner/Mazel.

Vernberg, E. M., & Johnston, C. (2001). Developmental considerations in the use of cognitive therapy for PTSD. *Journal of Cognitive Psychotherapy, 15*, 223–237.

Vernberg, E. M., La Greca, A. M., Silverman, W. K., & Prinstein, M. J. (1996). Prediction of posttraumatic stress symptoms in children after Hurricane Andrew. *Journal of Abnormal Psychology, 105*, 237–248.

Vernberg, E. M., & Varela, R. E. (2001). Posttraumatic stress disorder: A developmental perspective. In M. W. Vasey & M. R. Dadds (Eds.), *The developmental psychopathology of anxiety* (pp. 386–406). New York: Oxford University Press.

Vernberg, E. M., & Vogel, J. (1993). Interventions with children following disasters. *Journal of Clinical Child Psychology, 22*, 485–498.

4

MULTICULTURAL ISSUES IN THE RESPONSE OF CHILDREN TO DISASTERS

ALINE E. RABALAIS, KENNETH J. RUGGIERO, AND JOSEPH R. SCOTTI

A growing body of literature documents that natural and technological disasters are associated with a number of maladaptive reactions in child and adolescent populations, including posttraumatic stress disorder (PTSD; Ollendick & Hoffmann, 1982; Pfefferbaum, 1998; Saigh, Yasic, Sack, & Koplewicz, 1999). Examination of this body of work, however, reveals that relatively few empirical or conceptual efforts have focused specifically on the topic of multicultural issues in disaster-exposed children and youth. Instead, the literature reveals that Caucasian samples have received considerably greater research attention than have culturally and ethnically diverse populations. In light of the rapidly—and dramatically—changing demographics of the United States, it behooves the still predominantly Caucasian culture—both within the United States generally and within psychology specifically—to investigate and incorporate cultural and ethnic differences into the con-

Portions of this work were supported by a minority fellowship from the West Virginia University Office of Academic Affairs to Aline Rabalais and a National Institute of Mental Health research grant (1 R03 MH55533-01) to Joseph Scotti, both of which are gratefully acknowledged. The opinions expressed herein are not necessarily those of the supporting agencies.

73

sideration of the multiple variables that predict the differential response to traumatic events. This expansion of psychological variables must occur within both the research literature and at the level of individual case conceptualization. Thus, this chapter is a call for expanding the basic and applied research into the multiple and largely unaddressed, cultural and ethnic variables that influence the response of children to trauma.

The influence of risk and protective factors also is critical to evaluate within the disaster literature. Findings in the area of child and adolescent mental health have revealed that the development of psychological disorders is influenced by both protective and risk factors. Kimchi and Schaffner (1990), in summarizing the definition provided by Garmezy, state that "risk factors are those factors that, if present, increase the likelihood of a child developing an emotional or behavioral disorder [whereas] protective factors are those attributes of persons, environment, situations, and events that appear to temper predictions of psychopathology" (p. 476). A number of investigators have found that children who experience multiple, chronic stressors are at risk for developing mental disorders (Goodyer, 1988). Given the paucity of disaster studies that focus on multicultural issues, it is not surprising that empirical studies on risk and protective factors in diverse children and adolescents are scarce.

Given the limitations of the literature, we have three goals for this chapter. The first is to provide an overview of socioeconomic status (SES) and social support, two factors that may be relevant to ethnically diverse samples. We also propose that culture may serve as either a risk or a protective factor. A second goal is to summarize several studies of disasters among ethnically diverse, hurricane-exposed, American children to provide a background for how ethnicity might interact with risk and protective factors to affect the development of PTSD in children. Finally, we use the example of American Indian youth to demonstrate the need for further empirical investigation of cultural variables as potential risk and protective factors for PTSD. We close the paper with suggestions for future directions in research and clinical practice.

DEFINING RACE, ETHNICITY, AND CULTURE

Before progressing too far into a discussion of cultural issues in disaster research, it is important to define *culture*, *ethnicity*, and *race*, given that people often confuse the three terms. The study of human racial classification, which has largely become a social or political endeavor rather than one of biology, is based on distinguishing people by their genetically transmitted physical characteristics. Historically, race has been designated according to several (now archaic) classification terms (e.g., "Mongoloid" and "Negroid," which are no longer considered to be scientifically or politically acceptable terms).

The use of the term *race* has been largely replaced by the terms *culture* and *ethnicity*, which emphasize common history, nationality, or tradition rather than physical characteristics. The definitions of culture and ethnicity are difficult to disentangle, however. Shiang, Kjellander, Huang, and Bogumill (1998) note the multiple definitions and dimensions of each term and offer some clarification; they echo earlier observations by Dana (1993). Culture may be viewed as the beliefs, values, behaviors, shared history, and language (important for its own influence on, and reflection of, culture and worldviews; Harré, 1984) of a group of people at a particular time. Ethnicity may be taken as membership in a particular cultural group. This membership typically occurs by virtue of common background, geography, and physical characteristics, but it can be much more fluid than such happenstance. As Shiang et al. (1998) note, ethnicity may be assigned or claimed: One may be identified by others as being a member of an ethnic group on the basis of physical characteristics; one can assign oneself to an ethnic group; or one might be considered a member of one ethnic group, yet identify with certain cultural aspects of another group. Thus, a person's cultural membership is not always readily identifiable from that person's apparent ethnicity.

Even within the dominant Euro-American culture and presumably homogenous Caucasian ethnic group, our own experience with the predominantly Caucasian population of West Virginia reveals both subtle and startling differences between people in urban areas and the prototypical Appalachian culture of the rural sections of the state that present a range of challenges in assessment and treatment (e.g., fundamental religious beliefs, avoidance of mental health services, and a strong bond to the land; Mulder et al., 1994). Thus, within a complex and increasingly multicultural society, it is a vast oversimplification to assume certain cultural features on the basis of typical ethnic classifications.

RISK AND PROTECTIVE FACTORS

SES, social support, and culturally relevant beliefs and customs are just three of a large number of risk and protective factors that have been linked to psychological outcomes, such as temperament, genetics, gender, birth order, intelligence, and age (Kimchi & Schaffner, 1990; Saylor, Belter, & Stokes, 1997). We chose to focus this chapter on SES and social support, given that the two variables seem to be particularly influenced by cultural beliefs and customs.

Socioeconomic Status

SES is a summary variable representing multiple environmental factors that can affect psychopathology (Muralidharan & Sharma, 1971). It encompasses a variety of factors related to one's financial resources, such as type of occupation, level of education, and annual income. Additionally, a number of environmental conditions may be correlated with SES, such as exposure to crime-prone communities, substandard housing, toxic waste sites, and limited educational opportunities. Thus, cultural groups may be exposed to different types of environmental conditions that place them at risk for developing psychological problems.

In their review, Toomey and Christie (1990) found that parental unemployment (which is associated with low SES) has been linked with a number of problems in children, including increased exposure to child abuse, behavioral and academic difficulties, out-of-home placements, depression, worry, and anxiety. In another review, Gonzales and Kim (1997) concluded that poverty, rather than race, may be the primary predictor of mental health outcomes: They suggested that poverty-related risks include less effective parenting as a result of poor parental mental health and a high degree of family conflict. Furthermore, they noted that children who are members of specific ethnic minority groups within the United States (e.g., African Americans, Hispanic Americans, American Indian/Alaska Natives, and Southeast Asian Americans) have substantially lower SES than the general United States population; therefore, those groups may be at higher risk for a variety of psychological disorders.

Social Support

Social support also is related to mental health outcomes in children. Social support is a multidimensional construct that has been conceptualized in a variety of ways (Joseph, 1999). For instance, investigators have identified a number of sources of social support, including family, friends, and teachers. Investigators have divided support along the dimensions of *perceived* versus *received* support (Sarason, Sarason, & Pierce, 1995). Perceived support refers to a person's evaluation of supportive efforts and access to support (e.g., the belief that one's family provided adequate assistance). Received support refers to the objective properties of supportive efforts (e.g., the amount of financial assistance received). Although attempts have been made to distinguish whether perceived or received support is more strongly associated with mental health, Joseph (1999) suggested that current research has not added clarity, leading him to conclude that researchers need to study both forms of support. The literature on stress and coping shows that an adequate level of social support may serve as a protective factor, whereas deficiencies in social support can function as a risk factor for psychopathology. For instance, maintenance of healthy relationships with parents and peers has been associated with a lower likelihood of developing a psychiatric disorder in youth (Goodyer, 1988; Rutter, 1983).

Investigators have attempted to describe the processes by which social support acts as a protective factor against negative outcomes. Joseph (1999) cites two models describing how social support buffers against psychopathology and heightened stress. The stressor–support specificity model proposes that social support is most likely to serve as a protective factor when the type of support provided matches the type of support needed (Cohen & McKay, 1984; Cutrona & Russell, 1990). For instance, if a family's house is destroyed, the extended family members provide lodging. Similarly, the conservation of resources model proposed by Hobfoll, Dunahoo, and Monnier (1995) emphasizes that social support can serve as a means for restoring lost resources, thus promoting better psychological adjustment after the occurrence of a traumatic event.

Culturally Relevant Risk and Protective Factors

Both social support and SES may interact with cultural customs and beliefs to influence the development of psychopathology. Culture may be a risk factor when youth who are members of historically oppressed cultural groups (e.g., American Indians) experience a number of unique stressors (e.g., racial discrimination) that are not frequently encountered by socially advantaged children (e.g., Caucasians). As a result of the cumulative effect of a variety of stressors, some groups of children may be at greater risk for psychological problems (Goodyer, 1988). On a positive note, however, some cultural factors might protect against psychopathology. Maintenance of cultural ties (e.g., social support from important people in the community) may aid diverse youth in healthy coping efforts (Gonzales & Kim, 1997). Perhaps such cultural factors explain how seemingly socially and economically challenged youth are able to cope with stressors (e.g., disasters) as effectively as, if not more effectively than, children who are members of more advantaged cultural groups.

Prejudice and Discrimination

Prejudice and discrimination are two potential risk factors for negative mental health outcomes (Gonzales & Kim, 1997). Prejudiced beliefs and stereotypes may be verbalized in the form of derogatory racial slurs. A predisaster history of experiencing such slurs may make children and parents from ethnic minorities less likely to seek postdisaster assistance from what they perceive as hostile ethnic groups (e.g., predominantly Caucasian mental health providers). A history of experiencing prejudice also may interact with other factors to have a cumulative impact on stress level and psychopathology. Prejudiced beliefs also may lead to discriminatory actions. For instance, one cultural group (e.g., Caucasians) may restrict another cultural group's (e.g., Hispanic Americans) access to postdisaster financial aid or other forms of support. Gonzales and Kim (1997) have pointed out that the impact of discrimination "represents one of the least studied sources of stress for children and adolescents" (p. 497).

Acculturation Stress

Acculturation has been defined as the extent to which a person incorporates the values and practices of the majority culture into his or her daily life (McDonald, Morton, & Stewart, 1993). Acculturation may occur as the members of one cultural group (e.g., recent immigrants from Mexico) come into contact with the members of another cultural group (e.g., Caucasians). When this contact occurs, people from the minority group may experience stress as a result of both the migration process itself and the conflicts that arise with the majority culture, such as differences in values and customs (Berry & Kim, 1988; Gonzales & Kim, 1997), a situation known as *acculturation stress*. This form of stress, however, is not limited to recent immigrants. Some ethnic groups within the United States live in geographically or socially insular communities (e.g., American Indian reservation communities) and have limited contact with the majority culture. They may experience stress when confronted with majority-culture values and practices. For example, an American Indian might experience conflicting feelings about becoming an acculturated member of the Caucasian, professional community, thereby losing her connections to traditional American Indian values and customs (McNeil et al., 1997).

Although no empirical data describe a relation between acculturation stress and PTSD, McNeil, Porter, Zvolensky, Chaney, & Kee (2000) have made pioneering efforts in the measurement of generalized acculturation anxiety in American Indians. Specifically, they have created a self-report questionnaire (the Native American Cultural Involvement and Detachment Anxiety Questionnaire; McNeil et al., 2000) that measures acculturation-related anxiety. The relation between acculturation stress and postdisaster mental health outcomes, however, remains to be seen.

Cultural Beliefs and Customs

Another potential influence on mental health outcomes is participation in culturally sanctioned activities. Gonzales and Kim (1997) summarize the handful of studies suggesting several factors that may protect against negative psychological outcomes in specific cultural groups: positive parental or family relationships (African Americans and Hispanic Americans), reliance on extended kin networks (Hispanic Americans and African Americans), and spirituality (African Americans). Gonzales and Kim note a fourth protective factor: ethnic and racial socialization, which is multidimensional and includes the active teaching of cultural values, instillation of pride in one's culture, preparation of youth for coping with discrimination, and maintenance of cultural traditions. Cultures "create meaning systems that explain the causes of traumatic events"; those meanings, in turn, influence the manner in which emotional reactions are expressed (de Vries, 1996, p. 403). That is, cultural practices serve the function of providing culturally acceptable outlets for trauma-related emotional responses, and cultural support systems replenish lost material and emotional resources. Gonzales and Kim conclude their review by noting that a lack of empirical evidence prohibits drawing firm conclusions regarding the buffering effects of cultural factors. More research is clearly needed to establish whether specific cultural factors serve as moderators—or even mediators—of psychopathology, in general, and of the response to disasters, in particular.

REVIEW OF SELECTED STUDIES

With this overview of risk and protective factors in mind, we turn to selected studies that have examined child and adolescent hurricane survivors within the United States. For each study, we discuss inferences that can be drawn about the interaction between social support, SES, and cultural factors. Most studies that have examined disaster-exposed groups, regardless of country or disaster, have only compared ethnically homogenous exposed and nonexposed groups.[1] The existing studies are problematic because of their failure to include the necessary comparison groups for drawing conclusions about cultural differences. This section of the chapter therefore focuses on studies of North American hurricane survivors, which include limited data on differences among ethnic groups. Ultimately, what is needed are studies comparing two or more ethnic or cultural groups affected by the *same event* (not to similar events that occur at different places or times).

Hurricane Andrew (August 1992)

Several studies found no significant differences in psychopathology across ethnically diverse groups. Garrison and colleagues (1995) interviewed a sample of Hispanic American (n = 158), African American (n = 116), and Caucasian (n = 104) adolescents 6 months after Hurricane Andrew. The interviews consisted of a modified version of the Diagnostic Interview Schedule (Kilpatrick, Resnick, Saunders, & Best, 1989) that was administered over

---

[1]Examples include studies on a bush fire (McFarlane, Policansky, & Irwin, 1987), earthquakes (Azarian & Skriptchenko-Gregorian, 1998; Azarian, Skriptchenko-Gregorian, Miller, & Kraus, 1994; Goenjian et al., 1999; Yacoubian & Hacker, 1989), toxic waste disasters (Korol, Green, & Gleser, 1999), nuclear power plant accidents (Bromet, 1995; Havenaar et al., 1996; Kazakov, Demidchik, & Astakhova, 1992; van den Bout, Havenaar, & Meijler-Iljina, 1995; Williams, 1994), and transportation disasters (Milgram, Toubiana, Klingman, Raviv, & Goldstein, 1988; Winje, 1996). As key PTSD assessment measures were developed on English speakers, caution needs to be used in interpreting studies that have used these measures translating into widely different language—often without also back-translating the instrument (see Malekzai et al., 1996; Winje, 1996). Language and the interpretation of measures presents yet another cultural difference.

the telephone in order to obtain full PTSD diagnoses. Demographic information revealed that 44% of the reported family incomes were less than or equal to $25,000 per year; yet, analyses of the relation between income and ethnicity were not conducted. Approximately 7% of the youths reported symptoms consistent with a diagnosis of PTSD. Rates of PTSD symptoms were higher, but not significantly so, among African American (8%) and Hispanic American (6%) adolescents than among Caucasian adolescents (5%).

Shaw and colleagues (1995) compared students from two elementary schools in the wake of Hurricane Andrew, including Caucasian ($n = 39$), African American ($n = 21$), and Hispanic American ($n = 38$) children. One school (labeled *Hi-Impact*) received greater hurricane exposure; the other (labeled *Lo-Impact*) received relatively less exposure. The authors examined rates of posttraumatic stress (PTS) symptoms, rather than full PTSD diagnoses, and found that children at the Hi-Impact (87%) and Lo-Impact (80%) schools had similar rates of PTS symptoms, with no differences across ethnic groups.

Vernberg, La Greca, Silverman, and Prinstein (1996) examined PTS symptoms in an ethnically diverse sample of children 3 months after the hurricane. The sample ($N = 568$) comprised five groups: Caucasian (44%), Hispanic American (26%), African American (22%), Asian American (3%), and Unknown Ethnicity (5%). Using analysis of partial variance to test their conceptual model, four components were entered in the following sequence: (a) exposure to traumatic events, (b) child demographic characteristics, (c) access to perceived social support (from parents, classmates, teachers, and friends), and (d) coping. The model accounted for 62% of the variance in PTS symptoms; exposure accounted for the greatest proportion of variance, although all components were significant. Ethnicity did not achieve statistical significance, however.

In contrast to the aforementioned studies, several investigations have been able to identify ethnic differences in posthurricane symptomatology. Using the same sample of children studied by Vernberg et al. (1996), La Greca, Silverman, Vernberg, and Prinstein (1996) conducted a follow-up assessment 7 and 10 months posthurricane. In that study, a measure of major life events (e.g., divorce or death of family member) occurring between the initial and the 7-month measurement points was added to the original conceptual model. Analyses revealed that at 7 and 10 months postdisaster, all the variables in the model accounted for significant proportions of variance. In contrast to the results of Vernberg et al. (1996), however, African American and Hispanic American ethnicity were significant predictors of higher levels of PTS symptoms. Analyses of change in PTS symptoms over time also revealed that the children least likely to show a decrease in symptoms over time either had experienced a greater number of additional life stressors or were of African American or Hispanic American ethnicity. The authors suggest that this finding may reflect unmeasured differences among ethnic groups, such as limited availability of resources that might moderate the impact of stressors (e.g., money to rebuild).

La Greca, Silverman, and Wasserstein (1998) conducted a prospective study that examined whether predisaster behavioral and academic functioning predicted PTS symptoms. Participants ($N = 92$) were administered a variety of self-report measures 15 months before Hurricane Andrew and at 3 and 7 months posthurricane. The sample comprised Caucasians ($n = 45$), African Americans ($n = 35$), Hispanic Americans ($n = 11$), and one Asian American. Although the children were reported to have been "from lower-class to upper-middle-class neighborhoods" (La Greca et al., 1998, p. 885), the authors did not provide detailed information about the measures and procedures used to make that designation. Furthermore, La Greca et al. (1998) amended the Vernberg et al. (1996) model to include predisaster levels of anxiety, inattention, behavior problems, and academic functioning, and they excluded coping and social support. The results of regression analyses revealed that PTS symptoms 3 months posthurricane were predicted by level of exposure and predisaster ratings of anxiety, inattention, and academic performance. Ethnicity did not significantly predict PTS symptoms at the 3-month interval; however, African American ethnicity and predisaster anxiety levels did predict PTS symptoms at the 7-month interval. Ethnicity remained significant after controlling for the level of event exposure.

Finally, Wasserstein and La Greca (1998) investigated the relation between PTS symptoms and perceived social support with Caucasian ($n = 52$), African American ($n = 22$), and Hispanic (primarily Cuban American, $n = 15$) elementary school children. The authors reported that "precise information was not available on children's socioeconomic status" (Wasserstein & La Greca, 1998, p. 215). Results revealed that Hispanic children who reported perceiving a high level of parental conflict were more likely to endorse a greater number of PTS symptoms than either Hispanic children who reported perceiving a low level of parental conflict or Caucasian children who reported perceiving a high level of parental conflict. No other correlates of ethnicity were identified.

Hurricane Hugo (September 1989)

A number of studies have examined youth exposed to Hurricane Hugo. Belter, Dunn, and Jeney (1991) conducted an investigation, approximately 5 months posthurricane, with a sample of parents and their children from three elementary schools. Belter and colleagues found that families from School 1 and School 2 were exposed to "essentially the same" degree of damage, whereas those from School 3 "experienced a significantly lesser degree of damage" (Belter et al., 1991, p. 156). The damage estimates were based on parent descriptions of the amount of sustained home damage; however, the authors did not provide specific statistical data to support those estimates.

Although the sample was divided into Caucasian and non-Caucasian comparison groups, the number of participants was not clearly provided. PTS-related symptoms were measured using the parent and child self-report versions of the Reaction Index (see Norris & Riad, 1997). The results revealed an absence of statistically significant ethnic differences in the children's self-reported depressive and PTS symptoms. In contrast, the parents of non-Caucasian children reported a significantly higher level of PTS symptoms in their children than did Caucasian parents. This result should be interpreted in light of the general finding that the parents, across ethnic groups, gave significantly lower estimates of their children's level of PTS-related symptoms than did their children. When applying the Reaction Index clinical cutoff scores, 90% of the children, by their self-report, were classified as experiencing severe hurricane-related PTS symptoms; in sharp contrast, 69% of parents reported a severe level of PTS symptoms in their children. The findings suggest a higher level of agreement in the reporting of child symptoms between non-Caucasian parents and their children.

Ethnic differences in financial assistance and unemployment also were evident in the Belter et al. (1991) study: Non-Caucasian parents reported having received less financial assistance (e.g., funds from insurance companies). Such financial assistance might be considered a more objective measure of received social support. Non-Caucasian parents also reported being without an income and housing for longer periods of time than their Caucasian counterparts did. These findings bring the issue of discrimination in service delivery and employment opportunities to the forefront.

The Belter et al. (1991) study has implications for the relation among SES, level of exposure, and ethnicity. The authors reported that participants from School 1, who sustained significant home damage, were composed primarily of "middle- to lower-class" African Americans. In contrast, the participants from School 2, who sustained levels of home damage equal to the participants from School 1, were composed of "primarily middle- to upper-class" Caucasians. Finally, the participant group from School 3, which experienced less home damage, was composed of a "good range of socioeconomic status as well as racial backgrounds" (Belter et al., 1991, p. 156). Although African American children from School 1 had suffered the same amount of hurricane exposure as their Caucasian counterparts from School 2, they may have been more disadvantaged in several other respects: School 1 parents reported less social support (e.g., financial compensation), lower SES, and more extended periods of postdisaster unemployment and displacement from their homes than parents from School 2. If one accepts the data as presented, despite some reporting problems, then an interpretation of this study is that psychological adjustment of African American youth, despite being plagued by a greater number of pre- and postdisaster stressors, was no worse than that of their Caucasian peers. This finding is important because if it is replicated in other studies, it could suggest that unmeasured culture-specific buffers (e.g., family ties or parenting strategies) might have exerted a positive, protective influence on psychological adjustment.

Lonigan, Shannon, Finch, Daugherty, and Taylor (1991) conducted a study that measured symptomatology in a large sample of hurricane-exposed children and adolescents (N = 5,687) 3 months after the hurricane. Their diverse sample included Caucasians (n = 3,827), African Americans (n = 1,467), Asian Americans (n = 205), Hispanic Americans (n = 80), and "Others" (n = 108; primarily American Indians). Although the authors did not discuss the measurement or analysis of SES in great detail, they did assess hurricane-related parental unemployment. Specifically, unemployment, damage to home, and perceived hurricane severity were considered to be exposure variables and were used to classify participants into exposure groups (i.e., "mild," "moderate," and "high"). The analyses indicated that participants who experienced greater exposure to Hurricane Hugo reported higher anxiety levels and more PTS symptomatology. The authors also reported that in all three exposure groups, African American youth endorsed a greater number of PTS symptoms than Caucasian children. Interpretation of those findings, however, might be limited because the authors reported an overrepresentation of African American children in the "high" exposure group.

Using the same sample as Lonigan and colleagues (1991), Shannon, Lonigan, Finch, and Taylor (1994) more thoroughly examined the relation between ethnicity and PTS symptoms. They examined the endorsement of specific PTS symptoms and determined whether they corresponded to the diagnostic criteria outlined in the *DSM–III–R* (American Psychiatric Association, 1987). Although Criteria B (reexperiencing), C (avoidance), and D (hyperarousal) were examined, Criteria E (duration of symptoms) was not assessed. As a result, this study was not able to make formal PTSD diagnoses and instead identified the presence of a PTSD symptom profile. A PTSD syndrome diagnosis was said to be present if a participant met the *DSM–III–R* symptom criteria for each of the three symptom clusters.

Because of limited numbers of participants in some groups, Shannon and colleagues (1994) collapsed the data for several ethnic groups into three groups: Caucasians, African Americans, and Other Minorities. Analyses failed to reveal statistical differences among the three groups with respect to the presence of a PTSD syndrome diagnosis. Compared with the other groups, however, African Americans endorsed a significantly greater number of PTSD symptoms within each of the three symptom clusters and were more likely to report anhedonia than the Caucasian children. Also, African American children were more likely than Caucasian and other minority children to report attentional differences, a sense of foreshadowing (e.g., omens), and engaging in reckless or hazardous behavior.

One strength of the Shannon et al. (1994) study was a series of follow-up analyses to statistically control for a variety of potentially confounding factors that might have interacted with ethnicity. For example, the researchers used reported hurricane severity, degree of home damage, and continued displacement as control variables, thereby addressing concerns about the overrepresentation of highly exposed African American youth within the sample. Additionally, they controlled for one measure of SES (i.e., parent's occupation) as well as level of trait anxiety. Even after employing the control variables, they still found significant ethnic differences at the symptom-cluster and individual-symptom levels. The authors suggested that the findings may represent actual group differences in risk for developing PTSD; however, they also could be a result of demographic factors or reporting biases.

Summary and Implications of Disaster Research

In general, the studies reviewed here yielded mixed results with respect to the issue of ethnic differences in PTSD. Four of the nine studies found no statistically significant ethnic differences in PTSD symptomatology (Belter et al., 1991; Garrison et al., 1995; Shaw et al., 1995; Vernberg et al., 1996). The studies that did find differences suggested that African American and Hispanic American youth may be at higher risk for developing PTS symptomatology (La Greca et al., 1996, 1998; Lonigan et al., 1991; Shannon et al., 1994; Wasserstein & La Greca, 1998). Furthermore, two of those studies found that children from minority groups were less likely than Caucasian children to show a decrease in PTS symptoms over time (La Greca et al., 1996, 1998). A point to note here is that the studies varied with regard to the time at which the children were assessed following the event. The apparent ethnic differences appear to become evident at assessment points 7 to 10 months postevent.

Social support was meaningfully related to PTSD and ethnicity. Investigators found that low levels of perceived support predicted more severe levels of symptomatology (La Greca et al., 1996; Vernberg et al., 1996). Additionally, the Belter et al. (1991) study found that Caucasians reported receiving more financial assistance than did non-Caucasians. Finally, ethnic factors appeared to interact with social support in the Wasserstein and La Greca (1998) study, given that high levels of perceived parental conflict predicted higher levels of PTSD for Hispanic American youth than for Caucasian youth. Wasserstein and La Greca suggested that this finding might reflect a greater emphasis on family cohesiveness for Hispanic Americans relative to other cultural groups.

The impact of SES on PTSD symptomatology in children remains unclear. This conclusion is not surprising, given that few disaster-related studies have emphasized examining whether SES may affect both exposure to and response to trauma. We found that studies often incorporated measures of SES to describe sample characteristics or to divide participants into high- and low-exposure groups. Some studies also made general references to SES-related demographic factors (e.g., participants from upper-middle-class neighborhoods), but they did not give details about how those factors were measured. Consequently, no studies have adequately evaluated how SES might interact with ethnic differences to affect the expression of PTSD and related symptoms.

Our review also points to the need for further investigation of how cultural factors might interact with potential risk and protective factors. Although some studies found ethnic differences in rates of PTS symptoms, other studies did not support those results. The question then becomes, What may account for the mixed results? One possible explanation relates to limitations in research methodology. For instance, the overrepresentation of a particular ethnic group in "high-exposure" groups is problematic. The result might be to assume that PTSD symptomatology is a result of ethnicity rather than higher levels of exposure. Another possibility is that observed ethnic differences in rates of PTSD symptoms may reflect unmeasured risk and protective factors. For instance, children who are members of American minority groups may be from lower SES backgrounds, which in turn may be associated with exposure to a variety of stressors, such as lower parental support and dangerous living conditions. Also, culture-specific stressors, such as exposure to race-related discrimination, may have a cumulative impact with respect to the exacerbation of acute and chronic PTSD symptoms. La Greca and colleagues (1996) presented evidence in support of the cumulative impact of stressors: Their research found that a greater number of postdisaster life stressors, as well as African American and Hispanic American ethnicity, predicted a lower likelihood of recovering from PTS symptoms over the time course of their study. The higher numbers of postevent stressors may explain, in part, why ethnic differences in the response to a disaster begin to appear later (7 to 10 months postevent), rather than sooner (within 3 to 5 months); clearly, further research would be required to support such a contention.

Note that the lack of ethnic differences in rates of PTS symptomatology might be accounted for by unmeasured protective factors. For instance, the results of the Belter et al. (1991) study suggested that despite a number of disadvantages (i.e., lower SES, longer duration of home displacement and unemployment, and fewer financial resources), non-Caucasian youth fared no worse than their Caucasian counterparts with respect to PTS symptomatology. One plausible explanation for this finding is that culture-specific practices, such as support from key members of the African American community or involvement in religious activities, served as buffers against the development of psychopathology. Another possibility, however, is that differences in PTS symptoms may not have been observed because the study assessed symptoms at a single point 5 months postdisaster. Given the results of La Greca et al. (1998), it is possible that the participants in the Belter et al. (1991) study would have evidenced ethnic differences in PTS symptoms levels if they had been assessed 7 or more months postdisaster.

POSSIBLE RISK AND PROTECTIVE FACTORS
FOR AMERICAN INDIAN YOUTH

To date, there is only a small amount of empirical evidence that supports the importance of culturally relevant risk and protective factors in the expression of PTSD. To illustrate the potentially complex relations among risk factors, protective factors, and PTSD, we provide hypothetical examples that pertain to American Indian youth. The state of the disaster literature with respect to cultural issues is seriously underdeveloped at this time, particularly with respect to American Indian youth. As a result, our suggestions are based on the scant literature examining American Indian adults as well as the child and adolescent disaster literature. These examples and suggestions are intended to accomplish two goals: (a) to provide concrete examples of potential risk and protective factors in a specific cultural group and (b) to provide a springboard for generating future lines of empirical inquiry in the area of multicultural disaster research.

Studies of PTSD in American Indians

Before discussing risk and protective factors, we turn to the trauma literature on American Indians. A literature review by Rabalais, Scotti, and Larkin (2000) revealed only a handful of empirical investigations of PTSD in American Indians, most of which included adult participants. For instance, Robin, Chester, Rasmussen, Jaranson, and Goldman (1997) examined 247 adults who resided in a southwestern American Indian community. The results revealed that approximately 22% of the sample met criteria for a lifetime diagnosis of PTSD. Holm (1994), in a study of 170 American Indian veterans, found that 76% reported sleep disturbances and 64% experienced flashbacks. These figures are all dramatically higher than the 9% lifetime prevalence rate for PTSD found by Breslau and Davis (1992) in their study of 1,007 urban-dwelling adults (81% Caucasian, 19% African American).

The most comprehensive and methodologically rigorous study of cultural differences in PTSD to date is the American Indian Vietnam Veterans Project (AIVVP; National Center for PTSD and National Center for American Indian and Alaska Native Mental Health Research, 1996). This study showed that American Indians from the Northern Plains (31%) and from the Southwest (27%) had higher current PTSD prevalence rates than Hispanic Americans (30%), African Americans (21%), Caucasians (14%), Native Hawaiians (12%), and Japanese Americans (3%); similar patterns were found for lifetime prevalence. Jones, Dauphinais, Sack, and Somervell (1997) studied trauma-related symptoms in 109 American Indian adolescents who lived on a reservation located in the north central United States. In contrast to the higher rates in other studies, only 5% of that sample met diagnostic criteria for PTSD.

At this point, it is difficult to draw firm conclusions about rates of PTSD in American Indian youth compared with rates in other ethnic groups, given that so few studies include ample numbers of American Indians. Examination of the AIVVP study, however, suggests that American Indian veterans are clearly at a greater risk for developing PTSD than other cultural groups. The AIVVP was conducted with a random, national sample of veterans, giving further credibility to these findings. Although the results do not have direct implications for prevalence rates of PTSD in youth, they do suggest the possibility that American Indian children and adolescents may be at increased risk for PTSD following potentially traumatizing events.

Possible Risk Factors

As we have shown, people of low SES may be more prone to developing postdisaster psychopathology. Many American Indian youth fall into the low-SES category. In summarizing the 1973 census information, Yates (1987) reported that rates of unemployment on reservations ranged from 40% to 70%. Also, Gonzales and Kim (1997), summarizing the census information published in 1994 and 1995, found that the rate of childhood poverty for American Indians and Alaska Natives was 61%, compared with 43% for African Americans, 40% for Hispanic Americans, 16% for Asian Pacific Americans, and 12% for non-Hispanic Caucasians.

Impaired social support is another potential risk factor. High prevalence of psychiatric disorders in the adult, American Indian population may indirectly affect children. Rabalais et al. (2000) noted that general levels of psychopathology in American Indian communities have been estimated at 20% to 60% of the adult population (McShane, 1987; Pelz, Merskey, Brant, Patterson, & Heseltine, 1981; Robin, Chester, & Goldman, 1996). Alcohol problems and depression are of particular concern: Alcohol problems in a Pacific Northwest coastal tribe, for example, have been estimated at 27% (Shore, Kinzie, Hampson, & Pattison, 1973), and depression estimates range from 44% to 55% of adult clinical samples (Manson, Shore, & Bloom, 1985; Shore & Manson, 1981; Shore, Manson, Bloom, Keepers, & Neligh, 1987). It is likely that increased levels of parental distress may translate into less effective parenting strategies (Gordon et al., 1989; cf. Downey & Coyne, 1990).

Another stressor that may influence the risk of postdisaster psychopathology is the widespread loss of American Indian culture, which implies a loss of customs that could otherwise aid in one's ability to cope with potentially stressful situations (de Vries, 1996). This deculturation may be accompanied by increased levels of acculturation stress as American Indians continue to lose traditional American Indian social networks and customs and are exposed to the values, beliefs, and customs of the majority (Caucasian) culture. In the United States, the legacy of systematic destruction of American Indian culture was hastened by a long series of laws that made it illegal for American Indians to practice their own religious customs (Gagné, 1998; LaDue, 1994) and required American Indian children to be involuntarily removed from their parents' homes and placed in Protestant and Catholic missionary boarding schools. The result was a gradual erosion of cultural knowledge in youth, which has translated into a devastating loss of culture for future generations (Gagné, 1998). It was not until 1978, with the passing of the Indian Welfare Act and the Indian Religious Freedom Act, that American Indians were allowed to raise their own children and legally practice their native religions. American Indians have only within the past 25 years been afforded the rights that other Americans take for granted.

Possible Protective Factors

Although America Indian youth and their parents have suffered a long history of economic and cultural disenfranchisement, potential protective factors may provide a buffer against prejudice and psychopathology. The maintenance of family and community ties may serve as protective factors for American Indians, because the role of community in daily life is particularly important (LaDue, 1994). In fact, in communities where traditional American Indian values have been maintained, the concept of oneself as an individual is secondary to one's affiliation with the extended family, tribe, and community (Paniagua, 1994). This worldview is evidenced by respect for elders, an emphasis on sharing rather than competition, and allegiance to the community rather than to the self (Yates, 1987). This emphasis is expressed through community social events and religious rituals where American Indians can garner social support from an extended social network.

An example of a religious ritual that likely increases coping and protects against the development of trauma-related psychopathology in American Indians is the traditional sweat lodge, which encompasses rituals that are typically ceremonies of forgiveness and purification (Wilson, 1988). American Indian veterans may participate in these ceremonies as a way of coping with war-related distress (Silver & Wilson, 1990). A sweat lodge is a dome-shaped tent, which contains warmed rocks. The purification ceremony held within the interior is typically led by a traditional American Indian medicine person, a highly respected figure in the local American Indian community. Wilson outlines the possible benefits of this ceremony for treating PTSD symptoms such as social isolation, hyperarousal, and emotional avoidance. He suggests that the procedure is akin to group therapy in that it provides participants with social support and may serve as a source of physical relaxation. Several efforts to formally incorporate sweat lodges into treatment programs have used only Western models of mental health treatment (Scurfield, 1995; Silver & Wilson, 1990; Wilson, 1988). No empirical evidence supports the effectiveness of sweat lodges for treating PTSD, although descriptive reports of the perceived efficacy of these programs by both staff and participants have been overwhelmingly positive (Silver & Wilson, 1990).

Section Summary

At this point, one might wonder how risk and protective factors might interact to influence postdisaster reactions. None of the disaster-related investigations reviewed in this chapter included meaningful numbers of American Indians. As a result, it is difficult to draw conclusions about postdisaster rates of PTSD in American Indian youth. If future studies of disaster-exposed American Indian youth are conducted, they will need to assess the effects of pre- and postdisaster SES and social support. Given that many American Indians fall within a low-SES category, measurement of a range of variables related to SES may be particularly important for explaining potential elevations in PTSD symptomatology. Also, given that low social support has been linked to PTSD in several child and adolescent disaster studies, it is possible that American Indians who experience an erosion in extended family and community networks might be similarly affected when exposed to a disaster. In fact, disruptions in social support might be particularly problematic for reservation-based American Indian youth, given the strong emphasis on family and community cohesiveness on many reservations. The study by Belter et al. (1991), which revealed that family conflict was a particularly important risk factor for Hispanic American youth, suggests that family cohesiveness is more important for some ethnic groups than for others. We hypothesize that postdisaster erosion in social networks also may increase the risk of developing PTSD for American Indian youth.

FUTURE DIRECTIONS: RESEARCH

Despite multiple calls for the expansion of research that examines cultural and ethnic influences on the response to traumatic events, work in this area remains in its infancy, particularly in the case of children. Although the American Psychological Association (1993) has indicated that good, ethical practice considers culture when assessing and conceptualizing the mental problems of ethnically and culturally diverse clients, most studies focus on single measures of SES and the simple demographic of ethnicity (i.e., African American, Hispanic American, and Caucasian). The two factors, however, are only summary variables—exclusive reliance on them may result in stereotypical overgeneralizations about cultural or ethnic groups. Of course, researchers must begin somewhere, but it clearly would be a mistake to stop at this most basic level. Going beyond this level will be quite difficult, however, given that many researchers lack knowledge about the cultures that they hope to understand and accommodate in future research and clinical endeavors. Thus, the first step may be to foster greater representation of ethnically and culturally diverse researchers and clinicians within the ranks of psychology and, more specifically, within the field of traumatic stress (Sue, Bingham, Porché-Burke, & Vasquez, 1999). A second step would be to focus more attention on the empirical study of cultural factors.

To make broad generalizations about the interaction of culture, ethnicity, and disaster-related variables, we suggest some general guidelines for conducting empirical investigations. First, additional studies using ethnically diverse comparison groups need to be conducted with a variety of types of disasters (e.g., technological and natural disasters) and populations (e.g., heterogeneous and international samples). When examining diverse groups, it would be helpful to measure a wide range of demographic variables. For instance, SES variables of interest include family income, quality of housing, type of profession, and duration of employment. Such a wide range limits the possibility of oversampling from one domain of SES and drawing conclusions that are based on a restricted range of relevant variables. Similarly, investigators should assess a large number of environmental variables (e.g., risk of exposure to accidents and crime-ridden communities) that may correlate with SES variables. Given that the accumulation of daily hassles and stressful life events may negatively affect mental health (Goodyer, 1988; La Greca et al., 1996), it is important to assess chronic stressors both pre- and postdisaster.

Second, future studies should focus on measuring a variety of culturally relevant variables. For instance, quality of and access to culturally sanctioned sources of social support, such as extended kin networks for American Indians, might be assessed. Other cultural factors that might be measured are level of exposure to discriminatory behaviors, acculturation stress, and level of participation in culturally sanctioned social and religious activities. Finally, an effort should be made to identify, describe, and quantify culture-specific parenting strategies as well as beliefs about the expression of emotion. The expression of emotion is important because it could influence one's willingness to report distress, to engage in therapy, and to approach or avoid confronting trauma-related reactions. To assess culture-specific customs and patterns of social support, it is necessary to develop culturally sensitive interviews and self-report measures. The use of focus groups and key informants with a particular cultural group is one way to gather qualitative information about culture-specific variables. This information then can be used to design culturally sensitive and valid questionnaire items (Manson, 1997).

Finally, future studies will benefit from greater attention to measuring and statistically controlling for confounding variables in order to clarify the effect of culturally relevant anxiety, values, and beliefs on trauma-related psychopathology. Once data on culture-specific variables are gathered, it might be useful to conduct an extensive series of ethnic-group comparisons with respect to SES and other demographic factors, access to culturally relevant sources of social support, and participation in cultural activities. If significant differences among ethnic groups are found in one or more of those variables, then the variables should be controlled for using appropriate statistical techniques (e.g., analysis of partial variance), thereby making it possible to make meaningful statements about why groups differ as a function of ethnicity. Such methods might help clarify which risk and protective factors account for observed ethnic differences in trauma-related symptomatology.

This chapter has highlighted some important categories of cultural and ethnic variables that require further systematic study. Some of those variables may well fall within the rubric of the multilevel conservation of resources model (Hobfoll et al., 1995). This model includes several levels of social resources, such as one's cultural beliefs (individual), extended family social support networks (family), culturally relevant religious institutions (organization), and culturally valued ceremonies and customs (community). Other factors may need to be placed at even higher social levels in the conservation of resources model, such as one's worldview, perceptions of responsibility and control, and the aftermath of losing one's culture. Perhaps it also is now incumbent upon researchers in this field to begin to attend to the studies of cultural and ethnic differences that come from other fields of endeavor, such as sociology and cultural anthropology. Examination of the knowledge accumulated by those fields might assist in the identification and quantification of potentially critical factors that may either protect or place one at additional risk after exposure to traumatic events.

FUTURE DIRECTIONS: CLINICAL PRACTICE

Cultural and ethnic factors must be incorporated into functional analysis or case conceptualization models, as Evans and Paewai (1999) demonstrated in the case of the dominant (Caucasian European) and nondominant (indigenous Maori) cultures in Aotearoa/New Zealand. To determine the quality of individual case formulations in a bicultural context, Evans and Paewai provided a checklist of possible features that included the following elements:

- Evaluation of the person's cultural identity (i.e., ethnicity, as defined fluidly by Shiang et al., 1998);
- Description of the target complaint in the person's own idiom;
- The cultural context for specific triggers (e.g., discriminative stimuli, cues, and eliciting stimuli) for the target complaint;
- Cultural views of the unacceptability of the target complaint and the acceptability of alternative behavior;
- Conflicting demands of the different cultural contexts within which the person functions; and
- Perceptions of personal responsibility within the context of one's cultural and personal history of victimization.

Such features are consistent with the paradigmatic behavioral model of PTSD outlined elsewhere (see Scotti, Ruggiero, & Rabalais, this volume; Scotti, Beach, Northrop, Rode, & Forsyth, 1995). Evans and Paewai's (1999) checklist is important because it identifies the variables to be considered in an individual case conceptualization that is based on a paradigmatic behavioral model. Such variables include pretrauma history, perceptions of the traumatic event, behavioral repertoires (e.g., coping skills), social support, and the context within which clinical symptoms may be triggered. Cultural beliefs, behaviors, and worldviews can enter into the equation at any point. For instance, a worldview (see Dana, 1993) in which the person seeks mastery over nature (the typical Anglo American view) versus one of harmony with nature (American Indian) may well lead to different perceptions of helplessness and feelings of horror when confronted with a natural disaster. Such culturally related beliefs may influence one's emotional response to the disaster; treatment-seeking behavior; and reactions to mainstream, Western treatment approaches. Such a basic difference in worldview, which is likely to transcend the simple variable of ethnicity, has not been explored in traumatic stress studies.

A paradigmatic model also provides the basis for group research by pointing the way to factors within each element of the model that can be further investigated as well as links between the elements, all of which contribute to the differential response to traumatic events. We note that it remains highly likely that the single most important factor in any model of traumatic stress is the parameters of the event itself. Such models help us understand the additional factors that lead to the sometimes bewildering differential response to events and develop idiographic case conceptualizations that are based on factors identified through group research and issues raised in the individual case. Although DSM-based diagnoses facilitate communication among clinicians and researchers, they are structurally based: They list topographic classes of behavior that often have some research base indicating how the symptoms covary. Diagnoses, however, communicate neither the function of specific behaviors nor the functional relations among behaviors and the events to which they are causally related (Scotti, Morris, McNeil, & Hawkins, 1996). It may be relatively easy to see how school-refusal behavior in children that begins after an earthquake that occurred while they were in school might have the function of avoidance of anxiety-eliciting school-related stimuli; it also might be the case, however, that school refusal has other functions or comes under the control of other contingencies, such as maternal attention and overconcern in the wake of the event (i.e., positive reinforcement). In this instance, behavior with the same topography has different functions and, therefore, different implications for treatment.

One might think that functional analysis at this specific level need not consider cultural factors, but we disagree. As Evans and Paewai (1999) noted (see also Hayes & Toarmino, 1995), understanding the cultural differences in behavioral responses to different situations adds to the basic analysis of function, moving us to the more complex analysis of the functional relations between the multiple proximal and distal variables evident in the paradigmatic model. Thus, one might ask, What cultural differences in the perception of control over nature, individual and family responsibilities, group cohesion, and a range of personal and social resources interact with the basic features of an event and influence the individual response? This approach moves us to a complex, multidetermined model of functional relations that includes—but goes well beyond—the simple contingency analysis of approach–avoidance behavior.

CONCLUSIONS

We end our discussion by noting again that the search for important cultural and ethnic influences on the response to trauma is one that will help us refine our understanding of the differential effects of a wide range of variables. It also will help us develop an understanding of key features to evaluate in individual case conceptualizations that may otherwise go unaddressed, especially in the case of researchers and clinicians from the dominant culture who seek to understand and treat the traumatic stress responses of people from nondominant cultures.

It is critical that psychology and the field of traumatic stress recognize the radical shift in demographics that is occurring within the United States. We are rapidly moving from a largely Caucasian society with a Euro-American culture to a vastly diverse society in which racial and ethnic minorities will assume the majority by the year 2050, if not sooner (Sue et al., 1999). Moreover, the current great wave of immigration also brings many cultural features with it that are unfamiliar to mainstream America and, consequently, mainstream psychology. As Sue et al. note, a psychology built on the single perspective of the Euro-American culture will increasingly lose its relevance to the mainstream of society unless steps are taken now to purposely incorporate diversity into our science. Such diversity not only includes ethnicity and culture but also incorporates variation in gender, religiosity/spirituality, and sexual orientation. Sue et al. also note the largely "invisible" bias of ethnocentric monoculturalism that affects the field in many subtle ways, including the funding and conduct of ethnic minority research (Sue, 1999). It is important that we do not overlook this bias; in fact, we should combat it by actively studying issues of diversity and making them a primary focus of conceptual and empirical efforts.

REFERENCES

American Psychiatric Association. (1987). *Diagnostic and statistical manual for mental disorders* (3rd ed. rev.). Washington, DC: Author.

American Psychological Association, Office of Ethnic Minority Affairs. (1993). Guidelines for providers of psychological services to ethnic, linguistic, and culturally diverse populations. *American Psychologist, 48,* 45–48.

Azarian, A., & Skriptchenko-Gregorian, V. (1998). Traumatization and stress in child and adolescent victims of natural disasters. In T. W. Miller (Ed.), *Children of trauma: Stressful life events and their effects on children and adolescents* (International Universities Press Stress and Health Series Monograph 8, pp. 77–118). Madison, CT: International Universities Press.

Azarian, A., Skriptchenko-Gregorian, V., Miller, T., & Kraus, R. (1994). Childhood trauma in victims of the Armenian earthquake. *Journal of Contemporary Psychotherapy, 24,* 77–85.

Belter, R. W., Dunn, S. E., & Jeney, P. (1991). The psychological impact of Hurricane Hugo on children: A needs assessment. *Advances in Behaviour Research and Therapy, 13,* 155–161.

Berry, J. W., & Kim, U. (1988). Acculturation and mental health. In P. Dasen, J. W. Berry, & N. Sartorius (Eds.), *Health and cross-cultural psychology: Towards application* (pp. 207–236). London: Sage.

Breslau, N., & Davis, G. C. (1992). Posttraumatic stress disorder in an urban population of young adults: Risk factors and chronicity. *American Journal of Psychiatry, 149,* 671–675.

Bromet, E. J. (1995). Methodological issues in designing research on community-wide disasters with special reference to Chernobyl. In S. E. Hobfoll & M. W. de Vries (Eds.), *Extreme stress and communities: Impact and Intervention* (pp. 267–282). Dordrect, Netherlands: Kluwer Academic Publishers.

Cohen, S., & McKay, G. (1984). Social support, stress, and the buffering hypothesis: A theoretical analysis. In A. Baum, J. E. Singer, & S. E. Taylor (Eds.), *Handbook of psychology and health* (pp. 253–267). Hillsdale, NJ: Lawrence Erlbaum.

Cutrona, C. E., & Russell, D. W. (1990). Type of social support and specific stress: Toward a theory of optimal matching. In B. R. Sarason & I. G. Sarason (Eds.), *Social support: An interactional view* (pp. 319–366). New York: Wiley.

Dana, R. H. (1993). *Multicultural assessment perspectives for professional psychology.* Boston: Allyn and Bacon.

de Vries, M. W. (1996). Trauma in cultural perspective. In B. A. van der Kolk, A. C. McFarlane, & L. Weisaeth (Eds.), *Traumatic stress: The effects of overwhelming experience on mind, body, and society* (pp. 398–413). New York: Guilford Press.

Downey, G., & Coyne, J. C. (1990). Children of depressed parents: An integrative review. *Psychological Bulletin, 108,* 50–76.

Evans, I. M., & Paewai, M. K. (1999). Functional analysis in a bicultural context. *Behaviour Change, 16,* 20–36.

Gagné, M. (1998). The role of dependency and colonialism in generating trauma in First Nations citizens: The James Bay Cree. In Y. Danieli (Ed.), *International handbook of multigenerational legacies of trauma* (pp. 355–372). New York: Plenum Press.

Garrison, C., Bryant, E., Addy, C., Spurrier, P., Freedy, J., & Kilpatrick, D. (1995). Posttraumatic stress disorder in adolescents after Hurricane Andrew. *Journal of the American Academy of Child and Adolescent Psychiatry, 34,* 1193–1201.

Goenjian, A., Stilwell, B. M., Steinberg, A. M., Fairbanks, L. A., Galvin, M. R., Karayan, I., & Pynoos, R. S. (1999). Moral development and psychopathological interference in conscience functioning among adolescents after trauma. *Journal of the American Academy of Child and Adolescent Psychiatry, 38,* 376–384.

Gonzales, N., & Kim, L. (1997). Stress and coping in an ethnic minority context. In S. A. Wolchik & I. N. Sandler (Eds.), *Handbook of children's coping: Linking theory and intervention* (pp. 481–511). New York: Plenum Press.

Goodyer, I. M. (1988). Stress in childhood and adolescence. In S. Fisher & J. Reason (Eds.), *Handbook of life stress, cognition, and health* (pp. 23–40). New York: John Wiley & Sons.

Gordon, D., Burge, D., Hammen, C., Adrian, C., Jaenicke, C., & Hiroto, D. (1989). Observations of interactions of depressed women with their children. *American Journal of Psychiatry, 146,* 50–55.

Havenaar, J. M., van den Brink, W., van den Bout, J., Kasyanenko, A. P., Poelijoe, N. W., Wohlfarth, T., & Meijler-Iljina, L. I. (1996). Mental health problems in the Gomel region (Belarus): An analysis of risk factors in an area affected by the Chernobyl disaster. *Psychological Medicine, 26,* 845–855.

Hayes, S. C., & Toarmino, D. (1995). If behavioral principles are generally applicable, why is it necessary to understand cultural diversity? *The Behavior Therapist, 18,* 21–23.

Hobfoll, S. E., Dunahoo, C. A., & Monnier, J. (1995). Conservation of resources and traumatic stress. In J. R. Freedy & S. E. Hobfoll (Eds.), *Traumatic stress: From theory to practice* (pp. 29–47). New York: Plenum Press.

Holm, T. (1994). The national survey of American Indian Vietnam veterans. *American Indian and Alaska Native Mental Health Research, 6,* 18–28.

Jones, M. C., Dauphinais, P., Sack, W. H., & Somervell, P. D. (1997). Trauma-related symptomatology among American Indian adolescents. *Journal of Traumatic Stress, 10,* 163–173.

Joseph, S. (1999). Social support and mental health following trauma. In W. Yule (Ed.), *Post-traumatic stress disorders: Concepts and therapy* (pp. 71–91). New York: John Wiley & Sons.

Kazakov, V. S., Demidchik, E. P., & Astakhova, L. N. (1992). Childhood thyroid cancer after Chernobyl. *Nature, 359,* 21–22.

Kilpatrick, D., Resnick, H., Saunders, B., & Best, C. (1989). *The National Women's Study PTSD Module.* Charleston: Medical University of South Carolina, Department of Psychiatry and Behavioral Sciences, Crime Victims Research and Treatment Center.

Kimchi, J., & Schaffner, B. (1990). Childhood protective factors and stress risk. In L. E. Arnold (Ed.), *Childhood stress* (pp. 475–500). New York: John Wiley & Sons.

Korol, M., Green, B. L., & Gleser, G. C. (1999). Children's responses to a nuclear waste disaster: PTSD symptoms and outcome prediction. *Journal of the American Academy of Child and Adolescent Psychiatry, 38*, 368–375.

LaDue, R. (1994). Coyote returns: Twenty sweats does not an Indian expert make. *Women and Therapy, 15*, 93–111.

La Greca, A. M., Silverman, W. K., Vernberg, E. M., & Prinstein, M. J. (1996). Symptoms of posttraumatic stress in children after Hurricane Andrew: A prospective study. *Journal of Consulting and Clinical Psychology, 64*, 712–723.

La Greca, A. M., Silverman, W. K., & Wasserstein, S. B. (1998). Children's predisaster functioning as a predictor of posttraumatic stress following Hurricane Andrew. *Journal of Consulting and Clinical Psychology, 66*, 883–892.

Lonigan, C. J., Shannon, M. P., Finch, A. J., Daugherty, T. K., & Taylor, C. M. (1991). Children's symptom reactions to a natural disaster: Symptom severity and degree of exposure. *Advances in Behaviour Research and Therapy, 13*, 135–154.

Malekzai, A. S. B., Niazi, J. M., Paige, S. R., Hendricks, S. E., Fitzpatrick, D., Leuschen, M. P., & Millimet, C. R. (1996). Modification of CAPS-1 for diagnosis of PTSD in Afghan refugees. *Journal of Traumatic Stress, 9*, 891–898.

Manson, S. M. (1997). Ethnographic methods, cultural context, and mental illness: Bridging different ways of knowing and experience. *Ethos, 25*, 249–258.

Manson, S., Shore, J. H., & Bloom, J. D. (1985). The depressive experience in American Indian communities: A challenge for psychiatric theory and diagnosis. In A. Kleinman & B. Good (Eds.), *Culture and depression: Studies in anthropology and cross-cultural psychiatry of affect and disorder* (pp. 331–367). Los Angeles: University of California Press.

McDonald, J. D., Morton, R., & Stewart, C. (1993). Clinical concerns with American Indian patients. In L. VandeCreek, S. Knapp, & T. L. Jackson (Eds.), *Innovations in clinical practice: A sourcebook* (Vol. 12, pp. 437–454). Sarasota, FL: Professional Resource Press/Resource Exchange.

McFarlane, A. C., Policansky, S. K., & Irwin, C. (1987). A longitudinal study of the psychological morbidity in children due to a natural disaster. *Psychological Medicine, 17*, 727–738.

McNeil, D. W., Porter, C., Zvolensky, M. J., Chaney, J. M., & Kee, M. (2000). Assessment of culturally related anxiety in American Indians and Alaska Natives. *Behavior Therapy, 31*, 301–325.

McNeil, D. W., Zvolensky, M. J., Porter, C., Rabalais, A., McPherson, T., & Kee, M. (1997). Anxiety in American Indians and Alaska Natives: Identification and treatment. *Indian Health Service Primary Care Provider, 22*, 181–185.

McShane, D. (1987). Mental Health and North American Indian/Native communities: Cultural transactions, education, and regulation. *American Journal of Community Psychology, 15*, 95–116.

Milgram, N. A., Toubiana, Y. H., Klingman, A., Raviv, A., & Goldstein, I. (1988). Situational exposure and personal loss in acute and chronic stress reactions to a school bus disaster. *Journal of Traumatic Stress, 1*, 339–352.

Mulder, P. L., Daugherty, A., Teel, W., Midkiff, J., Murray, K., & Smith, L. (1994). Rural West Virginia: A cross cultural perspective with implications for clinical intervention. *West Virginia Journal of Psychological Research and Practice, 3,* 9–25.

Muralidharan, R., & Sharma, A. (1971). Manifest anxiety in Indian (Delhi) children. *Indian Educational Review, 6,* 67–78.

National Center for Post-Traumatic Stress Disorder and National Center for American Indian and Alaska Native Mental Health Research. (1996). *Matsunaga Vietnam Veterans Project* (Vol. 1, draft final report). Boston: Author.

Norris, F. H., & Riad, J. K. (1997). Standardized self-report measures of civilian trauma and posttraumatic stress disorder. In J. P. Wilson & T. M. Keane (Eds.), *Assessing psychological trauma and PTSD* (pp. 7–42). New York: Guilford Press.

Ollendick, D. G., & Hoffmann, J. (1982). Assessment of psychological reactions in disaster victims. *Journal of Community Psychology, 10,* 157–167.

Paniagua, F. A. (1994). *Assessing and treating culturally diverse clients: A practical guide.* Thousand Oaks, CA: Sage.

Pelz, M., Merskey, H., Brant, C., Patterson, P. G. R., & Heseltine, G. F. D. (1981). Clinical data from a psychiatric service to a group of Native people. *Canadian Journal of Psychiatry, 26,* 345–348.

Pfefferbaum, B. (1998). Caring for children affected by disaster. *Child and Adolescent Psychiatric Clinics of North America, 7,* 579–597.

Rabalais, A., Scotti, J. R., & Larkin, K. T. (2000). *Assessment and diagnosis of posttraumatic stress disorder in American Indians: Conceptual and methodological issues.* Manuscript submitted for publication.

Robin, R. W., Chester, D., & Goldman, D. (1996). Cumulative trauma and PTSD in American Indian communities. In A. J. Marsella, M. J. Friedman, E. T. Gerrity, & R. M. Scurfield (Eds.), *Ethnocultural aspects of posttraumatic stress disorder: Issues, research, and clinical applications* (pp. 239–253). Washington, DC: American Psychological Association.

Robin, R. W., Chester, B., Rasmussen, J. K., Jaranson, J. M., & Goldman, D. (1997). Prevalence and characteristics of trauma and posttraumatic stress disorder in a Southwestern American Indian community. *American Journal of Psychiatry, 154,* 1582–1588.

Rutter, M. (1983). Stress, coping and development: Some issues and some questions. In N. Garmezy & M. Rutter (Eds.), *Stress, coping, and development in children* (pp. 1–41). New York: McGraw-Hill.

Saigh, P. A., Yasic, A. E., Sack, W. H., & Koplewicz, H. S. (1999). Child-adolescent posttraumatic stress disorder: Prevalence, risk factors, and comorbidity. In P. A. Saigh & J. D. Bremner (Eds.), *Posttraumatic stress disorder: A comprehensive text* (pp. 18–43). Needham Heights, MA: Allyn & Bacon.

Sarason, I. G., Sarason, B. R., & Pierce, G. R. (1995). Stress and social support. In S. E. Hobfoll & M. W. de Vries (Eds.), *Extreme stress and communities: Impact and interventions* (pp. 179–197). Dordrect, Netherlands: Kluwer Academic Publishers.

Saylor, C. F., Belter, R., & Stokes, S. J. (1997). Children and families coping with disaster. In A. Wolchik & I. N. Sandler (Eds.), *Handbook of children's coping: Linking theory and intervention* (pp. 361–383). New York: Plenum Press.

Scotti, J. R., Beach, B. K., Northrop, L. M. E., Rode, C. A., & Forsyth, J. P. (1995). The psychological impact of accidental injury: A conceptual model for clinicians and researchers. In J. R. Freedy & S. E. Hobfoll (Eds.), *Traumatic stress: From theory to practice* (pp. 181–212). New York: Plenum Press.

Scotti, J. R., Morris, T. L., McNeil, C. B., & Hawkins, R. P. (1996). DSM-IV and disorders of childhood and adolescence: Can structural criteria be functional? *Journal of Consulting and Clinical Psychology, 64,* 1177–1191.

Scurfield, R. M. (1995). Healing the warrior: Admission of two American Indian war-veteran cohort groups to a specialized inpatient PTSD unit. *American Indian and Alaska Native Mental Health Research: Journal of the National Center, 6,* 1–22.

Shannon, M. P., Lonigan, C. J., Finch, A. J., & Taylor, C. M. (1994). Children exposed to disaster: I. Epidemiology of post-traumatic symptoms and symptoms profiles. *Journal of the American Academy of Child and Adolescent Psychiatry, 33,* 80–93.

Shaw, J. A., Applegate, B., Tanner, S., Perez, D., Rothe, E., Campo-Bowen, A. E., & Lahey, B. L. (1995). Psychological effects of Hurricane Andrew on an elementary school population. *Journal of the Academy of Child and Adolescent Psychiatry, 34,* 1185–1192.

Shiang, J., Kjellander, C., Huang, K., & Bogumill, S. (1998). Developing cultural competency in clinical practice: Treatment considerations for Chinese cultural groups in the United States. *Clinical Psychology: Science and Practice, 5,* 182–210.

Shore, J. H., Kinzie, J. D., Hampson, J. L., & Pattison, E. M. (1973). Psychiatric epidemiology of an Indian village. *Psychiatry, 36,* 70–81.

Shore, J. H., & Manson, S. M. (1981). Cross cultural studies of depression among American Indian and Alaska Natives. *White Cloud Journal, 2,* 5–12.

Shore, J. H., Manson, S. M., Bloom, J. D., Keepers, G., & Neligh, G. (1987). A pilot study of depression among American Indian patients with research diagnostic criteria. *American Indian and Alaska Native Mental Health Research: Journal of the National Center, 1,* 4–15.

Silver, S., & Wilson, J. (1990). Native American healing and purification rituals for war stress. In J. Wilson, Z. Harel, & B. Kahana (Eds.), *Human adaptation to stress: From the Holocaust to Vietnam* (pp. 337–356). New York: Plenum Press.

Sue, D. W., Bingham, R. P., Porché-Burke, L., & Vasquez, M. (1999). The diversification of psychology: A multicultural revolution. *American Psychologist, 54,* 1061–1069.

Sue, S. (1999). Science, ethnicity and bias: Where have we gone wrong? *American Psychologist, 54,* 1070–1077.

Toomey, B. G., & Christie, D. J. (1990). Social stressors in childhood: Poverty, discrimination, and catastrophic events. In L. E. Arnold (Ed.), *Childhood stress* (pp. 423–456). New York: John Wiley & Sons.

van den Bout, J., Havenaar, J. M., & Meijler-Iljina, L. I. (1995). Health problems in areas contaminated by the Chernobyl disaster: Radiation, traumatic stress, or chronic stress? In R. J. Kleber, C. R. Figley, & B. P. R. Gersons (Eds.), *Beyond trauma: Cultural and societal dynamics* (pp. 213–232). New York: Plenum Press.

Vernberg, E. M., La Greca, A. M., Silverman, W. K., & Prinstein, M. J. (1996). Prediction of posttraumatic stress symptoms in children after Hurricane Andrew. *Journal of Abnormal Psychology, 105,* 237–248.

Wasserstein, S. B., & La Greca, A. M. (1998). Hurricane Andrew: Parent conflict as a moderator of children's adjustment. *Hispanic Journal of Behavioral Sciences, 20,* 212–224.

Williams, D. (1994). Chernobyl, eight years on. *Nature, 371,* 556.

Wilson, J. P. (1988). Treating the Vietnam veteran. In F. M. Ochberg (Ed.), *Posttraumatic therapy and victims of violence* (pp. 254–277). New York: Brunner/Mazel.

Winje, D. (1996). Long-term outcome of trauma in adults: The psychological impact of a fatal bus accident. *Journal of Consulting and Clinical Psychology, 64,* 1037–1043.

Yacoubian, V. V., & Hacker, F. J. (1989). Reactions to disaster at a distance. *Bulletin of the Menninger Clinic, 53,* 331–339.

Yates, A. (1987). Current status and future directions of research on the American Indian child. *American Journal of Psychiatry, 144,* 1135–1142.

II

NATURAL DISASTERS

NATURAL DISASTERS: INTRODUCTION

ERIC M. VERNBERG

Natural disasters affect all regions of the world. In addition to injury and loss of life, they result in tremendous economic losses through property damage and disruptions in education, business, and government systems. The psychological toll exacted by this damage increases dramatically for children and adolescents who experience terror, hardship, and loss both during and after natural disasters.

The chapters in this section describe the growing empirical evidence of the relation between the level of traumatic exposure during natural disasters and trauma-related symptomatology. Evidence also increasingly shows that other important factors influencing disaster-related psychological outcomes include the level of disruption in day-to-day activities, access to social support, and coping efforts; interventions based on this evidence are being designed and evaluated. Although symptoms generally abate, some children and adolescents continue to experience substantial disaster-related symptoms for months or even years.

Results are preliminary, but researchers are laying important groundwork for evidence-based treatments and rigorous evaluation studies. It is becoming clear that interventions following natural disasters must, in most applications, take into account the large number of children affected. Paradigms for wide-scale screening for persistent symptom elevations are being developed and field tested, and initial attempts have been made to develop manualized, evidence-based interventions suitable for use with large numbers of people.

Chapter 5, by Annette La Greca and Mitchell Prinstein, focuses on hurricanes and earthquakes and touches briefly on the limited literature on tornadoes, lightning strikes, and volcanoes. These sudden, dramatic, and violent acts of nature can create widespread damage and high levels of exposure to life-threatening trauma and may require long periods of reconstruction and recovery. For children and adolescents caught in severe hurricanes, earthquakes, or tornadoes, these relatively brief displays of natural forces can transform a familiar environment into a jumbled pile of rubble. Normally confident and protective adults may show terror, shock, and fear. In the most unfortunate circumstances, children may witness deaths or serious injuries or be injured themselves.

La Greca and Prinstein describe the cumulative evidence showing that many children and adolescents living in heavily damaged areas experience significant disaster-related symptomatology for months after a tornado or hurricane. A substantial minority appear to develop chronic disaster-related symptoms. Among children who have truly catastrophic levels of trauma exposure during and after hurricanes and earthquakes, initial traumatic stress symptoms common in PTSD and separation anxiety disorder often are accompanied over time by serious levels of depression. La Greca and Prinstein describe early versions of manualized intervention materials for dealing with the aftermath of hurricanes and earthquakes.

Brett McDermott and Lyle Palmer give an excellent overview in chapter 6 of the aspects of wilderness area and wildfires that have a particularly strong impact on children and adolescents. Even children who do not lose their homes to fire may experience extended periods of worry and ambiguity about the progression of the fire; the possibility of evacuation; the safety of parents who continue to work in or commute through affected areas; and the fate of friends, neighbors, native animals, and pets. The limited research available on wildfires indicates that, as with other natural disasters, most children in affected areas report at least mild symptoms of stress reactions and a subset report moderate to severe distress months after the fires end. McDermott and Palmer's work has generated a model for school-based screenings to detect youth who are experiencing extreme reactions. The authors and their colleagues also have developed an evidence-based "guided workbook" to address troublesome aspects of the wildfire experience. The chapter describes those efforts and details an interesting attempt at service delivery in which parents worked with their children to complete the workbook, in consultation with a mental health worker.

Floods are a recurring problem in many regions. Dramatic flash floods from the sudden failure of dams or levies can cause terrible and sudden destruction, often with a high death toll (see also chapter 11), and rising water from excessive rainfall or melting snow represents a recurrent threat to many low-lying areas. In chapter 7, Gerard Jacobs, Jorge Boero, Randal Quevillon, Elizabeth Todd-Bazemore, Teri Elliott, and Gilbert Reyes describe their extensive work with Project Recovery in South Dakota in the years following the devastating Midwest floods of 1993.

Damage from rising water is often insidious. Buildings may remain standing when floodwaters recede, but mud, silt, mildew, and damage to electrical systems leave many families with a house full of ruined possessions and overwhelming cleanup and restoration tasks. In agricultural regions, growing seasons are lost from damaged equipment, ruined crops, and hopelessly muddy or flooded fields. Many livestock, pets, and other animals are often lost. The approach the authors developed in Project Recovery is striking in its careful attention to cultural factors, which range from community protocols for offering and accepting assistance from disaster mental health personnel to issues involved in working with an agricultural population of European Americans, Native Americans, and Latinos. Project staff gathered, developed, and distributed a great deal of child- and family-oriented material related specifically to floods, thus advancing the potential to develop and evaluate disaster-specific interventions. The bulk of the mental health intervention was delivered many months after the floods receded, bearing witness to the long-term strain, stress, and disruption caused by flooding.

Chapter 8, by Russell Jones and Thomas Ollendick, focuses on residential fires. These fires occur for many reasons, including natural forces (e.g., lightning); technological failures; and human acts, which may be intentional or unintentional. Unlike the widespread destruction from natural disasters, however, residential fires may affect only a single family in community at a time. Although fires' isolated occurrence may allow for greater community resources to be focused on the affected family, it also makes the experience seem unique and is therefore potentially stigmatizing.

Considering how often residential fires occur, surprisingly little systematic research has evaluated children's reactions to fires or psychosocial interventions following fires. Jones and Ollendick review research to date and describe early results from their ongoing efforts to assess the effects of residential fires and evaluate specific intervention strategies for children and adolescents.

All the chapters in this section demonstrate a progression toward increased scientific understanding of the impact of natural disasters on child and adolescent functioning. Intervention models are becoming increasingly well described and manualized, thereby allowing for more rigorous evaluations of effectiveness. A key theme underlies all work in this area: Exposure to trauma during disasters and the levels of loss, disruptions, and life adversity are unequivocally directly related to the severity of posttraumatic disturbances. Although disaster mental health efforts first must focus on reducing the likelihood of exposure through planning, preparation, and preventive efforts, equally important are efforts to reduce subsequent loss and disruption. Intervention efforts must be sustained for many months or even years in communities or with families in which exposure and devastation have reached catastrophic levels.

5

HURRICANES AND EARTHQUAKES

ANNETTE M. LA GRECA AND MITCHELL J. PRINSTEIN

Natural disasters can cause massive, widespread damage and destruction; fatalities and injuries; and severe disruption to families' and children's lives. Like many traumatic experiences, the psychological ramifications of disasters stem from their unpredictability, the severe potential for physical harm, and human vulnerability in the face of devastating forces of nature. These characteristics are particularly true for hurricanes and earthquakes, which are the primary focus of this chapter.[1]

Hurricanes include severe rains, winds, flooding, and occasionally tornadoes; the storms can extend over an area of up to 400 miles in diameter; the most severe weather is around the perimeter of the hurricane eye, which can be 20 to 30 miles wide. An average of five hurricanes strike the coast of the United States every 3 years, two of which will be classified as "major" storms, with winds exceeding 110 mph (American Red Cross, 1999). In the United States, hurricanes are most likely to occur between June and November; coastal states in the South and Southeast are most vulnerable to landfall. It is estimated that 80% to 90% of the population in those regions have not directly experienced a severe hurricane, however, and therefore may not

---

[1]This chapter also describes the sparse literature on tornadoes, lightning strikes, and volcano eruptions.

be prepared for a future hurricane (American Red Cross, 1999). Residents typically receive advance warning of an approaching hurricane—sometimes 1 or 2 weeks before the storm reaches land. The National Weather Service issues a hurricane *watch* when a storm is within 24 to 36 hours of possible landfall, and it issues a *warning* when the hurricane is within 24 hours of arrival (American Red Cross, 1999; National Oceanic and Atmospheric Administration [NOAA], 1998).

In contrast, earthquakes cannot be predicted, so residents cannot be warned before they strike (U.S. Geological Survey [USGS], 1995). Earthquakes are seismic waves in the earth's surface caused by the dislocation or disruption of the earth's crust. Worldwide, more than 20,000 detectable earthquakes occur each year; approximately 10% of them are in the United States (mostly in California and Alaska). Each year, approximately 20 earthquakes across the world could be destructive (i.e., having a magnitude of 7 or higher; USGS, 1995). Severe damage can occur up to 50 miles from an earthquake epicenter and may be caused by the earthquake itself or by any of the several aftershocks that typically follow. Aftershocks, by definition, are weaker than the initial earthquake, but they can occur frequently during the hours, weeks, or even months after the initial event (USGS, 2002). Most damage caused by earthquakes results from the failure of human-made physical structures (e.g., buildings and roadways), rather than the earthquake itself. Thus, the physical destruction caused by an earthquake varies greatly because damage is more directly related to the stability of constructed buildings or highways in the affected area.

Great variability also occurs in the damage caused by tornadoes because their path is typically arbitrary and unpredictable. Tornadoes most frequently occur during severe thunderstorms. In the United States, tornadoes are most likely to happen east of the Rocky Mountains during the spring or summer; however, in the past 40 years, tornadoes have been spotted in all 50 states (NOAA, 1998). Approximately 800 tornadoes occur each year, which together are responsible for 80 deaths and more than 1,500 injuries. Most tornadoes are relatively mild, however, almost one third are classified as "strong" with winds in the 110 to 205 miles per hour range; they account for 30% of tornado deaths. Another 2% are classified as "violent"; their winds exceed 205 miles per hour, and they are responsible for 70% of tornado deaths. A tornado's path of damage can be up to a mile wide and 50 miles long (NOAA, 1998). People in the path of a tornado often receive some warning of an impending tornado disaster. A tornado watch is issued when storm conditions make a tornado occurrence likely, and a tornado warning is issued upon sighting of a tornado.

These types of natural disasters differ in several ways that may be relevant for children's and families' physical safety and psychological responses. First, the predictability of a natural disaster affects families' opportunities for disaster-preparation activities. In the days preceding a hurricane, families are able to evaluate their level of risk, relocate if necessary, and make essential preparations to help minimize the damage to their homes, possessions, and lives. Families may also purchase items to help survive the aftermath of a hurricane, such as food and water, candles, flashlights or electric generators, and gas stoves. For other natural disasters, such as earthquakes, the opportunities for advance preparation are much more limited because little warning of the impending disaster is available, although families living in earthquake-prone areas may keep needed supplies on hand in case a disaster occurs.

Because earthquakes (and to some degree, tornadoes) are not predictable, they also may be associated with greater numbers of casualties and injuries than other types of disasters because people may not have the ability to get to a "safe place." High casualty rates can add substantially to the trauma and impact of these disasters. For example, following a devastating earthquake in Armenia, Pynoos and colleagues (1993) reported that many survivors said the worst part was hearing cries for help from friends and relatives trapped under the debris. In many instances, rescue was not possible, and the moans and cries went on for many days as the trapped people slowly died from thirst, starvation, and injury. This aspect of the earthquake and its aftermath added substantially to the psychological trauma associated with it.

A second factor distinguishing the various types of natural disasters has to do with their duration, which may directly relate to individual perceptions of life threat and, in turn, may predict postdisaster stress reactions (e.g., Vernberg, La Greca, Silverman, & Prinstein, 1996). The initial impact of an earthquake may last only a few minutes, and the most damaging aftershocks generally occur in the 2 hours thereafter (USGS, 1995). In contrast, families may spend 6 to 12 hours in protected rooms of their homes waiting for the threat of a tornado or hurricane to end.

Third, the number of victims affected by different types of natural disasters can vary widely, a characteristic that has implications for postdisaster recovery and resources. In widespread, community-based disasters, such as destructive hurricanes, considerable community support and assistance from outside sources (e.g., federal emergency workers) is available immediately following the event, although the rebuilding process may be extremely difficult and slow. The cost of rebuilding homes, schools, and businesses after Hurricane Andrew, for instance, exceeded $15 billion and lasted more than 2 years in many affected areas. In contrast, the effects of tornadoes and, sometimes, earthquakes are more localized. This characteristic may facilitate the rebuilding process because tornado victims' neighbors may be virtually unaffected by a storm that devastated only a fraction of the community; however, the tornado victims may be relatively isolated in their experiences of the disaster.

Regardless of those differences, the cost and disruption to victims caused by hurricanes and earthquakes is similarly tragic. In fact, according to the Federal Emergency Management Agency (FEMA; 2000), hurricanes and earthquakes have been the most costly natural disasters in the United States over a recent 10-year period (1989–1999), followed closely by floods. For example, FEMA spent nearly $7 billion following the Northridge earthquake in Southern California (1994), and the expenses of the American Red Cross exceeded $81 million following Hurricane Andrew in South Florida (1992). The high costs are a direct function of the extensive community destruction that resulted from those events.

As a consequence of such widespread destruction, families may be uprooted from their neighborhoods and required to adjust to the loss of their homes and personal belongings, the companionship of their friends and loved ones, and their security. Although media coverage of major disasters typically wanes within a few days or weeks, it may be months, if not years before disaster survivors are able to repair the physical damage to their homes and communities and reestablish their normal lives and routines. In the meantime, survivors' postdisaster experiences act as constant reminders of the trauma: Homes and schools may be overcrowded to accommodate relocated families and children; damaged buildings and rubble are visible throughout the neighborhood and may not be attended to for months; modern conveniences, such as electricity, telephone access, and clean water may be unavailable for weeks following the disaster; and the loss of relocated neighbors and classmates creates a social void that hinders opportunities for recreation and social support.

Not surprisingly, natural disasters can affect children's and adolescents' psychological functioning (Vogel & Vernberg, 1993), particularly when exposure to the disaster is high and postdisaster recovery is difficult. Consistent findings from the growing body of literature on children's disaster-related reactions have demonstrated that a substantial proportion of child and adolescent victims of natural disasters experience moderate to severe levels of psychological distress that may last for years following the disaster (Vogel & Vernberg, 1993). The first section below summarizes the literature on the effects of hurricanes and earthquakes on children and adolescents. Next is a brief overview of some of the key factors that correlate with or predict youngsters' disaster reactions. The final section of the chapter reviews information on intervention strategies for helping children cope with these destructive natural disasters.

EFFECTS OF HURRICANES AND EARTHQUAKES

Research on natural disasters depends on the occurrence of a disaster. Accordingly, relatively few studies on children's disaster adaptation have taken place. Over the past 30 years, however, common findings from a number of investigations have revealed that a strikingly large proportion of children and adolescents experience serious symptoms of psychological distress following hurricanes, earthquakes, and tornadoes. Table 5.1 summarizes

TABLE 5.1
Effects of Hurricanes, Earthquakes, and Other Selected Natural Disasters on Children and Adolescents

Disaster	Study	Participants (N and other characteristics)[a]	Measures[b]	Time postdisaster	Findings
Postimpact period (3 months or less postdisaster)					
Hurricane Hugo	Sullivan et al. (1991); Saylor et al. (1992)	N = 278 Age 2–6 (M = 4.2) 96% White; 2% Black; 2% Hispanic/ Other	Child Behavior Checklist (CBCL) items (parents) At 6 weeks posthurricane, parents indicated the number of severity of problems before and after the hurricane.	6 weeks	Number and severity of total problems increased after hurricane. Frequency of trauma-themed play increased after hurricane.
Hurricane Andrew	Shaw et al. (1995)	N = 144 Age 6–11 (M = 8.2) 57% of children in high-impact area; 43% in low-impact area	Reaction Index Teacher Report Form (teachers)	8 and 32 weeks	39% of children from low-impact area and 56% of children from high-impact area reported severe to very severe PTSD symptoms after 8 weeks. Disruptive behavior decreased after the disaster.
Earthquake	Papadatos et al. (1990)	N = 172 High school students	General Symptom Checklist Center for Epidemiologic Studies–Depression Scale (CESD)	2 weeks	34.9% of students indicated severe levels of symptoms; 69% of students reported severe depressive mood.

Table Continues

TABLE 5.1
(Continued)

Disaster	Study	Participants (N and other characteristics)[a]	Measures[b]	Time postdisaster	Findings
Lightning strike	Dollinger et al. (1984)	N = 87 Age 10–13 29 disaster-exposed and 58 matched controls 97% White; 82% male	Fear Checklist (child and mother reports) Projective story-writing assessment	1–2 months	Compared with controls, the disaster-exposed group exhibited significantly more storm-related fears according to child and mother reports. Disaster-exposed children also reported more fears of sleep, animals, noise and disasters, body penetration, death and dying, and enclosed spaces.
Volcano	Ronan (1997)	N = 113 Age 7–15 52% male; 30% asthmatic	Reaction Index Parent- and teacher-rated distress	1 month	Asthmatic children reported significantly more PTSD symptoms and were rated by parents and teachers as being more distressed than nonasthmatic children.

Recovery and reconstruction period (3 months to 1 year postdisaster)

Hurricane Hugo	Belter et al. (1991)	N = 220 Grades 3–5 Three schools ranging in ethnic diversity and SES	Reaction Index Children's Depression Inventory Eyberg Behavior Checklist (completed by parents for current and predisaster symptoms)	5 months	90% of children reported severe PTSD; 69% of parents reported their children exhibited severe PTSD. Children did not report elevated levels of depression. Some elevation of total PTSD symptoms was found, but still within normative range. Only parental reports of children's PTSD symptoms were associated with exposure variables.
	Lonigan et al. (1991, 1994); Shannon et al. (1994)	N = 5,687 Age 9–19 years (M = 14.02) 67.3% White; 25.8% Black; 3.6% Asian; 1.4% Hispanic; 1.9% Other	Reaction Index Revised Children's Manifest Anxiety Scale (RCMAS)	3 months	5.42% of children were found to have full PTSD. For those with PTSD, 51% exhibited a decline in school performance. Exposure was related to higher levels of trait anxiety. Factors related to PTSD symptoms were female gender, age (9–12), ethnicity (Black), and trait anxiety.

Table Continues

TABLE 5.1
(Continued)

Disaster	Study	Participants (*N* and other characteristics)[a]	Measures[b]	Time postdisaster	Findings
Hurricane Andrew	Garrison et al. (1995)	*N* = 400 Age 12–17 44% Hispanic; 33% Black; 19% White 40% of family incomes below $25,000	Diagnostic Interview Schedule for Children	6 months	7.3% of children were found to have full PTSD. Factors related to PTSD symptoms were female gender, fear of personal or others' safety, personal social or resource loss, lifetime exposure to violent or traumatic events, and life events since hurricane.
	La Greca et al. (1996); Prinstein et al. (1996); Vernberg et al. (1996)	*N* = 568 Grades 3–5 44% White; 26% Hispanic; 22% African American	Reaction Index Hurricane Exposure KidCope Life Events Schedule Social Support Scale for Children Children's Coping Assistance Scale	3 months, 7 months, and 10 months	30%, 18%, and 13% reported severe or very severe PTSD symptoms at 3, 7, and 10 months postdisaster, respectively. PTSD symptoms were prospectively predicted by perceived life threat, exposure to disaster, gender (female), more life events, less social support, and (more negative) coping.

Table Continues

Study	Sample	Measures	Assessment	Findings
La Greca et al. (1998)	N = 92, Grades 4–6, 54% boys, 49% White; 38% Black; 12% Hispanic; 1% Asian	Reaction Index, RCMAS, Teacher ratings of behavior and achievement, Peer ratings of behavior and achievement	15 months prehurricane; 3 and 7 months posthurricane	33% and 11% reported moderate to very severe PTSD at 3 months and 7 months postdisaster, respectively. Predisaster anxiety, inattention, conduct problems, and achievement predicted PTSD symptoms at 3 months. Only predisaster anxiety and ethnicity (Black) predicted PTSD symptoms at 7 months.
Warheit et al. (1996); Khoury et al. (1997)	N = 4,978, Middle-school students, 67% Hispanic; 17% Black; 16% White, 42%–45% low SES	A stress measure including worry, anxiety, irritability, and demoralization, Depression composite measure, Suicidal ideation item, Minor deviance	1 year prehurricane and 6 months posthurricane	Anxiety increased (pre- to postdisaster) in children with high exposure levels. Hurricane-related stress was significantly associated with posthurricane suicidality, after controlling for prehurricane suicidality. Hurricane-related stress was mild to moderately related to minor deviance.
Loma Prieta Earthquake				
Bradburn (1991)	N = 22, Age 10–12, 55% male, 77% Black; 23% White	Reaction Index	6–8 months	67% reported moderate PTSD; no severe cases. Proximity to collapsed highway was associated with PSTD symptoms.

Table Continues

TABLE 5.1
(Continued)

Disaster	Study	Participants (N and other characteristics)[a]	Measures[b]	Time postdisaster	Findings
Recovery and reconstruction period (1 year or more after the event)					
Hurricane Hugo	Garrison et al. (1993)	N = 1,264 Age 11–17; 93% ages 12–14 47% male 45% White; 55% Black	Symptom checklist, including PTSD subscale	1 year	2%–6% met full PTSD criteria. 20% exhibited reexperiencing symptoms. 9% exhibited avoidance symptoms. 18% exhibited hyperarousal symptoms. Gender (female), race (White), exposure to hurricane, and experiencing other violent trauma were associated with higher PTSD symptoms.
	Swenson et al. (1996)	N = 313 Age 2–6 (M = 4.2) 161 disaster-exposed participants; 170 controls 99% White	Emotional Distress Scale, including acting out, anxious and withdrawn, and fearful subscales	14 months	9% of children exhibited trauma themes in play or conversation, and 14% exhibited fear of storms or trauma reminders. Maternal distress, property damage, and life stressors since the hurricane were associated with onset and longevity of children's behavioral difficulties.

Hurricane Andrew	Shaw et al. (1995)	$N = 144$ Age 6–11 ($M = 8.2$) 57% in high-impact area; 43% in low-impact area	Reaction Index Teacher Report Form (teacher)	8 and 32 weeks	38% of children from the high-impact area continued to report severe to very severe PTSD at 32 weeks. Disruptive behavior decreased after the disaster and did not return to typical rates until 1 year postdisaster.
Northridge Earthquake	Asarnow (1999)	$N = 63$ Age 8.6–18.6 ($M = 13.7$) 60% male 84% White; 8% Hispanic; 2% Black; 6% Asian	Schedule for Affective Disorders and Schizophrenia for Children (child and parent) Reaction Index Earthquake Exposure Questionnaire Resource Questionnaire Coping Responses Inventory CDI RCMAS Social Adjustment Scale	1 year ($M = 1.22$ years postdisaster)	28.5% reported mild to moderate PTSD symptoms. Exposure (resource loss and perceived stress) predicted PTSD symptoms. Only predisaster anxiety disorder was a significant predictor of postdisaster PTSD symptoms. Higher PTSD scores were associated with frequent use of cognitive coping and with concurrent depression, general anxiety, and peer adjustment difficulties.

Table Continues

TABLE 5.1
(Continued)

Disaster	Study	Participants (N and other characteristics)[a]	Measures[b]	Time postdisaster	Findings
Armenian Earthquake	Goenjian et al. (1995); Pynoos et al. (1993)	N = 218 to 213 Age 8–16 (M = 12–13) 62% female Three cities at various distances from epicenter	Reaction Index Depression Self-Rating Scale Diagnostic Interview Schedule for Children (Separation Anxiety Disorder [SAD] scale)	1.5 years	Between 24% and 91% had severe or very severe symptoms on Reaction Index. PTSD was higher for children in cities closer to the epicenter, girls, children who experienced death of family member, and children with a greater number of depressive symptoms. SAD ranged from 23% to 49% of children in the 3 cities. Comorbidities were high.
Earthquake	Rustemli & Karanci (1996)	N = 44 Adolescents (M = 14.8–15.8 years) 36% male	Abbreviated form of Symptom Checklist (SCL-90-R)	16 months	Parents reported more distress than children. Parents' somatization was associated with child distress.
Tornado	Stoppelbein & Greening (2000)	N = 118 Age 7–17 41% male 99% White	Reaction Index CDI RCMAS	1 year	14% had severe or very severe PTSD. 3% had full PTSD diagnosis.

Note. Studies that lacked a child or adolescent focus (e.g., those that included a wide age range, such as age 5–80) were excluded. Multiple studies drawn from a single sample are grouped together.
[a]Missing subject characteristics were not reported in the original article.
[b]Measures are child-report unless otherwise indicated.

empirical studies on the effects of hurricanes, earthquakes, and tornadoes on children and adolescents. The studies are organized by the timing of the postdisaster assessment, and by the specific natural disaster (e.g., hurricane, earthquake, other). As can be seen in the table, only a few studies ($n = 6$) focused on the immediate or acute postimpact phase (i.e., less than 3 months postdisaster). Most investigations ($n = 20$) assessed children during the recovery and reconstruction phase, and most of those (60%) conducted assessments 3 months to 1 year postdisaster; the remainder conducted assessments more than 1 year postdisaster.

Most of the findings on children's reactions to natural disasters have come from studies of hurricane victims. Almost no data exist on children's responses to volcano eruptions or tornadoes. (See chapter 6 for information on children's reactions to wildfires and chapter 7 for information on children's reactions to floods.) Our review also revealed that most studies have focused on youngsters' symptoms of posttraumatic stress disorder (PTSD) or related anxiety symptoms.

Although a variety of measures have been used to evaluate youngsters' disaster reactions, studies suggest that the prevalence of symptoms of PTSD may be high. Typically, moderate to severe symptoms of PTSD are evident for approximately 30% to 50% of youth affected by devastating hurricanes (e.g., La Greca, Silverman, Vernberg, & Prinstein, 1996; Lonigan, Shannon, Finch, Daugherty, & Taylor, 1991; Shaw et al., 1995; Vernberg et al., 1996). Symptom rates may be as high as 90% of the children exposed to particularly gruesome aspects of hurricanes and earthquakes and their aftermath (e.g., Belter, Dunn, & Jeney, 1991; Pynoos et al., 1993). In addition, 5% to 10% of the children or adolescents surveyed may meet criteria for a full diagnosis of PTSD (e.g., Garrison et al., 1995; Shannon, Lonigan, Finch, & Taylor, 1994).

Although longitudinal studies are sparse, existing evidence suggests that rates of PTSD symptoms decline over the first year following natural disasters, such as hurricanes (e.g., La Greca et al., 1996; La Greca, Silverman, & Wasserstein, 1998). Nevertheless, even a year or more after hurricanes and earthquakes, many children continue to exhibit severe PTSD symptoms (e.g., Pynoos et al., 1993; Shaw et al., 1995; Swensen et al., 1996), and somewhere between 2% and 6% may meet criteria for a diagnosis of PTSD (Garrison, Weinrich, Hardin, Weinrich, & Wang, 1993). In a study of the earthquake in Armenia (Pynoos et al., 1993), up to 90% of youth reported severe PTSD symptoms 18 months following the disaster. Similar results have been obtained in studies that have examined PTSD-related symptoms, such as trauma-themed play, disaster-related storytelling, and specific fears related to disaster experiences (Dollinger, O'Donnell, & Staley, 1984; Saylor, Swenson, & Powell, 1992).

Thus far, no evidence suggests that the severity of children's responses varies across different types of natural disasters (i.e., hurricanes, earthquakes, or lightning strikes). Apart from the study of hurricanes, however, a paucity of data is available on other types of natural disasters for comparison. Indeed, only one empirical study looked at children's psychological responses to a volcano eruption; that report focused on comparisons between asthmatic and nonasthmatic children's PTSD reactions (Ronan, 1997). Also, only one empirical study could be found on children's reactions to a tornado; in that study, the children's reactions were reported primarily as a comparison for understanding the reactions of parentally bereaved children (Stoppelbein & Greening, 2000). Nevertheless, both reports revealed findings similar to past research on hurricanes and earthquakes. In addition, several case reports were published following the Vicksburg tornado of 1953. For instance, a group of psychiatrists described their clinical impressions of youth in the weeks following this disaster (Silber, Perry, & Bloch, 1958). The symptoms observed by the clinicians fit with current diagnoses of separation anxiety (i.e., fears of separation from adults and clinging), PTSD-related symptoms of reexperiencing (i.e., nightmares and disaster-themed games), avoidance (i.e., phobic avoidance of tornado reminders), hyperarousal (i.e., oversensitivity to sudden noises), and disaster-related fears (i.e., fears of open spaces and storms).

Also of interest are findings that certain PTSD symptoms are more prevalent than others following natural disasters. For example, studies have reported high rates of reexperiencing (e.g., intrusive thoughts or dreams about the disaster) following hurricanes (e.g., La Greca et al., 1996; Lonigan, Anthony, & Shannon, 1998; Shannon, Lonigan et al., 1994; Vernberg et al., 1996). In contrast, symptoms of avoidance or numbing (e.g., avoiding thoughts, feelings, conversations, or reminders about the disaster or a diminished interest in normal activities) are the least commonly reported aspects of PTSD in youth (Garrison et al., 1993; Lonigan et al., 1998), although those types of symptoms also may be difficult for children to recognize and describe.

Findings appear to confirm that the most common psychological reactions to hurricanes and earthquakes are consistent with current formulations of PTSD, but children may experience other types of symptoms as well. Studies suggest that children's total number of psychological or behavioral difficulties (e.g., anxiety, behavior problems, and inattention) appears to increase following a disaster (e.g., Belter et al., 1991; La Greca et al., 1998; Saylor et al., 1992; Shaw et al., 1995), at least in the short term (i.e., 3 months or less postdisaster). Other, less well studied postdisaster reactions include disaster-related fears (Dollinger et al., 1984), anxiety (La Greca et al., 1998; Lonigan et al., 1991), and depression (Nolen-Hoeksema & Morrow, 1991; Papadatos, Nikou, & Potamianos, 1990). Some evidence also indicates that disaster-related distress may be associated with increased suicidality (Warheit, Zimmerman, Khoury, Vega, & Gil, 1996). Finally, several investigations have revealed decreases in academic achievement following a disaster (e.g., La Greca et al., 1998; Shannon et al., 1994; Vincent, La Greca, Silverman, Wasserstein, & Prinstein, 1994), perhaps as a result of greater absenteeism and difficulties concentrating in school. Future studies would do well to examine multiple outcomes associated with children's disaster reactions. Moreover, efforts to distinguish between "normal" and "pathological" disaster reactions are needed. In this regard, it is noteworthy that the studies listed in Table 5.1 did not evaluate whether the youngsters showed signs of "impairment" in their day-to-day functioning. Impairment, however, was recently added to the diagnostic criteria for PTSD in the *Diagnostic and Statistical Manual of Mental Disorders, Fourth Edition* (DSM–IV; American Psychiatric Association, 1994) and should be considered in future work.

One key question that arises following natural disasters is whether the disaster itself causes psychological symptoms or whether youth who report such symptoms already evidence psychological problems. Because PTSD reactions are specific to traumatic experiences, evidence suggests that PTSD symptoms are directly associated with children's experience of a traumatic disaster. Nevertheless, a number of methodological limitations in this area of research may help explain some of the difficulty in obtaining valid assessments of disaster-related changes in children's psychological functioning.

One of the common limitations of investigations of youngsters' disaster reactions is the lack of a comparable, nonexposed comparison group. Some studies have addressed this issue by including a comparison group of youth who experienced the disaster in a milder form (e.g., Shaw et al., 1995). Other studies have included children with a wide range of disaster exposure and examined differences in symptoms as a function of level of disaster exposure (e.g., La Greca et al., 1996; Lonigan, Shannon, Taylor, Finch, & Sallee, 1994). Still other studies have compared rates of behavioral or emotional problems in disaster-affected children with those of normative samples to help document the elevated rates of symptoms among disaster victims (e.g., Belter et al., 1991). Together, such studies provide convincing evidence that disasters such as hurricanes and earthquakes, lead to stress reactions in youth.

Another common problem that plagues disaster research is that of documenting changes in children's functioning or stress symptoms that may result from exposure to a disaster. Given the sudden and unexpected nature of natural disasters, efforts to compare youngsters' pre- and postdisaster functioning have been limited by the use of retrospective reports of children's predisaster symptoms (e.g., Belter et al., 1991; Saylor et al., 1992). Such reports are subject to reporting bias and are likely influenced by the informant's own degree of psychological distress following a disaster. A few studies that have serendipitously collected predisaster data as part of an unrelated project on children's or adolescents' adjustment (e.g., La Greca et al., 1998; Nolen-Hoeksema & Morrow, 1991) have shown that disasters can alter youngsters' functioning. Such studies also suggest that certain predisaster characteristics (e.g., symptoms of anxiety and depression) may predispose youth to more severe disaster reactions (La Greca et al., 1998; Nolen-Hoeksema & Morrow, 1991).

Given the many difficulties associated with organizing and implementing large-scale investigations in the aftermath of catastrophic hurricanes and earthquakes, these limitations are often difficult to address. Nevertheless, the effects of disasters on children is an important area of child mental health research, one that has tremendous public health implications (American Psychological Association, 1995; Vernberg, 1994).

FACTORS THAT PREDICT (OR CORRELATE WITH) DISASTER-RELATED STRESS SYMPTOMS

The severity of children's reactions to disasters varies considerably, and a number of recent investigations of hurricanes and earthquakes have examined factors associated with those variations (e.g., La Greca et al., 1996; Lonigan et al., 1994; Pynoos et al., 1993). As highlighted in chapter 1, however, it is not always apparent whether the various "predictors" of children's postdisaster reactions are causal risk factors that play an active role in determining children's stress reactions or simply correlates of children's stress reactions. Nevertheless, existing research provides an initial framework for examining factors that may actively contribute to children's and adolescents' postdisaster adjustment. (See La Greca et al., 1996, and Vernberg et al., 1996, for a discussion of conceptual models to guide research on children's reactions to disasters; see also chapters 1 and 17 of this volume.)

A major emphasis of existing work on hurricanes and earthquakes has been to examine the type and severity of disaster experiences—or degree of "exposure" to the disaster—as predictors of disaster reactions. In particular, children's perceptions of life threat and their experiences of loss and life disruption following a major hurricane or earthquake are closely associated with symptoms of posttraumatic stress (e.g., Pynoos et al., 1993; Vernberg et al., 1996). Children from neighborhoods severely affected by a disaster (i.e., closer to an earthquake epicenter or the eye of a hurricane) experience more severe and prolonged PTSD symptoms than children from less severely affected neighborhoods or communities. This difference is likely a result of the greater life threat associated with being close to the disaster as well as the more extensive loss and destruction of property and belongings that come with proximity to a catastrophic natural disaster. For example, following Hurricane Andrew, approximately 60% of the children surveyed who were living in neighborhoods that were in the main path of the hurricane reported that they "thought they were going to die" during the storm, and high percentages of those children also reported damage to their homes and possessions (Vernberg et al., 1996). In turn, children's reports of life threat, loss, and disruption were significant predictors of the severity of PTSD symptoms at 3, 7, and 10 months posthurricane (La Greca et al., 1996). Pynoos and colleagues (1993) found that following an earthquake in which there was loss of life, PTSD symptoms were especially high among youngsters who experienced the death of a family member.

Another avenue of study has been to identify demographic factors that may help predict which children and adolescents are more at risk for severe PTSD reactions. In this regard, some studies have found that girls report more severe PTSD symptoms following hurricanes and earthquakes than boys do (e.g., Garrison et al., 1993, 1995; Pynoos et al., 1993; Shannon et al., 1994; Vernberg et al., 1996). Findings also suggest that ethnic minorities may exhibit a greater number of PTSD symptoms following these types of natural disasters (e.g., Shannon et al., 1994) although the likely mechanism for such findings has not been elucidated. It is possible that children from minority backgrounds live in less affluent households than nonminority youth and thus their families may lack the necessary financial resources and insurance coverage to rebuild their homes and lives after a destructive natural disaster (see also chapter 4). Findings also have revealed that young children may be at higher risk for PTSD symptoms than other children following a disaster (e.g., Lonigan et al., 1994), although it is unclear whether the risk stems from developmental differences in younger children's perceptions of natural disaster traumas or from the tendency of young children to engage in behavior that is more readily identifiable as symptoms of PTSD (i.e., trauma-themed play).

Some studies have attempted to examine preexisting psychosocial factors that might play a role in children's disaster reactions (e.g., La Greca et al., 1998). In this regard, children's predisaster levels of anxiety have been found to predict greater PTSD symptoms following hurricanes (La Greca et al., 1998). In addition, adolescents who have a history of experiencing other traumatic or violent events have reported more severe PTSD symptoms after hurricanes than those without prior trauma exposure (Garrison et al., 1993, 1995). Children who have low school achievement also may be more prone to reporting more severe PTSD symptoms after natural disasters than children with average or high achievement levels (Shannon et al., 1994; Vincent et al., 1994).

Finally, another set of factors that have been examined as predictors of children's postdisaster reactions are those associated with the postdisaster recovery environment, such as the availability of social support, the presence of other major life stressors, and the types of coping strategies children use to deal with the disaster. Following Hurricane Andrew, for example, children who reported high levels of social support from parents, friends, and teachers; few intervening life events; and low use of negative coping strategies were found to have less severe levels of PTSD symptoms 10 months after the disaster than those who reported less support, more life stress, and negative coping styles (La Greca et al., 1996). Children whose parents are highly distressed following hurricanes and earthquakes also appear to have a greater number of disaster-related problems than children whose parents are not so distressed (Rustemli & Karanei, 1996; Swensen et al., 1996). Such findings need to be interpreted cautiously, however, when parents are the informants for both their own and their children's adjustment.

In summary, efforts to understand the factors that predict disasters' effects on children and adolescents and that help mitigate their impact are promising, but relatively new. Further efforts to understand which children are most likely to be affected and the mechanisms that contribute to children's disaster reactions and adjustment will most likely require the development of sophisticated conceptual models that provide a foundation for understanding when and how to intervene (see chapter 1). Work in this area is just beginning (e.g., La Greca et al., 1996; Vernberg et al., 1996), and continued work is essential if treatment providers and researchers are to develop empirically sound intervention strategies. The next section discusses the current state of intervention efforts for children following hurricanes and earthquakes.

INTERVENTIONS FOLLOWING HURRICANES AND EARTHQUAKES

Several obstacles hinder the implementation of interventions following natural disasters, such as hurricanes and earthquakes. One major difficulty is that the significant people in children's lives—parents, teachers, and close friends—also may be affected by the disaster and thus may not be available to provide help and support. Parents and teachers also may minimize or underestimate children's distress following disasters, perhaps because they also are experiencing trauma. Moreover, supports from outside the community (e.g., the Red Cross or assistance from neighboring communities) that are available shortly after a disaster may dissipate quickly.

Obstacles exist to providing effective preventive services, such as developing disaster preparedness plans. Many communities do not perceive themselves to be vulnerable to disasters and therefore have done little to develop disaster plans. Even in high-risk areas for hurricanes , earthquakes, and tornadoes, communities vary widely in their development of disaster plans (Baum, 1987; Vernberg & Vogel, 1993). When Hurricane Andrew struck South Florida, for example, the local public schools did not have a formal disaster plan in place for dealing with children's mental health needs, despite being in a hurricane-prone area.

A critical factor impeding clinicians' ability to provide postdisaster interventions for children is the dearth of treatment outcome studies (Vernberg & Vogel, 1993). Treatment providers basically do not know when and how to best intervene, although some promising leads come from the growing literature on disasters' effects (reviewed above; see also chapters 1 and 3). This section of the chapter reviews current ideas on how to help children and adolescents following disasters. In general, the most promising interventions focus on processing the event, increasing social support, and improving problem solving along with coping with the event and its aftermath.

The following material on interventions for children and adolescents following disasters is organized by the length of time since the disaster. In general, interventions immediately following natural disasters are likely to be brief, universal, and community based. Interventions that extend past the initial, acute recovery phase (approximately the first 3 months after the disaster) focus increasingly on high-risk youth or those demonstrating persistent adjustment difficulties (see chapter 3).

Initial Recovery Period

The *initial impact phase* of a disaster begins with the onset of the event, extends through the end of the event, and concludes when an initial assessment of casualties and other loss is communicated to people directly affected by the disaster (Vernberg & Vogel, 1993, p. 486). Paramount during this brief period are efforts to restore children's sense of personal safety and security.

During the *short-term adaptation phase* (i.e., 24 hours or so after the event until approximately 3 months postdisaster), community- or school-based interventions that target youth in affected areas have been recommended (Vernberg & Vogel, 1993). Also, because children who evidence high levels of PTSD symptoms 3 months after a disaster (hurricane) appear to have high levels of PTSD symptoms up to 1 year after the event (La Greca et al., 1996), it may be desirable to identify and monitor early in this phase the youth who are most severely affected by the disaster.

As Vernberg and Vogel (1993) described, early interventions might include classroom and small-group activities, family approaches, and individual treatment. The purpose is to provide information and help normalize children's reactions to the disaster, provide a sense of safety and security, and help children return to a sense of routine and normalcy. During this time, efforts to provide information to helping professionals and the general public (e.g., fact sheets, web sites, and mass media) also are useful (Vernberg & Vogel, 1993). Exhibit 5.1 lists several resources for fact sheets and brochures that may be useful to children, parents, teachers, and mental health professionals in the aftermath of natural disasters.

During this initial recovery period (i.e., up to 3 months postdisaster), the types of interventions that have been evaluated primarily involve "debriefing" efforts. Debriefing, or critical incident stress debriefing (CISD), is a crisis intervention designed to relieve and prevent trauma-related distress in "normal" people who are experiencing abnormally stressful events or disasters (Chemtob, Tomas, Law, & Cremniter, 1997; Mitchell, 1983). Debriefings provide opportunities for children to ventilate feelings, normalize their re-

EXHIBIT 5.1
Helping Children Cope With Natural Disasters:
Selected Internet Resources

http://www.fema.gov/kids/	Child-oriented Web site on disasters developed by the Federal Emergency Management Association. It contains information on different types of disasters, how to prepare for them, and how to cope.
http://www.redcross.org/disaster/safety/guide.html	Brochure developed by the American Red Cross: *Talking About Disaster: Guide.* Check the Red Cross home page (http://www.redcross.org) for additional information and breaking news on disasters.
http://www.apa.org/practice/kids.html	Web site developed by the American Psychological Association (APA). Contains a fact sheet, "Helping Children Cope: A Guide to Helping Children Cope With the Stress of the Oklahoma City Explosion." Useful for a wide range of disasters. Check the APA home page (http://www.apa.org) for additional information and breaking news.
http://www.aacap.org	Web site of the American Academy of Child and Adolescent Psychiatry. Contains many fact sheets for children and families, including how to help children cope with disasters.
http://www.jmu.edu/psychologydept/4kids.htm	Contains disaster-related information for children from the Virginia Disaster Stress Intervention at James Madison University, Harrisonburg, VA.
http://www.disastertraining.org	Site provides adults with information to help children cope with natural disasters and violence.
http://www.mentalhealth.org	Web site for the Center for Mental Health Services. Contains information for communities and reference lists for practitioners on disaster interventions.
http://www.ncptsd.org	Web site for the National Center for PTSD. Includes manual for disaster mental health services.
http://www.aap.org	Web site for the American Academy of Pediatrics. Contains disaster intervention information for pediatricians.

sponses to the disaster, and learn about common psychological reactions in the context of a supportive group (Chemtob et al., 1997). At this point, however, little empirical support exists for the effectiveness of debriefing with children and adolescents or with adults (Rose & Bisson, 1998). In fact, some studies with adults suggest that CISD may be unhelpful following disasters (see Rose & Bisson, 1998). It is possible that multiple applications of CISD would be required to enhance its effectiveness (Horowitz, Schreiber, Hare, Walker, & Talley, 1999); brief, one-shot interventions are probably insufficient in length and scope to begin to address some of the multiple and cascading stressors that result from major disasters and may last for months or years.

At least in the short term, massage therapy has been shown to reduce symptoms of anxiety and depression among elementary school children following a hurricane. Field, Seligman, Scafidi, and Schanberg (1996) randomly assigned 60 children who displayed behavior problems and reported severe levels of PTSD symptoms 1 month after Hurricane Andrew to a massage therapy or video-attention control condition. The massage group received twice-weekly back massages for 30 minutes per session. Children in the control condition watched a video while sitting on the lap of a research assistant for a comparable amount of time. Children receiving massage reported less anxiety and depression, evidenced lower salivary cortisol levels (a measure of stress), and were observed to be more relaxed following treatment than the control children. Although further replication and follow-up would be desirable, the authors suggested that teaching parents to administer massage to their children might be useful in reducing children's distress following a traumatic natural disaster.

Aside from formal interventions, literature from the American Red Cross (1999) and other sources (Farberow & Frederick, 1978; FEMA, 1989; National Organization for Victim Assistance, 1991) recommends that parents, teachers, and mental health professionals encourage children and adolescents to express their feelings in developmentally appropriate ways after disasters, such as through discussions, drawings, storytelling, or journal writing. Those sources also suggest that adults should try to be aware of and sensitive to children's fears, worries, and concerns.

Efforts to return to "normal" roles and routines also may help youngsters renormalize their lives following disasters. Prinstein, La Greca, Vernberg, and Silverman (1996) found that children who reported high levels of assistance from parents, friends, and teachers in resuming their normal roles and routines during the first few months after Hurricane Andrew reported significantly fewer PTSD symptoms 7 months postdisaster. In our clinical experiences following Hurricane Andrew, several teachers told us that some children did not want to return home after school because things felt normal at school, whereas they still encountered considerable hurricane-related damage and destruction at home and in their neighborhoods. Those informal observations highlight the value of helping youth to normalize their lives following a natural disaster.

Long-Term Recovery Period

Few controlled investigations have been conducted of interventions for youth following disasters, even though a significant number of youth report moderate to severe levels of posttraumatic stress a year or more after a disaster (e.g., Green et al., 1994; Shaw, Applegate, & Schorr, 1996; Vincent, 1997). The studies described here may be especially pertinent for clinicians working with children and adolescents who have persistent and severe posttraumatic stress following a natural disaster: Such children may need more intensive, individualized interventions than are typically provided in school or community settings.

This section also describes promising intervention ideas that await further evaluation. The ideas are derived from community-based studies that have linked certain types of coping strategies and coping assistance with better child adjustment following disasters. The community-based studies suggest ways that teachers, counselors, or mental health professionals might enhance children's and adolescents' adjustment following large-scale, communitywide hurricanes and earthquakes.

Outcome Studies

Our literature search found only three controlled studies of child treatment following disasters or single-incident stressors (Goenjian et al., 1997; March, Amaya-Jackson, Murray, & Schulte, 1998; Yule & Canterbury, 1994), and only one is specific to natural disasters (Goenjian et al., 1997). Two of the studies used cognitive–behavioral therapy (CBT; March et al., 1998; Yule & Canterbury, 1994), and one developed a model of trauma- and grief-focused psychotherapy (Goenjian et al., 1997).

Central to both approaches is the notion that trauma victims need to be reexposed to the traumatic event (often through recalling images of the event) and allowed to "emotionally process" the event in a safe, controlled setting (see Foa, Steketee, & Rothbaum, 1989; Rachman, 1980). Exposure and emotional processing are thought to allow the person to habituate to the feared stimuli, reevaluate the probability of threat in feared situations, and change the negative valence associated with the fear responses (Foa, Rothbaum, Riggs, & Murdock, 1991). For example, a safe, controlled setting, sometimes paired with relaxation (e.g., March et al., 1998), can help a youngster gradually extinguish high levels of arousal to the traumatic event and trauma-related cues.

Goenjian and colleagues (1997) used brief trauma- and grief-focused psychotherapy administered in a school-based setting to treat symptoms of PTSD and depression among adolescents who were exposed to the 1988 Armenian earthquake. The earthquake devastated four cities and 350 villages in Armenia, killing at least 25,000 people. In Gumri, where the intervention took place, at least 18,000 people were killed and about 50% of the buildings were destroyed (Goenjian et al., 1997). Eighteen months after the earthquake, 64 youngsters (age 11 to 12, on average) participated in the intervention; 35 were treated, and 29 served as untreated controls. Another 18 months later, the youth were reevaluated for PTSD and depressive symptoms.

Treatment was conducted in classroom groups (four half-hour sessions) and individually (two 1-hour sessions) over a 3-week period. The most symptomatic adolescents received two additional individual treatment sessions.

In all cases, treatment was completed within 6 weeks. The trauma- and grief-focused psychotherapy included the following elements:

- Reconstructing and reprocessing the traumatic event (in part by clarifying distortions and misattributions) and addressing the resulting avoidance and maladaptations;
- Identifying traumatic reminders and assisting youth with developing tolerance and increasing social support during and after the reminders;
- Coping with stresses and adversities by encouraging proactive measures to cope with changes and losses that resulted from the disaster;
- Handling bereavement (e.g., by helping the bereaved reconstitute a nontraumatic mental image of the deceased person); and
- Assessing developmental impact by identifying missed developmental opportunities and promoting normal developmental tasks. (See Goenjian et al., 1997, for more details.)

By 3 years postdisaster, treated adolescents showed a significant decline in PTSD symptom scores relative to pretreatment levels, whereas controls showed a significant increase over time. Similarly, over the 18-month period following the start of treatment, the rates of "likely" PTSD cases decreased from 60% to 28% among treated adolescents but increased from 52% to 69% for the controls. Although treated adolescents showed no significant change in depressive symptoms over the 18-month period, control-group adolescents showed a significant increase in depression. Despite their promising results, the authors caution that further studies are needed to evaluate whether the results would generalize to youth with less severe trauma exposure (Goenjian et al., 1997).

Although they did not focus on natural disasters, March and colleagues (1998) evaluated the efficacy of group-administered CBT with 17 youths (ages 10 to 15) who experienced one or more stressors of sufficient magnitude to produce PTSD (e.g., car accidents, severe storms, accidental injury, gunshot injury, and fires). In some cases, the events happened to a loved one (e.g., death by assault). Before treatment, the youth reported mild to moderately severe PTSD (average duration, 1.5 to 2.5 years), anxiety, and depression. March and colleagues' 18-week Multi-Modality Trauma Treatment was adapted from CBT protocols for treating PTSD in adults (see Foa et al., 1991) and anxiety in children (Kendall, 1994). The treatment included the following components:

- Anxiety-management training;
- Relaxation training;
- Anger coping;
- Cognitive training for dealing with PTSD intrusions;

- Developing a stimulus hierarchy that is based on traumatic reminders; and
- Narrative, gradual "exposure" to the trauma along with corrective information regarding distortions and misattributions (see March et al., 1998).

To promote treatment generalization and relapse prevention, March and colleagues gave homework assignments. Of the 14 youth who completed treatment, 8 (57%) no longer met criteria for PTSD following treatment and 12 (86%) no longer met criteria at the 6-month follow-up. Similar improvements were observed for symptoms of depression, anxiety, and anger.

The two key studies (Goenjian et al., 1997; March et al., 1998) are promising and suggest that gradual exposure to traumatic events, with opportunities to reprocess the event in a reparative manner, is a critical component of treatments for PTSD following disasters. When conducting exposure-based treatments, is essential that the professional understand the child's "perception of the event, subjective meaning, level of exposure, and attributions of cause" (Amaya-Jackson & March, 1995, p. 291) and not terminate reprocessing until the child's arousal level has been returned to normal.

Associated treatment strategies also may be appropriate, depending on the nature of the trauma. Grief management (e.g., Goenjian et al., 1997) appears to be valuable for disasters that involve the death or loss of loved ones. Anger management may be appropriate when anger and behavior problems are a secondary problem, concurrent with PTSD.

One additional area of concern is how to help children and adolescents who have been exposed to multiple or chronic traumatic events. As the treatment literature develops further, more attention is needed to developing effective programs for children exposed to multiple traumatic events.

Community Studies

Although community-based interventions with children following disasters have not been evaluated systematically, empirical literature describes factors that play a role in the persistence of children's distress following natural disasters. The materials described in this section are consistent with that empirical research.

As noted earlier, certain factors have been found to predict children's PTSD symptoms over the year following natural disasters: levels of social support (from family, friends, and teachers), stressors and life events, and coping strategies (see La Greca et al., 1996; Vernberg et al., 1996). Thus, efforts to enhance children's social support networks, to reduce stress, and to cope effectively with ongoing stressors might be useful for helping children following disasters.

Building on those empirically based factors, La Greca, Vernberg, Silverman, Vogel, and Prinstein (1994) developed a school-based intervention manual to help children cope during the year following Hurricane Andrew.[2] The manual included "lessons" that teachers, counselors, or psychologists could use with children in disaster-affected areas to increase children's level of social support, especially from teachers and peers; identify stressors or ongoing problems that resulted from the disaster and that affected children's everyday lives; and promote positive methods for coping with ongoing stressors (and avoiding negative ones). Some lessons focused on how to help children cope with holidays (e.g., Thanksgiving) that are "different" because of the disaster (e.g., a child may have lost his or her home, possessions, or friends). Other lessons dealt with identifying ongoing stressors that bother children and help them develop ways to cope with those problems. To strengthen support networks and friendship ties in the classroom, children completed activities in small groups.

In addition to activities designed to promote coping and social support, the manual provides information on "risk factors" for PTSD symptoms, so that teachers, counselors, and psychologists can identify children with severe stress reactions early following the disaster. The manual also contains lessons on disaster preparation, so that children know what to do should another disaster strike.

As noted above, the specific components of this school-based program have received empirical support from the literature on factors that predict children's PTSD symptoms following hurricanes (e.g., La Greca et al., 1996; Swenson et al., 1996; Vernberg et al., 1996) and other traumatic events (see chapters 1, 6, 8, 14, and 16). Although the comprehensive program that is presented in the manual has not yet been evaluated, the manual has been distributed to thousands of schools, American Red Cross centers, and psychologists across the United States and abroad and has received favorable reviews. In fact, the manual was translated into Japanese (La Greca, Vernberg, Silverman, Vogel, & Prinstein, 1995) to help children cope with the aftermath of a devastating earthquake in Kobe, Japan. The manual also has been useful in other disasters, such as the bombing of the Alfred P. Murrah Federal Building in Oklahoma City in April 1995 (J. Gonzalez, personal communication, May 1995).

In another line of research, Prinstein et al. (1996) examined what children and families actually do to cope with disasters and how their coping relates to recovery. Such information could help develop evidence-based intervention efforts. In Prinstein and colleagues' study, more than 400 children in grades 3 to 5 were asked about the kinds of "coping assistance" (defined as the specific ways that others helped children cope with the trauma)

---

[2]Copies of *Helping Children Prepare for and Cope With Natural Disasters: A Manual for Professionals Working With Elementary School Children* can be obtained by writing to A. La Greca, Department of Psychology, P.O. Box 249229, University of Miami, Coral Gables, FL 33124. An abridged version of the manual, pertinent to all disasters is also available.

they received from parents, friends, and teachers following Hurricane Andrew. The frequency and type of coping assistance that children reported were then examined as a predictor of their PTSD symptoms. A review of disaster-related mental health materials resulted in three types of coping assistance being evaluated: *emotional processing* of the event (i.e., controlled and repeated exposure to reminders of the traumatic event); resuming normal *roles and routines*; and *distraction*. Children most often reported resuming normal roles and routine, followed by distraction and emotional processing. Children also reported receiving the most coping assistance from parents, followed by friends and teachers. Children reported emotionally processing the event (e.g., talking about it) significantly more often with friends than with parents or teachers, however.

Of particular interest in this study was the association between the types and sources of coping assistance and children's PTSD symptoms 7 months postdisaster. Children with moderate to very severe levels of PTSD symptoms reported more emotional processing and distraction than children with low to mild levels of symptoms did. In contrast, resuming normal roles and routines was significantly more frequent among children with low levels of PTSD symptoms. Furthermore, resuming normal roles and routines significantly predicted *declines* in children's PTSD levels from 7 to 10 months postdisaster (Prinstein & La Greca, 2002). Although further work of a prospective nature is needed, the findings highlight the importance of friends as well as family in helping children cope with the aftermath of a disaster. The studies additionally suggest that efforts to resume normal roles and routines (e.g., sharing usual activities with friends and keeping a similar home and school routine) may be especially beneficial to children following natural disasters.

Other community-based ideas for helping children and families cope with the long-term aftermath of disasters include having public ceremonies, memorials, or disaster-related rituals that provide an opportunity for survivors to remember the event and place it in context (Vernberg & Vogel, 1993). As noted in chapter 3 (also see Vernberg & Vogel, 1993), rituals serve several important psychological functions, including public expression of shared grief and support, reassurance that disaster victims are remembered, and an opportunity to review and reinterpret disaster experiences and to obtain closure on a difficult life event. The anniversary of an event is an especially common time for community-based ceremonies or rituals. For example, the local media in South Florida highlighted the 1-year anniversary of Hurricane Andrew with special television programs and newspaper articles that reviewed the disaster and the recovery period and emphasized the rebuilding and recovery process. Although little research has been conducted on the value of rituals, "the timelessness of human rites to mark deaths and tragedies bears witness to their appeal" (Vernberg & Vogel, 1993, p. 496). Rituals and commemorative activities are especially appealing for disasters that affect large numbers of children and families.

Summary

Little data are available on the efficacy or effectiveness of various interventions to help young disaster victims, although the literature suggests several important directions to pursue. In the immediate aftermath, efforts to reassure children, provide information, and "normalize" their reactions may be helpful. Parents, teachers, and clinicians might focus on identifying children with the most severe reactions, so that they can talk with them and provide additional help. Materials obtained from Web sites of mental health and government organizations (see Exhibit 5.1) contain resources (e.g., fact sheets, activities, information) that may facilitate this process. For large-scale communitywide disasters, efforts to deal with children and families in the community may be most productive; however, it also may be desirable to target youth who have severe reactions for additional services. Youth who are severely traumatized might benefit from the use of exposure-based, cognitive–behavioral treatments. These approaches hold promise for reducing levels of PTSD in children and adolescents exposed to traumatic disasters, especially when combined with other strategies for dealing with comorbid problems (e.g., grief and depression from the loss of a loved one).

CONCLUSIONS

This area of child mental health is relatively new. In future research, it is essential that consideration be given to developing disaster interventions that are developmentally appropriate and culturally sensitive, because those aspects of interventions have been overlooked (also see chapters 3 and 4 for suggestions). Helping children and their families cope with natural disasters and developing family-based strategies for those who are severely affected represent important avenues for further study. Other research needs include the development of interventions that take into account the particular phase of the recovery period (i.e., immediate, short-term, or long-term) and the type of disaster that has occurred (e.g., with or without mass casualties). Given that most people are not well prepared for disasters and their aftermath, efforts to develop networks of professionals (both researchers and clinicians) who are knowledgeable about disasters and their psychological effects on children and families in advance of a disaster might be valuable. Such professionals might provide mental health consultation to schools and communities following disasters and help improve the quality of assessment and treatment outcome research on the effects of disasters on children and youth.

REFERENCES

Amaya-Jackson, L., & March, J. S. (1995). Posttraumatic stress disorder. In J. S. March (Ed.), *Anxiety disorders in children and adolescents* (pp. 276–300). New York: Guilford Press.

American Psychiatric Association. (1994). *Diagnostic and statistical manual of mental disorders, 4th edition.* Washington, DC: Author.

American Psychological Association. (1995). *Resolution on children's psychological needs following disasters.* Washington, DC: Author.

American Red Cross. (1999). *Talking about disaster: Guide for standard messages.* Washington, DC: National Disaster Education Coalition.

Asarnow, J. (1999). When the earth stops shaking: Earthquake sequelae among children diagnosed for pre-earthquake psychopathology. *Journal of the American Academy of Child and Adolescent Psychiatry, 38,* 1016–1023.

Baum, A. (1987). Toxins, technology, and natural disasters. In G. R. VandenBos & B. K. Bryant (Eds.), *Cataclysms, crises, and catastrophes: Psychology in action* (pp. 7–53). Washington, DC: American Psychological Association.

Belter, R. W., Dunn, S. E., & Jeney, P. (1991). The psychological impact of Hurricane Hugo on children: A needs assessment. *Advances in Behaviour Research and Therapy, 13,* 155–161.

Bradburn, I. S. (1991). After the earth shook: Children's stress symptoms 6-8 months after a disaster. *Advances in Behavior Therapy and Research, 13,* 173–179.

Chemtob, C. M., Tomas, S., Law, W., & Cremniter, D. (1997). Postdisaster psychosocial intervention: A field study of the impact of debriefing on psychological distress. *American Journal of Psychiatry, 154,* 415–417.

Dollinger, S. J., O'Donnell, J. P., & Staley, A. A. (1984). Lightning-strike disaster: Effects on children's fears and worries. *Journal of Consulting and Clinical Psychology, 52,* 1028–1038.

Farberow, N., & Frederick, C. (1978). *Field manual for field service workers in disasters.* Rockville, MD: National Institute of Mental Health.

Federal Emergency Management Agency. (1989). *Coping with children's reactions to hurricanes and other disasters* (Document No. 1989 0-941-901). Washington, DC: U.S. Government Printing Office.

Federal Emergency Management Agency. (2000). *Disaster facts.* Retrieved March 10, 2001, from http://www.fema.gov/library/df_2.htm

Field, T., Seligman, S., Scafidi, F., & Schanberg, S. (1996). Alleviating posttraumatic stress in children following Hurricane Andrew. *Journal of Applied Developmental Psychology, 17,* 37–50.

Foa, E. B., Rothbaum, B. O., Riggs, D. S., & Murdock, T. B. (1991). Treatment of posttraumatic stress disorder in rape victims: A comparison between cognitive-behavioral procedures and counseling. *Journal of Consulting and Clinical Psychology, 59,* 715–723.

Foa, E. B., Steketee, G., & Rothbaum, B. O. (1989). Behavioral/cognitive conceptualization of posttraumatic stress disorder. *Behavior Therapy, 20*, 155–176.

Garrison, C. Z., Bryant, E. S., Addy, C. L., Spurrier, P. G., Freedy, J. R., & Kilpatrick, D. G. (1995). Posttraumatic stress disorder in adolescents after Hurricane Andrew. *Journal of the American Academy of Child and Adolescent Psychiatry, 34*, 1193–1201.

Garrison, C. Z., Weinrich, M. W., Hardin, S. B., Weinrich, S., & Wang, L. (1993). Posttraumatic stress disorder in adolescents after a hurricane. *American Journal of Epidemiology, 138*, 522–530.

Goenjian, A. K., Karayan, I., Pynoos, R. S., Minassian, D., Najarian, L. M., Steinberg, A. M., & Fairbanks, L. A. (1997). Outcome of psychotherapy among early adolescents after trauma. *American Journal of Psychiatry, 154*, 536–542.

Goenjian, A. K., Pynoos, R. S., Steinberg, A. M., Najarian, L. M., Asarnow, J. R., Karayan, I., Ghurabi, M., & Fairbanks, L. A. (1995). Psychiatric comorbidity in children after the 1988 earthquake in Armenia. *Journal of the American Academy of Child and Adolescent Psychiatry, 34*, 1174–1184.

Green, B. L., Korol, M. S., Grace, M. C., Vary, M. G., Kramer, T. L., Gleser, G. C., & Leonard, A. C. (1994). Children of disaster in the second decade: A 17-year follow-up of Buffalo Creek survivors. *Journal of the American Academy of Child and Adolescent Psychiatry, 33*, 71–79.

Horowitz, L. M., Schreiber, M. D., Hare, I., Walker, V. R., & Talley, A. L. (1999). *Psychological factors in emergency medical services for children.* Washington, DC: American Psychological Association.

Kendall, P. C. (1994). Treating anxiety disorders in children: Results of a randomized clinical trial. *Journal of Consulting and Clinical Psychology, 62*, 100–110.

Khoury, E. L., Warheit, G. J., Hargrove, M. C., Zimmerman, R. S., Vega, W. A., & Gil, A. G. (1997). The impact of Hurricane Andrew on deviant behavior among a multi-racial/ethnic sample of adolescents in Dade County, Florida: A longitudinal analysis. *Journal of Traumatic Stress, 10*, 71–91.

La Greca, A. M., Silverman, W. K., Vernberg, E. M., & Prinstein, M. J. (1996). Symptoms of posttraumatic stress after Hurricane Andrew: A prospective study. *Journal of Consulting and Clinical Psychology, 64*, 712–723.

La Greca, A. M., Silverman, W. K., & Wasserstein, S. B. (1998). Children's predisaster functioning as a predictor of posttraumatic stress following Hurricane Andrew. *Journal of Consulting and Clinical Psychology, 66*, 883–892.

La Greca, A. M., Vernberg, E. M., Silverman, W. K., Vogel, A., & Prinstein, M. J. (1994). *Helping children cope with natural disasters: A manual for school personnel.* Miami, FL: Author.

La Greca, A. M., Vernberg, E. M., Silverman, W. K., Vogel, A., & Prinstein, M. J. (1995). Japanese version: *Helping children.* Tokyo: Ashi.

Lonigan, C. J., Anthony, J. L., & Shannon, M. P. (1998). Diagnostic efficacy of posttraumatic symptoms in children exposed to disaster: *Journal of Clinical Child Psychology, 27*, 255–267.

Lonigan, C. J., Shannon, M. P., Finch, A. J., Daugherty, T. K., & Taylor, C. M. (1991). Children's reactions to a natural disaster: Symptom severity and degree of exposure. *Advances in Behaviour Research and Therapy, 13,* 135–154.

Lonigan, C. J., Shannon, M. P., Taylor, C. M., Finch, A. J., & Sallee, F. R. (1994). Children exposed to disaster: II. Risk factors for the development of post-traumatic symptomatology. *Journal of the American Academy of Child Psychiatry, 33,* 94–105.

March, J. S., Amaya-Jackson, L., Murray, M. C., & Schulte, A. (1998). Cognitive-behavioral psychotherapy for children and adolescents with posttraumatic stress disorder after a single-incident stressor. *Journal of the American Academy of Child and Adolescent Psychiatry, 37,* 585–593.

Mitchell, J. (1983). When disaster strikes: The critical incident stress debriefing process. *Journal of Emergency Medical Services, 8,* 36–39.

National Oceanic and Atmospheric Administration. (1994). *Hurricanes . . . Unleashing nature's fury: A preparedness guide.* Washington, DC: U.S. Department of Commerce.

National Oceanic and Atmospheric Administration. (1998). *Tornadoes . . . Nature's most violent storms: A preparedness guide.* Washington, DC: U.S. Department of Commerce.

National Organization for Victim Assistance. (1991). *Hurricane! Issues unique to hurricane disasters.* Washington, DC: Author.

Nolen-Hoeksema, S., & Morrow, J. (1991). A prospective study of depression and posttraumatic stress symptoms after a natural disaster: The 1989 Loma Prieta earthquake. *Journal of Personality and Social Psychology, 61,* 115–121.

Papadatos, Y., Nikou, K., & Potamianos, G. (1990). Evaluation of psychiatric morbidity following an earthquake. *International Journal of Social Psychiatry, 36,* 131–136.

Prinstein, M. J., & La Greca, A. M. (2002). *Children's coping assistance after a natural disaster: What predicts subsequent adjustment?* Manuscript in preparation.

Prinstein, M. J., La Greca, A. M., Vernberg, E. M., & Silverman, W. K. (1996). Children's coping assistance after a natural disaster. *Journal of Clinical Child Psychology, 25,* 463–475.

Pynoos, R. S., Goenjian, A., Tashjian, M., Karakashian, M., Manjikian, R., Manoukian, G., Steinberg, A. M., & Fairbanks, L. A. (1993). Post-traumatic stress reactions in children after the 1988 Armenian earthquake. *British Journal of Psychiatry, 163,* 239–247.

Rachman, S. (1980). Emotional processing. *Behaviour Research and Therapy, 18,* 51–60.

Ronan, K. R. (1997). The effects of a series of volcanic eruptions on emotional and behavioural functioning in children with asthma. *New Zealand Medical Journal, 110,* 145–147.

Rose, S., & Bisson, J. (1998). Brief early psychological interventions following trauma: a systematic review of the literature. *Journal of Traumatic Stress, 11,* 697–709.

Rustemli, A., & Karanei, A. N. (1996). Distress reactions and earthquake-related cognitions of parents and their adolescent children in a victimized population. *Journal of Social Behavior and Personality, 11*, 767–780.

Saylor, C. F., Swenson, C. C., & Powell, P. (1992). Hurricane Hugo blows down the broccoli: Preschoolers' post-disaster play and adjustment. *Child Psychiatry and Human Development, 22*, 139–149.

Shannon, M. P., Lonigan, C. J., Finch, A. J., & Taylor, C. M. (1994). Children exposed to disaster: I. Epidemiology of post-traumatic symptoms and symptom profiles. *Journal of the American Academy of Child and Adolescent Psychiatry, 33*, 80–93.

Shaw, J. A., Applegate, B., & Schorr, C. (1996). Twenty-one-month follow-up study of school-age children exposed to Hurricane Andrew. *Journal of the American Academy of Child and Adolescent Psychiatry, 35*, 359–364.

Shaw, J. A., Applegate, B., Tanner, S., Perez, D., Rothe, E., Campo-Bowen, A. E., & Lahey, B. L. (1995). Psychological effects of Hurricane Andrew on an elementary school population. *Journal of the American Academy of Child and Adolescent Psychiatry, 34*, 1185–1192.

Silber, E., Perry, S. E., & Bloch, D. A. (1958). Patterns of parent-child interaction in a disaster. *Psychiatry: Journal for the Study of Interpersonal Processes, 21*, 159–167.

Stoppelbein, L., & Greening, L. (2000). Posttraumatic stress symptoms in parentally bereaved children and adolescents. *Journal of the American Academy of Child and Adolescent Psychiatry, 39*, 1112–1119.

Sullivan, M. A., Saylor, C. F., & Foster, K. Y. (1991). Post-hurricane adjustment of preschoolers and their families. *Advances in Behaviour Research and Therapy, 13*, 163–171.

Swenson, C. C., Saylor, C. F., Powell, M. P., Stokes, S. J., Foster, K. Y., & Belter, R. W. (1996). Impact of a natural disaster on preschool children: Adjustment 14 months after a hurricane. *American Journal of Orthopsychiatry, 66*, 122–130.

United States Geological Survey. (1995). *Earthquakes.* Washington, DC: Author.

United States Geological Survey. (2002). *Earthquake Hazards Program: Earthquake glossary.* Retrieved February 13, 2002, from http://earthquake.usgs.gov/4kids/eqterms.html

Vernberg, E. M. (1994). Evaluating the effectiveness of school-based interventions after large scale disasters: An achievable goal? *Child, Youth, and Family Services Quarterly, 17*, 11–13.

Vernberg, E. M., La Greca, A. M., Silverman, W. K., & Prinstein, M. J. (1996). Predictors of children's post-disaster functioning following Hurricane Andrew. *Journal of Abnormal Psychology, 105*, 237–248.

Vernberg, E. M., & Vogel, J. M. (1993). Interventions with children after disasters. *Journal of Clinical Child Psychology, 22*, 485–498.

Vincent, N. R. (1997). *A follow-up to Hurricane Andrew: Children's reactions 42 months post-disaster.* Unpublished doctoral dissertation, University of Miami.

Vincent, N. R., La Greca, A. M., Silverman, W. K., Wasserstein, S., & Prinstein, M. J. (1994, August). *Predicting children's responses to natural disasters: Role of academic achievement.* Paper presented at the annual meeting of the American Psychological Association, Los Angeles, CA.

Vogel, J., & Vernberg, E. M. (1993). Children's psychological responses to disaster. *Journal of Clinical Child Psychology, 22,* 464–484.

Warheit, G. J., Zimmerman, R. S., Khoury, E. L., Vega, W. A., Gil, A. G. (1996). Disaster related stresses, depressive signs and symptoms, and suicidal ideation among a multi-racial/ethnic sample of adolescents: A longitudinal analysis. *Journal of Child Psychology and Psychiatry, 37,* 435–444.

Yule, W., & Canterbury, R. (1994). The treatment of posttraumatic stress disorder in children and adolescents. *International Review of Psychiatry, 6,* 141–151.

6

WILDERNESS AREA AND WILDFIRE DISASTERS: INSIGHTS FROM A CHILD AND ADOLESCENT SCREENING PROGRAM

BRETT M. MCDERMOTT AND LYLE J. PALMER

Wildfires may affect all types of vegetation and are probably part of all ecosystems, especially if the prerequisites for a fire exist (i.e., the presence of fuel that is sufficiently dry and a source of ignition; Martin, 1996). Lightning strikes are the most frequent cause of fire ignition, both historically (Scott, 1989) and in contemporary settings (Luke & McArthur, 1978). In the United States several fires during the 19th century burned more than 1 million acres. Fire-related mortality was significantly greater in the 19th century; for example, 1,500 lives in Wisconsin were lost in the Peshtigo fire of 1871. Contemporary records from the National Interagency Fire Center (Boise, Idaho) Web site include reports of nearly 7 million acres burned in wildland fires from January 1 to October 16, 2000. Devastating wildfires are a global phe-

The authors wish to acknowledge the dedication of Janet Cross and school psychologists in the Sutherland Shire of New South Wales and the vision of school principals and school authorities with responsibility in this area. Their participation made this project possible. Professor Einfeld (Sydney) gave valuable advice on research design. Lyle J. Palmer is a National Health and Medical Research Council of Australia Research Fellow and an Australian-American Educational Foundation Fulbright Fellow.

nomenon, with recent reports of major fires in Greece, Russia, Mexico, Spain, and Australia.

Large, destructive bushfires (the Australian term for both wilderness area and urban fringe wildfires) are common in the present Australian environment. Since 1957, when detailed recording of bushfires in the state of New South Wales began, bushfires leading to the loss of human life occurred in 1965, 1969, 1980, 1985, 1992, and 1994. The size of individual bushfires and the concomitant damage they cause vary greatly. The largest fires during this reporting period burnt 1,117,000 hectares of land. All Australian states are prone to summer bushfires. In terms of loss of life, the most serious thus far was the South Australian "Ash Wednesday" fire in 1983, in which 28 lives were lost on one day (see McFarlane & Raphael, 1984).

THE 1994 NEW SOUTH WALES BUSHFIRE DISASTER

The purpose of this chapter is to develop and evaluate an empirically supported rationale for a postdisaster intervention. Because empirical study of children's reactions to wilderness area fires is limited, it draws heavily on the Sutherland Bushfire Trauma Project (SBTP), an intersectoral, New South Wales (NSW) Departments of Health and School Education effort to document children's adjustment following a 1994 Australian bushfire disaster. Potentially important innovations are discussed, such as proactive postdisaster case recognition, which allow those with the greatest need to benefit from the limited resources available, and the employment of treatment tools, specifically a guided trauma workbook for young children and a group program for adolescents.

The summer bushfire "season" of 1993–1994 was one of the worst on record. From December 27, 1993, until January 16, 1994, more than 800 separate bushfires were reported. Fires burned in native vegetation around Sydney as well as in two major suburban areas. Unlike many disasters, which can be sudden, paroxysmal events, the bushfire disaster occurred over a period of 20 days. Details of the fires were seen or heard in hourly television and radio updates, and bushfires were the major item on nightly news bulletins. Smoke and ash were visible across much of the city of Sydney. About 800,000 hectares of land were burnt during this period, and 206 houses were destroyed. A state of emergency was declared, and 20,000 fire fighters, including volunteer brigades from all Australian states, assisted in the combating the fires. Miraculously, only four lives were lost during the disaster.

Children were especially distressed by the uncertainty inherent in the relationship between smoke and fire proximity. Smoke, ash, haze, and altered visibility were typical of the bushfire period, but wind shifts made fire proximity and actual danger often difficult to gauge. Conflicting opinions about whether to defend or leave the family home heightened family anxiety. Concerns about the fate of friends, neighbors, native animals, and pets were frequent. Many parents continued to attend their place of employment during the bushfire period, and children often expressed concern for the safety of the working parent. If report of actual fire danger was broadcast over the media or through police or state emergency personnel going door-to-door, the evacuation experience often exposed the child to images of the fire, including damage to vegetation, houses, or community infrastructure. Children also reported frightening noises, including emergency vehicles' sirens, shouting, the sound of burning vegetation, and trees exploding.

RATIONALE AND ORIGIN OF THE SBTP

The Sutherland Shire of southern Sydney, the site of the SBTP, was one of the areas most affected by the NSW bushfire disaster. In this area 86 houses were destroyed, 1 elementary school was completely razed, and 2 others were damaged. One life was lost. Approximately 3,600 children in grades 4 to 12 attended public schools in the affected area. One reason why this suburb was extensively affected was the woodland setting of the suburb, with houses often built to blend with the native environment. In addition, minimum clearing of native forest had occurred, and extensive valleys and deep gorges, although scenic, proved difficult terrain in which to fight a wildfire. Children in this area experienced dense smoke and ash and were more likely to witness an actual fire than in most other suburbs. Many children were evacuated literally minutes before their houses were destroyed. Some families survived in houses partially destroyed by the fire. Stories of "last-minute" parent–child separations, with one parent remaining with the house to combat an approaching fire, were common.

Schools were closed for the Australian summer vacation during the bushfire period. At the start of the 1994 school year, students in the Sutherland Shire had to traverse extensive tracts of blackened fire-damaged land to reach their schools. Early in the school year, Department of School Education staff expressed concern about the psychological well-being of some of their pupils. Many professionals provided anecdotal evidence of children appearing more anxious, an increase in separation difficulties among younger children, and children demonstrating an unwillingness to play outside the schoolroom during lunch and recess periods. Teachers complained that many students would not stop talking about the bushfire disaster.

To Sutherland Shire mental health professionals with some knowledge of the child trauma literature, such stories presented a microcosm of Benedek's period of "alarm" (Benedek, 1985). In Benedek's critique of the historical phases of awareness of emotional trauma, mental health professionals in the 1930s and 1940s became increasingly concerned about the adverse mental health consequences of children experiencing traumatic events. In the

Sutherland Shire in early 1994, an accumulation of anecdotal, experiential, and descriptive data suggested that a significant number of school students were experiencing posttraumatic mental health problems.

In response, an interdepartmental group of mental health, educational, nongovernment mental health, and pastoral practitioners was convened to discuss those issues and, if possible, devise a mental health response to the disaster, which was the greatest the area had experienced in living memory. (One of the authors of this chapter [McDermott] was a member of the working group.) The working group identified a series of issues that required clarification. Little was known regarding the likely number of children who might benefit from a postdisaster mental health intervention. Few existing mental health resources were available, and established mental health resources possessed little capacity to rapidly take on increased workloads. Last, few people had any expertise in providing a postdisaster mental health intervention to a potentially large group of children.

Before the SBTP formed, an expanding body of literature, including that describing children's responses following a natural disaster (McFarlane, 1987a, b; Shannon, Lonigan, Finch, & Taylor, 1994), was reporting that a significant proportion of children experienced symptoms of posttraumatic stress disorder (PTSD) following traumatic events. Scant literature discussed children and wildfires, although one questionnaire study following an Australian bushfire disaster reported that 13% of children experienced dreams or nightmares about the bushfire 8 months after the event (McFarlane, 1987a). Studies suggested that pathology was not restricted to the immediate postdisaster period; indeed, symptom chronicity appeared to be common. McFarlane (1987a) found that one third of children experienced persisting preoccupation with bushfire themes 26 months after the event. This finding is consistent with symptom chronicity reported after children's exposure to other traumatic events.

Some investigators had begun to take a broad developmental psychopathology approach to postdisaster research. At the time of the SBTP, detailed developmental models were not widely advocated (see Pynoos, Steinberg, & Wraith, 1995) and causal mechanisms, such as coping behavior (Vernberg, Silverman, LaGreca, & Prinstein, 1996), had yet to be integrated into postdisaster research. Studies assessing posttraumatic impairment in several domains, however, were beginning to report findings that included reduced academic performance (Kinzie, Sack, Angell, Manson, & Rath, 1986; Shannon et al., 1994), alterations in family functioning (McFarlane 1987a), and the identification of parents with significant psychopathology (Sack et al., 1994) in traumatized child groups.

A final issue considered important to the working group was the increasing evidence from child and adolescent mental health research suggesting that parents and teachers might significantly underreport a child's psychopathology. The tendency is probably secondary to the low parent–child concordance of internalizing symptoms (Hodges, Gordon, & Lennon, 1990; Rey, Schrader, & Morris-Yates, 1992; Verhulst & van der Ende, 1991). In the postdisaster context, parental reports of their children's internalizing psychopathology is exacerbated by children often consciously not wishing to burden their parents with their distress (Yule & Williams, 1990) or experiencing general difficulties talking to their parents following a trauma (Stallard & Law, 1993). Furthermore, parents may deny the presence of symptoms in their children (Burke, Borus, Burns, Millstein, & Beasley, 1982).

Drawing from existing research, the SBTP working group estimated that between 5% and 15% of children might report significant postdisaster psychopathology. In the local school context, that figure represented between 180 and 540 children. It was anticipated that those children might experience chronic symptoms and impairment in several domains, including academic achievement. The working group concluded that parents or teachers would be unlikely to identify all children who might benefit from a postdisaster mental health intervention. If an inclusive program was to be considered, a proactive case-finding procedure, such as screening for psychopathology, should be used. The concept of screening was attractive to the service providers in that screening would allow many children and parents to be reassured while providing the people in greatest need with more of the scarce resources available.

The recommendations endorsed by the working group included the following points:

- An effective intervention would require close collaboration between school and health authorities.
- Nongovernment and community participation would be encouraged and promoted.
- The school would be the most cost-effective point of assessment and service provision.
- Proactive screening for persistent postdisaster distress would assist in case identification, allow some assessment of service need, and provide data necessary to advocate for more services should they be necessary. Interventions would need to be developmentally meaningful.

The working group identified 19 elementary schools and 2 high schools that might be considered at greatest risk of having distressed children and adolescents. Ad hoc "at-risk" criteria were primarily related to perceived bushfire exposure. A school was considered at risk if the school had been directly damaged by the bushfire, if the fire had been in such proximity to the school that nearby structures were damaged, or if the school included students whose homes had been destroyed by the fire.

METHOD OF ASSESSMENT

The assessment battery chosen was that advocated by an experienced professional, both in print (Yule, 1992) and through personal communication. The self-report battery included a measure of trauma-related psychopathology, the Impact of Event Scale (IES; Horowitz, Wilner, & Alvarez, 1979); a measure of depressive symptoms, the Beck Depression Inventory (BDI; Birleson, 1981); and a measure of trait anxiety, the Revised Children's Manifest Anxiety Scale (RCMAS; Richmond & Reynolds, 1978). The IES had been used with both adolescents (Yule, 1992) and children as young as age 8 (Yule, Udwin, & Murdoch, 1990). Benefits of the battery included the self-report format; the breadth of assessed psychopathology; the acceptable psychometric properties of the scales; and the availability of comparison data from past studies, including cut-off scores for being in a "high risk for PTSD category" (Yule & Udwin, 1991; see McDermott & Palmer, 1999, for a more detailed report of the use of this battery in the bushfire project).

The assessment battery was piloted with 60 elementary school children (grades 4, 5, and 6). Two IES statements, "I was aware that I still had a lot of feelings about the bushfire, but I did not deal with them" and "My feelings about the bushfire were kind of numb," required clarification by more than 50% of students 8 years of age. Those questions were removed. The shortened IES used in the SBTP was designated as the IES-13.

The aim of this project was primarily to provide treatment to children in need. Financial resources were insufficient to undertake detailed research, and various schools and the Department of School Education were not willing to undertake research in the postdisaster environment. Approval was given to obtain some disaster-related information from parents, however. Information obtained included yes–no responses to questions regarding the child's location on the day of the bushfire, the child's verbalized perception of threat to self and parents, home damage, evacuation experience, and residential dislocation experience. High school students provided similar information by self-report.

Elementary and high school participants lived in an area in which 81% of residents were Australian born and only 0.03% were Australian Aboriginal or Torres Strait Islanders. The majority of non-Australian-born residents emigrated from an English-speaking country; this group composed 8.8% of the total population of the area. Immigrants from non-English-speaking European countries or Asia constituted 3.3% and 1.7%, respectively, of the area's population. Relatively few single-parent households (10.4%) were in the area. The area is considered "middle class," consistent with 46% of residents having obtained some postschool trade diploma or university qualification.

MAIN REACTIONS OF CHILDREN AND ADOLESCENTS

Postdisaster Psychopathology in Elementary School Children

Seventy-six percent of students from the elementary schools returned signed parental consent forms and subsequently participated in screening. Parents not giving consent to screening usually cited being "out of the area" during the fires and that the project therefore did not "apply" to them. High school students gave their own consent; however, parents could exercise an active, opting-out right. Ninety-seven percent of high school students agreed to participate.

A total of 602 elementary school students ages 8 to 12 ($M = 10.1$; $SD = 0.9$), of whom 54.6% ($n = 322$) were female and 45.4% ($n = 279$) were male, were screened. Six months after the bushfire disaster, the mean emotional distress score (the sum of IES-13 questions) was 12.60 (95% CI, 11.52–16.69). Most students reported some trauma-related symptoms, but 11.5% of the participants reported no symptoms at all. Modifying the cutoff advised by Horowitz and colleagues (1979) to accommodate the 13-question version of the scale, 12% of the sample ($n = 74$) experienced moderate to severe levels of distress symptoms (IES-13 > 36). IES-13 items that most frequently elicited an "often" response included "I tried to remove the bushfire from my memory"; "I tried not to think about the bushfire"; "Any reminder of the bushfire brought back feelings about the bushfire"; and "Pictures of the bushfire popped into my head." Only three IES-13 questions demonstrated a significant gender difference: Female students more commonly reported that "I had trouble with sleep because pictures or thoughts about the bushfire popped into my head"; "I had dreams about the bushfire"; and "Any reminder brought back feelings about the bushfires."

The mean Depression scale score of elementary school children was 6.48 ($SD = 4.99$). Using the BDI cutoff of 16 reported by Yule and Udwin (1991), 4.7% ($n = 44$) of the sample reported symptoms consistent with a depressive illness. The items most frequently validated by the participants were "I feel very bored" and "I am (not) easily cheered up." The mean Anxiety scale score was 15.90 (range = 18.49–19.31). Using the RCMAS cut-off of 19 cited by Yule and Udwin (1991), 14.1% ($n = 85$) of the sample reported symptoms consistent with high trait anxiety.

Multivariate analysis was used to investigate the relationship between children's emotional distress, depressive symptoms, and demographic and event-related variables. The anxiety score, depression score, experience of evacuation procedure, and perceived threat to parents were significant predictors of the child's emotional distress score, independently of other possible covariates. High symptom scores for anxiety and depression were associated with increased symptom scores for emotional distress. Neither gender nor age was significantly associated with emotional distress independently of the other covariates modeled. No significant cluster effect of school attended was observed (McDermott & Palmer, 1999).

The anxiety, emotional distress, and perceived threat to parents were significant predictors of depressive symptoms independent of other possible covariates. High symptom scores for anxiety and emotional distress were associated with increased symptom scores for depression. Neither gender nor age was significantly associated with the depression score independent of the other covariates modeled. As with the emotional distress model, no significant cluster effect of school attended was observed (McDermott & Palmer, 1999).

Findings Across the Elementary and High School Developmental Range

A total of 2,379 elementary and secondary school students, ages 8 to 19 ($M = 13.43$; $SD = 2.49$) were screened. The children were distributed evenly among grades 4 to 12 ($n = 183–329$ children per grade). The gender ratio was balanced (47.7% male). Six months after the bushfire disaster, the mean emotional distress score for high school students was 6.23 (95% CI, 5.88–6.60). The mean depression score for the group was 5.28 (95% CI, 5.08–5.49).

Multivariate modeling indicated that symptom scores for depression, perceived threat of death to self, perceived threat of death to parents, grade at school, and experience of evacuation during the week of the fires significantly predicted the emotional distress scores independent of the other possible covariates. Gender was not found to be a predictor of emotional distress. Symptom scores for depression demonstrated a nonlinear relationship with symptoms of emotional distress. Increased symptom scores for depression were associated with increased symptoms of emotional distress. Class in school also demonstrated a nonlinear relationship with symptom scores for emotional distress. Adjusted symptom scores were lowest in the lower and higher grades and highest in the middle grades (i.e., grades 7 to 9).

Multivariate modeling suggested that the emotional distress score, total anxiety score, grade at school, experience of evacuation during the week of the fires, and experience of evacuation on the day of fires to either a refuge or to friends or relatives were significant predictors of the depression score independent of the other possible covariates. Gender was not found to be a significant predictor of depression; however, evidence of a significant interaction between gender and grade at school was found. This finding suggested that depressive symptoms were systematically lower in males than in females across all school grades. Symptom scores for anxiety and emotional distress demonstrated a nonlinear relationship with symptom scores for depression. Class in school, a variable likely to reflect both chronological age and developmental maturity, also demonstrated a nonlinear relationship with symptom scores for depression: Adjusted symptom scores were highest in the lower and higher grades, and lowest in the middle grades (i.e., grades 8 to 10). Experience of evacuation on the day of fires to either a refuge or to friends or relatives also was associated with increased symptom scores for depression. Experience of evacuation during the week of the fires was associated with decreased symptom scores for depression. All reported associations of response variables with explanatory covariates were independent of the other possible covariates. Multivariate modeling of emotional distress and depressive psychopathology indicated no substantial clustering effects by school attended (McDermott & Palmer, 2001).

Special Client Groups: Young Elementary School Children

Both the work group members and the parents from the pilot school wished to include young elementary school students (i.e., grades 1–3; age approximately 6–8) in the screening procedure and any subsequent interventions. Given the age differentiation of children's mental capacities, an understandable lack of instruments was found for measuring PTSD symptoms in this age group. Existing approaches in the measurement of the psychopathology of young children rely on parental report of emotional and behavioral symptoms (Verhulst & Koot, 1995).

It was hypothesized that this group might be able to provide useful answers on a series of trauma-related questions in a simple yes–no format. Second, persistent posttraumatic psychopathology may be communicated by this group by drawing fire-related images in response to two neutral questions: (a) "Please draw a picture" and (b) "Please draw a picture of one of your dreams." The drawing exercises followed the trauma questionnaire and were extremely useful for postscreening debriefing and initiating discussion about the bushfire disaster. The pictures were not useful for screening children in "classroom-size" groups because of a strong contagion effect, whereby one child drawing a bushfire often led to many other students changing their pictures to bushfire-related themes.

Young elementary school students answered 20 yes–no questions. Some working-group members were concerned about asking this group of young children direct trauma-related questions. It was resolved that children would be presented with a drawing of a young person outside an intact house, with what appeared to be fire and smoke coming from a nearby hill. The person was named "Kerry," a name that can apply to either a boy or girl in Australia. Students were asked about Kerry's feelings (a) "at that time" and (b) "quite a long time after the fire." It was assumed that children would draw on their own experience, feelings, and cognitions to answer the questions about Kerry.

A total of 310 elementary school students ages 5 to 9 ($M = 8.20$; $SD = 4.62$) were screened with this procedure. Children were evenly distributed across first, second, and third grade. The gender ratio was balanced (49.7% female).

Most of the students felt that in response to the fire-related picture and vignette, Kerry would not be feeling "normal" (74.5%). They thought Kerry would be feeling either "frightened" (79%) or "sad" (68.1%). Few (10.6%) thought Kerry would feel "excited." Many elementary school children reported that Kerry was concerned about separation and loss issues. The children thought Kerry would be "worried the house would burn down" (81.4%), that Kerry's mother (48.5%), his or her father (47.8%), or Kerry (41.5%) might "die," that Kerry's mother (42.7%) or father (43.4%) might "go away," or that Kerry would be worried that he or she might be "left alone" (39.5%).

Despite the prompt, "It is now quite a long time after the fire," many children persisted in validating trauma-related answers for Kerry. Many children reported that Kerry still experienced "scary dreams about the fire" (59.7%), "during the day-time thinks a lot about the fire" (51.7%), and still tries "not to think about the fire" (66.1%); a smaller number reported that Kerry experienced headaches (38.6%) or stomach aches (36.8%). Many children reported that Kerry still experienced sleeping problems (48.7%). Although many children thought Kerry still felt "scared" (33.6%), that proportion dropped appreciably from the 79% who reported Kerry would initially feel frightened. Many children felt Kerry would be upset if someone talked about the fire (53.8%).

Some differences in responses were significant across school grades. Older, third-grade children thought significantly less often that Kerry would feel "normal" during the fire scenario (12.3% versus 24.5% in grade 2 and 39.2% in grade 1) and more often reported that Kerry would feel frightened (93.1% versus 30.0% in grade 2 and 44.6% in grade 1). Girls were significantly more likely to state that Kerry thought the fire would occur again (72.5% versus 56.9%). Girls also were more concerned that the house would "burn down" (89.0% versus 74.8%). Girls more often reported that Kerry would be concerned that her mother (54.5% versus 42.0%), father (54.5% versus 40.7%), or Kerry herself might die (47.2% versus 36.2%) and that Kerry would be "frightened" (85.0% versus 73.4%) and sad (74.3% versus 63.2%).

In summary, the use of the vignette and the Kerry character was well received by young children; no child became extremely distressed during the exercise. Many children thought Kerry would be frightened and concerned that the house would burn down. Many children also thought Kerry might still have nightmares and tried not to think about the fire. Some developmental and gender differences were found. Older children more often felt that Kerry would be frightened, and girls were more concerned than boys that the fire would occur again.

Special Client Groups: Children of Volunteer Firefighters

Of the children assessed, 25.6% (n = 154) of the elementary school students and 4.8% (n = 86) of the high school students had a parent who was a volunteer firefighter during the week of the bushfires. Anecdotal evidence suggests that those children may be at increased risk of emotional trauma because of the risks undertaken by the firefighter parent. Analysis of the SBTP data suggested that children of firefighters did have significantly higher emotional distress and depression scores than children whose parents were not firefighters. Multivariate analysis, however, suggested that having a parent who was a volunteer firefighter was not a significant predictor of emotional distress, anxiety, and depression scores once other important covariates had been adjusted.

POSTDISASTER COPING MATERIALS

Two interventions were offered to children and adolescents identified during the screening process. All elementary school students, including the young students (ages 5–8) used the guided therapy manual, *The Bushfire and Me: A Story of What happened to Me and My Family* (Storm, McDermott, & Finlayson, 1994). High school children were offered a group therapy program. Similar therapy principles guided the development of each resource, including the need to be developmentally appropriate and to be sympathetic to the major communication style of children. The guided workbook included pictures, drawings, cartoons, activities, and much free space. Such activities are consistent with established therapeutic communication strategies for children, as typified by Winnicott's Squiggle Game (Winnicott, 1971) and the use of drawings and play with traumatized children (Pynoos & Eth, 1986).

Description of the Materials and Considerations in Their Use

The professional backgrounds of the book authors were varied; as a result, both dynamic and cognitive–behavioral theory (the latter including information-processing theory; Chemtob, Roitblat, Hamada, Carlson, & Twentyman, 1988; Resick & Schnicke, 1992) influenced the workbook. It was conceptualized that children in the postdisaster environment often are confronted with the task of processing information that is dissonant with predisaster schemata relating to central issues such as safety of their home and their parents' ability to provide care and protection. Children therefore would experience difficulties in both the assimilation and accommodation of schemata-dissonant information following the disaster. This difficulty can be manifest in self-blame for the disaster, which is heightened by a child's tendency to regress to a more egocentric worldview. Accommodation difficulties may be manifest in schemata suggesting ongoing extreme danger from future disastrous events.

An important caveat in the use of both the guided workbook and the adolescent group program is that the resources were not meant to replace either the therapist or the parent. For instance, one treatment aim was that each child's workbook would be reviewed by a mental health professional at the end of every completed chapter. Second, both the workbook and group therapy were not seen as postdisaster panaceas. Parents, teachers, and mental health professionals were encouraged to identify children with either unremitting symptoms or persistent impairment; for those children, a more intensive and individualized treatment would be appropriate.

The guided workbook contained three sections. The introductory and final sections were primarily for parents and caregivers; those sections included factual information about the bushfire disaster and psychoeducational information summarizing the range of typical emotional responses exhibited by children after such a traumatic event. Guidelines were given as to why some children warrant a psychological intervention, whereas others do not.

The middle and largest section of the book was for children. The section began by introducing the reader to several cartoon characters who personified groups of people such as firefighters, who are often prominent during or after an Australian bushfire disaster. Cartoon characters included "Fire-fighting Pos" (possum), "Reporter Roo" (kangaroo), "Comfort Koala," and "Counselling Eagle." The characters were featured throughout the workbook and asked questions, made suggestions, described possible activities, and presented "Fact Boxes."

The structure of the workbook was a chronological progression from the predisaster period of normality, to predisaster apprehension, the actual disaster, the postdisaster aftermath, and transition points following the disaster. The latter included volunteer firefighters returning to their homes, children returning to school, and anniversary reactions. Chapter 1 focused on biographical details of the reader and practice using the workbook. Chapter 2, "Before the Bushfires," reminded readers that their life did not begin following the traumatic event. Chapters 3, "The Fire Came," and 4, "After the Bushfires," promoted intense reexperiencing of the traumatic event. Reexperiencing attempted to include trauma-related thoughts, feelings, and perceptions that may have been prominent during the disaster. Chapter 5, "People Who Helped," emphasized the positive aspect of volunteer and professional involvement in combating the disaster and assisting with recovery. Chapter 6, "Back to School," allowed children to share feelings and stories with friends, teachers, and others. The workbook discouraged feelings of loneliness or being singled out. The random nature of traumatic events was highlighted. Chapter 7, "Several Months Later," focused on community and ecological recovery. Chapter 8, "One Year Later," dealt both with the potentially distressing anniversary reactions and mastery in the form of active preparation for the ensuing summer bushfire season.

The adolescent group program comprised six 2-hour sessions with groups of 6 to 8 students and two therapists. The introductory session consisted of meeting participants and leaders and sharing expectations. Subsequent sessions included elements of trauma reexposure and testimony with other group participants and psychoeducation, including normalizing emotional and behavioral changes since the bushfire and skills acquisition. The latter included relaxation techniques, identifying and challenging unhelpful schemata and cognitions that had developed since the disaster, and gaining mastery by problem solving and preparing for future bushfire seasons.

Treatment Effectiveness

The implementation of "best practice" treatment outcome research in the postdisaster environment presents inherent difficulties. Research is often attempted in school systems and nongovernment and volunteer organizations, which are commonly without a tradition of rigorous service evaluation. The postdisaster environment, understandably, emphasizes the care of physical injury and the restoration of public utilities and community infrastructure. In such an environment, it is difficult to design, gain approval for, and implement treatment outcome research. Such was the case with the SBTP, although the local teaching hospital's ethics committee did grant permission for a randomized treatment trial of the SBTP treatment interventions. The committee agreed with the argument that children with emotional trauma warranted as detailed and rigorous an understanding of the efficacy of the proposed treatments as did other groups; however, funding was not available for even a rudimentary follow-up of psychopathology in the treatment group.

As a minimum evaluation, a detailed client satisfaction survey concerning the workbook and group program was undertaken. The questionnaire consisted of 10 questions with multiple-choice fields that were based on an existing instrument (Plapp & Rey, 1994). The survey was anonymous and sent to parents and children 1 month after completion of the workbook. Parent satisfaction with the workbook was high: 91% of parents ($n = 100$; 81% response rate) stated that the book helped their child "a great deal" or to "some extent." Ninety-seven percent of parents were "reasonably" or "very satisfied" with the book, and 97% found that the advice included was "reasonably" or "very useful"; 82% of parents felt a workbook was an "acceptable" treatment strategy. The remainder (18%) felt "neither bad nor good" about the approach. Many parents (42%) felt that the workbook helped them "a great deal" to talk to their child about the bushfires, whereas another 54% felt that talking to their child was aided to some extent. The great majority of parents (97%) reported that they would recommend the workbook to another family in a similar situation. The most prominent criticism was that many parents (57%) thought the book was too long. Parents of young elementary school children mostly reported that a separate, briefer, less sophisticated resource was required for the youngest ages.

Children also completed a satisfaction questionnaire independent of their parents. Most children (87%) felt that using the workbook generally helped and that it helped them talk about the bushfires (90%). Using the workbook in the home environment was felt to be a good idea (67%), and most respondents would "very much" (57%) or "to some extent" (26%) recommend the resource to another child. Children commented that their parents or caregivers often read the information in the workbook (89%) and that the parent or caregiver also often helped with workbook tasks (76%). Aspects of the workbook children most liked were the picture-coloring tasks (often bushfire-related pictures), the dialogue from the cartoon figures, and certificates they could remove and send to firefighters or other caring people to thank them for their help. Bushfire stories, empty pages to add their own work, feeling questions, and information boxes also were positively cited.

Project Limitations

One aim of the SBTP assessment protocol was to identify children who would benefit from a postdisaster psychological intervention. Substantial refinements are required before such an aim can be met. The SBTP assessment protocol was unidimensional; it focused on posttraumatic and depressive psychopathology. This approach was not consistent with findings from general child mental health research that impairment in several domains, rather than symptoms alone, is correlated with presentation for treatment (Cohen, 1995). Moreover, the SBTP did not incorporate causal mechanisms in risk prediction, such as measures of postdisaster coping (Vernberg et al., 1996); postdisaster perceptions of self-efficacy (Hardin, Weinrich, Weinrich, Hardin, & Garrison, 1994); internal causal attribution (Joseph, Brewin, Yule, & Williams, 1991); or perceived threat to self or significant others, such as parents (McDermott & Palmer, 1999). Future assessment batteries should include, along with measures of psychopathology, some measure of intrapsychic functioning and impairment in the social, school, and peer domains. Finally, the assessment battery chosen, although logistically bound to some questionnaire measure, also should include a random group for more detailed study with assessment tools possessing methodological rigor, such as semistructured interviews. A more potent methodology, given adequate resources, would be a two-stage screening procedure with self-report questionnaires identifying a group that required further more detailed assessment.

Treatment outcome research remains a substantial challenge to postdisaster mental health service providers. The current availability of manualized treatment programs, such as guided workbooks that are easily adapted to different traumatic events, allows more sophisticated comparative treatment designs. It is important that funding bodies (often state or federal disaster-relief funds) understand in principle the necessity for funding to be made available for longitudinal postdisaster follow up of victims and for outcome studies.

SUMMARY

The SBTP project and similar studies that have followed other large-scale disasters demonstrate that in the postdisaster environment, large numbers of children can be assessed using self-report questionnaires, often administered in the school environment. By restructuring the activities of school and nonschool mental health professionals and using a modest augmentation of existing funds, this project allowed children to be screened for postdisaster emotional distress and depression. By using therapy strategies other than an individual psychotherapy paradigm, large numbers of children were treated.

Although it primarily provides a psychological intervention, such a project also is capable of advancing knowledge in the field of children's trauma. In the sample, the reported prevalence of emotional distress in elementary school children was 12.3%. The high school student rate was 3.5%. Students in the middle grades (grades 7–9, approximate age 11–13) reported the highest symptom level. The rate of depression was 4.7% in elementary school children and 5.9% in high school students. Although comparison with young elementary school students is not possible given the methodology used, our experience suggests that such children are capable of providing trauma-related information about their feeling state, in either a simple written or a representational format. Further work in refining assessment procedures is required for this age group.

Results from this project also add to existing knowledge on the independent effects of trauma-related variables to postdisaster psychopathology. In students from grades 4 to 12, event exposure, evacuation experience, and perceived threat to self and parents all were significant independent contributors in multivariate models predicting both postdisaster emotional distress and depressive symptoms. School grade was itself an independent predictor of psychopathology, but the relationship was complex and nonlinear. Having a volunteer firefighter as a parent did not confer an increased risk of an adverse mental health outcome.

The interventions used in this project were well received by parents and children. Consistent with recovery from a traumatic event, parents and children reported being more able to talk about the traumatic event following the intervention. Parents and children reported that they would recommend the treatment resources to other families in similar need.

CONCLUSIONS

Wilderness area fires and wildfires in semiurban or substantially forested suburbs potentially traumatize significant numbers of children, usually more than can be treated by existing child and adolescent mental health services. To provide treatment resources for children with the greatest need, some form of postdisaster mental health case identification is needed. School-based screening can be an economically viable strategy that is well accepted by parents and teachers and should be given consideration. A confederate and collaborator in the school system is essential to gain sufficient acceptance to undertake large-scale mental health screening of children. The sophistication of screening should be increased in the future by adding trauma-related variables, such as measures of event exposure, evacuation and separation experience, and evidence of a child experiencing grief or postdisaster psychosocial impairment. A two-stage screening process with a more detailed mental health assessment for people identified by a screening procedure may prove viable.

Treatment recommendations include the development of treatment resources prior to a disaster. This strategy may be practical in that the area may be in a known natural disaster risk zone, such as a wildfire-prone area. In addition, treatments such as guided workbooks or brief group therapies should be developed for the large number of people with mild presentations. A treatment continuum should include intense, evidence-based treatments for moderately and severely affected children. Some resources should be available for children who have severely affected parents and caregivers, such as links to competent adult mental health service providers or systemic therapy approaches. Finally, consideration should be given to the incorporation of therapeutic messages from groups identified by children as positive role models in disasters. Certificates signed by the state's chief firefighter, stories from emergency personnel, and guided discussions with firefighters on how to make the family home safer for the following year were therapeutic initiatives that children found interesting, relevant, and empowering and promoted reexperiencing in a therapeutic setting.

REFERENCES

Benedek, E. P. (1985). Children and psychic trauma: A brief review of contemporary thinking. In S. Eth & R. Pynoos (Eds.), *Post traumatic stress disorder in children* (pp. 1–16). Washington, DC: American Psychiatric Association Press.

Birleson, P. (1981). The validity of depressive disorder in childhood and the development of a self rating scale: A research report. *Journal of Child Psychology and Psychiatry, 22,* 73–88.

Burke, J. D., Borus, J. F., Burns, B. J., Millstein, K. H., & Beasley, M. C. (1982). Changes in children's behaviour after a natural disaster. *American Journal of Psychiatry, 139,* 1010–1014.

Chemtob, C., Roitblat, H. L., Hamada, R. S., Carlson, J. G., & Twentyman, C. T. (1988). A cognitive action theory of post-traumatic stress disorder. *Journal of Anxiety Disorders, 2,* 253–275.

Cohen, D. J. (1995). Psychosocial therapies for children and adolescents: Overview and future directions. *Journal of Abnormal Child Psychology, 23,* 141–156.

Hardin, S. B., Weinrich, M., Weinrich, S., Hardin, T. L., & Garrison, C. (1994). Psychological distress of adolescents exposed to Hurricane Hugo. *Journal of Traumatic Stress, 7,* 427–440.

Hodges, K., Gordon, Y., & Lennon, M. P. (1990). Parent-child agreement on symptoms (CAS). *Journal of Child Psychology and Psychiatry, 31,* 427–436.

Horowitz, M. J., Wilner, N., & Alvarez, W. (1979). Impact of Event Scale: A measure of subjective stress. *Psychosomatic Medicine, 41,* 209–213.

Joseph, S. A., Brewin, C. R., Yule, W., & Williams, R. (1991). Causal attributions and psychiatric symptoms in survivors of the Herald of Free Enterprise disaster. *British Journal of Psychiatry, 159,* 542–546.

Kinzie, J. D., Sack, W. H., Angell, R. H., Manson, S., & Rath, B. (1986). The psychiatric effects of massive trauma on Cambodian children: I. The children. *Journal of the American Academy of Child and Adolescent Psychiatry, 25,* 370–376.

Luke, R. H., & McArthur, A. G. (1978). *Bushfires in Australia.* Canberra, ACT: Australian Government Publishing Service.

Martin, H. A. (1996). Wildfires in past ages. *Proceedings Linnean Society of New South Wales, 116,* 3–18.

McDermott, B. M., & Palmer, L. J. (1999). Post-disaster service provision following proactive identification of children with emotional distress and depression. *Australian and New Zealand Journal of Psychiatry, 33,* 855–863.

McDermott, B. M., & Palmer, L. J. (2001). *Post-disaster emotional distress, depression and Evert-related variables: Findings across child and adolescent developmental stages.* Manuscript submitted for publication.

McFarlane, A. C. (1987a). Posttraumatic phenomena in a longitudinal study of children following a natural disaster. *Journal of the American Academy of Child and Adolescent Psychiatry, 26,* 764–769.

McFarlane, A. C. (1987b). Family functioning and overprotection following a natural disaster: The longitudinal effects of post-traumatic morbidity. *Australian and New Zealand Journal of Psychiatry, 21,* 210–218.

McFarlane, A. C., & Raphael, B. (1984). Ash Wednesday: The effects of a fire. *Australian and New Zealand Journal of Psychiatry, 18,* 341–351.

Plapp, J. M., & Rey, J. M. (1994). Child and adolescent psychiatric services: Case audit and patient satisfaction. *Journal of Quality in Clinical Practice, 14,* 51–56.

Pynoos, R. S., & Eth, S. (1986). Witness to violence: The child interview. *Journal of the American Academy of Child and Adolescent Psychiatry, 25,* 306–319.

Pynoos, R. S., Steinberg, A. M., & Wraith, R. (1995). A developmental model of childhood traumatic stress. In D. Cicchetti & D. J. Cohen (Eds.), *Developmental psychopathology* (pp. 72–95). New York: Wiley.

Resick, P. A., & Schnicke, M. K. (1992). Cognitive processing therapy for sexual assault victims. *Journal of Consulting and Clinical Psychology, 60,* 748–756.

Rey, J. M., Schrader, E., & Morris-Yates, A. (1992). Parent-child agreement on children's behaviours reported by the child behaviour checklist (CBCL). *Journal of Adolescence*, 15, 219–230.

Richmond, C. R., & Reynolds, B. O. (1978). What I think and feel: A revised measure of children's manifest anxiety. *Journal of Abnormal Child Psychology*, 6, 271–280.

Sack, W. H., McSharry, S., Clarke, G. N., Kinney, R., Seeley, J., & Lewinsohn, P. (1994). The Khmer adolescent project I. Epidemiological findings in two generations of Cambodian adolescents. *Journal of Nervous and Mental Disease*, 182, 387–385.

Scott, A. C. (1989). Observations on the nature of Fusain. *International Journal of Coal Geology*, 12, 443–475.

Shannon, M., Lonigan, C. J., Finch, A. J., & Taylor, C. M. (1994). Children exposed to a disaster: Epidemiology of post traumatic symptoms and symptom profiles. *Journal of the American Academy of Child and Adolescent Psychiatry*, 33, 80–93.

Stallard, P., & Law, F. (1993). Screening and psychological debriefing of adolescent survivors of life threatening events. *British Journal of Psychiatry*, 163, 660–665.

Storm, V., McDermott, B. M., & Finlayson, D. (1994). *The Bushfire and me: A story of what happened to me and my family*. Sydney, Australia: New South Wales Department of Health.

Verhulst, F. C., & Koot, H. M. (1995). *The epidemiology of child and adolescent psychopathology*. Oxford, England: Oxford Medical Publications.

Verhulst, F. L., & van der Ende, J. (1991). Assessment of child psychopathology: Relationships between different methods, different informants and clinical judgment of severity. *Acta Psychiatrica Scandinavica*, 84, 155–159.

Vernberg, E. M., Silverman, W. K., La Greca, A. M., & Prinstein, M. J. (1996). Prediction of post traumatic stress symptoms in children after Hurricane Andrew. *Journal of Abnormal Psychology*, 105, 237–248.

Winnicott, D. W. (1971). *Therapeutic consultations in child psychiatry*. New York: Basic Books.

Yule, W. (1992). Post traumatic stress disorder in child survivors of shipping disasters: The sinking of the "Jupiter." *Psychotherapy and Psychosomatics*, 57, 200–205.

Yule, W., Udwin, O., & Murdoch, K. (1990). The "Jupiter's" sinking: Effects on children's fears, depression and anxiety. *Journal of Clinical Psychology and Psychiatry*, 131, 1051–1061.

Yule, W., & Udwin, O. (1991). Screening child survivors for PTSD: Experiences from the "Jupiter." *British Journal of Clinical Psychology*, 30, 131–138.

Yule, W., & Williams, R. (1990). Post traumatic stress reactions in children. *Journal of Traumatic Stress*, 3, 279–295.

7

FLOODS

GERARD A. JACOBS, JORGE V. BOERO, RANDAL P. QUEVILLON,
ELIZABETH TODD-BAZEMORE, TERI L. ELLIOTT, AND GILBERT REYES

This chapter provides information that can serve as a basis for disaster mental health planning for children affected by floods. It begins with a review of the literature on children and floods, then describes a crisis intervention program that served the needs of children affected by flooding. Finally, it provides recommendations for serving the mental health needs of children affected by floods or living in flood-vulnerable areas.

RESEARCH ON CHILDREN AND FLOODS

Buffalo Creek

In 1972 a mining company's slag dam gave way, unleashing a torrent of water down the 18-mile-long Buffalo Creek valley in West Virginia. Thousands were left homeless, and 125 people died. Survivors from 160 families initiated legal action against the mining company, including a claim for psychological damages (Titchener & Kapp, 1976). The effort to document the psychological impact of the flood for the trial was the impetus for much of the psychological assessment that followed. The Buffalo Creek flood may be the single most studied disaster in U.S. history. A number of studies included data on children (Erikson, 1976; Gleser, Green, & Winget, 1981; Green, Grace, Crespo da Silva, & Gleser, 1983; Green et al., 1991; Honig, Grace, Lindy, Newman, & Titchener, 1993; Newman, 1976; Titchener & Kapp, 1976), although the data are often sparse.

Representatives of both the plaintiffs and the mining company conducted assessments beginning in June 1973. Data from both sets of interviews were formalized using the Psychiatric Evaluation Form (PEF; Gleser et al., 1981). Green et al. (1983) presented evidence that the total score on the PEF constituted a valid tool for quantifying the psychiatric interviews, including data on construct validity and interrater and test–retest reliability.

Titchener and Kapp (1976) provided little information specifically on the children. They reported that more than 2 years after the flood, 90% of family members exhibited a set of disabling psychiatric symptoms which they dubbed the "Buffalo Creek Syndrome." This syndrome resulted both from the flood itself and the subsequent disruption of the community. It included anxiety, depression, changes in character and lifestyle, maladjustment, and developmental problems in children. Furthermore, the authors concluded that the survivors had minimized their distress.

Titchener and Kapp (1976) hypothesized that traumatic events of the magnitude of the Buffalo Creek flood can overwhelm anyone's coping resources and that pretrauma individual differences are reflected in the expression of the traumatic stress reaction. They noted that for some survivors, attempts at readjustment in the aftermath of the event actually resulted in further "psychologically disabling limitations" (p. 296). They felt that their data demonstrated that the initial traumatization did not subside with the passage of time; instead, the symptoms became more subtle.

Newman (1976) described in detail the survivor–plaintiff assessments with 11 children under age 12. Information from parent interviews was shared with the child interviewers before the children were seen. Newman reported that the children's stories had often been "submerged or inhibited" (p. 306) by more vocal family members until the child interviews. Fantasy-eliciting techniques, such as "three wishes," "draw-a-person," and "storytelling," were used to encourage children's expression of their stories. Newman concluded that the impact of the trauma was determined by a complex interaction of three factors: (a) the developmental level of the child, (b) the child's perception of the family's reactions to the disaster, and (c) direct exposure to the disaster. She also concluded that the children's experiences permanently affected their sense of self. This latter point seems like a premature conclusion because it was based on data only 2 years postdisaster; however, Newman also noted that the children seemed to maintain a sense of hope for the future far more than their parents did.

Erikson (1976) provided a lengthy sociological impression of the effects of the flooding but little detail on the basis or time frame of the descriptions. He indicated that the plaintiff children exhibited fear "beyond all measure—and perhaps even beyond all description" (p. 235). Children had many thoughts of and intrusive memories about the flood and the days following. Children slept clothed, and they experienced a general sense of a loss of safety. A general decline in the quality of community was observed, which Erikson believed stemmed in part from increased delinquency, "fooling around," and general moral decline on the part of the adolescents. Erikson argued that the changes were out of the norm of general societal changes in the same time frame. Nevertheless, the adolescent changes parallel those that occur in many adolescents in many communities across years of development. Without statistical evidence and a control group comparison, however, it is hard to be certain that the changes were part of a communal deterioration.

Gleser et al. (1981) provided brief summaries of the children's PEF data collected in both the plaintiffs' and the mining company's assessments. Children exhibited fewer symptoms than adults, and two thirds of the children had minimal to mild anxiety. The company's assessment, however, reported that 10% of the children had moderate to severe anxiety, whereas the plaintiffs' assessment reported 20% in that category. Furthermore, the plaintiffs' assessment reported that roughly 33% of the children had moderate to severe depression.

Green et al. (1991) reanalyzed the plaintiffs' and mining company's 1974 pediatric PEF data from 179 children for symptoms of posttraumatic stress disorder (PTSD), a diagnosis that did not exist in 1974. They reported that the incidence of PTSD was 37%. Symptoms increased significantly with age, from a mean of 2.7 for children ages 2 to 7 at the time of the flood to 3.5 for children who had been age 12 to 15. Denial (i.e., avoidance) was the most common category of symptoms. Boys had significantly more symptoms than girls. In a multiple correlation, life threat, gender, the mother's severity of psychiatric symptoms, an "irritable home environment," and a "depressed home environment" all correlated significantly with the number of PTSD symptoms in the children. Together, the variables accounted for 28% of the variance. Note, however, that the specific symptoms of PTSD were not systematically assessed in either of the two sets of evaluations. It is therefore hard to know how valid the results may be.

Honig et al. (1993) provided follow-up information on the data reported by Green et al. (1991) and Newman (1976). They reported data from a 1988 standardized interview of 99 of the 207 children originally interviewed in 1974 and a follow-up in 1990 with 15 children who were younger than 12 years of age at the time of the flood. Overall rates of PTSD for the children had declined from 37% to 5%. Levels of psychopathology also had declined and were no different from a control sample. The authors concluded, however, that the 1990 open-ended psychiatric interview provided evidence of long-term impact. They hypothesized that reactions to the traumatic stress experienced by the children in 1974 changed over time, becoming adult "patterns of adaptation" (p. 351). Whether the patterns were adaptive is debatable, but Honig et al. (1993) felt that the children still demonstrated clear effects of the trauma 18 years after the disaster.

Other Studies of Children and Floods

Some studies have examined the impact of other floods, but they, too, provide only a glimpse of the effects on children. The only mention of children in Hall and Landreth's (1975) description of the effects of the 1972 Rapid City, South Dakota flood, for example, was to note that children affected by the flood missed more school in the ensuing year. Studies that have focused on children's responses are described below.

Ollendick and Hoffman (1982) studied the responses of adults and children who experienced a flood in Rochester, Minnesota. They assessed the children's reactions in a single data collection using mothers' retrospective ratings of symptoms that were present shortly after the disaster and 8 months later at the time of the assessment. Roughly two thirds of the mothers reported that their children experienced emotional symptoms shortly after the disaster, and more than one third of the children still had emotional reactions at the time of the assessment.

Burke, Moccia, Borus, and Burns (1986) used clinician ratings to evaluate emotional distress in stories written by fifth-grade children. Nineteen children attended a church that served families in a Boston suburb flooded by a winter coastal storm surge and affected by the accompanying blizzard, and 28 children attended a church several miles inland that had been affected by the blizzard but not the flood. The stories were written 10 months after the blizzard and flood. There were no statistically significant differences between the groups for the full 13-item scale. The data from a 6-item subscale (generated post hoc), however, indicated significantly more emotional distress for children from the flooded neighborhood. In comparisons by gender, significant differences were reported only for girls. This latter finding is directly the opposite of the gender findings reported by Green et al. (1991).

Two communities in rural Missouri were flooded in late 1982 and early 1983 (Earls, Smith, Reich, & Jung, 1988; Reich & Earls, 1987). The flooding was complicated by a suspected major release of dioxin that was believed to have contaminated one of the communities. (The suspicion was allayed just before the data were collected.) Twenty of the 22 households with children ages 6 to 17 agreed to participate in the study.

In the first of the studies (Reich & Earls, 1987), the child and parent forms of the Diagnostic Interview for Children and Adolescents (DICA) and the Home Environment Interview for Children were used. School performance data were collected, and the teacher form of the Child Behavior Checklist was administered. Interviewers of the children and parents were blind to other results. Discrepancies between the parent and child versions of the DICA were resolved in meetings between Reich and Earls and the two interviewers.

Reich and Earls (1987) concluded that children's self-report was the most important single source of information in determining children's diagnoses. Children often reported symptoms of which parents were unaware. Monahon (1993) suggested that it is common for parents to minimize the distress experienced by children who have been traumatized; this tendency was more evident with increasing age of the children. The authors also reported that teacher ratings were important for behavioral diagnoses: A total of 53 diagnoses were determined for 32 children. Earls et al. (1988) added to those findings, indicating that children with preexisting psychiatric diagnoses were significantly more likely to experience problems following the flood. They did not find a significant relationship between the severity of exposure to the flooding and the emotional symptoms 1 year after the flood. This result is contrary to Newman's report (1976) on the children of Buffalo Creek.

Durkin, Khan, Davidson, Zaman, and Stein (1993) took advantage of a prospective study of 2- to 9-year-olds in a rural area of Bangladesh 6 months prior to a flood. Sixty-four children with disabilities and 140 other children who had been referred for additional testing in the earlier study were re-evaluated after the flood. In addition to an interview with the children, parents were asked to complete a child behavior screening instrument and a self-rating instrument regarding parental distress. The reassessment indicated a significant increase in aggressive behavior and encopresis or enuresis among the children.

In summary, five studies examined children's reactions to flooding. Although the methodologies, participant ages, and type and time of assessment varied, their results were generally congruent. Emotional distress was present shortly after and up to 1 year following the floods. Moreover, Reich and Earls (1987) noted that multiple sources of diagnostic information were valuable, particularly the children's self-reports. Moreover, Earls et al. (1988) noted that a significant relationship between exposure and emotional distress could not be established among their participants, in contrast to the findings of Newman (1976).

Methodological Notes

Numerous obstacles hinder conducting well-controlled studies in a postdisaster environment. Gaining access to participants in the aftermath of trauma is difficult, and it is important that those rushing to collect data not traumatize survivors a second time. Submitting general protocols to an institutional review board (IRB) on a prospective basis may obviate hurrying proposals through after a disaster. Following a disaster, researchers can provide the IRB with the specific details for the incident to be studied. Among the questions that need to be carefully addressed is whether one can adequately provide informed consent to participate in the aftermath of significant trauma. Ideally, everyone involved in the process has the welfare of the children as the first priority, and all research is designed to improve the understanding of children and disaster and enable more effective prevention or intervention for the future. Nevertheless, the people protecting access to the children and ensuring safe research designs need to be supported, not circumvented.

Following the bombing of the Alfred P. Murrah Federal Office Building in Oklahoma City, a single agency coordinated research on the psychological aftermath. Various research projects were combined, minimizing the number of times people were approached to provide data and coordinating the analyses of those data (see chapter 14). The American Psychological Association [APA] Task Force on the Mental Health Response to the Oklahoma City Bombing (1997) included among its recommendations that the "appropriate branch of state government should appoint a specific research university department or committee to be the coordinator of the mental health research for an incident. Ideally, this would be designated in the state disaster plan" (p. 54). The APA task force also recommended that

> [d]isaster researchers . . . begin to collaborate on a methodology allowing easy comparison of the findings of research following various disasters. . . . A "standardized" protocol would also allow more rapid IRB approval and investigation of the immediate psychological impact on a community. The use of a common core protocol to develop a common pool of data would not preclude individual teams from proposing to the coordinating university additional components for special research foci, but it would reduce the potential for repeatedly collecting identical data from those impacted by a disaster. In the long run, this will increase the willingness of individuals to participate, and thus improve the quality of the data, and thereby, the research itself. (APA, 1997, p. 54)

These recommendations seem particularly germane to research with children, given the challenges in gaining access to children and the variety of data collection strategies used in this literature.

Finally, it is important that research on the psychological aftermath of flood include data on children. Although the chaos that can characterize the aftermath of a flood and the protectiveness of parents and school officials may make studying children more difficult, it is important that there be sound scientific bases to the decisions made in serving the mental health needs of children affected by disaster.

CASE PROGRAM EXAMPLE: SOUTH DAKOTA'S PROJECT RECOVERY

The Midwest floods of 1993 began in South Dakota and spread throughout much of the Mississippi and Missouri basins. Thirty-nine of South Dakota's

66 counties, totaling 32,590 square miles, received a presidential disaster declaration. Only 2% of property owners had flood insurance, in part because much of the flooding was outside identified flood zones. Crop losses totaled $725 million.

Demographic Characteristics of the Affected Population

South Dakota was the second most impoverished state at that time. More than 5,000 families were affected. Population density ranged from 22 counties having fewer than 10 residents per square mile to Minnehaha County, which had 153 residents per square mile and includes the largest city in the state, Sioux Falls (population 110,000). The 39 counties included 9 of the 10 largest cities in the state. Vermillion, the 10th largest city in the state, had a population of less than 9,000. Vast cultural differences exist between the remote frontier agricultural areas and the urban and suburban counties.

Native Americans comprise about 7% of the state's population and are the largest ethnic minority in South Dakota. Five of the flooded counties included Native American reservations, including three bands of the Sioux nation. The single urban county had a large number of Native American residents and small populations of other ethnic minority groups. The remaining 33 counties were almost totally Caucasian.

The Design of Project Recovery

In June 1993 the Disaster Mental Health Institute[1] (DMHI) initiated discussions with the state's Divisions of Mental Health and Emergency Management to design a mental health response for the developing flooding. Initial designs called for a model centered on community mental health centers (CMHCs), but CMHC directors felt that providing the full response needed was beyond their capability, even with additional resources. Therefore, the DMHI was asked to direct the disaster mental health response to the flooding, and an "immediate services" (c.f., Myers, 1994) grant proposal for crisis intervention was submitted to the Federal Emergency Management Agency. Incomplete funding of the proposal, 22 counties added to the declared disaster area, and a 7-month delay in funding the "regular services grant" meant that resources were stretched thin.

The Division of Mental Health provided administrative oversight, worked closely with the DMHI to develop the project parameters, and provided broad direction and guidance to local CMHCs. The DMHI managed and provided day-to-day operations. Those activities included outreach and

---

[1]The Disaster Mental Health Group was founded and applied to become a regental institute in February 1993. The South Dakota Board of Regents approved its status as the Disaster Mental Health Institute in October 1993.

referral services throughout the affected area and education in disaster mental health for both mental health professionals (MHPs) and the public. The DMHI worked with the CMHCs and filled the void whenever their limitations prevented them from effectively delivering services to people affected by the storms and floods. CMHCs monitored the flood's impact on existing clients and provided some crisis counseling, particularly to those referred by DMHI outreach staff. The CMHCs also contributed to the project's public information and planning efforts.

The DMHI staff included three full-time and two part-time licensed psychologists, a licensed school counselor, up to 12 paraprofessional crisis counselors, and secretarial and support staff. About one third of the DMHI staff had themselves been directly affected by the flooding. The crisis counselors had a wide variety of experience and education, which ranged from bachelor's degrees to an "ABD"[2] in clinical psychology. The counselors completed up to 80 hours of intensive instruction, depending on their level of professional education, before beginning fieldwork. The training included 4 hours focused on the needs of children. They received weekly supervision from the MHPs and weekly support sessions with the consultants.

Project Recovery used five guiding principles:

1. Provision of professional services;
2. Use of a community psychology outreach model;
3. Focus on crisis intervention;
4. Support for Project Recovery staff; and
5. Special services for children and elders.

Provision of Professional Services

Because the program was directed and managed by psychologists, all client care and staff supervision were regulated by the ethical guidelines, professional standards, and state laws governing the activities of psychologists and their supervisees. Within the area of professional services were five guidelines for how professional services were to be delivered:

1. The competence of all staff providing services needed to be ensured, and the services themselves were required to be of appropriate quality. Providers were selected on the basis of their previous training and familiarity with the affected area, trained as and when necessary, and were provided regular supervision and professional backup.
2. Adequate informed consent required that clients had the capacity to give consent, were provided sufficient information describing the available services, and consented of their own

---

[2]"All but dissertation"—a doctoral student who has completed all requirements except the dissertation.

free will. This principle therefore prohibited "stealth psychology" (i.e., providing mental health services in such a manner as to deceive the recipient about their source or nature, for fear that the client might not seek or might reject mental health services). Children were not approached without the permission of either parents (for direct services) or school officials (for group educational sessions). The children themselves also gave consent before direct services or participation in any assessment.

3. Confidentiality applied to all information gained in the project's professional relationships with clients. Consequently, the project did not release information about a client to anyone without a signed release from the client. Exceptions to confidentiality specified in state law were, of course, respected.

4. Proper documentation was maintained by keeping adequate records to demonstrate that each client received appropriate services and that the ethical and legal responsibilities to each client were met.

5. Finally, cultural appropriateness was sought through cultural oversight by supervisors and by consultants for the entire program, selection of counselors familiar with the cultures of those who were to receive services, training in cultural awareness and sensitivity, and preparation of culturally appropriate informational materials. Agricultural, Native American, and Latino cultural consultants reviewed community outreach and counseling services. The flood counselors included a retired agricultural counselor, an agricultural mediator, two farmers, and a bilingual Native American who was an enrolled member of one of the affected tribes. Most of the flood counselors lived in frontier areas, and one was from the Sioux Falls area, the one metropolitan area in the declared counties.

Training in cultural awareness and sensitivity took place throughout Project Recovery. Initial training for flood counselors included workshops on rural, frontier, and agricultural culture as well as on Native American cultural awareness and sensitivity. The workshop sessions also were broadcast over interactive technology for MHPs in affected CMHCs. Weekly training sessions for flood counselors routinely included updates and question-and-answer periods on those topics. The cultural advisor and Native American flood counselor were available to counselors whenever needed.

Educational materials were prepared specifically for the agricultural community. Culturally appropriate brochures and pamphlets were developed in the Dakota and Lakota languages for the Native American communities. *After the Flood*, a common Spanish- and English-language flood coloring book

(Flood Support Services, 1990, 1994) was redrawn in cooperation with the original developers to reflect scenes characteristic of the northern plains. In addition, an entirely original version that was culturally appropriate for affected Native American reservations was developed in the Lakota and Dakota languages (Disaster Mental Health Institute, 1994).

Todd-Bazemore (1998) suggested that MHPs responding in culturally diverse communities consider factors that can significantly affect their ability to effectively deliver needed services. First, it is important to study the social and political history of the population in question, including the society within which they currently reside and their country or other community of origin. Additionally, existing and longstanding tensions between majority and minority community members may be exacerbated following a disaster. This tension may lead to increased community divisiveness and an unwillingness to provide or receive services from specific sectors of the community.

Second, MHPs need to become well acquainted with the appropriate cultural protocols for gaining entry to the community. Third, it is important for MHPs to assess the role of spiritual healing systems and cultural practices in the community. Fourth, mental health workers need to understand how the community conceptualizes health, illness, wellness, and healing. Fifth, mental health providers need to learn the standards of competency the community expects from service providers. Last, it is important for MHPs to assess the community's infrastructure for managing crises and long-term trauma, including basic health services.

Community Psychology Outreach Model

This strategy is particularly effective for serving both rural–frontier areas and communities affected by disaster (Jacobs, 1995; Quevillon & Jacobs, 1992). The project mailed periodic informational letters and materials to all 5,000 households during the 17 months of operation and made more than 16,000 phone calls to those households. Counselors visited nearly 800 homes by invitation from the families. Project staff worked with CMHC staff, community, agency, and government representatives throughout the region to coordinate activity. They also worked with school districts, Head Start and other preschool and child care programs, and the Agricultural Extension Service's youth program, "Project Rebound."

Focus on Crisis Intervention

One of the foci of the flood counselors' training was to accurately assess the needs of both adults and children directly affected by the flooding and to refer people to more traditional services if they required more than crisis intervention. More than 600 referrals were made to CMHCs for traditional mental health care, including only a handful of children. More than 900 families received regular counseling follow-up. Flood counselors were intensively trained regarding other resource and assistance programs available to those affected by the floods.

Support for the Project Recovery Staff

It has been well documented that disaster mental health staff can suffer cumulative stress as a result of their work (e.g., Figley, 1995). Self-care was one of the regular topics of the weekly staff training sessions. The two part-time consultant psychologists conducted weekly group support sessions for the staff, and individual sessions also were available.

Special Services for Children and Elders

Specific materials were developed for elders, and one flood counselor focused particularly on services to the elderly. Services focused on the needs of children were more extensive than for the elderly and are addressed in more detail below.

Services to Children

Children's cognitive–developmental perceptions of disaster events, together with their lack of ability and authority to control their environment, necessitate services that address their unique needs. The children's program was developed with the long-term goal of providing disaster mental health services to people age 18 and younger who were affected by the storms and floods of the summer of 1993. Its purpose was to serve individual children, to help the families better serve the needs of their children, and to assist the organizations that provided services to the children. The specific objectives of the program included providing training on children's reactions to disaster and disaster mental health interventions for children to MHPs, school and child care personnel, and parents; providing consultation to schools; and providing crisis intervention and referral services for children and families.

Training in disaster mental health for children was provided to project flood counselors and to CMHC, agency, and MHPs in private practice throughout the flood-affected area. Sections of the training included children's reactions to trauma, risk factors for traumatic stress, individuality of children's reactions, challenges of children's reactions, relationship of developmental stages to trauma reactions, and suggested interventions in working with children. The segment on interventions focused on community-based interventions, but it included a brief section on clinical interventions for community mental health professionals.

The structured interview used for first contacts with affected families and for home visits included specific assessments of the needs of children in the families. As part of their initial training, all crisis counselors were instructed in assessing the needs of and providing elementary crisis intervention services for children. They also were taught to recognize the limitations of their own training and when to refer clients to one of the project's supervising MHPs, a CMHC, or another agency with expertise in serving the mental health needs of children.

DMHI staff further participated in weekly training sessions that included frequent discussion of the same topics. Training in networking, home visit strategies, stress reactions, assistance agencies, advocacy, phasing down the operation, and service termination included discussions of services to children. In addition, the weekly update on resources and services available for affected families provided regular information on services for children.

Training for school and child care personnel was conducted at a number of levels, ranging from a statewide meeting of school superintendents to individual instruction with classroom teachers. A packet of materials was mailed to each of the school districts in the affected counties. The packets included the videotape *Children and Trauma: The School's Response* (Spofford et al., 1991) and the booklets *Helping Children Cope With a Traumatic Event* (DeWolfe, 1994), *Children and Disaster: A School Counselor's Handbook on How to Help* (Nordgren & Englund, 1994), and *Teen Stress: How to Cope When Disaster Strikes and Things Get Tough* (Wiemers, 1994). Schools in 24 of 39 counties requested assistance and consultation. An experienced school counselor followed up with the schools and focused on assisting teachers in preparing curricula that would provide children with an opportunity to process issues relating to the flooding. She also provided additional copies of the materials, including nearly 9,000 copies of the teen stress booklet. In addition, both flood crisis counselors and project MHPs provided consultation to Head Start programs and other child care facilities in the affected area.

Training for parents was provided primarily through educational handouts and home visits. Roughly 30,000 copies of *Helping Children Cope With a Traumatic Event* (DeWolfe, 1994) were distributed to households, schools, medical clinics, Head Start programs, community service agencies, among other organizations. Spanish-language versions of the booklet were distributed through migrant service offices.

The DMHI also collaborated with the Agricultural Extension Service, whose counselors offered schools disaster mental health consultation in much of the affected area. The DMHI provided the Extension Service with materials for distribution, and the Extension Service provided referrals to Project Recovery when appropriate.

It was common for school staff to fail to recognize links between children's behavior and the stress of the flooding. In one school, for example, teachers and administrators reported that none of the children were experiencing difficulties as a result of the flooding. They requested a consultation, however, for a high school student who had begun significant levels of acting out. The staff reported that the boy had never been in trouble before, and they acknowledged that the behavior had begun after the flooding started. They were certain, however, that the behavior was unrelated to the flooding.

In the counselor's first meeting with the boy he reported that he was experiencing tremendous stress because his family's farm had been seeded, flooded, reseeded, flooded, reseeded, and flooded a third time. (This was a common experience for farmers in much of the flooded area.) In addition to the high financial cost and labor of preparing the fields and seeding three times, no crop was harvested that year, resulting in the frustration of wasted labor as well as the hardship of the family's financial loss.

For many children it is difficult to recognize connections between acting-out behavior or negative emotions and traumatic events that may have occurred more than a year earlier. It may be somewhat easier to see the relationship from an outsider's perspective, however, if the pattern of behavior and emotions presents a stark contrast to previous experience with the child. If educators or providers know that a child has been exposed to a traumatic event, it is reasonable to examine the hypothesis that the changes being observed may be a result of the child's efforts to cope with that experience. Assessing for a history of trauma may provide important evidence in deciding on an effective response to children's problematic behavioral or emotional patterns.

RECOMMENDATIONS

It is not the purpose of this chapter to offer detailed recommendations for all the aspects of disaster mental health for children affected by flood. Consequently, we make only a few recommendations, which involve preparedness, assessment, and programs.

Preparedness

For many years people assumed that children were either immune to trauma or were so resilient that trauma's impact on them was minimal (Shelby, 1997). As a review of the literature on children and floods reveals, however, children may be strongly affected by exposure to floods. A concept frequently used to describe children's general reactions to these events is the "loss of a sense of safety" (e.g., APA Task Force, 1997; Greening & Dollinger, 1992). It has been noted, however, that children who are "adequately prepared" were more likely to have less severe and usually temporary reactions (Crabbs, 1981).

The cornerstone of disaster response is preparedness. Support for disaster preparation with children can perhaps most clearly be seen in the ubiquitous fire/tornado/earthquake drills in the nation's schools. A variety of Internet sites provide information to assist schools and families in designing programs to help children prepare for disaster. The National Weather Service (2000) provides information about preparing school emergency plans and education programs for severe weather. The California Governor's Office of Emergency Services (2000) provides similar information for earthquakes. The most comprehensive site seems to be that hosted by the American Red Cross (2000a), which provides information for families, schools, and corporations on preparing for a broad range of disasters. The site also includes downloadable brochures for families on how to prepare disaster kits. Visitors to the site may choose a Spanish-language version. All the sites emphasize physical safety, reducing injuries, and saving lives.

Disaster mental health has made great strides in recent decades. The emphasis, however, has been on preparing mental health professionals, governments, and mental health agencies for disaster response. The next step is to help those likely to be affected by disaster to prepare psychologically for such an event. Glenwick and Jason (1993) offered a similar perspective and described a variety of prevention programs.

Shelby's (1997) play therapy for children affected by flood provides insight into ways in which disaster-drill activities like those described above may provide a degree of psychological preparedness. Shelby reported that the sense of mastery experienced by the children returned a sense of control to them and helped them begin to rebuild a sense of safety. In Project Recovery, schools reported that some of the children who lived in areas that had been flooded prepared a list or even assembled a bag of things they wanted to rescue in the event of future flooding. Those spontaneous activities seemed to be a functional effort to regain a sense of control.

The American Red Cross (2000b) Internet site and brochure on developing family disaster kits provide a guide for helping children take control in preparing for disasters in a manner that is reminiscent of Shelby's play therapy. For children, knowing how to prepare for and respond to a flood may prevent the loss of a sense of safety and the disorientation experienced by some of the children of Buffalo Creek (Erikson, 1976).

Another tool with strong potential for developing psychological preparedness is psychological first aid (Kirk, 1993). This technique provides the general public with tools and strategies for coping with stress and psychological trauma in their own lives and in the lives of their family, friends, and neighbors. In June 1998 the International Federation of Red Cross and Red Crescent Societies trained the first group of international representatives to assist countries in developing psychological first-aid programs. It was presented as a model for implementing inexpensive psychological support for citizens affected by disasters as well as other stressful or traumatic events. The model's low initiation and maintenance costs make it a practical strategy for developing support programs, even in developing countries. Although the most important utility of psychological first aid may be in countries with few mental health resources, the low cost also means that it can be a practical addition to school and community programs, even when budgets are tightly constrained. If psychological first aid can become as prevalent as physical first aid, the public, including children, will have additional tools to cope with the psychological aspects of disaster. Moreover, those tools will be available during and in the immediate aftermath of the event. Just as with physical first aid, psychological first aid may obviate the need for professional assistance for some children affected by a disaster and help others cope until professional help arrives.

Assessment

It is laudable that most of the literature on children affected by flood includes data that are based on the direct assessment of the children. Lyons' (1987) review on PTSD in children concluded that parents are often unaware of the impact of stressful events on their children or may deny or downplay the impact. Pynoos and Nader (1988) reported that parents are more likely to underestimate the impact of traumatic events on their children shortly after the event but become more accurate after a year or more. Another possibility Lyons (1987) noted was that parents may simply not understand the salience of events for the children, a point shared by Aptekar and Boore (1990) and Pynoos and Nader (1990).

In conducting needs assessments, therefore, it is critically important that disaster mental health personnel attempt to obtain self-reports from children about their reaction to the events. Although parent and teacher reports may be informative, children's reports are likely to provide unique information about their perspective.

Response

The description of Project Recovery offered in this chapter provides an indication of many elements that need to be considered when designing an effective response program to serve the needs of children affected by flood. The features that characterize quality mental health services for children in daily life are much the same as those that lead to quality disaster mental health services: competent, well-trained, and well-supervised counselors and therapists who provide well-documented services to informed consumers in a culturally appropriate manner. Those hallmarks of professional mental health service will best serve the needs of children in the aftermath of flood.

REFERENCES

American Red Cross. (2000a). *Safety*. Retrieved February 29, 2000, from http://www.crossnet.org/disaster/safety

American Red Cross. (2000b). *Your family disaster plan*. Retrieved February 29, 2000, from http://www.crossnet.org/pubs/dspubs/genprep.html

American Psychological Association Task Force on the Mental Health Response to the Oklahoma City Bombing. (1997). *Final report*. Washington, DC: Author.

Aptekar, L., & Boore, J. A. (1990). The emotional effects of disaster on children: A review of the literature. *International Journal of Mental Health, 19*, 77–90.

Burke, J. D., Moccia, P., Borus, J. F., & Burns, B. J. (1986). Emotional distress in fifth-grade children ten months after a natural disaster. *Journal of the American Academy of Child Psychiatry, 25*, 536–541.

California Governor's Office of Emergency Services. (2000). *OES California*. Retrieved February 28, 2000, from http://www.oes.ca.gov/

Crabbs, M. A. (1981). School mental health services following an environmental disaster. *Journal of School Health, 51*, 165–167.

DeWolfe, D. (1994). *Helping children cope with a traumatic event*. Seattle, WA: King County Chapter, American Red Cross.

Disaster Mental Health Institute. (1994). *Min hiyaye oyasin (All about floods)*. Vermillion, SD: Author.

Durkin, M. S., Khan, N., Davidson, L. L., Zaman, S. S., & Stein, Z. A. (1993). The effects of a natural disaster on child behavior: Evidence for posttraumatic stress. *American Journal of Public Health, 83*, 1549–1553.

Earls, F., Smith, E., Reich, W., & Jung, K. G. (1988). Investigating psychopathological consequences of a disaster in children: A pilot study incorporating a structured diagnostic interview. *Journal of the American Academy of Child and Adolescent Psychiatry, 27*, 90–95.

Erikson, K. T. (1976). *Everything in its path*. New York: Simon & Schuster.

Figley, C. R. (Ed.). (1995). *Compassion fatigue*. New York: Brunner/Mazel.

Flood Support Services. (1990). *My flood book (Mi libro de inundacion): Activities for children*. Olympia, Washington: Washington State Mental Health Division.

Flood Support Services. (1994). *My flood book (Mi libro de inundacion): Activities for children*. Olympia, Washington: Washington State Mental Health Division.

Glenwick, D. S., & Jason, L. A. (Eds.). (1993). *Promoting health and mental health in children, youth, and families*. New York: Springer.

Gleser, G. C., Green, B. L., & Winget, C. N. (1981). *Prolonged psychosocial effects of disaster: A study of Buffalo Creek*. New York: Academic Press.

Green, B. L., Grace, M. C., Crespo da Silva, L., & Gleser, G. C. (1983). Use of the Psychiatric Evaluation Form to quantify children's interview data. *Journal of Consulting and Clinical Psychology, 51*, 353–359.

Green, B. L., Korol, M., Grace, M. C., Vary, M. G., Leonard, A. C., Gleser, G. C., & Smithson-Cohen, S. (1991). Children and disaster: Age, gender, and parental effects on PTSD symptoms. *Journal of the American Academy of Child and Adolescent Psychiatry, 30*, 945–951.

Greening, L., & Dollinger, S. J. (1992). Illusions (and shattered illusions) of invulnerability: Adolescents in natural disaster. *Journal of Traumatic Stress, 5*, 63–75.

Hall, P. S., & Landreth, P. W. (1975). Assessing some long term consequences of a natural disaster. *Mass Emergencies, 1*, 55–61.

Honig, R. G., Grace, M. C., Lindy, J., Newman, C. J., & Titchener, J. L. (1993). Portraits of survival: A twenty-year follow-up of the children of Buffalo Creek. *Psychoanalytic Study of the Child, 48*, 327–335.

Jacobs, G. A. (1995). The development of a national plan for disaster mental health. *Professional Psychology: Research and Practice, 26*, 543–549.

Kirk, U. (1993). *Psychological first aid–and other human support.* Copenhagen, Denmark: Danish Red Cross.

Lyons, J. A. (1987). Posttraumatic stress disorder in children and adolescents: A review of the literature. *Developmental and Behavioral Pediatrics, 8*, 349–356.

Monahon, C. (1993). *Children and trauma: A guide for parents and professionals.* San Francisco: Jossey-Bass.

Myers, D. (1994). *Disaster response and recovery: A handbook for mental health professionals* (DHHS Publication No. SMA 94-3010). Washington, DC: U.S. Government Printing Office.

National Weather Service. (2000). *A guide to developing a severe weather emergency plan for schools.* Retrieved February 29, 2000, from http://www.nws.noaa.gov/er/lwx/swep/index.htm.

Newman, C. J. (1976). Children of disaster: Clinical observations at Buffalo Creek. *American Journal of Psychiatry, 133*, 306–312.

Nordgren, J. C., & Englund, N. (1994). *Children and disaster: A school counselor's handbook on how to help.* Vermillion, SD: Disaster Mental Health Institute.

Ollendick, D. G., & Hoffman, S. M. (1982). Assessment of psychological reactions in disaster victims. *Journal of Community Psychology, 10*, 157–167.

Pynoos, R. S., & Nader, K. (1988). Psychological first aid and treatment approach to children exposed to community violence: Research implications. *Journal of Traumatic Stress, 1*, 445–473.

Pynoos, R. S., & Nader, K. (1990). Children's exposure to violence and traumatic death. *Psychiatric Annals, 20*, 334–344.

Quevillon, R. P., & Jacobs, G. A. (1992). Treatment issues in mental health responses to disaster. In L. VandeCreek, S. Knapp, & T. Jackson (Eds.), *Innovations in clinical practice: A source book* (Vol. 11, pp. 403–411). Sarasota, FL: Professional Resource Press.

Reich, W., & Earls, F. (1987). Rules for making psychiatric diagnoses in children on the basis of multiple sources of information: Preliminary strategies. *Journal of Abnormal Child Psychology, 15*, 601–616.

Shelby, J. S. (1997). Rubble, disruption, and tears: Helping young survivors of natural disaster. In H. G. Kaduson, D. Cangelosi, & C. E. Schaefer (Eds.), *The playing cure: Individualized play therapy for specific childhood traumas* (pp. 143–169). Northvale, NJ: Jason Aronson.

Spofford, E., Hiley-Young, B., Myers, D., & Fernandez, N. (Producers), & Thierman, E., & Schwartz, M. (Directors). (1991). *Children and trauma: The school's response* [Videotape]. Rockville MD: Center for Mental Health Services.

Titchener, J. L., & Kapp, F. T. (1976). Family and character change at Buffalo Creek. *American Journal of Psychiatry, 133,* 295–299.

Todd-Bazemore, E. (1998, June). *Long term mental health care after disaster for groups with special needs.* Paper presented at Innovations in Disaster Mental Health, Rapid City, SD.

Wiemers, K. S. (1994). *Teen stress: How to cope when disaster strikes and things get tough.* Vermillion, SD: Disaster Mental Health Institute.

8

RESIDENTIAL FIRES

RUSSELL T. JONES AND THOMAS H. OLLENDICK

National statistics suggest that 1 in 5 families will experience a fire in their homes at some point in time and that a significant minority of families will experience repeated fires. In 1997 it was reported that 500,000 residential fires occur each year and result in approximately 5,000 deaths and 21,000 injuries (Greenberg & Keane, 1997). Burn injuries resulting from residential fires in the United States are estimated at 600,000 to 750,000 incidents per year (Snyder & Saigh, 1984) and are the third leading cause of death for children (Tarnowski, 1994). The people most likely to be injured by fire are children and adolescents, particularly those from low-income families (Tarnowski, 1994). According to Stoddard, Norman, Murphy, and Beardslee (1989), 25% to 35% of burn-injured children develop posttraumatic stress disorder (PTSD) and more than 50% display significant PTSD symptoms. Unfortunately, research has not yet disentangled the relations among those demographic variables. Although a number of research investigations have studied fire emergency responding (Holmes & Jones, 1996; Jones, 1980; Jones, Ollendick, & Shinske, 1989; Jones, Van Hasselt, & Sisson, 1984; Randall &

This chapter was supported in part by National Institute of Mental Health Grant RO1-MH431304, awarded to Russell T. Jones and Thomas H. Ollendick. Support was also provided by the Georgia Firefighters' Burn Foundation Grant 433849 and the Federal Emergency Management Agency Grant 425441, both awarded to Russell T. Jones.

Jones, 1994), few have examined the potentially deleterious consequences of fire emergencies on children and their families.

DEFINITION OF THE EVENT

Residential fire can be conceptualized as either a technological (i.e., human made) disaster or a natural disaster, as in the case of wildfire. Characteristics of fire often include: powerful impact, unpredictability, low controllability, threat, terror, and horror. Although several of those characteristics also are associated with natural disasters (Foa, Steketee, & Rothbaum, 1989; Jones & Barlow, 1990), the fact that residential fires usually occur in isolation may lead to greater levels of psychological distress (Bernstein, 1990).

Characteristics that are somewhat unique to fire have been shown to be correlated with survivors' functioning, including exposure to noxious fumes, toxic gases, fire appearance (Bickman, Edelman, & McDaniel, 1977), and potential for severe harm and injury (Bickman et al., 1977; Phillips, 1978). Perhaps the best way to define the event is through "the eyes of a child." Below is a quote from a transcription of a child's report when returning home following a fire:

> When we got to the house, the street was covered with fire trucks. I couldn't really see the house because of all the smoke, the wind blew the smoke and it drifted back. I saw how a big chunk of the house was gone. I still wasn't upset at that point, I was really shocked. It was too much like a bad dream story and I would wake up from it any second. Almost everything was gone. There was still smoke, and everything was covered in black soot or tar. Our pets had all died.

REVIEW OF THE LITERATURE

Although little attention has been given to the study of the consequences of fire for children, adolescents, and their families, this section provides an account of the studies that have been conducted. Krim (1983) carried out one of the initial studies examining the impact of residential fire on children. Symptoms including inability to eat or sleep, nervousness, anxiety, depression, and denial were reported. Many reactions parallel those reported in the disaster literature as resulting from large-scale disasters, such as floods and hurricanes. The postdisaster state of mental health of mother and child was significantly related to the extent of damage or loss incurred. Although the data are preliminary in nature, they shed some light on the mental health consequences of fire.

Between March 1987 and January 1988, Jones and Ribbe (1991) conducted a pilot study targeting 20 survivors of residential fires and obtained similar results to those of Krim (1983). Eight children and adolescents (ages 4 to 15) and 12 adults (ages 21 to 68) participated. During individual interviews, a child and adult version of the Fire Questionnaire (Jones & Ribbe, 1988) was used to obtain participants' experiences. Information concerning the individual's behavior prior to the fire (i.e., location in the home and time of fire), behavior during the fire (i.e., panic, cognitions, and fear of injury), and consequences of the fire (i.e., loss, injury, and depression) was obtained. Findings from this study illustrated two important points: (a) that a person's psychological reaction to residential fire can be reliably documented, and (b) that several symptoms related to PTSD were expressed by the fire survivors.

On the basis of those findings, Jones and Ribbe (1991) next studied 25 male adolescents who were residents in a dormitory that burned and compared them with 13 adolescent males who were not residents of the dormitory. Using selected portions of the Diagnostic Interview for Children and Adolescents, Revised Version (DICA-R; Reich & Welner, 1990) and the Horowitz Impact of Events Scale (Horowitz, Wilner, & Alvarez, 1979), the consequences of the fire were determined. Two primary findings were documented. First, and somewhat unexpectedly, stress symptomatology, as measured by the Horowitz scale, proved substantial in both groups even 4 months postdisaster. Second, the adolescents whose dorm was burned reported significantly greater levels of PTSD symptoms, as determined by the diagnostic interview, than those whose dorm had not burned. Additionally, assessment of premorbid functioning with reference to several disorders, including oppositional defiant disorder, conduct disorder, overanxious disorder, and major affective disorder (past and present), revealed no significant differences between the two groups. At 1-year follow-up, however, significant drops in PTSD symptoms in both groups were observed.

Using a similar methodology, elevated levels of PTSD symptomatology were evidenced between a group of children whose homes had been destroyed by wildfires and a group whose homes were unaffected (Jones, Ribbe, & Cunningham, 1994). Both groups lived in the same city. No significant differences were obtained between the two groups and the number of symptoms reported for oppositional defiant disorder, conduct disorder, overanxious disorder, past or present major affective disorder, and PTSD. Those who lost their homes met significantly more criteria for PTSD, however. Of the group of children who had lost their homes, two met the criteria for PTSD, whereas one of the children from the control group met such criteria. Results from this study were consistent with earlier reports suggesting that various degrees of psychosocial distress do indeed result from fire-related disaster.

Greenberg (1994) examined 12 children ages 6 to 17, all of whom had been involved in separate residential fires. Consistent with Heider's attribution theory, children sought reasons for the fire. They attributed responsibility of the fire to others, particularly neighbors. Although actual diagnostic assessments were not administered, symptoms of anxiety, depression, sleep disturbance, hyperalertness, guilt, and lack of concentration were reported. Unfortunately, no measure of the degree of intensity of these symptoms was obtained. All children reported fear of the fire as well as apprehension of another fire occurring in their home. Nine of the 12 children reported withdrawing from regular activities and friends. Half of the parents rated their child's adjustment following the fire as "not normal." Children's perception of their parent's reaction to the fire indicated that they desired to "protect" their parents. That is, nine children reported that they knew how worried their parents were, and six indicated that they (their parents) were not "handling things well." In summary, the data also suggested that children and adolescents experience various levels of distress following fire disaster.

March, Amaya-Jackson, Terry, & Costanzo (1997) used a population-based sampling strategy to assess the impact of an industrial fire on 1,400 children and adolescents. Nine months following a major fire at a chicken-processing plant, in which 25 people were killed and 56 workers were seriously injured, posttraumatic symptomatology (PTS) was obtained using the Self-Reported Post-Traumatic Symptomatology modeled on the Frederick Reaction Index (Frederick, 1985; Pynoos et al., 1987). Additionally, measures of depression (Children's Depression Inventory [CDI]; Kovacs, 1985), anxiety (Revised Children's Manifest Anxiety Scale; Reynolds & Paget, 1981), locus of control (Nowicki-Strickland measures; Nowicki & Strickland, 1973) and features of attention-deficit hyperactivity disorder and oppositional defiant disorder (Hyperactivity Index from the Conners' Teacher Rating Scale; Conners, 1995) were administered. Results demonstrated that PTS and comorbid internalizing and externalizing symptoms were directly related to levels of exposure, that race and gender had variable effects on risk for PTS and comorbid symptoms, and that PTS was positively correlated with comorbid symptoms.

SHORTCOMINGS OF EXISTING LITERATURE

Notwithstanding the reports from both the child and adult literature, fire disaster research has many shortcomings. One shortcoming is the failure to consistently account for survivors' premorbid psychopathology. Evidence indicates that children with psychiatric disorders before a residential fire are more likely to develop PTSD symptomatology (Patterson et al., 1993) and are more likely to be burn victims (Tarnowski, 1994). In fact, reported estimates on the prevalence of previous psychiatric illness among burn patients range from 28% (Brezel, Kassenbrock, & Stein, 1988) to 75% (Davidson & Brown, 1985). Not only are people with premorbid psychopathological disorders at a higher risk of sustaining burn injuries than their nondisordered counterparts, they also are more likely to have longer, more extensive recovery periods that could affect their adjustment (Patterson et al., 1993). Furthermore, females are at a greater risk for maladjustment than males (Pruzinsky & Doctor, 1994). Therefore, assessment of levels of premorbid functioning is important.

Another significant shortcoming is that children's reactions to fires and other disasters are frequently not obtained from children themselves; rather, parents typically report on their children's distress (Green, Grace, Crespo da Silva, & Glesner, 1983). Those reports are problematic because parents often underestimate the level of distress experienced by their children (Earls, Smith, Reich, & Jung, 1988). Thus, direct reports from child survivors themselves are necessary.

Two related shortcomings stem from the lack of standardized assessment instruments when assessing survivors of disasters (McNally, 1991) and the lack of a theoretical model to guide investigations in the disaster field (Green et al., 1991; Jones et al., 1994). These issues will be considered in some detail in the sections that follow.

CONCEPTUAL MODELS

A glaring omission in the literature is that of a comprehensive, conceptually driven, theoretical model of the consequences of fire across the lifespan. Disasters afford unique opportunities for theory development inasmuch as they typically have an immediate onset and are relatively short in duration (Green, 1993; Solomon, 1989). In our work, we have used two models to guide our thinking during the development as well as the conduct of our present investigation: the psychosocial model of disaster (Korol, Green, & Grace, 1999) and the conservation of resources model (Hobfoll, 1989). The psychosocial model is discussed below.

Psychosocial Model of Disaster

In Korol et al.'s (1999) psychosocial model of disaster, four primary factors are identified and hypothesized to interact to determine both short-term functioning and long-term adaptation to the "traumatic event." Those factors include characteristics of the stressor (i.e., loss and life threat), cognitive processing of the event (i.e., magical thinking and appraisal), individual characteristics of the child (i.e., age and sex), and characteristics of the environment (i.e., reactions of family members). The strength of this model is its attempt to conceptualize and account for child and adolescent functioning following major disasters. Unlike previous models in the disaster literature, which examined adult reactions to disaster, the Korol et al. model uses a developmental perspective in which children's reactions also can be explored. Empirical support for each of the model's four factors, derived from earlier findings in the general child disaster literature as well as some of our own efforts, is briefly discussed next.

Empirical Support for Each Factor

Among several important factors that fall under this heading are exposure to the event, degree of displacement resulting from the event, amount of physical disruption, and degree of life threat and bereavement (Korol et al., 1999). Perhaps the most objective factor is exposure, which has been found to be significantly related to heightened levels of psychological distress in several studies (La Greca, Silverman, Vernberg, & Prinstein, 1996; Pynoos et al., 1987) supporting a dose–response relationship.

Cognitive processing of the stressor is a primary factor hypothesized to affect short-term response and long-term adaptation to the fire. A major aspect of the "stress response," as Green (1990) articulated, is the perception and the immediate appraisal of the event. Although this variable may be difficult to assess in young children as a result of developmental limitations, the need to explore this relatively ignored area of children's cognitive functioning is clear. Evidence suggests a meaningful role of coping processes in mediating child and adolescent functioning across a variety of conditions (Compas & Epping, 1993; Folkman & Lazarus, 1985). Earlier work in our lab suggested that appraisal of the "changeability" or secondary appraisal of a situation may influence performance as well (Randall & Jones, 1994).

Literature on natural and technological disasters dating back some years indicates that reactions to traumatic events vary with age. The degree of distress exhibited by preschoolers is consistently lower than that observed at other developmental levels. Children and adolescents report a variety of symptoms, including traumatic anxiety reactions, nightmares, and sleep disorders (Newman, 1976); specific fears (Milne, 1977); and anxiety and depression (Burke, Borus, Burnes, Millstein, & Beasley, 1986). Several investigators have maintained that adolescents' symptomatology is often more similar to that of adults than that of younger children (D. G. Ollendick & Hoffman, 1982; Terr, 1985).

With respect to PTSD symptoms, early reports suggested no differences among youths of various developmental levels (Terr, 1981). Terr (1983) maintained that distress was relatively independent of age. Later reports suggested variation in distress among preschoolers, school-aged children, and adolescents (Eth, Silverstein, & Pynoos, 1985). Internalizing behaviors, including somatic complaints and separation anxiety, were more likely to be reported among preschoolers, whereas actual symptoms of PTSD were reported among school-aged children. Lyons (1991) found that adolescents reported extreme levels of both internalizing and externalizing behaviors. They also reported increased levels of anxiety, dysphoria, aggressive behavior, acting out, substance abuse, and decreased energy (Eth et al., 1985). Recently, however, researchers have reported that posttraumatic symptomatology in children and adolescents closely resembles that of adults (Earls et al., 1988; March, 1990; March & Amaya-Jackson, 1994).

With reference to gender, several reports have documented the fact that females are more likely than males to develop the full PTSD syndrome (Breslau, Davis, Andreski, & Peterson, 1991; Helzer, Robins, & McEvoy, 1987). Korol (1990), however, suggested that an age-by-gender interaction may exist: Middle-age (8–11) boys and adolescent girls show more total PTSD symptoms and intrusion symptoms than do boys and girls in other age groups. Explanations for those gender differences are yet to be clearly ascertained in the child disaster area.

The role of the environment has been shown to have a major impact on individual functioning during and following disasters. Specifically, parental reactions and family cohesiveness following traumatic events affect children's functioning. Children's reactions to traumatic events may be more a function of their parents' reactions (typically the mother) than the event itself (Kinston & Rosser, 1974). McFarlane (1987) reported that mothers' reactions to disaster were better predictors of children's PTSD than children's direct exposure to the disaster itself. Melamed and Siegel (1980) also reported that parental anxiety was correlated with poor adjustment of children. Likewise, Pynoos, Nader, Frederick, Gonda, and Stuber (1988) stated that children were likely to respond similarly to adults in both the nature and frequency of grief reactions up to 1 year following the incident. Similar findings were also observed by other investigators (Jones & Ribbe, 1991; Korol et al., 1999).

Regarding family cohesiveness, a small number of studies have examined dimensions of family structure to determine its impact on children's postdisaster functioning. McFarlane (1987) showed a relatively strong correlation between family functioning and children's psychopathology 8 months following bushfires in Australia. Similarly, Green et al. (1991) found a meaningful effect of family atmosphere on children's postdisaster functioning.

An additional characteristic of the environment is social support. One reason that some people may not develop PTSD or related symptomatology is that they have a strong social support network. Families are usually the most used source of support available to trauma victims both at the time of impact and after the disaster (Kaniasty, Norris, & Murrell, 1990). A strong social support network may act as a buffer to postdisaster distress. The Stress Buffer Model presented by Kaniasty and Norris (1993) suggests that social support protects disaster victims from the negative consequences of stressful conditions. When faced with stress, people have a greater tendency to affiliate with others who may offer support. When expected help is not received, however, greater resentment is felt toward relatives and friends than toward strangers (Kaniasty et al., 1990).

In summary, because of the wealth of findings supporting the need to examine these characteristics, we initially adopted Korol et al.'s (1999) psychosocial model of disaster. We set out to determine the exact nature of the relationship among the four factors as well as their short- and long-term impact on the recovery of fire survivors.

DEVELOPMENT AND APPLICATION OF A CONCEPTUAL MODEL FOR UNDERSTANDING CHILDREN'S REACTIONS TO RESIDENTIAL FIRES

Past studies often quite narrowly defined loss, which is a major contributor to psychological distress. For example, Green (1990) and Korol et al. (1999) defined it as sudden loss of a loved one. In an attempt to obtain a more robust measure of loss, we adopted Hobfoll's (1989) Conservation of Resources Model. This model, which focuses on critical social and personal characteristics, provided us with a more comprehensive means of assessing loss. Hobfoll maintained that resources are conceptualized as tools that facilitate successful interaction with the environment. The absence of such tools will result in acute negative emotional experiences. Additionally, prolonged emotional distress will occur if losses are not effectively compensated through individual, social, and communitywide efforts.

The four categories of loss for adults are *objects* (e.g., car, home, and possessions), *conditions* (e.g., employment, marriage, and parenthood), *personal characteristics* (e.g., sense of meaning and purpose, self-esteem, and self-efficacy), and *energies* (e.g., knowledge and skills, money, and time). Similar categories were devised for children in a modified scale for youngsters (Freedy, Shaw, Jarrell, & Masters, 1992). The conservation of resources model therefore enabled us to examine loss from both adults' and children's perspectives.

We propose a model that is based on recent work of La Greca and her colleagues (1996). They maintain, as we do, that predictors of response to trauma in children include preexisting child characteristics (i.e., ethnicity, gender, and age). Additionally, the amount of exposure to the traumatic event, degree of life threat during the event, and amount of property loss and disruption following the event are hypothesized to predict outcome. Last, efforts to process and cope with the event and characteristics of the postdisaster environment (i.e., major life events and social support from parents, friends, classmates, and teachers) also may affect postdisaster functioning.

More specifically, consistent with Baron and Kenny (1986), we view coping and social support as quantitative variables that affect the direction and strength of the relation between the independent variable (the fire) and the dependent variable (distress). That is, following the event, the fire affects the moderators of coping and social support which then influence the outcome. Additionally, we maintain that the fire interacts with specific moderators (i.e., demographics, negative life events, parental functioning, and family environment) to produce the effect on coping and social support, which then influences the effect on outcome.

We also maintain that those moderators affect the recovery process following the fire and that solid theoretical arguments can be made for those relationships. For example, regarding coping, we hypothesize that increased levels of avoidance coping following the fire will result in greater levels of distress. Females are hypothesized to exhibit greater levels of avoidance coping and to be at greater risk for elevated levels of distress than males are. A primary goal of our investigation is to examine these and related hypotheses.

We also contend, as articulated by Holmbeck (1997), that each aspect of the coping process (appraisal, coping self-efficacy, and coping), may be viewed as moderators. That is, when fire survivors are asked to indicate their levels and types of coping for example, in *direct response* to the fire (i.e., "How did you cope with the fire?"), coping is being conceptualized as a moderator. Similarly, when respondents are asked, "How do you generally cope with difficult situations?", coping is again viewed as a moderator. This relationship also exists with the variable of social support where measures of support in *direct and general response* to the fire are conceptualized as moderators. Our goal is to empirically test portions of this more refined model.

With this model in mind, we now turn to a description of the sample of children and families participating in our large-scale NIMH-funded project on residential fires. To date, we have interviewed 100 families from a four-state area (Virginia, West Virginia, North Carolina, and South Carolina). We have recently added a new site in the Atlanta, Georgia area. Names and addresses of families are obtained from a variety of sources, including fire departments, schools, mental health centers, hospitals, newspapers, and the American Red Cross. If the family includes a child or adolescent between ages 7 and 17, the parent is contacted by letter (or phone) and asked to participate in the study. Only one child or adolescent in each family is targeted for inclusion. If more than one child or adolescent is in the family, the child whose birth date (month and day) is closest to the date of the fire is selected. Additional inclusion criteria for the children are average intellectual ability (as documented by school-administered ability tests) and actual residence in the home with the caregiver. Absence from the home during the actual fire, however, does not preclude participation. Many children may be in school, church, camp, staying at a friend's house, or attending other activities during the time of the fire. Families in which a member dies during the fire or receives serious burns or injuries are included, but families whose homes are burned as a result of documented arson are not included in the study because of potential litigation in such cases (see Table 8.1 for a summary of relevant demographics).

The average and median age of the children was 12 years. Fifty-four percent of the children were girls, and 46% were boys; 54% of the children

TABLE 8.1
Relevant Demographics and Identifying Information

Family race (*N* = 100)
  48% European American
  42% African American
  3% Hispanic American
  2% Biracial/other ethnic background
Income
  Median = $20,000
Head of household
  55% headed by single parents
Education
  53% did not complete high school
Home during fire
  51% of mothers were home during fire
  49% of mothers were not home during fire
Dwellings
  10% condominiums/townhouses
  25% apartments
  13% trailers
    49% own
    51% rent
Degree of damage
  50% completely destroyed
Dollar loss
  A few thousand to over $100,000; 61% of families had minimal insurance coverage

were at home at the time of the fire. Approximately 30% thought they would die during the fire, 10% saw some member of the family get hurt or burned, and another 10% lost a family pet in the fire.

All in all, the residential fires ranged considerably in the extent and amount of loss. The experiences of the children and their parents varied extensively as well. Furthermore, the characteristics of the families varied widely; as a result, we believe a representative sample of families experiencing residential fire was obtained. The project is still ongoing and has the ultimate goal of recruiting 150 families.

METHODS OF ASSESSMENT

Our assessment methods closely followed our theoretical model examining four primary factors in the prediction of both short- and long-term outcomes of residential fires. Multimethod assessment (Ollendick & Hersen, 1984, 1993) was used to assess each of Korol et al.'s (1999) four factors. Measures used to assess each factor represent an optimal assessment package in that both the emotional and the behavioral responses of the children to the fires were systematically captured. Additionally, we obtained parent, teacher, and peer assessments of the children. Instruments used to assess each of the four factors are briefly described in the sections that follow.

Characteristics of the Stressor

The stressor itself was measured in two ways: exposure to the fire and loss associated with the fire. To measure degree of exposure, we devised the Fire-Related Traumatic Experiences questionnaire (Jones & Ollendick, 1996). In a semistructured interview, children responded to questions about whether they were at home during the fire, actually saw and experienced the fire, were close to the fire, got hurt or burned during the fire, thought they might die during the fire, or saw other people (e.g., siblings or other relatives) or their pets get hurt or burned during the fire. This measure was designed to obtain a direct index of exposure to the stressful event.

Loss was measured through a modified version of Freedy's Resource Loss Scale (Freedy et al., 1992). It included factors labeled Object Loss and Personal Resource Loss and tapped a wide range of events. Children appeared to understand the concept of loss and provided us with a rich array of comments about specific losses and how those losses affected their lives.

Characteristics of the Children

Demographic variables such as age, sex, ethnicity, family structure, and socioeconomic status of the families were obtained from the parents. In addition, structured diagnostic interviews were conducted with the children and their parents to determine preexisting psychiatric disorders that might make the children more vulnerable to adverse reactions to the fire. For this purpose, we used the computerized versions of the DICA. Parents and children (age 8 or older) were interviewed separately but concurrently. Interviews took between 1 and 1.5 hours to complete. From the interviews, we obtained both current and past diagnoses, as defined in the *Diagnostic and Statistical Manual of Mental Disorders, Fourth Edition* (*DSM–IV*; American Psychiatric Association, 1994), of major anxiety and affective disorders as well as disruptive behavior disorders, such as oppositional defiant disorder and conduct disorder.

In addition to these variables, children's attributional style was measured using the 48-item Children's Attributional Style Questionnaire (Kaslow, Tannenbaum, & Seligman, 1978). This well-validated questionnaire obtained measures of internal, stable, and global attributions for positive and negative events that occur to the child.

Characteristics of the Environment

In this domain, we obtained measures of psychopathology in the parents; family environment; parenting styles; and social support from peers, teachers, and parents. Two measures of parental psychopathology were used: a symptom checklist and a diagnostic interview conducted with the parents themselves. The Brief Symptom Inventory (Derogatis, 1983) assessed the intensity of nine psychological and somatic symptoms and was used as a measure of current psychological distress in the parents. The Anxiety Disorders Interview Schedule (Di Nardo, Brown, & Barlow, 1994) was used to obtain a measure of current and past psychiatric disorders in the parents. Only the PTSD and Specific Phobia modules were administered. Psychopathology in the parents was measured because earlier studies have suggested that parental disorder may serve as a vulnerability factor for their children. We set out to determine the impact of parent psychopathology on the child's adjustment subsequent to the fire.

Family environment was measured by the Family Environment Scale (Moos & Moos, 1981), which is designed to assess interpersonal relationships and basic organizational structure related to different facets of the family environment (i.e., cohesion, expressiveness, conflict, and control). It provides an evaluation of the emotional supportiveness and control in the family environment.

To assess parenting style, we adapted McFarlane's (1987) work with children who survived bush fires. We asked parents two questions to determine the level of concern they had for their child following the fire. Finally, support was measured with an abbreviated Social Support Scale (Dubow & Ullman, 1989) and by three additional support items designed specifically for this study. The Dubow scale provided an index of general support from parents, teachers, and friends, whereas the remaining three items provided an index of support regarding the fire.

Children's Cognitive Processing

Measures of appraisal and coping were obtained to determine the child's appraisal of the fire and how he or she coped with the fire itself. Previous research (Randall & Jones, in press) has suggested that those cognitive dimensions are related to adjustment following trauma. Primary and secondary appraisals were measured by items added to the Fire Questionnaire (Jones & Ribbe, 1988) designed for this study.

Coping was measured in three ways. First, a Coping Efficacy questionnaire was devised, modeled after one used by Ayers, Sandler, West, and Roosa (1996). Coping was also measured with Ayers and colleagues' (1996) How I Coped Under Pressure Scale. This 45-item scale has 11 factors measuring coping dimensions such as direct problem solving, expressing feelings, avoidant actions, cognitive avoidance, problem-focused support, and emotion-focused support. In response to the various items inquiring how much the child engages in particular actions, children respond with "not at all," "a little," "somewhat," and "a lot." Finally, coping was measured through the 32-item Religious Coping Activities Scale (Pargament et al., 1990).

Outcome Measures

Multiple measures from different informants were used to assess responses to the fire. First, the computerized version of the DICA was used to assess current disorders (as well as past disorders). Separate but concurrent interviews were conducted with the child and her or his parents. In particular, we were most interested in the presence of major anxiety and affective disorders in the children as a result of the fire (e.g., PTSD, specific phobia, separation anxiety disorder, and major depressive disorder).

In addition, both parent- and teacher-completed measures of behavior were obtained using the Achenbach (1991) Child Behavior Checklist. This 118-item behavior problem checklist provides measures of both internalizing and externalizing behavior problems. We were particularly interested in the Anxiety/Depression, Somatic, and Social Withdrawal scales.

Various self-report measures were also administered, including the 15-item Children's Reaction to Traumatic Events Scale (Jones, 1996), the 37-item Revised Children's Manifest Anxiety Scale (Reynolds & Richmond, 1985), the 80-item Fear Survey Schedule for Children-Revised (Ollendick, 1983), and the 27-item CDI (Kovacs, 1985). These self-report measures have been used frequently in trauma research and provide the child with an opportunity to express a variety of negative mood states associated with the trauma. For the most part, they are highly reliable and valid instruments.

Finally, archival data from a variety of community sources were obtained. School records and physician visit records were examined in an attempt to obtain indices of academic, social, and health functioning. We hoped that the data would provide us with a direct measure of outcomes that might be viewed as secondary to the experience of trauma.

REACTIONS OF THE CHILDREN TO RESIDENTIAL FIRES

Both qualitative and quantitative responses were obtained from the children and their parents. Qualitative information was obtained during the Fire Questionnaire interview, which was conducted separately with the children and the parents. Approximately 30% of the children felt they should have been able to do something to prevent the fire from occurring, and 18% felt the fire was their fault. Moreover, 16% of the children felt they could have done more to stop the fire. A full 85% reported that they had never experienced anything as bad as the fire, and 22% reported that they had *not* been trained in fire-safety skills. Clearly, a significant minority of the children reported a negative reaction to the fire. In reference to primary appraisal, 49% felt a lot of fear at the time of the fire, whereas another 27% felt at least some fear; in reference to secondary appraisal, only 6% felt they could control the fire "a lot," and another 24% felt they could control the fire "some."

Taken together, the findings suggest that the children perceived the fire as an uncontrollable event. Coping strategies varied, and no one strategy appeared to characterize the children. They reported both problem-focused and emotion-focused coping strategies; some of them used religious coping more than others. In general, the children felt their coping efforts subsequent to the fire had worked quite well.

Quantitative information on outcome was obtained from the various standardized instruments. On the Children's Reaction to Traumatic Events Scale (Jones, 1996), the mean response for both the total score (22.80) and the avoidance score (13.19) placed the children in the moderate range of distress. On both indices, scores ranged considerably; about one half of the youngsters were in the severe range of distress. Items such as "I kept seeing it over and over in my mind," "I tried not to talk about it," and "I tried not to think about it" were endorsed frequently by the children. Although mean scores on the self-report measures of fear, anxiety, and depression did not differ from normative means, the range of scores varied considerably on the measures. For example, one third to one half of the children scored in the clinical range on the measures (i.e., greater than one standard deviation above the normative mean), suggesting heightened levels of negative affectivity in a subset of our children.

On the DICA, children reported heightened levels of both depression and PTSD symptoms, although only 10 children (10%) met criteria for major depressive disorder and 9 children (9%) met criteria for PTSD. Still, the average child reported 2.6 symptoms of depression (range = 0–9) and 2.3 symptoms of PTSD (range = 0–15). On the parent DICA, similar rates of symptomatology and diagnosis were obtained. On the Child Behavior Checklist, however, both the Internalizing and Externalizing T-scores centered on 50, although once again considerable variability was present.

Inasmuch as our theoretical model proposed the role of parental and familial factors in moderating child outcomes following a residential fire, we also examined family environment, parenting practices, and parent psychopathology. On the Family Environment Scale, as reported by the parents, none of the scales were in the clinical range; the Cohesion, Conflict, and Control subscales, however, were marginally elevated. Responses on the scales suggest that the families reported issues involving being cohesive while experiencing conflict and lack of control. The differences were not significant, however. The nature of those issues may be reflected in the parenting-style reports of the parents. On that measure, a significant number of parents reported heightened levels of vigilance and concern about their children. In response to the question, "Since the fire, do you worry more about the possibility of harm coming to your children?" 29% responded "some more" and 40% indicated "a lot more." Similarly, in response to the question, "Since the fire, do you need to know where your children are more than before?" 13% reported needing to know "some more" and 42% indicated needing to know "a lot more." We hypothesize that this need to know more about the child's whereabouts and to have more worry about harm befalling them serves to produce conflict and control in the family. At the same time, this heightened vigilance may be perceived by the parents as engendering a tight-knit and close family, resulting in reported levels of enmeshment. Of course, our speculations await empirical test and scrutiny.

Finally, we anticipated heightened levels of psychopathology in our parents. Unexpectedly, such was not the case. We found trends suggesting a heightened global severity index on the Brief Symptom Inventory, however ($t = 59.4$, approaching one standard deviation above the normative mean). Still, a range of scores was evident, and some of our parents clearly were in the clinical range (e.g., t-test scores of 80).

The overriding conclusion to be drawn from our qualitative and quantitative findings is that children and their parents respond in a highly variable manner to fire. We are currently undertaking hierarchical regression analyses in an attempt to understand those differences and relate them to outcome. Already, however, we know that some myths will fall by the wayside. For example, it does not appear to make a difference whether the family was home during the fire, nor does it seem to matter whether the home was a total loss or whether the loss was extensive in dollar amount. It appears that response to residential fires is highly idiosyncratic and highly subjective; that is, a person living in a trailer and working at a nighttime job during an evening fire may well experience the same "subjective" loss as a person living in a $200,000 home and asleep in the home at the time of the fire. Although both homes might be a total loss, both parents and children might respond similarly.

PREPARATORY AND POSTDISASTER COPING MATERIAL

Although several groups and agencies have made a number of efforts to target functioning prior to residential fire (i.e., the American Red Cross, the Federal Emergency Management Agency, and the NFPA (National Fire Protection Association), no published, empirically supported interventions have targeted survivors of residential fire. Some of our preliminary efforts examining fire survivors have been encouraging, however. This section provides a brief overview of a research program that served as the conceptual and empirical foundation of another pilot study; we then present some preliminary findings from the study.

In an attempt to improve upon a strategy shown to enhance children's substance-refusal behavior (Corbin, Jones, & Schulman, 1993) as well as reduce fire-related fears, a strategy entitled Rehearsal-Plus (R+) was devised. This strategy, developed by Jones (Jones & Randall, 1994), was based on both behavioral and cognitive conceptualizations. The approach fosters specific skills through behavioral techniques (i.e., modeling and positive reinforcement) and enhances knowledge through manipulating cognitive processes (i.e., beliefs). Its major elements consist of a behavioral component, which uses behavioral techniques to foster desired skills, and a cognitive component, in which elaborative rehearsal is used to modify specific cognitive processes (i.e., expectations, beliefs, appraisals, and attributions), which in turn enhance learning, retention, and appreciation of such skills (Craik & Watkins, 1973). Although the initial version of the R+ procedure was similar to other stress-reducing strategies, such as stress inoculation, it had several important distinctions. Although stress inoculation is typically a general procedure that includes components of deep-muscle relaxation, self-statements, construction of a hierarchy, and presentation of educational information, the R+ strategy targeted specific stimuli (i.e., chains of behavioral responses and fire-related fear) and elaborative rehearsal, in which a developmentally appropriate rationale was provided to enhance behavioral and cognitive functioning.

One of the primary goals of the study was to integrate the behavioral and cognitive components during training. Unlike a number of behavioral change procedures that have used cognitive aids that often are not accompanied by governing conceptual schemes (Rosenthal & Downs, 1985), the R+ procedure was clearly derived from behavioral and cognitive conceptualizations. Indeed, a series of preliminary studies stemming from this framework have shown desired outcomes (i.e., Hillman, Jones, & Farmer, 1986; Jones, McDonald, Fiore, Arrington, & Randall, 1990; Jones, Ollendick, McLaughlin, & Williams, 1989; Williams & Jones, 1989). Therefore, we felt survivors of fire could benefit from this procedure. Hence, two child survivors of a residential fire were treated using the R+ strategy in combination with systematic desensitization and deep-muscle relaxation.

Participants in this study were an 11-year-old boy (John) and his 7-year-old sister (Jane), both from a white middle-class family. The family of five was forced to relocate while repairs were being made to their home following an early morning fire. The mother reported that John was experiencing difficulty resulting from the fire, including nightmares and flashbacks of the fire. In addition, increased levels of anxiety were noted when he was in the presence of various fire-related stimuli (i.e., sounds of sirens and emergency scenes on television).

A multimethod assessment strategy was used for both John and his sister prior to and following treatment. Primary assessment instruments consisted of the Fire Questionnaire, the CDI, the Horowitz scale, and the DICA. Additionally, the Fire Emergency Behavioral Situations Scale (Jones, 1988) was used to assess emergency functioning. Generally, elevated levels of distress were noted in both children at pretesting. Physiological assessment of heart rate and GSR (Galvanic Skin Response) in response to fire-related stimuli also was obtained. Although John's reactivity was greater than Jane's, both showed marked increase within this modality. Unfortunately, posttreatment physiological data were not collected.

Formal treatment consisted of eight weekly, 50-minute sessions at the Child Study Center. The major components of the treatment were the R+ strategy, deep-muscle relaxation, and systematic desensitization. Although all three components were administered to John, Jane received only R+.

R+ (Reprocessing the Event)

Briefly, components of the R+ strategy were enlisted during the first two sessions, in which the primary focus of treatment was to reduce the children's immediate fear and anxiety of fire. A goal of the cognitive component was to provide the children with valid and adaptive ways of thinking about (i.e., reprocessing) the event, such as not feeling guilty for actions during the fire, feeling comfortable about being upset, and discussing feelings. An opportunity was provided for each child to discuss the event, during which time they were assisted in their reprocessing at developmentally appropriate levels. We had found in earlier studies that this strategy led to meaningful ways of coping with fire-related fears.

We assisted the children in "challenging" several perceptions and beliefs related to their functioning during and following the fire. For example, both children initially reported that they should not be afraid or upset shortly after the fire, that they should not discuss their experiences with their parents and others, and that they should avoid situations and things that remind them of the fire. Additionally, John reported that he should feel guilty for not acting more appropriately during the fire (e.g., assisting others out of the house). Given that one of the goals of the R+ procedure was to modify maladaptive cognitions, we provided the children with more adaptive ways of thinking about this event. For example, they were told that it was "okay and normal" to be scared shortly following a fire and that it was "okay and helpful" to discuss their feelings and experiences with their parents and others. They also were encouraged to not inadvertently reinforce their fears by avoiding fire-related stimuli. In fact, they were told to visit their home (accompanied with a parent) while it was being repaired.

To further process the event, they were allowed to draw pictures of fearful scenes related to the fire and encouraged to discuss their thoughts and feelings. Following this phase of treatment, given that Jane consistently stated that she was not experiencing any symptoms of fear or anxiety at this point,

John became the targeted subject. The following steps were taken to treat his problem behavior. Consistent with Barlow and Lehman's (1996) recommendation to treat specific symptoms, each of John's symptoms was targeted, so reducing his avoidance of fire-related stimuli (including fear of returning to the burned home), flashbacks, hyperarousal, hyperalertness, sleeping difficulties, and sensation of smelling smoke in the absence of fire became the focus of this phase. We also targeted his general anxiety surrounding fire-related stimuli portrayed on television, storms, hearing sirens in route to and from school, and evacuation fire drills at school. A 14-item, thematic hierarchy comprising the symptoms was devised with John over a 3-week period. Subjective units of distress ratings (i.e., a 10-item subjective units of distress scale) were obtained for each scene.

Deep-Muscle Relaxation and Systematic Desensitization

John was trained in deep-muscle relaxation over a 3-week period. The relaxation script for children devised by Ollendick and Cerny (1981) was used to ensure developmentally appropriate wording and behavior. His parents were allowed to observe the first session in order to learn the procedure. They were given a homework assignment to practice the relaxation at least four times per week with John.

The third component of treatment was systematic desensitization proper where John was first relaxed and presented with scenes from the previously constructed hierarchy. This phase extended for two sessions. SUDS ratings indicated that a high level of effectiveness was achieved with this procedure.

R+ (Development and Retention of Skills)

The final aspect of treatment focused on development and retention of fire-evacuation skills. The rationale for this training was primarily based on John's report that he had "feelings of guilt for not knowing what to do during the fire." He stated that he "panicked." For example, shortly after discovering the fire, he ran upstairs to warn his sisters, who were asleep. He then immediately returned to the living room and sat in the middle of the floor and cried. Therefore, we reasoned that mastery of appropriate skills would greatly enhance his sense of efficacy in the event of another fire as well as in related stressful situations. Both John and Jane were taught the steps necessary to evacuate a burning house. Consistent with the R+ strategy, following a demonstration of each step, they were allowed to behaviorally practice the steps. After demonstration of each step, rationale for the procedure was provided. Training took place over four sessions.

A goal of the cognitive component was to provide the children with valid ways of reprocessing the event. Although no objective assessment of the children's cognitions was obtained, use of the cognitive component during the first two sessions appears to have led to meaningful ways of processing and coping with the fire and resulting trauma.

Several interesting findings were obtained for symptom reduction. Although neither John nor Jane showed clinically significant levels of depression at pretest, Jane showed a drop from 9 at pretest to 0 at posttest, and John's initial score of 6 dropped to 4 on the CDI. As hypothesized, results on the Horowitz scale showed significant drops across both children. John's pretest scores of 31 for Intrusion and 23 for Avoidance dropped to 0 in both categories at posttest. Jane showed similar results: Her pretest scores of 25 for Intrusion and 23 for Avoidance also dropped to 0 in both categories at posttest.

Both children demonstrated significant drops in each PTSD symptom cluster. Jane's pretest scores of 6 for Reexperiencing, 4 for Avoidance, and 4 for Increased Arousal all fell to 0 on the posttest. John also reported significant drops in PTSD symptomatology: His pretest scores of 6 for Reexperiencing, 5 for Avoidance, and 4 for Increased Arousal fell to 1 for Reexperiencing and 0 on the other scales. As hypothesized, posttest scores evidenced significant increases in both appropriate evacuation skills and providing rationales for each child. Although not objectively assessed in this investigation, the increase in behavior and knowledge may have led to increases in self-efficacy.

A major shortcoming of this pilot study is that one cannot separate out the relative impact of each component (deep-muscle relaxation, systematic desensitization, and R+) of treatment on outcome. Additionally, it is not clear why Jane had reductions in symptomatology, given that she did not receive two components of the treatment package (deep-muscle relaxation and systematic desensitization) hypothesized to change behavior. Also, a question is raised concerning the reliability and validity of assessment of this nature with children younger than age 8. Results for John, however, are encouraging. Nonetheless, as an initial attempt at treating survivors of fire, this treatment package seems like a potentially plausible first step and one worth examining in a more controlled manner.

CONCLUSIONS

In summary, we have attempted to highlight the potentially deleterious consequences of fire emergencies on children and their families. Although our preliminary findings do not provide a clear picture of the nature or course of these consequences, we feel that important progress is being made in this understudied area. The important next step, intervention, is yet to be systematically explored. However, our data set and early intervention efforts may provide insight into this domain.

REFERENCES

Achenbach, T. M. (1991). *Integrative guide for the 1991 CBCL 14-18, YSR, and TRF profiles*. Burlington: University of Vermont Department of Psychiatry.

American Psychiatric Association. (1994). *Diagnostic and statistical manual of mental disorders* (4th ed.). Washington, DC: Author.

Ayers, T. S., Sandler, I. N., West, S. G., & Roosa, M. W. (1996). A dispositional and situational assessment of children's coping: Testing alternative models of coping. *Journal of Personality, 64*, 923–958.

Barlow, D. H., & Lehman, C. L. (1996). Advances in the psychosocial treatment of anxiety disorders: Implications for national health care. *Archives of General Psychiatry, 53*, 727–735.

Baron, R. M., & Kenny, D. A. (1986). The moderator–mediator variable distinction in social psychological research: Conceptual, strategic, and statistical considerations. *Journal of Personality and Social psychology, (51)*6, 1173–1182.

Bernstein, N. R. (1990). Fire. In J. D. Noshpitz & R. D. Coddington (Eds.), *Stressors and the adjustment disorders* (pp. 260–277). New York: John Wiley & Sons.

Bickman, L., Edelman, P., & McDaniel, M. (1977). *A model of human behavior in a fire emergency* (NBS-GCR-78420). Washington, DC: Center for Fire Research.

Breslau, N., Davis, G., Andreski, P., & Peterson, E. (1991). Traumatic events and post-traumatic stress disorder in an urban population of young adults. *Archives of General Psychiatry, 48*, 216–222.

Brezel, B. S., Kassenbrock, J. M., & Stein, J. M. (1988). Burns in substance abusers and in neurologically and mentally impaired patients. *Journal of Burn Care and Rehabilitation, 9*, 169–171.

Burke, J. D., Borus, J. F., Burnes, B. J., Millstein, K. H., & Beasley, M. C. (1986). Changes in children's behavior after a natural disaster. *American Journal of Psychiatry, 139*, 1010–1014.

Compas, B. E., & Epping, J. E. (1993). Stress and coping in children and families: Implications for children coping with disaster. In C. F. Saylor (Ed.), *Children and disasters* (pp. 11–28). New York: Plenum Press.

Conners, C. (1995). *Conners' rating scales*. Toronto, CA: Multi-Health Systems.

Corbin, S., Jones, R. T., & Schulman, R. S. (1993). Drug refusal behavior: The relative efficacy of skills-based and information-based treatment. *Journal of Pediatric Psychology, 18*, 769–784.

Craik, F. I., & Watkins, M. J. (1973). The role of rehearsal in short-term memory. *Journal of Verbal Learning and Verbal Behavior, 12*, 599–607.

Davidson, T. I., & Brown, L. C. (1985). Self-inflicted burns: A 5-year retrospective study. *Burns, 11*, 157–160.

Derogatis, L. R. (1983). *SCL-90-R: Administration, scoring and procedures manual-II*. Towson, MD: Clinical Psychometric Research.

Di Nardo, P. A., Brown, T. A., & Barlow, D. H. (1994). *Anxiety disorders interview schedule for DSM-IV (ADIS-IV)*. Albany, NY: Graywind Publications.

Dubow, E. F., & Ullman, D. G. (1989). Assessing social support in elementary school children: The Survey of Children's Social Support. *Journal of Clinical Child Psychology, 18,* 52–64.

Earls, F., Smith, E., Reich, W., & Jung, K. G. (1988). Investigating psychopathological consequences of a disaster on children: A pilot study incorporating a structured diagnostic interview. *Journal of the American Academy of Child and Adolescent Psychiatry, 27,* 90–95.

Eth, S., Silverstein, S., & Pynoos, R. S. (1985). Mental health consultation to a preschool following the murder of a mother and child. *Hospital and Community Psychiatry, 36,* 73–76.

Foa, E. B., Steketee, G. S., & Rothbaum, B. O. (1989). Behavioral cognitive conceptualizations of post-traumatic stress disorder. *Behavior Therapy, 20,* 155–157.

Folkman, S., & Lazarus, K. S. (1985). If it changes it must be a process: A study of emotion and coping during three stages of a college examination. *Journal of Personality and Social Psychology, 48,* 150–170.

Frederick, C. J. (1985). *Children traumatized by catastrophic situations.* Washington, DC: American Psychiatric Press.

Freedy, J. R., Shaw, D. L., Jarrell, M. P., & Masters, C. R. (1992). Towards an understanding of the psychological impact of natural disasters: An application of the conservation of resource model. *Journal of Traumatic Stress, 5,* 441–454.

Green, B., Korol, M., Vary, M., Leonard, A., Gleser, G., & Smitson-Cohen, S. (1991). Children and disaster: Age, gender, and parental effects on PTSD symptoms. *Journal of the American Academy of Child and Adolescent Psychiatry, 30,* 945–951.

Green, B. L. (1990). Defining trauma: Terminology and genetic stressor dimensions. *Journal of Applied Social Psychology, 20,* 1632–1642.

Green, B. L. (1993). Disasters and post traumatic stress disorder. In J. R. T. Davidson & E. B. Foa (Eds.), *Post traumatic stress disorder: DSM-IV and beyond* (pp. 75–97). Washington, DC: American Psychiatric Press.

Green, B. L., Grace, M. C., Crespo da Silva, L., & Glesner, G. C. (1983). Use of the psychiatric evaluation form to quantify children's interview data. *Journal of Consulting and Clinical Psychology, 51,* 353–359.

Greenberg, H. S. (1994). Responses of children and adolescents to a fire in their homes. *Child and Adolescent Social Work, 11,* 475–492.

Greenberg, H. S., & Keane, A. (1997). A social work perspective of childhood trauma after a residential fire. *Social Work in Education, 19,* 11–22.

Helzer, J. E., Robins, L. N., & McEvoy, L. (1987). Post-traumatic stress disorder in the general population: Findings of the epidemiological catchment area survey. *New England Journal of Medicine, 317,* 1630–1634.

Hillman, H. S., Jones, R. T., & Farmer, L. (1986). The acquisition and maintenance of fire emergency skills: Effects of rationale and behavioral practice. *Journal of Pediatric Psychology, 11,* 247–258.

Hobfoll, S. E. (1989). Conservation of resources: A new attempt at conceptualizing stress. *American Psychologist, 44,* 513–524.

Holmbeck, G. N. (1997). Toward technological, conceptual, and statistical clarity in the study of mediators: Examples from the child–clinical and pediatric psychology literatures. *Journal of Consulting and Clinical Psychology, 65*, 599–610.

Holmes, G. S., & Jones, R. T. (1996). Fire evacuation skills: Cognitive behavioral versus computer mediated instruction. *Fire Technology, 31*, 50–64.

Horowitz, M. J., Wilner, N., & Alvarez, W. (1979). Impact of events scale: A measure of subjective stress. *Psychosomatic Medicine, 41*, 209–218.

Jones, J. C., & Barlow, D. H. (1990). The etiology of post-traumatic stress disorder. *Clinical Psychology Review, 10*, 299–328.

Jones, R. T. (1980). Teaching children how to make emergency telephone calls. *Journal of Black Psychology, 6*, 81–93.

Jones, R. T. (1988). The Fire Emergency Behavioral Situations Scale. In M. Hersen & A. S. Bellack (Eds.), *Dictionary of behavioral assessment techniques* (pp. 224–226). New York: Pergamon Press.

Jones, R. T. (1996). Child's reaction to traumatic events scale (CRTES). Assessing traumatic experiences in children. In J. P. Wilson & T. Keane (Eds.), *Assessing psychological trauma and PTSD* (pp. 291–298). New York: Guilford Press.

Jones, R. T., McDonald, D. W., Fiore, M. F., Arrington, T., & Randall, J. (1990). A primary preventive approach to children's drug refusal behavior: The impact of rehearsal-plus. *Journal of Pediatric Psychology, 15*, 211–223.

Jones, R. T., & Ollendick, T. H. (1996). *The fire-related traumatic experiences questionnaire.* Unpublished manuscript. Virginia Polytechnic Institute and State University, Blacksburg.

Jones, R. T., Ollendick, T. H., & McLaughlin, K. J., & Williams, C. E. (1989). Elaborative and behavioral rehearsal in the acquisition of fire emergency skills and the reduction of fear of fire. *Behavior Therapy, 20*, 93–101.

Jones, R. T., Ollendick, T. H., & Shinske, F. K. (1989). The role of behavioral versus cognitive variables in skill acquisition. *Behavior Therapy, 20*, 293–302.

Jones, R. T., & Randall, J. (1994). Rehearsal-plus: Coping with fire emergencies and reducing fire-related fears. *Fire Technology, 30*, 432–444.

Jones, R. T., & Ribbe, D. P. (1988). *The child fire questionnaire.* Unpublished manuscript. Virginia Polytechnic Institute and State University, Blacksburg.

Jones, R. T., & Ribbe, D. P. (1991). Child, adolescent and adult victims of residential fire. *Behavior Modification, 139*, 560–580.

Jones, R. T., Ribbe, D. P., & Cunningham, P. (1994). Psychosocial correlates of fire disaster among children and adolescents. *Journal of Traumatic Stress, 7*, 117–122.

Jones, R. T., Van Hasselt, V. B., & Sisson, L. A. (1984). Emergency fire safety skills: A study with blind adolescents. *Behavior Modification, 8*, 59–78.

Kaniasty, K. Z., & Norris, F. H. (1993). A test of the social support deterioration model in the context of natural disaster. *Journal of Personality and Social Psychology, 64*, 395–408.

Kaniasty, K. Z., Norris, F. H., & Murrell, S. A. (1990). Received and perceived social support following natural disaster. *Journal of Applied Social Psychology, 20*, 85–114.

Kaslow, N. J., Tannenbaum, R. L., & Seligman, M. E. P. (1978). *The KASTAN: A children's attributional style questionnaire.* Unpublished manuscript, University of Pennsylvania, Philadelphia.

Kinston, W., & Rosser, R. (1974). Disaster: Effects on mental and physical state. *Journal of Psychosomatic Research, 18*, 437–456.

Korol, M. S. (1990). *Children's psychological responses to a nuclear waste disaster in Fernald, Ohio.* Unpublished doctoral dissertation, University of Cincinnati.

Korol, M. S., Green, B. L., & Grace, M. C. (1999). Developmental analysis of the psychosocial impact of disaster on children: A review. *Journal of the American Academy of Child and Adolescent Psychiatry, 38*, 368–375.

Kovacs, M. (1985). CDI (The Children's Depression Inventory). *Psychopharmacology Bulletin, 21*, 995–998.

Krim, A. (1983). *Families after urban fire: Disaster intervention* (Publication No. MH29197). Washington, DC: National Institute of Mental Health.

La Greca, A. M., Silverman, W. K., Vernberg, E. M., & Prinstein, M. J. (1996). Symptoms of posttraumatic stress in children after Hurricane Andrew: A prospective study. *Journal of Consulting and Clinical Psychology, 64*, 712–723.

Lyons, J. A. (1991). Issues to consider in assessing the effects of trauma: Introduction. *Journal of Traumatic Stress, 4*, 3–6.

March, J. S. (1990). The nosology of post-traumatic stress disorder. *Journal of Anxiety Disorders, 4*, 61–82.

March, J., & Amaya-Jackson, L. (1994). Post-traumatic stress disorder in children and adolescents. *PTSD Research Quarterly, 4*, 1–7.

March, J. S., Amaya-Jackson, L., Terry, R., & Costanzo, P. (1997). Posttraumatic symptomatology in children and adolescents after an industrial fire. *Journal of the American Academy of Child and Adolescent Psychiatry, 36*, 1080–1088.

McFarlane, A. C. (1987). Family functioning and overprotection following a natural disaster: The longitudinal effects of post-traumatic morbidity. *Australian and New Zealand Journal of Psychiatry, 21*, 210–216.

McNally, R. J. (1991). Assessment of post traumatic stress disorder in children. *Psychological Assessment: A Journal of Consulting and Clinical Psychology, 3*, 531–537.

Melamed, B. G., & Siegel, L. J. (Eds.). (1980). *Behavioral medicine, Vol. 6: Practical applications in health care.* New York: Springer.

Milne, G. C. T. (1977). Some consequences of the evacuation for adult victims. *Australian Journal of Psychology, 12*, 39–54.

Moos, R. H., & Moos, B. S. (1981). *Family Environment Scale.* Palo Alto, CA: Consulting Psychologists Press.

Newman, C. J. (1976). Children of disaster: Clinical observations at Buffalo Creek. *American Journal of Psychiatry, 133*, 306–312.

Nowicki, S., & Strickland, B. (1973). A locus of control scale for children. *Journal of Consulting and Clinical Psychology, 40,* 148–154.

Ollendick, D. G., & Hoffman, S. M. (1982). Assessment of psychological reactions in disaster victims. *Journal of Community Psychology, 10,* 157–167.

Ollendick, T. H. (1983). Reliability and validity of the Revised Fear Survey Schedule for Children (FSSC-R). *Behaviour Research and Therapy, 21,* 685–692.

Ollendick, T. H., & Cerny, J. A. (1981). *Clinical behavior therapy with children.* New York: Plenum Press.

Ollendick, T. H., & Hersen, M. (Eds.). (1984). *Child behavioral assessment: Principles and procedures.* New York: Pergamon Press.

Ollendick, T. H., & Hersen, M. (1993). Child and adolescent behavioral assessment. In T. H. Ollendick & M. Hersen (Eds.), *Handbook of child and adolescent assessment* (pp. 3–14). New York: Pergamon Press.

Pargament, K. I., Ensing, K. F., Olsen, H., Reilly, B., van Haitsma, K., & Warren, R. (1990). God help me: I. Religious coping efforts as predictors of the outcomes to significant negative life events. *American Journal of Community Psychology, 18,* 793–824.

Patterson, D. R., Everett, J. J., Bombardier, C. H., Questad, K. A., Lee, V. K., & Marvin, J. A. (1993). Psychological effects of severe burn injuries. *Psychological Bulletin, 113,* 362–378.

Phillips, A. W. (1978). The effects of smoke on human behavior: A review of the literature. *Fire Journal, 72,* 69–78.

Pruzinsky, T., & Doctor, M. (1994). Body images and pediatric burn injury. In K. J. Tarnowski (Ed.), *Behavioral aspects of pediatric burns* (pp. 169–191). New York: Plenum Press.

Pynoos, R. S., Frederick, C., Nader, K., Assoyo, W., Steinberg, A., Eth, S., Nunez, F., & Fairbanks, L. (1987). Life threat and post-traumatic stress in school-age children. *Archives of General Psychiatry, 44,* 1057–1063.

Pynoos, R. S., Nader, K., Frederick, C., Gonda, L., & Stuber, M. (1988). Grief reactions in school-age children following a sniper attack at school. In E. Chigier (Ed.), *Grief and bereavement in contemporary society, Vol. 1: Psychodynamics* (pp. 29–41). London: Freud Publishing House.

Randall, J. S., & Jones, R. T. (1994). Teaching children fire safety skills. *Fire Technology, 29,* 268–280.

Randall, J. S., & Jones, R. T. (in press). The role of developmental levels and appraisals on children and adolescent coping processes in fire emergencies. *Fire Engineering.*

Reich, W., & Welner, Z. (1990). *Diagnostic Interview for Children and Adolescents—Revised.* St. Louis, MO: Washington University.

Reynolds, C. R., & Paget, K. D. (1981). Factor analysis of the Revised Children's Manifest Anxiety Scale for blacks, whites, males and females with a national normative sample. *Journal of Consulting and Clinical Psychology, 49,* 352–359.

Reynolds, C. R., & Richmond, B. O. (1985). *Revised Children's Manifest Anxiety Scale*. Los Angeles: Western Psychological Services.

Rosenthal, T. L., & Downs, A. (1985). Cognitive aids in teaching and treating advances in behavior. *Behaviour Research and Therapy, 7*, 1–53.

Snyder, C. C., & Saigh, P. A. (1984). Burn injuries in children. In V. C. Kelley (Ed.), *Practice of Pediatrics I* (pp. 1–13). New York: Harper & Row.

Solomon, S. D. (1989). Research issues in assessing disaster's effects. In R. Gist & B. Lubin (Eds.), *Psychosocial aspects of disaster* (pp. 308–340). New York: John Wiley & Sons.

Stoddard, F. J., Norman, D. K., Murphy, J. M., & Beardslee, W. R. (1989). Psychiatric outcome of burned children and adolescents. *Journal of American Academic Child Adolescent Psychiatry, 28*, 589–595.

Tarnowski, K. J. (Ed.). (1994). *Behavioral aspects of pediatric burns*. New York: Plenum Press.

Terr, L. C. (1981). Psychic trauma in children: Observations following the Chowchilla school bus kidnapping. *American Journal of Psychiatry, 138*, 14–19.

Terr, L. C. (1983). Chowchilla revisited: The effects of psychic trauma four years after a school bus kidnapping. *American Journal of Psychiatry, 140*, 1543–1550.

Terr, L. C. (1985). Psychic trauma in children and adolescents. *Psychiatric Clinics of North America, 8*, 815–835.

Williams, C. E., & Jones, R. T. (1989). Impact of self-instructions on response maintenance and children's fear of fire. *Journal of Clinical Psychology, 18*, 84–89.

III

HUMAN-MADE AND TECHNOLOGICAL DISASTERS

HUMAN-MADE AND TECHNOLOGICAL DISASTERS: INTRODUCTION

MICHAEL C. ROBERTS

Up to this point, the volume has focused on disasters and events that are considered "natural," whereas Part III shifts the focus to trauma that results from human actions interacting with technology by examining the effects of toxic waste spills, nuclear accidents, dam breaks and flooding, transportation disasters, and motor vehicle crashes. The effects of technological disasters may be large or small. For example, large-scale transportation disasters, such as ship sinkings or plane crashes, may involve many casualties at a single time in one venue. However, motor vehicle injuries and deaths are much more frequent than any other type of transportation disaster and involve many more humans annually, but individual motor vehicle crashes involve a small number of people and are distributed across venues and time. As the chapters in Part III show, the psychological impact of technological disasters should not be presumed to correlate with the number of people or the physical magnitude at the time.

Human-made and technological disasters typically do not include intentional acts to psychologically or physically harm another person. Often they are attributed to human error in the design or the use of a technology (e.g., the release of radioactive isotopes from nuclear power plants and failure of dams). The role of human negligence in exacerbating or moderating the psychological impact of the traumatic events is unclear.

In chapter 9, Minhnoi Wroble and Andrew Baum examine the psychological consequences of technological catastrophes, which are unique in that the physical manifestations of the incident (e.g., toxic gases or nuclear radiation) may be invisible and the consequences (e.g., cancer) measured in terms of statistical probabilities. Specifically, Wroble and Baum examine the technology failures at the Three Mile Island (Pennsylvania) nuclear reactor and the Chernobyl (Ukraine) nuclear power plant. They look at the consequences of chemical leaks from three hazardous waste disposal sites. In addition to the research on the potential harm to physical health engendered by the incidents, a small amount of research has investigated the effects on a range of psychological variables. Wroble and Baum conclude that the children involved in the technological disasters they studied do not demonstrate a serious adverse effect on psychological functioning, although they did have some symptoms. The authors note that the most reliable predictor of a child's response to technological disasters is the psychological well-being of his or her parents. Long-term psychological effects, however, may result from the chronic physical threat resulting from toxic exposure.

Chapter 10, by William Yule, Orlee Udwin, and Derek Bolton, examines the effects on children and adolescents of disasters involving transportation systems. Yule and his colleagues review the research conducted following children's involvement in bus crashes in Norway and Israel, the capsizing of a ferry crossing the English Channel, and the sinking of an educational cruise ship. They conclude that following transportation disasters, posttraumatic stress disorder (PTSD) and other psychological symptoms increase in children. In addition to summarizing the research into the children's psychiatric symptoms, the authors describe issues involved in intervention and treatment efforts. Unfortunately, systematic empirical studies have not been undertaken on treatment following mass transportation accidents. The authors conclude that because transportation disasters will continue to occur in our highly mobile society, a great deal more work is needed to gain a fuller understanding of the psychological importance of these events and the outcomes of interventions following transportation disasters.

In chapter 11, Mindy Korol, Teresa Kramer, Mary Grace, and Bonnie Green discuss the results of an empirical study of children and families affected by a West Virginia dam collapse that caused widespread death and injury and required physical relocation of the survivors. Early reports on the disaster aftermath indicated that some children exhibited moderate to severe psychological stress. This chapter, written 17 years after the dam collapse, summarizes evidence indicating that children's postdisaster reactions were influenced by various characteristics, such as age, gender, family environment, and parental responses to the disaster. Symptom severity ameliorated over time and as the children developed, but the authors found that PTSD remained present among the survivors at a higher than normal rate. This study is significant for being one of the few to follow disaster survivors longitudinally.

Finally, in chapter 12, Joseph Scotti, Kenneth Ruggiero, and Aline Rabalais focus on car crashes, which are far more common in children's lives than mass transportation disasters are. Despite the multitude of car crashes each year, which often result in death and serious injuries to passengers, research on the postevent adjustment of child survivors is sparse. The authors present case examples of children in various situations related to motor vehicle crashes and examine the children's emotional and behavioral functioning. They then outline a paradigmatic model of PTSD related to the motor vehicle collisions in which death or injury occurred. The authors suggest that their conceptualization can help guide treatment strategies for trauma-exposed children and adolescents. They note, however, that no developed literature provides empirical support for treatment of the type of PTSD that results from motor vehicle crashes.

Humans of all ages interact with now basic and advanced technology daily. While some people may perceive technological disasters or events to be inevitable or chance occurances, physical and psychological injury are not driven by fate. Certainly, the response of society to the psychological impact of human-made and technological disasters should equate to the attention given to the physical impact.

9

TOXIC WASTE SPILLS AND NUCLEAR ACCIDENTS

MINHNOI C. WROBLE AND ANDREW BAUM

Environmental contamination has become a major public health problem that threatens the health and well-being of many adults and children. Largely the result of industrial and technological accidents and faulty storage of toxic chemicals, contamination hazards have become increasingly common and appear to cause long-lasting stress and anxiety. Many nuclear accidents and incidents of toxic waste release are the result of human error, malfunctions, or oversights, but the causes are complex. Three Mile Island, for example, was believed to result from the "complexity of the system" (Thompson, 1985, pp. 63–64), rather than simply human error, mechanical failure, design, or the safety procedures in place, even though system operators made errors and mechanical failures did occur. In essence, the accident was a result of a series of human, institutional, and technological failures initiated by equipment malfunction and exacerbated by training, decision making, and a failure to understand the situation quickly (Thompson, 1985, pp. 43–79).

The human and technological causes of environmental contamination are important because they interact with the threatening aspects of technological breakdown and toxic exposure and engender chronic stress that may follow technological accidents or catastrophes. This chapter addresses the stressful consequences of toxic accidents and contamination in children exposed to what are often called *toxic* or *technological* disasters. These accidents reveal that even well-tested safety systems can generate unfortunate, unanticipated errors and reduce confidence in and perceived safety of critical technological networks.

Nearly all accidents involving nuclear materials or toxic waste affect nearby families and children. Stress associated with nuclear or toxic contamination appears to be more persistent and disruptive than many other forms of family stress, and some theorists have argued that unlike normal stressful situations in families, the threats associated with technological contamination are often invisible, unpredictable, and chronic (Ellis, Greenberg, Murphy, & Reusser, 1992). Furthermore, notification of the problem is often delayed, thereby creating a history of unknown family risk (Ellis et al., 1992). The uncertainty associated with toxic events exists on several levels, including whether people were exposed, whether exposure was sufficient to cause health problems, whether people will develop exposure-related diseases or conditions, and whether they will experience new exposures. The uncertainties experienced by adults and children who have been exposed to these contaminants can heighten feelings of powerlessness and a lack of control that, in turn, may be associated with higher levels of stress (Vyner, 1988). It has been argued that technological contaminants challenge a family's sense of control and their beliefs concerning the safety of their home and neighborhood (Edelstein, 1988). In addition to eroding perceptions of control, the incidents can cause families to experience alienation, isolation, and stigmatization from their larger community by nonresidents (Edelstein, 1988). Because many sources of uncertainty are involved in most technological disasters, lasting worry has been found in communities that have been affected by those accidents (e.g., Baum, Gatchel, & Schaeffer, 1983; Bromet, Parkinson, & Dunn, 1990; Edelstein, 1988).

Although many studies have examined stress consequences of technological accidents in adults, few have carefully examined the response of children to these accidents. Anecdotal reports from parents of children living near hazardous waste facilities or nuclear power plants suggest that children suffer levels of stress that are similar to their parents' (i.e., Havenaar et al., 1996). Parents report that their children have fears of death and often have nightmares about technological accidents (Unger, Wandersman, & Hallman, 1992). Observational studies have found that fears and anxiety specific to nuclear disaster can become internalized in children as young as age 4 or 5 and can become an increasing concern in preadolescent (i.e., ages 10–12) and adolescent children (Parens, 1988). The findings underscore the importance of psychological trauma and stress in children and draw attention to the relatively understudied state of this area.

Like their parents' responses, children's emotional response to disasters appears to be related to the degree of violence produced by the incident, the extent to which the child was involved in the aftermath of the event, and beliefs concerning the cause of the disaster (Aptekar & Boore, 1990). In general, more violence or overt threat, greater proximity to the accident, and negative beliefs about the accident are associated with more negative mood. Moreover, the developmental level of the child (e.g., Handford et al., 1986; Laube & Murphy, 1985) and the child's mental health prior to the event (e.g., Ursano, 1987) appear to be associated with his or her response to highly threatening events. Separation from parents (Aptekar & Boore, 1990) and the reaction of important adults (i.e., parents) to the event (e.g., Freud & Burlingham, 1944; McFarlane, 1986) also are related to children's emotional and behavioral response following traumatic events.

This chapter explores the response of children to technological disasters, such as nuclear accidents and toxic waste disposal. The literature is organized around three toxic accidents that have posed substantial threat to local residents. As noted above, few studies have carefully examined children's responses to toxic accidents and disasters, but some work has been done following the disasters at the Three Mile Island and Chernobyl nuclear power plants and the Fernald, Ohio, toxic waste site. Our discussion of children's responses to technological disaster and toxins includes evidence directly from children as well as from parents regarding their children. Unfortunately, this limited research literature has not addressed the interaction between parents' response to the accident and the resulting response and psychological or behavioral outcome of their children. The importance of this interaction in the mental health of children following nuclear and toxic waste accidents will be considered.

THREE MILE ISLAND

On March 28, 1979, the worst commercial nuclear accident in the United States took place. A series of malfunctions occurred in the cooling system of the Unit 2 reactor at the Three Mile Island (TMI) nuclear power plant near Middletown, Pennsylvania. Errors or oversights by plant personnel, in combination with mechanical errors, resulted in a partial meltdown of Unit 2's reactor core. Hundreds of thousands of gallons of radioactive water overflowed onto the floor of the adjacent containment building, and radioactive steam was released into the atmosphere as a result of the accident. Radioactive gases also were trapped in the containment building until they were released into the atmosphere approximately 16 months after the accident. Despite the damage to the reactor core, no loss of life, direct injury, or property damage was reported at the plant or in the neighborhoods surrounding the plant. The accident itself was a relatively brief episode and, although dangerous and unprecedented, was far less disastrous than the human reactions to the accident and decontamination of the facility would later suggest.

In fact, this contained accident led to widespread fear and distress, evacuations, and poorly managed reporting of events and hazards. For a week or more, TMI held the nation's attention, inspired large-scale evacuations, and caused considerable stress.

Beyond the initial incident, residents of nearby Middletown (and other areas) dealt with the clean-up operation and increased media attention that revealed prior incidences of exposure had been unnoticed by residents neighboring TMI. For instance, as a part of the clean-up operation in 1980, radioactive gases were vented from TMI. In light of this event, the media revealed that many reactors had been designed to release low levels of radioactive gases on a regular basis (Smith, 1993). The process of cleaning up the accident, including removing the radioactive water, nuclear fuel, and damaged reactor core, took many years and was in and out of the news, reinforcing old fears and introducing new ones. Each operation brought fears of new exposures and reminded area residents about the possible exposures in the past. Distrust and worry continued as the events unfolded.

Despite opposition from segments of the community, the reactor in Unit 1 of TMI was restarted in October 1985. The reactor had been off-line during the 1979 accident and did not experience an accident. Despite its relatively good safety record, however, the restart of the undamaged Unit 1 reactor was controversial. In March 1990, a leak in one of the steam generators of Unit 1 forced the reactor to be shut down for more than a week (Lengeman, 1990). The continued worries concerning the current reactor operation, the previous accident, and previous exposure, combined with a report of increased incidence of cancer (i.e., leukemia) in the local area (Rowe, 1997), has helped to establish persistent stress in many people living near TMI.

Children and TMI

Families who participated in studies examining the effect of TMI on children were sampled from larger, longitudinal TMI studies (i.e., Cornely & Bromet, 1986; Handford et al., 1986). The larger studies focused primarily on the mental health effects of the TMI accident in adults (see Handford et al., 1986). Children and their families sampled from the original TMI studies were interviewed between 1.5 and 2.5 years after the TMI reactor incident. Children ranged from 2.5 to 19 years old at the time of the accident.

Some studies have suggested that the TMI accident had relatively few effects on area children. Cornely and Bromet (1986) examined behavioral problems in 565 toddlers (ages 2.5–3.5) using maternal interviews and measuring maternal responses to the Behavior Screening Questionnaire (Richman & Graham, 1971). In addition mothers' mental health and level of stress were examined. Responses of TMI mothers ($n = 291$) were compared with responses of mothers who lived near comparison nuclear ($n = 148$) or fossil fuel ($n = 126$) plants. No differences were found in the prevalence of behavior problems among children at the three sites. Children of TMI did not differ from children in other communities in symptoms of anxiety; sleep problems; or behavioral problems, such as overactivity and management difficulties. Across all three samples, relatively few mothers (less than 5%) reported major behavioral problems in their children.

Although few mothers reported behavioral problems in their toddlers, the investigators also examined the effects of maternal stress and mental health on children's behavior (Cornely & Bromet, 1986). History of psychiatric disorder and current psychiatric symptomatology were related to child behavior among TMI-area children, although stress specifically related to TMI was not associated with maternal reports of child behavior problems. In the control groups, current psychiatric symptoms and economic problems were associated with reports of child behavior problems.

A second study conducted with children of the TMI area (Handford et al., 1986) examined anxiety and intensity of child-reaction scores to the TMI accident in 35 children who ranged in age from 6 to 19 (M = 13.2). Medical and psychiatric histories of the children and parents were collected. Children's recall and experience during the TMI incident and self-report of anxiety were examined along with parent reports of child behavioral problems and parent distress and mood. Children and parents from TMI were compared with a published normal range of responses for each measure, rather than a control sample of parents and children.

For the child report measures, diagnoses of psychiatric disorders in the TMI children were not substantially different from their reported incidence in the general population (11%). Although the data suggested comparable levels of psychopathology among TMI-area children and the general population, nearly two thirds of the 35 children living near TMI reported that they were frightened during the incident. A year and a half after the accident, children living in Middletown reported greater anxiety than is typical in the general population; however, scores were still lower than anxiety scores from a population of children hospitalized for anxiety disorders.

Data reflecting children's responses concerning TMI suggested widespread fear during the accident, but only a third of the parents reported observing fear or anxiety in their children (Handford et al., 1986). Consistent with Cornely and Bromet's (1986) study, parent assessment of behavioral problems revealed few problems in the TMI children. These data raise the possibility that children in the TMI area were more severely affected by the accident and parental reports did not accurately reflect children's distress. When parental response to TMI was assessed in combination with the child's responses, children's reactions were most severe when parents' responses to TMI differed from each other. Thus, if one parent responded to the TMI incident with high levels of distress and negative mood but the other parent did not, the child was more likely to experience distress after the TMI accident (Handford et al., 1986).

This limited literature and lack of clear conclusions from the data that are available make firm conclusions difficult to draw. Parental reports suggest that children living near TMI were not strongly affected by the accident. Although most school-aged children reported being fearful or anxious as a result of the events surrounding the TMI accident (Handford et al., 1986), those anxieties did not translate into an abnormally high incidence of psychiatric disorders (Handford et al., 1986) or externalizing behaviors (Cornely & Bromet, 1986). In fact, few parents reported behavioral problems in either toddlers or school-aged children, and the incidence of psychiatric diagnoses was consistent with published norms for similar age groups (Handford et al., 1986). The most consistent finding was the relation between parent response to TMI and the intensity of child response. In the Cornely and Bromet (1986) and Handford et al. (1986) studies, current parental psychiatric symptoms or distress was related to greater child responses to the event.

THE CHERNOBYL DISASTER

On April 26, 1986, one of the four reactors at the Chernobyl nuclear power plant exploded in the Ukraine of the former USSR. The explosion of the reactor sent burning debris and sparks into the air that set off numerous fires and explosions in other areas of the compound. Hundreds of tons of radioactive dust were released into the air and dispersed throughout Eastern Europe and Scandinavia. As in the case of TMI, initial information about the Chernobyl accident was inaccurate or inconsistent, and official reactions featured denial and understatement. Public announcements of the accident were not made until after alarming background radioactivity readings in the Scandinavian countries made it apparent to the rest of the world that a large-scale nuclear accident was occurring somewhere in the Soviet Union. After the dust settled and many years had passed, the extent of the Chernobyl accident was revealed. In the end, at least 30 of the workers involved in the clean-up efforts died (Henshaw, 1996), although thousands of other deaths have been linked to the accident at Chernobyl. The radiation released from the Chernobyl accident amounted to 200 times the radiation released by the combination of the atomic bombs dropped on Hiroshima and Nagasaki in 1945 (Henshaw, 1996).

Although an initial announcement was made concerning the nuclear fallout, precautionary measures, such as staying inside and eating canned food, were not publicized for nearly a week. Furthermore, much information made available about the extent of the Chernobyl disaster was not released for more than 2 years. A great deal of uneasiness was created through the release of partial truths and unsubstantiated assurances along with rumors of high rates of miscarriage and prominent birth defects in animals. For example, federal agents minimized the magnitude and severity of the accident, yet the same agents strongly advised pregnant women to have abortions (Havenaar, 1996). The presence of contradictory information and an increasing mistrust of government officials dramatically changed the lifestyle of Chernobyl children and families.

Beyond the stress created by the accident, the period after the accident was chaotic at best. Families not evacuated from the area surrounding Chernobyl spent little time outdoors and were not allowed to eat home-grown foods. The restrictions on foods and activities during times of economic hardship and food shortage contributed to deteriorated physical conditions and developmental delays in children (Havenaar, 1996). Of the families that were evacuated, many were evacuated twice; once from the town of Pripyat (adjacent to the Chernobyl reactor), then from the towns to which they were first evacuated because the contaminated area was found to include the initial relocation areas (Bromet, 1995). Eventually many of the evacuees were placed in temporary residences in Kiev. The temporary relocation also was problematic because the temporary papers given to the evacuees meant that they could be relocated again at any time. Stress associated with evacuation was exacerbated by limitations in adequate housing in the new cities and difficulty in the attainment of health care, because the government required such extensive paperwork for people exposed to the Chernobyl accident (Bromet, 1995).

In general, children and families exposed to the Chernobyl accident experienced many sources of stress. First, the families were exposed to potentially dangerous radioactivity before the evacuation orders were given. The same kinds of uncertainty as were likely present at TMI were relevant here as well, with perhaps a greater likelihood that people had sustained potentially dangerous exposures. In addition, families had to endure the losses created by the evacuation and relocation process that required families to leave their possessions and neighborhoods behind. Children and families also had to endure the continued stigma attached to them as a result of the accident. Many of their new neighbors, classmates, and peers viewed the relocated people as "contaminated" and "objects of fear" (Bromet, 1995, p. 277). Finally, the stress that children of Chernobyl experienced may have been compounded by their parents' ability (or inability) to cope with those stressors. In fact, parental mental health is often cited as the most important risk factor for child psychopathology (Rutter, 1985).

Families and Chernobyl

Although registries of the families evacuated from the 30-kilometer area surrounding Chernobyl were kept by each of the affected republics (i.e., Ukraine, Russia, and Belarus), scientists apparently have not been given access to much of the registry information. As a result, many people sampled for independent studies were selected on the basis of convenience. For instance, a number of schools in Kiev were used to explore psychological and behavioral differences between the children who had been evacuated from the Chernobyl area (specifically Pripyat) and children living in Kiev at the time of the accident (Bromet, 1995). Other comparisons were made between evacuated area residents and people living within the high-radiation zone but more distant from Chernobyl (e.g., Kiev and Gomel). Comparisons also contrasted evacuees with families who lived in cities outside the immediate danger areas for radiation exposure (e.g., Tver, north of Moscow).

The International Chernobyl Project examined the health status of five groups of people who remained in contaminated villages outside the Chernobyl nuclear disaster and compared them with residents of "uncontaminated" villages (International Advisory Committee, 1991). The comparison villages not contaminated by radiation were heavily contaminated by pesticides, however. The groups included 2-year-old children born in 1988; 5-year-old children born in 1986; 10-year-old children born in 1980; and 40- and 60-year-old adults born in 1950 and 1930, respectively. Measures of relative health, psychological distress, and psychopathology were included but were not extensive. Findings indicated that psychological stress was more prevalent in the villages contaminated by the Chernobyl accident, but no differences among villages were found on other measures of physical or psychological health (International Advisory Committee, 1991).

As noted, a good deal of distrust was generated by the accident, and the International Chernobyl Project (International Advisory Committee, 1991) found evidence of this distrust. Many citizens in the contaminated area believed the Soviet government had limited the reporting of results. Exposed adults and children anecdotally reported many more ailments and health complications than were reported by the government-sponsored International Chernobyl Project. In general, mothers of exposed children and doctors treating the exposed children reported many somatic symptoms in the children of Chernobyl (Havenaar, 1996). Some children were reportedly sick for long periods of time and missed long periods of school (Havenaar, 1996). Consistent with other studies that examined sustained trauma in children (e.g., Aptekar & Boore, 1990; McLeer, Deblinger, Atkins, Foa, & Ralphe, 1988), a wide range of somatic, anxiety, mood, and externalizing symptoms were observed in the children (Bromet, 1995).

Beyond these anecdotal reports of somatic and anxiety symptoms in the Chernobyl children, little evidence bearing on the experiences of these children has been published. More specific study of the effects of the trauma associated with the nuclear disaster and relocation process on the children of Chernobyl compared evacuated children from Pripyat with children in Kiev (Bromet, 1995). The comparison group of children sustained more stress than most children because of the exposure risks associated with the accident, but because of sampling limitations in nearby schools, the Kiev schoolchildren were used as a convenience sample. At this writing, the data have not been published. Evidence of physical health effects of the disaster on children have been reported, including an increased incidence of thyroid diseases (Henshaw, 1996; Nau, 1994) and DNA mutations in children born after the Chernobyl accident (Sternberg, 1996). Data on children's psychological and emotional reactions to the disaster are not available.

Independent of the International Chernobyl Project reports, some studies have found evidence of psychopathology across exposed and nonexposed groups of adults 6 years after the Chernobyl disaster (Havenaar et al., 1997). For example, Havenaar et al. (1996) found that approximately 35% of the exposed population was diagnosed with a psychiatric disorder as defined by the *Diagnostic and Statistical Manual of Mental Disorders, Third Edition, Revised* (*DSM–III–R*; American Psychiatric Association, 1987). Significantly higher levels of depression and posttraumatic stress disorder (PTSD) were found in exposed adults (from the region near Chernobyl) than in adults from a nonexposed sample in Tver. Especially high rates of affective (16.5%) and anxiety (12.6%) disorders were present in the adult populations 6 years after the accident (Havenaar et al., 1996). Contrary to expectations, anxiety disorders were higher in the nonexposed group, whereas affective disorders were higher in the exposed group (Havenaar, 1996). Consistent with data from the TMI accident (e.g., Bromet et al., 1990; Dew, Bromet, & Schulberg, 1987), psychological disorders were most prevalent in exposed mothers with children under age 18 (Havenaar et al., 1996; Havenaar et al., 1997).

Beyond those studies, few systematic investigations of the impact of the Chernobyl disaster on the mental health of adults exposed to the Chernobyl disaster have been reported. Because of limited access to this population, information concerning the mental health of the children of Chernobyl is largely limited to a few Russian studies and secondhand reports from mothers and physicians. The anecdotal reports suggest elevations in physical complaints, psychological distress (higher anxiety and negative mood), and behavioral problems in the Chernobyl children (Havenaar, 1996).

TOXIC WASTE: LOVE CANAL, WOBURN, AND FERNALD

Unlike the abrupt nature of the nuclear accidents previously discussed, unmasking hazardous toxic waste facilities or disposal sites generally unfolds over a long period of time. In recent decades, a number of toxic waste sites have been discovered, including Love Canal, New York; Woburn, Massachusetts; and Fernald, Ohio. In both Love Canal and Woburn, residential neighborhoods were built on sites previously used for toxic chemical disposal. Love Canal, near Niagara Falls, New York, was the first major toxic waste disposal site to be discovered and cleaned up by the Environmental Protection Agency (EPA). More than 200 chemicals were identified at the waste site, many of which had seeped from their original containment facilities into the soil and indoor air supply of homes and schools (Paigen, Goldman, Magnant, Highland, & Steegmann, 1987).

More than 200 families were evacuated from Love Canal in 1978, when reports exposed the extent to which neighborhood creeks, school yards, and air inside the school and nearby homes were contaminated (Paigen et al., 1987). The initial evacuees only included families living nearest the old chemical disposal site. Residents living in the surrounding area were not initially advised to evacuate, but they continued to suffer from both the toxins in the environment and the stress of living in a known contaminated neighborhood (Holden, 1980). Many of the Love Canal families reported psychological and psychosomatic problems such as depression, irritability, dizziness, fatigue, insomnia, and extremity numbness (Holden, 1980).

Because of the publicity surrounding Love Canal, many communities sought to find and expose potentially hazardous landfills and waste facilities in their local area. In Woburn, for example, rumors of higher than average childhood leukemia rates led residents to request an investigation into possible chemical exposure from an old (early 20th century) chemical production plant. The resulting Woburn studies uncovered a possible risk of toxic exposure but did not confirm that the elevations in risk for toxic exposure resulted in an increase in childhood cancers (Cutler et al., 1986).

As was the case in Woburn and at Love Canal, many toxic waste sites have been discovered in recent decades. Unfortunately, much of the research examining the effects of living near toxic waste disposal sites has been limited to the physical health of children (i.e., growth in Love Canal; Paigen et al., 1987) or prevalence of cancer in children from the exposed community (i.e., Cutler et al., 1986). To date, only one study has examined the effects of toxic waste exposure on the mental health of children: Korol, Green, and Gleser (1999) examined PTSD in children exposed to the Fernald contamination.

Fernald

In October 1984, residents of Fernald learned that a neighboring U.S. Department of Energy (DoE) Feed Materials Production Center (FMPC) had been negligent in its disposal and storage of toxic waste. The FMPC processed materials for nuclear weapons and served as a toxic waste storage site for nuclear waste for nearly 40 years. The Environmental Protection Agency (EPA) declared that the FMPC was one of the nation's worst emitters of radioactive materials (Carpenter, 1986). It had processed uranium for the DoE, and for decades the plant had been spewing thousands of pounds of radioactive dust over the Ohio countryside. Furthermore, the plant had permitted toxic by-products to leak into the ground, eventually poisoning the Fernald area water supply.

Many families and landowners in the 5-mile radius of the plant were clearly at risk for stress related to their exposure to radioactive waste, the health hazards associated with radiation exposure, and the decline in their community resulting from the depreciation of their property. Moreover, the government did not take an active role in providing health care and aid to the families in the immediate contamination area. As a result, many Fernald residents filed a class-action lawsuit against the management company and company that ran the uranium plant for the DoE (Feiberg, 1990). Although the relative levels of exposure experienced by the residents of Fernald remains unknown, a monetary settlement was reached in 1989.

Family Response to Fernald

Korol et al. (1999) examined psychological distress and PTSD symptoms in children from the Fernald toxic waste disaster. A total of 120 children and 91 parents from the Fernald families were compared with a demographically similar sample of 60 children and 41 parents from Carmargo, Ohio (Northeast Cincinnati suburb). The Fernald children were divided into three age groups: 7- to 9-year-olds, 10- to 12-year-olds, and 13- to 15-year-olds. Severity of stress in response to the Fernald incident was assessed using an open-ended questionnaire for the children (modeled after Handford et al., 1986). Additionally, the child's developmental level, depression (Children's Depression Inventory; Kovacs & Beck, 1977), and PTSD (Child PTSD Reaction Index; PTSDRI, Pynoos, Frederick, & Nader, 1987) were assessed using appropriate measures. Parents assessed child PTSD symptoms (Fernald only), children's somatic symptoms, family life events, and parents' somatic symptoms (as measured by the Symptom Checklist-90-Revised [SCL-90-R]; Derogatis, 1983).

No differences were found between the Fernald and Carmargo children for depression or somatic symptoms (Korol et al., 1999). Using the general psychological measures, the Fernald children did not appear to exhibit an elevated level of psychological distress. Although the Fernald children were not at risk for elevated levels of psychological distress and depression, age differences in reporting the stressfulness of the situation were found. Older children appraised the events surrounding the Fernald incident as more stressful than younger Fernald children.

PTSD symptomatology was assessed only in the Fernald sample. Although PTSD symptoms were relatively infrequent, significant differences were found across sex and age. Reports of PTSD symptoms were more common in older girls, whereas the total number of symptoms and the number of intrusion symptoms were less frequent in older boys. Parent ratings of child PTSD symptoms were similar to the child response data, but children reported nearly twice as many symptoms as their parents reported. Although Fernald and Carmargo parents did not differ in psychological functioning, parents' distress (as measured by the SCL-90-R) was related to child psychological functioning and PTSD symptoms in the Fernald children.

Consistent with previous research at TMI (e.g., Cornely & Bromet, 1986) little psychological impairment was found in the sample of Fernald children. Variability was found in the children's subjective stressful experience of the incident, but severity ratings of stress and reports of psychological distress experienced as a result of the incident were relatively low in the Fernald children. The findings in the Fernald study are compatible with previous research (e.g., Green et al., 1991) that found consistent associations between the level of exposure and PTSD symptoms. The Fernald children did not experience a concrete threat to their lives, however, and their lives were relatively undisrupted compared with findings of other studies examining PTSD in children. Children's PTSD symptoms were related to parent symptom reporting.

CONCLUSIONS

Empirical work reflected in the small research literature on this topic suggests that children are not severely affected by these disasters/accidents. The source and nature of threats associated with toxic or nuclear catastrophes may not be sufficiently concrete or clear to children to produce distress. This finding may be particularly true for young children, who may not fully understand the threats associated with toxic hazards. To a large extent, the threats are subtle: Toxic chemicals and radiation can cause cancers and genetic mutations that may affect a range of heritable traits. Whether young children understand the consequences of such exposures or appreciate the long-term threats conveyed by mutagenic compounds is not known, but it is unlikely that they are affected by the possibility of birth defects in their offspring or cancers in them or their families in the same way adults or older children are affected. The specific characteristics of toxic hazards that appear to give rise to unusual, prolonged distress in adult victims, paradoxically, may lessen the extent to which children experience threat and stress.

Given the likely continued expansion of the technological networks that support the 21st-century lifestyle, it is almost certain that accidents like these will continue to occur and more leaking landfills will be found. Adults respond to these events with greater chronic stress and dysfunction than they do to more immediate, powerful natural disasters (Baum, 1987). Exposures to toxic hazards are likely to have effects on children that can continue into adulthood. For all of those reasons, more extensive study and a better understanding of how children perceive, interpret, and cope with toxic and nuclear accidents is urgently needed.

REFERENCES

American Psychiatric Association. (1987). *Diagnostic and statistical manual of mental disorders* (3rd ed. rev.). Washington, DC: Author.

Aptekar, L., & Boore, J. A. (1990). The emotional effects of disaster on children: A review of the literature. *International Journal of Mental Health, 19,* 77–90.

Baum, A. (1987). Toxins, technology, and natural disasters. In G. R. VandenBos, & B. K. Bryant (Eds.), *Cataclysms, crises, and catastrophes: Psychology in action: Vol. 6. The master lectures* (pp. 5–53). Washington, DC: American Psychological Association.

Baum, A., Gatchel, R. J., & Schaeffer, M. A. (1983). Emotional, behavioral, and physiological effects of chronic stress at Three Mile Island. *Journal of Consulting and Clinical Psychology, 51,* 565–572.

Bromet, E. J. (1995). Methodological issues in designing research on community-wide disasters with special reference to Chernobyl. In S. E. Hobfoll & M. W. de Vries (Eds.), *Extreme stress and communities: Impact and intervention* (pp. 267–282). Dordrect, Netherlands: Kluwer Academic Publishers.

Bromet, E. J., Parkinson, D. K., & Dunn, L. O. (1990). Long-term mental health consequences of the accident at Three Mile Island. *International Journal of Mental Health, 19,* 48–60.

Carpenter, T. (1986). *Fernald Fact Sheet Summary.* Washington, DC: Government Accountability Project, Cincinnati Nuclear Weapons Freeze Campaign.

Cohen, S., & Bromet, E. J. (1992). Maternal predictors of behavioral disturbance in preschool children: A research note. *Journal of Child Psychology and Psychiatry and Allied Disciplines, 33,* 941–946.

Cornely, P., & Bromet, E. (1986). Prevalence of behavior problems in three-year-old children living near Three Mile Island: A comparative analysis. *Journal of Child Psychology and Psychiatry, 27,* 489–498.

Cutler, J. J., Parker, G. S., Rosen, S., Prenney, B., Healey, R., & Caldwell, G. G. (1986). Childhood leukemia in Woburn, Massachusetts. *Public Health Reports, 101,* 201–205.

Derogatis, L. R. (1983). *SCL-90-R: Administration, scoring, and procedures manual-II* (2nd ed.). Towson, MD: Clinical Psychometric Research.

Dew, M. A., Bromet, E. J., & Schulberg, H. C. (1987). Application of a temporal persistence model to community residents' long-term beliefs about the Three Mile Island nuclear accident. *Journal of Applied Social Psychology, 17,* 1071–1091.

Edelstein, M. R. (1988). *Contaminated communities: The social and psychological impacts of residential toxic exposure.* Boulder, CO: Westview.

Ellis, P., Greenberg, S., Murphy, B. C., & Reusser, J. W. (1992). Environmentally contaminated families: Therapeutic considerations. *American Journal of Orthopsychiatry, 62,* 44–54.

Feiberg, K. R. (1990). In the shadow of Fernald: Who should pay the victims? *Brookings Review, 8,* 41–47.

Freud, A., & Burlingham, D. (1944). *War and children*. New York: International Universities Press.

Green, B. L., Korol, M. S., Grace, M. C., Vary, M. G., Leonard, A. C., Gleser, G. C., & Smitson-Cohen, S. (1991). Children and disaster: Age, gender, and parental effects on PTSD symptoms. *Journal of the American Academy of Child and Adolescent Psychiatry, 30*, 945–951.

Handford, H. A., Mayes, S. D., Mattison, R. E., Humphrey, F. J., Bagnato, S., Bixler, E. O., & Kales, J. D. (1986). Child and parent reaction to the Three Mile Island nuclear accident. *Journal of the American Academy of Child Psychiatry, 25*, 346–356.

Havenaar, J. M. (1996). *After Chernobyl: Psychological factors affecting health after a nuclear disaster*. Amsterdam: The University Hospital.

Havenaar, J. M., van den Brink, W., van den Bout, J., Kasyanenko, A. P., Poelijoe, N. W., Wohlfarth, T., & Meijler-Iljina, L. I. (1996). Mental health problems in the Gomel region (Belarus): An analysis of risk factors in an area affected by the Chernobyl disaster. *Psychological Medicine, 26*, 845–855.

Havenaar, J. M., Rumyantzenva, G. M., van den Brink, W., Poelijoe, N. W., van den Bout, J., van Engeland, H., & Koeter, M. W. J. (1997). Long-term mental health effects of the Chernobyl disaster: An epidemiologic survey in two former Soviet regions. *American Journal of Psychiatry, 154*, 1605–1607.

Henshaw, D. L. (1996). Chernobyl 10 years on. *British Medical Journal, 312*, 1052–1054.

Holden, C. (1980). Love Canal residents under stress: Psychological effects may be greater than physical harm. *Science, 208*, 1242–1244.

International Advisory Committee. (1991). *The International Chernobyl Project: An Overview*. Vienna: International Atomic Energy Association.

Korol, M., Green, B. L., & Gleser, G. C. (1999). Children's responses to a nuclear waste disaster: PTSD symptoms and outcome prediction. *Journal of the American Academy of Child and Adolescent Psychiatry, 38*, 368–375.

Kovacs, M., & Beck, A. T. (1977). An empirical-clinical approach, a definition of childhood depression. In J. G. Schulterbrandt & A. Raskin (Eds.), *Depression in childhood: Diagnosis, treatment, and conceptual models* (pp. 1–26). New York: Raven Press.

Laube, J., & Murphy, S. A. (1985). *Perspectives on disaster recovery*. Norwalk, CT: Appleton-Century-Crofts.

Lengeman, W. I. (1990). Back at TMI. *Environmental Action, 21*, 10.

McFarlane, A. C. (1986). Long-term psychiatric morbidity after a natural disaster. *Medical Journal of Australia, 145*, 561–566.

McLeer, S. V., Deblinger, E., Atkins, M. S., Foa, E. B., & Ralphe, D. L. (1988). Post-traumatic stress disorder in sexually abused children. *American Academy of Child and Adolescent Psychiatry, 27*, 650–654.

Nau, J. Y. (1994). Reports on Chernobyl effects. *Lancet, 344*, 184.

Paigen, B., Goldman, L. R., Magnant, M. M., Highland, J. H., & Steegmann, A. T. (1987). Growth of children living near the hazardous waste site, Love Canal. *Human Biology, 59*, 489–508.

Parens, H. (1988). Psychoanalytic explorations of the impact of the threat of nuclear disaster on the young. In H. B. Levine, D. Jacobs, & L. J. Rubin (Eds.), *Psychoanalysis and the nuclear threat: Clinical and theoretical studies* (pp. 223–244). Hillsdale, NJ: The Analytic Press.

Pynoos, R., Frederick, C., & Nader, N. (1987). Life threat and posttraumatic stress in school-age children. *Archives of General Psychiatry, 44*, 1057–1063.

Richman, N., & Graham, P. J. (1971). A behavioral screening questionnaire for use with 3-year-old children: Preliminary findings. *Journal of Child Psychology and Psychiatry, 12*, 5–33.

Rowe, P. M. (1997). Three Mile Island cancers linked to radiation. *Lancet, 349*, 625.

Rutter, M. (1985). Resilience in the face of adversity: Protective factors and resistance to psychiatric disorder. *British Journal of Psychiatry, 147*, 589–611.

Smith, G. (1993). The deadly legacy of "America's Chernobyl." *Earth Island Journal, 8*, 24.

Sternberg, S. (1996). Radiation damages Chernobyl children. *Science News, 149*, 260.

Thompson, J. (1985). *Psychological aspects of nuclear war.* New York: John Wiley & Sons.

Unger, D. G., Wandersman, A., & Hallman, W. (1992). Living near a hazardous waste facility: Coping with individual and family distress. *American Journal of Orthopsychiatry, 62*, 55–70.

Ursano, R. J. (1987). Posttraumatic stress disorder: The stressor criterion. *Journal of Nervous and Mental Disease, 175*, 273–275.

Vyner, H. (1988). *Invisible trauma: The psychosocial effects of the invisible contaminants.* Lexington, MA: D.C. Health.

10

MASS TRANSPORTATION DISASTERS

WILLIAM YULE, ORLEE UDWIN, AND DEREK BOLTON

Before the 20th century, transportation was by foot, by horse and horse-drawn vehicles and, of course, by boat. During the 19th century, rail came into use for transportation. Undoubtedly many accidents occurred, and one can assume that some were life threatening. Given both the slow speed of travel and the low value put on children's lives in previous centuries, however, people seemed to take little interest in the effects of such accidents. Even mass transport of people in dangerous sailing ships evoked little study and no clamour for reducing any psychopathology that resulted.

Thus, mass transportation disasters are a phenomenon peculiar to the 20th and 21st centuries. As the Victorians developed the steam engine and the railways, railway accidents occurred, and slowly it was realized that such accidents carried an increased risk of "nervous problems." Those risks, however, were mainly discussed in relation to the effects on adults, and the phenomenon of "railway spine" entered the nomenclature (Trimble, 1981). In the past 20 years, researchers have taken interest in studying the effects of accidents and disasters on children, particularly the effects of road traffic accidents on children (see chapter 12, this volume). Surprisingly, no studies of the effects of airplane disasters on children have taken place, probably because children generally do not travel as frequently by air and when such disasters occur, children generally do not survive.

Less than 15 years' worth of methodologically adequate studies have examined transportation disasters as they relate to children. This chapter reviews the few studies of group accidents in buses and coaches, and then describes the findings from two ship disasters in which the authors have been heavily involved. It describes issues concerning long-term outcomes and the need for better treatment studies. The chapter pays particular attention to how the research has contributed to professionals' understanding of the etiology, maintenance, and treatment of posttraumatic stress disorder (PTSD) in children and young people.

COACH AND BUS ACCIDENTS

When children are involved in transportation disasters, such as bus crashes that result in serious injuries and deaths, they are likely to be exposed to life threat as well as witness death and injury in others, including friends or family members. Moreover, when children are involved in transportation disasters, they are more likely to be going on a long journey and, therefore, to be separated from their parents and families at the time of the accident. Children may be cared for in a foreign environment should the accident happen abroad, and it may be some time before they can be reunited with their parents and return to the familiar surroundings of home and school.

Stallard and Law (1993) assessed seven adolescents who had been involved in a school minibus accident in which they received minor injuries. Six months later, when they were assessed and given brief therapy, they reported intrusive thoughts about the accident, feelings of acute anxiety and panic attacks, and a heightened awareness of danger when travelling in motor vehicles. They reported difficulties with concentrating in school, and a number found it difficult to talk with their parents.

Casswell (1997) described the aftermath of an accident in which a school bus was hit by a lorry (truck). The bus driver and one pupil were killed. Thirty-four of the survivors were assessed 9 to 15 months after the accident; as a group, they reported high scores on the Impact of Event Scale (IES; Horowitz, Wilner, & Alvarez, 1979). Around 1 in 6 of the children were found to be at high risk of developing PTSD.

Winje and Ulvik (1998) reported a 3-year follow-up of Swedish children who survived a fatal school bus crash in Norway in August 1988. The 11 child and 7 adult survivors were all badly injured and treated in Bergen before returning to Sweden. Data were gathered on the survivors and other members of their families 1 and 3 years after the accident. Unfortunately, the survivors and their relatives were regarded by the investigators as being traumatized, and the groups were not reported separately. Moreover, the investigators altered the scaling of the IES, making it difficult to compare with other findings; nevertheless, some general observations are possible. Most of the children showed high levels of intrusion and avoidance 1 year after the accident, with the reported distress dropping markedly by 3 years. No delayed reactions were found. Those who had suffered loss showed higher scores on intrusion. No age or gender differences were found in this small sample. Fathers' mental health ratings were not related to those of the children, but mothers' ratings were; in particular, their ratings on intrusion were significantly correlated to the children's ratings on intrusion.

The study by Winje and Ulvik (1998) raises the important issue of how parental reactions relate to and may modify children's reactions. In general, when parents and children experience the same traumatic event, reasonably strong correlations have been found between parent and child ratings on various instruments. In cross-sectional studies, this finding has sometimes been taken to indicate that all the children's reactions are mediated by the parents' reactions (McFarlane, 1987). One has to be careful in drawing such causal conclusions from cross-sectional data, however, particularly when the mother has made the ratings of both her own and her child's reactions. In one of our studies in Bosnia, we found that direct exposure to war trauma accounted for more variance in child distress than the mother's own stress reactions, although the latter did make a small contribution.

Apart from Winje and Ulvik's (1998) study, two other studies of road accidents have addressed whether parental presence in the same accident was associated with greater or lesser degrees of distress in the child (Ellis, Stores, & Mayou, 1998; Perrin, Yule, & Smith, 1996). Unfortunately, the studies used slightly different methodologies and came to opposite conclusions, so the question of whether parental presence is a protective factor or a risk factor remains unresolved.

In June 1985, 415 seventh graders in Israel departed in 13 buses for their annual school trip. They were age 13 at the time. One bus was hit by a train on a level crossing, and three adults and 19 pupils from the same class were killed. Fourteen other child passengers were badly injured. Children in three buses witnessed the crash; children in nine other buses, all on the same outing, did not witness the crash but heard that their school friends had been killed. Milgram, Toubiana, Klingman, Raviv, and Goldstein (1988) studied 108 children from the 3 buses who witnessed the crash, 302 from the other 9 buses, and 265 control participants from uninvolved schools. The children completed questionnaires at 1 week and at 9 months after the accident. In the first week, only half of the exposed children exhibited mild or minimal stress reactions. Rates of acute distress were as high in those who saw the accident as in those who did not witness the accident, and both groups showed significantly greater distress than the control group.

Although data were gathered on only 286 members of the exposed group at follow up, they were representative of the original total group. Their ratings showed a marked drop in distress by 9 months. A strong relationship was found between initial and follow-up scores. In the interim, all the children had been offered help with their reactions to the accident. Most children wanted to have the tragedy properly remembered by a permanent memorial. A significant minority reported fear of going on the following annual bus outing, and about 5% reported generalized fear of travelling by bus.

Seven years later, Tyano et al. (1996) took advantage of Israel's universal conscription to mount a long-term follow-up study of the effects of this bus crash on 389 conscripts when they did their National Service. In addition to assessing 9 *high-exposure* survivors, 74 *moderate-exposure* survivors from the three buses at the site of the accident, and 223 *low-exposure* survivors from the remaining nine buses, the investigators also studied a control group from a school that was not involved in the accident. The high-exposure group was found to report significantly higher levels of distress and higher levels of PTSD symptoms at the 7-year follow up. Although all groups reported that they were functioning equally well in the military, the high-exposure group reported the highest rates of help-seeking from the military mental health services—indeed, all three exposed groups reported far higher levels of help seeking than did the control participants (12% to 17% vs. 1%).

This unique 7-year follow up of a bus accident showed that directly exposed adolescents experienced higher rates of PTSD symptoms, depression, phobic anxiety, somatization, and psychoticism than their nonexposed counterparts; they also sought more mental health services at follow-up. The investigators were surprised at the absence of a strong exposure and "near miss" effect. When studied at 9 months after the accident, the same children had shown no relationship between proximity to the crash or to risk of physical injury and their ratings of distress. The finding is puzzling and out of keeping with much of the other literature on the severity of the stressor and subsequent distress. As the authors indicated, it may be that the early intervention offered to the survivors was effective among the less distressed children and so affected later correlations (Toubiana, Milgram, Strich, & Edelstein, 1988).

SHIPPING DISASTERS

Capsize of the *Herald of Free Enterprise*

On March 6, 1987, a cross-channel ferry, the *Herald of Free Enterprise*, set sail from Zeebrugge in Belgium to return to Dover, England, with nearly 400 people on board. Unknown to the captain, the bow doors had been left open; as the ship picked up speed, it took on water, making it so inherently unstable that it capsized just outside the harbour. Half the people on board died. Yule and his colleagues studied the survivors over a number of years.

At the time, little literature could guide one in making comprehensive assessments of children and adolescents caught up in such a disaster. We therefore arranged to see all the children, together with other members of their families, and undertook broad-based, semistructured clinical interviews. To those we added self-completion measures of depression (Birleson, 1981), anxiety (Reynolds & Richmond, 1978), and trauma-related symptomatology using the 15-item version of the IES. We were surprised by the high levels of distress found in the children; they scored every bit as high as Horowitz's adult PTSD patients. The children older than age 8 all found the questionnaires relevant to their experiences. By using standard measures, we were able to challenge the then widely held view that children are so resilient that the category of PTSD was not needed to encapsulate the phenomenology they reported. As we later argued, that conclusion had been based on early studies that relied on adult reports and had never asked children what they actually felt.

We presented our early findings together with a description of the therapeutic groups we ran in parallel for child and adult survivors (Yule & Williams, 1990). That experience convinced us of the value of group interventions, even when the child passengers had not been part of a cohesive group prior to the accident. Tracking the children informally over the next few years showed a slow but steady resolution of their difficulties, although 6 years later, they still reported considerable residual symptoms.

The *Jupiter* Sinking

Two years later, on October 21, 1988, a party of nearly 400 British schoolchildren were on board the cruise ship *Jupiter* bound for an educational cruise in the Eastern Mediterranean. As it left Athens harbour, the *Jupiter* was struck by a container ship, the *Adige*. It was holed below the water line and sank within 45 minutes. Two tugs came out from Pireaus Harbour and jammed themselves against the side of the *Jupiter* to keep it afloat as long as possible so that children could scramble over to other vessels to safety. Unfortunately, two of the rescuers were crushed during this maneuver. Their bodies were hurriedly hauled on board a tug and covered, but many of the distraught teenagers, who were on their first long-distance journey from home, saw the bodies. Of the passengers, one girl and one teacher were unaccounted for, presumed drowned. Their bodies were never recovered, a situation that intensified the distress of many of the survivors.

Five months after the event, we were asked to screen all the children who were involved in a legal suit against the owners of the container ship, and we were able to get screening data on 334 of the survivors. On the basis of our experience with children from the *Herald* and from numerous individual disasters, we decided to use a battery consisting of the IES, the Beck Depression Scale (Birleson, 1981), the Revised Children's Manifest Anxiety Scale (Reynolds & Richmond, 1978), and a 98-item version of the Fear Survey Schedule for Children Revised (Yule & Udwin, 1991).

The results of this 5-month screen showed high levels of distress. In one school we were able to obtain data on the survivors, those who had wanted to go on the cruise but had not gotten a place, those who had never showed interest in going, and control participants from a matched school nearby. We found an exposure–response relationship: The girls who had missed getting a place on the trip had distress scores between those of the survivors (who scored highest) and those who had never wanted to go on the trip (who scored lowest). The control participants in the uninvolved school scored lowest. Thus, the "near miss" group behaved as most people would expect—unlike the children in the Israeli bus crash (Milgram et al., 1988; Tyano et al., 1996). Nearly 100 of the highest risk children were individually assessed by this chapter's authors, confirming a high rate of PTSD.

The data gathered in the first few years after the disaster allowed us to examine in detail the psychometric properties of the scales used and helped shape our revision of the IES. We dropped two of the items that children had difficulty understanding, because they both contained double negatives (Yule, ten Bruggencatte, & Joseph, 1994; Dyregrov & Yule, 1995; Yule, 1997). Detailed study of subgroups of survivors demonstrated that adolescents showed similar patterns of attributions as adults (Joseph, Brewin, Yule, & Williams, 1993), a finding that related to the pattern of presentation of their symptoms. Good social support was found to be an important protective factor associated with reduction in distress (Joseph, Yule, Williams, & Andrews, 1993).

We looked at the pattern of fears in the survivors. Following Dollinger, O'Donnell, and Staley's (1984) methodology, we grouped the fears according to whether they shared any characteristics with what the children had experienced in the sinking. Good agreement occurred between judges as to which fears were related to the disaster and which were not. Although the level of self-reported fears was higher among the survivors than among the controls (but not statistically significantly so), a highly significant increase was found in the number of disaster-related fears reported. In part, this finding is confirmatory evidence that some fears are acquired through conditioning (Yule, Udwin, & Murdoch, 1990). The finding also has major implications for treatment (see below).

The *Jupiter* Follow-Up Study

We undertook a 5- to 7-year follow-up of the *Jupiter* survivors. By then, most of the adolescents had left school and were either in tertiary education or working. We were interested not only in how their psychopathology had developed over the years but also in how they were negotiating the crucial changes into adulthood in work as well as intimate relationships. The methodology of our study is detailed in Yule et al. (2000) and Bolton, O'Ryan, Udwin, Boyle, & Yule (2000). We managed to trace 331 of approximately

400 survivors (no accessible list of all survivors was available); 217 agreed to participate fully, and a further 30 agreed to return some questionnaires. Thus, we interviewed 57% of those identified (66% of those whom we managed to contact). We also interviewed 87 control particpants—young people who had attended the same schools but who were not involved directly in the accident.

In addition to completing similar questionnaires to those they had completed earlier, all the participants were individually interviewed using the Clinician Administered PTSD Scale (Blake et al., 1990; Weathers, Ruscio, & Keane, 1999). They were also interviewed on the Retrospective Experiences and Child and Adolescent Psychology Interview (RECAP; Holmshaw & Simonoff, 1996). The measures allowed us to compare the survivor and control groups on a wide range of predisaster mental health risk factors. We used the Schedule for Affective Disorders and Schizophrenia Lifetime Version (Spitzer & Endicott, 1975) to assess general psychopathology and its course since the disaster. Additional items were inserted to update the interview to allow for diagnoses according to the *Diagnostic and Statistical Manual of Mental Disorders, Fourth Edition* (DSM–IV; American Psychiatric Association, 1994). All interviews were audiotaped, and satisfactory agreement was found between the interviews conducted by research workers and clinicians.

No differences were found between the survivors and the control group on any of the 16 variables relating to predisaster psychosocial risk. Thus, any differences to emerge between the survivors and the control participants in terms of psychopathology after the accident can reasonably be seen as related to the event. Of the survivors, 51.5% developed PTSD at some time after the disaster, compared with only 3.4% of the control group. Most of the survivors who developed PTSD did so in the first few weeks after the accident. Around 10% had a delayed onset, defined as developing PTSD at least 6 months after the sinking. Half developed PTSD around the anniversary of the disaster. In most cases, these children had a number of stress symptoms but failed to reach strict criteria for the diagnosis beforehand. The duration of PTSD was also measured. In 30% of the survivors, PTSD lasted less than 1 year; in 16.4% it lasted 1 to 2 years; in 12.6% it lasted 2 to 3 years; in 6.3% it lasted 3 to 4 years; in 8.1% it lasted 4 to 5 years; and in 26.1% it lasted more than 5 years. Indeed, 38 cases still had PTSD at follow up, meaning that PTSD was still present in 17.5% of the sample. Put another way, of the 111 who developed PTSD, 34.2% still had it 5 to 7 years later.

We can therefore draw a number of conclusions with a fair degree of certainty. First, PTSD occurred in just over half of the adolescents who survived this disaster. Thus, PTSD may not be as rare as was once thought. Second, few cases of delayed onset occurred. Indeed, few absolutely new cases occurred, in the sense that most of those who had PTSD had had troubling symptoms prior to developing one or two additional symptoms, which then placed them above threshold for the strict diagnosis. Third, once adolescents developed PTSD they remained above diagnostic threshold for 5 to 7 years in 34% of cases. Thus, PTSD in childhood is not a transient phenomenon that all affected children will grow out of. Indeed, children and adolescents can be resilient, but they can also develop and continue to suffer from quite debilitating disorders. Fourth, proportionally more females than males developed PTSD (56.6% vs. 36.2%).

Turning to consider the rates of other disorders, excluding PTSD, we found that in the 5 to 8 years after the accident, the survivors reported significantly higher rates of specific phobia (23.6% vs. 9.2%), panic disorder (12.0% vs. 2.3%), separation anxiety (6.8% vs. 0%), and major depression (34.3% vs. 17.2%) than the control participants. Looking more crudely at collapsed categories (and still excluding diagnoses of PTSD), we found that survivors reported higher rates on any anxiety disorder (40.7% vs. 18.4%) and any affective disorder (38.4% vs. 17.4%). The survivors reported a total rate of 56.5% for any psychopathology excluding PTSD, compared with a rate of 34.5% in the control group. Gender differences were apparent in the disorders. Female survivors reported significantly higher rates on separation anxiety (9.3% vs. 0%), any anxiety disorder (47.8% vs. 19.3%), any affective disorder (42.8% vs. 26.3%), and any psychopathology (excluding PTSD; 61.6% vs. 42.1%). In general, the survivors who developed PTSD had higher rates of other disorders as well.

If we look at the picture at the time of follow up and compare point prevalence rates of the various DSM-defined disorders, we find that apart from specific phobia, no significant increases occurred in specific categories. Statistically significant differences remained between survivors and control participants in rates of combined categories; however, Rates of any anxiety disorder were 24.1% among survivors versus 9.2% among the control participants, and rates of any psychopathology were 26.0% for survivors but 10.3% for controls. Looking at the time course for the disorders overrepresented among the survivors, we found that specific phobia lasted for many years. In contrast, most recovered from major depression within 1 year and from panic disorder and separation anxiety within 2 years. We tried to examine whether major depression was primary or secondary to PTSD and found that 61 children developed both disorders; in 57 cases the depression developed at the same time or after the PTSD. In 21 cases (more than one third), the onset of major depression was not only after the onset of PTSD but also after recovering from PTSD.

RISK FACTORS FOR STRESS REACTIONS

The design of our study and the large number of survivors we managed to trace and interview provided us with an unique opportunity to study risk factors for the presence, duration and severity of PTSD (Udwin, Boyle, Yule,

Bolton, & O'Ryan, 2000). As noted earlier, just more than half of the 217 adolescents followed over a 5- to 7-year period developed PTSD, enough for meaningful statistical analyses. Following Winje and Ulvik (1998), we considered factors that appear to mediate the development and maintenance of traumatic stress reactions under three headings: factors associated with the traumatic experience itself; factors associated with the individual child; and postdisaster factors, including the child's recovery environment and family characteristics.

The mediating variables we examined were grouped into three categories. *Predisaster risk factors* were drawn from the RECAP interview, and *disaster-related factors* were based on survivors' own audiotaped accounts of the accident, paying particular attention to real and perceived threat to life and multiple traumas. Care was taken to elicit where the children had been on board, how they had got off the ship, whether they had been in the sea, whether they were separated from friends, and whether they sustained physical injuries. Interviewers probed for subjective factors, such as thinking they might not escape, thinking they might die, and feeling extreme fear. Regarding *postdisaster factors*, survivors were asked about their immediate and long-term reactions. The Ways of Coping Questionnaire–Short Form (Folkman & Lazarus, 1988) was used together with the Life Event Scale (Masten, Neeman, & Andenas, 1994) and the Social Support Scale (Joseph, Andrews, Williams, & Yule, 1992). We also had available 5-month screening measures on most of the children.

We used various logistic regression analyses to test which of the variables best predicted the presence, duration, and severity of PTSD. The development of PTSD was best predicted by being female, having learning difficulties and mental health problems in childhood, and having experienced violence in the home during earlier childhood. Other childhood difficulties and parent separation or divorce were *not* related to developing PTSD after the accident. The data suggested that prior experience of sexual abuse was a risk factor, but the numbers were too small to reach significance.

In terms of experiences during the disaster, those who were trapped in the ship, who had to jump into the water, who saw blood, and who received injuries all had higher risk of developing PTSD. Likewise, the risk was greater if the survivors thought at the time that they might die or had moderate to severe feelings of fear or panic. As for the aftermath, people who had significant amnesia or feelings of guilt were more likely to develop PTSD. High scores on subsequent life events or low scores on coping strategies were also risk factors. Finally, participants' high scores on the IES, depression, and anxiety 5 months after the disaster were also strongly related to developing PTSD.

Most of the associations were expected. The important finding was that we could test their relative importance in one analysis. Six variables emerged as the best predictors for developing PTSD. Two were "objective factors" relating to the accident (i.e., having seen blood and having been trapped), three were "subjective factors" (i.e., thinking they would not escape, reports of panicking, and recollections of intense fear at the time), and the last variable consisted of high scores on the Revised Children's Manifest Anxiety Scale at 5 months postdisaster. Those who scored high on these factors were 1.1 to 3.7 times more likely than the remainder to develop PTSD.

Parallel analyses were conducted to predict the duration and the severity of the PTSD. Duration was best predicted by three variables: ratings of social relationship difficulties in childhood, illness in childhood, and depression scores at 5 months postdisaster. Survivors who scored high on these factors were 1.08 to 5.16 times more likely to have PTSD that lasted 2 years or more. Severity of PTSD was best predicted by having had a separation anxiety in earlier childhood, a high depression score at 5 months, and not receiving help and support at school. The last point indicates that in general, when schools did provide help, children seemed to do better. Unfortunately, this accident occurred in 1988, when schools were generally not well prepared to assess risk and develop contingency plans to deal with critical incidents. Having assessed many survivors, we are aware that the sort of help that was offered turned out to be patchy and rarely matched clinical evidence of survivors' symptoms.

It is interesting to see that both objective factors and subjective appraisals exert influences on whether someone will develop PTSD after an accident and that earlier adjustment and experiences also play important roles. The difference between risk indices and risk factors is that the early (i.e., 5-month) measures of distress are really indicators rather than causes of the pattern of disorder. Even so, the measures can be easily, quickly, and cheaply obtained; our findings therefore have implications for screening high-risk survivors following a large-scale disaster in situations of limited mental health resources.

Most of the *Jupiter* survivors were age 14 or 15 at the time of the accident. As a result, it was not possible to examine the role of age and developmental stage as risk factors. Adolescence is often viewed as a high-risk period for experiences of trauma and an inherently stressful stage of development. In general, though, studies have yielded inconsistent findings on the influence of age on the extent to which children are affected by disasters. Vogel and Vernberg (1993) point to a number of mediators of age differences in disaster reactions, which may help explain the inconsistencies. They include age-related changes in appraisal of the disaster, coping strategies, and children's beliefs about determinants of control over events.

INTERVENTION AND TREATMENT

Apart from the study by Stallard and Law (1993), which showed good effects of two sessions of cognitive–behavioral therapy "de-briefing" given many months after a school coach accident, no reports have been published of treatment especially for survivors of mass transportation disasters. Yule and Williams (1990) described the groups they ran for children and parents who survived the *Herald of Free Enterprise* capsize, but those were essentially pragmatic attempts at help and not designed as controlled trials of previously developed treatments.

Before looking briefly at the current state of the art of treating PTSD in children, let us look at the particular aspects of mass transportation disasters that must be taken into consideration in mounting a therapeutic response. The first consideration is whether the children are travelling alone, with an organized group with whom they already have a relationship, or with their parents or other trusted adults. These factors are important because the sheer practicalities of organizing treatment in groups for people who are widely geographically scattered are immense, particularly if the children develop travel phobias and are expected to travel long distances to the group.

If the accident occurs a long way from home and if the parents are not part of the group on board the ship or bus, the question of reuniting children and families arises. The need for children to be near their parents is very strong and characteristic of a normal reaction after threat. In most cases of crashes a long way from home, tour organizers assume that the children should be returned home as quickly as possible and reunited there, but that is not necessarily the best approach. Such action means the children are removed from the site of the accident before they have become clear in their own minds as to what happened. Their parents have not seen the site and therefore cannot help the children desensitize to it. They will not know the relevance of casual details that the child recalls and therefore will not be able to help as much as they might otherwise. The presence of their parents—their "safety signal"—at the scene of the accident may do more to counteract children's anxiety than any number of imaginal exposure sessions. This idea is conjecture, but it is spelled out here to challenge the automatic response so prevalent at present. In our view, such accident-management strategies should be subjected to empirical test.

Although a number of case reports of treatment of children with PTSD have been published, few accounts of randomized controlled studies are available. For the most part, treatment approaches are predominantly cognitive–behavioral and appear to consist of adaptations of approaches used with adults (Smith, Perrin, & Yule, 1998; Yule, 1991).

Critical incident stress debriefing techniques have been adapted for use with groups of children following a variety of traumas (Dyregrov, 1991). This structured crisis intervention approach was used with some children following the *Jupiter* sinking, with good effects on lowering the levels of intrusion and of fears (Yule & Udwin, 1991). Stallard and Law (1993) used two debriefing sessions to reduce distress in girls who survived a school bus crash. Casswell (1997) also reported good results from debriefing following a school bus crash, although data were not systematically gathered.

Group treatments are to be preferred as a first line of intervention when large numbers of survivors are involved. Gillis (1993) suggests that groups of six to eight are optimum and advises that separate groups be run for boys and girls. Different types of incidents, however, are likely to require different responses from professionals (Galante & Foa, 1986; Yule & Williams, 1990), and it is too soon to pontificate on what should be a standard approach.

Individual treatment centers mainly on cognitive–behavioral therapies that aim to help survivors both make sense of what happened and master their feelings of anxiety and helplessness. Drug treatments, judiciously used, occasionally may have a place in dealing with high levels of anxiety and depression. Asking children to draw their experiences can be useful in helping them recall both the event and the emotions associated with it (Blom, 1986; Galante & Foa; 1986; Newman, 1976; Pynoos & Eth, 1986). Merely drawing the trauma, however, is not a sufficient therapy. A recent study from the former Yugoslavia, where great emphasis was placed on getting children to express their emotions through drawing, found that 6 months after having had structured sessions on drawing and other expressive techniques, no measurable change occurred in children's adjustment on a whole range of self-report measures of stress reactions (Bunjevac & Kuterovac, 1994).

Saigh (1986) was one of the first to provide clinical evidence that, as Rachman (1980) had predicted, there were dangers in using standard systematic desensitization approaches because the length of exposure sessions may be too short to permit adequate habituation of anxiety. It should also be remembered that children may be frightened by the vividness of their memories, and relaxation training may only serve to intensify the vividness. The theoretical aspects of exposure therapy in treating PTSD in children are discussed elsewhere (Saigh, Yule, & Inamdar, 1996).

Eye movement desensitization and reprocessing (EMDR) treatment has generated considerable interest and scepticism (Shapiro, 1995; Smith & Yule, 1999). Few published accounts of its use with children and adolescents exist. As with all techniques that have no clear rationale, caution must be exercised. If, as claimed, symptomatic relief can be attained in a few brief sessions, then the approach needs to be carefully evaluated. Because there does seem to be a different quality to the memories of a trauma that at the same time appear to be locked in, vivid, and unchangeable by merely talking about them, then any technique that will allow emotional processing to proceed must be examined. Some examples of using EMDR with child survivors of road traffic accidents are given in Yule (1999).

When trauma affects a large number of children at once, as in an accident at school, a public health approach to dealing with the emergency is required, such as contingency planning (Pynoos, Goenjian, & Steinberg, 1995). Schools need to plan ahead not only to deal with large-scale disasters but also to respond to the needs of children after threatening incidents that affect only a few of them. Thus, a number of texts have now been written especially for schools to help them develop contingency plans to deal with the effects of a disaster (Johnson, 1993; Klingman, 1993; Yule & Gold, 1993). The British Child Accident Prevention Trust has recently published leaflets containing advice for professionals, parents, and children themselves and describing the main emotional reactions to accidents and some of the first aid that can be followed, in the hope that emotional difficulties will not become entrenched (Child Accident Prevention Trust, 1998).

CONCLUSIONS

Although surprisingly few empirical studies of child survivors of mass transportation disasters have been conducted, those that exist do show the value of using standard assessment instruments to assess the children's reactions. The data thus far strongly indicate that following any life-threatening transportation disaster, a high incidence of both PTSD and other serious mental health problems is likely to occur. Most cases will manifest in the first few weeks. Indeed, the strength of distress in the early days is a good indicator of high risk of developing PTSD and of having it for a long time. There are very few cases of delayed onset and most seem to be of children newly crossing the diagnostic threshold, having been symptomatic for a long time, rather than de novo disorders. Once developed, PTSD is likely to remain for up to 7 years in a third of the affected cases.

Survivors manifest a broad range of problems after a disaster, including specific fears of traveling. It is an anomaly of the current *DSM* system that if someone has a PTSD diagnosis, one cannot also diagnose a specific travel phobia. This limitation needs to be recognized for the needless technicality that it is. The travel phobia is no less real and requires treatment in its own right. Often it involves a loss of trust in any other person being in charge of the survivor and requires different treatment from simple exposure.

The literature points to our lack of understanding of how child and family reactions interact in the maintenance of the distress. This aspect should be a fruitful source of research over the next few years. The "near miss" phenomenon is poorly understood; the *Jupiter* findings and the Israeli bus findings are contradictory.

Sadly, mass transportation disasters will continue to happen. The challenge is for the international community of traumatic stress clinical researchers to develop protocols that will both help identify better interventions and also contribute to our understanding of human reactions to disasters.

REFERENCES

American Psychiatric Association. (1994). *Diagnostic and Statistical manual of mental disorders* (4th ed.). Washington, DC: Author.

Birleson, P. (1981). The validity of depressive disorder in childhood and the development of a self-rating scale. *Journal of Child Psychology and Psychiatry, 22,* 73–88.

Blake, D. D., Weathers, F. W., Nagy, L. M., Kaloupek, D. G., Klauminzer, G., Charney, D. S., & Keane, T. M. (1990). A clinician's rating scale for assessing current and lifetime PTSD: The CAPS-1. *The Behavioral Therapist, 13,* 187–188.

Blom, G. E. (1986). A school disaster—intervention and research aspects. *Journal of the American Academy of Child Psychiatry, 25,* 336–345.

Bolton, D., O'Ryan, D., Udwin, O., Boyle, S., & Yule, W. (2000). The long-term psychological effects of a disaster experienced in adolescence: II. General psychopathology. *Journal of Child Psychology and Psychiatry, 41,* 513–523.

Bunjevac, T., & Kuterovac, G. (1994). *Report on the results of psychological evaluation of the art therapy program in schools in Hercegovina.* Zagreb, Croatia: United Nations International Children's Emergency Fund (UNICEF).

Casswell, G. (1997). Learning from the aftermath: The response of mental health workers to a school-bus crash. *Clinical Child Psychology and Psychiatry, 2,* 517–523.

Child Accident Prevention Trust. (1998). *Providing emotional support to children and families after an accident.* London: Author.

Dollinger, S. J., O'Donnell, J. P., & Staley, A. A. (1984). Lightning-strike disaster: Effects on children's fears and worries. *Journal of Consulting and Clinical Psychology, 52,* 1028–1038.

Dyregrov, A. (1991). *Grief in children: A handbook for adults.* London: Jessica Kingsley.

Dyregrov, A., & Yule, W. (1995, May). *Screening measures—the development of the UNICEF screening battery.* Paper presented at the 4th European Conference on Traumatic Stress, Paris.

Ellis, A. J., Stores, G., & Mayou, R. A. (1998). Psychological consequences of road traffic accidents in children. *European Journal of Child and Adolescent Psychiatry, 7,* 61–68.

Folkman, S., & Lazarus, R. S. (1988). Coping as a mediator of emotion. *Journal of Personality and Social Psychology, 54,* 466–475.

Galante, R., & Foa, D. (1986). An epidemiological study of psychic trauma and treatment effectiveness after a natural disaster. *Journal of the American Academy of Child Psychiatry, 25,* 357–363.

Gillis, H. M. (1993). Individual and small-group psychotherapy for children involved in trauma and disaster. In C. F. Saylor (Ed.), *Children and disasters* (pp. 165–186). New York: Plenum Press.

Holmshaw, J., & Simonoff, E. (1996). Retrospective recall of childhood psychopathology. *International Journal of Methods in Psychiatric Research, 6,* 79–88.

Horowitz, M. J., Wilner, N., & Alvarez, W. (1979). Impact of Event Scale: A measure of subjective stress. *Psychosomatic Medicine, 41,* 209–218.

Johnson, K. (1993). *School crisis management: A team training guide.* Alameda, CA: Hunter House.

Joseph, S., Andrews, B., Williams, R., & Yule, W. (1992). Crisis support and psychiatric symptomatology in adult survivors of the Jupiter cruise ship disaster. *British Journal of Clinical Psychology, 31*, 63–73.

Joseph, S., Brewin, C., Yule, W., & Williams, R. (1993). Causal attributions and post-traumatic symptoms in adolescent survivors of a disaster. *Journal of Child Psychology and Psychiatry, 34*, 247–253.

Joseph, S., Yule, W., Williams, R., & Andrews, B. (1993). Crisis support in the aftermath of a disaster: A longitudinal perspective. *British Journal of Clinical Psychology, 32*, 177–185.

Klingman, A. (1993). School-based interventions following a disaster. In C. F. Saylor (Ed.), *Children and disasters* (pp. 187–210). New York: Plenum Press.

Masten, A. S., Neeman, J., & Andenas, S. (1994). Life events and adjustment in adolescents: The significance of event independence, desirability and chronicity. *Journal of Research on Adolescence, 4*, 71–97.

McFarlane, A. C. (1987). Posttraumatic phenomena in a longitudinal study of children following a natural disaster. *Journal of the American Academy of Child and Adolescent Psychiatry, 26*, 764–769.

Milgram, N. A., Toubiana, Y. H., Klingman, A., Raviv, A., & Goldstein, I. (1988). Situational exposure and personal loss in children's acute and chronic stress reactions to a school bus disaster. *Journal of Traumatic Stress, 1*, 339–352.

Newman, C. J. (1976). Children of disaster: Clinical observation at Buffalo Creek. *American Journal of Psychiatry, 133*, 306–312.

Perrin, S., Yule, W., & Smith, P. (1996, November). *Post-traumatic stress in children as a function of sibling and parental exposure to the trauma.* Paper presented at the 12th Annual Convention of the International Society for Traumatic Stress Studies, San Francisco.

Pynoos, R. S., & Eth, S. (1986). Witness to violence: The child interview. *Journal of the American Academy of Child Psychiatry, 25*, 306–319.

Pynoos, R. S., Goenjian, A., & Steinberg, A. (1995). Strategies of disaster interventions for children and adolescents. In S. E. Hobfoll and M. de Vries (Eds.), *Extreme stress and communities: Impact and intervention* (pp. 445–471). Dordrecht, Netherlands: Kluwer.

Rachman, S. (1980). Emotional processing. *Behaviour Research and Therapy, 18*, 51–60.

Reynolds, C. R., & Richmond, B. O. (1978). What I think and feel: A revised measure of children's manifest anxiety. *Journal of Abnormal Child Psychology, 6*, 271–280.

Saigh, P. A. (1986). In vitro flooding in the treatment of a 6-year-old boy's posttraumatic stress disorder. *Behaviour Research and Therapy, 24*, 685–688.

Saigh, P. A., Yule, W., & Inamdar, S. C. (1996). Imaginal flooding of traumatized children and adolescents. *Journal of School Psychology, 34*, 163–183.

Shapiro, F. (1995). *Eye movement desensitization and reprocessing: Basic principles, protocols and procedures.* New York: Guilford Press.

Smith, P., Perrin, S., & Yule, W. (1998). Post traumatic stress disorders. In P. Graham (Ed.), *Cognitive behaviour therapy for children and families* (pp. 127–140). Cambridge Monograph Series in Child and Adolescent Psychiatry. Cambridge, UK: Cambridge University Press.

Smith, P. A., & Yule, W. (1999). Eye movement desensitization and reprocessing therapy (EMDR) and other rapid treatments. In Yule, W. (Ed.), *Post traumatic stress disorder* (pp. 267–284). Chichester: Wiley

Spitzer, R. L., & Endicott, J. (1975). *Schedule for affective disorders and schizophrenia.* New York: Biometrics Research.

Stallard, P., & Law, F. (1993). Screening and psychological debriefing of adolescent survivors of life-threatening events. *British Journal of Psychiatry, 163,* 660–665.

Toubiana, Y. H., Milgram, N. A., Strich, J., & Edelstein, A. (1988). Crisis intervention in a school community disaster. *Journal of Community Psychology, 16,* 228–240.

Trimble, M. (1981). *Post-traumatic neurosis: From railway spine to whiplash.* New York: Wiley.

Tyano, S., Iancu, I., Solomon, Z., Sever, J., Goldstein, I., Touviana, Y., & Bleich, A. (1996). Seven-year follow-up of child survivors of a bus-train collision. *Journal of the American Academy of Child and Adolescent Psychiatry, 35,* 365–373.

Udwin, O., Boyle, S., Yule, W., Bolton, D., & O'Ryan, D. (2000). Risk and protective factors for long term psychological effects of a disaster experienced in adolescence: Predictors of post traumatic stress disorder. *Journal of Child Psychology and Psychiatry, 41,* 969–979.

Vogel, J. M., & Vernberg, E. M. (1993). Part I: Children's psychological responses to disasters. *Journal of Clinical Child Psychology, 22,* 464–484.

Weathers, F. W., Ruscio, A. M., & Keane, T. M. (1999). Psychometric properties of nine scoring rules for the Clinician-Administered Post-Traumatic Stress Disorder Scale. *Psychological Assessment, 11,* 124–133.

Winje, D., & Ulvik, A. (1998). Long-term outcome of trauma in children: The psychological consequences of a bus accident. *Journal of Child Psychology and Psychiatry, 39,* 635–642.

Yule, W. (1991). Working with children following disasters. In M. Herbert (Ed.), *Clinical child psychology: Social learning, development and behaviour* (pp. 349–363). Chichester, UK: Wiley.

Yule, W. (1997). Anxiety, depression and post-traumatic stress in childhood. In I. Sclare (Ed.), *Child psychology portfolio.* Windsor, UK: NFER-Nelson.

Yule, W. (1999). Treatment of PTSD in children following road traffic accidents. In A. J. Hickling & E. B. Blanchard (Eds.), *The international handbook of road accidents and psychological trauma: Current understanding treatment and law* (pp. 375–387). Amsterdam: Elsevier.

Yule, W., Bolton, D., Udwin, O., Boyle, S., O'Ryan, D., & Nurrish, J. (2000). The long-term psychological effects of a disaster experienced in adolescence: I. The incidence and course of PTSD. *Journal of Child Psychology and Psychiatry, 41,* 503–512.

Yule, W., & Gold, A. (1993). *Wise before the event: Coping with crises in schools.* London: Calouste Gulbenkian Foundation.

Yule, W., ten Bruggencatte, S., & Joseph, S. (1994). Principal components analysis of the Impact of Events Scale in children who survived a shipping disaster. *Personality and Individual Differences, 16,* 685–691.

Yule, W., & Udwin, O. (1991). Screening child survivors for post-traumatic stress disorders: Experiences from the "Jupiter" sinking. *British Journal of Clinical Psychology, 30,* 131–138.

Yule, W., Udwin, O., & Murdoch, K. (1990). The "Jupiter" sinking: Effects on children's fears, depression and anxiety. *Journal of Child Psychology and Psychiatry, 31,* 1051–1061.

Yule, W., & Williams, R. (1990). Post traumatic stress reactions in children. *Journal of Traumatic Stress, 3,* 279–295.

11

DAM BREAK: LONG-TERM FOLLOW-UP OF CHILDREN EXPOSED TO THE BUFFALO CREEK DISASTER

MINDY KOROL, TERESA L. KRAMER, MARY C. GRACE, AND BONNIE L. GREEN

Studies of the Buffalo Creek dam collapse disaster, which occurred in 1972, provided some of the earliest comprehensive quantitative psychological data on disaster survivors. The follow-up of this event over several decades also represents one of the longest term longitudinal studies of disaster survivors. Although the time frame of these studies (early 1970s to mid-1980s) precluded the early assessment of some of the symptoms that are the focus in modern studies (e.g., posttraumatic stress disorder [PTSD] entered the psychiatric nomenclature in 1980), the evaluations included quantitative assessments of several dimensions of exposure as well as a range of outcomes. Both parent and child exposure and reactions were assessed. The original assessments took place in the context of a lawsuit, with the disadvantage

We would like to acknowledge everyone who worked on this series of studies over a period of 20 years. In particular, we would like to thank James Titchener, who was the lead clinician for the adults in the original study; Janet Newman, who led the clinical evaluations of the children; and Goldine Gleser, who developed the research project associated with the original evaluations. We also wish to acknowledge Jacob Lindy, Fred Kapp, Carolyn Winget, Mark Vary, Anthony Leonard, and Sheila Smitson-Cohen for their critical roles in specific aspects of the project.

that participants' motives may have included secondary gain. The advantages of this context, however, were that a large portion of the community was represented and that evaluations from both sides of the suit were available for assessment purposes. Detailed descriptions of the event itself, as well as its impact on the community, can be found in Erikson (1976); Stern (1976) provides a detailed account of the mounting of the legal case.

This chapter describes the empirical investigation of the experiences and reactions of a sample of exposed children who were ages 2 to 15 at the time of the disaster. They were originally assessed in 1974 (at ages 4 to 17), approximately 2 years postdisaster, and they were reassessed approximately 15 years later. The original clinical descriptions of the children and their responses at 2 years are detailed in Newman (1976); Titchener and Kapp (1976) described the reactions of their parents. The original assessments in the quantitative study were based in part on interviews that served as the basis for these descriptions. We did not conduct psychological interventions for the children or their parents, and no organized intervention efforts took place in the community following the disaster, primarily because of a lack of resources. The data, however, were rich with implications for such interventions, and we address those possibilities in the discussion.

THE DISASTER

The Buffalo Creek valley is in Logan County, West Virginia. It is a narrow, 18-mile stretch in the Appalachian Mountains composed of many small, unincorporated villages, only 6 to 8 houses wide in many spots. In the early 1970s, the residents made their living primarily through the coal mining industry, including mining itself and businesses supporting this industry in the local community. Early on Saturday morning, February 26, 1972, after several days of heavy rain, a slag dam built by the Pittston Coal Mining Company collapsed, pouring millions of gallons of water and black coal waste into the valley below. After 20 minutes, the flood waters receded. In their wake, 125 people were dead, thousands were left homeless, and the landscape and community were devastated. It was many weeks before the worst of the debris was cleared away (Erikson, 1976). (See chapter 7 for additional information on the disaster.)

A number of residents felt that the fault for the disaster lay with the coal company that had constructed the unstable dam. They filed a class action lawsuit against the company that included claims of "psychic impairment" as well as property damage and wrongful death. The Department of Psychiatry at the University of Cincinnati College of Medicine participated in the suit on the side of the plaintiffs and conducted extensive psychiatric interviews on all adult and child plaintiffs. A psychiatrist for the defense also examined all parties to the suit. The interviews took place between 18 and

26 months (approximately 1 to 2 years) postflood. The suit was settled out of court (Stern, 1976) in the summer of 1974, and awards for psychological damages were made to the plaintiffs.

Design of the Original Study

The original sample of Buffalo Creek participants, all plaintiffs in the lawsuit against Pittston Coal Company, consisted of 381 adults (175 men and 206 women) age 16 and older (including 81 late adolescents and young adults ages 16 to 20) and 207 children. At the time of the disaster, 51 children were between ages 2 and 7 (27 boys and 24 girls), 74 children were between ages 8 and 11 (43 boys and 31 girls), and 82 children were between ages 12 and 15 (35 boys and 47 girls). At the time of the assessments, they were approximately 2 years older. Twenty-three children were under age 2 in 1972.

Assessments consisted of two interviews for each litigant, one conducted by a neuropsychiatrist working for the defense and one conducted by a team of mental health professionals working for the plaintiffs. Interviews for the defense were conducted in the neuropsychiatrist's office in Charleston, WV (approximately 1.5 hours from Buffalo Creek), an average of 1.5 years postflood, whereas those for the plaintiff's side were conducted in the participants' homes approximately 2 years postflood.

Interview data were quantified using the Psychiatric Evaluation Form (PEF; Endicott & Spitzer, 1972; Spitzer, Endicott, Mesnikoff, & Cohen, 1968), ratings by research staff, and impairment ratings by clinicians (Gleser, Green, & Winget, 1981). Several validity checks were conducted among the assessment measures to substantiate their appropriateness for children. The PEF typically is based on a structured interview and yields scores on 19 subscales (aspects of psychopathology) and one score of overall severity, all of which are based on 6-point scales with high scores indicating greater impairment (1 = *no impairment*; 6 = *extreme impairment*). The original reports were based on semistructured interviews; although this format did not guarantee coverage of all areas, interviewers tended to cover the major categories. Three major symptom clusters on the PEF were identified rationally and empirically: (a) anxiety, which combined the Somatic Concerns and Anxiety subscales; (b) depression, which combined the Social Isolation, Depression, Daily Routine Impairment, and Suicidal Thoughts subscales; and (c) belligerence, which combined the Belligerence and Antisocial subscales. A rating of overall severity previously mentioned was included as well. Despite the different perspectives and attributions of the two interviews, relationships between the ratings were highly significant. Thus, scores from the two sides of the lawsuit were averaged for analyses (Gleser et al., 1981).

Because PTSD was not an official diagnosis in 1974, its symptoms were not systematically investigated in the original study. The neuropsychiatrist for the defense routinely inquired about flood-specific phobia symptoms and other possible stress-related symptoms, however, and the mental health professionals for the plaintiffs' lawyers were looking for symptoms of "traumatic neurosis." As a result, many PTSD symptoms were routinely assessed. Thus, as part of the preparation for the follow-up study of the children, PTSD symptoms at 2 years were rated on the basis of the two original evaluations for each of 179 children (92 boys and 87 girls). Some interviews were insufficiently complete to allow the ratings. Forty-three children were in the younger age group (ages 2 to 7 at the time of the flood), 64 children were in the middle age group (ages 5 to 11 at the time of the flood), and 72 children were in the older age group (ages 12 to 15 at the time of the flood). Symptoms were based on the 1987 criteria for PTSD from the *Diagnostic and Statistical Manual for Mental Disorders, Third Edition, Revised* (DSM–III–R; American Psychiatric Association, 1987).

A work sheet was developed and tested to gather the symptoms from both reports. Symptoms were grouped into intrusive, denial, and arousal categories in accordance with *DSM–III–R* criteria. To test reliability, 20 children were scored by two raters. Because not all the symptoms were separately explored, giving a diagnosis of PTSD was not appropriate; however, an estimate was made of how many children might have received the diagnosis if it had been systematically investigated and in the nomenclature at the time. Therefore, children showing one intrusion symptom, one denial symptom, and one arousal symptom were labeled "probable" PTSD.

Data related to flood stressors, parental functioning, and family atmosphere collected at the time of the original study were used for predictive purposes. Two indices for flood stressors were developed. Initial Flood Stress, or Life Threat, consisted of a 6-point scale measuring degree of warning about the collapse, contact with flood waters, separations from family, and exposure to the elements. Loss was a 5-point scale ranging from no loss (0) to loss of a close family member (4). More than half of the sample had lost at least a close friend, and more than one fourth had lost extended family. More than one third had come close to death or watched helplessly while others they knew were carried to their death (Gleser et al., 1981). Parent functioning was operationalized as the average PEF overall severity rating from the two original parental reports. Family atmosphere included four dimensional ratings (depressed-gloomy, irritable, violent, supportive) of atmosphere in the home.

Design of the 17-Year Follow-Up Study

The *exposed* sample consisted of 99 young adults who were in the Buffalo Creek dam collapse and were child plaintiffs initially seen in 1974 (Gleser et al., 1981; Green et al., 1991). The participants represented 48% of the original sample of 207 children who were between ages 2 and 15 at the time of the disaster. Children were located from information provided by their parents along with information from community informants. Because the study was not originally designed as longitudinal, no traditional tracking procedures had been used. Even so, information on 91% of the original sample was obtained. Of the people approached to participate ($N = 132$), 100 (76%) agreed. One participant completed only self-report data and was not included in the sample. Because almost all the children in Buffalo Creek were part of a lawsuit, it was not possible to include nonlitigants in the exposed group.

The *comparison* sample consisted of 46 young adults from a community in eastern Kentucky that was similar demographically and culturally to Buffalo Creek. Participants were recruited by knocking on doors in appropriate neighborhoods, by asking people already participating for names of friends or neighbors, and by having community informants post notices at several places of employment. Thus, this was a sample of convenience rather than one representative of the region, but it was matched as closely as possible demographically to the Buffalo Creek target group.

A research team of eight members made four trips to the Buffalo Creek area and two to the comparison area in Kentucky. Assessments were usually conducted in participants' homes. A subset who had moved away from the region were interviewed by telephone. The participants gave verbal informed consent and later signed the written consent when they mailed the self-report questionnaires back.

The research team had clinical interviewing experience and extensive training on the Structured Clinical Interview for *DSM–III–R*, Nonpatient Version (SCID; Spitzer, Williams, Gibbon, & First, 1989) and the PEF. The SCID covers the primary Axis I diagnoses from the *DSM–III–R* for both past and present diagnoses as well as antisocial personality disorder. The SCID PTSD section was added to the usual diagnoses assessed. SCID interviews were conducted individually with each participant. The PEF ratings were completed by the interviewer at the end of the SCID interview. Also, flood stressor information collected at the time of the original study was reviewed with participants.

Self-report measures included the Symptom Checklist-90-R (SCL-90-R; Derogatis, 1983) and the Impact of Event Scale (IES; Horowitz, Wilner, & Alvarez, 1979; Zilberg, Weiss, & Horowitz, 1982). The SCL-90-R is a self-report measure on which participants rate their experience of each of 90 symptoms during the past month along a 5-point scale from "*not at all*" (0) to "extremely" (4). It yields a global severity index (GSI) and nine subscale scores. Twelve additional PTSD-related items used in previous trauma-related research (Green et al., 1990) were added to the checklist; they were not included in the calculation of the GSI but were examined as a separate subscale. The IES is an assessment of the current response to a stressful life event (i.e., the dam collapse). It consists of 15 statements which respondents rate on a 5-point scale from "*not at all*" (0) to "*often*" (4) for how frequently each was true for them during the past week. The IES yields Intrusion and Avoidance subscale scores consistent with Horowitz's (1976, 1986) theoretical model for stress-response syndromes.

Design of the 17-Year Follow-Up Psychoanalytic Case Study

A small subset ($n = 15$) of the 99 young adults participating in the follow-up study agreed to participate in an extensive, semistructured, psychodynamic interview conducted by a team of seven psychiatrists (six analysts and four child psychiatrists). The participants were selected on the basis of their availability during the short data collection period. Nine of the interviews were audiotaped, and six were videotaped. The interviewing team determined that the videotaped interviews provided significantly richer data than the audiotaped interviews, especially with regard to the interviewer–interviewee interaction. As a result, the six videotaped interviews were chosen for closer examination. The PSTD symptoms elicited by the interview were assessed (Honig, Grace, Lindy, Newman, & Titchener, 1999), and the interviews were analyzed from a psychoanalytic developmental perspective (Honig, Grace, Lindy, Newman, & Titchener, 1993).

Findings of the Original Study

Ratings of overall severity on the PEF (based on the average of the two reports for the child litigants) yielded both age and gender effects. Approximately 10% of the children in the younger age group were rated as having moderate to severe levels of psychological distress 1.5 to 2 years postdisaster, and approximately 45% were rated as having no psychological distress. A high incidence (about 20%) of regressive toileting behaviors was found, however. Approximately 18% of the children in the middle group (ages 8 to 11) were rated as having moderate to severe levels of psychological distress, and approximately 36% were rated as having no psychological distress. Approximately 30% of the children in the older age group were rated as having moderate to severe levels of psychological distress; approximately 22% had no psychological distress.

With regard to PTSD symptoms, 37% of the children fit the criteria for a "probable PTSD" diagnosis because they experienced at least one symptom each of intrusion, denial, and arousal (Green et al., 1991). This figure is quite similar to the figure of 32% of participants who at follow-up reported a lifetime diagnosis of disaster-related PTSD on the SCID (see below) using the entire range of symptom criteria, suggesting that the 37% figure derived from the earlier interviews was an appropriate estimate. The most frequent symptom reported was the intrusion symptom of psychological distress at exposure to or thinking about events resembling some aspect of the flood (65%). The next most frequent symptoms were the denial symptoms of re-

TABLE 11.1
Average PTSD Symptom Estimates by Age Group for Original Study

	Age 2–7	Age 8–11	Age 12–15	Total
Symptom	$N = 43$	$N = 64$	$N = 72$	$N = 179$
Intrusion	1.21	1.53	1.39	1.40
Denial*	0.63	1.14	1.19	1.04
Arousal	0.91	1.06	1.25	1.10
Total PTSD symptoms**	2.74	3.73	3.83	3.54

Note. $*p < .05$ for age difference. $** p < .01$ for age difference.

stricted social range (40%) and restricted range of affect (39%) and the arousal symptom of irritability or anger outbursts (37%). Also common were the intrusion symptoms of sleep disturbance when it rains (30%) and flood-related bad dreams or nightmares (30%). All 11 other symptom frequencies fell at or below 22%; 6 symptom frequencies were at or below 8% (Green et al., 1991).

Overall severity and depression cluster symptoms scores on the PEF increased linearly with age: The older children showed more overall distress (2.8 on PEF overall severity rating) and depression symptom cluster ratings (1.7) than the middle age group, who in turn showed more overall distress (2.3) and depression symptom cluster ratings (1.6) than the younger age group (2.0 and 1.2), respectively. No differences were found in anxiety symptom cluster ratings among age groups (all age groups had 1.8 rating). The older age group (1.5), however, showed higher ratings on the belligerence symptom cluster than the other age groups (both = 1.2). Gender effects indicated that girls (of all age groups) scored significantly higher on the psychiatric ratings of overall severity and symptom clusters of anxiety and depression and lower on ratings of belligerence than same-age boys (Gleser et al., 1981).

Analyses revealed age and gender effects but no significant interaction, so the main effects are displayed separately. Table 11.1 shows the average number of PTSD symptoms by age group and for the three separate symptom categories. With regard to developmental differences, the youngest group showed the fewest symptoms overall as well as the fewest denial symptoms. The children showed an average of approximately one symptom in each category. The prevalence of "probable PTSD" diagnosis was 30% for the younger, 39% for the middle, and 39% for the older age groups, indicating no statistical significance.

Table 11.2 shows the average PTSD symptoms by gender. Significant differences were found in total PTSD symptoms and in denial symptoms: Girls showed higher symptom levels than boys. Intrusion symptoms approached significance. The average number of PTSD symptoms rated was 3.11 for boys and 3.99 for girls. Similarly, girls were somewhat more likely to receive a "probable PTSD" diagnosis (44% vs. 30%; Green et al., 1991).

TABLE 11.2
Average PTSD Symptom Estimates by Gender for Original Study

Symptom	Boys $n = 92$	Girls $n = 87$
Intrusion	1.26	1.54
Denial*	0.75	1.34
Arousal	1.10	1.10
Total PTSD symptoms**	3.11	3.99

Note. *$p < .07$ for gender difference. ** $p < .01$ for gender difference.

Correlations between stressor variables and PEF scales showed that for the children in all three age groups ($n = 207$), Life Threat was significantly related to Overall Severity, Anxiety, and Depression (but not Belligerence), and Loss was significantly related to Overall Severity and Anxiety. To further explore predictive factors, hierarchical multiple regression analyses were conducted separately for boys and girls. The following factors were entered into the analysis in the order indicated: stressor variables, demographic variables (age and race), parent's psychopathology (i.e., PEF overall severity), and family atmosphere. Older children ($n = 66$), who were between ages 16 and 20 at the time of the flood, also were included in the analyses, yielding a total of 273 children; the analyses were conducted separately by gender. Focusing on the overall severity rating, disaster exposure, and age significantly contributed to outcome prediction for both genders. For boys, father's overall severity rating and a supportive family atmosphere contributed incrementally to prediction of the child's overall severity rating. For girls, mother's overall severity rating and a violent family atmosphere were the significant incremental predictors (Gleser et al., 1981).

Prediction of PTSD symptoms was examined in boys and girls combined using the 154 children with complete data. With regard to stressors, Life Threat was a significant predictor of PTSD symptoms, but Loss did not predict. Both age group and gender were related to PTSD, but age group did not add significant predictive power over and above Life Threat and gender. Both mother and father's Overall Severity ratings were related to PTSD symptoms, but father's functioning contributed only marginally after accounting for the mother's functioning. Both irritable and depressed family atmosphere significantly predicted PTSD symptoms; irritable atmosphere had the most predictive power. Thus, stressor experiences, demographic variables, parental reactions, and aspects of the family atmosphere all significantly contributed to the children's postdisaster functioning (Green et al., 1991).

Findings of the 17-Year Follow-Up Study

Demographic information for the 99 young adults in the Buffalo Creek sample indicated that the sample was fairly well distributed across the three age groups, although it had a slightly higher representation of those origi-

TABLE 11.3
Changes in Select Scales of the Psychiatric Evaluation Form (PEF) From
Original Study to 17-Year Follow-Up

	Original	Follow-up		
PEF Subscale	*M*	*M*	*t*	*p*
Anxiety	2.48	1.44	10.26	< .01
Depression	1.88	1.65	1.80	NS
Belligerence	1.62	1.03	8.72	< .01
Somatic Concerns	1.25	1.04	3.56	< .01
Agitation	1.46	1.15	4.14	< .01
Suicidal Thoughts	1.00	1.06	2.16	< .04
Drug Abuse	1.00	1.16	2.84	< .01
Alcohol Abuse	1.00	1.23	2.90	< .01
Overall Severity	2.17	1.59	4.67	< .01

Note. N = 95–98; NS = not significant.

nally in the youngest group. Although women were slightly overrepresented in the follow-up (62% vs. 49%), ethnic representation was nearly identical (73% White in the original study vs. 75% White in the follow-up). When those who were followed up were compared with those who were not in the follow-up group on their original levels of psychopathology, those who participated in the follow-up were rated as *less* impaired on the 1974 PEF overall severity (M = 2.16 vs. M = 2.43). No differences were found between the groups on the 1974 PSTD symptoms. The PEF subscales that significantly differentiated participants from nonparticipants were Belligerence, Alcohol Abuse, and Suspicion; those not followed up were more impaired. This finding is not surprising because the symptom clusters reflect characteristics that would likely reduce willingness to participate in research.

To assess changes over time, PEF ratings between the original study and the follow-up were compared (see Table 11.3). The two ratings were not significantly correlated, so there was no association between earlier to the later scores. Thus, the findings indicate only gross trends for the sample as a whole. Overall Severity, Anxiety, Belligerence, Somatic Concerns, and Agitation decreased significantly over the 17-year period. No significant change in depression occurred, but Alcohol Abuse, Drug Abuse, and Suicidal Thoughts increased significantly over time (Green et al., 1994). The SCID yielded diagnostic prevalence data for any time postdisaster as well as current (i.e., time of follow-up). The lifetime rate of disaster-related PTSD for the sample was 32%; the rate at follow-up was 7%. Nondisaster PTSD showed a lifetime rate of 6% and a current rate of 4%. The rate of postdisaster major depression was 33%, and the current rate was 13%. Alcohol and Drug Abuse showed lifetime rates of 18% but current rates of only 6% and 3%, respectively (Green et al., 1994).

Analyses for age group and gender for present status on the PEF, SCID, SCL-90-R, and IES showed no significant age group effects. The number of

PTSD symptoms, as measured by the SCID, approached significance, however; the oldest group showed more symptoms (3.1) than the youngest (1.9) and the middle (1.3) groups. Significant gender effects were found: Women showed higher symptom levels and scored significantly higher than men on the PEF subscales of Anxiety and Social Isolation. They also showed a trend toward higher rates of depression (18% vs. 5%) and PTSD (12% vs. 0%). Also notable is that all the current PTSD cases were women. Commensurate with this, women scored higher on the IES self-report for both the intrusion and avoidance dimensions.

Exposure was not strongly related to current functioning, and it predicted primarily PTSD symptoms. The analyses evaluated specific stressor experiences. PEF overall severity was predicted by loss of an immediate family member. IES intrusion and avoidance were predicted by loss of relatives, and IES intrusion was predicted by degree of warning and by being blocked in trying to escape. Prolonged exposure to the elements predicted less IES avoidance, and injury predicted the number of PTSD symptoms.

For the purposes of comparing the Buffalo Creek participants to a demographically similar sample, only those who had stayed in the valley or the surrounding area ($n = 50$) were used in the analyses. The one demographic difference between the two samples occurred for marital status: The Buffalo Creek residents were more likely to be married (60% vs. 48%) and the Kentucky residents were more likely to be single (35% vs. 18%). The two groups were quite similar with regard to current functioning and in most areas of past functioning as well. Although the Buffalo Creek sample showed somewhat higher rates of current anxiety (Generalized Anxiety Disorder, 8% vs. 0%) and major depression (36% vs. 29%) than the other group, lifetime rate of PTSD was the only significant difference between groups; the Buffalo Creek sample showed higher rates (34% vs. 7%; Green et al., 1994).

Findings of the 17-Year Follow-Up Psychoanalytic Case Study

The number of PTSD symptoms elicited in each of the six videotaped semistructured interviews of the young adults who were children at the time of the flood were recorded and compared with the results (blind to the interviewers) of the PTSD symptoms for the same adults as elicited by the SCID in a previous study (Green et al., 1994). The results indicated that 67% ($n = 4$) of the participants showed PTSD symptoms in the psychodynamic interview that were not evident in the SCID interview; 33% ($n = 2$) showed PTSD symptoms in the SCID interview that were not evident in the psychodynamic interview. Of the 25 total PTSD symptoms elicited by both methods together, 18 were evident only in the clinical interviews and 3 were evident only in the research-oriented interviews. The 18 symptoms that emerged through the clinical method consisted of 5 intrusion symptoms (Cluster B of the DSM–III–R criteria), 9 avoidance or denial symptoms (Cluster C), and 4 arousal symptoms (Cluster D), thus suggesting that avoidance symptoms may be especially more accessible in a clinical psychodynamic format. Also notable was that 67% ($n = 4$) of the young adults interviewed reported flood-related symptoms of survivor guilt, obsessive feelings of responsibility, persistent rage toward perpetrators, preoccupation with death thoughts, and counterphobic behavior toward physical danger that were not part of the DSM–III–R PTSD criteria.

The in-depth psychoanalytic evaluations of four of the videotaped interviews examined the participants' initial coping responses to the flood and followed their course. What appeared to be critical was whether the coping response consolidated or involved the integration of adaptive behaviors related to the traumatic experience (Honig et al., 1993). Consolidation appeared to contribute to resiliency and healthy adult psychological functioning; lack of consolidation seemed to contribute to a risk for chronic PTSD. Also revealed in the analysis was that the family's response to the flood seemed closely associated with their self-reported adaptive coping styles and behavior patterns.

DISCUSSION

The extensive interviews conducted with the young survivors of the Buffalo Creek Dam collapse at 1 to 2 years postflood and again at 17 years postflood represent the first longitudinal study of traumatic stress reactions in a community sample. At the initial evaluation, approximately 10% to 30% of children and adolescents exhibited moderate-to-severe levels of overall psychological distress. Moreover, 37% of all children fit the criteria for a probable diagnosis of PTSD, experiencing at least one symptom of intrusion, denial, and arousal. Factors influencing children's postdisaster reactions have been accounted for in a conceptual model initially developed by Korol (1990) and Green et al. (1991). The factors include characteristics of the stressor, characteristics of the child, characteristics of the postdisaster environment, and the child's efforts to process and cope with the ensuing distress. By assessing each domain, mental health specialists can identify children at risk and intervene more quickly to prevent the onset or persistence of problems.

In our studies, prevalence of symptoms was most strongly associated with age, gender, experiences of the flood, parental functioning, and family environment. Specifically, older children showed more overall distress, depressive symptoms, and belligerence than younger children; they also reported more symptoms of PTSD. Girls of all age groups scored higher on overall severity and symptom clusters of anxiety and depression, but they had lower ratings of belligerence compared with boys of the same age. Child symptoms also were associated with parental psychopathology and family atmosphere, although those factors had differential effects, depending on the age and gender of the child. Finally, aspects of the flood, including Life Threat and Loss, were associated with more severe symptoms of depression or PTSD.

The findings have important implications for the assessment and treatment of children, adolescents, and their families who are exposed to sudden, catastrophic, and communitywide trauma. Consistent with the developmental literature, children react differently to events depending on their cognitive capabilities (Pynoos & Eth, 1985). A second possibility is that older children are better able to express their distress, whereas younger children engage in more regressive or avoidant behaviors that are not easily associated with the original trauma (Drell, Siegel, & Gaensbauer, 1993). Regardless, assessments of children exposed to trauma should be tailored to their age and cognitive level and consist of multiple methods of evaluation, including observation, self- and parental report, and projective techniques (e.g., play and artwork; Pfefferbaum, 1997). It was particularly useful in our research to use parental report of specific behaviors, such as soiling and wetting the bed at night, or onset of unusual fears and concerns. Older children were asked directly about symptoms using structured interview techniques and validated measures. Although we also attempted to collect information about preexisting functioning from medical and school records, our difficulty in obtaining the data retrospectively precluded analyses of such data. It is extremely important, however, for clinician or mental health specialists to inquire about a child's predisaster functioning from multiple sources, because research has indicated that premorbid academic difficulties and psychological problems are predictive of worse outcomes (La Greca, Vernberg, Silverman, & Prinstein, 1996).

The pattern of symptoms observed in girls and boys is consistent with observed differences in child psychopathology: Girls (especially older girls) are more likely to exhibit internalizing disorders, such as depression and anxiety, and boys are more likely to exhibit externalizing disorders, such as behavioral and socialization problems. Girls also appear to be at higher risk for developing and maintaining specific symptoms of a posttraumatic stress response, a finding consistent with similar studies focusing on the sequelae of disasters (Giaconia et al., 1995; Lonigan, Shannon, Finch, Daugherty, & Taylor, 1991; Shannon, Lonigan, Finch, & Taylor, 1994). Boys' tendency to act out, however, may be an attempt to avoid thoughts and feelings about the original trauma, thereby masking their distress to others. It is important for clinicians to recognize gender differences and assess the interaction between gender and a child's coping style, availability and use of social support, and expectations for recovery (Pfefferbaum, 1997).

Parental response and family environment also significantly influenced boys' and girls' symptoms following the dam collapse. Multiple studies have demonstrated this relationship (cf., Cohen, 1998), clearly indicating a need to evaluate the child within the context of his or her immediate environment. In large-scale disasters, each family member endures the trauma, although their individual experiences may differ depending on their physical location, position within the family (e.g., an older child may have accepted responsibility for a younger child), and subjective appraisal of the event. Because each person is affected to some extent, functioning and roles within the family may become disturbed in the aftermath, producing disruptions in attachment and growth (Miller, 1999). It was undoubtedly positive that few of the children in the sample lost parents in the dam collapse. Because it occurred early on a Saturday, most families were together and tended to escape (or die) as a family. A great deal of destruction of the psychological community (Erikson, 1976) occurred, however, which resulted in the absence of a benevolent recovery environment. Those losses can have a significant impact on the healing capacity of all family members, but they may be most influential for the adults or caregivers, who also must cope with financial, housing, and employment issues. These circumstances can lead to impaired caretaking, lack of parental responsiveness, and impairment in role functioning, further contributing to the child's anxiety or depression (Pynoos, 1994). Clinicians who assess the role of the parent and functioning of the family will be better prepared to intervene on behalf of the child. Our findings support the work of several authors who have proposed crisis intervention models involving all members of the family to understand the trauma, identify and mobilize potential resources, and develop and use problem-solving skills (Harris, 1991).

Finally, exposure to the event also predicted the severity of symptoms in the children of Buffalo Creek, a finding that provides additional support for clinical interviews that evaluate the child's perception of what happened, including life-threatening circumstances, loss, environmental disruption, separation from family and friends, and self-blame or guilt. Almost 2 decades after the flood, the severity of symptoms had dissipated in the people who were children at the time of the dam collapse. Although the Buffalo Creek group showed somewhat higher rates of current anxiety and depression than the comparison group, the lifetime rate of PTSD was the only significant difference between the two. Only 7% of the Buffalo Creek group had a current diagnosis of disaster-related PTSD, according to the SCID interviews. Two thirds of the participants, however, revealed some PTSD symptoms when a thorough, psychodynamically oriented interview was conducted (Honig et al., 1999).

Although symptoms had decreased by the 17-year follow up, the extent to which symptoms persisted in this group through adolescence and into early adulthood is unknown. We only asked about lifetime and current symptoms and did not evaluate how or whether symptoms waxed and waned over the years. Of particular concern were the characteristics of cases lost to follow-up (i.e., those who were not interviewed had exhibited greater overall severity and higher rates of Belligerence, Alcohol Abuse, and Suspicion than those who were interviewed). Whether they continued to have these problems is unknown. Moreover, their unwillingness to participate may reflect a tendency toward avoidance behaviors characteristic of PTSD, suggesting the possibility of higher rates of the disorder than indicated by our follow-up sample.

Unfortunately, we did not obtain information on treatment received by either group. Harvey (1996) proposed an ecological model that groups trauma survivors into four categories: those who do and do not receive clinical intervention and those who do and do not recover. Because of limited mental health resources available in the area, it is highly unlikely that a large number of children in Buffalo Creek received intensive counseling following the flood. We therefore presume that most interviewed children were those who received no clinical intervention but nonetheless recovered from debilitating symptoms. Although this conclusion supports the theory of resiliency in children, we did not evaluate persistent personality disturbances, which many have theorized develop in response to trauma and its aftermath (Pynoos, 1994). We also have no information on people who did or did not receive treatment and continued to function poorly. This area of research is largely unexamined and requires careful consideration of the quality, quantity, accessibility, affordability, and cultural sensitivity of mental health treatment as well as the short- and long-term efficacy of various interventions.

Because our objective in entering Buffalo Creek was not therapeutic in nature, we did not conduct interventions per se, although our presence probably affected the community in several ways. First, the interviews may have served as a form of late "debriefing" by offering residents the opportunity to communicate their feelings. Most notably, the components of our work mirroring debriefing efforts included discussion about the event and the child's responses to it, exploration of feelings and thoughts, and promotion of support from interviewers and family members. Over the course of the studies, the researchers served as historians by promoting storytelling in an empathic environment. Conversely, the interviewers may have served as reminders of the event, thereby intensifying posttrauma symptoms.

In addition, our original studies were conducted as part of a lawsuit in which Buffalo Creek residents were seeking corporate responsibility and damages for the dam collapse. Despite this context, at follow-up we had some difficulty accessing residents, who, quite naturally, maintained a suspiciousness of outsiders. Our team frequently encountered the "trauma membrane," a protective stance of survivors to minimize intrusions and maintain privacy during the aftermath of a disaster (Lindy, Grace, & Green, 1981). Consequently, we often relied on naturally occurring support systems (e.g., churches and schools) to gain access in this rural community and provide referrals when appropriate. This "trauma membrane" is a particular challenge for mental health professionals attempting to assist disaster survivors without formal emergency response networks or established support systems within the community.

In summary, the Buffalo Creek dam collapse devastated a community, killing 125 people and leaving children and families bereaved, without homes, and sometimes separated from one another. The studies described herein represent the first longitudinal effort to identify symptoms in a cohort of young survivors and follow them into adulthood. Although significant symptoms were noted almost 2 years following the disaster, most of the participants of the follow-up study had recovered by adulthood. Both prospective and longitudinal studies are needed to examine the effects of trauma on children and their families, particularly the effectiveness of early identification and prevention, mental health treatment, and school-based intervention programs.

REFERENCES

American Psychiatric Association. (1987). *Diagnostic and statistical manual of mental disorders* (3rd ed. rev.). Washington DC: Author.

Cohen, J. A. (1998). Practice parameters for the assessment and treatment of children and adolescents with posttraumatic stress disorder. *Journal of the American Academy of Child and Adolescent Psychiatry, 37* (Suppl. 10), 4–26.

Derogatis, L. R. (1983). *SCL-90-R: Administration, scoring, and procedures manual-II* (2nd ed.). Towson, MD: Clinical Psychometric Research.

Drell, M. J., Siegel, C. H., & Gaensbauer, T. J. (1993). Posttraumatic stress disorder. In C.H. Zeanah (Ed.), *Handbook of infant mental health* (pp. 291–304). New York: Guilford Press.

Endicott, J., & Spitzer, R. (1972). What! Another rating scale? The psychiatric evaluation form. *Journal of Nervous and Mental Disease, 154,* 88–104.

Erikson, K. T. (1976). Loss of communality at Buffalo Creek. *American Journal of Psychiatry, 133,* 302–305.

Giaconia, R. M., Reinherz, H. Z., Silverman, A. B., Pakiz, B., Frost, A. K., & Cohen, E. (1995). Traumas and posttraumatic stress disorder in a community population of older adolescents. *Journal of the American Academy of Child and Adolescent Psychiatry, 34,* 1369–1380.

Gleser, G. C., Green, B. L, & Winget, C. (1981). *Prolonged psychological effects of disaster: A study of Buffalo Creek.* New York: Academic Press.

Green, B. L., Grace, M. C., Lindy, J. D., Gleser, G. C., Leonard, A. C., & Kramer, T. L. (1990). Buffalo Creek Survivors in the second decade: Comparison with unexposed and nonlitigant groups. *Journal of Applied Social Psychology, 20,* 1033–1050.

Green, B. L., Grace, M. C., Vary, M. G., Kramer, T. L., Gleser, G. C., & Leonard, A. C. (1994). Children of disaster in the second decade: A 17-year follow-up of the Buffalo Creek survivors. *Journal of the American Academy of Child and Adolescent Psychiatry, 33,* 71–79.

Green, B. L., Korol, M., Grace, M. C., Vary, M. G., Leonard, A. C., Gleser, G. C., & Smitson-Cohen, S. (1991). Children and disaster: Age, gender, and parental effects on PTSD symptoms. *Journal of the American Academy of Child and Adolescent Psychiatry, 30,* 945–951.

Harris, C. J. (1991). A family crisis-intervention model for the treatment of post-traumatic stress reaction. *Journal of Traumatic Stress, 4,* 195–208.

Harvey, M. R. (1996). An ecological view of psychological trauma and trauma recovery. *Journal of Traumatic Stress, 9,* 3–24.

Honig, R. G., Grace M. C., Lindy, J. D., Newman, C. J., & Titchener, J. L. (1993). Portraits of survival: A twenty year follow-up of the Buffalo Creek flood. *Psychoanalytic Study of the Child, 48,* 327–355.

Honig, R. G., Grace M. C., Lindy, J. D., Newman, C. J., & Titchener, J. L. (1999). Assessing long-term effects of trauma: Diagnosing symptoms of avoidance in numbing. *American Journal of Psychiatry, 156,* 483–485.

Horowitz, M. J. (1976). *Stress response syndromes.* New York: Jason Aronson.

Horowitz, M. J. (1986). *Stress response syndromes* (2nd ed.). New York: Jason Aronson.

Horowitz, M. J., Wilner, N., & Alvarez, W. (1979). Impact of event scale: A measure of subjective stress. *Psychosomatic Medicine, 41,* 209–218.

Korol, M. S. (1990). *Children's psychological responses to a nuclear waste disaster in Fernald, Ohio.* Unpublished doctoral dissertation, University of Cincinnati, Ohio.

La Greca, A. M., Vernberg, E. M., Silverman, W. K., & Prinstein, M. J. (1996). Symptoms of posttraumatic stress in children after Hurricane Andrew: A prospective study. *Journal of Consulting and Clinical Psychology, 64,* 712–723.

Lindy, J. D., Grace, M. C., & Green, B. L. (1981). Survivors: Outreach to a reluctant population. *American Journal of Orthopsychiatry, 51,* 468–478.

Lonigan, C. J., Shannon, M. P., Finch, A. J., Daugherty, T. K., & Taylor, C. M. (1991). Children's reactions to a natural disaster: Symptom severity and degree of exposure. *Advanced Behavioral Research Therapy, 13,* 135–154.

Miller, L. (1999). Treating posttraumatic stress disorder in children and families: Basic principles and clinical applications. *American Journal of Family Therapy, 27,* 21–34.

Newman, C. J. (1976). Children of disaster: Clinical observations at Buffalo Creek. *American Journal of Psychiatry, 133,* 306–312.

Pfefferbaum, B. (1997). Posttraumatic stress disorder in children: A review of the past 10 years. *Journal of the American Academy of Child and Adolescent Psychiatry, 36,* 1503–1511.

Pynoos, R. S. (Ed.). (1994). *Posttraumatic stress disorder: A clinical overview.* Lutherville, MD: Sidran Press.

Pynoos, R. S., & Eth, S. (1985). Developmental perspective on psychic trauma in childhood. In C. Figley (Ed.), *Trauma and its wake* (pp. 36–52). New York: Brunner/Mazel.

Shannon, M. P., Lonigan, C. J., Finch, A. J., & Taylor, C. M. (1994). Children exposed to disaster: I. Epidemiology of posttraumatic symptoms and symptom profiles. *Journal of the American Academy of Child and Adolescent Psychiatry, 33,* 80–93.

Spitzer, R. L., Endicott, J., Mesnikoff, A. M., & Cohen, M. S. (1968). *The psychiatric evaluation form.* New York: New York State Psychiatric Institute, Biometrics Research Department.

Spitzer, R. L., Williams, J. B., Gibbon, M., & First, M. B. (1989). *Structured clinical interview for the DSM-III-R: Non-patient version.* New York: New York State Psychiatric Institute, Biometrics Research Department.

Stern, G. M. (1976). *The Buffalo Creek disaster: The story of the survivors' unprecedented lawsuit.* New York: Random House.

Titchener, J. L., & Kapp, F. T. (1976). Family and character change at Buffalo Creek. *American Journal of Psychiatry, 133,* 295–299.

Zilberg, N. J., Weiss, D. S., & Horowitz, M. J. (1982). Impact of event scale: A cross validation study and some empirical evidence supporting a conceptual model of stress response syndromes. *Journal of Consulting and Clinical Psychology, 50,* 407–414.

12

THE TRAUMATIC IMPACT OF MOTOR VEHICLE ACCIDENTS

JOSEPH R. SCOTTI, KENNETH J. RUGGIERO, AND ALINE E. RABALAIS

A discussion of the traumatic impact of motor vehicle accidents (MVAs) on children necessarily begins with a comment on the scope of the problem and how common this event is in our daily lives. *Healthy People 2000* (U.S. Department of Health and Human Services [HHS], 1991), which sets national health promotion and disease prevention objectives, notes that the overall rate of accidental injury in 1987 was 34.5 per 100,000 people. The rate is higher among males than females: Males are 2.5 times more likely to die from an unintentional injury than females. American Indians and Alaska Natives have disproportionately higher death rates from injury than the general U.S. population (about 2.5 times higher generally, and even higher on western reservations), followed by African American males and Caucasian males. Rice, MacKenzie, and Associates (1989) determined that nearly 57 million Americans experienced an accidental injury in 1985 and that unintentional injuries accounted for approximately 84% of injury-related hospi-

Portions of this work were supported by a National Institute of Mental Health research grant (1 R03 MH55533-01) to Joseph Scotti, and a minority fellowship from the West Virginia University Office of Academic Affairs to Aline Rabalais, both of which are gratefully acknowledged. The opinions expressed herein are not necessarily those of the supporting agencies.

talizations (see also Sosin, Sacks, & Sattin, 1992); about 28% of those injuries resulted from motor vehicle crashes. With regard to MVAs alone, *Healthy People 2000* set as an objective for the year 2000 a reduction in deaths caused by MVAs to no more than 16.8 per 100,000 people, which is a decrease from the 1987 age-adjusted rate of 18.8 per 100,000. For children age 14 and younger, the target was set as 5.5 deaths per 100,000 (from 6.2); and for youth ages 15 to 24 years, the target was 33.0 (from 36.9). The 1996 vehicle crash data from the U.S. Department of Transportation (DOT) suggest that those goals may well be met, even exceeded, although increases and decreases vary from year to year (National Highway Traffic Safety Administration [NHTSA], 1996).

What the focus on crash fatality data do not capture is the number of people who survive motor vehicle crashes, whether or not a fatality occurred in a given crash. The DOT data for 1996 reveal that 6.8 million crashes occurred in the United States that year; one third of them (2.3 million) resulted in injury to at least one person, and less than 1% resulted in the death of at least one person (NHTSA, 1996). A closer look shows that approximately 413,000 children age 15 and younger (671 per 100,000) and 953,000 youth ages 16 to 24 (2,938 per 100,000) were injured in MVAs in 1996. This figure only represents the reported physical injuries from 1 year's worth of crashes and does not include the resulting distress that may be evident in any crash. That psychological and behavioral distress is the focus of this chapter.

OVERVIEW OF STUDIES ON CHILDREN AND MVAS

Research Literature

Rather surprisingly, only a handful of studies exist on the psychological and behavioral consequences for children who have been exposed to MVAs. Two are descriptive accounts of children who showed a range of symptoms, including difficulty concentrating; increased crying; depressed, irritable, and regressive behavior; somatic complaints; and insomnia and nightmares following bus–train collisions (Milgram, Toubiana, Klingman, Raviv, & Goldstein, 1988; Tuckman, 1973). Jones and Peterson (1993) provided a case report of a 3-year-old girl with posttraumatic stress disorder (PTSD; e.g., nightmares, anxiety, avoidance of vehicles, and aggressive play) following an MVA, even though she was not injured. Her father, however, had some minor injuries, and their vehicle was beyond repair following impact with a truck. A number of other descriptive reports have been published (e.g., Casswell, 1997; Stallard & Law, 1993; Thompson, McArdle, & Dunne, 1993; Winje & Ulvik, 1998), which serve only to point out the rather dismal lack of large-scale empirical studies of this common event.

Several attempts at systematic evaluations have been made. Canterbury and Yule (1997) and Ellis, Stores, and Mayou (1998) followed children after admission to hospital emergency rooms as a result of MVAs. Of a sample of 28 children in the first study, about 16% had symptoms suggestive of PTSD. Of the 45 children in the latter study, about one third were experiencing symptoms indicative of significant distress. Studies using formal diagnostic interviews have found PTSD rates of around 15% 2 to 6 months postaccident (DiGallo, Barton, & Parry-Jones, 1997; Mirza, Bhadrinath, Goodyer, & Gilmour, 1998). As Stallard (1999) points out, however, those studies are fraught with methodological problems that limit the conclusions that can be drawn, including the absence of appropriate control groups, a focus on PTSD rather than a range of possible pathological responses, reliance on self-report questionnaires, and the failure to exclude other diagnoses. We would add to this list the lack of a measure documenting the characteristics and severity of the MVAs (see the discussion of accident severity, below). Finally, no published research, to date, has taken the step of bringing MVA-exposed children into the clinical research laboratory for the purpose of a comprehensive, multimodal assessment.

Clearly, a pressing need exists for the systematic and empirical study of the types of behavioral and psychological responses that children may exhibit following exposure to MVAs. Beyond simply establishing the range of responses that can be expected in children post-MVA, multiple factors may increase either risk or resiliency in children, a topic for which virtually no information exists. Several of those factors are highlighted in the following case illustrations.

Illustrative Cases of the Response of Children to MVAs

In our clinical and research endeavors at the Department of Psychology at West Virginia University, we have encountered a number of child survivors of MVAs that cover a range of crash severity. Some of those cases have been involved in our grant-funded research (Scotti, Mullen James, & Rode, 1999) on child accident survivors; others have presented in the Quin Curtis Center, the departmental outpatient clinic for research, service, and graduate training; still others were first encountered through our research and then referred to the clinic as a result of their clinical needs. The next sections describe several cases in brief, to which we refer throughout the remainder of the chapter.

Brandon

Brandon, age 11, was driving an all-terrain vehicle (ATV) without a helmet during a weekend visitation with his father. The ATV flipped over during the outing, and Brandon sustained minor bruises and lacerations to his arms and legs. The parents were in the early stages of a divorce and a related custody battle when the accident occurred. The mother claimed that the accident demonstrated that the father was not providing sufficient supervision of Brandon because he allowed the child to drive an ATV without a helmet, and she claimed that Brandon was subsequently experiencing symptoms of PTSD. Evaluation failed to substantiate such symptoms, although other clear sources of distress for Brandon were found, notably the break-up of the family.

Sammy and Pammy

Sammy and Pammy were 8-year-old fraternal twins. Neither had been in a car accident themselves; however, both of their parents had died in a MVA 18 months prior to their presenting at our clinic. The children were being raised by an aunt and uncle (the deceased father's sister and brother-in-law), who had adopted them. The adoptive parents noted that the children were "clingy," concerned about "things" happening to the adoptive parents when they were not together, and reticent to discuss their deceased parents. The successful course of therapy involved fostering open discussion between the children and the adoptive parents (who, in fact, were even more reluctant to discuss the deceased parents) and behavior therapy (i.e., graduated exposure; Hagopian & Slifer, 1993) for the symptoms of separation anxiety.

Charley and Nathan

Charley, age 3, and Nathan, age 7, were both in an accident 6 months prior to their first visit to the clinic. Their mother, age 35, was driving on a wet road with many sharp turns and skidded off the road into a ditch. The mother's arm was caught between the steering wheel and the door for about 20 minutes until help arrived. Her arm and face were covered with multiple minor pinpoint cuts caused by the shattering of the window glass. As the rain poured in the car, the mother was helpless as blood flowed from her seemingly serious head wounds; the uninjured children screamed in distress until helped arrived. All the injuries were revealed to be quite minor and quickly healed. Both the parents and Nathan were born in South Africa but had been in the United States for 5 years. The mother was unemployed and was very submissive—even passive—particularly in the presence of her husband who was unconcerned, even dismissive, about the apparent distress of his family (he only came to the first session). Nathan could vividly describe the accident, but Charley could not and claimed not to remember it. The mother reported, however, that *both* children were distressed whenever she drove, especially in rainy weather, but not when the father drove. The children indicated that their father insisted on their being quiet "all the time."

Robbie

Robbie was a 7-year old African American boy whose family was devoutly Christian. He attended a religious school and many church-run after-school activities (e.g., Bible study several times per week). He had been involved in a mild rear-end collision (which resulted in a dented bumper and smashed taillight but no physical injuries), in which his mother had been driving on a wet road and was struck from behind by a light truck. Subsequently, Robbie was resistant to entering the car, and when coaxed to ride in the car he was hypervigilant (especially to the sound of squealing brakes and of coming to stop signs where another vehicle might fail to stop). He was highly critical of his mother's driving, as evidenced in repeated remarks to be careful and to keep both of her hands on the steering wheel at all times, to which she complied. A critical aspect of this case was the perspective by the family that God had played a role in allowing the accident and that a resolution, in part, involved prayer.

Danielle

Danielle, age 10, and her mother, age 43, were in the same MVA involving a head-on collision with a car that had swerved into their lane. Both mother and daughter experienced severe bruising, largely from the restraint of the seatbelts, and lacerations to their head and arms. The mother claimed that Danielle had been experiencing a great deal of distress since the accident. Evaluation of the daughter, however, failed to reveal any distress other than some concern about a small, barely noticeable, scar in her hairline. We subsequently treated the mother with implosive therapy (Westrup, Kalish, & Scotti, 1997; see also Lyons & Scotti, 1995), an imaginal exposure technique that is an empirically validated intervention for PTSD (Chambless et al., 1998). Work with the mother focused on her serious symptoms of PTSD as well as guilt concerning the daughter's scar (even though it was the father who had been driving the vehicle) and eventually revealed both her own history of prior physical abuse trauma and a troubled marriage.

Marcy and Lucien

Marcy, age 12, and Lucien, age 18, had been in a serious crash that involved sideswiping an oncoming vehicle, rolling over repeatedly, and being ejected from the car. Lucien, who was driving, experienced severe head trauma, resulting in some decrement in his cognitive functioning and impulse control. Notably, Lucien had no memory of the accident and thus experienced no accident-related symptoms. He did, however, report guilt and a sense of responsibility for the injuries that his sister, Marcy, experienced. Marcy's hand was crushed in the accident and had required repeated corrective surgeries and physical therapy, which was still ongoing 1 year postaccident. She also sustained a facial laceration that left a noticeable 4-inch scar. Finally, Marcy was experiencing the full range of PTSD symptoms and major depression, which was significantly interfering with her sleep, ability to travel to school, and attention to and completion of schoolwork. Marcy also reported intense anger that her brother appeared unaffected by the accident.

These six case examples demonstrate the range of both accident severity and differential response that most clinicians treating children and families are likely to see. As is a common issue in the study of PTSD, it should be clear that the single most important feature is the severity of the accident itself (Blanchard & Hickling, 1997; Carlson, 1997). It also should be clear, however, that the same event can have different effects on the people experiencing it for numerous reasons. Most notable in the case examples are the different effects likely to come with developmental age, family relationships, extent of injury, and head trauma. In an attempt to pull those and other issues together, the next section presents a conceptual model to assist clinicians in evaluating the multiple contributors to the response to MVAs. This model also can form the basis of a functional analysis that can aid in both diagnosis and treatment of individual cases.

A PARADIGMATIC MODEL OF ACCIDENT-RELATED PTSD

Overview of the Model

The literature on traumatic stress has grown considerably over the past 20 years, to the point that it is quite clear that single-factor models (e.g., learning theory, cognitive processing, biological factors, and genetic predisposition) alone cannot adequately explain the complex variables at play in the response to traumatic events (see Freedy & Donkervoet, 1995). As Scotti, Beach, Northrop, Rode, and Forsyth (1995) noted, even if the greatest percentage of variance in the response to trauma is accounted for by event severity, such models do not adequately explain the idiographic—or differential—response of people to traumatic events. One can probably think of an accident so severe that virtually no one could walk away completely unaffected, but short of that line, the range of response is incredibly varied and sometimes bewilderingly inexplicable.

In their work on the psychological impact of accidental injury, Scotti and colleagues (1995) proposed a paradigmatic behavioral model of accident-related PTSD. The model was derived from similar framework models developed by Staats and his colleagues (Eifert, Beach, & Wilson, 1998; Eifert & Evans, 1990; Staats, 1993). The utility of this model, aside from bringing together diverse perspectives and sources of data into one conceptually unified model (i.e., a paradigm), is the linking together of relevant variables into a dynamic system that contains sufficient flexibility to incorporate idiographic differences within a comprehensive framework. The framework thus serves as a basis for additional research focusing either on single components or on the linking of one or more components. It also serves as a heuristic for conceptualizing the etiological and maintaining factors for individual cases.

This framework forms a *clinical functional analysis* (see Haynes & O'Brien, 2000; Scotti, Morris, McNeil, & Hawkins, 1996), which is a model for integrating the multiple interrelated factors that set the occasion for and maintain a set of behaviors, be they overt motor, covert cognitive, or physiological responses. Such an analysis should help identify appropriate intervention strategies.

Table 12.1 summarizes the six critical elements of this model, each of which is thoroughly described elsewhere (Scotti et al., 1995). The elements of the model involve multiple factors (e.g., biological, genetic, behavioral, and psychological) across several levels of analysis (e.g., biochemistry, behavioral principles, social environment, and culture and ethnicity). The model is dynamic, rather than static: The elements of the model reciprocally interact with each other over time. Psychological vulnerabilities and acquired or learned biological vulnerabilities affect each other against the background of prior learning, biological and genetic predispositions, the traumatic event, and the current situational features and stressors. Cultural and ethnic influences also can be readily incorporated here (see chapter 4, this volume). Through continuous evolution and interaction with each other, the elements produce the present symptomatic responses, which may be of sufficient number, intensity, and duration to meet criteria for a diagnosable disorder.

Applying the Model in Case Conceptualization

Table 12.1 provides a number of references supporting the features of the model. Interested readers are encouraged to review Scotti et al. (1995) and related models by Staats and colleagues (Eifert, Beach, & Wilson, 1998; Eifert & Evans, 1990; Staats, 1993) for a fuller explication of this model. Here we highlight the usefulness of the model by reference to aspects of the cases of Marcy and Lucien.

Recall that Marcy and Lucien are sister and brother. Thus, one may suppose a fairly high degree of similarity (certainly much higher than for unrelated people raised in different households, but not as high as in the cases of Sammy and Pammy) in their biological and genetic predispositions as well as in their basic family background and relationships. Their unlearned or genetic biological vulnerability includes a family history of depression and no report of prior pathology or significant behavior problems, although gender may account for some important differences. Their original learning and historical antecedents include high family cohesion; same socioeconomic status and cultural and ethnic background; no history of exposure to other traumatic events; excellent academic achievement, but at different grade levels; a 6-year age difference that may reflect different levels of maturity, coping skills, and peer relationships; and different gender roles.

TABLE 12.1
Critical Elements of a Paradigmatic Model of Posttraumatic Stress
Disorder for Children Exposed to Motor Vehicle Accidents

Element	Description	Examples	Sample References
Original learning (historical antecedents)	Individual learning history prior to the event of interest	• Age and developmental history • Prior trauma • Family cohesion • Education (grade level, achievement) • Socioeconomic status • Cultural and ethnic background • Prior psychopathology (child and family) • Coping skills (e.g., emotion-focused vs. problem-focused coping styles)	• Bramsen, Dirkzwager, & van der Ploeg, 2000 • Deblinger, Taub, Maedel, Lippmann, & Stauffer, 1997 • Harvey & Bryant, 1999 • La Greca, Silverman, & Wasserstein, 1998
Unlearned genetic and biological vulnerability	Genetically based characteristics and biological differences	• Family history of anxiety disorders, alcohol abuse, depression, or attention deficit–hyperactivity that may have a genetic or biological link • High baseline levels of autonomic arousal • Physiological reactivity	• Freedy & Donkervoet, 1995
Accident or trauma learning and characteristics	Features of the event and the person's exposure to and role in it	• Extent of injury to self or others • Death of others • Degree of vehicle and other property damage • Time to heal from injuries • Suddenness or unpredictability of the event • Perceived role in the event (i.e., guilt and blame, cultural views of responsibility)	• Foa, Zinbarg, & Rothbaum, 1992 • Ruggiero, McLeer, & Dixon, 2000 • Vernberg, La Greca, Silverman, & Prinstein, 1996

Table Continues

TABLE 12.1
(Continued)

Element	Description	Examples	Sample References
Present situational factors	Presence of stimuli related to the event and situational factors (including behavioral contingencies)	• Salience of event-related stimuli (e.g., the sights, sounds, smells, tastes, and physical sensations that occurred during the event) • Event-related and generalized stimuli (e.g., loud, sudden noises, such as banging metal or horn blasts; smells of blood or gasoline; the sensation of sudden stops or taking a turn too fast when riding in a vehicle; and riding a bus to school) • Family cohesion/discord • Social support (family, friends, neighbors, teachers, community, culture) • School-related stressors (e.g., entering the next grade or a new school) • Extracurricular activities	• Lyons & Scotti, 1995 • Vernberg et al., 1996 • Whiffen, Judd, & Aube, 1999
Acquired or learned biological vulnerability	Physical and physiological changes as a result of the event	• Conditioned autonomic arousal • Changes in neurotransmitter and hormonal levels • Loss of limbs or decreased functioning • Traumatic brain injury	• van der Kolk & Saporta, 1993 • Wang & Mason, 1999

Table Continues

TABLE 12.1
(Continued)

Element	Description	Examples	Sample References
Psychological vulnerability	Deficient and inappropriate behavioral repertoires in each of three domains (i.e., emotional–motivational, language–cognitive, sensory–motor)	Emotional–motivational: • Intense physiological arousal in presence of event-related stimuli • Hypervigilance for event-related cues Language–cognitive: • Selective attention to threat cues • Problem-solving deficits Sensory–motor: • Avoiding event-related stimuli and situations • Deficient social skills and social support–seeking behaviors	• Difede & Barocas, 1999
Present symptomatic responses	The symptomatic responses (potentially diagnosable as a disorder) that result from the interactions, over time, of the critical elements in the model	Emotional–motivational: • Hyperarousal, inability to relax, and irritability • Loss of interest and emotional numbing • Fears and phobias Language–cognitive: • Reexperiencing (intrusive thoughts, nightmares) • Concentration difficulties • Avoiding discussion of the event Sensory-motor: • Restlessness • Active avoidance behavior (e.g., refusing to ride in cars or buses) • Avoiding peers and friends	• Perrin, Smith, & Yule, 2000

Marcy and Lucien experienced the same traumatic event—the rollover of their vehicle—but from somewhat different perspectives and with rather different immediate outcomes. Lucien, the driver, was hospitalized, in a coma, and near death for several weeks. Upon recovery from the coma, he had no memory of the accident and experienced significant cognitive and motor deficits due to traumatic brain injury (i.e., acquired or learned biological vulnerability). Marcy, however, was conscious during the entire event and experienced significant physical pain both while awaiting emergency medical assistance and during the recovery from multiple surgeries on her hand and related physical therapy. Lucien felt a sense of guilt and responsibility for the accident that interacted with the fact that he could not recall it. Thus, he felt oddly in the situation of being responsible for something that he could not recall doing. Marcy recalled the event all too vividly, including Lucien's role in causing the accident, and was intensely angry and blaming. In essence then, key aspects of the same accident (i.e., accident-related stimuli, type and extent of injury, blame, and guilt) were experienced quite differently by this brother and sister.

As a result of the different views of the same event and different types of injury, the stage was set for rather different outcomes. Lucien slowly recovered cognitive and motor functioning; he was able to return to school and attain a grade point average similar to that which he had prior to the accident. He did require the use of new learning strategies and found himself experiencing concentration difficulties (which appeared to be more related to traumatic brain injury than to PTSD), but the strategies were working for him. He returned to driving without any problem, once declared medically able to do so, and was not bothered by any reminders of the event. In fact, other than his interactions with Marcy, he gave the accident little to no thought at all. Marcy, in comparison, was highly phobic of riding in a car and reported high autonomic arousal much of the time, particularly in response to event-related stimuli, for which she was hypervigilant. It was soon evident that Marcy met criteria for PTSD as well as major depression. Marcy, as opposed to Lucien, withdrew from her family and peer-support network and was irritable when people attempted to draw her out of this isolation. Lucien was older and more mature and took an active, "problem-focused" approach to resolving the issues resulting from the accident. Marcy was younger, less skilled in general problem solving, and relatively "emotion-focused" in terms of coping skills. Thus, her isolation and being overwhelmed with reminders of the event left her feeling increasingly depressed and helpless to remediate the situation. She had difficulty returning to school—travel to school was a major barrier—and was quickly falling behind in her work.

In this way, components of the paradigmatic model (present situation, acquired or learned biological vulnerability, and psychological vulnerability) were interacting with historical and unlearned genetic and biological vulnerabilities to produce the current symptomatic picture, one that differed rather dramatically for the two siblings. Lucien was successfully and positively adjusting to the lingering effects of a traumatic brain injury and had no evidence of a complicating psychological disorder. Marcy, however, demonstrated full-blown PTSD and depression—perhaps more endogenous (i.e., biological) than exogenous (i.e., situational), reflecting the family history of depression). Adding to her difficulties was the need to address her own medical problems and facial disfigurement while entering the highly self-conscious period of puberty. The paradigmatic model was thus able to link a number of important clinical features to form two rather different case conceptualizations for two siblings. Treatment for Lucien focused on cognitive rehabilitation from the effects of traumatic brain injury along with some education targeting how he could support his sister in the face of her anger at him. Marcy's intervention plan had separate medical and psychological components. She required continued medical treatment, including physical therapy and plastic surgery; her psychological therapy focused on imaginal exposure (see Lyons & Scotti, 1995), desensitization to trauma-related stimuli, and the development of additional problem-focused coping skills and strategies for seeking social support. Her family physician prescribed antidepressant medication in consultation with the treating psychologist.

This example thus shows the clinical usefulness of the paradigmatic model in developing a complex analysis that is based on a interactive systems approach (Evans, 1985), a model that can then be "tested" at two critical levels. The first is the usefulness of the analysis in the assessment and treatment of individual cases. At this level, the conceptualization calls for the gathering of specific assessment information and points toward individualized treatments. The success of the intervention is then gauged by repeated assessment; the analysis is adjusted as new information demands, and intervention is redesigned accordingly (Evans, 1985; Haynes & O'Brien, 2000; Scotti & Morris, 2000). The second critical level is in the gathering of data to provide general support for the usefulness of a paradigmatic model in conceptualizing and drawing together what is known about the traumatic impact on children of MVAs. It is to this level that we now turn.

CONSIDERATIONS FOR DEVELOPING A PARADIGMATIC MODEL FOR CHILD MVA SURVIVORS

Table 12.1 refers the reader to what we know from the traumatic stress literature about the multiple elements that link within a paradigmatic model of PTSD. We expect that many elements are the same or highly similar for children involved in MVAs, but perhaps we can let the data speak for themselves. What is likely most critical—and, unfortunately, least researched—is the influence of developmental level and the multitude of interrelated variables that the construct of development subsumes (e.g., education, problem-solving skills, intelligence, language, social relationships, and memory for events) on the response to traumatic MVAs. Thus, our goal is to look at the available data on child survivors of MVAs and begin to outline a number of features that may be important to investigate in further clinical and research efforts. Our framework here is the paradigmatic behavior model, within which we discuss a number of variables in turn, providing data for some and educated speculation for others.

Accident Characteristics

The traumatic event itself is incorporated into the paradigmatic behavioral model within the element in Table 12.1 labeled *accident or trauma learning and characteristics*. The most critical feature of such an event (and the subsequent response) is its severity, even though the most extreme events do not invariably set the stage for traumatic stress symptoms (Carlson, 1997; Davidson & Foa, 1991), as is shown in our case examples. In the case of MVAs, as in other types of events, some critical features of event severity appear to be the extent of injury to self; witnessing the injury or death of others, particularly gruesome death by decapitation or dismemberment; the frequency of such events (i.e., single event vs. a history of multiple accidents); extent of damage to the vehicle(s) and other property; and perceptions of blame. Those categories of event descriptors, among others, are not dissimilar from those found in the general trauma literature (Scotti et al., 1995), and they led our research group to develop a scale for evaluating accident severity. Not surprisingly, the scale contains items that are similar to those found on a well-established scale for exposure to trauma: the Combat Exposure Scale (Keane et al., 1989).

The initial development of the Accident Characteristics Identification Scale (AcCIDentS; Scotti et al., 1992) examined research participants' descriptions of their "worst" accidents using the items found on a standard MVA reporting form. The data were used to identify the items that distinguished between participants on the basis of their level of accident-related symptomatology (Scotti et al., 1992). In initial research with college students (mean age = 22), several key accident characteristics were statistically related to distress, even though, on average, the accident in question had occurred 4 years previously. The features included major irreparable damage to the vehicle; having hit a fixed object (versus another vehicle); having sustained injuries, especially bruises or open wounds; the severity of the injury, as judged by the time needed for healing; the number of other people injured or killed in the accident; and fear of being injured or killed at the time of the accident. Compared with a mild-accident group and a no-accident control group (which did not differ from each other), participants who scored higher on the AcCIDentS (i.e., above the cut-off between "mild" and "severe" accidents) also scored significantly higher on current level of fear of driving, a measure of depression, and three measures of posttraumatic stress symptoms: the Impact of Event Scale (IES; Horowitz, Wilner, & Alvarez, 1979), the Keane PTSD Scale (Keane, Malloy, & Fairbank, 1984; Lyons & Scotti, 1994;

Scotti, Veltum-Sturges, & Lyons, 1996), and the Mississippi Scale (modified for civilian events; Keane, Caddell, & Taylor, 1988; Stamm, 1996).

In subsequent grant-funded research (Scotti et al., 1999; see also Mullen, Annan, Myers, & Scotti, 1997; Mullen, Rode, & Scotti, 1997), our group has used the AcCIDENTS with children ages 7 to 13 in several multidimensional studies of the effects of MVAs. Rode (1997), in a small subsample ($n = 14$) of our study of child MVA survivors, found significant positive correlations between scores on the AcCIDENTS and general and PTSD-specific symptoms on a diagnostic interview; self-report measures of depression and anxiety; total score on the IES, which appears more related to intrusive than avoidant symptoms; and parental self-report of symptoms (Symptom Checklist-90-Revised; Derogatis, 1983). Mullen James (1999), in a separate subsample of 45 children from our larger study, divided 30 accident-exposed children into distressed and nondistressed groups on the basis of IES scores. The distressed children had significantly higher scores than the nondistressed children on the AcCIDENTS as well as higher scores on measures of depression, general anxiety, child behavior problems (both internalizing and externalizing), and fear of riding in cars; they also had more diagnoses of accident-related PTSD. As in Rode (1997), most of the measures of symptomatology also were correlated significantly and positively with increasing accident severity.

Thus, the data from our use of the AcCIDENTS with child and young adult accident survivors provide good evidence that certain features of MVAs can be quantified and shown to be related to symptomatic response, even in cases in which full-blown PTSD may not be evident. Note that we have developed both child and parent versions of the AcCIDENTS, which have good agreement with each other (Mullen James, 1999). In the child version of the AcCIDENTS, we include several line drawings to assist children in completing the rating scales. Blanchard and Hickling (1997) offer a motor vehicle interview that covers a number of the same variables and could be used with parents, but it would need to be modified for use with children.

Aside from the characteristics of a particular accident, it is important to evaluate the number of other accidents and the full range of other traumatic events to which children have been exposed. A wide range of interviews and checklists exists for this purpose (e.g., Stamm, 1996). Evidence suggests that cumulative trauma has a nonlinear relation with psychological and behavioral distress in adults (Annan, Mullen, Scotti, & Morris, 1997; Herman, 1992); little is known about the effects on children of multiple events. Research by Mueser et al. (1998) suggests that the number of different types of trauma, along with a history of childhood sexual abuse, is a strong predictor of PTSD in adults with severe mental illness. With children, Ford et al. (1999) showed a relation between oppositional defiant disorder and a history of victimization trauma (e.g., sexual abuse), but not nonvictimization trauma (e.g., accidents); although Cobb, Cairns, Miles, and Cairns (1995) showed a relation between accidental injury and childhood aggression. The need for further research is clear.

Symptom Assessment in Children

Standard assessments of behavioral, cognitive, and physiological symptoms, both in response to the event in question and otherwise, and various measures of coping skills and interactional styles fall within both the elements of psychological vulnerability and present symptomatic response in the paradigmatic model shown in Table 12.1. Given the general lack of large-group studies with children on MVA-related trauma and the differences in how trauma-related symptoms may emerge in children versus adults, we feel that the present strategy should be to conduct the broadest assessment possible within those areas. Thus, in our clinical and research efforts we have used a range of measures, including the IES, the Child Depression Inventory (Kovacs, 1985), the Children's Manifest Anxiety Scale-Revised (Reynolds & Richmond, 1978), the Child Behavior Checklist (child and parent versions; Achenbach, 1991), and parental and child diagnostic interviews. The utility of this range of assessment devices in the evaluation of the response to MVAs can be seen in our work reported by Rode (1997) and Mullen James (1999), above (see also Stallard, 1999). Note that Ford et al. (2000) observed an overlap between symptoms of attention deficit–hyperactivity disorder and PTSD, notably in hyperarousal and hypervigilance, suggesting the need for careful differential diagnosis.

Of course, it is critical to evaluate a range of posttraumatic stress symptoms, for which a wide variety of scales developed specifically for children are available, as can be seen in the compilation edited by Stamm (1996) and the reviews by Nader (1997), Carlson (1997), and March (1999). A quick review of the child MVA literature shows the IES (or adaptations of it) to be the most consistently used measure of traumatic stress response in children. It should be noted that the original IES includes only avoidant and intrusive symptoms; an updated version (Weiss & Marmar, 1997) includes arousal symptoms, making it more compatible with criteria in the *Diagnostic and Statistical Manual of Mental Disorders, Fourth Edition* (DSM–IV; American Psychiatric Association, 1994). No known uses of the modified IES with child accident survivors exist, however.

Beyond standard psychometric measures, the anxiety and trauma literature also has used direct measures of psychophysiological arousal and selective attention to threat-related stimuli. We next turn to a discussion of those means of assessment with child accident survivors.

Clinical Stroop Task

The original Stroop (1935) color-naming task involved participants naming—as accurately and quickly as they could—the five different colors in which a set of five color names were printed on cards; the color of the ink and the color name were different (e.g., when seeing the word "blue" printed in red ink, the participant would say "red"). In the clinical Stroop task, fear- or trauma-relevant words are printed in different colors; the participant is to ignore the word and say the color. The clinical Stroop task has been used in a number of studies of anxiety and traumatic stress with adults (e.g., Foa, Feske, Murdock, Kozak, & McCarthy, 1991; Mathews & MacLeod, 1985; McNally, Kaspi, Riemann, & Zeitlin, 1990). The consistent outcome of clinical Stroop studies is the significantly longer response times to color-name trauma-relevant words by people who are both trauma-exposed and distressed (i.e., trauma survivors with PTSD versus trauma survivors without PTSD and nontraumatized control participants). This *Stroop effect* is typically explained in terms of information processing or selective attention, but it may be more parsimoniously conceptualized as behavioral disruption resulting from conditioned emotional responses (Mullen James, 1999; Scotti, 1992).

The Stroop effect has been demonstrated with children (Green & McKenna, 1993; Kindt, Brosschot, & Everaerd, 1997; Martin, Horder, & Jones, 1992), but to our knowledge it has not been attempted with child trauma survivors until recently. In our research program, Mullen James (1999) reported on our use of a clinical Stroop task in which we presented four groups of words: (a) MVA-related words (e.g., "crash"); (b) school stress-related words (e.g., "test"); (c) neutral household-related words (e.g., "kitchen"); and (d) the standard control stimuli of colored Xs (i.e., XXXXX). Children who had been in relatively severe accidents (as determined by the ACCIDENTS) showed the expected Stroop effect, in which color-naming times were longer for accident-related words than any other word category. In working with children, it is critically important to be aware that the Stroop effect is related to reading level (Horn & Manis, 1987); only children reading at or above the fourth-grade level demonstrated the effect in our work. This grade-level effect is likely due to the acquisition of reading fluency and the over-learning of the reading response by that grade level (Mullen James, 1999).

At the present time, the clinical Stroop task is primarily a research instrument, rather than a clinical assessment device. We conducted a pre- and post-Stroop assessment with one of our clients (Robbie, described above), however, and found a decrease in the Stroop effect (i.e., faster and more accurate naming of the colors, despite the accident-related content of the words) following treatment. Of course, this single-case example needs to be evaluated with due caution.

Psychophysiological Assessment

Unlike the adult literature on MVAs, which largely comes from the work of Blanchard and colleagues (see Blanchard & Hickling, 1997), we have not come across any psychophysiological assessment studies of child accident survivors (see also Klorman, 2000). The studies by Mullen James

(1999) and Rode (1997) are embedded within our grant-funded project that is looking at the multimodal assessment of children involved in accidents, which includes our measure of accident severity, standard self-report and interview measures of distress, a laboratory measure of behavioral disruption (i.e., the clinical Stroop task), and psychophysiological measures (i.e., heart rate and skin conductance). We have measured psychophysiological reactivity in response to audiotaped vignettes (i.e., accident, school-stress, and neutral scenes). Unfortunately, the data are still under analysis and cannot be reported at this time (Scotti et al., 1999). Our accumulating experience with this method indicates that it is generally feasible in the assessment of child accident survivors. We have found that young children, however, have rather more difficulty not only remaining sufficiently still for the assessment but staying seated for the requisite baseline and stimulus phases of the evaluation, despite our making the phases less than 5 minutes in duration. Although it is presently a research tool, it might eventually be possible for clinicians to conduct pre- and posttreatment assessment with such methods or even to monitor physiological arousal during imaginal or in vivo exposure treatment sessions using the newest highly portable monitoring equipment.

Developmental Issues

The case examples above demonstrate the age range that is included when one refers to "child" MVA survivors. Although not a numerically large range (birth to age 21), the developmental differences that must be considered within both the original learning and psychological vulnerability elements of the model are enormous and well beyond the scope of this chapter. A few of these developmental issues, however, bear mentioning.

The first issue includes the usual considerations when evaluating and treating children: developmental norms, the contexts within which presenting problems occur, the reliability and validity of assessment devices across different age groups as well as the agreement of parent and child reports, and consideration of whether the client is the child or the parent (Scotti & Morris, 2000).

A second consideration, particularly in forthcoming research on child MVA survivors, is models of developmental psychopathology. Popper, Ross, and Jennings (2000) discuss three ways to approach psychopathology from a developmental perspective: (a) deviations from age-appropriate norms, which is the most typical approach taken to date; (b) exaggerations of typical development; and (c) behavior that is pathological because it interferes with typical development (i.e., social, intellectual, academic, etc.). The latter two views are likely to be most relevant to the response to trauma, and the third is of the greatest concern—and the greatest unknown—for child MVA survivors (see Pynoos, Steinberg, & Goenjian, 1996).

We have found it important to consider two other issues with child survivors: memory of the event and bereavement, as described in the following sections.

Memory of the Event

The case of Charley and Nathan illustrates how a young child may report not having any memory of an MVA that they are known to have experienced. Of course, one can only judge the child's memory by what he or she verbally reports. Of interest, however, is how Charley exhibited symptoms similar to those of his older brother when in the presence of both his brother and mother. One might ask, "Does this behavior reflect event-associated remembering or the modeling of his brother's behavior, which appeared to be dependent on the presence of the mother (as opposed to the father)?" Alternatively, does one need to be able to describe events verbally to be affected by them? Pynoos et al. (1996) discussed the differences in the organization and experience of memory in younger versus older children, event narratives, and the issue of "false memory syndrome." The evidence to date suggests that children are likely to remember traumatic events of the severity typically encountered in MVAs, that older children are somewhat better at recall than younger children, and that recall and accuracy diminish over time, as with any memory (Peterson, 1999; Peterson & Rideout, 1998; see also Elliott, 1997). This developmental issue likely interacts with the characteristics of the event and subsequent psychological vulnerabilities and symptom presentation. For example, Bahrick, Parker, Fivush, and Levitt (1998) found that 3-year-old children recalled less than 4-year-old children about their experience of Hurricane Andrew and that children who had a moderate level of exposure to the storm recalled more details about their experience of the hurricane than did children with either high or low exposure levels.

Bereavement

The issue of bereavement is barely covered in the case of adult survivors of accidents (Lehman, Lang, Wortman, & Sorenson, 1989; Lehman, Wortman, & Williams, 1987) and is even less so with children (see Lehman et al., 1989; Yule, 1999), despite its importance in elements of our model, such as psychological vulnerability (e.g., depression) and present situational factors (e.g., social and familial support). We include bereavement under a discussion of developmental issues because of the likely differences in the responses of children (versus adults) to the death of a family member and the complications to further development that are created by the death of a parent.

What we have seen clinically is typified by the avoidant responses seen in the case of Sammy and Pammy, where no one, child or adult, wanted to discuss the deceased for fear of upsetting the other. It became clear in our work with this case that both sides needed to discuss the death of their loved ones. Thus, conceptualizing the issue within an exposure model, the successful course of therapy consisted of having the parties bring memorabilia to the session and discuss their fond memories of the children's parents. Contrary to the expectations of the adults, this approach appeared related to improved child behavior (i.e., the children became less clingy and separation anxious). The adults admitted to benefits for themselves as well.

Family, Cultural, and Ethnic Factors

We simply do not know much about the relation between various aspects of culture and ethnicity and the impact of trauma in general (see chapter 4, this volume), let alone in the case of MVAs. Two recent comprehensive texts entirely devoted to research on MVAs (Blanchard & Hickling, 1997; Hickling & Blanchard, 1999) and heavily focused on adult survivors scarcely mention cultural and ethnic differences and familial factors.

The cases of Robbie and of Charley and Nathan illustrate some of the difficulty that begins to ensue when considering ethnic and cultural differences, particularly on a case-by-case basis. Some authors (Dana, 1993; Sue, Bingham, Porché-Burke, &Vasquez, 1999) note the differences in spirituality and general worldview across cultures and ethnicity. One temptation, then, is to begin to think that the religiosity of Robbie's family was related to their African American ethnic tradition, when it may be more related to the traditional Appalachian culture in which they lived (Mulder et al., 1994). In either case, their spirituality needed to be incorporated into our treatment efforts (e.g., rather than reinforcing the passive view of "leaving it up to God to solve their problems," giving them an active view of "God helps those who help themselves"). The spirituality and cohesiveness of Robbie's family was in stark contrast to the apparent lack of those features in Charley and Nathan's family. These cases raise the issue that it may be as problematic to assume the presence of certain cultural features on the basis of apparent ethnicity as it is to ignore them; either error is an overgeneralization that may stem from "ethnocentric monoculturalism" (Sue et al., 1999). It is thus important to consider such features but to do so within a flexible framework such as the one proposed here (see also Evans & Paewai, 1999; chapter 4, this volume). We also need to be aware that we know virtually nothing about the variability in the response to trauma across various cultures; it may be that certain symptoms are differentially expressed according to what is considered normal and abnormal within that culture (see Rabalais, Scotti, & Larkin, 2000; Scotti & Morris, 2000).

The cases of Robbie, Brandon, and Charley and Nathan also demonstrate differences in the level of family cohesion, or support, a factor that may affect the response to events. Consider the cases of Sammy and Pammy, whose parents died in an MVA. Subsequently, the young children were raised by relatives who themselves were having difficulty discussing the death of the parents, negatively affecting support for the children and their resolution of the event. As Garmezy and Rutter (1983) demonstrated, the family environment can have both protective and damaging effects on children's responses to stressful life events. Watson and Gross (2000) summarized the multiple factors that come under the heading of "family determinants," including issues of defining the family unit in present society, parenting styles and attachment, parental psychopathology, separation and divorce, homelessness, and socioeconomic status. Although preliminary results from Rode (1997) suggested a relation between parental self-report of pathology, several child measures of distress, and the child's rating of accident severity, and between measures of family cohesion and support and child distress, we know little about the role of family in the response of children to MVAs. One need only consider the cases of Brandon and Danielle to see the complex interrelations of those variables, which fall into several elements of the paradigmatic behavioral model, including original learning, present situation, and present symptomatic responses.

Acquired Biological Vulnerability

The evidence has been accumulating for some years in the adult trauma literature as to the biological and neurological changes that ensue following trauma, especially repeated trauma (see Freedy & Hobfoll, 1995; van der Kolk, McFarlane, & Weisaeth, 1996; van der Kolk & Saporta, 1993). Many PTSD symptoms have been linked to various brain structures (e.g., the *locus coeruleus*), neurotransmitters, and hormones (e.g., noradrenaline and adrenocorticotropin), findings that have multiple implications for psychopharmacological treatment. The effects of biological responses to stress on the developing brains of young children at various developmental stages is poorly understood (Pynoos et al., 1996). Studies suggest, however, that trauma early in the life cycle has "long-term effects on the neurochemical response to stress" (van der Kolk & Saporta, 1993, p. 27). It is completely unknown how this effect may show itself in the behavior of children, particularly in response to single but potentially severe stressors, such as an MVA, compared with repeated trauma, such as child sexual abuse. The potential exists for a cascading effect, in which elevated levels of arousal are related to a range of disorders, including anxiety, hyperactivity, and conduct, that may detrimentally affect academic achievement, social skill development, and a host of related skills and outcomes. Thus, for children, this element of the paradigmatic model (i.e., acquired or learned biological vulnerability) has implications for other aspects, including psychological vulnerability and present symptomatic responses.

Traumatic Head Injury

The case of Lucien illustrates the effect of head injury, the most obvious of acquired biological vulnerabilities, on child survivors of MVAs. An interesting predicament in the case of MVA trauma is that the symptoms of head injury overlap to a fairly high degree with those of PTSD, including memory problems, difficulties with attention and concentration, emotional lability, irritability and disinhibition, loss of interest, social avoidance, insomnia, depression, anxiety, and fatigue (Davidoff, Laibstain, Kessler, & Mark, 1988; Horton, 1993; Jacobson, 1999; Scotti et al., 1992). The time course is likely to differ for the two conditions. The symptoms of mild postconcussive head injury may onset quickly and be relatively brief in duration (i.e., within hours or days of the event and lasting weeks to months), while the clinical picture for PTSD—by definition—onsets after several months and may last for years. In the case of severe head injury, however, the differences can become blurred (Davidoff et al., 1988). Thus, it is highly advisable that clinicians treating MVA survivors ensure that a medical evaluation for head injury has been completed, especially when any physical trauma to the head has been reported.

In the case of Lucien, the head injury resulted in a lack of memory (postconcussive amnesia) for the event, and therefore, a lack of the necessary condition for PTSD (although this is a debated point; Jacobson, 1999). This memory loss would seem to be a source of relief for the accident survivor, yet in many cases, the lack of memory for an event is a grave source of distress. Head injury often implies brain damage, so another complicating factor is ensuring a proper neuropsychological evaluation that leads to a rehabilitation plan for overcoming or accommodating any continuing cognitive and motor deficits. Although the effects of severe head trauma are self-evident, it is still debated as to whether milder head injury has a lasting negative impact on children (Satz et al., 1997).

Behavioral Contingencies

Typical case presentations reveal the role of event-related stimuli (e.g., cars, smell of gasoline, similar weather, sudden movement, or loud sounds; see the present situational factors category in Table 12.1) in eliciting arousal and maintaining escape and avoidance behavior. Several of our clinical case illustrations demonstrate how MVA-precipitated anxious responding also can come under the control of behavioral contingencies unrelated to the MVA (i.e., present symptomatic responses). In the case of Robbie, we presumed that the onset of several anxiety responses (e.g., hypervigilant behavior in cars and requests for mother to exhibit "safer" driving behavior) coincided with the occurrence of the MVA. In-session observations, however, additionally suggested that maternal attention generally functioned as a reinforcer for Robbie's behavior under a variety of circumstances. Thus, although it is likely that post-MVA instances of anxious responding in cars initially were maintained by negative reinforcement through escape from MVA-related cues, maternal attention that fairly reliably followed those responses likely contributed to the maintenance of the symptoms through positive reinforcement. If treatment services had not been accessed, it is plausible that these and other forms of apparently anxious behavior eventually may have come fully under the control of positively reinforcing events (e.g., maternal attention). For those reasons, we attributed Robbie's symptom reduction over the course of treatment to the combined effects of escape extinction (i.e., a lack of opportunity to escape MVA-related cues), extinction (i.e., withholding maternal attention by ignoring anxious responses), and differential reinforcement of alternative behavior (i.e., maternal attention contingent upon nonanxious behavior in the presence of MVA-related cues).

The case of Charley and Nathan further illustrates the potential role that behavioral contingencies unrelated to the event may have on children's responses to a potentially traumatic MVA. With the two brothers, initial inspection of the presenting concerns and the contextual factors that predicted anxiety-related responding (e.g., mother vs. father driving) led to hypotheses similar to those in the case of Robbie. For instance, the reported absence of child "distress" when the father was driving may have reflected a lack of trauma-relevant cues to which the children might otherwise respond (i.e., mother or rain), or it may have been indicative of a history of paternally implemented punishing contingencies in response to behavior that is not "quiet." Thus, the children's apparent lack of distress in the presence of their father may reflect an instance of rule following rather than an absence of trauma-relevant responding. Clearly, it is important for clinicians to assess circumstances under which a child's behavior may come under the control of behavioral contingencies *unrelated* to the MVA. As with the examples presented here, the effects of such contingencies may aid in the persistence of trauma-relevant responding, or they may obscure (as in the case of parent-implemented punishment for trauma-related distress) the identification of MVA-related cues that are critical for appropriate case conceptualization.

Legal Issues

Blanchard and Hickling (1997) and Hickling and Blanchard (1999) cover well the legal issues that coincide with MVAs, including insurance, lawsuits, and malingering. Although largely an issue for adults, children can be drawn into legal matters, partly as witnesses to the event, but mostly as compensable victims (see Mitrany, 1993). Although less likely to occur in a deliberate manner, children may "malinger" for the secondary effects that ensue, as in our discussion of the case of Robbie. It also is possible that they may be encouraged to "elaborate" on their symptoms by parents involved in lawsuits (or custody battles, as in Brandon's case). Thus, it is important to evaluate the ongoing nature of any legal issues and to spend some time alone with a child survivor of an MVA to evaluate his or her report in the absence of the child's parents. The case of Brandon illustrates a complicating issue for children. We were asked to evaluate for the effects of his accident and testify about our findings in court during a divorce and custody battle. In his case, no effects were apparent, but consider the conflict encountered by a child who is experiencing distress and whose report of it determines which parent he or she may live with, a predicament reminiscent of cases of child abuse. Such issues fall within elements of the model that describe symptomatic responses and situational factors.

APPLYING THE PARADIGMATIC BEHAVIORAL MODEL IN TREATMENT

The outcome of a comprehensive paradigmatic behavioral conceptualization, such as the one presented in this chapter, should be the linking of elements that point toward effective treatment strategies for individual cases. Trauma-exposed youth may express a variety of concerns upon presentation for treatment (i.e., the present symptomatic responses). Those concerns primarily include symptoms of anxiety, depression, and PTSD (Yule, 1998), but they also may coincide with several other forms of psychopathology (Perrin, Smith, & Yule, 2000). For this reason, comprehensive assessment, as we have described here (e.g., functional assessment; administration of broadband rating-scale instruments; diagnostic interviews; and more intensive forms of evaluation, such as the clinical Stroop task and psychophysiological assessment), is recommended to facilitate treatment selection. Once practitioners move beyond assessment, however, the underdeveloped trauma-relevant treatment-outcome literature offers little information pertaining to empirically supported interventions that are effective with children (Ruggiero, Morris, & Scotti, 2001). Although some controlled clinical trials have been conducted with trauma-exposed youth (e.g., Cohen & Mannarino, 1996), few have targeted populations other than sexually abused children, and no studies with randomized control groups have targeted the symptoms of PTSD (Ruggiero et al., 2001).

Three open trials represent the highest level of methodological rigor currently available in the child-focused treatment-outcome literature. Trauma-relevant criteria for inclusion differed across the studies, which included recruitment of children exposed to sexual abuse (Deblinger, McLeer, & Henry, 1990), an earthquake (Goenjian et al., 1997), and a range of single-incident stressors (March, Amaya-Jackson, Murray, & Schulte, 1998). Each open trial offered preliminary support for the efficacy of cognitive–behavioral interventions with trauma-exposed youth. Such interventions typically include various anxiety-management techniques (e.g., relaxation exercises, education, and role plays) and exposure-based procedures (e.g., in vivo and imaginal or verbal exposure in the form of systematic desensitization, graduated exposure, or flooding). To date, the efficacy of nonbehavioral (e.g., psychodynamic and hypnotherapeutic) forms of psychosocial treatment for children has not been assessed with research of adequate methodological rigor (Ruggiero et al., 2001). Before implementing any form of treatment with trauma-exposed children, mental health professionals should consider a variety of factors, particularly developmental variables (Pynoos, 1993) and ethical issues (Saigh, Yasik, Oberfield, & Inamdar, 1999), along with the range of issues that we have raised here.

A number of single-case treatment reports have described success with a range of strategies with MVA survivors:

- Age-appropriate exposure through play therapy along with distraction and redirection techniques with a 3-year-old girl (Jones & Peterson, 1993);
- Fluoxetine with a 2.5-year-old girl with a specific fear of cars (Avci, Diler, & Tamam, 1998);
- Guided fantasy (imagery) and relaxation in the context of family therapy with an 8-year-old female survivor of two accidents (Stedman & Murphey, 1984);
- Parent-implemented in vivo deconditioning of a fear of loud noises with a 3-year-old girl following an MVA (Stableford, 1979); and
- Eye movement desensitization and reprocessing (EMDR) with two boys, ages 7 and 12 (Yule, 1999).

We also note the recent development of virtual reality–based exposure (Rothbaum, Hodges, & Smith, 1999), which has been shown to be useful with adults with fears of flying or driving. The potential here for use with children is enormous, both for the ability to control the presentation of stimuli while maintaining safety and the likely high interest of children in a computer-based intervention.

With regard to the clinical cases introduced earlier, attempts were made to use conceptually sound and empirically supported interventions. Additionally, treatment selection was informed by various levels of assessment (see Hawkins, 1979). For instance, in the case of Robbie, administration of a structured interview and rating-scale instruments was followed by a functional assessment that facilitated the identification of MVA-relevant anxiety-eliciting cues as well as behavioral contingencies (e.g., maternal attention) that potentially maintained anxiety-related responding. In particular, functional assessment results led us to piece together an intervention package that focused on the extinction of anxious responding in the presence of relevant cues (e.g., riding in the car), punishment (through maternal ignoring) of anxious responding that may have served an attention-seeking function, and positive reinforcement (e.g., maternal praise) for nonanxious behavior. Gradual in vivo exposure to MVA-related stimuli was used for purposes of extinction, including having Robbie engage in deep-breathing relaxation and self-distraction (e.g., toy play and drawing) while riding in the family car. Additionally, age-appropriate supplemental forms of exposure were used with Robbie, including drawing the accident scene and recreating the scene with toy cars and action figures. Finally, we used parent training in behavior management skills to promote the use of punishment and positive reinforcement to facilitate further behavior change. Taken together, use of the interventions appeared related to significant reductions in reported anxiety-related responding. At 6 months post-intervention, Robbie continued to be free of problems related to traveling in cars.

CONCLUSIONS

We hope that this chapter has not only served to highlight the sparseness of research on child survivors of MVAs but also has pointed to key directions that the developing empirical literature might take. We have conceptualized the needed work within a paradigmatic behavioral model as a way to provide a framework within which to unite seemingly disparate elements of the research and clinical efforts that are needed. Such a model can link efforts in the areas of developmental psychopathology, event characteristics, culture and ethnicity, and biological factors (unlearned and acquired), among others, such that each holds relevance to the others. Given the paucity of existing research, the paradigmatic behavioral model also equips the practicing clinician with a framework for an individual case conceptualization by aiding in the consideration of the multiple issues that may be relevant with a given child.

One direction that we hope further research and clinical efforts might take is the early identification and treatment of children who have been in accidents and are at risk for developing a range of problems. Such an effort has been one goal of the work in our research group, which is focusing on the development of the ACCIDENTS and using it to predict outcomes. Completion of such work might allow for easy risk screening that is based on accident and family characteristics and could direct at-risk children into preventive treatment programs. The field as a whole has some distance to travel before reaching that point and, indeed, before successfully identifying and treating children who already need such services. The next few years promise an exponential increase in such efforts.

REFERENCES

Achenbach, T. M. (1991). *Manual for the Child Behavior Checklist/4-18 and 1991 profile*. Burlington: University of Vermont, Department of Psychiatry.

American Psychiatric Association. (1994). *Diagnostic and statistical manual of mental disorders* (4th ed.). Washington, DC: Author.

Annan, S. L., Mullen, K. B., Scotti, J. R., & Morris, T. L. (1997, November). *Cumulative effects of traumatic events on PTSD: Results from a community sample*. Poster presented at the 31st annual convention of the Association for Advancement of Behavior Therapy, Miami Beach, FL.

Avci, A., Diler, R. S., & Tamam, L. (1998). Fluoxetine treatment in a 2.5-year-old girl. *Journal of the American Academy of Child and Adolescent Psychiatry, 37*, 901–902.

Bahrick, L. E., Parker, J. F., Fivush, R., & Levitt, M. (1998). The effects of stress on young children's memory for a natural disaster. *Journal of Experimental Psychology: Applied, 4*, 308–331.

Blanchard, E. B., & Hickling, E. J. (1997). *After the crash: Assessment and treatment of motor vehicle accident survivors*. Washington, DC: American Psychological Association.

Bramsen, I., Dirkzwager, A. J. E., & van der Ploeg, H. M. (2000). Predeployment personality traits and exposure to trauma as predictors of posttraumatic stress symptoms: A prospective study of former peacekeepers. *American Journal of Psychiatry, 157*, 1115–1119.

Canterbury, R., & Yule, W. (1997). The effects in children of road accidents. In M. Mitchel (Ed.), *The aftermath of road accidents: Psychological, social, and legal consequences of an everyday trauma* (pp. 375–387). London, UK: Routledge.

Carlson, E. B. (1997). *Trauma assessments: A clinician's guide*. New York: Guilford Press.

Casswell, G. (1997). Learning from the aftermath: The responses of mental health workers to a school-bus crash. *Clinical Child Psychology and Psychiatry, 2*, 517–523.

Chambless, D. L., Baker, M. J., Baucom, D. H., Beutler, L. E., Calhoun, K. S., Crits-Cristoph, P., Daiuto, A., DeRubeis, R., Detweiler, J., Haaga, D. A. F., Bennett-Johnson, S., McCurry, S., Mueser, K. T., Pope, K. S., Sanderson, W. C., Shoham, V., Stickle, T., Williams, D. A., & Woody, S. R. (1998). Update on empirically validated therapies, II. *The Clinical Psychologist, 51*(1), 3–16.

Cobb, B. K., Cairns, B. D., Miles, M. S., & Cairns, R. B. (1995). A longitudinal study of the role of sociodemographic factors and childhood aggression on adolescent injury and "close calls." *Journal of Adolescent Health, 17*, 381–388.

Cohen, J. A., & Mannarino, A. P. (1996). A treatment outcome study for sexually abused preschool children: Initial findings. *Journal of the American Academy of Child and Adolescent Psychiatry, 35*, 42–50.

Dana, R. H. (1993). *Multicultural assessment perspectives for professional psychology*. Boston: Allyn and Bacon.

Davidoff, D. A., Laibstain, D. F., Kessler, H. R., & Mark, V. H. (1988). Neurobehavioral sequelae of minor head injury: A consideration of post-concussive syndrome versus post-traumatic stress disorder. *Cognitive Rehabilitation*, 6, 8–13.

Davidson, J. R. T., & Foa, E. B. (1991). Diagnostic issues in posttraumatic stress disorder: Considerations for the DSM-IV. *Journal of Abnormal Psychology, 100*, 346–355.

Deblinger, E., McLeer, S. V., & Henry, D. (1990). Cognitive behavioral treatment for sexually abused children suffering post-traumatic stress: Preliminary findings. *Journal of the American Academy of Child and Adolescent Psychiatry, 29*, 747–752.

Deblinger, E., Taub, B., Maedel, A. B., Lippmann, J., & Stauffer, L. B. (1997). Psychosocial factors predicting parent reported symptomatology in sexually abused children. *Journal of Child Sexual Abuse, 6*, 35–49.

Derogatis, L. R. (1983). *SCL-90-R: Administration, scoring and procedures manual-II*. Towson, MD: Clinical Psychometric Research.

Difede, J., & Barocas, D. (1999). Acute intrusive and avoidant PTSD symptoms as predictors of chronic PTSD following burn injury. *Journal of Traumatic Stress, 12*, 363–369.

DiGallo, A., Barton, J., & Parry-Jones, W. L. I. (1997). Road traffic accidents: Early psychological consequences in children and adolescents. *British Journal of Psychiatry, 170*, 358–362.

Eifert, G. H., Beach, B. K., & Wilson, P. H. (1998). Depression: Behavioral principles and implications for treatment and relapse prevention. In J. J. Plaud & G. H. Eifert (Eds.), *From behavior theory to behavior therapy* (pp. 68–97). Needham Heights, MA: Allyn and Bacon.

Eifert, G. H., & Evans, I. M. (Eds.). (1990). *Unifying behavior therapy: Contributions of paradigmatic behaviorism*. New York: Springer.

Elliott, D. M. (1997). Traumatic events: Prevalence and delayed recall in the general population. *Journal of Consulting and Clinical Psychology, 65*, 811–820.

Ellis, A., Stores, G., & Mayou, R. (1998). Psychological consequences of road traffic accidents in children. *European Child and Adolescent Psychiatry, 7*, 61–68.

Evans, I. M. (1985). Building systems models as a strategy for target behavior selection in clinical assessment. *Behavioral Assessment, 7*, 21–32.

Evans, I. M., & Paewai, M. K. (1999). Functional analysis in a bicultural context. *Behaviour Change, 16*, 20–36.

Foa, E. B., Feske, U., Murdock, T. B., Kozak, M. J., & McCarthy, P. R. (1991). Processing of threat-related information in rape-victims. *Journal of Abnormal Psychology, 100*, 156–162.

Foa, E. B., Zinbarg, R., & Rothbaum, B. O. (1992). Uncontrollability and unpredictability in post-traumatic stress disorder: An animal model. *Psychological Bulletin, 112*, 218–238.

Ford, J. D., Racusin, R., Daviss, W. B., Ellis, C. G., Thomas, J., Rogers, K., Reiser, J., Schiffman, J., & Sengupta, A. (1999). Trauma exposure among children with oppositional defiant disorder and attention deficit-hyperactivity disorder. *Journal of Consulting and Clinical Psychology, 67,* 786–789.

Ford, J. D., Racusin, R., Ellis, C. G., Daviss, W. B., Reiser, J., Fleischer, A., & Thomas, J. (2000). Child maltreatment, other trauma exposure and posttraumatic symptomatology among children with oppositional defiant and attention deficit hyperactivity disorders. *Child Maltreatment: Journal of the American Professional Society on the Abuse of Children, 5,* 205–217.

Freedy, J. R., & Donkervoet, J. C. (1995). Traumatic stress: An overview of the field. In J. R. Freedy & S. E. Hobfoll (Eds.), *Traumatic stress: From theory to practice* (pp. 3–28). New York: Plenum Press.

Freedy, J. R., & Hobfoll, S. E. (Eds.). (1995). *Traumatic stress: From theory to practice.* New York: Plenum Press.

Garmezy, N., & Rutter, M. (1983). *Stress, coping, and development in children.* New York: McGraw-Hill.

Goenjian, A. K., Karayan, I., Pynoos, R. S., Minassian, D., Najarian, L. M., Steinberg, A. M., & Fairbanks, L. A. (1997). Outcome of psychotherapy among early adolescents after trauma. *American Journal of Psychiatry, 154,* 536–542.

Green, M., & McKenna, F. P. (1993). Developmental onset of eating related color-naming interference. *International Journal of Eating Disorders, 13,* 391–397.

Hagopian, L. P., & Slifer, K. J. (1993). Treatment of separation anxiety disorder with graduated exposure and reinforcement targeting school attendance: A controlled case study. *Journal of Anxiety Disorders, 7,* 271–280.

Harvey, A. G., & Bryant, R. A. (1999). Predictors of acute stress following motor vehicle accidents. *Journal of Traumatic Stress, 12,* 519–525.

Hawkins, R. P. (1979). The functions of assessment: Implications for selection and development of devices for assessing repertoires in clinical, educational, and other settings. *Journal of Applied Behavior Analysis, 12,* 501–516.

Haynes, S. N., & O'Brien, W. H. (2000). *Principles and practice of behavioral assessment.* New York: Kluwer Academic/Plenum Press.

Herman, J. K. (1992). Complex PTSD: A syndrome in survivors of prolonged and repeated trauma. *Journal of Traumatic Stress, 5,* 377–391.

Hickling, E. J., & Blanchard, E. B. (Eds.). (1999). *Road traffic accidents and psychological trauma: Current understanding, treatment, and law.* Oxford, UK: Elsevier.

Horn, C. C., & Manis, F. (1987). Development of automatic and speeded reading of printed words. *Journal of Experimental Child Psychology, 44,* 92–108.

Horowitz, M. J., Wilner, N., & Alvarez, W. (1979). Impact of Event Scale: A measure of subjective distress. *Psychosomatic Medicine, 41,* 209–218.

Horton, A. M., Jr. (1993). Posttraumatic stress disorder and mild head trauma: Follow-up of a case study. *Perceptual and Motor Skills, 76,* 243–246.

Jacobson, R. (1999). Road traffic accidents and the mind: The post-concussional syndrome. In E. J. Hickling & E. B. Blanchard (Eds.), *Road traffic accidents and psychological trauma: Current understanding, treatment, and law* (pp. 89–116). Oxford, UK: Elsevier.

Jones, R. W., & Peterson, L. W. (1993). Post traumatic stress disorder in a child following an automobile accident. *Journal of Family Practice, 36,* 223–225.

Keane, T. M., Caddell, J. M., & Taylor, K. L. (1988). Mississippi Scale for Combat-Related Posttraumatic Stress Disorder: Three studies in reliability and validity. *Journal of Consulting and Clinical Psychology, 56,* 85–90.

Keane, T. M., Fairbank, J. A., Caddell, J. M., Zimering, R. T., Taylor, K. L., & Mora, C. A. (1989). Clinical evaluation of a measure to assess combat exposure. *Psychological Assessment: A Journal of Consulting and Clinical Psychology, 1,* 53–55.

Keane, T. M., Malloy, P. F., & Fairbank, J. A. (1984). Empirical development of an MMPI subscale for the assessment of combat-related posttraumatic stress disorder. *Journal of Consulting and Clinical Psychology, 52,* 888–891.

Kindt, M., Brosschot, J. F., & Everaerd, W. (1997). Cognitive processing biases of children in a real life stress condition and a neutral situation. *Journal of Experimental Child Psychology, 64,* 79–97.

Klorman, R. (2000). Psychophysiological research on childhood psychopathology. In M. Hersen & R. T. Ammerman (Eds.), *Advanced abnormal child psychology* (2nd ed., pp. 57–80). Hillsdale, NJ: Lawrence Erlbaum.

Kovacs, M. (1985). The Children's Depression Inventory (CDI). *Psychopharmacological Bulletin, 21,* 995–998.

La Greca, A. M., Silverman, W. K., & Wasserstein, S. B. (1998). Children's predisaster functioning as a predictor of posttraumatic stress following Hurricane Andrew. *Journal of Consulting and Clinical Psychology, 66,* 883–892.

Lehman, D. R., Lang, E. L., Wortman, C. B., & Sorenson, S. B. (1989). Long-term effects of sudden bereavement: Marital and parent-child relationships and children's reactions. *Journal of Family Psychology, 2,* 344–367.

Lehman, D. R., Wortman, C. B., & Williams, A. F. (1987). Long-term effects of losing a child or spouse in a motor vehicle crash. *Journal of Personality and Social Psychology, 52,* 218–231.

Lyons, J. A., & Scotti, J. R. (1994). Comparability of two administration formats of the Keane Posttraumatic Stress Disorder Scale. *Psychological Assessment, 6,* 209–211.

Lyons, J. A., & Scotti, J. R. (1995). Behavioral treatment of a motor vehicle accident survivor: An illustrative case of direct therapeutic exposure. *Cognitive and Behavioral Practice, 2,* 343–364.

March, J. S. (1999). Assessment of pediatric posttraumatic stress disorder. In P. A. Saigh & J. D. Bremner (Eds.), *Posttraumatic stress disorder: A comprehensive text* (pp. 199–218). Needham Heights, MA: Allyn and Bacon.

March, J. S., Amaya-Jackson, L., Murray, M. C., & Schulte, A. (1998). Cognitive-behavioral psychotherapy for children and adolescents with posttraumatic stress disorder after a single-incident stressor. *Journal of the American Academy of Child and Adolescent Psychiatry, 37,* 585–593.

Martin, M., & Horder, P., & Jones, G. V. (1992). Integral bias in naming of phobia related words. *Cognition and Emotion, 6,* 479–486.

Mathews, A., & MacLeod, C. (1985). Selective processing of threat cues in anxiety states. *Behaviour Research and Therapy, 23*, 563–569.

McNally, R. J., Kaspi, S. P., Riemann, B. C., & Zeitlin, S. B. (1990). Selective processing of threat cues in posttraumatic stress disorder. *Journal of Abnormal Psychology, 99*, 398–402.

Milgram, N. A., Toubiana, Y. H., Klingman, A., Raviv, A., & Goldstein, I. (1988). Situational exposure and personal loss in children's acute and chronic stress reactions to a school bus disaster. *Journal of Traumatic Stress, 1*, 339–352.

Mirza, K. A. H., Bhadrinath, B. R., Goodyer, I. M., & Gilmour, C. (1998). Posttraumatic stress disorder in children and adolescents following road traffic accidents. *British Journal of Psychiatry, 172*, 443–447.

Mitrany, E. (1993). The expert opinion of the child and adolescent psychiatrist: A review of 140 lawsuits of minors involved in accidents. *Medicine and Law, 12*, 311–315.

Mueser, K. T., Goodman, L. B., Trumbetta, S. L., Rosenberg, S. D., Osher, F. C., Vidaver, R., Auciello, P., & Foy, D. W. (1998). Trauma and posttraumatic stress disorder in severe mental illness. *Journal of Consulting and Clinical Psychology, 66*, 493–499.

Mulder, P. L., Daugherty, A., Teel, W., Midkiff, J., Murray, K., & Smith, L. (1994). Rural West Virginia: A cross cultural perspective with implications for clinical intervention. *West Virginia Journal of Psychological Research and Practice, 3*, 9–25.

Mullen James, K. (1999). *Measuring behavioral disruption in children who have been in motor vehicle accidents.* Unpublished doctoral dissertation, Department of Psychology, West Virginia University, Morgantown.

Mullen, K. B., Annan, S. L., Myers, M., & Scotti, J. R. (1997, November). *Measuring behavioral disruption in children who have been in motor vehicle accidents: Clinical use of the Stroop task.* Poster presented at the 31st annual convention of the Association for Advancement of Behavior Therapy, Miami Beach, FL.

Mullen, K. B., Rode, C., & Scotti, J. R. (1997, March). Children exposed to MVAs: Assessment of effects. In C. L. Masia & T. L. Morris (Chairs), *Assessment of anxiety disorders in youth: Innovative techniques for comprehensive assessments of anxiety symptomatology.* Symposium presented at the 17th annual convention of the Anxiety Disorders Association of America, New Orleans, LA.

Nader, K. O. (1997). Assessing traumatic experiences in children. In J. P. Wilson & T. M. Keane (Eds.), *Assessing psychological trauma and PTSD* (pp. 291–348). New York: Guilford Press.

National Highway Traffic Safety Administration. (1996). *Traffic safety facts 1996.* Retrieved December 12, 2001, from, http://www.nhtsa.dot.gov/people/ncsa/TSF96Contents.html

Perrin, S., Smith, P., & Yule, W. (2000). Practitioner review: The assessment and treatment of post-traumatic stress disorder in children and adolescents. *Journal of Child Psychology and Psychiatry and Allied Disciplines, 41*, 277–289.

Peterson, C. (1999). Children's memory for medical emergencies: Two years later. *Developmental Psychology, 35*, 1493–1506.

Peterson, C., & Rideout, R. (1998). Memory for medical emergencies experienced by 1- and 2-year-olds. *Developmental Psychology, 34,* 1059–1072.

Popper, S. D., Ross, S., & Jennings, K. D. (2000). Development and psychopathology. In M. Hersen & R. T. Ammerman (Eds.), *Advanced abnormal child psychology* (2nd ed., pp. 47–56). Hillsdale, NJ: Lawrence Erlbaum.

Pynoos, R. S. (1993). Traumatic stress and developmental psychopathology in children and adolescents. In J. M. Oldham, M. B. Riba, & A. Tasman (Eds.), *The American Psychiatric Press review of psychiatry, Vol. 12* (pp. 205–238). Washington DC: American Psychiatric Press.

Pynoos, R. S., Steinberg, A. M., & Goenjian, A. (1996). Traumatic stress in childhood and adolescence: Recent developments and current controversies. In B. van der Kolk, A. C. McFarlane, & L. Weisaeth (Eds.), *Traumatic stress: The effects of overwhelming experience on mind, body, and society* (pp. 331–358). New York: Guilford Press.

Rabalais, A., Scotti, J. R., & Larkin, K. T. (2000). *Assessment and diagnosis of posttraumatic stress disorder in American Indians: Conceptual and methodological issues.* Manuscript submitted for publication.

Reynolds, C. R., & Richmond, B. O. (1978). What I Think and Feel: A revised measure of children's manifest anxiety. *Journal of Abnormal Child Psychology, 6,* 271–280.

Rice, D. P., MacKenzie, E. J., & Associates. (1989). *Cost of injury in the United States: A report to Congress.* San Francisco: University of California, Institute for Health and Aging and The Johns Hopkins University, Injury Prevention Center.

Rode, C. A. (1997). Psychological reactions of children following exposure to motor vehicle accidents. *Dissertation Abstracts International, 58*(05), 2697. (UMI No. 9734403)

Rothbaum, B. O., Hodges, L., & Smith, S. (1999). Virtual reality exposure therapy abbreviated treatment manual: Fear of flying application. *Cognitive and Behavioral Practice, 6,* 234– 244.

Ruggiero, K. J., McLeer, S. V., & Dixon, J. F. (2000). Sexual abuse characteristics associated with survivor psychopathology. *Child Abuse and Neglect, 24,* 951–964.

Ruggiero, K. J., Morris, T. L., & Scotti, J. R. (2001). Treatment for children with posttraumatic stress disorder: Current status and future directions. *Clinical Psychology: Science and Practice, 8,* 210–227.

Saigh, P. A., Yasik, A. E., Oberfield, R. A., & Inamdar, S. C. (1999). Behavioral treatment of child-adolescent posttraumatic stress disorder. In P. A. Saigh & J. D. Bremner (Eds.), *Posttraumatic stress disorder: A comprehensive text* (pp. 354–375). Needham Heights, MA: Allyn & Bacon.

Satz, P., Zaucha, K., Asarnow, R., McCleary, C., Light, R., & Becker, D. (1997). Mild head injury in children and adolescents: A review of studies (1970–1995). *Psychological Bulletin, 122,* 107–131.

Scotti, J. R. (1992). An analysis of several parameters of conditioned fear in combat-related post-traumatic stress disorder: Serial cues, contexts, conditioning trials, and avoidance behaviors. *Dissertation Abstracts International, 53*(2), 1076B–1077B. (UMI No. 9217704)

Scotti, J. R., Beach, B. K., Northrop, L. M. E., Rode, C. A., & Forsyth, J. P. (1995). The psychological impact of accidental injury: A conceptual model for clinicians and researchers. In J. R. Freedy & S. E. Hobfoll (Eds.), *Traumatic stress: From theory to practice* (pp. 181–212). New York: Plenum Press.

Scotti, J. R., & Morris, T. M. (2000). Diagnosis and classification. In M. Hersen & R. T. Ammerman (Eds.), *Advanced abnormal child psychology* (2nd ed., pp. 15–32). Hillsdale, NJ: Lawrence Erlbaum.

Scotti, J. R., Morris, T. L., McNeil, C. B., & Hawkins, R. P. (1996). DSM-IV and disorders of childhood and adolescence: Can structural criteria be functional? *Journal of Consulting and Clinical Psychology, 64*, 1177–1191.

Scotti, J. R., Mullen James, K., & Rode, C. A. (1999). [Children exposed to MVAs: Assessment of effects]. Unpublished raw data.

Scotti, J. R., Veltum-Sturges, L., & Lyons, J. A. (1996). The Keane PTSD Scale extracted from the MMPI: Sensitivity and specificity with Vietnam veterans. *Journal of Traumatic Stress, 9*, 643–650.

Scotti, J. R., Wilhelm, K. L., Northrop, L. M. E., Price, G., Vittimberga, G. L., Ridley, J., Cornell, K., Stukey, G. S., Beach, B. K., Mickey, G. H., & Forsyth, J. (1992, November). *An investigation of post-traumatic stress disorder in vehicular accident survivors.* Poster presented at the 26th annual convention of the Association for Advancement of Behavior Therapy, Boston, MA.

Sosin, D. M., Sacks, J. J., & Sattin, R. W. (1992). Causes of nonfatal injuries in the United States, 1986. *Accident Analysis and Prevention, 24*, 685–687.

Staats, A. W. (1993). Personality theory, abnormal psychology, and psychological measurement: A psychological behaviorism. *Behavior Modification, 17*, 8–42.

Stableford, W. (1979). Parental treatment of a child's noise phobia. *Journal of Behavior Therapy and Experimental Psychiatry, 10*, 159–160.

Stallard, P. (1999). Children and young people: The neglected victims of road traffic accidents. In E. J. Hickling & E. B. Blanchard (Eds.), *Road traffic accidents and psychological trauma: Current understanding, treatment, and law* (pp. 117–127). Oxford, UK: Elsevier.

Stallard, P., & Law, F. (1993). Screening and psychological debriefing of adolescent survivors of life-threatening events. *British Journal of Psychiatry, 163*, 660–665.

Stamm, B. H. (Ed.). (1996). *Measurement of stress, trauma, and adaptation.* Lutherville, MD: Sidran.

Stedman, J. M., & Murphey, J. (1984). Dealing with specific child phobias during the course of family therapy: An alternative to systematic desensitization. *Family Therapy, 11*, 55–60.

Stroop, J. R. (1935). Studies of interference in serial verbal reactions. *Journal of Experimental Psychology, 18*, 643–661.

Sue, D. W., Bingham, R. P., Porché-Burke, L., & Vasquez, M. (1999). The diversification of psychology: A multicultural revolution. *American Psychologist, 54*, 1061–1069.

Thompson, A., McArdle, P., & Dunne, F. (1993). Psychiatric consequences of road traffic accidents: Children may be seriously affected. *British Medical Journal, 307*, 1282–1283.

Tuckman, A. J. (1973). Disasters and mental health intervention. *Community Mental Health Journal, 9*, 151–157.

U.S. Department of Health and Human Services. (1991). *Healthy people 2000: National health promotion and disease prevention objective: Full report with commentary* (DHHS Publication No. PHS 91-50212). Washington, DC: U.S. Government Printing Office.

van der Kolk, B. A., McFarlane, A. C., & Weisaeth, L. (Eds.). (1996). *Traumatic stress: The effects of overwhelming experience on mind, body, and society*. New York: Guilford Press.

van der Kolk, B. A., & Saporta, J. (1993). Biological response to psychic trauma. In J. P. Wilson & B. Raphael (Eds.), *International handbook of traumatic stress syndromes* (pp. 25–33). New York: Plenum Press.

Vernberg, E. M., La Greca, A. M., Silverman, W. K., & Prinstein, M. J. (1996). Prediction of posttraumatic stress symptoms in children after Hurricane Andrew. *Journal of Abnormal Psychology, 105*, 237–248.

Wang, S., & Mason, J. (1999). Elevations of serum T-sub-3 levels and their association with symptoms in World War II veterans with combat-related posttraumatic stress disorder: Replication of findings in Vietnam combat veterans. *Psychosomatic Medicine, 61*, 131–138.

Watson, G. S., & Gross, A. M. (2000). Familial determinants. In M. Hersen & R. T. Ammerman (Eds.), *Advanced abnormal child psychology* (2nd ed., pp. 81–99). Hillsdale, NJ: Lawrence Erlbaum.

Weiss, D. S., & Marmar, C. R. (1997). The Impact of Event Scale-Revised. In J. P. Wilson & T. M. Keane (Eds.), *Assessing psychological trauma and PTSD* (pp. 399–411). New York: Guilford Press.

Westrup, D., Kalish, K. D., & Scotti, J. R. (1997, November). *MVA-related PTSD treated with implosion: Use of the paradigmatic model*. Poster presented at the 31st annual convention of the Association for Advancement of Behavior Therapy, Miami Beach, FL.

Whiffen, V. E., Judd, M. E., & Aube, J. A. (1999). Intimate relationships moderate the association between childhood sexual abuse and depression. *Journal of Interpersonal Violence, 14*, 940–954.

Winje, D., & Ulvik, A. (1998). Long-term outcome of trauma in children: The psychological consequences of a bus accident. *Journal of Child Psychology and Psychiatry and Allied Disciplines, 39*, 635–642.

Yule, W. (1998). Posttraumatic stress disorder in children and its treatment. In T. W. Miller (Ed.), *Children of trauma: Stressful life events and their effects on children and adolescents* (pp. 219–243). Madison, CT: International Universities Press.

Yule, W. (1999). Treatment of PTSD in children following road traffic accidents. In E. J. Hickling & E. B. Blanchard (Eds.), *Road traffic accidents and psychological trauma: Current understanding, treatment, and law* (pp. 375–387). Oxford, UK: Elsevier.

IV

ACTS OF VIOLENCE

ACTS OF VIOLENCE: INTRODUCTION

ANNETTE M. LA GRECA AND WENDY K. SILVERMAN

For at least the past 15 years, violence in the United States has been considered a public health epidemic (U.S. Department of Health and Human Services, 1986). Despite tremendous concern about this epidemic (Cooke & Laub, 1998), it took the tragic April 1999 shooting of 14 students and 1 teacher at Columbine High School in Littleton, Colorado, to move Congress and the Administration to request the first-ever *Surgeon General's Report on Youth Violence* (U.S. Public Health Service [PHS], 2000). This report describes youth violence as a "high-visibility, high-priority concern in every sector of U.S. society. No community, whether affluent or poor, urban, suburban, or rural, is immune from its devastating effects" (p. 1). The report focuses on the scope of the problem of violence, its causes, and how to prevent it.

As is apparent from the Surgeon General's report (PHS, 2000), many children and adolescents in the United States and around the world are witnesses to or victims of acts of violence. In addition to this serious concern, children and adolescents may be affected by violence resulting from terrorism or war. Part IV, the last section of this volume, turns to "disasters" of violence: sniper shootings, hostage takings, terrorism, war, and community violence. All of these situations have the potential to cause serious injury and death and often involve violent bereavement—that is, the sudden and unexpected loss of loved ones through acts of violence.

Violence-related disasters have been consistently linked to posttraumatic stress disorder (PTSD) and related symptoms in children, adolescents, and adults. In fact, it was the war-related trauma evidenced by Vietnam War veterans that led to the inclusion of the diagnostic category of PTSD in the third edition of the *Diagnostic and Statistical Manual of Mental Disorders* (American Psychiatric Association, 1980). As the chapters in this section show, acts of violence may lead to PTSD in children and youth as well as to comorbid problems with anxiety and depression.

The violence-oriented disasters covered in this section contain many elements that are thought to contribute to traumatization—notably, the threat to one's life or bodily integrity (see chapter 1). In addition, incidents of violence contain other characteristics that have been associated with severe trauma (see Green, 1990), including severe physical harm or injury; experience of intentional harm or injury; exposure to the grotesque; the violent, sudden loss of a loved one; and witnessing or learning of violence to a loved one. Thus, their potential for causing severe and persistent stress reactions is high.

School shootings have received substantial media attention, especially following the shooting at Columbine High School and the 2001 shooting at Santana High School near San Diego, California. The shootings occurred in middle-class, even affluent, neighborhoods thought to be safe and generally "immune" to acts of violence. Such events seriously challenge youngsters' sense of security and safety. As Kathleen Nader and Christine Mello discuss in chapter 13, issues of trust and betrayal become paramount following shootings and hostage-takings. If violence is perpetrated by a neighbor, classmate, or someone who looks "average," children may not know whom to trust or how to evaluate who is dangerous. If violence is perpetrated by an unknown assailant, the experience may challenge children's beliefs that adults can and will protect them.

In addition, violent injury has been associated with severe and persistent stress symptoms in children and adolescents; as a result, they may require special attention and intervention following violent events. As Nader and Mello note, perhaps the best way to prevent the deleterious effects of shootings and hostage-takings in school settings may be to have a prepared environment and staff. In some communities, schools have worked with law enforcement agencies to develop crisis-management plans and have even conducted crisis drills involving school lockdowns or evacuations (see, e.g., Brooks, Schiraldi, & Ziedenberg, 2000) to test their procedures. Such preventive measures may help prevent violent incidents from escalating and may protect youth from physical and psychological harm when violence breaks out in school-based settings.

Until recently, most Americans had not been exposed directly to the effects of terrorism, nor did they believe terrorist activities would ever happen in the United States. The bombing of the Alfred P. Murrah Federal Building in Oklahoma City in April 1995 changed those perceptions forever, and the September 11, 2001, attacks on the World Trade Center and the Pentagon traumatized thousands of people across the United States. As Robin Gurwitch, Karen Sitterle, Bruce Young, and Betty Pfefferbaum describe in chapter 14, the bombing of the Murrah Building was the largest act of terrorism on U.S. soil at that time, and it precipitated some of the first investigations of the effects of terrorism on children in the United States.

Gurwitch and her colleagues found that PTSD symptoms were fairly common among children and adolescents following the bombing of the Murrah Building; they were most likely to occur among those who had a close relationship with someone who was killed or injured by the bombing. The media coverage of the bombing event, its aftermath, and the subsequent criminal trials was unrelenting, especially in Oklahoma City, and PTSD symptoms were found to be higher among youth who spent much of their television time watching bombing-related programming. The authors elaborate on how events following the bombing (i.e., the criminal proceedings and trials) took their toll on the victims and families who lost loved ones. The closed-circuit televised viewing of the federal execution of the person found guilty for the Oklahoma City bombing, Timothy McVeigh, in June 2001, further intensified the wide-ranging psychological reactions of the victims, their families, and those who lost family members. Those reactions included relief, a sense of disbelief, shock at "confronting" the perpetrator via camera, and lack of closure for the devastating distress caused by the bombing (CNN, 2001).

One disturbing finding that emerged from Gurwitch and colleagues' work was that few of the elementary children surveyed reported having contact with a counselor to discuss the bombing (Gurwitch & Pfefferbaum, 1999). Given that most children received no systematic help from a mental health professional to deal with their reactions soon after the bombing, it is reasonable to assume that most children also received little or no attention to deal with the events that occurred subsequent to the bombing (e.g., the trial and the execution). The authors suggest that the crisis-intervention model is too narrow and too brief; moreover, it fails to recognize the various psychological experiences that victims likely go through as different phases of the event unfold. Gurwitch and her colleagues call for ongoing involvement of mental health professionals who have expertise in working with traumatized individuals and communities.

Children under the "stress of war" is the topic of chapter 15, by Avigdor Klingman. Like other violent disasters, war presents many risk factors for PTSD and other mental health effects, such as severe physical harm and the sudden loss of loved ones. Unlike most other disasters, however, wars are usually preceded by an extended warning period and are prolonged events that may last for months or years.

Klingman points out that children exhibit wide-ranging accommodations to war situations and reports that only a minority of children go on to develop chronic PTSD after war. Klingman also reports, however, that growing up in a war-affected community appears to promote aggressive behavior in some children, and he further notes that one potential consequence of the long duration of some wars (e.g., the conflicts in Israel and Northern Ireland) is that children may minimize or habituate to war-related distress.

Because wars affect entire communities, Klingman maintains that communitywide interventions should take precedence over individual therapeutic interventions. In fact, he emphasizes that the extended warning periods that typically precede wars are an important time for initiating school-based preventive interventions, particularly interventions that teach coping skills and stress inoculation skills. Resources such as the media, the Internet, and the telephone may be useful as large-scale alternative support systems, especially because they may be accessible to children and families who are housebound. Moreover, Klingman points out that during and immediately following wartime, individual therapeutic interventions may be limited by practical considerations (e.g., a shortage of professionals, geographic distances, and physical dangers of traveling).

In chapter 16, the final chapter of Part IV, Janis Kupersmidt, Ariana Shahinfar, and Mary Ellen Voegler-Lee focus on community violence. The high rate of community violence in the United States has had a profound impact on youth. The nation's young people, particularly those from low socioeconomic and urban communities, are increasingly exposed to extreme acts of crime or violence, either as witnesses or victims. As a result, many young people are at risk for experiencing myriad disturbing psychological symptoms. Unfortunately, crime and violence have become so much a part of the culture of modern American life that exposure to such traumatic events among many youth has become the norm. Consequently, youth frequently do not recognize the effects of that exposure as problems.

The authors summarize the issues that arise in the aftermath of youth exposure to community violence. Specifically, they explore the relation between exposure to community violence and various aspects of children's functioning (e.g., academic, social, cognitive, psychological). Because youth who have witnessed or have been victims of community violence experience high levels of distress, the authors further highlight the need for effective interventions that can be used in the aftermath of children's exposure to crime and violence. They discuss the direction that needs to be taken in developing effective interventions, focusing particularly on the factors that *mediate* or *moderate* the effects of community violence, such as coping processes, perceptions of neighborhood safety, intrusive thinking, and social information–processing skills.

This last chapter also underscores the potential value of intervening at multiple levels: individual, family, community, and society. Interventions that can be easily implemented in the schools seem paramount: Schoolchildren are at greatest risk for exposure to community violence, yet they often are least likely to seek help through traditional modes of intervention, such as mental health clinics. Schools not only are excellent sites for delivering services to children and their families but also present an outstanding opportunity for addressing some important correlates of violence, such as academic failure and peer rejection.

In conclusion, a few general observations from the research reviewed in this section are worth highlighting. One is that violence-related disasters have been extremely difficult to study; findings regarding which children are most affected and why are just beginning to emerge. This area of study might benefit from the application of conceptual models that examine predictors of children's reactions in a systematic manner and include mediators and moderators of outcomes.

In addition, the current knowledge base for treating children and adolescents affected by violence-oriented disasters is extremely limited. This observation extends to preventive interventions and is consistent with the Surgeon General's report on Youth Violence (PHS, 2000), which indicated that relatively little is known about the effectiveness of youth violence prevention programs currently in use.

A final observation is that a "one-size-fits-all" approach to dealing with the aftermath of violent events is likely to yield less than optimal results. Not only are children's stress reactions likely to vary as a function of the different factors discussed in chapter 1 of this volume, but their reactions and psychological needs also are likely to vary, depending on the phase of the situation. Furthermore, as underscored in each chapter, one must look beyond PTSD when assessing children and developing interventions.

We hope that the chapters in this section will stimulate further thinking about how to help children following acts of violence and how to better study important associated issues.

REFERENCES

American Psychiatric Association. (1980). *Diagnostic and Statistical Manual of Mental Disorders* (3rd ed.). Washington, DC: Author.

Brooks, K., Schiraldi, V., & Ziedenberg, J. (2000). *School house hype: Two years later*. Retrieved April 12, 2001, from http://www.cjcj.org/schoolhousehype/shh2.html

Cable News Network. (2001). *In depth specials: The execution of Timothy McVeigh*. Retrieved February 25, 2002, from http://www.cnn.com/specials/2001/okc/

Cooke, P. J., & Laub, J. H. (1998). The unprecedented epidemic in youth violence. In M. Tonry & M. H. Moore (Eds.), *Youth violence. Crime and justice: A review of research* (Vol. 24, pp. 27–64). Chicago: University of Chicago Press.

Green, B. L. (1990). Defining trauma: Terminology and generic stressor dimensions. *Journal of Applied Social Psychology, 20*, 1632–1642.

Gurwitch, R. H., & Pfefferbaum, B. (1999). *The impact of trauma and disaster on young children.* Paper presented at the annual Children's Mental Health Care Conference, Tulsa, OK.

U.S. Public Health Service. (2000). *Youth violence: A report of the Surgeon General.* Retrieved April 12, 2002, from http://www.surgeongeneral.gov/library/youthviolence/report.html

U.S. Department of Health and Human Services. (1986). *Surgeon General's workshop on violence and public health* (DHHS Publication No. HRS-D-MC 86-1). Washington, DC: U.S. Government Printing Office.

13

SHOOTINGS, HOSTAGE TAKINGS, AND CHILDREN

KATHLEEN NADER AND
CHRISTINE MELLO

Multiple incidents of violence against youths occur yearly. In addition, dramatic instances of mass violence toward youths have changed over the past 2 decades. In the 1970s and 1980s, highly publicized shootings and hostage takings of children in the United States were most often committed by intruding adults (e.g., the Chowchilla school bus kidnapping; armed attacks on elementary schools in Chicago, Los Angeles, and Stockton, California, and on a fast-food restaurant in San Ysidro, California; a hostage taking and suicide in Orange, California; and a hostage bomber in Wyoming). In the 1990s, highly publicized events were more often committed by students shooting other students (e.g., in Pearl, Mississippi; West Paducah, Kentucky; Jonesboro, Arkansas; Edinboro, Pennsylvania; Springfield, Oregon; and Columbine, Colorado). Hostage takings and shootings of groups of children often last less than 24 hours and end in violence (e.g., shootings, bombings, or knifings). Consequently, shootings and hostage takings have both similarities and differences.

Statistics regarding violent crimes and children are generally incomplete.[1] Approximately 3,000 children die from gunfire each year (Donahue, Schiraldi, & Ziedenberg, 1998); of this group, 90% of children under age 12 and 75% from ages 12 to 17 are killed by adults. Although violent assaults increased substantially in the 1990s, arrest rates for murder increased from 1980 to 1993 and declined through 1997 (Snyder & Sickmund, 1999). From 1993 to 1998, the number of youths arrested for committing homicides decreased from 3,092 to 1,354 (Brooks, Schiraldi, & Ziedenberg, 2000). The Gun-Free Schools Act of 1994 requires expulsion of students carrying guns to schools. During the 1996–1997 school year, 5,724 students were expelled (Brooks et al., 2000), and in the 1997–1998 school year, 3,927 students were expelled for carrying guns to school (Sinclair, 1999).

Age and Gender

Most samples of schoolchildren suggest that violent victimizations increase by age grouping; incidents are least common in elementary school and most common in high school (Brooks et al., 2000; Kaufman et al., 1999; National School Safety Center [NSSC], 1999). Victimization rates were higher for boys than girls on but not off campus (Kaufman et al., 1999). Although still far lower than the number of boys, the number of girls arrested for committing violent crimes more than doubled between 1985 and 1995 (Evans, 2000). Age-based violent crime index arrest rates peak in the late teens and early twenties and consistently decline through older age groups (Snyder & Sickmund, 1999). Decreases in violent crime rates may be related to lower populations in peak age groups.

Location

Following increases in school shootings, school safety has come into question. Yet, from 1992 to 1999, fatal and nonfatal victimization rates were higher off school campuses than on campuses (Kaufman et al., 1999). For example, in 1998 students ages 12 to 18 were victims of 253,000 serious nonfatal violent crimes at school and 550,000 away from school (Kaufman et al., 2000). Urban students were more vulnerable than suburban or rural students both on and off campus (Kaufman et al., 1999).

From the 1992–1993 to the 1998–1999 school year, the number of deaths per year from school shootings fluctuated as follows: 55, 51, 20, 35, 25, 43,

---

[1]Response rates for statistics that are based on surveys vary from 52% to less than 70%. School statistics are generally compiled from law enforcement sources and school surveys over the course of 2 years following a school term.

and 26 (Donahue et al., 1998; Brooks et al., 2000). During the 1997–1998 year, 60 school-associated violent deaths (43 shootings and a total of 2,752 homicides of children ages 5 to 19 occurred in the United States (Kaufman et al., 2000). The number of violent injuries during each time period is significantly greater than the number of deaths. Seven to 8% of students sampled were threatened or injured with a weapon on school property in 1993, 1995, 1997, and 1998 (Kaufman et al., 1999, 2000). In a 1996–1997 report, the percentages of physical attacks with a weapon were 2% in elementary schools, 12% in middle schools, and 13% in high schools (Obmascik, 2000). Although school shootings have undermined our faith in school safety, the incidence of violence is higher off campus than on campus. The number of people affected by these deaths is greater still.

PREVENTION AND PREPARATION

Prevention of the deleterious results of violent trauma includes a prepared environment and staff. Mayer and Leone (1999) compared schools with "secure buildings"[2] and schools with a rule enforcement policy. Schools in which the rules and consequences of breaching them were emphasized and fairly applied reported lower rates of victimization and disorder than schools with secure buildings. The researchers were unable to differentiate, however, between schools with preexisting high levels of violence and those with low levels. Secure building practices may have been implemented in schools with higher levels of violence. Studies of schools with equal violence rates are needed to ascertain whether installation of metal detectors, video equipment, locked doors, or personal search systems have effectively prevented the entry of dangerous people and weapons.

It is essential that school personnel be armed with knowledge that may save lives and prevent the unnecessary escalation of posttrauma symptoms (Capotorto, 1985; Fuselier, 1988). School personnel should know (a) the school layout and safe locations; (b) the cultural environment; (c) strengths and weaknesses in youths and staff that may affect their behavior in stressful events; (d) communication methods understood only by staff; (e) factors that increase risk of injury, traumatization or other adverse emotional responses; (f) the signs of danger; and (g) the necessities of physical and emotional survival under siege. For example, knowing a child's usual behavior under stress can prepare adults to direct the child appropriately during a crisis. Understanding risk factors permits adults to protect children from circumstances that may escalate symptoms (e.g., see the section on "Risk and Protective Factors").

---

[2]Schools that have implemented security procedures and equipment (e.g., metal detectors, search systems, locked doors, and surveillance cameras).

Many hostage victims have commented on the mistake of not having a plan outlining the appropriate conduct to maintain during hostage situations (Capotorto, 1985). In a number of communities, schools and law enforcement have worked together to map school grounds and plot responses to violent outbreaks; they have implemented crisis drills that involve lockdowns, evacuations, or both (Brooks et al., 2000). Some police departments recommend training teachers in methods of self-defense so that a murderer may be prevented from inflicting multiple victimizations.

Risk Factors for Committing Violence or Suicide

Interviews and assessments of numerous violent youths (e.g., Garbarino, 1999; Gibbs & Roche, 1999) have resulted in lists of risk factors and warning signals for committing violence or suicide (American Academy of Child and Adolescent Psychiatry [AACAP], 1999; American Psychological Association [APA], 1999; NSSC, 1999). Identification of potentially violent youths, however, is a complex process fraught with difficulties (Sewell & Mendelsohn, 2000). In fact, attackers do not fit a single descriptive or demographic profile (Fein & Vossekuil, 2000). Many identified characteristics of attackers are found in the general population and among nonviolent people. Moreover, lists of risk factors, in combination with the climate of fear resulting from school shootings, have sometimes resulted in loss of confidentiality, punishment for mere allegations, excessive punishment for minor offenses or even thoughtless remarks, and discriminative practices (Brooks et al., 2000; Sewell & Mendelsohn, 2000). Although failure to identify someone who will behave violently may have fatal consequences, no method of identification has proven fully effective. Falsely identifying an adolescent as potentially violent may negatively affect the adolescent's development. The "heightened emphasis on peer regard leaves adolescents vulnerable to emotional and social debilitation in the face of any experience that impugns their social position" (Sewell & Mendelsohn, 2000, p. 159).

The U.S. Departments of Education and Justice recommend policies and procedures that ensure that school staff and students use early warning signs only for preliminary identification and referral purposes and that only trained professionals diagnose a student in consultation with the child's parents or guardians (Dwyer & Osher, 2000). Many schools have assembled a team of trained professionals who provide consultation, evaluation, and intervention for students who are struggling academically, behaviorally, and socially, including students who exhibit early warning signs (Dwyer & Osher, 2000). Availability for informal consultation, not having a waiting list, and maintaining students' and parents' confidentiality is essential to ensuring effectiveness, personal rights, and willing informants (Dwyer & Osher, 2000).

Overlooked warning signals prior to school shootings of the past decade suggest the need for awareness (Egan, 2000). Among the signs and factors observed in individual youths who have committed school violence (or suicide) are stressful life experiences (e.g., previous trauma, parent marital breakup), biological factors (e.g., brain injury, genetic factors), and the absence of emotional support or personal validation (AACAP, 1999; Bonilla, 2000; NSSC, 1999). Many of the items on the risk lists (e.g., bullying, humiliation, and extreme stress) warrant benign intervention. For example, the prevalence of traumatic experiences and symptoms or mental health disturbances among perpetrators of mass violence suggests the need for effective and timely interventions for traumatized and disturbed youths. Mood disorders are occurring at younger ages, and the incidence of depression and suicide have risen (Egan, 2000). The combination of easy access to weapons, a violent pop culture, and the possibility of ending a tortured life in a blaze of terror have been factors in school shootings (Egan, 2000).

Remedying situations of risk rather than labeling youths may better protect youths without worsening risk factors such as humiliation and isolation. Furlong, Morrison, and Dear (1994) translated risk factors into major risk areas for schools. Among the risk areas are (a) life threat; (b) physical harm; (c) personal–social intimidation and menace; (d) individual isolation and rejection; (e) limited opportunities and support; (f) issues of diversity, success, and productivity; (g) issues of personal and social self-determination; (h) harsh and stressful life conditions; and (i) need for support personnel (Bonilla, 2000; Furlong et al., 1994).

Assessing threat (rather than profiling youths) must include attention to issues of youth and milieu. Adolescence is a time of turmoil and disequilibrium that is fraught with anxiety and tension. Imaginable violent acts are currently readily available through the media and the accessibility of weaponry (Sewell & Mendelsohn, 2000). Moreover, social environmental forces, such as implicit or explicit tolerance of intimidation, humiliation, or ostracization, permit resentment, anger, and vigilante justice to flourish (Vernberg & Twemlow, 2000).

WHAT TO DO DURING AN EVENT

Each violent occurrence must be assessed individually, and every rule and guideline has its exceptions. The duration of the situation, the location and nature of the trauma, and the personalities involved all can differ. A main goal in both shootings and hostage situations is survival (Capotorto, 1985).

Shootings

When an intruder enters the building, someone pulls a gun, or a gun goes off, law enforcement officials currently recommend a system of classroom "lockdown" (Brooks et al., 2000). Lockdown includes locking the classroom door; turning off lights; and moving students away from windows, into protected areas and out of sight. This practice removes visible or available targets.

Although it is essential to assess each situation individually, a few general guidelines apply when an assailant is actually in a classroom. During a hostage situation or under sniper fire, it is important that adults maintain responsibility for the course of the experience to prevent children's increased guilt, emotional proximity, and symptoms (see "Risk and Protective Factors"). As much as possible, children should be protected from viewing traumatic images (e.g., bloody or mutilated bodies). If a child is directed to do something or has to make a decision about what must be done, adults should act to protect the child from any emotional sense of responsibility as long as it can be done without creating increased stress or hostility in the assailant.

Hostage Situations

Hostage situations may last from a fraction of a day to prolonged captivity. Among the motivations identified for taking hostages are to right a perceived wrong, to prove power (or overcome powerlessness), to generate publicity or resources, to coerce the release of group members, or to ensure safety during a criminal act or a protest. People who are mentally disturbed may take hostages as a manifestation of their illness (e.g., as a result of hallucinations or delusions; Fuselier, 1988; J. Kelley, personal communication, March 26, 2000). In hostage situations, psychological domination is based on systematic and repetitive traumatization, disempowerment, and disconnection. The perpetrator instills fear of death and gratitude for being allowed to live; destroys the victim's sense of autonomy through scrutiny and control; and increases his or her own power over victims by isolating them from information, emotional support, and material aid. Terror, isolation, intermittent reward, and enforced dependency may create submissiveness and compliance (Herman, 1992; Jenkins, 1985).

A number of traumatic situations (e.g., gang membership and child abuse) may include prolonged emotional captivity (Herman, 1992). For example, 1 year after a shooting at his elementary school, a boy from inner-city Los Angeles described being forced to join a gang (Nader, Pynoos, Fairbanks, & Frederick, 1990). His friend had been killed for refusing to join; anyone who tried to leave the gang was killed. In the gang, he was exposed to multiple shootings in which he was sometimes required to participate.

Prolonged Captivity

During prolonged captivity, a person's ability to maintain a sense of autonomy and avoid morbid contemplation may depend on important coping mechanisms such as psychological constriction (e.g., dissociation, denial, fantasy, thought suppression, accepting contradictory beliefs), humor, and humanization of the victim to the captor (Herman, 1992; Ochberg &

Soskis, 1982). Those efforts may be assisted by setting individual goals; fantasizing about remembered objects (e.g., friends, favorite foods, and situations); maintaining faith in God, colleagues, negotiators and family; and focusing on maintaining health (e.g., eating and exercising; Jenkins, 1985; Niehous, 1985). In hostage situations of shorter duration that involve children, however, survival and the prevention of exposure to trauma or guilt-inducing experiences are priorities. Although an assailant's concern for the hostage's safety and survival may increase chances of survival, the hostage's caring for the assailant may complicate traumatic response and recovery.

In prolonged hostage situations, adults are advised to make themselves more human to the hostage taker (Jenkins, 1985; Niehous, 1985). Although specific difficulties may arise when *hostage syndrome* develops (e.g., hostages may give inaccurate information or later refuse to testify; see "Sympathy or Attachment to the Perpetrator," below), captors' positive feelings enhance hostages' chances of survival (Fuselier, 1988). Ongoing harmless communication may assist this process (Jenkins, 1985; Niehous, 1985). Assessment must be made within each individual situation, however. Bombs, guns, and other weapons are dangerous, despite any goodwill from assailants. In one school hostage situation involving a bomb, a female hostage taker who seemed to care about the children inadvertently set off the bomb. In a number of incidents at schools, people with mental disturbance have shot at those who moved and attracted their attention. Thus, talking or even subtle interaction may be impossible (e.g., Hough et al., 1989; Schwarz & Kowalski, 1991a).

Although sometimes disagreeing with a captor may be acceptable during prolonged captivity, becoming abusive toward captors is inadvisable (Niehous, 1985). Aggravating or startling the hostage taker can be dangerous regardless of the length of the event. For example, when a group of children unknowingly tried to enter a classroom held hostage (Nader, 1998), the hostage taker became agitated, accidentally firing the gun and barely missing a child. In her agitation, the woman immediately shot herself in front of the children. A more outwardly hostile intruder may have fired directly at the children and teacher.

Hostage negotiations require specific preparation and professionalism and should be left to trained professionals (Capotorto, 1985). Although successful negotiator traits have been identified, outcome also depends on a number of uncontrollable variables (Fuselier, 1988). Psychologists have served as consultants to negotiators by providing an objective presence to assess negotiator mental status; to assess the motives and personality of the hostage taker; and to provide training in methods of coping with stress and fatigue, interviewing and communicating skills, and understanding hostage syndrome (Fuselier, 1988).

Phases of a Hostage Situation

A hostage situation resulting in a student killing fellow students is extremely dangerous because of the preexisting relationships. To enhance chances of survival, Jack Kelley, a police and wartime hostage negotiator, recommends training school staff to respond to each stage of a hostage situation (J. Kelley, personal communication, March 26, 2000). A number of models of hostage stages have been proposed (Crelinsten & Szabo, 1979). Kelley proposed a model described below (J. Kelley, personal communication, March 26, 2000).

In the *initial hostage-taking stage* (Phase 1), emotions are elevated and reasoning capacity is diminished. Kelley (J. Kelley, personal communication, March 26, 2000) suggested that this stage is one of the two times in which hostages are at greatest risk. Unexpected reactions by hostages may have dire consequences (Capotorto, 1985). In this stage, the hostage taker acts to secure control of hostages and to convince hostages that he or she is in control (Kelley, 2000). Whether a hostage might put the hostage taker at a disadvantage by resisting is a complex question; resistance may be gravely dangerous (Capotorto, 1985). Negotiators will need to quickly interview people with close ties to the hostage taker (Kelley, 2000).

In the still-chaotic *crisis stage* (Phase 2), the hostage taker may behave emotionally and irrationally, threaten, and use hostages' welfare to press for demands (Kelley, 2000). Responding authorities will organize, evaluate, and position officers at the scene. School hostage situations, however, may resolve (frequently with deaths) by this stage. In this phase, some captors are positively influenced if victims rapidly overcome shock and regain dignity (Capotorto, 1985). In contrast are hostage situations in which children held by a mentally disturbed person were shot when they drew attention to themselves (Hough et al., 1989; Schwarz & Kowalski, 1992).

Kelley describes the *accommodation stage* (Phase 3) as the most productive of all the stages. The situation often has settled into a routine, and the hostage taker may have calmed. Negotiators should be making progress toward resolution (Kelley, 2000). During this phase, if given the opportunity to be released, it is essential that hostages leave. Reactions such as guilt for leaving others, empathy for captors or fear of authorities may make hostages reluctant to leave when released during a long hostage incident (Kelley, 2000).

Kelley's final, *surrender stage* (Phase 4) becomes a crisis stage for negotiations. If all goes well, all hostages will have been released, and the hostage taker will have realized the futility of continuing the situation. In most cases, the hostage taker becomes suicidal and must be dealt with as a danger to himself as well as to others (Kelley, 2000).

AFTERMATH OF HOSTAGE SITUATIONS AND SHOOTINGS

After hostage situations or shootings, children need assistance to resume a sense of normalcy and safety. Initial posttrauma interventions include taking care of concrete needs and providing protection (Ochberg &

Soskis, 1982), such as moving children to safety, caring for physical injuries, and protecting them from additional horrible perceptions (sights, sounds, smells) or upsetting reminders. Physical locations and other reminders of the traumatic episode often provoke strong reactions. Protecting children requires more than guarding against physical dangers; for example, media interviews may worsen symptoms, cause stigmatization, or enhance celebrity (Ochberg & Soskis, 1982; Swiss & Giller, 1993). The reasons to avoid enhancing the celebrity of the offender are obvious. Enhancing the celebrity of victims may result in regrets for emotional statements or demeanor, in a subsequent sense of "falling from grace" or in a sense of having been exploited. Families of victims may need assistance in recognizing symptoms; late effects; and residual, possibly disabling attachments to hostage holders and other assailants (Ochberg & Soskis, 1982).

Assessment

When assessing the reactions of children, it is best to gather information from multiple sources in order to accurately measure the full range of their symptoms (Nader, 1997a). Clinical and statistical evidence suggest that symptoms may fluctuate over time with or without treatment. For example, children in the Los Angeles sniper attack reported more guilt and avoidance of reminders at 1 and 14 months than at 6 months following the event (Nader et al., 1990). Children may report fewer symptoms than they manifest 1 to 2 years after an event, but they may become more adept at reporting symptoms with age, maturity, and treatment (Nader, 2001). Some symptoms may appear immediately (e.g., sleep disturbance), whereas others may have a delayed onset (e.g., behavior problems; Frederick, 1985; Schwarz & Kowalski, 1992). Some evidence indicates that as intrusive recollections decrease, reactivity to reminders and physiological reactivity may increase (North, Smith, & Spitznagel, 1997).

Traumatic Reactions

A number of measures are available for the assessment of childhood and adult traumatic reactions (see chapter 2, this volume; Wilson & Keane, 1997). A few questionnaires examine symptoms in addition to those of posttraumatic stress disorder (PTSD). Although important, the assessment of PTSD is insufficient to measure the long-term effects of trauma or treatment. Research is needed to determine the development of patterns of thought, behavior, and interaction that result (and may change over time) from specific traumatic impressions and experiences in combination with specific child characteristics (Nader, 2001). These identified individual results of traumatic experience as well as PTSD must be measured over time into adulthood. One individualized measure, goal attainment scaling (GAS; Hogue, 1994; Kiresuk, Smith, & Cardillo, 1994), may serve as a model in developing a method of individualized assessment. Rather than rate all patients on the same fixed set of psychiatric symptoms, GAS requires the development of outcome scales specifically tailored to the individual or group whose progress is to be measured and the examination of those characteristics, behaviors, or symptoms that intervention is intended to change or alleviate (or prevent). It enlists a 5-point Level of Attainment scale and additional scales with specific indicators of each level of success for identified goals (Kiresuk et al., 1994). Accurately identifying the experiences and impressions that will affect the long-term results of treatment and the patterns that result from them is a prerequisite to the effectiveness of this method of measuring outcome. It is important to identify child qualities (e.g., personality and temperament) before and after traumatic exposure to be able to determine trauma's effects on children with these characteristics (Nader, 2001).

Assessment of Risk of Violence

Assessment tools have been developed to predict dangerousness, for example, in mentally disordered people or previous offenders (e.g., the Violence Risk Assessment Guide and the Psychopathy Checklist Revised; Litwack & Schlesinger, 1999). Although studies have shown that some instruments or clinician assessments have demonstrated a better-than-chance ability to predict future violence, all the assessment methods have proven imperfect. Future nonoffenders have been identified as being at risk of committing violence, and future offenders have not been identified (Litwack & Schlesinger, 1999).

The accuracy of lists developed to identify students at risk of committing violence remains untested. Proposed risk factors for violence must be studied for their degree of association with various levels of violence over various time periods (Litwack & Schlesinger, 1999). The proportion of all students with identified characteristics who will later perpetrate extreme violence and the proportion of violent offenders who have previously exhibited those characteristics is unknown (Sewell & Mendelsohn, 2000). Moreover, the extent to which each individual warning sign or risk factor is associated with extreme violent actions is not clear (Sewell & Mendelsohn, 2000). In checklists, purported signs of violence occurring frequently or infrequently among youthful populations appear as equally weighted indicators. Sewell and Mendelsohn (2000) suggest that checklist items that logically appear to have a higher predictive validity (e.g., inappropriate use of firearms, patterns of aggression or intimidation, and threats of violence) are themselves violent behaviors, which, even at a low level, merit intervention.

Risk and Protective Factors

Although some traumatic exposures are likely to result in traumatic response regardless of risk or protective factors, a few factors have been found to provide a measure of protection or increased risk for children exposed to shootings and hostage takings. Increased physical or emotional proximity to traumatic phenomena during or after a shooting or hostage taking increases risk of traumatic and associated reactions. Exposure to horrible sounds, images, and smells; guilt, shame, or self-blame; and knowing a deceased victim well have been associated with increased symptoms (Nader et al., 1990; Pynoos et al., 1987; Schwarz & Kowalski, 1991a). For example, children exposed to ongoing violence in south central Los Angeles reported increased symptoms with greater proximity to gunfire and injury and increased acquaintance with the deceased child (Nader et al., 1990; Pynoos et al., 1987). Unexposed children with some emotional involvement in the attack (e.g., a relationship or unresolved interactions with the deceased) had greater symptoms than others without exposure. Similarly, the PTSD reactions of children held hostage in their classrooms by people who were mentally disturbed in Evanston, IL, and Paris, France, were associated with the children's levels of subjective involvement during the event (Schwarz & Kowalski, 1991b; Vila, Porche, & Mouren-Simeoni, 1999).

Severe violent injury has been a factor in the persistence of symptoms (Rozensky, Sloan, Schwarz, & Kowalski, 1993). For example, injured adolescents held by terrorists in their classrooms continued to exhibit symptoms 17 years after the event (Desivilya, Gal, & Ayalon, 1996). Children with severe injuries fared worst in their long-term adjustments.

In addition to event factors (e.g., horrible sights and endangerment), other factors have been associated with increased reactions or future vulnerabilities. They include family factors (e.g., psychopathology and previous trauma), child factors (e.g., a sensitive nature and difficult temperament), and other factors that reduce emotional distance or increase vulnerability (Carey & McDevitt, 1995; Nader, 2001; Pynoos et al., 1987). After a sniper attack, increased symptoms were found in siblings whose father was mentally disturbed (Pynoos et al., 1987). After a hostage taking, children described by their mothers as "sensitive" had more symptoms than other children (Nader, 1998).

Protection from traumatic sights, sounds, and responsibilities (for events and outcomes) and opportunities for successful actions, resolution of response, and healthy development may serve as protective factors in children's traumatic reactions. Ignorance of the magnitude of the occurrence may prevent or reduce response (Pynoos et al., 1987). For example, the child who walked across a playground reading while a sniper shot and thought he heard firecrackers was not traumatized (Pynoos et al., 1987). Individual cases of hostage takings and shootings involving children suggest that good emotional health in youth and family prior to a traumatic experience may make recovery easier. Guilt has been associated with increased symptoms (Pynoos et al., 1987). Assigning culpability for the event and its outcomes to an external source, feeling protected, and believing that adults are in control during and after the event can prevent the escalation of symptoms. Increasing a child's (or adult's) sense of responsibility increases risk and may significantly worsen symptomatic level. For example, after being urged to pray for her and to ask her not to shoot herself, children felt guilty for not helping the woman who held them hostage and then killed herself (Nader, 1998).

Children who believe they have behaved competently during a traumatic event or have successfully resolved previous traumas have exhibited fewer symptoms than other children with similar exposures (Nader, 1998; Pynoos et al., 1987). For example, a boy who had resolved a previous trauma in therapy reported fewer symptoms than his peers after they were held hostage and watched the hostage taker shoot herself. Moreover, clinical evidence suggests that when, in the course of treatment, children recognize their successful actions during an event, they experience an increased sense of competence and some symptomatic relief (Nader, 1997b).

A single posttrauma psychological debriefing or screening interview may not prevent disorders but may mitigate the escalation of symptoms. Children screened for their traumatic reactions within a month of exposure to a school sniper attack using the Child Post Traumatic Stress Reaction Index (Frederick, Pynoos, & Nader, 1992) had significantly fewer symptoms 14 months after the event than children screened for the first time 14 months after the event (Nader, 1997a). In 1995, 29 children and their teacher were taken and held hostage for 2 hours in a French elementary school classroom. Twenty-six of the children held hostage and 21 of 22 children from another classroom participated in the study. Psychological debriefing (Allen & Bloom, 1994; Blom, 1986) was conducted the evening after the event, and 6 weeks later. Seven of the 26 children (27%) who were taken hostage at one time or another developed full PTSD. The rate of subclinical PTSD evolved from 24% (6 of 25 children) at 2 months to 34% (8 of 24 children) at 4 months, 32% (6 of 17 children) evaluated at 7 months, and 38% (8 of 21) evaluated at 18 months. Although psychological debriefing did not prevent PTSD, nondebriefed children had the worst outcomes (Vila et al., 1999). The clinical course for children who received specialized treatment for PTSD was "good" to "very good" (Vila et al., 1999).

THE IMPACT OF SHOOTINGS AND HOSTAGE TAKINGS

Children and adolescents who are exposed to violent traumatic events are at risk of mental health disturbances, disturbances of thought and behavior, reduced quality of life, disrupted developmental progressions, thwarted confidence and goal accomplishment, and future aggression or victimization (APA, 1999; Nader, 1998; Nader et al., 1990; Pynoos et al., 1987; Terr, 1979).

Individual Differences in Reactions to Shootings and Hostage Takings

Differences among children and their families during and after traumatic events are influenced by cultural heritage; community mores and style; parental personalities, education levels, parenting styles, and experience; child's personality, temperament, education, and life experiences; and socioeconomic issues. This chapter elaborates on only a few of those issues.

Culture

Understanding cultural issues is important to the resolution of community response (Dubrow & Nader, 1999), to accurate psychological assessment (Marsella, Friedman, Gerrity, & Scurfield, 1996), and to effective treatment interventions (Heras, 1992). For some children, families, and communities, it is important to use both modern and traditional intervention methods. For example, John did not see the sniper who shot and killed his best friend while they were leaving school. He was unable to recover from this traumatic loss until he observed his Native American traditional practices in addition to completing psychotherapy. After a sniper attack in a California community with many southeast Asian children, Buddhist purification ceremonies on the school grounds reduced school and community anxieties (Dubrow & Nader, 1999).

Family styles of understanding and coping with shootings and hostage takings differ among and within cultures. For example, following a sniper attack on an elementary school in a Black and Hispanic community, parents of both cultures were protective of their children. No significant differences in symptoms were found between children in the cultures; however, in one culture, family cohesiveness could be more often characterized as "you and me against the world" (e.g., families often expressed anger and desires to fight back), whereas in the other culture, the walls of home seemed to serve as a barrier against the external world (e.g., families expressed fears and described staying inside and together more). Some exceptions were found to this general occurrence; for example, although one girl was from the first culture (partially as a result of her mother's previous rape and assault), her family fit the second description better.

Primary concerns and life stresses may differ among cultures. For example, the 1984 Los Angeles sniper attack and 1987 Orange County hostage taking represent incidents in two very different California neighborhoods, one a predominantly Black and Hispanic, inner-city neighborhood with ongoing violence, and the other a predominantly upper-middle-class Caucasian neighborhood in which concerns were often related to family socioeconomic status. Following the hostage taking of her fifth-grade class, Ann's severe traumatic response was complicated by two concerns: (a) being one of the few children of a single parent and (b) the unavailability of her working mother to provide the additionally needed support.

Personality and Temperament

Studies of shootings and hostage takings have suggested differences in traumatic reactions according to personality or temperament factors (Nader, 1998; Schwarz & Kowalski, 1992). Reviewing studies of adult twins in war (True et al., 1993), Carey and McDevitt (1995) suggested that temperament is a likely factor in traumatic response.

Information related to childhood trauma and personality or temperament is problematic and limited. Pretrauma ratings of personality or temperament are rarely available, and trauma has led to alterations in personality (Terr, 1991). Thus, traits found in association with PTSD may be a result of trauma rather than a cause of symptoms. For example, Schwarz and Kowalski (1992) found an association for adults between PTSD levels and guilt and resentment, insecurity, and psychasthenia. Children and adolescents who were previously secure, confident, and otherwise normal, however, have been markedly affected by exposure to shootings and hostage takings. Traits such as insecurity, found present after a shooting or hostage taking, may either be a factor in a child's increased vulnerability to traumatization or may be a result of the trauma.

Characteristics of the Event

Specific characteristics of shootings and hostage events contribute to the short- and long-term consequences of this form of traumatic exposure. In general, the nature, intensity, and personal impact of an event affect the intensity and nature of response (Carey & McDevitt, 1995). In addition to the full range of PTSD symptoms, details of a traumatic event become embedded in aspects of life following the event. They may shape or become a part of sensitivity to traumatic reminders, reenactments or patterns of behavior, affective or conduct disturbances, biological patterns, or vulnerabilities (Nader, 1998, 2001; Suomi & Levine, 1998). Episodic, perceptual, emotional, or kinesthetic details of the event may become triggers for emotions or behaviors. For example, a teacher who runs for safety may feel guilty for not running toward children to assist them; subsequently, he or she may no longer be able to run daily for health and relaxation without thinking of the event.

In addition to reenactments and heightened reactivity to reminders, aspects of the event may translate later into symptoms less obviously related to the traumatic experience. For example, even after moving to a safe community from one of ongoing violence, a girl exposed to a school shooting began to jump for cover or freeze whenever she heard a loud bang. As a young adult, loud noises raised her blood pressure and resulted in irritability and reduced stress tolerance.

Violence vs. Natural Disasters

After intentional human violence, issues of human accountability, trust, and betrayal become prominent in the course of response and recovery. With a natural disaster, adults and older children understand that the traumatic action is the result of impersonal natural forces. For any disaster, people may ask "Why me?" or look for the personal or spiritual meaning of the experience.

Children traumatized by nonviolent disasters may lose faith in the protection and power of adults, a supreme being, or both. Violence introduces issues of trust and whom to trust. If violence is perpetrated by a neighbor (e.g., Pynoos et al., 1987) or someone who looks like an average person, it becomes difficult to determine who is dangerous. Even with an unknown assailant, a level of betrayal is involved in that a fellow human has created terror and inflicted personal harm. The affects of these actions are even more problematic for preschool and elementary-school age children, who still believe that adults know best and will protect them (Stillwell, Galvin, & Kopta, 1991).

Violence may intensify or add to trauma's deleterious effects on trust, moral development, and sense of ongoing safety, (Garbarino, Kostelny, & Dubrow, 1991; Terr, 1991). For example, children exposed to severe ongoing violence may develop a changed moral code in which self-preservation is primary (Garbarino, 1999) or may develop a dual identity as victim and perpetrator (Parson, 1997). Consequently, they may commit violence that to them is necessary (e.g., to prevent future harm from another person) but to the outsider seems meaningless (e.g., after the disagreement appeared to be resolved).

Single Event vs. Ongoing Events

Researchers continue to examine the differences between single incidents and ongoing traumas (Nader, 1997b; Terr, 1991). Although treatment methods are designed specifically or primarily for one or the other (Cohen, 1999; Nader, 2001; Parson, 1997), the differences between traumatic events and their effects are not as simple as whether they are single incidents or ongoing experiences (Nader, 1997b). A number of factors affect the nature of traumatic response, including personal history, whether the source or impetus of the trauma is personal or impersonal, and the nature of the experience.

For children exposed to ongoing traumas, arousal symptoms may become modulated over time and reappear episodically (Realmuto et al., 1992). Children who endure repeated similar events may tend to merge similar incidents into a representative memory (Howe, 1997). Clinical experience, however, suggests that particular experiences may be recalled distinctly. For example, certain segments of a shooting or hostage event or a particular shooting (in areas of ongoing violence) are remembered as separate episodes.

Prolonged Captivity

Symptoms found after single incidents may become more pronounced after multiple or ongoing traumas (e.g., prolonged captivity; Herman, 1992; Terr, 1991). The intensified symptoms involve issues of trust; shame, self-loathing, and failure; rage; hopelessness; and constrictions in the capacity to actively engage with the world. Constriction may be accompanied by ingrained attitudes, such as feeling watched or thwarted, and feeling that the penalty for failure is severe or that personal initiative equates to insubordination (Herman, 1992). These attitudes persist outside captivity, although many symptoms may fade or change over time. Ongoing or episodic arousal may persist (Herman, 1992; Realmuto et al., 1992). Some former hostages have delayed reactions; some experience profound changes in health, personality, lifestyle, and outlook. Family members also suffer (e.g., through breakdowns, miscarriage, or substance abuse; Jenkins, 1985).

Defenses developed during the hostage experience may affect communication in and out of treatment. Former captives often feel critical of their own performances during captivity (e.g., for being captured, for cooperating, or for not escaping) and expect the same criticism from others. They often feel a strong need to retell their stories but fear judgment. Survivors feel on trial and, in a way, *are* on trial because of a frequently believed notion that bad things happen to people who deserve them or because of fear that persuades us to blame the victim (Jenkins, 1985).

Like other trauma victims, captives become attached to those with whom they have endured the experience (Herman, 1992; Nader, 1997b; Ochberg & Soskis, 1982). After isolation, captives may develop a sort of "psychological infantilism" with the perpetrator (Symonds, 1980). In and out of therapeutic sessions, survivors may oscillate between intense attachment and isolated withdrawal and have a sense that in all relationships, life and death issues are at stake (Herman, 1992).

Brief Captivity

Hostage experiences of shorter duration may elicit some of the symptoms and intensity levels of both single traumatic incidents and prolonged captivity, depending on the circumstances of the event (e.g., Nader, 1998). The symptomatic results of increased time held hostage may be affected by a number of factors (e.g., degree of perceived life threat). In a hostage taking of elementary school children and teachers that did not result in deaths or injury, Jessee, Strickland, and Ladewig (1992) found an association between length of time held hostage and negative behaviors (e.g., arousal symptoms, fears and anxiety, increased attachment, and undesirable classroom behaviors). In an airplane hijacking that resulted in three deaths, however, children and adults released early who feared they would be shot as soon as they left the plane reported increased symptoms (Cremniter et al., 1997).

Even a few minutes can be a long time under siege when bloody injuries and intense fears are a part of the experience. Protection, attachment, endearing oneself to the assailant, and so forth are affected by the particular intruder, the group held hostage, the situation, and other variables. For example, in the 1-day school hostage situation in which the woman accidentally set off the bomb, a number of children had some positive feelings toward the female captor because she was kind to the children and tried to calm the male captor.

TREATMENT OF SURVIVORS

Hostage situations are similar to shootings in their psychological impact. Most treatment methods address traumatic impressions through review of the event. Following a prolonged hostage experience, issues of personal power, reduction of helplessness, nurturance versus isolation, planning for the future, expression of anger, channeling rage into productive activity, and diminishing life and work stress are among the foci of treatment (Fuselier, 1988). Similar issues are dealt with in treatment of youth following brief shootings and hostage takings.

It is important to treat all the symptoms along with the specific disorder and experience of the individual child (Nader, 2001; Terr, 2001). Understanding the complexity of response is essential when trauma and grief interact and when aspects of the event exacerbate or complicate response (e.g., with traumatic attachments; Eth & Pynoos, 1985; Nader, 1996). Rage and other intense symptoms sometimes must be addressed after some progress, often more than once. Moreover, clinical evidence suggests that as physical recovery increases and a child is free to attend to other trauma matters, some symptoms may increase (Nader, 1997b).

Treatment for Shooting and Hostage Experience

In addition to psychotherapeutic treatment, individual assessment of children by a skilled and sensitive interviewer has reduced symptoms (Nader, 1997a) as well as determined treatment needs. Although not tested specifically for shootings and hostage takings, methods used for a variety of traumas (including shootings and hostage takings), in pre- and posttreatment assessments, have successfully reduced traumatic symptoms and have been clinically observed to increase confidence. Among those methods are cognitive–behavioral therapy (Cohen, 1999; March, Amaya-Jackson, Foa, & Treadwell,

1999) and play therapy (Nader, 2001). Most methods include adjunct treatments (see "Adjunct Treatment," below).

Mental health professionals have become fairly adept at measuring and reducing the symptoms of trauma (e.g., PTSD, anxiety, depression, and impaired confidence) found in children 1 to 3 years after an event. To enhance the long-term successes of psychological interventions, the field must improve its knowledge of specific individual outcomes for children with specific types of experiences, traumatic impressions, temperaments, personality styles, histories, and family circumstances (Carey & McDevitt, 1995; Nader, 2001). A cooperative effort between teachers, parents, and mental health professionals can assist this knowledge.

Systematic studies over years are needed to assess symptoms and trauma-related patterns of thought and behavior as they change or affect life. Evaluations of the similarities and differences between events also are needed. For example, will youths hiding in a small office during a shooting with 15 deaths, 22 injuries, and shooters and bombs inside the school building (Columbine, CO; Obmascik, 2000) fare worse over time than children hidden in closets or under tables inside a school while a sniper shoots from across the street, killing 2 and injuring 13 on the playground (Nader et al., 1990; Pynoos et al., 1987)?

Treatment for Violent Offenders

For delinquent youth with serious offenses, two successful treatment models have been identified (National Institute of Mental Health, 2000). One is multisystemic therapy, a home-based treatment program with a particular focus on changing the peers with whom a youth associates, identifying family strengths, and developing natural support systems for the youth. The other model is therapeutic foster care, a community-based intervention for chronically offending delinquents. Carefully selected therapeutic foster parents are supported with research-based procedures for working with chronic delinquents in their homes. Treatment typically lasts 6 to 7 months.

Adjunct Treatment

School and community violence affects the entire community adversely (Frederick, 1985). Incidents have been followed by increases in interpersonal violence, juvenile criminal bookings, somatic complaints, mental illness, and substance abuse (Frederick, 1985; Nader, 1997a). Moreover, violence may result in a loss of communality and needed support (Frederick, 1985). Adults with risk factors (e.g., exposure and previous trauma) may experience symptoms (Schwarz & Kowalski, 1991a). Traumatized parents and teachers often have more difficulty engaging in their normal roles with children (e.g., teaching, grading, disciplining, and protecting). Traumatized or not, parents often minimize their children's reactions (Terr, 2001; Webb, 1994). Parents, teachers, students, support staff, and administrators will need assistance from clinicians to understand the needs of affected children. Treatment programs by experienced clinicians generally address the needs of the child in context (Nader, 2001). Assisting the adults in the child's personal milieu is important to both the child's and the community's recovery.

Most methods of treatment for childhood trauma include one or more adjunct treatment methods (e.g., peer or support groups; family, conjoint, or parent meetings; and school or larger community interventions; Nader, 2001; Pope, Campbell, & Kurtz, 1992; Terr, 2001). The adjunct methods are used to treat adults in the child's environment, to assist the child with special needs (e.g., to function in the classroom, with grief or injury), or to address specific issues (e.g., generalized fears and reenactments). For example, individual, family, and community fear and arousal levels have been diminished by psychoeducational group meetings (e.g., parent or community meetings or classroom interventions; Nader, 1997b). Support groups have assisted parents of traumatized and injured children and have assisted grieving children and parents.

Traumatic Impressions

As a consequence of physiological and psychological phenomena during traumatic events, multiple impressions register or imprint themselves with intensity and may become interlinked. The details will represent themselves in and out of therapy in the form of attitudes, thoughts, behavior, relationship patterns, and automatic reactions (Nader, 2001; Terr, 1979). When children's impressions and desires to act during an event go unresolved, the result can be major changes in behavior and personality. This situation may be particularly true after fearing or witnessing deaths during shootings or hostage takings; issues of human betrayal and desires to intervene or retaliate may be pronounced. For example, lack of resolution of a traumatically imprinted desire for retaliation or intervention, or identification with the aggressor, may result in increased aggression or inhibition (Nader, 2001; Terr, 1979). Some intense traumatic impressions (e.g., wishes, urges, and emotions) remain in the psyche as strong urges to express and must be intensely expressed. Consequent repeated behaviors may emerge in the survivor acutely or over time and may endanger or frustrate the survivor or those with whom the survivor interacts. Clinical evidence suggests that in treatment sessions, those wishes, urges, and emotions can be expressed with intensity and without harm and can be resolved (Nader, 2001).

Sympathy or Attachment to the Perpetrator

Attachment to the perpetrator of a crime, often called the "Stockholm Syndrome," or "hostage syndrome" most often has been associated with prolonged captivity and isolation (Fuselier, 1988; Herman, 1992; Ochberg & Soskis, 1982). Hostage syndrome includes the hostages' negative feelings toward authorities, hostages' positive feelings toward captors, and captors' positive feelings toward hostage(s) (Fuselier, 1988; Ochberg, 1980). Strentz (1982) suggested that this syndrome is a function of time and depends on the interaction of hostages and hostage takers. The exception occurs when (a) victims have negative contact (especially physical abuse without the ability to rationalize its occurrence) with hostage takers who do not evidence concern for them, or (b) victims have minimal contact with hostage takers. For example, refugee children interviewed in Los Angeles and Croatia who endured prolonged captivity that entailed much abuse (e.g., beatings, burnings, or witnessing murder or injury of significant others) and no reward did not report or exhibit attachment to their captors. Individual victims of the San Ysidro siege and massacre in a fast-food restaurant, who had no direct contact with their captor and waited fearfully as he shot many to death, did not exhibit hostage syndrome. Individual cases of single or family hostage takings suggest that the syndrome can be avoided despite the victims' dependence on the captor and the captor's best efforts to befriend the surviving victims. For example, the surviving daughter of a family held captive for days after mistakenly entering a drug transaction exhibited no hostage syndrome. The captor spent periods chatting and flirting with her and claimed her family was alive but drugged. Most of the time, she was bound and isolated from him and her family.

In contrast, hostages who felt sympathy for their captors, regardless of time before release, have developed aspects of hostage syndrome (Strentz, 1982). This finding has proven true in violent situations of relatively short duration in which children have had face-to-face contact with the assailant. For example, elementary school children were both angry and sorry for a woman who held them hostage at school, complained of poor treatment by doctors and then shot herself in front of them (Nader, 1997b). In situations in which a child has felt some responsibility for or felt sorry for a perpetrator or other culpable person (e.g., because the perpetrator died or caused harm by accident), the child will need to express both positive and negative emotions toward the perpetrator. This expression can be accomplished by allowing the child to separate feelings of sadness and empathy from those of anger and by giving the opportunity to express and address each set of emotions.

CONCLUSIONS

Each shooting and hostage-taking situation is unique and must be considered individually. Nevertheless, the situations have similarities that can help students, faculty, and administrative staff prepare for them. Research indicates that actions taken during these traumatic events can affect posttrauma symptoms and adjustment. Preparation is essential to enhance the chances of physical and psychological safety. For example, it is essential to recognize the phases of a hostage situation, to avoid angering an assailant, to remove children from a shooter's sight and attention, and to stop the violence in a manner that minimizes physical and psychological injury. For children, it is important, when possible, to minimize traumatic impressions, promote competence, protect them from taking on responsibility for outcomes, and minimize the loss of trust. Following traumatic events, the communities affected and the people involved need support and interventions. Thorough assessment of community and individual needs assists the development of appropriate intervention plans. Consideration of culture and individual differences is essential in providing appropriate assessment and therapeutic support. A number of methods are available for treating childhood trauma. It is essential to look beyond PTSD when assessing children and interventions. Continued research is needed regarding the interaction of time, personality, temperament, and specific traumatic experiences and impressions and their impact on the outcomes of treatment.

REFERENCES

Allen, S. N., & Bloom, S. L. (1994). Group and family treatment of post-traumatic stress disorder. *Psychiatric Clinics of North America, 17*, 425–437.

American Academy of Child and Adolescent Psychiatry. (1999). *Understanding violent behavior in children and adolescents*. Retrieved January 5, 2000, from http://www.aacap.org/publications/factsfam/behavior.htm

American Psychological Association. (1999). *Warning signs of teen violence*. Retrieved November 16, 1999, from http://www.helping.apa.org/warningsigns/recognizing.html

Blom, G. E. (1986). A school disaster: Intervention and research aspects. *Journal of American Academy of Child Adolescent Psychiatry, 25*, 336–345.

Bonilla, D. (Ed.). (2000). *School violence*. New York: H. W. Wilson.

Brooks, K., Schiraldi, V., & Ziedenberg, J. (2000). *School house hype: Two years later*. Retrieved September 20, 2000, from http://www.cjcj.org/schoolhousehype.html

Capotorto, G. (1985). Avoiding capture and surviving captivity. In B. Jenkins (Ed.), *Terrorism and personal protection* (pp. 395–406). Boston: Butterworth.

Carey, W. B., & McDevitt, S. C. (1995). *Coping with children's temperament*. New York: Basic Books.

Cohen, J. (1999). Treatment of traumatized children. *Trauma therapy audio series*. Thousand Oaks, CA: Sage Publications.

Crelinsten, R. D., & Szabo, D. (1979). *Hostage-taking*. Lexington, MA: Lexington Books.

Cremniter, D., Crocq, L., Louville, P., Batista, G., Grande, C., Lambert, Y., & Chemtob, C. M. (1997). Posttraumatic reactions of hostages after an aircraft hijacking. *Journal of Nervous and Mental Disease, 185,* 344–346.

Desivilya, H. S., Gal, R., & Ayalon, O. (1996). Extent of victimization, traumatic stress symptoms, and adjustment of terrorist assault survivors: A long-term follow-up. *Journal of Traumatic Stress, 9,* 881–889.

Donahue, E., Schiraldi, V., & Ziedenberg, J. (1998). *School house hype: The school shootings and the real risks kids face in America.* Washington, DC: The Justice Policy Institute.

Dubrow, N., & Nader, K. (1999). Consultations amidst trauma and loss: Recognizing and honoring differences. In K. Nader, N. Dubrow, & B. Stamm (Eds.), *Honoring differences: Cultural issues in the treatment of traumatic stress* (pp. 1–19). Philadelphia: Taylor and Francis.

Dwyer, K., & Osher, D. (2000). *Safeguarding our children: An action guide.* Washington, DC: U.S. Department of Education and U.S. Department of Justice.

Egan, T. (2000). From adolescent angst to shooting up schools. In D. Bonilla (Ed.), *School violence* (pp. 69–77). New York: H. W. Wilson.

Eth, S., & Pynoos, R. (1985). Interaction of trauma and grief in childhood. In S. Eth & R. Pynoos (Eds.), *Post-traumatic stress disorder in children* (pp. 169–186). Washington, DC: American Psychiatric Press.

Evans, H. (2000). Young, female and turning deadly. In D. Bonilla (Ed.), *School violence* (pp. 51–55). New York: H. W. Wilson.

Fein, R., & Vossekuil, B. (2000). *Protective intelligence and threat assessment investigations* (Document No. NCJ 179981). Washington, DC: U.S. Department of Justice.

Frederick, C. J. (1985). Children traumatized by catastrophic situations. In S. Eth & R. S. Pynoos (Eds.), *Post-traumatic stress disorder in children* (pp. 71–99). Washington, DC: American Psychiatric Press.

Frederick, C., Pynoos, R., & Nader, K. (1992). *Childhood Post-Traumatic Stress Reaction Index.* Unpublished copyrighted instrument for measuring childhood trauma levels.

Furlong, M. J., Morrison, G. M., & Dear, J. D. (1994). Addressing school violence as part of schools' educational mission. *Preventing School Failure, 38,* 10–26.

Fuselier, G. D. (1988). Hostage negotiation consultant: Emerging role for the clinical psychologist. *Professional Psychology: Research and Practice, 19*(2), 175–179.

Garbarino, J. (1999). *Lost boys: Why our sons turn violent and how we can save them.* New York: The Free Press.

Garbarino, J., Kostelny, K., & Dubrow, N. (1991). What children can tell us about living in danger. *American Psychologist, 46,* 376–383.

Gibbs, N., & Roche, T. (1999, December 20). The columbine tapes [Special report]. *Time Magazine, 154*(25).

Gun-Free Schools Act of 1994, 20 U.S.C. § 14601 (1994).

Heras, P. (1992). Cultural considerations in the assessment and treatment of child sexual abuse. *Journal of Child Sexual Abuse, 1*, 119–132.

Herman, J. L. (1992). Captivity. In J. L. Herman (Ed.), *Trauma and recovery* (pp. 74–95). New York: Basic Books.

Hogue, T. E. (1994). Goal attainment scaling: A measure of clinical impact and risk assessment. *Issues of Criminological and Legal Psychology, 21*, 96–102.

Hough, R. L., Vega, W., Valle, R., Kolody, B., del Castillo, R. G., & Tarke, H. (1989). Mental health consequences of the San Ysidro McDonald's massacre: A community study. *Journal of Traumatic Stress, 3*, 71–92.

Howe, M. L., (1997). Children's memory for traumatic experiences. *Learning and Individual Differences, 9*, 153–174.

Jenkins, B. M. (1985). Reentry. In B. Jenkins (Ed.), *Terrorism and personal protection* (pp. 426–433). Boston: Butterworth.

Jessee, P. O., Strickland, M. P., & Ladewig, B. H. (1992). The aftereffects of a hostage situation on children's behavior. *American Journal of Orthopsychiatry, 62*(2), 309–312.

Kaufman, P., Chen, X., Choy, S., Ruddy, S. A., Miller, A. K., Chandler, K. A., Chapman, C. D., Rand, M. R., & Klaus, P. (1999). *Indicators of school crime and safety, 1999* (Publication Nos. NCES 1999-057 & NCJ-178906). Washington, DC: U.S. Department of Education and U.S. Department of Justice.

Kaufman, P., Chen, X., Choy, S. P., Ruddy, S. A., Miller, A. K., Fleury, J. K., Chandler, K. A., Rand, M. R., Klaus, P., & Planty, M. G. (2000). Indicators of school crime and safety, 2000. Washington, DC: U.S. Department of Education, Office of Educational Research and Improvement (NCES 2001–017) and U.S. Department of Justice, Office of Justice Programs (NCJ 184176).

Kiresuk, T. J., Smith, A., & Cardillo, J. E. (Eds.). (1994). *Goal Attainment Scaling: Applications, theory, and measurement*. Hillsdale, NJ: Erlbaum Associates.

Litwack, T. R., & Schlesinger, L. B. (1999). Dangerousness risk assessments: Research, legal, and clinical considerations. In A. K. Hess & I. B. Weiner (Eds.), *Handbook of forensic psychology* (2nd ed., pp. 171–217). New York: Wiley & Sons.

March, J., Amaya-Jackson, L., Foa, E., & Treadwell, K. (1999). *Trauma focused coping treatment of pediatric post-traumatic stress disorder after single-incident trauma* (Version 1.0). Unpublished manuscript.

Marsella, A. J., Friedman, M. J., Gerrity, E. T., & Scurfield, R. M. (Eds.). (1996). *Ethnocultural aspects of posttraumatic stress disorder: Issues, research, and clinical applications*. Washington, DC: American Psychological Association.

Mayer, M. J., & Leone, P. E. (1999). A structural analysis of school violence and disruption: Implications for creating safer schools. *Education and Treatment of Children, 22*(3), 333–356.

Nader, K. (1996). Children's exposure to violence and disaster. In C. A. Corr & D. M. Corr (Eds.), *Handbook of childhood death and bereavement* (pp. 201–222). New York: Springer.

Nader, K. (1997a). Assessing traumatic experiences in children. In J. Wilson, & T. Keane (Eds.), *Assessing psychological trauma and PTSD* (pp. 291–348). New York: Guilford Press.

Nader, K. (1997b). Treating traumatic grief in systems. In C. Figley, B. Bride, & N. Mazza (Eds.), *Death and trauma: The traumatology of grieving* (pp. 159–192). London: Taylor & Francis.

Nader, K. (1998). Violence: Effects of a parents' previous trauma on currently traumatized children. In Y. Danieli (Ed.), *An international handbook of multigenerational legacies of trauma* (pp. 571–583). New York: Plenum Press.

Nader, K. (2001). Treatment methods for childhood trauma. In J. P. Wilson, M. Friedman, & J. Lindy (Eds.), *Treating psychological trauma and PTSD* (pp. 278–334). New York: Guilford Press.

Nader, K., Pynoos, R., Fairbanks, L., & Frederick, C. (1990). Children's PTSD reactions one year after a sniper attack at their school. *American Journal of Psychiatry, 147*, 1526–1530.

National Institute of Mental Health. (2000). *Youth in a difficult world* [Fact sheet]. (NIH Publication No. 01-4587). Retrieved December 15, 2000, from, http://www.nimh.nih.gov/publicat/youthdif.cfm

National School Safety Center. (1999). *School associated violent deaths*. Retrieved November 16, 1999, from http://www.nssc1.org/savd/savd.pdf

Niehous, W. F. (1985). Surviving captivity II: The hostage's point of view. In B. Jenkins (Ed.), *Terrorism and personal protection* (pp. 423–425). Boston: Butterworth.

North, C. S., Smith, E. M., & Spitznagel, E. L. (1997). One-year follow-up of survivors of a mass shooting. *American Journal of Psychiatry, 154*, 1696–1702.

Ochberg, F. M. (1980). Victims of terrorism. *Journal of Clinical Psychiatry, 41*, 73–75.

Ochberg, F., & Soskis, D. (1982). Planning for the future: Means and ends. In F. Ochberg & D. Soskis (Eds.), *Victims of terrorism* (pp. 173–190). Boulder, CO: Westview Press.

Obmascik, M. (2000). Colorado, world mourns deaths at Columbine High. In D. Bonilla (Ed.), *School violence* (pp. 40–45). New York: H. W. Wilson.

Parson, E. R. (1997). Post-traumatic child therapy (P-TCT): Assessment and treatment factors in clinic work with inner-city children exposed to catastrophic community violence. *Journal of Interpersonal Violence, 12*, 172–194.

Pope, L., Campbell, M., & Kurtz, P. (1992). Hostage crisis: A school-based interdisciplinary approach to posttraumatic stress disorder. *Social Work in Education, 14*, 227–233.

Pynoos, R., Frederick, C., Nader, K., Arroyo, W., Eth, S., Nunez, W., Steinberg, A., & Fairbanks, L. (1987). Life threat and posttraumatic stress in school age children. *Archives of General Psychiatry, 44*, 1057–1063.

Realmuto, G. M., Masten, A., Carole, L. F., Hubbard, J., Groteluschen, A., & Chun, B. (1992). Adolescent survivors of massive childhood trauma in Cambodia: Life events and current symptoms. *Journal of Traumatic Stress, 5*, 589–599.

Rozensky, R. H., Sloan, I. H., Schwarz, E. D., & Kowalski, J. M. (1993). Psychological response of children to shootings and hostage situations. In C. F. Saylor (Ed.), *Children and disasters* (pp. 123–136). New York: Plenum Press.

Schwarz, E., & Kowalski, J. (1991a). Malignant memories: PTSD in children and adults after a school shooting. *Journal of the American Academy of Child and Adolescent Psychiatry, 30,* 936–944.

Schwarz, E., & Kowalski, J. (1991b). Posttraumatic stress disorder after a school shooting: Effects of symptom threshold selection and diagnosis by DSM-III, DSM-III-R, or proposed DSM-IV. *American Journal of Psychiatry, 148,* 592–597.

Schwarz, E., & Kowalski, J. (1992). Personality characteristics and posttraumatic stress symptoms after a school shooting. *Journal of Nervous and Mental Diseases, 180,* 735–737.

Sewell, K., & Mendelsohn, M. (2000). Profiling potentially violent youth: Statistical and conceptual problems. *Children's Services: Social Policy, Research, and Practice, 3,* 147–169.

Sinclair, B. (1999). *Report on state implementation of the Gun-Free Schools Act—School year 1997–98.* Retrieved December 30, 1999, from http://www.ed.gov/offices/OESE/SDFS/GFSA/index.html

Snyder, H. M. , & Sickmund, M. (1999). Juvenile offenders and victims: 1999 national report (Report no. NCJ 178257). Washington, DC: Office of Juvenile Justice and Delinquency Prevention.

Stilwell, B. M., Galvin, M., & Kopta, S. M. (1991). Conceptualization of conscience in normal children and adolescents, ages 5 to 17. *Journal of the American Academy of Child and Adolescent Psychiatry, 30,* 16–21.

Strentz, T. (1982). The Stockholm syndrome: Law enforcement policy and hostage behavior. In F. Ochberg & D. Soskis (Eds.), *Victims of terrorism* (pp. 149–163). Boulder, CO: Westview Press.

Suomi, S. J., & Levine, S. (1998). Psychobiology of intergenerational effects of trauma. In Y. Danielli (Ed.), *International handbook of multigenerational legacies of trauma* (pp. 623–637). New York: Plenum Press.

Swiss, S., & Giller, J. E. (1993). Rape as a crime of war: A medical perspective. *Journal of the American Medical Association, 270,* 612–615.

Symonds, M. (1980). The second injury to victims. *Evaluation and Change* [Special issue, Spring], 36–38.

Terr, L. (1979). Children of Chowchilla: Study of psychic trauma. *Psychoanalytic Study of the Child, 34,* 547–623.

Terr, L. (1991). Childhood traumas: An outline and overview. *American Journal of Psychiatry, 148,* 10–20.

Terr, L. C. (2001). Childhood posttraumatic stress disorder. In G. O. Gabbard (Ed.), *Treatment of psychiatric disorders* (3rd ed., Vol. 1, pp. 293–306). Washington, DC: American Psychiatric Press.

True, W. R., Rice, J., Eisen, S. A., Heath, S. C., Goldberg, V., Lyons, M. V., & Nowak, J. (1993). A twin study of genetic and environmental contribution to liability for post-traumatic stress symptoms. *Archives of General Psychiatry, 50*, 257–264.

Vernberg, E. M., & Twemlow, S. W. (2000). Profiling potentially violent youth: Comments and observations. *Children's Services: Social Policy, Research, and Practice, 3*, 171–173.

Vila, G., Porche, L., & Mouren-Simeoni, M. (1999). An 18-month longitudinal study of posttraumatic disorders in children who were taken hostage in their school. *Psychosomatic Medicine, 61*, 746–754.

Webb, N. B. (1994). School based assessment and crisis intervention with kindergarten children following the New York world trade center bombing. *Crisis Interventions, 1*, 47–59.

Wilson, J., & Keane, T. (Eds.). (1997). *Assessing psychological trauma and PTSD*. New York: Guilford Press.

14

THE AFTERMATH OF TERRORISM

ROBIN H. GURWITCH, KAREN A. SITTERLE,
BRUCE H. YOUNG, AND BETTY PFEFFERBAUM

The insidious reality of terrorism is that that anyone, anytime, anywhere can be a target. No one is immune; no one is safe. Terrorism is a vicious and violent strategy intended to kill innocent people and designed to intimidate and control a group or a nation by the threat of random murder. The traumatic impact of terrorism is greatly magnified because it is of human design. The intention of terrorists is to demoralize their targets, to undermine a community's sense of security, and to violate the belief that one's self, loved ones, and others are safe from harm. Victims are chosen precisely because they are helpless and defenseless; for this reason, children are often the targets of terrorist attacks.

Terrorism is an extreme form of trauma. All victims of violence may develop an acute sense of personal vulnerability and live in distressful expectation of harm; however, the extreme magnitude of violence involved in terrorist acts may undermine the cornerstones of possible recovery environments (e.g., home and family, peer group and school, and community). Moreover, terrorism's effects extends far beyond its direct victims to include secondary (e.g., helpers) and tertiary victims (e.g., relatives and next of kin). Increased media coverage, shared values, and identification with the victim also can extend victimization to an entire community or a nation. The unique and frightful characteristics of terrorism require special consideration because they necessarily inform and shape services provided by helping professionals in the aftermath.

Until recently, Americans perceived terrorism as something that happened in faraway places. Over the past decade, however, American lives have been greatly affected by events such as the bombings of Pan Am Flight 103, the World Trade Center, two American embassies in Africa, and the Alfred P. Murrah Federal Building in Oklahoma City. The September 11, 2001, terrorist attacks that destroyed the World Trade Center towers, damaged the Pentagon, and caused a plane crash in Pennsylvania forever changed America's perception of invulnerability. In all the events, children were either killed or seriously injured or had a parent who was either killed or seriously injured; many more were at risk for injury.

This chapter examines issues related to helping children cope with the effects of terrorist violence. We begin with a review of the emerging literature reporting the effects of exposure to terrorism. Next we summarize our work involving the impact on children of the Oklahoma City bombing. This discussion is followed by a review of recent intervention efforts, the challenges in implementing such programs, and the recommendations regarding future intervention program development. Last, because the reality of terrorism in America is a relatively new phenomenon and terrorist actions toward Americans are increasing, implications for public policy are addressed.

THE EFFECTS OF TERRORIST ACTS OF VIOLENCE ON CHILDREN: LITERATURE REVIEW

Discussion of terrorism in this chapter is confined to intentional acts of violence designed to intimidate or coerce others for political or social objectives and in which the impact on children is the focus. The literature reveals a continuum of violent activities that are classified as acts of terrorism. Terrorism ranges from isolated violent acts in peaceful countries (e.g., the Oklahoma City bombing) to serial terrorist acts in countries locked in political strife (e.g., bombings, kidnappings, and hostage-taking situations in Israel). The research also covers various methods used by terrorists. Some terrorists strike from afar with bombs, remaining hidden. Other terrorists use direct, face-to-face confrontations to attack civilians and take hostages. Moreover, unlike conventional war, political terrorism may be long term and random and often involves schools, homes, and neighborhoods (Swenson & Klingman, 1993). Consequently, children frequently are subjected to terrorist actions, leading to a state of "continuous traumatic stress syndrome" (Straker & the Sanctuaries Team, 1987). It remains to be investigated how this state will apply to children in the aftermath of recent terrorist events, the ongoing issues of alert, threats of invisible agent attacks, and the war on terrorism.

Most of the research with children has been conducted in response to situations in which a society is constantly exposed to violence, making terrorism a more common occurrence. The early literature, which is largely anecdotal or involves clinical case studies, was conducted in response to the frequent terrorist attacks on the Israeli civilian population, particularly during the 1970s and 1980s (Ayalon, 1982, 1983a,b, 1993; Fields, 1982). Those studies, as a body of work, indicate that children who are exposed to terrorism are deeply affected by that experience. However, structured assessments of posttraumatic stress (PTS) or posttraumatic stress disorder (PTSD) are not present in much of this early work because PTSD did not become a formal diagnostic entity until 1980 (American Psychiatric Association, 1980). Measures available for use with children also were not available to researchers at the time of the early studies.

Ayalon (1993) summarized the effects of 15 terrorist attacks occurring in the years 1974 to 1980, many of which involved kidnapping and face-to-face killing of Israeli civilians in the years. The attacks varied in duration (ranging from a few moments to a number of days) and in the number of people who were killed (which ranged from 1 to 38). In some cases, the victims were murdered at the onset of the attack. In others, they were held as hostages until their liberation by force through a military operation. Victims ranged in age from infants to adults and in kinship. In certain cases, attacks were directed toward an entire family, and in others the victims were captured in the company of peers, friends, or strangers. Many of the children were wounded, and almost all were eyewitness to murder. Ayalon's studies documented how children exposed to terror through terrorist attacks suffer symptoms indicative of what we now term *posttraumatic stress reactions* as well as other psychological difficulties, including depression, anxiety, and long-term psychological effects and disturbances in development.

Work in recent years has focused on psychological disturbances associated with PTSD using structured assessments with well-established criteria. Studies vary tremendously as to the methods used to assess PTS; no two studies use the same methodology. Across the studies, rates of PTSD in children exposed to terrorist events range from 28% to 50%. Similar to the Ayalon studies (Ayalon, 1983a,b), several reports also have documented other psychological difficulties, including depression, anxiety, and disturbances in behavior and development (Elbedour, Baker, Shalhoub-Kevorkian, Irwin, & Belmaker, 1999; Trappler & Friedman, 1996). The findings are fairly consistent across diverse political and ethnic groups.

Risk Factors Associated With Obvious PTSD in Children

Physical Injury or Witnessing Death and Physical Injury

High rates of PTS have been found in studies in which exposure includes physical injury or witnessing death and physical injury of others.

Desivilya, Gal, and Ayalon (1996) interviewed adolescent survivors of the Ma'alot terrorist attack in 1974 in Israel. This incident involved 120 high school children who were seized and taken hostage by armed Palestinian guerillas. The seizure lasted 16 hours; 22 of the children were killed, and many were wounded, some severely. The results indicated that survivors who had sustained severe injuries revealed poorer long-term adjustment and more distress than their counterparts who were not wounded or had mild injuries.

Trappler and Friedman (1996) examined the effects of a politically motivated terrorist shooting incident in New York, where a gunman specifically targeted a Hasidic group of male adolescents. One student was killed, another was critically injured, and many shots were fired. Highly significant differences were found between survivors and a comparison group of students attending the same school but who were not present at the shooting. Survivors suffered from moderate depression, severe anxiety, and moderate-to-severe PTS symptoms. The investigators found that 28% of the survivors were diagnosed with PTSD as well as concurrent major depression.

Degree of Exposure

Almqvist and Brandell-Forsberg (1997) specifically investigated whether the degree of traumatic exposure to terrorist-type actions is related to the prevalence of PTSD. In their study of Iranian preschool children, parents were asked to describe their children's exposure to different events, which ranged from severe direct exposure to war (i.e., violence) to indirect exposure to war (e.g., through television or hearsay). Almqvist and Brandell-Forsberg found that the degree of traumatic exposure was strongly related to the prevalence of PTSD. Children who were eyewitness to assaults on parents or were within approximately 55 yards of bomb explosions developed PTSD much more frequently than children who did not see violent acts, although they were exposed to air-raid bombardments in their neighborhoods. Most children were with one or both of their parents when they were exposed to severe traumatic events. The study's authors suggest that children with severe exposure to organized violence are at even greater risk for developing PTS symptomatology when their parents have been similarly exposed, because effective parenting is potentially compromised. Concerns of safety because of genocide actions were also predictive of PTS symptoms in Rwandan children (Dyregrov, Gupta, Gjestan, & Mukanohelli, 2000). With the thousands of children and adults directly impacted by the attacks of September 11, 2001, the relationship between exposure and symptom development needs closer examination.

Relationship to the Victim

Another critical factor placing children at risk is the child's relationship with the victim. Children appear to be most affected by incidents that involve people who are close to them (Pynoos & Eth, 1985). The highest rates of

PTSD have been found in studies in which children have lost a parent. Elbedour and colleagues (1999) found that more than one third (34.4%) of the children whose fathers were massacred while praying in a Muslim mosque met the criteria for PTSD on the Clinician-Administered PTSD Scale (Blake et al., 1990). Girls (50%) displayed greater PTSD symptomatology than boys (23.1%). Depression was also a significant feature among all subjects.

Similarly, evidence indicates that witnessing the death or injury of a close friend is particularly traumatic (Ayalon, 1993; Trappler & Friedman, 1996). In the previously mentioned study by Trappler and Friedman (1996), high school students who witnessed the shooting death of one classmate and the critical injury of another exhibited high rates of PTSD (28%), which were unremitting 1 year later. The violent death of a loved one appears to be particularly difficult, placing children at risk for significant symptoms associated with both trauma and loss. Again, with the magnitude of lives lost (many of them parents) in recent terrorist attacks against the United States, the risk of an extraordinary number of children developing PTSD must be addressed.

Parental Reactions and Distress

The literature on disaster and young children emphasizes the impact of parental involvement in mediating stress reactions. Two reviews (American Academy of Child and Adolescent Psychiatry [AACAP], 1998; Cohen, Berliner, & Mannarino, 2000) point out that numerous studies have documented a relationship between children's PTSD symptoms and family support and parental emotional reaction to the trauma. Specifically, across a variety of disasters, family support mitigates the development of PTSD in children. Conversely, the presence of parental distress about the traumatic event and the presence of parental psychiatric disorders predicted higher levels of PTSD in children (Cohen et al., 2000). How well parents and caregivers cope with a traumatic event has been described as the best predictor of how children will cope (Lyons, 1987).

The Long-Term Effects on Children of Exposure to Terrorism

The long-term effects of terrorism include high rates of unremitting PTSD in children (Almqvist & Brandell-Forsberg, 1997; Ayalon, 1993; Desivilya, Gal, & Ayalon, 1996; Elbedour et al., 1999; Trappler & Friedman, 1996). Almqvist and Brandell-Forsberg (1997) reported that preschool children who were initially diagnosed with PTSD (1 year postevent) continued to exhibit PTSD at follow-up (3.5 years postevent). Children who did not initially meet PTSD criteria tended to show a decrease in their psychological symptoms with time, although 2.5 years later more than 80% still showed some behavioral disorders (e.g., aggressiveness, generalized fear, irritability, peer problems, sleep disturbance, misbehavior, and restlessness). Similarly, in the Trappler and Friedman (1996) study, follow-up data (10 months postevent) indicated that adolescent survivors with other diagnoses (e.g., depression, anxiety, or adjustment disorder without PTSD) appeared to be recovering, whereas adolescents diagnosed with PTSD continued to show symptoms and functional impairment despite additional individual psychological treatment. The "long arm" of extreme victimization also was documented by Desivilya et al. (1996), who investigated survivors exposed to terrorism as children 17 years after the event. Their findings indicated that the effects of a traumatic face-to-face encounter with terrorism that involved mass casualties were quite pervasive and long lasting. Most survivors experienced some form of traumatic stress symptoms even 17 years after the terrorist assault.

In summary, the findings suggest that once a child develops PTSD, the psychological difficulties are likely to be severe, to follow a chronic course, and to be difficult to resolve even with treatment. Children who do not develop PTSD, however, are also at risk and may develop other significant behavioral and developmental difficulties (Ayalon, 1982; Cohen, Berliner, & March, 2000; Macksoud, Dyregrov & Raundalen, 1993; March, 1999). Political terrorism has other far-reaching, long-term effects on the psychosocial development of children (Macksoud et al., 1993). The constant unpredictability of political violence and acts of terrorism can alter children's sense of security, inhibit their ability to enjoy life in general, increase catastrophic expectations of the future, and destroy their ability to trust themselves and others (Ayalon, 1982; Lyons, 1987; Melville & Lykes, 1992).

TERRORIST BOMBING IN OKLAHOMA CITY

Many of the findings on the effects of terrorism on children are similar to findings of the effect of violence in general on children (Osofsky, 1997). The conclusions about terrorism, until recently, primarily involved investigations of children who frequently were exposed to violence in their surroundings. The bombing in Oklahoma City brought about one of the first investigations of how terrorism affects children who live in a country relatively free from large-scale, single-incident acts of violence. Until the destruction of the World Trade Center and the attack on the Pentagon on September 11, 2001, the bombing of the Murrah Federal Building in Oklahoma City on April 19, 1995, was the largest act of terrorism on American soil. Insights and lessons learned form this event may lead to a better understanding of the impact of terrorism on children. The Murrah Federal Building was nine stories high with a daycare center located on the second floor. The blast not only destroyed the federal building but also damaged 800 buildings and businesses in the area surrounding the explosion, including the adjacent YMCA, which also housed a day care facility. Miles from "ground zero," people reported shaking of buildings and hearing the blast. Within 1 mile of the site, glass breakage in buildings was evident (Oklahoma State Department of Health [OSDH], 1996; Sitterle & Gurwitch, 1999). The statistics related to this terrorist action were shattering. One hundred and sixty-eight people lost their lives, including 19 children. The blast left 30 children orphaned; 219 other children lost one parent. Area hospitals treated 442 people, 83 of whom required admission. Private physicians treated an additional 233 people. Among the injured were approximately 50 children from the adjacent YMCA day care facility. Because of the damage, 562 people were left homeless, and congregations in surrounding churches had to find new places to worship (OSDH, 1996).

With this unprecedented event came extensive media coverage. Cameras and crews were at the site, in the area, at the hospitals, and in the air within moments of the blast. The city and, indeed, the nation became riveted to the images of the aftermath of a terrorist incident that heretofore had been unimaginable. In Oklahoma City, coverage on television and in the press was fairly continuous for several weeks.

The immediate response to the bombing lasted 17 days. This large-scale response involved multiple agencies from local, state, and federal levels and involved thousands of law enforcement, fire department, emergency, and medical service personnel. An extensive mental health response was provided to the victims, their families, the rescue workers, and the community (American Psychological Association, 1997; Sitterle, 1995; Sitterle & Gurwitch, 1999). Here we summarize the findings from several of our research investigations examining children's responses to the bombing. The studies, taken together, examine the effects of the event on three different groups of children: (a) young children from the day care center adjacent to the bomb site; (b) elementary, middle, and high school children from the Oklahoma City Public Schools; and (c) middle school children living 100 miles away from the bomb site.

A Study of Preschool Children at the Bomb Site

Approximately 6 months after the terrorist bombing, Gurwitch and colleagues (Gurwitch, Pfefferbaum, & Leftwich, in press) evaluated 11 children ages 2 to 6 from the YMCA day care center adjacent to the bomb site and their mothers. No one in the day care center died or suffered serious or life-threatening injuries from the bombing; however, most sustained multiple cuts and bruises from the falling debris and glass. The children were exposed to chaos and constant media attention while they were evacuated from the destroyed building and in the aftermath of the event. Each mother completed a battery of questionnaires including the Structured Clinical Interview for DSM–IV (First, Spitzer, Gibbon, & Williams, 1997), which was also adapted for parental report of children's reactions; an unstructured play observation was conducted with each child. Although mothers endorsed many symptoms of PTSD, they reported few in their children. However, members of the mental health team and center staff observed signs of traumatic stress including posttraumatic play, increased startle responses, and sleep problems (Gurwitch et al., in press). These observations support other findings that parents underestimate their children's reactions (Almqvist & Brandell-Forsberg, 1997).

The objective findings were supported by informal assessments of infants, children, and families from the YMCA day care facility who were relocated to another center in Oklahoma City. A team of mental health providers headed by Robin Gurwitch collected qualitative data in the first 6 months following the bombing. Information was obtained from individual and group debriefings, educational and crisis intervention sessions with parents, and day care staff, and several debriefing sessions held with the children. Observations of the children were compared with staff reports and parent interviews about the children's behaviors.

Based on these informal assessments, infants and young children did display many PTS symptoms. Reactions noted in the young children included reexperiencing the event, as evidenced by extensive posttraumatic play and peer discussions of the bombing. Hyperarousal and an increased startle response were reported and observed in both infants and preschool children. Behaviors identified as disturbances in functioning included problems with sleep, increased irritability, and regressive behaviors, such as a return to the pacifier or bottle. The behavior changes were noted in children across the age range. The preschool children did not appear to avoid activities or people that served as reminders of the bombing but, instead, seemed to embrace opportunities to interact with the staff and first responders and play games that were reminiscent of the event. Restricted range of affect and a sense of a foreshortened future were relatively absent in reports from caregivers and professional observations of the children (Gurwitch & Pfefferbaum, 1999; Gurwitch et al., in press; Gurwitch, Tassey, Sitterle, & Pfefferbaum, 1998).

Informal feedback was obtained from staff and parents after debriefing and educational sessions. They reported that the information about normal reactions to trauma helped reduce their stress and noted that their concerns related to behavior changes seen in the children also diminished after discussing concerns with team members. Finally, they reported increased confidence in their abilities to address the children's behaviors and concerns (Gurwitch et al., in press).

In summary, formal and qualitative data from the infant and preschool sample mirrors findings in young children reported after other types of trauma, including natural disasters and shootings (cf. Gurwitch, Sullivan, & Long, 1998; Vogel & Vernberg, 1993). The observed increased startle response also supports Perry's (1997) findings of changes in the startle response following an intense trauma.

Responses of School-Age Children and Adolescents Following the Bombing

Concerns about the level of exposure to the bombing and potential clinical problems in Oklahoma youth, both locally and in the surrounding areas, prompted our research team to perform a clinical needs assessment. The studies reported here form part of a larger assessment designed to identify school-age children who were at risk and in need of treatment. Here we report the results from middle and high school children at 7 weeks after the blast and elementary school children at 8 to 10 months after the bombing. The clinical needs assessment procedure was generally the same for both groups of participants and is outlined below.

Clinical Needs Assessment Procedure

The Clinical Needs Assessment instrument consisted of 56 items and, in consultation with Robert Pynoos, was designed specifically for the Oklahoma City bombing study. Variables included direct exposure through physical proximity to the blast (physical exposure), as measured by two items asking participants if they heard or felt the explosion. Indirect exposure through bomb-related television viewing (television exposure) was assessed by a single-item: "How much bomb-related TV did you watch?" Personal loss and consequences (emotional exposure) examined the child's relationship to people who were killed or injured. Other items targeted difficulty handling the demands of home and school and whether the children had sought counseling.

A 12-item measure was used to assess retrospective reports of initial arousal and fear. This measure was adapted from scales developed for this use by Freedy, Kilpatrick, and Resnick (1993) and Wang, Pynoos, James, and Wang (1994). The measure of PTS was adapted from the Impact of Event Scale-Revised (IES-R; Weiss & Marmar, 1997). The IES-R consists of 22 items representing the three PTSD symptom clusters. It includes items measuring intrusion and avoidance from the Impact of Event Scale (Horowitz, Winler, & Alvarez, 1979) and items assessing arousal added by Weiss and Marmar (1997). Participants were asked to rate the frequency of occurrence of 22 symptoms in "the past seven days" on a scale with four response options: *not at all*, *rarely*, *sometimes*, and *often*. The PTS symptom score was a summation of all items on this scale.

Middle and High School Students

Seven weeks after the terrorist bombing, approximately 3,200 middle and high school students completed the clinical needs assessment. The students were largely minority youths, and although all socioeconomic levels were represented, students from lower socioeconomic status families predominated. Girls (56.5%) outnumbered boys (43.5%), and lower grade students predominated—more than 78% of the children attended grades 6 to 8.

Results revealed that more than 60% of the students heard and felt the explosion, a finding that was not surprising given the proximity of the schools to the bomb site. The impact of indirect exposure (as a result of viewing bomb-related events and images on television) also was extensive. Two thirds (66.6%) of the students reported that "most" or "all" of their television viewing was bomb related (Pfefferbaum, Nixon, Krug, et al., 1999; Pfefferbaum et al, 2000).

A large number of children in our sample reported emotional exposure by knowing someone injured or killed in the blast. More than one third of the students reported knowing someone killed, and more than 40% of the children reported knowing someone injured. Within the bereaved group of children, 49 students reported that an immediate family member (e.g., parent or sibling) was killed, and 81 children said that a family member had been injured. Interestingly, 330 students reported attending at least one bomb-related funeral; of this group, 107 attended more than one funeral (Pfefferbaum, Nixon, Krug, et al., 1999). The results are consistent with a random-digit dial telephone survey of adults residing in Oklahoma City in which more than one third reported knowing someone killed or injured in the blast (Smith, Christiansen, Vincent, & Hann, 1999) and thus underscore the communitywide nature of this terrorist event (Sitterle & Gurwitch, 1999).

To further examine the effects of traumatic loss, three groups of children experiencing loss across a spectrum of relationships were compared: children who lost (a) an immediate family member (either a parent or sibling); (b) a relative outside the immediate family; or (c) a friend or acquaintance. The three groups of bereaved children were compared with peers who did not know anyone killed (i.e., *nonbereaved* peers). Comparisons of the bereaved groups with the nonbereaved groups are included in the discussion that follows (Pfefferbaum, Nixon, Tucker, et al., 1999).

Seven weeks after the bombing, 62.8% of the total sample reported that they still worried about themselves or their families and 14.7% of the children reported that they still did not feel safe "at all." Comparison of the bereaved and nonbereaved children revealed that more than 33% of those who lost an immediate family member reported not feeling safe at all, whereas only 11.9% of those who lost no one reported a similar response. When asked about current worries about self or family, 75% of those who lost a parent or sibling and 73.8% of those who lost another relative reported some level of worry. In contrast, 40% of those reporting no loss reported no worry. Bereaved children also were significantly more likely than nonbereaved children to report that the bombing changed life at home and school. When groups were compared, those reporting the loss of an immediate family member were more likely than other bereaved groups to "strongly agree" with statements reflecting changes at home and school.

Significant gender differences were found in the total sample; girls reported higher levels of PTS symptoms than did boys. PTS symptoms were examined in relation to exposure as a result of personal loss (i.e., knowing someone killed or injured). Predictably, students who reported that their parents or siblings were killed or injured exhibited more symptoms of PTS than their counterparts. An unexpected finding, however, was that children reporting a sibling killed or injured endorsed the greatest number of PTS symptoms, followed next by those reporting a parent killed or injured. Similarly, children reporting a sibling injured had significantly higher PTS symptoms than all other groups.

One of the findings in our work has been the influence of bomb-related television exposure on PTS symptomatology. Most of the children in the sample reported that in the aftermath of the bombing, "most" or "all" of their television viewing was bomb related, and television exposure correlated with PTS symptoms at 7 weeks. The impact of media exposure was further examined by studying youth with no physical or interpersonal exposure. Those who reported high levels of television exposure were more symptomatic at 7 weeks than those with less television exposure (Pfefferbaum et al., 2001).

In our sample, the retrospective report of arousal at the time of the blast was highly predictive of the total PTS symptoms and symptom cluster scores at 7 weeks. In addition, in our sample, the retrospective report of symptoms associated with arousal at the time of the blast was highly predictive of levels of PTS symptoms and symptom cluster scores at 7 weeks. Of note, television exposure was shown to be a stronger predictor of PTS for the full middle school sample than either physical or emotional exposure (Pfefferbaum et al., 2001).

Counseling services were available in the public schools and in city and state agencies (Pfefferbaum, Call, & Sconzo, 1999). These were available to students identified by parents, school personnel, or the students themselves as needing mental health services in the aftermath of the bombing. Only 6.8% of the total sample reported that they had had contact with a counselor or clergy for mental health support. When examined by loss, approximately 40% of the students who lost an immediate family member, 15% of those who lost another relative, and 8% of those who lost a friend or acquaintance had been seen by a counselor (Pfefferbaum, Nixon, Krug, et al., 1999).

Elementary School Students

Approximately 1,150 elementary school children (grades 3–5) in the Oklahoma City Public School system completed the clinical needs assessment 8 to 10 months after the bombing (Cote, Leftwich, Gurwitch, & Pfefferbaum, 1999; Gurwitch & Pfefferbaum, 1999). The sample had approximately equivalent numbers of boys and girls and equivalent grade distribution. Race also reflected the school system demographics— most of the children were African American.

Nearly one fourth of the children reported that a family member or relative was killed or injured, and almost 30% of children reported knowing a friend or acquaintance who was killed or injured in the blast. As expected, the closer the relationship a child had with someone killed or injured by the bombing (i.e., higher level of interpersonal exposure), the greater the PTS symptoms endorsed on the IES-R. Girls tended to have higher IES-R scores than did boys (Gurwitch, Leftwich, Pfefferbaum, & Pynoos, 2000).

Close to 1 year after the bombing, nearly 5% of the elementary school children reported that they were experiencing clinically significant levels of PTS as a result of the bombing. Nearly one third of the children continued to be concerned about family members, and one fifth had trouble calming down after a bombing reminder. Similar to the data collected from the middle and high school students 7 weeks after the bombing, the students reporting all or most of their television viewing to have been bomb related had significantly higher PTS symptoms than students reporting little to no bombing-related television. At the time of the survey, media attention had turned to the criminal proceedings. Much of this television coverage revolved around the trial and provided frequent images of the original blast, those wounded and killed, and the destruction of the building. Almost two thirds of the children reported distress surrounding their feelings toward the perpetrator(s) of the event. Unfortunately, 8 to 10 months after the bombing, although less than one third of the children reported contact with a counselor to discuss the bombing, many children reported continuing distress (Gurwitch & Pfefferbaum, 1999).

Middle School Students 100 Miles From the Bombing

Two years after the terrorist action, Pfefferbaum and colleagues (2000) investigated the impact of the Oklahoma City bombing on middle school students residing in a community 100 miles from Oklahoma City. The children had no direct physical or interpersonal exposure, but approximately one third of children reported having a friend who knew someone killed or injured in the incident. Media exposure and, to a lesser extent, indirect interpersonal exposure were significant predictors of PTS symptomatology. Two years after the event, almost 20% of the sample reported current bomb-related symptoms that impaired their functioning at home or school.

Discussion of Findings and Clinical Implications

In summary, the results of our research on children's responses to the bombing in Oklahoma City indicate that the ripple effect of terrorism affects literally thousands of innocent children. These children experienced emotional reactions and may be at risk for long-term difficulties. Large numbers of children reported high rates of PTS symptoms, and more than one third of the total sample (i.e., more than 1,000 children) reported knowing someone killed in the explosion. Our finding that the degree of exposure, here defined as knowing someone killed or injured, is an important risk factor in the development of PTS symptoms after trauma. It is consistent with other studies of children and disaster (e.g., Pynoos et al., 1987).

Many children in our sample may have been both traumatized and bereaved. The violent death of a loved one appears to be particularly difficult in that trauma and grief reactions may interact. Pynoos and colleagues (Pynoos & Nader, 1988; Pynoos, Steinberg, & Goenjian, 1996; Pynoos, Zisook, & Foy, 1995) noted that a significant problem in the child trauma literature has been a failure to differentiate between PTS symptoms and symptoms of grief and their interaction resulting in traumatic bereavement. In their studies involving children exposed to violence and loss (both of which are risk factors in terrorism), Pynoos (1992) and Goenjian (Goenjian et al., 1997) found evidence of PTS symptoms, grief reactions, complicated grief, and bereavement-related depression. Those authors have described how PTS complicates the grieving process and interferes with children's efforts to address the loss and adapt to subsequent life changes. It is important to evaluate the interaction of trauma and grief in future research on terrorism because they have significant treatment implications (Gurwitch & Kees, in press).

Futhermore, initial experience (e.g., arousal) with the bombing was predictive of symptoms almost 2 months later. Although the preschool children did not show evidence of avoidance, those symptoms were strongly endorsed by children in the elementary school grades, suggesting a developmental progression of PTS symptoms (Gurwitch et al., 2000). Indeed, many researchers (e.g., Green et al., 1991; Terr, 1985) see age and developmental level as two factors to be considered in working with children after a trauma. For example, an adolescent's understanding of death following terrorist actions will likely be different from a preschool child's understanding of the same event.

Gender differences, as seen in the data collected from Oklahoma City, also have been supported in the literature (Garrison et al., 1995; Green et al., 1991; Shannon, Lonigan, Finch, & Taylor, 1994), but that finding is not consistent (Blom, 1986; Nader, Pynoos, Fairbanks, Al-Ajeel, & Al-Asfour, 1993; Shaw et al., 1995). It is possible that the type of trauma or disaster experienced may affect gender differences. Another possibility may be that girls are more likely to internalize symptoms associated with PTS, whereas boys show more of an externalized expression, which is not addressed by the current PTSD criteria. Additional controlled research is needed to explain discrepant findings.

Across all ages, the role of television exposure also appeared to be a significant risk factor in the development of PTS symptoms (Gurwitch & Pfefferbaum, 1999; Pfefferbaum et al., 2001). Television has become an essential tool for learning about events in our world. As children increase their exposure to world events through this medium, it seems critical for researchers to empirically examine the issue of how children are affected by graphic media coverage of traumatic events. Our research indicates that media and television coverage can be an important secondary source of exposure to trauma. Children who were not directly exposed to the bombing, either by physical proximity or by having a parent, sibling, relative, or friend injured or killed, but who endorsed extensive television viewing of the bombing also endorsed a greater number of PTS symptoms than those with less viewing. It is as though, through the media, children experience vicarious exposure that may be as significant a traumatic stressor as direct experience. This idea parallels much of the emerging literature on the traumatic impact on children of witnessing violence (Osofsky, 1997; Pynoos, 1992). It may be that being a passive observer in a community victimized by terrorism, even by viewing it on television, affects young children and places them at risk for the development of significant levels of PTS.

The findings related to television viewing of children in a distant Oklahoma community may in part be explained by a classification scheme for trauma-related conditions not associated with direct threat that has been proposed by Terr and colleagues (1999). They described a range of perceptual and interpersonal involvement in children following the *Challenger* disaster. Perceptual involvement may occur through direct witnessing, media coverage, and hearing about an incident. Interpersonal involvement may range from a direct personal relationship with a victim to various indirect relationships. Images and reports surrounding the attacks of September 11 riveted the nation and the world, and the coverage continues. As it made a difference in children's reactions after Oklahoma City, it is imperative that the effects of the reporting on September 11 and related ongoing actions be investigated. Questions for future research may involve not only the quantity of the viewing of the trauma but the quality. For example, a potential moderating factor, such as discussing the images and information with adults, may temper the negative impact of this type of exposure on children's PTS reactions.

Clearly, our research indicates that our understanding of who constitutes the victims of communitywide acts of violence, such as terrorism, needs to be broadened. Our findings suggest that the circle of impact is far greater than might initially be expected and point to the strong need for professionals to actively screen *all* children within an affected community, not just the children who have been directly and personally affected. Since September 11, 2001, anecdotal accounts of children's distress have been reported from across the country. It is important to be proactive in identifying such children, rather than wait for them to come to the attention of concerned parents or school personnel, who may themselves be similarly affected.

Terrorism is of human design and criminal in nature. The data from the Oklahoma City schoolchildren indicated that their feelings toward the perpetrators of the trauma were distressing. After the attacks in New York City, Robin Gurwitch talked with children from the affected area and the children shared incidents of hate talk toward classmates of Middle Eastern descent.

We recommend that future examinations of children's responses to terrorism include an assessment of feelings related to the perpetrators as well as their faith in the criminal justice system. Perhaps assessments of PTS symptoms at times surrounding criminal proceedings are warranted, because such proceedings may serve as significant reminders and television is likely to convey many images and stories surrounding the terrorist actions. Ongoing monitoring of peer interactions and hate talk is also recommended.

The universal screening revealed a large percentage of children endorsing PTS symptoms who never had contact with mental health personnel. The data underscore the difficulties of relying on parents and school personnel alone to accurately identify all children at risk after a trauma. The lack of identification and, therefore, lack of intervention may place children at increased risk for development of PTS symptoms and related difficulties in the future.

U.S. EMBASSY BOMBINGS IN EAST AFRICA

Shortly after the terrorist bombing in Oklahoma City, two other terrorist events involving U.S. embassies in East Africa occurred (Nairobi, Kenya, and Dar es Salaam, Tanzania). The events exposed U.S. vulnerability to international terrorism abroad. In Nairobi, more than 200 people were killed and more than 5,000 were injured. The casualties, for the most part, spared children from direct physical exposure. Far fewer people were killed or injured in the nearly simultaneous explosion in Dar es Salaam, but the Embassy was totally destroyed.

"Operation Recovery" was established to respond to the mental health needs in Nairobi. This effort was swift and benefited from consultation with mental health disaster response specialists from around the world, including experts from Oklahoma City (Betty Pfefferbaum). Operation Recovery provided crisis and support services, outreach, and public education. The U.S. Agency for International Development later established a similar effort through the Kenya Red Cross Society and the International Federation of the Red Cross and Red Crescent Societies. Children were seen in school settings as well as treatment facilities throughout the community.

Preliminary analysis of a sample of almost 300 children surveyed within 1 year of the Nairobi bombing revealed high levels of interpersonal exposure associated with increased bomb-related PTS symptomatology, similar to the findings of the children in Oklahoma City. In contrast to Oklahoma City, however, danger is a way of life in Nairobi. Natural disasters, crime, and political violence are common. In addition, PTS symptoms associated with a prior traumatic event were an important predictor in the development of bomb-related PTS symptomatology in the Nairobi school sample (B. Pfefferbaum & C. North, personal communication, November, 2000).

Clearly, the potential exists for serious long-term psychological sequelae for children exposed to terrorism. A review of the current literature suggests that the natural course of PTSD in children is not uniform (AACAP, 1998). Although symptoms may remit in many children, symptoms may persist for significant periods of time in a substantial proportion of others. Identifying the critical risk factors that may predict how a child reacts to traumatic stressors and what impact intervention efforts may have on long-term outcome is, therefore, essential to furthering our work with children and trauma. No studies have measured the efficacy of interventions following terrorist acts of violence; the methodological challenge of measuring the efficacy of such multivariate programs is formidable (Cohen et al., 2000). Thus, systematic interventions with children following terrorist events are guided more by clinical principles and related findings than by treatment outcome studies.

Intervention Model for Children Affected by Violent Acts of Terrorism

Effective mental health interventions following catastrophic events, including violent acts of terrorism, should be theoretically and empirically informed, developmentally appropriate, and shaped by survivor's needs (AACAP, 1998; Cohen et al., 2000; Pynoos, Steinberg, & Wraith, 1995). Moreover, interventions need to match the temporal phases of the traumatic event. The essential components in response to communitywide acts of terrorism should include (a) early community-based intervention; (b) clinical needs assessment to identify children at risk; (c) multimodel, trauma-loss-focused treatment programs; and (d) program evaluation of treatment efficacy.

Early Community-Based Intervention

Interventions during the initial aftermath, when the needs of survivors are primarily related to safety and physical health, are necessarily pragmatic in nature and different from interventions when life threat and physical hardship are not imminent. During the immediate aftermath of a terrorist event, children not only need to be in a safe environment, they also need to *feel* safe and to know the whereabouts and the safety of parents, siblings, and other loved ones. They need adequate food, rest, and sleep. Correspondingly, mental health interventions at this phase may be understood as "psychological first aid" (Pynoos & Nader, 1988; Young, 1998).

The objectives of psychological first aid include the establishment of safety (both objective and subjective), stress-related symptom reduction, restoration of rest and sleep, and connection to social support and caregivers (e.g., family, clergy, primary care physicians, teachers, and protectors, such as police; Pynoos & Nader, 1988; Young, 1998). For example, a psychological first aid program was developed as a crisis intervention program for children; it expands the critical incident stress debriefing (CISD) model (Mitchell, 1983) to include two to three sessions (Pynoos & Nader, 1988). This program emphasizes clarifying the facts about the traumatic event, normalizing children's PTS reactions, encouraging expression of feelings, and teaching problem-solving techniques. Other adaptations of this debriefing model may include the use of art and other media to facilitate the child's expression of feelings. An essential component is screening children for significant psychological difficulties and referral for intensive and ongoing treatment.

Children who are most in need of psychological first aid include those who exhibit extreme anxiety, dissociative symptoms (i.e., experience of the world as dreamlike, detachment, derealization, and depersonalization), uncontrollable intense grief, inability to sleep or eat, or extreme cognitive impairment (e.g., confusion, poor concentration, and impaired decision making). In general, all children survivors will benefit from some degree of psychological first aid.

Young, Ford, Ruzek, Friedman, and Gusman (1998) suggested ways of helping survivors in the immediate aftermath of a disaster that are applicable to children. They include six central principles: (a) ensuring children's basic survival and comfort resources (e.g., food, shelter, and clothing); (b) ensuring basic personal space (e.g., privacy, quiet, and space for personal effects); (c) addressing physical health problems or concerns; (d) reassuring safety and the whereabouts and status of loved ones and friends; (e) reconnecting children with loved ones, friends, and trusted other persons; and (f) helping children and families take practical steps to resolve instrumental problems caused by the terrorist event.

In the weeks following the terrorist event, mental health interventions may still be pragmatic in that they help children and families take practical steps to resume ordinary day-to-day life; that is, normal family, student, community, and work roles. During this time, other forms of early intervention may be appropriate, including formal clinical assessment, one-to-one counseling, and brief treatment.

In the aftermath of traumatic events, the most commonly used early clinical intervention is debriefing. Several models of debriefing have been described (e.g., Armstrong, O'Callahan, & Marmar, 1991; Dyregrov, 1989; Raphael, 1986; Young, 1998), although CISD (Mitchell, 1983) is the best known and most widely delivered model. The current practice of routinely providing debriefing to children exposed to community disaster and violence, however, deserves further examination (Cohen et al., 2000; Foa, 2001; Gurwitch, 2001). For one, serious questions have been raised about the efficacy of psychological debriefing with adults. Randomized trials have failed to demonstrate that debriefing prevents subsequent PTSD, and evidence indicates that it sometimes has iatrogenic impact on adults (Bisson, 1997; Rose, Brewin, Andrews, & Kirk, 1999). It is possible that too much information about harmful trauma consequences or the reliving aspect of some approaches to debriefing actually sensitizes recipients instead of alleviating distress.

Second, because of the severity of traumatic exposure associated with terrorism, it is even less likely that either short-term crisis intervention or debriefing procedures will be powerful enough mediators to mitigate stress reactions.

Even if debriefing does not prove effective in the prevention of PTS, it is possible that debriefing methods may achieve other important outcomes if used in the context of a comprehensive intervention program. Participant ratings of perceived helpfulness are consistently high across studies, although such ratings are uncorrelated with levels of PTS symptoms and other psychological distress (Carr, Lewin, Webster, & Kenardy, 1997). Debriefings also can help provide education, identify children at risk, and determine those in need of in-depth evaluation or treatment.

Communitywide Screening of Children At Risk

Several studies have found that parents and teachers tend to minimize children's trauma-related reactions (Almqvist & Brandell-Forsberg, 1997; Handford et al., 1986). Parents and teachers may misunderstand the impact of the trauma in their desire to reassure themselves that children are not harmed in any way or to relieve vicarious distress over the child's experience. Parents and caregivers may misinterpret reactions such as ongoing discussions of the event or posttraumatic play as signs of effectively processing the trauma. If adults are experiencing distress about a trauma, such as the recent terrorist attacks in the U.S., they may not be able to recognize similar distress in their children. If children sense distress in the significant adults in their lives, they may minimize reactions in hopes of not further upsetting their caregivers or teachers. Finally, many salient PTS symptoms may not be readily observable, such as emotional constriction, withdrawal, or dissociation. We believe sufficient evidence supports the use of universal screening of children to identify those at risk following a terrorist event. Systematic community-based screening of children is most easily conducted in settings such as schools (public and private), neighborhood centers, or primary care settings. The screening information then can be used to identify children at risk, determine children in need of trauma-related services, guide outreach efforts, and plan specialized treatment programs tailored to the unique needs of the children, their families, and the community. Moreover, the screening data can provide pretreatment baseline data for evaluating a treatment program's effectiveness.

The consensus on the most effective means of assessing children following trauma continues to be debated (AACAP, 1998; Cohen et al., 2000). Many self-report and structured interviews for assessing children are available and can be used to systematically screen children and identify those in need of treatment. Although a review of trauma assessment instruments for children are beyond the scope of this chapter, they are available in literature (AACAP, 1998; Carlson, 1997; March, 1999; see also chapter 2, this volume). A second issue in the assessment of PTS in children is related to current diagnostic criteria. No consensus exists about the "typical" presentation of PTSD in young children (Cohen, 1998). Unfortunately, the diagnostic construct of PTSD, as currently defined by the *Diagnostic and Statistical Manual of Mental Disorders, Fourth Edition* (American Psychiatric Association, 1994) fails to take into account some important developmental considerations. Young children who are experiencing acute or chronic stress reactions may present relatively few PTSD symptoms because nearly half of the diagnostic symptoms require verbal descriptions of the experience and internal states that exceed a young child's cognitive and language skills (Scheeringa, Zeanah, Drell, & Larrieu, 1995). This requirement may account for why children are likely to have symptoms but rarely receive a diagnosis of PTSD following a traumatic event (Cohen et al., 2000; Gurwitch et al., 2000).

The UCLA Trauma Psychiatry Program has developed a systematic screening procedure that is currently being used in the Pasadena, California, schools with adolescents exposed to community violence and traumatic loss (Saltzman, Pynoos, Layne, Steinberg, & Aisenberg, 1999). This screening, which is one component of a school-based trauma- and grief-focused psychotherapy program, has been adapted from the programs used following the Armenian earthquake (Goenjian et al., 1997) with adolescent victims of community violence, and in postwar Bosnia (Layne, Pynoos, & Cardenas, 2001). The purpose of the schoolwide screening is to identify students who have experienced significant trauma or loss and exhibit symptoms of PTSD, depression, and complicated grief. The screening, which is administered in a group format, is a self-report instrument and includes measures of exposure, PTSD symptoms, depressive symptoms, and normal and complicated grief reactions. In addition, various indices are used to assess school performance, including grade point average, number of classes failed, number of suspensions, and teacher reports of behavioral difficulties. As this screening evolves, it may be useful to add indices related to change in participation in extracurricular activities and interactions with peers. Furthermore, since children may be anxious or depressed following trauma, screenings should also incorporate these issues (Cohen, Berliner, & March, 2000; March, 1999).

Students endorsing significant exposure to violence or traumatic loss or who evidence significant PTSD, depression, or complicated grief symptoms during the screening process are then triaged for further assessment on an individual basis. This clinical evaluation involves a semistructured assessment to obtain a detailed understanding of the child's traumatic exposure, endorsed symptoms, and level of impairment across settings. Furthermore, the interview is used to identify major psychiatric disorders and substance abuse, suicidality, homicidality, and issues requiring intervention outside of the treatment program.

Challenges and Obstacles in Screening Children

Access to victims, especially children, in the aftermath of traumatic events can be particularly difficult. Protective boundaries often form around survivors (Lindy & Grace, 1986; Young, 1990), making both access to victims and recruitment into studies difficult, especially when either involve children. When trauma is a terrorist action, the boundaries between systemic methods to assess the impact and the victims may be even more impenetrable. For example, following the Oklahoma City bombing, efforts were made to screen all children in the Oklahoma City public school system. Although the superintendent was supportive of this need, ultimate decisions were left to local school principals and individual classroom teachers. Several refused to participate, stating with assurance that all children at risk had already been identified by school personnel and school services. Given our findings that most of the Oklahoma City Public School children assessed showed PTS symptoms and that less than one third of elementary school students had been in contact with a mental health professional, it is believed that many children in need of services were never identified (Gurwitch & Pfefferbaum, 1999). Some children also may minimize their reactions in an effort to protect their parents and other adults from knowing how badly the trauma has affected them (AACAP, 1998; Cohen et al., 2000; Yule & Williams, 1990). It is therefore critical to educate and enlist the support of those involved in leadership and decision-making positions within the setting in which the screening is to be conducted as well as the support of the child's parents and caregivers. The challenges to a universal screening may be especially daunting in the face of the September 11, 2001, tragedy. With thousands of children being directly impacted and thousands potentially indirectly affected, it is imperative that we overcome barriers that may hinder identification of children in need of services.

Community-Based Trauma and Loss Programs

Communitywide interventions are necessarily complex and require multimodal programs with extended community involvement because the effects of traumatization extend into many domains of a child's life, such as family, school, peers, and health. As the literature and our research indicate, terrorist attacks create extreme stress reactions in children and therefore require a level of family, community, and professional support that far exceeds crisis intervention models alone.

Despite the lack of treatment outcome studies with children exposed to terrorist acts of violence, the empirical evidence and clinical consensus support the use of "trauma-focused interventions" in the treatment of PTSD in children (Berliner, 1997; Cohen, 1998; Cohen et al., 2000, Cohen & Mannarino, 1996; Deblinger, Lippman, & Steer, 1996; Frederick, 1996; Goenjian et al., 1997). The current state of knowledge indicates that the essential components of trauma-specific treatment should include psychoeducation about trauma, anxiety management, and cognitive coping skills; exposure (i.e., directly addressing the trauma); correcting the child's inaccurate and maladaptive attributions; and a parallel treatment for parents and caregivers.

One program that incorporates all of those components is the UCLA School-Based Trauma/Grief-Focused Psychotherapy Program developed by Pynoos, Saltzman, and colleagues (Saltzman et al., 1999), outlined previously. Early outcome data for this program is promising; participants show reduction in symptoms and improved academic performance and school behavior (Saltzman et al., 1999). This program has recently been refined for use with traumatically bereaved children in New York City (Layne, Saltzman, & Pynoos, 2001; Pynoos, personal communication, November, 2001).

Rescue! An Emergency Handbook (Ayalon, 1978) is a manualized program for educators and mental health professionals to use specifically to support children in the aftermath of a terrorist attack or following a "near miss." The program has been accepted by the Israeli Ministry of Education for widespread use throughout the education system in Israel and was used extensively in the northern border areas. It includes a wide variety of tools that are oriented to the development of coping skills in emotionally expressive, cognitive, and behavioral areas by means of work in groups, bibliotherapy, creative expression through writing and play, simulated situations, drama, and guided-imagination exercises that are suitable for all age groups. Ayalon (1993) stresses that such crisis intervention strategies should be initiated immediately, should be provided on-site, and should use a community intervention approach. No treatment outcome data on the handbook is currently in the literature.

Following the bombing in Oklahoma City, Gurwitch and Messenbaugh (2001) developed a manualized treatment program for use following communitywide traumatic events, including acts of terrorist violence. The program, *Healing After Trauma Skills* (HATS), benefited from the work of La Greca, Vernberg, Silverman, Vogel, and Prinstein (1994) following Hurricane Andrew and of Storm, McDermott, and Finlayson (1994) after the Australian bushfires. HATS, which is primarily for children ages 5 to 12, incorporates educational material on basic safety skills in the face of disasters, psychoeducation, and treatment exercises to address symptoms and behavioral difficulties associated with trauma and loss. This systematic program is conducted by mental health professionals or school personnel and relies on a group format, although it may be used individually. Other key components include active involvement and participation of parents and caregivers. Perhaps one of the most important features of the HATS manual is the inclusion of the child's parents or guardians. These home-based exercises are included because they can have a significant impact on the child's adjustment. Although HATS is based on theoretical and empirical findings related to children and trauma and disaster, well-designed research studies are needed to determine the program's effectiveness.

Immediately after the terrorist attacks of September 11, 2001, the American Red Cross developed classroom materials to help children cope. The materials are grade-specific exercises that can be easily incorporated into the school curricula (American Red Cross, 2001). La Greca, Sevin, and Sevin (2001) also developed a manual for parents to use with their children to address the events and aftermath of the terrorist actions. Evaluation of these materials will be important.

In summary, the literature on treatment interventions following violent acts of terrorism is sparse. Assessments, interventions, and manuals to aid in working with victims of terrorist events are being developed, but work is needed to determine the efficacy of those approaches. A few currently being implemented and evaluated are showing success (Goenjian et al., 1997; Layne, Pynoos, et al., 2001; Murphy, Pynoos, & James, 1997; Saltzman et al., 1999). Drawing on these established programs may serve as an important first step in developing effective interventions with children impacted by communitywide terrorist events.

Public Policy Implications

The magnitude and severity of emotional difficulties that follow terrorist incidents require specialized multimodal clinical interventions that are responsive to children's needs at different temporal phases following the traumatic event. It is critical that mental health public policies be similarly developed and match the phases of survivors and their families' needs during the long course of recovery.

Typically, a crisis intervention model has been advocated by federal agencies following large-scale community events, including terrorist events (Meyers, 1994). Such a model was used following the Oklahoma City bombing (Pfefferbaum, Call, & Sconzo, 1999) as well as following the events of September 11, 2001 (e.g., Project Liberty and Project Phoenix). Until recently, the federal laws designed to provide funding for the long-term emotional needs of victim groups exposed to large-scale violent acts or traumatic loss have been inadequate (American Psychological Association, 1997). Moreover, the intervention model supported by those grants was a brief crisis intervention model that depends largely on paraprofessionals and mental health professionals with little training in disaster, trauma, or grief counseling. Unfortunately, both qualitative and quantitative data appearing in the literature indicate that the needs of people affected by a terrorist event, particularly children, are long lasting and are unlikely to be mitigated by a crisis intervention approach alone (Almqvist & Brandell-Forsberg, 1997; Trappler & Friedman, 1996). In the aftermath of community violence, many factors may inadvertently contribute to the underestimation of those in need. For example, empirical findings indicate that parents and teachers tend to underestimate or minimize the extent and severity of children's emotional reactions following traumatic events. We therefore support the recommendation of several experts (AACAP, 1998; March, Amaya-Jackson, Murry, & Schulte, 1998; Saltzman et al., 1999) for needs assessment screening to be conducted (i.e., in schools and primary care settings) following violent acts such as a terrorist incident. We recognize that communitywide implementation of this recommendation would require policy decisions at multiple levels, including state and local school boards, as well as the federal agencies that control the funds for these endeavors. But, as Cohen, Berliner, and March (2000) note, it makes no sense to identify children at risk and then not have effective services available.

In the wake of recent events, mental health services are evolving. Monies are currently available through federal agencies, foundations, and charities to help children impacted by the September 11, 2001 attacks. Unfortunately, these services may not reach all children in need. Certainly, because of the potential impact of media coverage on the development of PTSD symptoms in children, assessment and intervention services need to be further expanded. Federal agencies, such as the Federal Emergency Management Agency and the Center for Mental Health Services, may need to reevaluate the availability and the distribution of monies following communitywide acts of violence like terrorism. In summary, we suggest that terrorist events be treated as a separate category. Funds for mental health needs may wax and wane after an event. For example, funding for initial screenings and the development of specialized interventions may be high, then reduced following the interventions. Funds for mental health services may need to be reactivated later to help victims cope with the reminders, anniversaries, and new issues raised by the judicial phase of the terrorist action, and the ongoing war on terrorism. Therefore, funding should be targeted to the needs of survivors and families throughout their recovery.

Currently, people providing intervention services to high-risk children may not have sufficient training to provide for their needs. Children may have depression, anxiety disorders, and bereavement issues. The lack of experience and training to recognize significant problems may be one reason so few children were referred for mental health services beyond minimal crisis counseling following the Oklahoma City bombing. We recommend that standards for mental health providers be established for people working with children following a terrorist incident. A triage system may be useful for professionals. For example, licensed professionals with high levels of training may supervise and guide the screening and assessment; planning, design, and implementation of specialized treatment interventions; and program evaluation. Licensed professionals with debriefing training and experience could aid in the initial crisis and early intervention efforts. School personnel and other counselors could be trained to provide brief manualized interventions in the schools; on-going assessment to determine continued need for services would be conducted. Finally, licensed professionals with expertise in traumatic loss and complicated bereavement could provide services for children needing intensive treatment.

CONCLUSIONS

In conclusion, given the levels of terrorism around the world and their impact on Americans here and abroad, provision of effective mental health assistance to the children directly touched by such events is an urgent public health need. The young, innocent victims of this extreme form of trauma suffer high rates of PTSD with comorbid symptoms of depression and long-term behavioral and developmental disturbances. Moreover, our research on the Oklahoma City bombing indicates that the ripple effect of terrorism extends far into the community and can affect large numbers of children, who are often the indirect, hidden victims. This is the likely case in the face of the recent terrorist attacks against the United States. As stated previously, we believe that the growing body of clinical work and research underscores the need for a systematic public mental health approach using comprehensive screening, specialized trauma and traumatic bereavement grief-focused interventions, and multimodal outcome evaluations. Only in this way will we make significant strides in our understanding of how terrorism affects its youngest victims.

REFERENCES

Almqvist, K., & Brandell-Forsberg, M. (1997). Refugee children in Sweden: Posttraumatic stress disorder in Iranian preschool children exposed to organized violence. *Child Abuse and Neglect, 21*, 351–366.

American Academy of Child and Adolescent Psychiatry. (1998). Practice parameters for the assessment and treatment of children with posttraumatic stress disorder. *Journal of the American Academy of Child and Adolescent Psychiatry, 37*(10 Suppl.), 4S–26S.

American Psychiatric Association. (1980). *Diagnostic and statistical manual of mental disorders* (3rd ed.). Washington, DC: Author.

American Psychiatric Association. (1994). *Diagnostic and statistical manual of mental disorders* (4th ed.) Washington, DC: Author.

American Psychological Association. (1997). *Final report: Task force on the mental health response to the Oklahoma City bombing.* Washington, DC: Author.

American Red Cross (2001). *Facing fear: Helping young people deal with terrorism and tragic events.* Falls Church, VA: Author.

Armstrong, K., O'Callahan, W., & Marmar, C. R. (1991). Debriefing Red Cross disaster personnel: The Multiple Stressor Debriefing model. *Journal of Traumatic Stress, 4*, 581–593.

Ayalon, O. (1978). *Rescue! An emergency handbook*. Haifa, Israel: University of Haifa Press.

Ayalon, O. (1982). Children as hostages. *Practitioner, 226*, 1773–1781.

Ayalon, O. (1983a). Coping with terrorism: The Israeli case. In D. Meichenbaum & M. Jaremko (Eds.), *Stress reduction and prevention* (pp. 293–340). New York: Plenum Press.

Ayalon, O. (1983b). Face to face with terrorists. In A. Cohen (Ed.), *Education as encounter* (pp. 81–102). Haifa, Israel: University of Haifa Press.

Ayalon, O. (1993). Posttraumatic stress recovery of terrorist survivors. In J. Wilson & B. Raphael (Eds.), *International handbook of traumatic stress syndromes* (pp. 855–866). New York: Plenum Press.

Berliner, L. (1997). Intervention with children who experience trauma. In D. Cicchetti & S. Toth (Eds.), *The effects of trauma and the developmental process* (pp. 491–514). New York: Wiley.

Bisson, J. (1997). Is post-traumatic stress disorder preventable? *Journal of Mental Health, 6*, 109–111.

Blake, D., Weathers, F., Nagy, L., Kaloupek, D., Klauminzer, G., Charney, C., & Keane, T. (1990). A clinical rating scale for assessing current and lifetime PTSD: The CAPS-1. *Behavioral Therapist, 13*, 187–188.

Blom, G. (1986). A school disaster—intervention and research aspect. *Journal of the American Academy of Child and Adolescent Psychiatry, 25*, 336–345.

Carlson, E. B. (1997). *Trauma assessments: A clinician's guide*. New York: Guilford Press.

Carr, V. J., Lewin, T. J., Webster, R. A., & Kenardy, J. (1997). A synthesis of findings from the Quake Impact Study: A two-year investigation of the psychological sequelae of the 1989 Newcastle Earthquake. *International Journal of Social Psychiatry and Psychiatric Epidemiology, 32*, 123–136.

Cohen, J. A. (1998). Practice parameters for the assessment and treatment of children and adolescents with posttraumatic stress disorder. *Journal of the American Academy of Child and Adolescent Psychiatry, 37*(10 Suppl.), 4S–26S.

Cohen, J. A., Berliner, L., & Mannarino, A. P. (2000). Treating traumatized children: A research review and synthesis. *Trauma, Violence, and Abuse: A Review Journal, 1*, 29–46.

Cohen, J. A., Berliner, L., & March, J. S. (2000). Treatment of children and adolescents. In E. B. Foa & T. M. Keane (Eds.), *Effective treatments for PTSD: Practice guidelines from the International Society for Traumatic Stress Studies* (pp. 106–138). New York: Guilford Press.

Cohen, J. A., & Mannarino, A. P. (1996). A treatment outcome study for sexually abused preschool children: Initial findings. *Journal of the American Academy of Child and Adolescent Psychiatry, 35*, 42–50.

Cote, M. P., Leftwich, M. J. T., Gurwitch, R. H., & Pfefferbaum, B. (1999, April). *Post-traumatic stress symptomatology in young children following the Oklahoma City bombing*. Paper presented at the annual meeting of the Southwestern Psychological Association, Albuquerque, NM.

Deblinger, E., Lippman, J., & Steer, R. (1996). Sexually abused children suffering post-traumatic stress symptoms: Initial treatment outcome findings. *Child Maltreatment, 1*, 310–321.

Desivilya, H., Gal, R., & Ayalon, O. (1996). Long-term effects of trauma in adolescence: Comparison between survivors of a terrorist attack and control counterparts. *Anxiety, Stress, and Coping, 9*, 1135–1150.

Dyregrov, A. (1989). Caring for helpers in disaster situations: Psychological debriefing. *Disaster Management, 2*, 25–30.

Dyregrov, A., Gupta, L., Gjestad, R., & Mukanohelli, E. (2000). Trauma exposure and psychological reactions to genocide among Rwandan children. *Journal of Traumatic Stress, 13*, 3–21.

Elbedour, S., Baker, A., Shalhoub-Kevorkian, N., Irwin, M., & Belmaker, R. (1999). Psychological responses in family members after the Hebron massacre. *Depression and Anxiety, 9*, 27–31.

Fields, R. (1982). Research on the victims of terrorism. In F. Ochberg & D. Soskis (Eds.), *Victims of terrorism* (pp. 137–171). Boulder, CO: Westview.

First, M. B., Spitzer, R. L., Gibbon, M., & Williams, J. B. (1997). *Structured clinical interview for DSM–IV axis I disorders, clinical version.* Washington, DC: American Psychiatric Press.

Foa, E. B. (2001, November). *Early interventions for trauma: Possibilities and pitfalls.* Paper presented at the annual meeting of the Association for the Advancement of Behavior Therapy, Philadelphia, PA.

Frederick, W. N. (1996). Clinical considerations of empirical treatment studies of abused children. *Child Maltreatment, 1*, 343–347.

Freedy, J. R., Kilpatrick, D. G., & Resnick, H. S. (1993). Natural disaster and mental health: Theory, assessment and intervention. *Journal of Social Behavior and Personality, 8*, 49–103.

Garrison, C., Bryant, E., Addy, C., Spurrier, P., Freedy, J., & Kilpatrick, D. (1995). Posttraumatic stress disorder in adolescents after Hurricane Andrew. *Journal of American Academy of Child and Adolescent Psychiatry, 34*, 1193–1201.

Goenjian, A., Karayan, I., Pynoos, R. S., Minassian, D., Najarian, L., Steinberg, A., & Fairbanks, L. (1997). Outcome of psychotherapy among pre-adolescents after the 1988 earthquake in Armenia. *American Journal of Psychiatry, 154*, 536–542.

Green, B., Korol, M., Grace, M., Vary, M., Leonard, A., Gleser, G., & Smitson-Cohen, S. (1991). Children and disaster: Age, gender, and parental effects on PTSD symptoms. *Journal of American Academy Child and Adolescent Psychiatry, 30*, 945–951.

Gurwitch, R. H. (2001, November). The impact of trauma and disasters on children. In S. Batten & M. Polusny (Chairs), *In the wake of terror: Science-based guidelines for mental health professionals.* Paper presented at the annual meeting of the Association for the Advancement of Behavior Therapy, Philadelphia, PA.

Gurwitch, R. H., & Kees, M. (in press). In the face of tragedy: Placing children's trauma in a new context. *Cognitive and Behavioral Practice.*

Gurwitch, R. H., Leftwich, M. J. T., Pfefferbaum, B., & Pynoos, R. (2000, March). *The roles of age and gender on children's reactions to trauma and disaster: The Oklahoma City bombing*. Paper presented at the third world conference for the International Society for Traumatic Stress Studies, Melbourne, Australia.

Gurwitch, R. H., & Messenbaugh, A. (2001). *Healing after trauma skills: A manual for professionals, teachers, and families working with children after trauma/disaster*. Oklahoma City: Children's Medical Research Foundation.

Gurwitch, R. H., & Pfefferbaum, B. (1999, February). *Children and trauma: Lessons from the Oklahoma City bombing*. Paper presented at the Rocky Mountain Region Disaster Mental Health Conference, Laramie, WY.

Gurwitch, R. H., Pfefferbaum, B., & Leftwich, M. J. T. (in press). The impact of terrorism on children: Considerations for a new era. *Journal of Trauma Practice*.

Gurwitch, R. H., Sullivan, M. A., & Long, P. (1998). The impact of trauma and disaster on young children. *Psychiatric Clinics of North America, 7*, 19–32.

Gurwitch, R. H., Tassey, J., Sitterle, K., & Pfefferbaum, B. (1998, February). *Special issues of children in man-made disasters*. Paper presented at the workshop Children's emergencies in disasters: A national emergency medical services for children, Orlando, FL.

Handford, H., Mayes, S., Mattison, R., Frederick, H., Bagnato, S., Bixler, E., & Kales, J. (1986). Child and parent reactions to the Three Mile Island nuclear accident. *Journal of American Academy of Child Psychiatry, 35*, 346–356.

Horowitz, M., Winler, N., & Alvarez, W. (1979). Impact of Event Scale: A measure of subjective stress. *Psychosomatic Medicine, 41*, 209–218.

La Greca, A. M., Sevin, S. W., & Sevin, E. L. (2001). *Helping America cope: A guide to help parents and children cope with the September 11th terrorist attacks*. Coral Gables, FL: 7-Dippity.

La Greca, A. M., Vernberg, E. M., Silverman, W. K., Vogel, A., & Prinstein, M. J. (1994). *Helping children prepare for and cope with natural disasters: A manual for professionals working with elementary school children*. Miami, FL: Author.

Layne, S., Pynoos, R. S., & Cardenas, J. (2001). Wounded adolescence: School-based group psychotherapy for adolescents who sustained or witnessed violent injury. In M. Shafir & S. Shafir (Eds.), *School Violence: Contributing factors, management, and prevention* Washington, DC: American Psychiatric Press.

Layne, C. M., Saltzman, W. R., & Pynoos, R. S., (2001). *Trauma/grief-focused group psychotherapy program*. Unpublished manuscript.

Lindy, J., & Grace, M. (1986). The recovery environment: Continuing stressor versus a healing psychological space. In B. J. Sowder & M. Lystad (Eds.), *Disasters and mental health: Contemporary perspectives and innovations in services to disaster victims*. Washington, DC: American Psychiatric Press.

Lyons, J. A. (1987). Posttraumatic stress disorder in children and adolescents: A review of the literature. *Developmental and Behavioral Pediatrics, 8*, 349–356.

Macksoud, M., Dyregrov, A., & Raundalen, M. (1993). Traumatic war experiences and their effects on children. In B. Raphael & J. P. Wilson (Eds.), *International handbook of traumatic stress syndromes* (pp. 625–633). New York: Plenum Press.

March, J. (1999). Assessment of pediatric posttraumatic stress disorder. In P. A. Saigh & J. D. Bremner (Eds.), *Posttraumatic stress disorder: A comprehensive text* (pp. 199–218). Needham Heights, MA: Allyn & Bacon.

March, J., Amaya-Jackson, L., Murry, M., & Schulte, A. (1998). Cognitive behavioral psychotherapy for children and adolescents with posttraumatic stress disorder following a single incident stressor. *Journal of the American Academy of Child and Adolescent Psychiatry, 37,* 585–593.

Melville, M., & Lykes, M. B. (1992). Guatemalan Indian children and the sociocultural effects of government-sponsored terrorism. *Social Science Medicine, 34,* 533–548.

Meyers, D. (1994). *Disaster response and recovery: A handbook for mental health professionals.* (Publication No. SMA 94–3010). Washington, DC: U.S. Department of Health and Human Services.

Mitchell, J. T. (1983). When disaster strikes . . . The critical incident stress debriefing process. *Journal of Emergency Medical Services, 8,* 36–39.

Murphy, L., Pynoos, R. S., & James, C. (1997). The trauma/grief-focused group psychotherapy module of an elementary school-based violence prevention/intervention program. In J. D. Osofsky (Ed.), *Children in a violent society* (pp. 223–255). New York: Guilford Press.

Nader, K., Pynoos, R. S., Fairbanks, L., Al-Ajeel, M., & Al-Asfour, A. (1993). A preliminary study of PTSD and grief among the children of Kuwait following the Gulf crisis. *British Journal of Clinical Psychology, 32,* 407–427.

Oklahoma State Department of Health. (1996). *Injury update: Investigation of physical injuries directly associated with the Oklahoma City bombing. A report to Oklahoma injury surveillance participants.* Oklahoma City, OK: Injury Prevention Service.

Osofsky, J. D. (1997). Children and youth violence: An overview of the issues. In J. D. Osofsky (Ed.), *Children in a violent society* (pp. 3–31). New York: Guilford Press.

Perry, B. (1997, April). *Childhood trauma and neurological and physical development.* Presented at the Oklahoma Department of Mental Health and Substance Abuse Services training conference, Oklahoma City, OK.

Pfefferbaum, B., Call, J., & Sconzo, G. (1999). Mental health services for children in the first two years after the 1995 Oklahoma City terrorist bombing. *Psychiatric Services, 50,* 956–958.

Pfefferbaum, B., Nixon, S., Krug, R., Tivis, R., Moore, V., Brown, J., Pynoos, R., Foy, D., & Gurwitch, R. H. (1999). Clinical needs assessment of middle and high school students following the 1995 Oklahoma City bombing. *American Journal of Psychiatry, 156,* 1069–1074.

Pfefferbaum, B., Nixon, S., Tivis, R., Doughty, D., Pynoos, R., Gurwitch, R. H., & Foy, D. (2001). Television exposure in children after a terrorist incident. *Psychiatry, 64,* 202–211.

Pfefferbaum, B., Nixon, S., Tucker, P., Tivis, R., Moore, V., Gurwitch, R. H., Pynoos, R., & Geis, H. (1999). Posttraumatic stress responses in bereaved children after the Oklahoma City bombing. *Journal of the American Academy of Child and Adolescent Psychiatry, 38,* 1372–1379.

Pfefferbaum, B., Seale, T., McDonald, N., Brandt, E., Rainwater, S., Maynard, B., Meierhoefer, B., & Miller, P. (2000). Posttraumatic stress two years after the Oklahoma City bombing in youths geographically distant from the explosion. *Psychiatry, 63,* 358–370.

Pynoos, R. S. (1992). Grief and trauma in children and adolescents. *Bereavement Care, 1,* 2–10.

Pynoos, R. S., & Eth, S. (1985). Children traumatized by witnessing acts of personal violence: Homicide, rape or suicidal behavior. In S. Eth & R. Pynoos (Eds.), *Posttraumatic stress disorder in children* (pp. 17–44). Washington, DC: American Psychiatric Press.

Pynoos, R. S., Frederick, C., Nader, K., Arroyo, W., Steinberg, A., Eth, S., Nunez, E., & Fairbanks, L. (1987). Life threat and posttraumatic stress in school-age children. *Archives of General Psychiatry, 44,* 1057–1063.

Pynoos, R. S., & Nader, K. (1988). Psychological first aid and treatment approach to children exposed to community violence: Research implications. *Journal of Traumatic Stress, 1,* 445–473.

Pynoos, R. S., Steinberg, A. M., & Goenjian, A. (1996). Traumatic stress in children and adolescents: Recent trends and current controversies. In B. van der Kolk, A. McFarlane, & L. Wiesaeth (Eds.), *Traumatic stress: The effects of overwhelming experience on mind, body, and society* (pp. 331–358). New York: Guilford Press.

Pynoos, R. S., Steinberg, A., & Wraith, R. (1995). A developmental model of childhood traumatic stress. In D. Cicchetti & D. J. Cohen (Eds.), *Manual of developmental psychopathology* (pp. 72–95). New York: Wiley.

Pynoos, R. S., Zisook, S., & Foy, D. W. (1995, July). *Traumatic bereavement vs. posttraumatic stress disorder.* Paper presented at the Oklahoma Department of Mental Health and Substance Abuse Services training conference, Oklahoma City, OK.

Raphael, B. (1986). *When disaster strikes. How individuals and communities cope with catastrophe.* New York: Basic Books.

Rose, S., Brewin, C., Andrews, A., & Kirk, M. (1999). A randomized controlled trial of individual psychological debriefing for victims of violent crime. *Psychological Medicine.*

Saltzman, W., Pynoos, R. S., Layne, C., Steinberg, A., & Aisenberg, E. (1999). *School-based trauma-grief focused psychotherapy program for youth exposed to community violence.* Unpublished manuscript.

Scheeringa, M. S., Zeanah, C., Drell, M., & Larrieu, J. (1995). Two approaches to diagnosing posttraumatic stress disorder in infancy and early childhood. *Journal of the American Academy of Child and Adolescent Psychiatry, 34,* 191–200.

Shannon, M., Lonigan, C., Finch, A., & Taylor, C. (1994). Children exposed to disaster, I: Epidemiology of posttraumatic symptoms and symptom profiles. *Journal of the American Academy of Child and Adolescent Psychiatry, 33*, 80–93.

Shaw, J., Applegate, B., Tanner, S., Perez, D., Rothe, E., Campo-Bowen, A., & Lahey, B. (1995). Psychological effects of Hurricane Andrew on an elementary school population. *Journal of American Academy of Child and Adolescent Psychiatry, 34*, 1185–1192.

Sitterle, K. A. (1995). Mental health services at the Compassion Center: The Oklahoma City bombing. *National Center for PTSD Quarterly, 5*, 20–23.

Sitterle, K. A., & Gurwitch, R. H. (1999). The terrorist bombing in Oklahoma City. In E. S. Zinner & M. B. Williams (Eds.), *When a community weeps: Case studies in group survivorship* (pp. 160–189). Ann Arbor, MI: Taylor & Francis.

Smith, D., Christiansen, E., Vincent, R., & Hann, N. (1999). Population effects of the bombing of Oklahoma City. *Journal of the Oklahoma State Medical Association, 92*, 193–198.

Storm, V., McDermott, B., & Finlayson, D. (1994). *The bushfire and me*. Newtown, Australia: VBD Publications.

Straker, G., & the Sanctuaries Team (1987). The continuous traumatic stress syndrome: The single therapeutic interview. *Psychology and Sociology, 8*, 48–56.

Swenson, C., & Klingman, A. (1993). Children and war. In C. F. Saylor (Ed.), *Children and disasters* (pp. 137–163). New York: Plenum Press

Terr, L., Bloch, D., Michel, B., Shi, H., Reinhardt, J., & Metayer, S. (1999). Children's symptoms in the wake of Challenger: A field study of distant-traumatic effects and an outline of related conditions. *American Journal of Psychiatry, 156*, 1536–1544.

Terr, L. C. (1985). Children traumatized in small groups. In W. Eth and R. S. Pynoos (Eds.), *Post-traumatic stress disorder in children*. Washington, DC: American Psychiatric Press.

Trappler, B., & Friedman, S. (1996). Posttraumatic stress disorder in survivors of the Brooklyn Bridge shooting. *American Journal of Psychiatry, 153*, 705–707.

Vogel, J. M., & Vernberg, E. M. (1993). Task force report, part 1: Children's psychological responses to disasters. *Journal of Clinical Child Psychology, 22*, 464–484.

Wang, A., Pynoos, R. S., James, Q., & Wang, M. (1994, October). *Los Angeles earthquake, 1994: School district reduction of trauma effects*. Paper presented at the annual meeting of the American Academy of Child and Adolescent Psychiatry, New York.

Weiss, D., & Marmar, C. (1997). The Impact of Event Scale–Revised. In J. Wilson & T. Keane (Eds.), *Assessing psychological trauma and PTSD* (pp. 399–411). New York: Guilford Press.

Young, B. H. (1990, October). *VA outreach to Santa Cruz County: Respecting the trauma membrane*. Symposium presented at the Annual Meeting of the International Society for Traumatic Stress Studies, New Orleans, LA.

Young, B. H. (1998). Evaluating stress debriefing: Some considerations. *Emergency Management Support Network, 4*, 2.

Young, B. H., Ford, J. D., Ruzek, J. I., Friedman, M., & Gusman, F. D. (1998). *Disaster mental health services: A guide for clinicians and administrators.* Palo Alto, CA: National Center for Post Traumatic Stress Disorder.

Yule, W., & Williams, R. (1990). Posttraumatic stress reactions in children. *Journal of Traumatic Stress, 3,* 279–295.

15

CHILDREN UNDER STRESS OF WAR

AVIGDOR KLINGMAN

The urgency of addressing the special needs of children in wartime increases as the focus of contemporary wars shifts from fights between armies over military objectives to wars that substantially disrupt the lives of civilians. The recent Balkan conflict, an active and brutal war in the midst of an otherwise peaceful Europe, presented many aspects of such contemporary "conventional" wars (e.g., Berk, 1998). In other contemporary wars, however, long-range high-technology weapons capable of carrying chemical and biological warheads "surgically" remove specific civilian targets, devastating civilians and their environment. The Persian Gulf War illustrates such an "unconventional" war. All Israeli children were rushed to sealed rooms, forced to wear gas masks (infants and toddlers were confined in protective carriers), and shared with the rest of the family the uncertainty about the types of missiles (i.e., conventional, chemical, or bacteriological) as well as their local targets.

Wars, unlike most other disasters, are usually preceded by an extended warning period and are prolonged disasters, lasting for weeks, months, or years. Mental health interventions therefore can be initiated to prevent psychological and psychosocial sequelae both prior to and during war's course. This chapter describes how wars affect children, summarizes the major finding about children's responses, and reports on some relatively effective communitywide and individualized interventions.

359

THE IMPACT OF WAR ON CHILDREN

It is generally accepted that war-related experiences expose children to unacceptably high levels of stressors during a critical time in their psychosocial development. War events may inflict a setback in psychosocial development, notably hindering interpersonal trust, elevating anxiety levels, and curtailing the threshold for stress endurance (Kaffman & Elizur, 1979; Raphael & Wilson, 1993). Children have been intimidated or horrified, killed, injured, tortured, imprisoned, physically and sexually abused, forcefully recruited to participate in violent acts against fellow villagers and even their own families, malnourished, disabled, physically separated from their families, displaced, and orphaned by present-day armed conflicts. Uncertainties about the types of damage and the duration of the war add to the impact on children as well as their caregivers. Children also suffer the most when basic infrastructures (i.e., economy, public health, medicine, education, and social services) collapse. When state-operated facilities for vulnerable children (e.g., institutions for children with mental retardation and development disabilities) have to be closed, sending children back home imposes unbearable strain on their parents and, in some cases, means returning children to places from which they were rejected or places they suffered physical or sexual abuse (Solomon, 1995).

Individual children's lives also may be disrupted when a parent is sent to fight overseas, as was the case in the participation of American armed forces in the Vietnam and Gulf Wars (Figley, 1993; Hobfoll et al., 1991). The vivid images of war and destruction are brought home by television and add to the child's worries.

Drastic changes in daily routines during wartime result in children's being confined indoors for most (if not all) of the day, limiting play and other recreational activities and promoting feelings of isolation and boredom. Their sleep may be interrupted by sojourns to shelters or sealed rooms. Some must take over the responsibilities of an absent parent. Parental absence can disrupt family life after the return as well as during the separation.

Permanent loss of a parent demands great emotional adjustment, particularly when excessive strain on the remaining parent diminishes the attention and quality of care the child receives. Not talking about the death at home, for example, may reinforce the child's denial and avoidance of the event, which, in turn, may undermine the mourning process. A missing parent poses a special challenge because no concrete evidence of the death, such as a funeral, burial place, or designated period of mourning, is available. Children may fantasize excessively about the missing parent's return, and it is advisable to provide such children with the near certainty of the missing parent's death so that the mourning process can proceed (Green & Kocijan-Hercigonja, 1998).

Physical injuries to children may cause loss of control, loss of self-image, dependency, stigma, isolation, abandonment, and anger. Even minor wounds can create considerable risk for posttrauma disorders in children. The injured parts of the body may act as a constant reminder of the trauma and interfere with the processing and resolution of traumatic experiences. Some children have a tendency to dwell on the death and injuries of other family members and fellow victims, rather than on their own injuries. Adolescents may be particularly traumatized by their wounds because for them, the smallest imperfection is of enormous significance (Bronfman, Campis, & Koocher, 1998; Green & Kocijan-Hercigonja, 1998).

The prolonged closure of schools deprives children of educational opportunities as well as additional school-related activities and routines that signify life stability (e.g., important regular social ties, social support of their peers, the reassurance of their teachers, and the steadying influence of familiar structures and routines). Schools often reopen before the dangers have entirely passed; as a result, lessons may be interrupted by various emergencies. Pupils must deal with fears, anxiety, fatigue, lack of concentration and, for some, a parent's absence.

Home is a symbol of familiarity, intimacy, and inviolability of the self; thus, the loss of a home has a deep personal meaning for children. Losing their home also involves losing significant social ties and support. Children may arrive at evacuation centers or refugee campsites in a state of shock. When exposed to crowded and unsanitary conditions of refugee camps, they may experience high health risks. Unfamiliarity with the new surroundings, impaired parenting, and the lack of privacy place additional burdens on them. Refugees are likely to encounter difficulties adjusting to life in an unfamiliar culture and to new language; refugee children also may face teasing and bullying when entering new school systems.

BEHAVIORAL AND PSYCHOLOGICAL RESPONSES

Studies conducted while fighting was still in progress (Klingman, 2001b) and immediately following wars have revealed high levels of stress symptoms, anxiety, and depression; high levels of exposure lead to greater subjective distress for children (Solomon, 1995). Commonly reported stress reactions include fears, anxiety, hypersensitivity, moderate levels of depression, and increased dependency on parents (Yule, Perrin, & Smith, 2001). Predominant emotional reactions in human-made disasters tend to be rage, hatred, and despair, whereas in other disasters (e.g., natural disasters), they tend to be frustration, helplessness, and acceptance. Children's war-related modes of coping point predominantly to affect regulation, whereas in other disasters coping tends more toward reappraisal of the situation (Gal, 1998).

War-related posttraumatic stress disorder (PTSD) prevalence estimates for children and adolescents varied between studies. The prevalence ranges from about 8% to 75% (Saigh, Green, & Korol, 1996). Predictors of PTSD in wartime include levels of personal (firsthand) exposure to war, proximity to traumatized people, subjective impact of the trauma, and negative social support structures after war (Shields, Erdal, Skrinjaric, & Majic, 1999). A wide spectrum of individual responses occur, and most studies of psychopathology report that only a minority of children go on to develop chronic PTSD.

The growing literature suggests that children's psychological reactions may differ from those of adults in that the responses may be more transient and less severe. Studies of Israeli and Palestinian children and children from Northern Ireland indicated a notable decrease in stress reaction with lapse of time (e.g., Klingman, 1992a; Lyons, 1971; Punamaki & Suleiman, 1990). Residual stress reactions were detected, particularly among children with high immediate stress reactions and with high degrees of stress exposure (Solomon, 1995). When extremely violent war events directly touch a child's nuclear family, the psychological effects may become serious. A study of the long-term impact 20 years after a terrorist attack involving the seizure of Israeli high school students as hostages (Desivilya, Gal, & Ayalon, 1996) revealed that although most survivors exhibited relatively high levels of adaptation, the traumatic experience at adolescence had a long-lasting effect on the survivors' adult life. This effect has been noted in intrapersonal and interpersonal domains, as well as in their emotional response in emergency situations, such as the Gulf War.

Several studies have found that children with high exposure to a war reported significantly more adverse emotional, cognitive, and physiological symptoms than those residing in areas less exposed to war events and may sustain more long-term damage (Klingman, 1992a; Rosenthal & Levy-Shiff, 1993; Schwartzwald, Weisenberg, Waysman, Solomon, & Klingman, 1993). Our experience is that some children evacuated to safer environs apparently remain highly anxious; changing the physical distance to the war does not necessarily change the psychological distance to it (see Solomon, 1995, pp. 34–35, with regard to older populations).

As for gender differences, studies have reported greater distress levels for girls than for boys (Klingman, Sagi, & Raviv, 1993; Macksoud & Nazar, 1993; Swenson & Klingman, 1993). Girls reported receiving higher levels of social support than boys; girls who reported receiving low levels of social support had the highest levels of psychological distress (e.g., Llabre & Hadi, 1994). Thus, although girls may be at greater risk of distress, that risk may be minimized by enhancing levels of social support and permitting them to express their feelings and fears to others while they confront and deal with reminders of war experience.

Somatic and health indicators are affected by trauma. Studies with Kuwaiti children following the Gulf War showed a link between proximity to war violence and increased self-reported somatic symptoms and complaints. Diastolic blood pressure was associated with the level of exposure to trauma

(Llabre & Hadi, 1994), and an inverse relationship was found between the presence of reexperiencing symptoms and somatic complaints (Nader & Fairbanks, 1994).

Growing up in a war-affected community may promote aggressive behavior in children, at least in some cultural contexts (Garbarino, Kostelny, & Dubrow, 1991; McCloskey & Southwick, 1996). Children's experience of war-related trauma has been linked to an increase in aggressiveness, some increase in juvenile delinquency (see review by Muldoon & Cairns, 1999), and problems with impulse control (Nader & Fairbanks, 1994; Nader et al., 1993). A broad range of daily activities, such as reckless and inconsiderate driving and externalization of rage toward authority figures, is seen in the war-torn Israeli society (Klingman, Sagi, & Raviv, 1993).

Rosenthal and Levy-Shiff (1993), who studied the reaction of infants and toddlers during the Gulf War, found that many of the children initially displayed strong negative reactions to the state of alarm. As the war progressed, about one third of the children became increasingly distressed when being placed in their sealed tents (because infants cannot use gas masks, parents had to put them in protective, semi-sealed, gas-proof tentlike covers). Those who showed the strongest distress in the early days of the war continued to show strong distress to its end. This finding indicates that even young children are vulnerable, yet they also manifest rudimentary attempts at coping. The results also showed habituation patterns similar to those displayed by older children. Older toddlers reacted more strongly but adjusted more quickly than infants and younger toddlers and exhibited more intense emotional responses to the sealed room and more habit changes over time than their juniors; over time, however, they were less likely to show adjustment disturbances, coped better with the siren and the confinement in the sealed room, and were more likely to engage in war-related play and to entertain their families with "witty jokes." Apparently, even the limited increase in maturity enabled toddlers to cope better in the long run than the infants.

Adolescents are less dependent than young children on their parents and tend to respond more to the world beyond their families. Developmental psychologists are increasingly recognizing that late adolescence is a time when sociopolitical influences on identity are particularly powerful. A political ideology and commitment may help buffer the experience of war by allowing adolescents to interpret their experiences as a "necessary evil" that must be endured if ideological objectives are to be achieved (Garbarino & Kostelny, 1993; Muldoon & Cairns, 1999).

Following the war in Bosnia and Croatia, it was noted that many adolescent refugees refused to return home, in direct conflict with their parents' wishes. This refusal could be explained by the greater educational opportunities in their host country together with the developmental need for independence; it also could be that their homes had become reminders of their traumatic war experiences (Green & Kocijan-Hercigonja, 1998).

COPING AND ADAPTATION

The impact of war stress on children depends considerably on both personal coping capacity and environmental support. Young children's resilience depends considerably on their parents' stress absorption and their parents' and significant others' support, whereas individual dispositions and interpretations of their situational (and environmental) control play a greater part for older children and adolescents. For adolescents, war often brings out a strength and energy unlike anything seen at other times.

Coping behaviors can be directed at managing the stressor itself (i.e., active or problem-focused coping), avoiding the stressor (i.e., avoidance coping), and reducing the aversive emotional reactions resulting from exposure to stress (i.e., emotion-focused or palliative coping; Lazarus & Folkman, 1984). During war, problem-focused coping is concentrated in actions to improve safety. Behaviors designed to reduce the emotional impact of the situation (i.e., avoidance and emotion-focused coping) become vital in low-control situations to help reduce or relieve anxiety. A number of studies have revealed that children minimize the distress induced by disaster situations and wars through distancing, distraction, disengagement, wishful thinking, or denial (Compas, Nakarne, & Fondacavo, 1988; Solomon, 1995) in an attempt to encapsulate and isolate the scary feelings of war (Klingman, 2001b; Schwartzwald et al., 1993). Defensiveness may offer temporary protection when the situation cannot be controlled, allowing the children the needed time to assimilate the experience. Palliative coping may facilitate habituation to their emotions, thereby freeing children for later use of problem-focused coping (Klingman & Kupermintz, 1994).

Young people's habituation phenomenon was noted for Israeli (Klingman, 1992a; Solomon, 1995) and Northern Ireland (Muldoon, Trew, & McWhirter, 1998) children. In general, children exhibited surprisingly wide-ranging acclimation to the war situations under investigation (Klingman, Sagi, & Raviv, 1993). It is possible, however, that habituation may be a coping mechanism that is more available to those not directly hit or who experience war from a relative safe distance (Muldoon & Cairns, 1999). Also, the cost of a high level of habituation in the long run has yet to be studied.

Clinical observations indicate that children with a cause were better able to focus some of their energy in a positive capacity (e.g., caring for the disabled), rather than feel lonely, isolated, or without purpose. A cause creates a central life theme and thus enhances a sense of communality, creates a commitment to cooperate and take some action when possible (thus enhancing a sense of control over one's destiny), and enables a focus on a better future. Research suggests that for older children, ideology may contribute to coping in warlike situations (Cairns & Dawes, 1996; Klingman, 2001a; Muldoon & Cairns, 1999; Punamaki, 1996): Adolescents are able to make use of ideology as a personal resource and as a resource of resilience (Elder,

1980; Punamaki, 1989). Conversely, when ideological commitment turns rigid (e.g., through propaganda), it may exacerbate and sustain justification of violent acts by children; in some places older children become active protagonists of war as a result (Muldoon & Cairns, 1999). Thus, it is important to consider the extent to which children should be exposed to ideological propaganda. It also was suggested that religion and prayer may have an instrumental meaning attached to them (Zeidner, 1992).

Sense of humor promotes coping with emotional strain by enhancing "esprit de corps" and providing mental insulation against being overwhelmed. In war, humor allows immediate and spontaneous catharsis without directly revealing specific personal fears; a partial denial of fears; and a sense of mastery through reframing (e.g., by changing the meaning of frightening objects), making some sense of a chaotic experience (e.g., suggesting humorous alternative explanation), letting out aggression towards the enemy, and strengthening group togetherness and morale (Nevo, 1994).

Staying active, as through involvement in helpful behaviors (Hobfoll et al., 1991), can help children (especially the young) gain a sense of mastery and control over their lives despite the ordeal and keep their minds off the dangers and the war. Specifically, they should be trained in the most effective personal steps or measures to be taken against war dangers; taught basic, age-relevant, activities they can help with at home, in school, and in the community; encouraged to take part (however small) in the solutions in their own families, thereby avoiding the victim role; and encouraged to remain active. For example, many Israeli children in the Gulf War were actively involved in sealing windows, taping up the doors of a designated sealed room, and helping younger siblings or the elders on with their gas masks. Adolescents volunteered as helpers in local hospitals (e.g., for simple secretarial work, to help carry stretchers, to rinse chemical substances from casualties, and to help with elementary first aid). In Bosnia, children in garden clubs were encouraged to plant flowers and protect plants from being ruined or stolen, teenagers volunteered to go into hospitals and tutor nonambulatory children, and older children were provided with materials to build a playground for their siblings (Berk, 1998). Children were encouraged to get engaged in art work and art exhibition. The activities enabled them to ventilate feelings and kept them occupied, active, and creative as well (Shilo-Cohen, 1993). In other cases, channeling energy into doing may include writing letters to troops, engaging in sports, and becoming occupied with hobbies.

Children must gain positive expectations. The lack of (or the limited) experience with the adversities of war and the war being a protracted crisis, may lead children to exaggerate their problems and prevent them from seeing "light at the end of the tunnel" (Hobfoll et al., 1991). Children therefore should be helped to not catastrophize and encouraged to gain perspective and view situational setbacks and psychological lapses as part of a "normal" process of a war.

The long-term prognosis for children exposed to war hinges, in large measure, on the ability of the adult community to be psychologically available to children, to reassure and protect them, and to clarify and interpret the experience (Garbarino & Kostelny, 1993). Although experiencing helplessness and exposure to violence are likely to cause regression in youngsters' development (e.g., delays in attaining independence, identity formation, establishing trust, and intimacy), such patterns can be minimized by the availability of a highly cohesive support system (Caplan, 1964; Garmezy, 1985; Klingman, 2001a; Ziv & Israeli, 1973). For those experiencing long-term separation from both parents, the mobilization of community resources is vital.

Studies of children exposed to war in England during World War II (Freud & Burlingham, 1943; Janis, 1951) showed that the level of emotional upset displayed by the adults in the child's life (and not the war situation itself) was the best predictor of children's response. Children were more distressed by separation from the parents than by exposure to bombings or witnessing destruction, injury, or death. Even those who experienced constant bombings did not seem adversely affected, provided that they remained with their mothers or mother substitutes and the familiar routines continued. More recent studies have supported this by showing a mediating, or buffering, role for parents of preschool as well as school-age children exposed to traumatic war events (Bat-Zion & Levy-Shiff, 1993; Laor et al., 1997). Thus, children will show more resiliency if parents are close by, are able to make them feel that everything possible is being done to guard their safety, maintain (at least some) day-to-day care routines, and project high morale. If parents are apprehensive and overwhelmed by the threat of war, children are bound to regard the entire world as a threatening and insecure place. It is when they feel that grownups cannot be depended on to assume full responsibility for their security that they become extremely anxious and insecure. When parents are not available, other primary caregivers can play a part in buffering the experience of war for children; however, amid war this protective role is often performed not only by adults but also (and sometimes solely) by older siblings.

Children who grow up during war need to "make sense" of their experiences; thus, telling them about the war is important. Once children know or feel that a danger exists, they need to have a concrete picture of how the adults around them will deal with the dangers. School-age children may demand to know exactly what lies ahead of them and what they will be expected to do; talking about and imagining events in a gradual, controlled way before they happen often can forestall the fears. The events they see portrayed in the media should be discussed and explained while maintaining as calm, confident, and reassuring an attitude as possible under the circumstances. A map indicating where the war is occurring at the time can be examined with older children. The experience of hearing war-related topics spoken of by significant others in a calm and reasonable manner helps relieve children from hidden worries and is reassuring. Overwhelmed by the war, adults must guard against vivid descriptions of their own fears when in the presence of young children. Monitoring young children's television viewing is important, and it is best for adults to watch with them.

Some children distance themselves, whereas others show remarkable willingness to talk about their deeply troubling war experiences and welcome the opportunity to do so (Berman, 1999). Preschoolers' fears often are based on (at least partial) misunderstandings and misinterpretation of the complex information they hear discussed. Although explanations may be beyond them, they may be calmed by a bedtime story, an extra cookie, a night light, and the knowledge that a significant other is close by. Children (especially older ones) should be helped to understand at least some of the factors that led to the war and the types of weapons that are involved. They should be instructed about situation-specific precautions, safety measures, and family emergency plans, but they also should be allowed to communicate their concerns and ventilate their fears and worries in a supportive and positive context.

THE CONTINUITY PRINCIPLE

Consistent with the major findings from disaster and trauma research, Omer and Alon (1994) suggested and developed the *continuity principle* to provide concrete applicable guidelines for decision making and treatment under severe conditions The continuity principle proved to be acceptable and helpful during the Gulf War in Israel to professionals from different orientations and organizations. It stipulates that throughout all stages of the war cycle, intervention should be aimed at preserving and restoring continuities that had been disrupted as a result of war. The more an intervention is built on the child's existing individual, familial, organizational, and communal (e.g., schools, neighborhood support services) strengths and resources, the more effective it will be in counteracting the disruptive effects of war. Every available material, every person, and every event can become "therapeutic" if used to help a child advance in the direction of bridging some breach in continuity (Alon & Levine Bar-Yoseph, 1994). Intervention methods should be swift and as simple as possible, and they should have a clear goal of normalization of stress reactions.

Restoring *personal (historical) continuity* includes seeing to the child's basic needs, orienting the child to what led to the war and the plans for him or her for the near future, encouraging the child to talk about the experience until as clear and full a picture as possible is obtained, ascribing meaning to and reframing the situation and the child's emotional responses as being a normal transitory process of adaptation, and clearly presenting positive expectations. The mental anguish is gradually processed and integrated into the child's perceived world: The life before the war, the war itself, its meaning, the child's response to it, and the child's life after the war become part of a meaningful continuum rather than remain fragmented in disconnected segments.

Restoring *interpersonal continuity* involves establishing or enhancing interpersonal support with significant others. Restoration of social bonds includes the enhancement of solidarity of the group; such bonds provide the strongest protection against despair and an antidote to war experiences.

Restoring *functional continuity* on the personal level involves encouraging even minimal and simple situation-specific activities that can be executed at a given time by the child as well as resuming (whenever possible) the child's prewar home routines and duties.

Restoring *organizational continuity* means taking action to rebuild the child's sense of order and continuity in the familiar neighborhood. In this context, school reopening serves to restore the child's feelings of belonging and relative stability.

Provided that schools are reopened, disaster mental health teams guided by the continuity principle approach children in their respective schools and give priority to helping the school system resume active roles, and return quickly to routine functioning (however partial in view of the circumstances). In this way the communication channels between the school and the existing, precrisis community support services are reestablished. Through the school system, mental health teams can reach out to families to advise them on proper situation-specific versus negative (e.g., sit mesmerized rewatching traumatic scenes over and over again) reactions of children and on desirable ways of coping they can encourage and reinforce.

COMMUNITYWIDE PREVENTIVE INTERVENTIONS

Children experience a war communally, or collectively; therefore, a communitywide preventive intervention approach takes priority over individual therapeutic interventions under the circumstances. Because war is usually preceded by a warning period, school-based anticipatory intervention is indicated (Caplan, 1964; Klingman, 1978). *Anticipatory coping strategy* refers to premeditative efforts to manage (i.e., reduce, minimize, master, or tolerate) an impending stressful transaction (Lazarus & Folkman, 1984). Initiating stress-inoculation (Meichenbaum & Cameron, 1983) school programs (Klingman, 1978, 1993) specifically designed to deal with aspects of the impending war may reduce the physical and psychological effects of war. Gas mask preparedness, a communitywide, war-related anticipatory coping program with school-age children, was initiated before the Gulf War in Israel. Preparedness ensured that children were familiar with the gas masks and other protective measures against chemical fallout and became competent in using them. The school-based anticipatory guidance consisted of an educational phase; a skills-training phase, which involved demonstrating the equipment and instructing how to use the protective kit; and a few standardized (i.e., controlled gradual exposure) training sessions. Through the simulations of donning, learning to fasten, and breathing through the gas masks, pupils gained a sense of control and expected themselves to withstand the threat of unconventional warfare effectively should it erupt. Moreover, they were able to help train siblings and older people at home; many children were helpful at home during the war.

Because the conventional face-to-face outreach to children and parents is often impractical, the media, the Internet and the telephone serve as large-scale alternative support systems. They allow easy access for children and parents who are housebound or otherwise limited in their ability to travel as a result of war circumstances. During the Gulf War, telephone emergency hotlines operated in Israel. The hotlines served to disseminate situation-specific psychological information, behavioral guidance, and suggestions for anxiety-reduction techniques (Gilat, Lobel, & Gill, 1998; Klingman, 1992b; Noy, 1992; Raviv, 1993). The media were involved in addressing the plethora of mental health issues. This was done directly, by interviewing psychologists to provide a dynamic look at stress response and advice on what mental health messages could be passed to the children at different developmental stages, and indirectly, through children's most popular programs. For example, characters and puppets from the local version of *Sesame Street* transmitted psychological messages aimed at helping children cope with their fears and anxieties (Raviv, 1993).

The Internet also should be considered a means for children's retrieval of information and for communications. It enables fast, home-based access to (a) frequently updated, age-tailored information regarding physical safety measures and expected psychological reactions, (b) age-appropriate coping suggestions, (c) one-time advice/consultation, (d) participation in peer support groups through chat rooms, (e) e-mail communication, (f) relaxing interactive entertainment (e.g., games), and (g) distance learning.

People may choose coping strategies from their resources and "fit" them to meet the demands placed on them by war situations as they unfold (Hobfoll & Lilly, 1993). Thus, children should be encouraged within the preventive approach (Klingman, 2002) to explore various internal and external resources. They should be shown how to be flexible and how to accommodate those resources to their personal encounter with war events.

Along those lines, a broad-spectrum, highly flexible, multidimensional coping and resilience intervention program was developed for group crisis intervention in war for the Israeli school system (Lahad, 1997; Lahad &

Abraham, 1983). The intervention format follows Lazarus' (1976, 1989) multimodal therapy approach and relates to six major modalities (using the acronym BASIC Ph): Beliefs (e.g., hope, self-esteem, locus of control, attitudes, value clarification, and meaning), Affect (e.g., sharing of experience, verbal and nonverbal expression of feelings, and debriefing), Social (e.g., group sharing of experience, peer and family support, support-seeking, role taking, and assertiveness training), Imagery (e.g., calming imagery and guided fantasy), Cognition (e.g., information, reframing, and problem solving), and Physiology (e.g., relaxation, exercise, recreational activities, rest, sleep, and proper diet). Children are offered all modalities and can potentially use any of them. Because each child has a preferred mode (e.g., a child whose primary coping style is Social–Imagery), he or she may be helped to use it (e.g., to seek support from imaginary figures, such as Superman). Within each modality, adaptive skills are presented, encouraged, and directly "learned" through shared experience (e.g., situation-specific tasks, art work, and bibliotherapy), shared group discussion, and ongoing communication between children. This program was reported to have immediate situational benefits following terrorist attacks (Shacham, 1996).

This and other resiliency-enhancing intervention programs can be initiated by local organizations, especially when schools are closed. For example, Croatian librarians helped children cope with the consequences of war by providing bibliotherapy workshops (Sabljak, 1999); similarly, Israeli museums organized "paint the war" workshops during the height of the Gulf War (Shilo-Cohen, 1993).

A communitywide outreach in wartime is best delivered through a "pyramid" procedure, whereby a core of mental health workers are debriefed and guided in group; they, in turn, train a large group of caregivers who train teachers and parents (Gal, 1998; Macksoud, Haber, & Cohen, 1996). A lesson from recent wars is that it is important to help caregivers before expecting them to help children—caregivers often are feeling overwhelmed or even traumatized themselves. Such a "helping the helpers" program was organized for helpers in the former Yugoslavia; it involved intensive training in various trauma-relief issues along with debriefing sessions that dealt with the helpers' stresses and burnout (Gal, 1998).

THERAPEUTIC INTERVENTIONS

Possibilities for direct individual treatment during the war (and immediately following it) are limited because therapists face numerous environmental as well as psychological and cultural obstacles. Whenever individual treatments are possible, their frequency and duration are influenced by logistical factors more than therapeutic considerations and by the relative shortage of professionals, geographical distances, and physical danger in traveling. When it is possible to reach out for acute cases, the intervention (adhering to the continuity principle) should not be "personality-and-developmentally" focused but "circumstances-and-present-and-future" oriented (Alon & Levine Bar-Yoseph, 1994). Interventions frequently oscillate between a focus on problems in daily living and exploration of traumatic war experiences. Creating a safe environment and strengthening the child's feelings of safety and trust take priority. The most widely used and, apparently, effective approaches are short-term, trauma-focused (as opposed to child-focused) interventions that provide reassurance and support while gradually, often indirectly, exploring the war experiences. Subsequently, the child is helped to gradually uncover the traumatic war experiences to make some sense of the overwhelming experiences and to identify and express the underlying affect necessary for the healing process to take place. The interventions often combine selected elements of both dynamic and cognitive–behavioral therapies. The intervention must be age-appropriate and conducted at the child's own pace to avoid a premature flooding of fresh memories that are too overwhelming. (See chapter 14 for additional information on premature flooding of fresh memories; Gurwitch et al. discuss children's reexperiencing and provide empirical findings on the age and gender effects and implications for PTSD symptomatology.)

To treat young children effectively, therapists need the full cooperation and compliance of both the child and the parent(s). Moreover, children's fears often reflect their mother's fear (Barrios & Hartman, 1988); therefore, the intervention with the child is usually complemented by guidance, counseling, or therapy with the child's parents (especially the mother). Klingman (1992c) reported a case study of a 5-year-old Israeli boy who refused to put on his gas mask during the Gulf War. The parent's difficulty with his behavior (i.e., anger tantrums, noncompliance, and removal of the gas mask when forced to put it on) was complicated by the urgency of the situation, the high probability of chemical or bacteriological missile warheads, and the parents' extreme anxiety about their own safety. A short-term, family focused, cognitive–behavioral intervention was the method of choice. At intake, the interview centered on ventilation and clarification of feelings, a review and analysis of the child's behavior, elaboration of the relevancy of behavioral principles for compliance, and development of a contract agreement (45 minutes). The parents were instructed, step-by-step, to record their child's behavior for the baseline and control phases and to use story reading, play, and cognitive–behavioral modification on the targeted noncompliant behaviors in the home. The results supported the application of the combined procedure of contact desensitization and cognitive–behavioral prompts through bibliotherapy, play, and behavior modification. The findings highlight the use of the child's parents in the natural setting (home) within a 3-day, short-term, emergency crisis intervention in the midst of a war.

Closely following the continuity principle, Alon and Levine Bar-Yoseph (1994) presented a 10-session case study with a family whose apartment house had been targeted in a terrorist attack. The two sons, ages 6 and 9, narrowly escaped, losing one another in the process. A family debriefing session, in which each member recounted his or her action during and after the assault, was held in the home of the mother's family of origin. The combined vivid picture was depicted in diagrams and broadened as a result of the therapist's questions to include thoughts and emotions, revealing and emphasizing everyone's courage and resourcefulness. The parents were asked to serve as "co-therapists" and coaches for their children between sessions (i.e., to assume habitual roles). The children's freedom of movement in their own home was reestablished by conjointly making a hierarchy of fear of the rooms (that the terrorists had occupied), training the children in moving from room to room singing a special "song of fear" (a humorously lamenting, wailing song improvised by the psychotherapist), and teaching self-hypnosis for relaxation and better sleep. Family routine and cohesiveness was reinforced (e.g., each of the sessions would usually start with the joint family-and-therapist lunch under the pretext that the therapist came from a distant city and needed some refreshment). Although not systematically assessed, a 2-year follow-up showed satisfactory adjustment. This case study represents the use of the continuity principle (Klingman, 2001a; Omer & Alon, 1994) in a situation-specific secondary prevention intervention, and it illustrates that principles drawn from work with soldiers exposed to combat stress (i.e., treatment mode based on immediacy, proximity, and expectancy [Salmon, 1919]) are applicable to posttrauma intervention with children.

Ronen (1996) reported a specific combination of group-based exposure therapy and self-control for the treatment of ten 8- to 11-year-old Israeli children 4 to 6 weeks following the end of the Gulf War. All children evidenced anxiety reactions as an outcome of the war situation and features of preexisting separation anxiety disorders that continued or intensified throughout the war. The children and their parents attended a 45-minute individualized family intake, two 90-minute group intervention sessions (the second one a week after the first), and a follow-up group session held 6 to 8 weeks after the second treatment session. The parents were encouraged to call the therapist whenever needed. The treatment package consisted of a combination of self-control methods for changing a personal belief system and self-guided graduated exposure skills for decreasing fear and anxiety. The postintervention outcomes attest to noticeable improvement in postwar behaviors (for all participants) and previous separation anxiety behaviors and to participants' increased ability to be responsible for their own changes: The children found solutions to their problems, and most families did not require more than two long sessions before being able to conduct the rest of the treatment themselves. Although the study lacked controlled outcome evaluation as well as a follow-up assessment, the preliminary findings, nevertheless, suggest that self-guided, self-controlled, exposure therapy may facilitate improvement in war-related reactions.

Because it is possible that people become conditioned to react to frightening stimuli in certain chance ways, classical conditioning treatment (e.g., systematic desensitization and flooding) can be effective with PTSD cases. Saigh (1987b,c, 1989) carried out a number of clinical interventions using imaginal flooding with 10- to 14-year-old traumatized Lebanese youth. Traumatic scenes were identified and verbally presented. Stimulus and response imagery cues were employed during the flooding process. Stimulus cues involved the visual, auditory, tactile, and olfactory components of each scene; response cues involved the behavioral and cognitive aspects of the scene (for a case example, see also Saigh, 2002). In another case, Saigh (1987a) examined and treated a 14-year-old Lebanese boy who had been abducted and tortured and who met the criteria for PTSD. The boy went through imaginal flooding process consisting of 10 minutes of therapist-directed deep-muscle relaxation exercises and a subsequent 60 minutes of therapeutic stimulation, wherein he was instructed to imagine particular details of anxiety-evoking scenes. Posttreatment and 4-month follow-up assessments reflected clinically significant treatment gains with respect to self-reported anxiety, depression, and misconduct.

Given that young children are not able to imagine some traumatic material, follow the detailed relaxation instructions, or tolerate in vivo (flooding) presentations (see chapter 14), alternative strategies can be used. For example, preschool children can be encouraged first to express their traumatic experiences nonverbally and indirectly by playing freely with dolls and puppets or creating drawings and artwork; those activities inevitably may be shaped by the child's exposure to the war trauma. They then can be helped to put the anxiety-ridden play and art contents into words and thus may be gradually helped to experience a sense of mastery concerning their past traumatic experiences (Green & Kocijan-Hercigonja, 1998). Trauma-reminiscent prompts and soundtracks of (progressively closer) shell and rocket explosions (Saigh, Yule, & Inamdar, 1996) can be used later.

Adopting a family-centered approach, rather than a child-focused approach, was the method of choice for focusing on American military families (Figley, 1993). Jurich (1983) suggested that families of Vietnam veterans often exhibited an enmeshed parent–child relationship and used a five-stage treatment plan that accommodated children's individual styles.

ASSESSMENT CONSIDERATIONS

Research on children's responses to war and on therapeutic intervention with children in war has been much sparser on the whole than the study of adults. This difference is attributed to the methodological, ethical, and practical problems entailed in studying children (Jensen, 1996; Klingman, 1992a,

1993, 2001b; Klingman, Sagi, & Raviv, 1993). It also is difficult to draw defini-
tive empirical conclusions from some of the research, given the inevitable absence of control groups in wartime. The responses of young children to war
have been the least studied as a result of the difficulties inherent in assessing
children too young to fill in questionnaires or even to speak; conducting well-
controlled, objective behavioral observations during wartime; and relying
heavily on the observations of parents, whose objectivity and accuracy are inevitably in question because of their involvement with their children and possible projection of their own anxieties on their children.

To counteract a number of the possible methodological flaws of the
conventional paper-and-pencil questionnaire procedure, Zeidner, Klingman,
and Itskovitz (1993) adapted a clinically oriented, semiprojective assessment
procedure for group administration to investigate young schoolchildren's responses to the war situation a few days after the end of the Gulf War. The
measure consists of pictorial stimuli designed to elicit children's preconscious
thematic contents; the stimuli (i.e., pictures representing images of children,
parents, and teachers in the natural settings) are accompanied by printed
open-ended questions that elicit the children's perceptions, attitudes, anxieties, and fears. Because it is a group-administered instrument, each group is
to be debriefed after completing the questionnaires. Almqvist and Brandell-
Forsberg (1995) reported an assessment procedure for preschool children.
They used the Erica method (Sjolund, 1981), a standardized modified version of Lowenfeld's (1950) World Technique, with Iranian refugee children.
This assessment procedure included structured tasks, questions, and observation relating to reenacted play (consisting of miniature toys and 20 small
wooden dolls of different sizes). The researchers encouraged the children to
make traumatic references, explain the situations they were performing, and
talk about their dramatized memories. Berman (1999) assessed refugee children of war using an audiotaped interviewing approach that, unlike a traditional interview format, followed a theoretical and methodological perspective that encouraged children to "name their reality," critically reflect on
that reality, and consider strategies for changing that reality if desired.

Keeping in mind the methodological constraints embedded in those
procedures, they nevertheless further our understanding of young children's
affective reactions and coping in war circumstances. Moreover, the procedures appear to engage children's interest, ensure a high level of motivation,
and minimize evaluative anxiety. In addition, they have therapeutic value in
themselves because they serve as an outlet for ventilation of children's fears
and anxieties.

CONCLUSIONS

Sadly, wars are likely to be part of the human experience for many years
to come. This chapter describes what is known about children's reactions to

war. Through understanding children's responses to war, it becomes possible to determine the most effective ways of helping them cope. Young children are influenced most heavily by the attitudes and actual responses of their caregivers. Therefore, it is important for children not to be separated from their natural support system and for preventive intervention efforts to be aimed first at providing caregivers with the resourcefulness to help children adapt to the altered circumstances that war presents. For older children and adolescents, both parents and educators play a vital role in buffering the experience of war and determining children's responses to the adversities of war; educators have particular opportunities to integrate preventive measures in the context of wide-ranging curricula.

As to resiliency, without minimizing the high psychological costs of war to children, the chapter has addressed the substantial evidence suggesting that most children cope successfully and manage to adapt despite the circumstances they encounter and the core resources that account for their adaptation. The evidence from studies of communities in war suggests some positive role of war stress, such as when people experience cohesiveness with their family and peers more than they did before or when they initiate successful and, sometimes, courageous behaviors that bolster their self-esteem.

War usually can be predicted some time before its onset, and it usually lasts long enough for mental health professionals to offer guidance to parents, schools, and other community (e.g., media) resources both before the war's full impact and throughout its course. The research findings highlight the importance of adapting coping strategies to the demands of the often-changing war situation. Alternating between palliative strategies and active coping to regulate emotional stress seems to serve people best.

One last note: The astonishing velocity with which technological innovations are now introduced and their popularity with children call for their use in preventive intervention for wartime (Klingman, 2002). Every effort should be made to mobilize all the mental health communication resources available to help children prepare for and cope with the ravages of war.

REFERENCES

Almqvist, K., & Brandell-Forsberg, M. (1995). Iranian refugee children in Sweden. *American Journal of Orthopsychiatry, 65*, 225–237.

Alon, N., & Levine Bar-Yoseph, T. (1994). An approach to the treatment of post-traumatic stress disorders (PTSD). In P. Clarkson & M. Pokorny (Eds.), *The handbook of psychotherapy* (pp. 451–469). New York: Routledge.

Barrios, B. A., & Hartman, D. P. (1988). Fears and anxieties. In E. J. Mash & L. G. Terdal (Eds.), *Behavioral assessment of childhood disorders* (2nd ed., pp. 196–262). New York: Guilford Press.

Bat-Zion, N., & Levy-Shiff, R. (1993). Children in war: Stress and coping reactions under the threat of the Scud missile attacks and the effect of proximity. In L. A.

Leavitt & N. A. Fox (Eds.), *The psychological effects of war and violence on children* (pp. 143–161). Hillsdale, NJ: Lawrence Erlbaum.

Berk, J. H. (1998). Trauma and resilience during war: A look at the children and humanitarian aid workers of Bosnia. *Psychoanalytic Review, 85*, 639–658.

Berman, H. (1999). Stories of growing up amid violence by refugee children of war and children of battered women living in Canada. *Image: Journal of Nursing Scholarship, 31*, 57–63.

Bronfman, E., Campis, B., & Koocher, G. P. (1998). Helping children to cope: Clinical issues for acutely injured and medically traumatized children. *Professional Psychology: Research and Practice, 29*, 574–581.

Cairns, E., & Dawes, A. (1996). Children ethic and political violence: A commentary. *Child Development, 67*, 129–139.

Caplan, G. (1964). *Principles of preventive psychiatry.* New York: Basic Books.

Compas, B. E., Nakarne, V. L., & Fondacavo, K. M. (1988). Coping with stressful events in older children and younger adolescents. *Journal of Consulting and Clinical Psychology, 56*, 405–411.

Desivilya, H. S., Gal, R., & Ayalon, O. (1996). Long-term effects of trauma in adolescence: Comparison between survivors of a terrorist attack and control counterparts. *Anxiety, Stress, and Coping, 9*, 135–150.

Elder, G. (1980). Adolescence in historical perspective. In J. Adelson (Ed.), *Handbook of adolescent psychology* (pp. 3–46). New York: Wiley.

Figley, C. R. (1993). War-related stress and family-centred intervention: American children and the Gulf War. In L. A. Leavitt, & N. A. Fox (Eds.), *The psychological effects of war and violence on children* (pp. 339–356). Hillsdale, NJ: Lawrence Erlbaum.

Freud, A., & Burlingham, D. (1943). *War and children.* New York: International University Press.

Gal, R. (1998). Colleagues in distress: "Helping the helpers." *International Review of Psychiatry, 10*, 234–238.

Garbarino, J., & Kostelny, K. (1993). Children's response to war: What do we know? In L. A. Leavitt & N. A. Fox (Eds.), *The psychological effects of war and violence on children* (pp. 23–39). Hillsdale, NJ: Lawrence Erlbaum.

Garbarino, J., Kostelny, K., & Dubrow, N. (1991). *No place to be a child: Growing up in a war zone.* New York: Lexington Books.

Garmezy, N. (1985). Stress resilient children: The search for protective factors. In J. E. Stevenson (Ed.), *Recent research in developmental psychopathology* (pp. 213–223). Oxford, UK: Pergamon Press.

Gilat, I., Lobel, T. E., & Gil, T. (1998). Characteristics of calls to Israeli hotlines during the Gulf War. *American Journal of Community Psychology, 26*, 697–704.

Green, A. H., & Kocijan-Hercigonja, D. (1998). Stress and coping in children traumatized by war. *Journal of the American Academy of Psychoanalysis, 26*, 585–597.

Hobfoll, S. E., & Lilly, R. S. (1993). Resource conservation as a strategy for community psychology. *Journal of Community Psychology, 21*, 128–148.

Hobfoll, S. E., Spielberger, C. D., Breznitz, S., Figley, C., Folkman, S., Lepper-Green, B., Meichenbaum, D., Milgram, N. A., Sandler, I., Sarason, I., & van der Kolk, B. (1991). War-related stress. *American Psychologist, 46*, 848–855.

Janis, I. L. (1951). *Air war and emotion stress.* New York: McGraw-Hill.

Jensen, P. S. (1996). Practical approaches to research with children in violent settings. In R. J. Apfel & B. Simon (Eds.), *Minefields in their hearts: The mental health of children in war and communal violence* (pp. 206–217). New Haven, CT: Yale University Press.

Jurich, A. P. (1983). The Saigon of the family's mind: Family therapy with families of Vietnam veterans. *Journal of Marital and Family Therapy, 9*, 355–363.

Kaffman, M., & Elizur, E. (1979). Children's bereavement reactions following death of the father. *International Journal of Family Therapy, 1*, 203–229.

Klingman, A. (1978). Children in stress: Anticipatory guidance in the framework of the educational system. *Personnel and Guidance Journal, 57*, 22–26.

Klingman, A. (1992a). Stress reactions of Israeli youth during the gulf war: A quantitative study. *Professional Psychology: Research and Practice, 23*, 521–527.

Klingman, A. (1992b). The contribution of school mental health services to community-wide emergency reorganization and management during the 1991 Gulf War. *School Psychology International, 13*, 195–206.

Klingman, A. (1992c). The effect of parent-implemented crisis intervention: A real-life emergency involving a child's refusal to use a gas-mask. *Journal of Clinical Child Psychology, 21*, 70–75.

Klingman, A. (1993). School based intervention following a disaster. In C. F. Saylor (Ed.), *Children and disaster* (pp. 187–210). New York: Plenum Press.

Klingman, A. (2001a). Prevention of anxiety disorders: The case of post-traumatic stress disorder. In W. K. Silverman & P. D. A. Treffers (Eds.), *Anxiety disorders in children and adolescents: Research, assessment, and intervention* (pp. 368–391). Cambridge, UK: Cambridge University Press.

Klingman, A. (2001b). Stress reactions and adaptation of Israeli school-age children evacuated from homes during massive missile attacks. *Stress, Anxiety, and Coping, 14*, 1–14.

Klingman, A. (2002). School and war. In S. E. Brock, P. J. Lazarus, & S. R. Jimerson (Eds.), *Best practices in school crisis prevention and intervention* (pp. 577–598). Bethesda, MD: National Association of School Psychologists.

Klingman, A., & Kupermintz, H. (1994). Response style and self-control under Scud missile attacks: The case of the sealed room situation during the 1991 Gulf War. *Journal of Traumatic Stress, 7*, 415–426.

Klingman, A., Sagi, A., & Raviv, A. (1993). The effect of war on Israeli children. In L. A. Leavitt & N. A. Fox (Eds.), *The psychological effects of war and violence on children* (pp. 75–92). Hillsdale, NJ: Lawrence Erlbaum.

Lahad, M. (1997). BASIC Ph.: The story of coping resources. In M. Lahad & A. Cohen (Eds.), *Community stress prevention* (Vols. 1 & 2, pp. 117–145). Kiryat Shmona, Israel: Community Stress Prevention Center.

Lahad, M., & Abraham, A. (1983). Hachanat Morim Vetalmidim Lehitmodedoot Im Matzaviey Lachatz: Tochnit Ruv-maymadit [Preparing teachers and pupils for coping with stress situations: A multi-modal program]. *Psychologia Veyeuttz Bachinuch, 16,* 196–210.

Laor, N., Wolmer, L., Mayers, L., Gershon, A., Weizman, R., & Cohen, D. J. (1997). Israeli preschool children under Scuds: A 30-month follow-up. *Child and Adolescent Psychiatry, 36,* 349–355.

Lazarus, A. A. (1976). *Multimodal behavior therapy.* New York: Springer.

Lazarus, A. A. (1989). *The practice of multimodal therapy: Systematic, comprehensive and effective psychotherapy.* Baltimore: Johns Hopkins University Press.

Lazarus, R. S., & Folkman, S. (1984). *Stress, appraisal, and coping.* New York: Springer.

Llabre, M. M., & Hadi, F. (1994). Health-related aspects of the gulf crisis experience of Kuwaiti boys and girls. *Anxiety, Stress, and Coping, 7,* 217–228.

Lowenfeld, M. (1950). The nature and use of the Lowenfeld World Technique in work with children and adults. *Journal of Psychology, 30,* 325–331.

Lyons H. A. (1971). Psychiatric sequelae of the Belfast riots. *Psychiatry, 118,* 265–273.

Macksoud, M. S., Haber, J. L., & Cohen, L. (1996). Assessing the impact of war and children. In R. J. Apfel & B. Simon (Eds.), *Minefields in their hearts: The mental health of children in war and communal violence* (pp. 218–230). New Haven: Yale University Press.

Macksoud, M. S., & Nazer, F. A. (1993). *The impact of the Iraqi occupation on the psychological development of children in Kuwait* [Tech. Rep.]. Kuwait City: Kuwait Society for the Advancement of Arab Children.

McCloskey, L. A., & Southwick, K. (1996). Psychosocial problems in refugee children exposed to war. *Pediatrics, 97,* 394–397.

Meichenbaum, D., & Cameron, R. (1983). Stress inoculation training: Toward a general paradigm for training coping skills. In D. Meichenbaum & M. E. Jaremko (Eds.), *Stress reduction and prevention* (pp. 115– 154). New York: Plenum Press.

Muldoon, O., & Cairns, E. (1999). Children, young people, and war: Learning to cope. In E. Frydenberg (Ed.), *Learning to cope: Developing as a person in complex societies* (pp. 322–337). Oxford, UK: Oxford University Press.

Muldoon, O., Trew, K., & McWhirter, L. (1998). Children's response to negative life events in Northern Ireland: A ten year comparison. *European Child and Adolescent Psychiatry, 7,* 36–41.

Nader, K., Pynoos, R., Fairbanks, L., Frederick, C., Al-Ajeel, M., & Al-Asfour, A. (1993). A preliminary study of PTSD and grief among the children of Kuwait following the Gulf crisis. *British Journal of Clinical Psychology, 32,* 407–416.

Nader, K. O., & Fairbanks, L. A. (1994). The suppression of re-experiencing: Impulse control and somatic symptoms in children following traumatic exposure. *Anxiety, Stress, and Coping, 7,* 229–239.

Nevo, O. (1994). Troomat Hapsichologia Shel Hahumor Beisrael Bemilchemet Hamifratz [The psychological contribution of humor in Israel during the Gulf War]. *Psychologia, 4,* 41–50.

Noy, B. (1992). The open line for students in the Gulf War. *School Psychology International, 13*, 207–227.

Omer, H., & Alon, N. (1994). The continuity principle: A unified approach to disaster and trauma. *American Journal of Community Psychology, 22*, 273–283.

Punamaki, R. L. (1989). Factors affecting the mental health of Palestinian children exposed to political violence. *International Journal of Mental Health, 18*, 63–69.

Punamaki, R. L. (1996). Can ideological commitment protect children's psychosocial well-being in situations of political violence? *Child Development, 67*, 55–69.

Punamaki, R. L., & Suleiman, R. (1990). Predictors and effectiveness of coping with political violence among Palestinian children. *British Journal of Social Psychology, 29*, 67–77.

Raphael, B., & Wilson, J. P. (Eds.). (1993). *International handbook of traumatic stress syndromes.* New York: Plenum Press.

Raviv, A. (1993). The use of hotline and media interventions in Israel during the Gulf War. In L. A. Leavitt & N. A. Fox (Eds.), *The psychological effects of war and violence on children* (pp. 319–337). Hillsdale, NJ: Lawrence Erlbaum.

Ronen, T. (1996). Self-control exposure therapy for children's anxieties: A preliminary report. *Child and Family Behavior Therapy, 18*, 1–17.

Rosenthal, M., & Levy-Shiff, R. (1993). Threat of missile attacks in the Gulf War: Mothers' perceptions of young children's reactions. *American Journal of Orthopsychiatry, 63*, 241–254.

Sabljak, L. (1999). How librarians help children overcome the consequences of the war in Croatia. In O. Ayalon, M. Lahad, & A. Cohen (Eds.), *Community stress prevention* (Vol. 4, pp. 34–40). Jerusalem, Israel: Ministry of Education, Psychological and Counseling Service.

Saigh, P. A. (1987a). In vitro flooding of an adolescent's posttraumatic stress disorder. *Journal of Clinical Child Psychology, 16*, 147–150.

Saigh, P. A. (1987b). In-vitro flooding of a childhood posttraumatic stress disorder. *School Psychology Review, 16*, 203–211.

Saigh, P. A. (1987c). In-vitro flooding of a childhood posttraumatic stress disorder: A systematic replication. *Professional School Psychology, 2*, 133–145.

Saigh, P. A. (1989). The development and validation of the children's posttraumatic stress disorder inventory. *International Journal of Special Education, 4*, 75–84.

Saigh, P. A. (1996). Posttraumatic stress disorder among children and adolescents: An introduction. *Journal of School Psychology, 34*, 103–105.

Saigh, P. A. (2002). School and war. In S. E. Brock, P. J. Lazarus, & S. R. Jimerson (Eds.), *Best practices in school crisis prevention and intervention* (pp. 639–652). Bethesda, MD: National Association of School Psychologists.

Saigh, P. A., Green, B. L., & Korol, M. (1996). The history and prevalence of posttraumatic stress disorder with special reference to children and adolescents. *Journal of School Psychology, 34*, 107–131.

Saigh, P. A., Yule, W., & Inamdar, S. C. (1996). Imaginal flooding of traumatized children and adolescents. *Journal of School Psychology, 34*, 163–183.

Salmon, T. W. (1919). The war neuroses and their lessons. *New York Journal of Medicine, 59*, 933–934.

Schwartzwald, J., Weisenberg, M., Waysman, M., Solomon, Z., & Klingman, A. (1993). Stress reaction of school-age children to the bombardment by Scud missiles. *Journal of Abnormal Psychology, 102*, 404–410.

Shacham, Y. (1996). *Stress reactions and activating coping resources: A comparison between children who remained under Katyusha rocket shelling and children who were evacuated to a safe haven.* Unpublished doctoral dissertation, Newport University, Newport Beach, CA.

Shields, J., Erdal, K., Skrinjaric, J., & Majic, G. (1999). Post-traumatic stress symptomatology among health care professionals in Croatia. *American Journal of Orthopsychiatry, 64*, 529–535.

Shilo-Cohen, N. (1993). Israeli children paint war. In L. A. Leavitt & N. A. Fox (Eds.), *The psychological effects of war and violence on children* (pp. 93–107). Hillsdale, NJ: Lawrence Erlbaum.

Sjolund, M. (1981). Play diagnosis and therapy in Sweden: The Erica-Method. *Journal of Clinical Psychology, 37*, 322–325.

Solomon, Z. (1995). *Coping with war-induced stress.* New York: Plenum Press.

Swenson, C. C., & Klingman, A. (1993). Children and war. In C. F. Saylor (Ed.), *Children and disasters* (pp. 137–163). New York: Plenum Press.

Yule, W., Perrin, S., & Smith, P. (2001). Traumatic events and post-traumatic stress disorder. In W. K. Silverman & P. A. Treffers (Eds.), *Anxiety disorders in children and adolescents: Research, assessment, and intervention* (pp. 212–234). Cambridge, UK: Cambridge University Press.

Zeidner, M. (1992). Coping with disaster: The case of Israeli adolescents under threat of missile attack. *Journal of Youth and Adolescence, 22*, 89–108.

Zeidner, M., Klingman, A., & Itskovitz, R. (1993). Children's reactions and coping under threat of missile attack: A semi-projective assessment procedure. *Journal of Personality Assessment, 60*, 435–457.

Ziv, A., & Israeli, R. (1973). Effects of bombardment of the manifest anxiety level of children living in Kibbutzim. *Journal of Consulting and Clinical Psychology, 40*, 287–291.

16

CHILDREN'S EXPOSURE TO COMMUNITY VIOLENCE

JANIS B. KUPERSMIDT, ARIANA SHAHINFAR,
AND MARY ELLEN VOEGLER-LEE

Over the past decade, the problem of community violence in this country has become a top priority for mental health professionals, researchers, educators, policy makers, and politicians alike (see Elliott & Tolan, 1999). Community violence has been defined as the presence of violence and violence-related events within a person's proximal environment (Shahinfar, Fox, & Leavitt, 2000). This definition encompasses exposure that occurs in or around the home, school, or neighborhood; may involve physical as well as threatened harm; may be witnessed, heard about, or experienced; and may involve known or unknown perpetrators. Violence threatens the safety of children and their families in a place where safety is crucial: their everyday environment. Evidence from both anecdotal and large-scale studies indicates that the psychological, cognitive, and behavioral health of American children is suffering as the result of exposure to trauma within their communities (e.g., Allen, Jones, Seidman, & Aber, 1999; Garbarino, 1999; Horn &

This work was funded in part by a University Research Council Grant from the University of North Carolina at Chapel Hill to the first author and an Intra-University Research Grant from La Salle University awarded to the second author.

Trickett, 1998; Howard, Cross, Li, & Huang, 1999; Kliewer, Lepore, Oskin, & Johnson, 1998; Margolin & Gordis, 2000; Shahinfar et al., 2000). Many children have suffered as victims of or witnesses to violence; still others have suffered through hearing about the loss or hurt caused to someone they know.

Several features distinguish community violence from the other types of trauma discussed in this book. The natural disasters described in the second section of this book are, by definition, time-limited events that are unlikely to recur in the same geographic area. Community violence, in contrast, presents as a chronic threat that often is concentrated in particular parts of our country—most often, the inner cities. Although not all children living in inner-city or other potentially violent environments are continually exposed to violent incidents, the nature of community violence presents a threat that continually challenges children's and parents' sense of safety (Garbarino, 1999; Osofsky, 1995).

The technological disasters that are covered in the third section of this book also differ substantially from community violence. Both are caused by humans; however, the former is generally the result of human miscalculation or technological malfunction, whereas the latter generates from intentional and harmful acts of one person against another.

The chapters included in this section also include acts of human-made, intentional violence, but community violence may be distinguished from war violence (see Klingman, chapter 15), hostage taking (see Nader, chapter 13), and other terrorist activities (see Gurwitch, chapter 14) by its lack of ideological purpose. The other types of violence included in this section generally are based on ideological beliefs and are goal-directed in their intent. Ideology is important insofar as it assigns purpose to the violence; ideological purpose also has been shown to serve as a protective factor in moderating the traumatic effects of war (Liddell, Kemp, & Moema, 1993). Community violence, however, often appears as a series of random acts, and lacks an ideological framework from which to understand the occurrence of such violence. Although some have argued that gang violence shares some qualities with wartime behavior in that both represent conflict between two opposing sides (Garbarino, Kostelny, & Dubrow, 1991), the victims of gang violence often are innocent bystanders who are not privy to the goals of such "turf wars." Such violence therefore appears to the community to be senseless and random.

Our purpose in this chapter is twofold: (a) to trace and review the development of the literature on children's exposure to community violence and (b) to use a coping framework through which to generate ideas for helping children who have been exposed to community violence. We begin by examining the prevalence of children's exposure to community violence. We next consider the psychological, cognitive, and behavioral outcomes that have been identified as correlates of such exposure, then conclude by examining how the stress and coping literature may be applied to understanding children's responses to exposure to violence. Within this discussion we consider factors that serve to mediate or moderate children's experiences with community violence and how those factors are useful in designing interventions to help children cope with exposure to community violence.

PREVALENCE OF CHILDREN'S EXPOSURE TO COMMUNITY VIOLENCE

Since its recognition as a public health problem (Rosenberg & Fenley, 1991; Rosenberg, O'Carroll, & Powell, 1992), the issue of community violence has received a great deal of attention in the psychological and psychiatric literatures. The first phase of studying any new phenomenon is to gather information on the incidence and prevalence of the problem. The early data-gathering phase of community violence research was marked by survey interviews of children, adolescents, and their parents in an effort to document the prevalence of children's exposure to violence. The estimates of children's witnessing of and victimization by community violence gleaned from the surveys of primarily inner-city children revealed that children and adolescents report exposure to significant amounts of community violence.

A survey conducted in Washington, DC, revealed that 61% of a sample of first- and second-grade children and 72% of fifth- and sixth-grade children reported witnessing the perpetration of violence within their community (Richters & Martinez, 1993). In Chicago, a similar survey revealed that one third of a sample of school-age children reported witnessing a homicide and two thirds reported witnessing a serious assault (Bell & Jenkins, 1991). In New Orleans, 91% of 9- to 12-year-olds reported that they had witnessed at least one violent incident (Osofsky, Wewers, Hann, & Fick, 1993). In Boston, 69% of adolescents between ages 13 and 19 reported witnessing violence, and 37% reported experiencing threats (Hausman, Spivak, & Prothrow-Stith, 1994). In Miami, 93% of high school students surveyed reported having witnessed at least one violent event, and 44% reported having been a victim of at least one violent event (Berman, Kurtines, Silverman, & Serafini, 1996). In Baltimore, 67% of youths ages 12 to 24 reported knowing someone who had been shot, and 23% reported witnessing murder (Gladstein, Rusonis, & Heald, 1992). In Detroit, 22% of adolescents and young adults between ages 14 and 23 reported witnessing a murder, and 9% reported witnessing more than one murder (Schubiner, Scott, & Tzelepis, 1993).

Those prevalence rates extend to young children as well. In Washington, DC, a study of preschool children preparing to enter Head Start found that 78% of the children reported that they had either witnessed or been a victim of at least one violent event (Shahinfar et al., 2000). High rates of community violence exposure also have been reported by children who live in rural areas (Martin, Gordon, & Kupersmidt, 1995). Thus, exposure to violence has become pervasive across our society and is not just restricted to adolescents or children living in inner cities.

Methodological Issues

Although the numbers are sobering, several factors related to methodological variation across studies must be considered when examining the statistics regarding the prevalence of children's exposure to community violence. The first of those factors is the issue of who offered the report of violence exposure—namely, whether the child, parent, or both were interviewed. In general, studies in which both child and parent reports have been considered have found low concordance between the rates of exposure reported by the two sources; parents generally underestimate children's reports of their own exposure (Hill & Jones, 1997; Howard et al., 1999; Richters & Martinez, 1993; Schwarz & Kowalski, 1991; Shahinfar et al., 2000).

Some have suggested that underestimation of exposure is a particular problem when parents offer reports on their older children and adolescents, because parents generally spend less time with older children than with younger (Howard et al., 1999). Researchers have interpreted the lack of concordance between parents' and older children's reports of exposure in several ways. First, parents may be unaware of their older children's exposure to violence (Richters & Martinez, 1993). Alternatively, parents may repress information as either a passive or active coping strategy (Richters & Martinez, 1993). Both explanations assume that children are the best reporters of their own experiences with violence. Allen and her colleagues (1999), however, have suggested that older children may overreport because they are confused between violence-related fantasies and memories of actual occurrences, particularly in cases in which adolescent reporters may be seeking identification with the glamorized image of violence created by the media.

With regard to younger children, several alternatives have been suggested to explain the discordance between parent and child reports of exposure. First, it has been suggested that young children may be unable to distinguish between events that were actually witnessed and those only heard about (Richters & Martinez, 1993) or between fantasy and reality reports of violence (Shahinfar et al., 2000). Indeed, children of preschool and early school age are still developing their ability to distinguish between reality and other cognitive processes, such as imagination (Flavell, 1993). Others have suggested the possibility that inflated reports of exposure may be related to a difference between parent and child perceptions of what constitutes violence (Shahinfar et al., 2000), a problem that could account for older children's lack of consistency with parental reports as well.

A second factor to consider when interpreting the statistics regarding the prevalence of children's exposure to violence is that the instruments used in the surveys have varied widely across studies. For example, although some researchers have assessed violence exposure using a small number of true–false questions incorporated into a measure of stressful life events (e.g., Attar, Guerra, & Tolan, 1994), others have collected reports of exposure to many different types of violence-related events and asked the respondents to indicate when and how often those events occurred and whether the events had been witnessed, heard about, or experienced (e.g., Richters & Martinez, 1993).

A third methodological problem is that although violence researchers have acknowledged that exposure to violence has the potential to vary along several dimensions, including the result of the violence, the level of severity, the proximity at which exposure occurs, and the relationship of the victim or perpetrator to the child (e.g., Allen et al., 1999; Pynoos et al., 1987; Richters & Martinez, 1993), many researchers have not systematically gathered data that allows for distinctions among those dimensions. For example, even among studies that have essentially considered the same elements of violence (e.g., robbery, beating, shooting, stabbing, and drug dealing), some have combined witnessing and victimization into single questions, whereas others have gathered separate information on the modality of exposure and have found different correlates for victims versus witnesses (e.g., Martin, Gordon, & Kupersmidt, 1995; Shahinfar et al., 2000; Shahinfar, Kupersmidt, & Matza, 2001).

In a related vein, most studies that have considered the psychometric properties of violence exposure inventories have identified categories of exposure that are based on the severity of the event to which the child has been exposed (e.g., Hastings & Kelley, 1997; Selner-O'Hagan, Kindlon, Buka, Raudenbush, & Earls, 1998; Shahinfar et al., 2000; Shahinfar et al., 2001), yet few studies have examined the correlates of these conceptually and statistically distinct categories of exposure. The problem with methodologies that rely on broad questioning regarding exposure is that they leave little room for the sensitivity necessary to explore how various types of violence exposure affect children in various ways.

Despite a lack of consistency with regard to the measures used and the methods by which prevalence information has been collected, agreement exists across studies that violence exposure is a serious problem for children living in dangerous environments. Whether considering parent or child reports of exposure, the numbers that have been generated are alarming. With greater agreement on which characteristics of exposure are most important will come greater precision in identifying and linking particular outcomes to particular types of exposure.

CORRELATES OF CHILDREN'S EXPOSURE TO COMMUNITY VIOLENCE

Given the alarmingly high prevalence rates of community violence exposure in children, investigators recently have begun to examine the correlates of exposure with children's functioning. Most of the studies reviewed to date are correlational in design. Nonetheless, the studies are important in that they have consistently demonstrated significant links between children's exposure to violence and a number of negative psychological, behavioral, cognitive, and academic outcomes.

Impact of Exposure to Chronic Community Violence Versus Acute Trauma Exposure

Unlike children who are affected by single, acute events such as disasters, children who are chronically exposed to violence within their immediate environment do not necessarily experience and react to a particular precipitating incident. When violence is part of the norm of everyday life for children, it may affect virtually all aspects of their life and environment and may not be time limited in its presence. For example, when urban elementary school children were asked to draw pictures of "what happens" in their neighborhoods, the children presented a graphic gallery of shootings, stabbings, fights, and drug deals (Lewis, Brown, Jones, & Osofsky, 1994). In an environment in which those incidents are frequent, it is methodologically challenging to link children's responses to any one particular incident; instead, a pattern of experiences and responses may be observed.

Psychological Functioning

A number of studies have examined the relation between exposure to community violence and psychological functioning. In their study of violence exposure among 6- to 12-year-old urban children, Freeman, Mokros, and Poznanski (1993) reported a significant positive relation between reports of exposure to violence and depression. Others have demonstrated significant associations between parent and child reports of violence exposure and distress symptoms such as anger, anxiety, sleep problems, and increased fears (Fitzpatrick & Boldizar, 1993; Martinez & Richters, 1993; Singer, Anglin, Song, & Lunghofer, 1995). Also, Martin et al. (1995) reported a significant relation between witnessing community violence and internalizing behavior problems.

Many of the symptoms that children exposed to violence report parallel those experienced by people with posttraumatic stress disorder (PTSD; Bell & Jenkins, 1993; Berton & Stabb, 1996; Cicchetti & Lynch, 1993; Martinez & Richters, 1993). Commonly reported symptoms of PTSD in traumatized children include reenactment, avoidance, numbing, hypervigilance, and sleep disturbances (Terr, 1991). Such symptoms have been reported not only in children who have been victims of violence but also in those who have witnessed or heard about traumatic events without actually experiencing physical injury themselves (Applebaum & Burns, 1991; Malmquist, 1986; Saigh, 1991).

Behavioral Functioning

Although it has been adequately argued that children who are exposed to community violence experience some of the classic posttrauma symptoms, increased attention traditionally has been paid to the externalizing behaviors associated with violence exposure. This focus on externalizing symptoms among children exposed to violence has resulted both from the urgency with which aggression must be addressed in social situations (Mills & Rubin, 1990) as well as the high degree of stability that has been demonstrated for those behaviors (Loeber, 1982; Moffitt, 1990).

In general, the results of studies of violence-exposed children suggest that they are more likely to display behavioral problems than their nonexposed peers are. For example, in a study of urban primary and secondary students, Bell and Jenkins (1993) found reports of violence exposure to be associated with increased fighting behavior among boys and young children. Similarly, Schubiner et al. (1993) demonstrated that children who had been victims of violence were at greater risk for involvement in the perpetration of violence. Martin et al. (1995) reported that children who had been victims of community violence were more likely to carry a weapon and to have elevated externalizing behavioral problems. At least one longitudinal investigation has demonstrated that community violence exposure was related to antisocial behavior and increased aggression in adolescents, after controlling for earlier aggression (Gorman-Smith & Tolan, 1998).

Social Cognitive Functioning

Evidence from the social cognitive literature suggests that violence exposure may play a role in children's development of maladaptive social information–processing patterns (e.g., Dodge, Bates, & Pettit, 1990; Huesmann, 1998). Theories regarding the development of social cognitive processes in aggression grew out of the social learning model of behavioral development (Bandura, 1973, 1986), which posits that exposure to aggressive role models will increase a child's chance for developing aggressive behavior problems. Several studies have shown that the social information–processing patterns that are characteristic of aggressive children are shaped by experiences within the family, particularly harsh discipline (Dodge, Lochman, Harnish, Bates, & Pettit, 1997; Weiss, Dodge, Bates, & Pettit, 1992) and maltreatment (Dodge, Bates, & Pettit, 1990; Smetana & Kelly, 1989; Spacarelli, Coatsworth, & Bowden, 1995). Others have found that social cognitive processes may serve as moderators that compensate for maltreatment status (Downey & Walker, 1989).

Recent evidence has indicated that exposure to violence within the community also may play a role in the development of social cognitions supportive of aggressive behavior (Shahinfar et al., 2001). Berkowitz (1993) has suggested that highly aggressive personalities develop out of an atmosphere of continuous, strong, and adverse influences. The chronic exposure to violence that has been documented in many American cities may provide a better test of the influence of violence exposure on cognitive patterns and aggression development than violence that occurs in only one context (e.g., domestic violence that occurs in the home).

Social Functioning

Although little is known about the impact of community violence exposure on children's social functioning, one study investigated this relationship. Schwartz and Proctor (2000) examined the social adjustment of fourth-through sixth-grade inner-city children who had experienced various degrees of violence exposure. They found that children who were victims of violence evidenced numerous negative social outcomes, including aggressive behavior, peer rejection, and bullying by peers (Schwartz & Proctor, 2000). In contrast, children who witnessed violence but were not themselves victimized exhibited aggressive behavior but were not rejected or bullied by peers. In addition to providing important information regarding the social functioning of youth exposed to community violence, the findings highlight distinct correlates for children as a function of the modality of their exposure to violence (i.e., victim vs. witness).

Academic Functioning

Children exposed to community violence have been argued to be at risk for academic problems (see Garbarino, Dubrow, Kostelny, & Pardo, 1992; Mazza & Overstreet, 2000). Indeed, several researchers have found that exposure to community violence predicted poor academic performance, although those studies focused only on children and adolescents who experienced severe violence exposure, such as the murder of a family member (Dyson, 1989) or the witnessing of a shooting or stabbing (Schwab-Stone et al., 1995). One possible explanation for the link between violence exposure and poor academic functioning among severely traumatized children may be that the problems with concentration often experienced by children with manifestations of PTSD preclude full effort and participation in the academic arena (e.g., Pynoos & Nader, 1988). As such, PTSD could be described as a mediator between violence exposure and poor academic performance in children who have been traumatized severely enough to display symptoms of PTSD. This theory, however, has not been directly tested and reported in the literature.

One recent study, which examined mild forms of community violence exposure in addition to the severe types described above, also indicated a significant, albeit weak, relation between total exposure and academic functioning (Overstreet & Braun, 1999). Interestingly, the relation between exposure and poor academic performance in this study was exacerbated for children whose families emphasized an achievement orientation. This finding suggests that violence exposure may display its strongest effects in the areas we particularly value.

Summary

Together with the data from prevalence research, the work on outcomes related to children's reactions to violence exposure has proven fruitful for descriptive purposes toward documenting the salience of community violence in the lives of children. The two lines of research, now fairly firmly established, provide the foundation on which to build a picture of factors that may mediate or moderate the relations between violence exposure on negative outcomes.

FACTORS THAT MEDIATE OR MODERATE THE EFFECTS OF COMMUNITY VIOLENCE

Despite the fact that this area of research is relatively new, several studies have begun to examine factors that may mediate or moderate the effects of community violence exposure on negative outcomes in children. Six basic sets of factors were located in the literature, including research on coping processes, perceptions of neighborhood safety, intrusive thinking, social support, emotional dysregulation, and social information–processing skills.

Coping With Community Violence

In a recent review of the literature on how children cope with stress, Compas, Connor, Saltzman, Thomsen, and Wadsworth (2001) found an extensive literature on how children cope with self-reported and general stressors, but no studies that specifically examined how children cope with exposure to community violence. The general pattern of findings suggests that problem-focused, or *engaged*, coping (i.e., trying to fix or solve the problem or an orientation toward the stressor) is associated with reduced levels of internalizing and externalizing symptoms; however, several studies indicated the opposite relation between style of coping and adjustment. Engaged coping used in the context of stressors that were subjectively or objectively reported to be uncontrollable by the child was associated with poorer adjustment. The findings suggest the importance of understanding the context of coping in addition to the child's coping methods or strategies.

Emotion-focused coping strategies, or *disengagement*, (i.e., focusing on one's thoughts or feelings about the stressor or avoiding the source of stress) were uniformly associated with poorer adjustment. Compas and colleagues (2001) interpreted the findings to suggest that attempts to regulate or change one's emotions to cope with stress are not the problematic aspects of coping. Instead, they note that it is the child's "disengagement with the stressor or one's emotions, negative cognitions about the self and the situation, and unregulated release or ventilation of emotions that are most consistently associated with more symptoms and lower competence" (p. 24). We located one study that examined the role of positive and negative coping styles in predicting PTSD symptoms for children who had been exposed to crime and violence. Berman and colleagues (1996) found that increased use of a negative coping style (i.e., distraction, withdrawal, criticizing self, blaming others, wishful thinking, and resignation) was associated with increased PTSD symptomatology. Their findings are consistent with the general findings reported by Compas et al. (2001) regarding the negative effects of using disengagement strategies.

Our knowledge of coping mediators is best developed in the literatures on coping with other types of stressors, such as illness and chronic diseases. Four classes of mediators have been consistently identified in the adult coping literature, including social support (Cohen & Wills, 1985); individual sense of control (Parkes, 1984); optimism (Scheier, Weintraub, & Carver, 1986), and sense of humor (Martin & Lefcourt, 1983). Most of these mediators have not been thoroughly examined in studies of children's coping or of children exposed to violence. Thus, the applicability of those findings to children's coping with community violence is not certain. Further examination of these factors is an important direction for future research.

Perceptions of Neighborhood Safety

One study examined how safe children felt in their neighborhoods. Overstreet and Braun (2000) reported that children's perceptions of neighborhood safety mediated the negative effects of community violence exposure on posttraumatic stress symptoms. They also found that family conflict served as a mediator of adjustment. These findings have two implications. First, they are consistent with a cumulative stress model, which suggests that exposure to violence in multiple settings (i.e., both the home and the community) may have a particularly deleterious effect on children. Second, they are consistent with conceptualizations of the emergence of posttraumatic stress symptoms in relation to perceptions of threat and danger. The findings suggest important directions for future research in understanding the mediating role of cognitions in the development of posttraumatic stress symptoms.

Intrusive Thinking

Kliewer, Lepore, Oskin, and Johnson (1998) examined the role of cognitive processes in children's adjustment following violence exposure in a sample of 8- to 12-year-old children. They found that the presence of intrusive thinking (i.e., the occurrence of mental images that were unpleasant and uncontrollable) served to mediate the effect of violence exposure on anxiety and depressive symptoms (Kliewer et al., 1998). The findings further highlight the importance of examining the impact of cognitions on children's adjustment to experiencing traumatic events.

Social Support

The role of both familial and extrafamilial social support in mediating or moderating children's adjustment has been investigated in a number of studies of children exposed to community violence. In their examination of maternal social support, Kliewer et al. (1998) found that the presence of support moderated children's adjustment following violence exposure. That is, children whose mothers provided support were better adjusted than those receiving little maternal support. Specifically, Kliewer et al. found that the availability of unencumbered, supportive opportunities to talk about violence exposure was particularly helpful to children. Likewise, perceptions of availability of support from social network members predicted fewer PTSD symptoms for high school children (Berman et al., 1996).

The importance of social support, in general, as a mediator of the effects of community violence on internalizing and externalizing symptomatology also was reported for a clinical sample of adolescents (Muller, Goebel-Fabbri, Diamond, & Dinklage, 2000), but it was not found as a moderator for a low-income sample of African American 10- to 15-year-olds (Overstreet, Dempsey, Graham, & Moely, 1999). The discrepancy in findings across those studies suggests that the relative importance of social support may vary as a function of age, ethnic group, and social class of the child as well as the person providing the support, and it therefore requires additional study.

Emotion Dysregulation and Social Information–Processing Skills

Schwartz and Proctor (2000) examined mediators of social adjustment in fourth- through sixth-grade inner-city children. They distinguished between mediators associated with victimization and those associated with witnessing violence. They found that for children who were victims of violence, emotion dysregulation mediated social adjustment. Emotion dysregulation included affective lability, intensity, valence, flexibility, and situational appropriateness. Social outcomes included aggressive behavior, peer rejection, and bullying by peers. In contrast, for witnesses to community violence and aggressive behavior, social information–processing deficits mediated social adjustment. Social information processing included positive evaluation of aggressive behavior, positive outcome expectancies for aggressive behavior, and perceived self-efficacy for aggressive behavior. Similarly, Shahinfar et al. (2001) examined the relation between different types of violence exposure and social information–processing mechanisms in a sample of highly aggressive incarcerated male adolescents. They reported that victimization by severe violence was related to early stages in the social information–processing model, including positive beliefs about aggression, problems with the interpretation of ambiguous social cues, and hostile social goals. Conversely, witnessing severe violence was related to later stages in the social information–processing model, including perceived positive outcomes for the use of aggression. Taken together, the studies suggest that emotional and social cognitive processes of children are differentially related to the type of violence exposure. These provocative findings highlight the importance of differentiating children's experiences with violence exposure to better develop our theories about the processes associated with negative outcomes.

TREATMENT OF CHILDREN EXPOSED TO COMMUNITY VIOLENCE

The high rates of children's exposure to community violence in our society and the strong links to posttraumatic stress and other mental health problems in exposed children suggest the urgent need for the development of empirically validated treatment programs. In fact, Robert Pynoos was quoted by Sahagun (1999) as saying, "Children exposed to violence and disaster deserve at least the same ongoing psychological treatment we provide firemen and police officers." This need is true for both the victims and the witnesses; however, evidence-based treatment programs for children exposed to community violence were not located in the literature.

Intervention programs aimed at helping children cope with stress were the basis for the treatment recommendations described below. Monat and Lazarus (1991) have categorized such intervention programs according to their purpose, which can include altering the environment or lifestyle of the target child, altering the personality of the child or his or her perception of the event, or altering the child's biological responses to the stressor. Most intervention efforts, to date, have been directed to the latter two goals and focus on environmental intervention for prevention purposes and cognitive–behavioral types of intervention for treatment purposes.

Evidence from research with children with severe mental health problems suggests that effective treatment must occur on a number of levels (e.g., child, family, and community). The following sections discuss treatment strategies at each level.

Child-Focused Interventions

At the child level, the importance of providing opportunities for the child to talk about his or her experiences cannot be overstated. In addition, it is important to assess and address such qualities as the child's perception of neighborhood and school safety, the presence of intrusive thinking, and social information–processing skills. Clinicians also can apply this information to the therapy process, an indication that creating repeated opportunities for children to talk about their trauma experiences may be fundamental to the therapeutic process. Other potential goals for intervention with violence-exposed children include those that promote and enhance adequate coping skills, emotional regulation skills, optimism, an internal locus of control, and a sense of humor.

We did not locate evidence-based programs specific to the treatment of violence-exposed children; however, March, Amaya-Jackson, Murray, and Schulte (1998) developed the Multi-Modality Trauma Treatment (MMTT), an innovative, manualized treatment program for youth experiencing PTSD following a single-incident stressor. The use of this treatment model has not been applied directly to children experiencing community violence, but MMTT appears to be promising for the treatment of violence-exposed youth. The program uses modules to address many of the mediators reported in the literature review above, including anxiety management, anger coping, cognitive training, exposure, and relapse prevention. MMTT is designed to be used in both clinic and school settings, and it can be used with individuals or groups of children.

Several evidence-based programs and a growing clinical literature are available for assisting children exposed to chronic stressors, such as domestic violence, as well as children who have been the victim of physical or sexual abuse (Kolko, 1998). Notably, the two literatures (i.e., scientific and clinical) are quite consistent with each other. For example, both literatures recommend using expressive art therapies that include the use of storytelling, drawing, and coloring books. In addition, with young children, both literatures recommend using play or dramatic play incorporating blocks, hand puppets, and figures as a way of "talking" about exposure to the stressor.

In general, the main treatment goal for children who are young and may not be especially verbal is to tell the story often and in a wide variety of ways to supportive others. Storytelling can be out loud, in pictures, through radio play (pretending to be a radio announcer), with puppets, or with toys. It is hypothesized that such storytelling helps validate feelings and contribute to desensitizing and destigmatizing the child. It is further recommended that storytelling and therapeutic interventions include (a) having the child identify and discuss the feelings associated with the events, (b) supporting the child in knowing that his or her feelings are a normal and natural reaction to experiencing trauma, and (c) explaining to the child that every person's reaction to violence is unique and that it is okay if his or her feelings about it differ from those of a friend, sibling, or someone else. Also, it may be necessary to communicate to the child the message that he or she may never "get over" the feeling, so that the child is not worried if the feeling does not go away quickly. It may be important to reassure the child that he or she will be able to perform in school, with friends and family, and in other places, even if the bad feelings continue. For some children who are chronically exposed to community violence, it also might be useful to role play planning and coping skills to prevent or reduce the impact of reexposure.

Family-Focused Interventions

In addition to treatment at the child level, intervention must occur at the family level. Given the helplessness that the parents of children exposed to community violence often feel, involving parents in the child's treatment can allow them to learn ways to assist their child's coping efforts. Osofsky (1997) stated that parents can help their children by reestablishing a sense of order and routine in their lives, providing the children with an explanation of the event that is appropriate to the child's developmental stage, and responding to the child's fears and worries with as much reassurance as possible. Kliewer et al.'s (1998) finding of the importance of parental social support suggests that parents should be taught how to provide such support, including helping their children express their thoughts and feelings and supporting the children's use of prosocial coping skills. Parents also can be taught ways to reduce their children's reexposure to community violence. In addition, intervening with parents can provide support to parents who themselves feel overwhelmed by their children's exposure. Assisting the parents' own coping can allow them, in turn, to better support their children. Finally, Overstreet and Braun's (2000) identification of family conflict as a mediator of adjustment suggested that problems within the family system serve as an additional risk factor for maladjustment following exposure. The presence of family conflict can be assessed in the context of family sessions, and steps then can be taken to reduce the conflict.

Community Interventions

The third level of intervention occurs at the community level and includes the school, neighborhood, and health care settings. The school setting could serve as the primary community resource for intervention, given that it provides a structured and consistent environment for the child. It is also a natural environment for children rather than a clinic-based setting. Normalizing children's experiences and getting them back to a predictable, stable, normal routine can be a critical component of successful adaptation after trauma exposure. Such interventions as March and colleagues' (1998)

MMTT program could be used regularly in schools after proper screening and assessment for trauma reactions.

Another implication of the research findings is that school personnel can monitor children for adverse reactions to known incidents of exposure as well as for changes in performance or behavior. For example, Pynoos et al. (1993) reported marked changes in behavior that arose in direct proportion to the amount of exposure, damage, and injury to a child. Thus, teachers and other school personnel can be taught basic debriefing techniques as well as case-detection or case-finding skills for early identification purposes. Teachers also can be prepared with predisaster training in how disasters affect children and the importance of communicating the facts about a disaster to children. Thoroughly and accurately addressing children's questions and fears has been found to result in a reduction in children's anxiety.

In addition to intervention in the school setting, a number of new programs aimed at the neighborhood level are involving police in their efforts to reduce children's exposure to community violence. A promising program in New Haven, Connecticut, trains police officers to identify issues related to youth's exposure to violence so that the officers can address those issues in the field when working with exposed children (Osofsky, 1997). In addition, the inclusion of police officers in prevention and intervention efforts provides a positive police presence for children. It is expected that this program will promote an increased perception of neighborhood safety among children. Given that a decreased sense of safety was identified as a mediator of adjustment difficulties (Overstreet & Braun, 2000), this intervention might offset adjustment difficulties in exposed youth. In addition, the efforts are intended to prevent reexposure to community violence.

The health care system represents another community area in which youth might be helped. Physicians can play an important role in identifying children in need of services. Children can be screened as part of a routine medical examination. The child and his or her parent or caregiver should be asked about prior exposure to violence, both as a witness and as a victim, and should be screened for trauma reactions. Pediatricians or family medicine physicians can refer children to appropriate mental health services either within the community or their school.

Social Policy Recommendations

Finally, Osofsky (1997) provides social policy recommendations regarding children's exposure to community violence. She recommends changing the image of violence from acceptable to disdained and unacceptable, educating the public more generally on the effects of violence exposure on children and how to protect children from exposure, and assisting communities with developing local prevention and intervention efforts. She also recommends creating sane and safe gun laws and creating specific resources for treatment intervention for exposed children.

CONCLUSIONS

Until now, community violence research has been successful in drawing attention to the prevalence of and risks associated with children's exposure to violence, particularly in urban areas. The question that remains concerns the implications of such research: Now that we know that community violence is placing a substantial number of children at risk for behavioral and psychological distress, what do we do about it? The answer lies in preventive intervention, both stopping violence before it occurs and building on children's protective resources to prevent exposure and its negative effects.

REFERENCES

Allen, L., Jones, S. M., Seidman, E., & Aber, J. L. (1999). Organization of exposure to violence among urban adolescents. In D. J. Flannery & C. R. Huff (Eds.), *Youth violence: Prevention, intervention, and social policy* (pp. 119–141). Washington, DC: American Psychiatric Press.

Applebaum, D. R., & Burns, G. L. (1991). Unexpected childhood death: Posttraumatic stress disorder in surviving siblings and parents. *Journal of Clinical Child Psychology, 20,* 114–120.

Attar, B. K., Guerra, N. G., & Tolan, P. H. (1994). Neighborhood disadvantage, stressful life events, and adjustment in urban elementary-school children. *Journal of Clinical Child Psychology, 23,* 391–400.

Bandura, A. (1973). *Aggression: A social learning theory analysis.* New York: Prentice Hall.

Bandura, A. (1986). *Social foundations of thought and action.* Englewood Cliffs, NJ: Prentice Hall.

Bell, C. C., & Jenkins, E. J. (1991). Traumatic stress and children. *Journal of Health Care for the Poor and Underserved, 2,* 175–185.

Bell, C. C., & Jenkins, E. J. (1993). Community violence and children on Chicago's Southside. *Psychiatry: Interpersonal and Biological Processes, 56,* 47–54.

Berkowitz, L. (1993). *Aggression: Its causes, consequences, and control.* New York: McGraw-Hill.

Berman, S. L., Kurtines, W. M., Silverman, W. K., & Serafini, L. T. (1996). The impact of exposure to crime and violence on urban youth. *American Journal of Orthopsychiatry, 66,* 329–336.

Berton, M. W., & Stabb, S. D. (1996). Exposure to violence and post-traumatic stress disorder in urban adolescents. *Adolescence, 31,* 122, 489–498.

Cicchetti, D., & Lynch, M. (1993). Toward an ecological/transactional model of community violence and child maltreatment: Consequences for children's development. *Psychiatry: Interpersonal and Biological Processes, 56,* 96–118.

Cohen, S., & Wills, T. A. (1985). Stress, social support, and the buffering hypothesis. *Psychological Bulletin, 98,* 310–357.

Compas, B. E., Connor, J. K., Saltzman, H., Thomsen, A. H., & Wadsworth, M. E. (2001). Coping with stress during childhood and adolescence: Problems, progress and potential in theory and research. *Psychological Bulletin, 127,* 87–127.

Dodge, K. A., Bates, J. E., & Pettit, G. A. (1990). Mechanisms in the cycle of violence. *Science, 250,* 1678–1683.

Dodge, K. A., Lochman, J., Harnish, J., Bates, J., & Pettit, G. (1997). Reactive and proactive aggression in school children and psychiatrically-impaired chronically assaultive youth. *Journal of Abnormal Psychology, 106,* 37–51.

Downey, G., & Walker, E. (1989). Social cognition and adjustment in children at risk for psychopathology. *Developmental Psychology, 25,* 835–845.

Dyson, J. L. (1989). The effect of family violence on children's academic performance and behavior. *Journal of the National Medical Association, 82,* 17–22.

Elliott, D. S., & Tolan, P. H. (1999). Youth violence prevention, intervention, and social policy: An overview. In D. J. Flannery & C. R. Huff (Eds.), *Youth violence: Prevention, intervention, and social policy* (pp. 3–46). Washington, DC: American Psychiatric Press.

Fitzpatrick, K. M., & Boldizar, J. P. (1993). The prevalence and consequences of exposure to violence among African-American youth. *Journal of the American Academy of Child and Adolescent Psychiatry, 32,* 424–430.

Flavell, J. H. (1993). Young children's understanding of thinking and consciousness. *Current Directions in Psychological Science, 2,* 40–43.

Freeman, L. M., Mokros, H., & Poznanski, E. O. (1993). Violent events reported by urban school-aged children: Characteristics and depression correlates. *Journal of the American Academy of Child and Adolescent Psychiatry, 32,* 419–423.

Garbarino, J. (1999). The effects of community violence on children. In L. Balter & C. Tamis-LeMonda (Eds.), *Child psychology: A handbook of contemporary issues* (pp. 412–425). Philadelphia: Taylor & Francis.

Garbarino, J., Dubrow, N., Kostelny, K., & Pardo, C. (1992). *Children in danger: Coping with the consequences of community violence.* San Francisco: Jossey-Bass.

Garbarino, J., Kostelny, K., & Dubrow, N. (1991). What children can tell us about living in danger. *American Psychologist, 46,* 376–383.

Gladstein, J., Rusonis, E. S., & Heald, F. P. (1992). A comparison of inner-city and upper-middle class youths' exposure to violence. *Journal of Adolescent Health, 13,* 275–280.

Gorman-Smith, D., & Tolan, P. (1998). The role of exposure to community violence and developmental problems among inner-city youth. *Development and Psychopathology, 10,* 101–116.

Hastings, T. L., & Kelley, M. L. (1997). Development and validation of the Screen for Adolescent Violence Exposure (SAVE). *Journal of Abnormal Child Psychology, 25*, 511–520.

Hausman, A. J., Spivak, H., & Prothrow-Stith, D. (1994). Adolescents' knowledge and attitudes about and experience with violence. *Journal of Adolescent Health, 15*, 400–406.

Hill, H. M., & Jones, L. P. (1997). Children's and parents' perceptions of children's exposure to violence in urban neighborhoods. *Journal of the National Medical Association, 89*, 270–276.

Horn, J. L., & Trickett, P. K. (1998). Community violence and child development: A review of research. In P. K. Trickett & C. J. Schellenbach (Eds.), *Violence against children in the family and the community* (pp. 103–138). Washington, DC: American Psychological Association.

Howard, D. E., Cross, S. I., Li, X., & Huang, W. (1999). Parent-youth concordance regarding violence exposure: Relationship to youth psychosocial functioning. *Journal of Adolescent Health, 25*, 396–406.

Huesmann, L. R. (1998, July). *An information processing theory for understanding the interaction of emotions and cognitions in the development and instigation of aggressive behavior.* Presidential address at the International Society for Research on Aggression, Ramapo College, Mahwah, NJ.

Kliewer, W., Lepore, S. J., Oskin, D., & Johnson, P. D. (1998). The role of social and cognitive processes in children's adjustment to community violence. *Journal of Consulting and Clinical Psychology, 66*, 199–209.

Kolko, D. (1998). Treatment and intervention for child victims of violence. In P. K. Trickett & C. J. Schellenbach (Eds.), *Violence against children in the family and the community* (pp. 213–249). Washington, DC: American Psychological Association Press.

Lewis, M., Brown, M., Jones, C., & Osofsky, J. D. (1994). *Drawings as a method of assessment and research for children exposed to chronic community violence.* Unpublished manuscript, Louisiana State University Medical Center, New Orleans.

Liddell, C., Kemp, J., & Moema, M. (1993). The young lions: South African children and youth in political struggle. In L. A. Leavitt & N. A. Fox (Eds.), *The psychological impact of war and violence on children* (pp. 199–214). Hillsdale, NJ: Erlbaum.

Loeber, R. (1982). The stability of antisocial and delinquent child behavior. *Child Development, 53*, 1431–1446.

Malmquist, C. P. (1986). Children who witness parental murder: Posttraumatic aspects. *Journal of the American Academy of Child Psychiatry, 25*, 320–325.

March, J. S., Amaya-Jackson, L., Murray, M. C., & Schulte, A. (1998). Cognitive-behavioral psychotherapy for children and adolescents with posttraumatic stress disorder after a single-incident stressor. *Journal of the American Academy of Child and Adolescent Psychiatry, 37*, 585–593.

Margolin, G., & Gordis, E. B. (2000). The effects of family and community violence on children. *Annual Review of Psychology, 51*, 445–479.

Martin, R. A., & Lefcourt, H. M. (1983). Sense of humor as a moderator of the relation between stressors and moods. *Journal of Personality and Social Psychology, 45*, 1313–1324.

Martin, S. L., Gordon, T. E., & Kupersmidt, J. B. (1995). Survey of exposure to violence among the children of migrant and seasonal farm workers. *Public Health Reports, 110*, 268–276.

Martinez, P., & Richters, J. E. (1993). The NIMH Community Violence Project: II. Children's distress symptoms associated with violence exposure. *Psychiatry: Interpersonal and Biological Processes, 56*, 22–35.

Mazza, J. J., & Overstreet, S. (2000). Children and adolescents exposed to community violence: A mental health perspective for school psychologists. *School Psychology Review, 29*, 86–101.

Mills, R. S. L., & Rubin, K. H. (1990). Parental beliefs about problematic social behaviors in early childhood. *Child Development, 61*, 138–151.

Moffitt, T. E. (1990). Juvenile delinquency and attention deficit disorder: Boys' developmental trajectories from age 3 to 15. *Child Development, 61*, 893–910.

Monat, A., & Lazarus, R. S. (Eds.). (1991). *Stress and coping: An anthology* (3rd ed.). New York: Columbia University Press.

Muller, R. T., Goebel-Fabbri, A. E., Diamond, T., & Dinklage, D. K. (2000). Social support and the relationship between family and community violence exposure and psychopathology among high risk adolescents. *Child Abuse and Neglect, 24*, 449–464.

Osofsky, J. D. (1995). The effects of exposure to violence on young children. *American Psychologist, 50*, 782–788.

Osofsky, J. (Ed.). (1997). *Children in a violent society*. New York: Guilford Press.

Osofsky, J. D., Wewers, S., Hann, D. M., & Fick, A. C. (1993). Chronic community violence: What is happening to our children? *Psychiatry: Interpersonal and Biological Processes, 56*, 36–45.

Overstreet, S., & Braun, S. (1999). A preliminary examination of the relation between exposure to community violence and academic functioning. *School Psychology Quarterly, 14*, 380–396.

Overstreet, S., & Braun, S. (2000). Exposure to community violence and post-traumatic stress symptoms: Mediating factors. *American Journal of Orthopsychiatry, 70*, 263–271.

Overstreet, S., Dempsey, M., Graham, D., & Moely, B. (1999). Availability of family support as a moderator of exposure to community violence. *Journal of Clinical Child Psychology, 28*, 151–159.

Parkes, K. R. (1984). Locus of control, cognitive appraisal, and coping in stressful episodes. *Journal of Personality and Social Psychology, 46*, 655–668.

Pynoos, R. S., Frederick, C., Nader, K., Arroyo, W., Steinberg, A., Eth, S., Nunez, F., & Fairbanks, L. (1987). Life threat and post-traumatic stress in school-age children. *Archives of General Psychiatry, 44*, 1057–1063.

Pynoos, R. S., Goenjian, A., Tashjian, M., Karakashian, M., Manjikian, R., Manoukian, G., Steinberg, A. M., & Fairbanks, L. A. (1993). Post-traumatic stress reactions in children after the 1988 Armenian earthquake. *British Journal of Psychiatry, 163,* 239–247.

Pynoos, R. S., & Nader, K. (1988). Psychological first aid and treatment approach to children exposed to community violence: Research implications. *Journal of Traumatic Stress, 1,* 445–473.

Richters, J. E., & Martinez, P. (1993). The NIMH Community Violence Project: I. Children as victims and witnesses to violence. *Psychiatry: Interpersonal and Biological Processes, 56,* 7–21.

Rosenberg, , M. L., & Fenley, M. A. (1991). *Violence in America: A public health approach.* New York: Oxford University Press.

Rosenberg, M. L., O'Carroll, P., & Powell, K. (1992). Let's be clear: Violence is a public health problem. *Journal of the American Medical Association, 267,* 3071–3072.

Sahagun, L. (1999, September 28). Children's legacy of violence: Schools are seeing more and more youngsters haunted by killings and other crimes in their lives. *Los Angeles Times,* p. 1.

Saigh, P. A. (1991). The development of posttraumatic stress following four different types of traumatization. *Behaviour Research and Therapy, 29,* 213–216.

Scheier, M. F., Weintraub, J. K., & Carver, C. S. (1986). Coping with stress: Divergent strategies of optimists and pessimists. *Journal of Personality and Social Psychology, 51,* 1257–1264.

Schubiner, H., Scott, R., & Tzelepis, A. (1993). Exposure to violence among inner-city youth. *Journal of Adolescent Health, 14,* 214–219.

Schwab-Stone, M., Ayers, T., Kasprow, W., Voyce, C., Barone, C., Shriver, T., & Weissberg, R. (1995). No safe haven: A study of violence exposure in an urban community. *Journal of the American Academy of Child and Adolescent Psychiatry, 34,* 1343–1352.

Schwartz, D., & Proctor, L. J. (2000). Community violence exposure and children's social adjustment in the school peer group: The mediating roles of emotional regulation and social cognition. *Journal of Consulting and Clinical Psychology, 68,* 670–683.

Schwarz, E. D., & Kowalski, J. M. (1991). Malignant memories: PTSD in children and adults after a school shooting. *Journal of the American Academy of Child and Adolescent Psychiatry, 30,* 936–944.

Selner-O'Hagan, M. B., Kindlon, D. J., Buka, S. L., Raudenbush, S. W., & Earls, F. J. (1998). Assessing exposure to violence in urban youth. *Journal of Child Psychology and Psychiatry, 39,* 215–224.

Shahinfar, A., Fox, N. A., & Leavitt, L. (2000). Preschool children's exposure to violence: Relation of behavior problems to parent and child reports. *American Journal of Orthopsychiatry, 70,* 115–125.

Shahinfar, A., Kupersmidt, J. B., & Matza, L. S. (2001). The relation between exposure to violence and social information–processing among incarcerated adolescents. *Journal of Abnormal Psychology, 110,* 136–141.

Singer, M. I., Anglin, T. M., Song, L., & Lunghofer, L. (1995). Adolescents' exposure to violence and associated symptoms of psychological trauma. *Journal of the American Medical Association, 273*, 477–482.

Smetana, J. G., & Kelly, M. (1989). Social cognition in maltreated children. In D. Cicchetti & V. Carlson (Eds.), *Child maltreatment: Theory and research on the causes and consequences of child abuse and neglect* (pp. 620–645). New York: Cambridge University Press.

Spacarelli, S., Coatsworth, J. D., & Bowden, B. S. (1995). Exposure to serious family violence among incarcerated boys: Its association with violent offending and potential mediating variables. *Violence and Victims, 10*, 163–182.

Terr, L. C. (1991). Childhood traumas: An outline and overview. *American Journal of Psychiatry, 148*, 10–20.

Weiss, B., Dodge, K. A., Bates, J. E., & Pettit, G. A. (1992). Some consequences of early harsh discipline: Child aggression and a maladaptive social information processing style. *Child Development, 63*, 1321–1335.

V

CONCLUSIONS AND IMPLICATIONS

17

CHILDREN AND DISASTERS: FUTURE DIRECTIONS FOR RESEARCH AND PUBLIC POLICY

ANNETTE M. LA GRECA, WENDY K. SILVERMAN,
ERIC M. VERNBERG, AND MICHAEL C. ROBERTS

Child-focused disaster research is a relatively new area of study, one that has grown substantially in recent years and will continue to develop in the recent aftermath of the September 11th terrorist attacks in New York and Washington, DC. This text, with its chapters on children's reactions across the full spectrum of disasters and terrorism, is a testament to the fact that child-focused disaster research has never been as vibrant and active as it is now. As reflected in this volume, the first generation of studies focused predominantly on documenting children's and adolescents' reactions to disasters and identifying factors that correlate with or predict severe disaster reactions. Studies have begun to examine interventions for youngsters following disasters, although this line of research is still in a preliminary stage. The field has yet to develop empirically supported interventions for children and youth following disasters, although "good leads" have been derived from clinical observations and from empirical findings on factors that predict disaster outcomes. A broadened research agenda, however, is needed to advance our understanding of how children are affected by disasters, which youth are most at risk, and when and how to intervene.

This concluding chapter highlights several key issues, including the need for researchers and clinicians in the child mental health field to help advance knowledge of the effects of disasters on children and youth and to develop and evaluate empirically based treatments for child disaster victims. Also emphasized is the importance of researchers and clinicians becoming advocates for children's needs following disasters and becoming attentive to public policy issues. Accordingly, this chapter focuses predominantly on future research needs as well as issues in public policy.

SETTING A RESEARCH AGENDA

Until recently, a number of obstacles have hindered child-focused disaster research. One has been a widely held (but erroneous) view that children did not display significant clinical reactions in the aftermath of disasters or, if they did, their reactions were transitory, fleeting, and relatively innocuous. As this book makes clear, children and adolescents do have significant reactions that have the potential to interfere with their current and future psychological adjustment. Those old beliefs no longer need to impede research progress.

Certain obstacles, however, continue to hinder research and practice in this area. A critical problem has to do with the practical difficulties of accessing disaster-affected communities, which often are disorganized and chaotic after a disaster strikes. This disorganization makes it exceedingly difficult to organize and implement research following disasters or to intervene in a systematic manner. Another problem is the lack of properly trained mental health providers and researchers. Few graduate programs offer coursework and training opportunities related to children and disasters.[1] As a result, few professionals in communities affected by disasters may have the knowledge and expertise to guide research and interventions with children and youth after disasters. Although disaster-response networks, such as the one sponsored by the American Psychological Association (APA; 2001), have been established, the available mental health providers in the network may be more attuned to the needs of adult disaster victims than to those of the children and youth who are affected.

On a conceptual level, a major obstacle to understanding disasters' effects on children has been the absence of theories and models for directing research and intervention efforts. This issue was discussed in chapter 1 and is highlighted in the discussion below.

---

[1]The University of South Dakota has an APA-accredited program in clinical psychology with a training track in disaster mental health (for information, see http://www.usd.edu/dmhi).

Understanding and Predicting Children's and Adolescents' Disaster Reactions

When disasters strike, a sizable proportion of children react; for many children and youth, the reactions can be severe and distressing. The research findings described in this volume indicate that considerable progress has been made in recognizing the importance of particular variables (or sets of variables) in understanding children's reactions to disasters. Those variables are beginning to form the core of a conceptual model intended to guide research in the child disaster field (see chapter 1; La Greca, Silverman, Vernberg, & Prinstein, 1996; Vernberg & Varela, 2001); they include aspects of the disaster experience, child characteristics, and aspects of the recovery environment. For example, the extent and intensity of exposure is now known to be key to predicting children's psychological reactions. Similarly, child characteristics such as age, gender, and ethnicity, as well as aspects of the postrecovery environment, such as social support and family functioning, have been identified as important predictors of some of the variation in children's disaster reactions. At the same time, those relationships are likely to be complex and multifaceted, and further work is needed to understand how those predictors vary across different disasters, different ages of children, and different points in time.

Continued progress in child-focused disaster research will be assisted by efforts to develop and evaluate comprehensive conceptual models of the ways exposure to highly traumatic disasters in childhood and adolescence influence developmental processes. In this effort, the symptoms of posttraumatic stress disorder (PTSD) are important outcomes, but they are not the only possible outcomes to consider. The larger issue is to understand how traumatic exposure (through disasters) at various points in the developmental period affects developmental trajectories in multiple domains, including biological, cognitive, behavioral, and interpersonal functioning.

Put simply, the field needs to move beyond asking what factors predict outcomes and begin to ask *why certain variables are important* and by what processes certain variables influence children's reactions. We also need to ask *how those processes vary* as a function of children's development. The task of asking and answering those questions is challenging and complex. It may require new ways of thinking in order to adapt existing theories to explain children's disaster reactions or to develop new theories that are specific to children and disasters. Addressing those questions also may entail using new or alternative data gathering procedures to test the theories and, most likely, complex statistical procedures (e.g., growth curve modeling and structural equation modeling) to analyze the data.

As a way of thinking more broadly about how and why different factors might contribute to children's disaster reactions, we adapted a useful table from Kazdin (1999) that pertained to child psychotherapy research (see Table 17.1).

TABLE 17.1
Summary of Key Concepts Involved in Understanding the Relationships Among Variables in Disaster Research

Variables That Relate to or Predict Disaster Outcomes (i.e., Antecedents)

Variable Type	Description
Correlates	Variables that are associated with disaster outcomes at a given point in time; however, no direct evidence indicates that the variables precede the outcomes. Examples might include levels of distress, coping, or anxiety that are measured concurrently with outcomes.
Risk factor	A variable or characteristic that is antecedent to and increases the likelihood of an outcome of interest (e.g., PTSD symptoms). It is a correlate in which the time sequence is established. Examples include levels of anxiety or academic functioning that are measured prior to disasters.
Marker	A stable characteristic or trait that is considered a risk factor but is not directly (causally) related to the outcome. Examples include age, gender, and ethnicity.
Causal risk factor	A variable that influences, either directly or through other variables, the outcome. Change in a causal risk factor leads to a change in outcome. Examples might include children's levels of exposure to disasters or sustaining a serious injury during a disaster.

Variables That Influence the Direction or Magnitude of the Relation Between Predictors and Outcomes

Variable Type	Description
Moderator	A variable that influences the relation of two variables of interest. The relation between the variables changes or differs as a function of some other variable. For example, the relation between disaster exposure and PTSD symptoms might be influenced by children's gender, age, ethnicity, or availability of social support.
Protective factor	A characteristic that reduces the likelihood of a particular outcome (e.g., PTSD symptoms) among people who are at risk. The relation between the risk factor and the outcome is altered by the presence of some other characteristic (e.g., social support, coping skills, or family adjustment). Protective factors are moderators, but they are worth distinguishing because of their importance for clinical interventions.

Variables That Explain How Antecedents Exert Their Influence

Variable Type	Description
Mediator	The process, mechanism, or means through which a variable produces a particular outcome. Beyond knowing that A may cause B, the mechanism elaborates precisely what happens to cause that result (e.g., cognitively,

Table Continues

TABLE 17.1
(Continued)

affectively, interpersonally, or biologically). For example, exposure to disasters may cause PTSD symptoms through a variety of mechanisms, such as biological changes in arousal levels, conditioned fears, and so forth.

Note. Adapted from "Current (Lack Of) Status of Theory in Child and Adolescent Psychotherapy Research," by A. E. Kazdin, 1999, *Journal of Clinical Child Psychology, 28,* 533–543. Copyright © 1999 by the American Psychological Association. Adapted with permission.

As modified for the context of children and disasters, the table depicts the various levels of understanding that are needed to ultimately advance "why" questions about children's disaster reactions.

Risk Factor

The chapters in this book indicate that research efforts have focused primarily on variables associated with children's disaster reactions at a given point in time (i.e., correlates) and variables that precede children's disaster reactions (i.e., risk factors). Little is known about the other concepts that are depicted in Table 17.1. For example, little is known about *markers* of influence; that is, stable child characteristics or traits that are part of the clinical picture of postdisaster reactions yet are unlikely to be related in a direct or causal way. As reflected in several chapters, child characteristics, such as ethnicity and gender, may represent markers for children's disaster reactions. As also noted in the chapters, however, research findings on the markers have been inconsistent across studies. Moreover, markers do not provide explanations for differences in children's and adolescents' responses.

Even less is known about causal risk factors; that is, risk factors that precede and directly or indirectly influence children's reactions. In that regard, children's level of disaster exposure appears to be a causal factor in children's disaster reactions and is perhaps the most well studied causal risk factor. Children's predisaster anxiety also holds potential as a causal risk factor for children's postdisaster reactions (e.g., La Greca, Silverman, & Wasserstein, 1998), although evidence is scant at this point. Much more work is needed in this aspect of "theory building" to appreciate which children and youth are at most risk for developing severe postdisaster stress reactions and how to prevent or ameliorate those reactions.

Moderating Variables

To provide explanations for differences in children's responses, research needs to move beyond "main effects" models and begin to consider the complex ways in which variables interact in producing children's reactions (i.e., moderating variables). Moderating variables influence the direction, magnitude, and nature of the association between risk factors and outcomes (e.g., PTSD symptoms). For example, the availability of social support may moderate the association between children's exposure to disasters and their PTSD symptoms, such that those with high levels of exposure and high levels of social support may fare much better than those with high levels of exposure and low levels of social support. Among children with low levels of disaster exposure, however, levels of social support may not be important to predicting children's PTSD.

An important moderating variable that has been neglected in most disaster-related research is children's developmental level. Few studies have examined developmental issues in determining children's postdisaster reactions (see chapter 1), and when variables such as age have been considered, they rarely are evaluated as moderators of outcomes. Nevertheless, ample reason exists to believe that children's developmental level has multiple and profound effects on the ways in which disasters are experienced as well as on the possible outcomes disasters elicit. Vernberg and Varela (2001) have described how developmental features can influence subjective aspects of traumatic exposure. For example, the ability to accurately interpret the degree of threat posed by objective events emerges gradually with age. The threshold and tolerance for arousal also is related to age (van der Kolk, 1997). Inhibition of the startle reflex is still developing in middle childhood, and the ability to attend to multiple dimensions of experience (e.g., internal cues and environmental signals) improves with age. As a result of those developmental trends, young children may be terrified by events that produce mild fear in adolescents or adults, or they may attend more selectively or idiosyncratically to signals of threat. This example serves to emphasize the importance of considering children's developmental level as a moderating variable in child-focused disaster research. To date, initial conceptual models of children's disaster reactions (see chapter 1) have not addressed development as an important moderating variable in understanding disaster risk and outcome, although some efforts to highlight important developmental concerns are evident (see Vernberg & Varela, 2001).

Related to the concept of moderators is the concept of protective factors. Protective factors are moderators that reduce the risk of showing the undesired outcome (i.e., PTSD reactions; Kazdin, 1999). Several chapters in this volume suggest that adaptive parental reactions and adaptive child coping are associated with fewer PTSD symptoms in children following disasters compared with those whose parents react poorly or who themselves have problems with adaptive coping. In this regard, the two variables hold promise as potential protective factors. The variables have not directly been studied as moderating variables (i.e., in interaction with other variables of interest), however. Research on potential protective factors for child disaster victims is scant and warrants further consideration.

Another potential moderator (and protective factor) to consider in future research on disasters is families' economic resources, particularly after destructive natural disasters, such as hurricanes, earthquakes, and floods, which require substantial rebuilding of homes and neighborhoods. Economic resources may be related to the course of children's postdisaster psychological recovery in several important ways. As Vernberg and Varela (2001) noted, rebuilding and repairing damage brought about by disasters typically occurs more rapidly for families with good property insurance coverage and other financial assets. Poor families are less likely to have adequate personal property insurance, are more likely to work in service jobs that are often disrupted following widespread disasters, and may have fewer options for housing and child care than their more affluent counterparts. The lack of adequate (or any) mental health insurance for low-income families also decreases access to mental health services that may help children and families cope with traumatic events. Although research has not directly addressed the role of families' economic resources as a moderator of children's postdisaster reactions, some indirect evidence supports its important role. Specifically, in developing countries psychiatric morbidity following natural disasters is much higher than in developed countries, and the level of exposure to trauma is much higher for similar types of disasters (Goenjian et al., 1995; see Vernberg & Varela, 2001).

In general, the identification of moderating variables, including protective factors, is of critical importance because the variables suggest that different causal paths or trajectories occur as a function of the moderating variable (Kazdin, 1999; also see Holmbeck, 1997). It also is critical that the selection of variables to be evaluated as potential moderators is based on empirical or theoretical grounds. Otherwise, the selection of variables can be endless.

Although the evaluation of factors that moderate children's disaster reactions is important, this type of research is challenging. Among other things, adequate evaluation of moderators requires studies of sufficient power (i.e., large sample sizes) to allow for detection of significant interaction effects.

Mediating Variables

The final level depicted in Table 17.1 pertains to *mediators*, or the mechanisms by which exposure to disasters may produce a particular outcome (e.g., PTSD symptoms, depression, or anxiety); that is, what is the process or combination of processes (e.g., cognitive, affective, interpersonal, or biological) that lead to the development of a particular set of postdisaster reactions in a given group of children?

Although many areas may be useful to pursue, one important avenue for investigation is that of the biobehavioral processes that likely underlie children's disaster reactions. Although understudied in the child disaster literature, some provocative findings on biological processes related to arousal and threat (e.g., startle responses and sensitized neural responses) and emotional regulation suggest potentially fruitful areas for future research on mediational processes. For example, findings by Ornitz and Pynoos (1989) suggest that acute traumatic exposure interferes with the development of inhibitory control over the startle reflex, thereby increasing sensitivity to fear-producing stimuli. In particular, disaster exposure may reduce the threshold for producing startle, leading children who have been exposed to disaster-related trauma to have frequent and interfering episodes of overarousal or hyperarousal when confronted with a wide range of trauma stimuli (see Vernberg & Varela, 2001). In this example, the lowered threshold for producing a startle response is the biological process that potentially mediates children's disaster reactions. In all likelihood, this biological process works in combination with other processes (both biological and nonbiological) to elicit children's disaster reactions. Thus, the study of mediational processes can be quite complex (see Kazdin, 1999).

A further nuance in understanding the mediational processes that underlie children's disaster reactions is that different types of mediators for different types of exposures are likely to exist. In the community violence area, for example, different mediational processes have been identified for exposure to violence through direct victimization versus exposure to violence through witnessing violence (Schwartz & Proctor, 2000; see also chapter 16). In the case of direct victimization, impairment in emotion regulation (e.g., soothing self-talk, cognitive strategies for reframing upsetting events, and shifting attention from provocative stimuli) mediated children's social adjustment (e.g., aggressive behavior, peer rejection, and bullying). In contrast, among children who witnessed violence, social information–processing deficits (e.g., misattribution of others' intentions or beliefs that aggression leads to positive outcomes) mediated the linkage between exposure and children's aggressive behavior. Such findings underscore how important it is for researchers to recognize that different processes (i.e., emotional and cognitive processes for community violence) are related to different types of exposure. Moreover, different processes also may underlie different disaster *reactions* (e.g., PTSD versus depression), and those processes may differ as a function of other variables, such as gender and development (i.e., moderating variables). Thus, evaluating mediational processes is a complex undertaking (also see Kazdin, 1999).

Nevertheless, this issue of mediational processes represents the most critical and important issue for the next generation of research on understanding children's disaster reactions. A better understanding of mediational processes is critical for theory development. It also is critical for the development of appropriate and effective disaster-related interventions. More specifically, knowing the variables that mediate children's disaster responses will help improve the design and delivery of psychosocial interventions, because the knowledge will render interventions that are maximally effective. Once the specific mediators that result in children's disaster responses are known, those variables can be included as components in interventions, and the variables found not to mediate can be excluded.

Issues in Assessment

Understanding children's disaster reactions and planning appropriate interventions require that researchers and clinicians become sensitive to issues of what, how, and when to assess. Moreover, the assessment of children's and adolescents' disaster-related reactions needs to be developmentally appropriate and culturally sensitive.

It is critical that future research in the area of assessment show sensitivity to the issue of development. Specifically, there needs to be increased sensitivity to the notion that many manifestations of children's behaviors following disasters are likely to be indicative of adaptation that may (or may not) be stage specific; other manifestations are likely to be indicative of pathological adaptation that may (or may not) be stage specific. Furthermore, although some behaviors may require intervention, others may be self-corrective. The current knowledge base does not provide mental health professionals with sufficient information to adequately know whether children's behaviors following disasters are clearly adaptive or pathologic and whether they require intervention.

In addition to the need to assess children's postdisaster reactions from a developmental perspective, similar sensitivity to development is needed in assessing children's resources for processing, organizing, and integration of disaster-related information, both in adaptive and maladaptive ways. Such a developmentally sensitive approach to assessment would involve measuring children's adaptive and maladaptive behaviors and competence or incompetence within the context of crucial developmental tasks (Carlson & Garber, 1986). For example, following disasters, how well do children handle entry into their peer group; separation from loved ones; and manage new situations, such as new schools? This type of assessment approach would shift the focus of assessment away from symptoms and disorders to impairment in important areas of children's lives (e.g., school, peers, and family). Such a shift would be more reflective of clinical reality, because typically it is *not* simply the manifestation of symptoms that leads to a child referral for clinical services; rather, it is the impairment that results from the symptoms (Angold, Costello, Farmer, Burns, & Erkanli, 1999). Large-scale studies that gather normative data for boys and girls of different age groups across different ethnic and racial groups and that rely on broad assessments within a developmental perspective are needed if the field is to progress. This type of assessment approach also would include developmental variations that are likely to exist in children's postdisaster recovery environments and the likely different functions or roles that support agents (parents, teachers, peers) play in children's lives in the aftermath of a disaster.

Aside from developmental issues, some consideration needs to be given to the use and integration of categorical and dimensional approaches to evaluating children's disaster reactions. The chapters in this text have shown that studies have typically used either categorical (i.e., diagnoses from the *Diagnostic and Statistical Manual of Mental Disorders*; American Psychiatric Association, 1994) or dimensional (i.e., level of children's stress symptoms) approach to assessing children's disaster reactions. Yet, *both* approaches to assessment have a place in child disaster research. Future research that integrates the two approaches would be desirable. It also would be desirable to specify the situations for which each approach is most appropriate. For example, a categorical approach might be particularly important for use with clinical samples of children, whereas the dimensional approach might be particularly valuable when assessing community samples of children affected by disasters. A similar point holds with respect to sources of information during the assessment processes. Most studies have relied on using either children or parents as the main informant for child functioning. Both children and parents, however, provide valuable information. Future research might focus on the ways in which various sources might best be integrated and used in various contexts for various purposes.

In addition, assessments of children's disaster reactions and factors influencing those reactions need to consider children's cultural context. Little, if any, work has been conducted on the appropriateness of the most widely used child disaster measures for use with culturally diverse populations. Research is needed that not only addresses the psychometric properties of child disaster measures in different cultural groups but also considers the acceptability and suitability of the measures. Such research is likely to suggest ways in which child disaster measures might need to be modified or adapted to ensure a culturally competent assessment. For children who are not primarily English speaking, translations and back-translations of measures are needed, as is evaluation of their appropriateness and psychometric properties.

Research Issues Specific to Interventions

Greater recognition of the mental health needs of children and adolescents affected by disasters has led to the development of an ever-increasing array of intervention strategies. This is a positive step, yet disaster intervention research, for the most part, remains in an early phase. Kazdin and Kendall (1998) articulated key steps in the process of developing truly evidence-based treatments for children and adolescents. This blueprint can be applied to gauge the current state of disaster mental health interventions and identify priorities for the next generation of intervention studies (Exhibit 17.1). Most intervention research in disaster mental health thus far addresses one or more

EXHIBIT 17.1
Steps Toward Developing Evidence-Based Disaster Mental Health Interventions

1. *Conceptualization of the disaster-related dysfunction.* Propose key areas, processes, and mechanisms that contribute to the development, onset, and escalation of dysfunction.
2. *Research on processes related to disaster-related dysfunction.* Conduct studies to test proposed processes and mechanisms in relation to the dysfunction.
3. *Conceptualization of intervention.* Propose key areas, processes, and mechanisms through which intervention may achieve its effects. Describe how the interventions relate to those processes and mechanisms.
4. *Specification of intervention.* Operationalize the procedures, preferably in manual form, that specify how changes in key processes are accomplished. Provide material to codify the procedures sufficiently to permit assessment of treatment integrity and to allow replication in research and practice.
5. *Tests of treatment outcome.* Conduct direct tests of the impact of interventions, drawing on diverse designs (e.g., open or uncontrolled studies, single-case designs, and clinical trials) and types of studies (e.g., dismantling and comparative outcomes studies).
6. *Tests of treatment processes.* Carry out studies to identify whether the intervention techniques actually affect the processes that are critical to the model.
7. *Tests of the boundary conditions and moderators.* Examine child, parent, family, therapist, and other factors that influence intervention outcomes.

Note. Adapted from "Current Progress and Future Plans for Developing Effective Treatments: Comments and Perspectives," by A. E. Kazdin and P. C. Kendall, 1998, *Journal of Clinical Child Psychology, 27,* 217–226. Copyright © 1998 by the American Psychological Association. Adapted with permission.

of the first four steps shown in the exhibit, which pertain primarily to conceptualizing disaster-related dysfunction and intervention approaches and gathering evidence on the processes thought to contribute to dysfunction. Tests of interventions, including assessment of outcomes, proof that the intervention affects proposed key processes or mechanisms, and evaluation of factors affecting treatment outcomes, are just beginning to be reported in most instances.

On the positive side, many intervention strategies are reaching a stage where manualization is possible (Exhibit 17.1, Step 4). Manualization is a crucial step in the process of conducting rigorous evaluations of efficacy and effectiveness. It is imperative to document what interventions are delivered and how delivery is accomplished, both to allow meaningful evaluation and to facilitate training, dissemination, and replication of effective approaches. Examples of manualized, or nearly manualized, treatments are described in many chapters, including chapters 5, 6, 10, 12, and 14.

It is helpful to consider the current status of intervention research for different phases of disasters (i.e., preimpact, impact, recoil, postimpact, and recovery and reconstruction; see chapters 1 and 3). In light of convincing evidence that events during the impact phase account for much of child and adolescent postdisaster symptomatology, interventions intended to limit psychological harm in this critical period deserve high priority. The interventions may begin in the preimpact phase, in the form of child-oriented disaster-preparedness efforts, and during the impact and recoil phases, by prompting the use of safety and psychological coping skills taught in the preimpact phase. Klingman (chapter 15) provides a glimpse of the sophisticated integration of preimpact planning and impact- and recoil-phase interventions that can be accomplished when effort is devoted to this task. He also gives clues about how the effectiveness of such interventions can be evaluated. Much more research could be done in this area; it could generate a tremendous payoff for public health and safety. Unfortunately, support for this type of careful preparation and activation when disaster strikes remains the exception.

Crisis intervention and other efforts to promote child mental health soon after disasters (i.e., in the recoil and postimpact phases) appear to be offered much more frequently now than in the recent past. The efforts are laudable examples of the mental health community's compassion and concern for children and adolescents who have been exposed to trauma. To sustain and refine those efforts, much more research must be done to evaluate which interventions produce measurable benefits, both in the short run and beyond. Resources for child-focused disaster mental health generally are scarce, and real danger lies in devoting a large portion of available funds to support interventions that have little evidence for efficacy (e.g., wide-scale debriefing and group counseling sessions) when research indicates that resource loss, ongoing disruptions to roles and routines, and parental distress have a strong influence on recovery from trauma. As argued by Omer and Alon (1994), it may be more beneficial to concentrate resources on disseminating information, fostering continuities, and trusting families and communities to make good decisions during periods of crisis (see chapters 3 and 15).

Research on mental health interventions for children following disasters is most advanced for the recovery-and-reconstruction phase. This situation is understandable: As a disaster moves further into the past, the sense of crisis and upheaval diminishes. By this phase, it is easier to distinguish between persistent and transitory disaster-related distress. Also, more time is available to complete the long process of planning, applying for funds, training staff, and gaining approval for intervention research. Most of the manualized or nearly manualized interventions available thus far belong to this phase, and preliminary trials have been accomplished in a few instances (chapter 3; see also Cohen, Mannarino, Berliner, & Deblinger, 2000; Smith, Perrin, & Yule, 1999). Among highly traumatized children and adolescents, ample evidence indicates the need for symptom-focused treatment, and additional controlled studies seem achievable over the next several years.

In addition to developing specific treatment protocols, intervention research must continue to address key issues such as service delivery models, treatment acceptability, and developmental and cultural factors. Cost-effectiveness also is an important issue, especially when large numbers of children and adolescents have experienced extreme trauma. Screenings of disaster-exposed populations routinely identify substantial numbers of symptomatic children many months after the disaster has supposedly ended. At the time of screening, most children identified have received no formal treatment for disaster-related distress. If preliminary evidence of treatment effectiveness is supported by further research, early screening could become an extremely important component of mental health services.

Reaching affected children and their families and gaining cooperation in treatment requires creative, culturally sensitive service delivery models. Strategies for creating sensitive systems of care for children have been described in recent years (see chapters 4 and 7). A next step is to investigate the success of different approaches and promote the use of effective strategies. Effective systems of care in disaster mental health seem likely to include specific symptom-focused treatments as well as attention to other factors that contribute to disaster-related distress. Continued strains related to resource loss, social support depletion, and despair clearly contribute to ongoing mental health difficulties for children and adolescents. Mental health services must be accompanied by instrumental assistance, economic support, and social support for families who are left in the debris long after the disaster is over for most people in the community.

PUBLIC POLICY TO MEET PSYCHOLOGICAL NEEDS IN DISASTERS

Public policies set the conditions by which attention can be directed to the psychological needs of children and their families affected by disaster. That is, policies made by decision makers at different levels of government and by nongovernmental organizations (e.g., the Red Cross and American Psychological Association [APA]) can enhance society's ability to respond appropriately to disasters and their aftermath. As mental health professionals integrally involved in these issues, psychologists should take a lead role in advocating for public and private policy initiatives to better meet the needs of children and families following disasters.

The chapters in this volume occasionally touch on policies affecting research and clinical activities in various disasters. Throughout this book, particularly in this section, we take as our charter the APA's resolution, *The Psychological Needs of Children Exposed to Disasters* (adopted February, 1995; DeLeon, 1995). Specifically, we endorse the following as an aspirational goal:

> Resolved, that the Council of Representatives of the APA finds and declares that the development and implementation of a national strategy to prevent and treat the psychological dysfunction resulting from the exposure of children and their families to disasters is a matter of the

highest priority, and supports the establishment of policies to maintain their psychological well-being. (DeLeon, 1995, pp. 675–678)

This section presents several considerations for public policy changes and enhancements.

First, greater attention should be given to recognizing and raising awareness of the psychological needs of children, adolescents, and families affected by disasters. Recognition of those needs should include the range of trauma and stressors. Specifically, the next revision of the *Healthy People* report should include the psychological needs of children and families for the promotion of health and prevention of problems in the United States (some existing health objectives are related, but the document does not include a comprehensive public policy statement on the subject).

Second, public and private funding for research and clinical interventions is needed to enhance responsibility to children in disaster situations, both immediately and over the long term. Appropriate research funds should be made available through the Center for Mental Health Services, the Federal Emergency Management Administration, the Red Cross, and other voluntary assistance organizations and agencies.

Third, the training of mental health specialists (viz., psychologists, social workers, and psychiatrists) in disaster work should be provided in graduate education and recur throughout the professional's career in continuing education. Credentialing of proficiency expertise should be considered for those serving children and families after trauma and disaster. Additionally, training on mental health needs following disasters should be implemented in medical training (viz., pediatrics and family practice) to ensure adequate screening and identification of problems and referral mechanisms to qualified mental health care providers. One professional psychological organization has established a network for response through national, state, and local psychological associations (viz., the APA's Disaster Response Network; Aguilera & Planchon, 1995; APA, 2001; Carll, 1994; Jacobs, 1995; Yeast, 1994). This effort requires more attention during training to meeting the psychological needs of children and families, particularly postdisaster counseling and support. Another professional organization for pediatricians, the American Academy of Pediatrics (AAP), has created the CHILDisaster Network for volunteer participation of child health professionals (AAP, 2001). Noting the need to improve psychological health outcomes for children affected by disaster, this network supports training in advance to create preparedness, rather than just organize professionals reacting after a disaster. Psychologists have been actively sought by this network to participate, and interorganizational agreements should be developed between the AAP and APA or its subunits.

Fourth, a research agenda (as outlined in this chapter) should be pursued to provide an empirical foundation for understanding children's responses to disaster and effective ways to provide psychological relief. The current grant system for funding mental health services and research for emergency and disaster recovery needs to be streamlined. The goal of research and interventions following disasters should be to use empirically supported assessments, counseling, and treatment. Empirical research findings should be systematically translated into easy-to-use materials for practitioners faced with emergent situations. An information exchange network could be established to help researchers and clinicians interact and provide easily accessible information for professionals as well as the public.

Fifth, every locality and state needs to develop mental health disaster-preparedness plans and should be encouraged to do so. All agencies, including community mental health centers and schools, should annually review and update their emergency response plans, paying great attention to psychological issues of children and adolescents. Disaster-preparedness plans need to include mental health organizations, especially those that attend to the special needs of children (see Athey, O'Malley, Henderson, & Ball, 1997). Agencies involved in those plans (e.g., schools, community mental health centers, and hospitals) and that provide mental health services should consider practicing their emergency response plans, as is typically done by emergency medical services and city or county emergency management offices to test organization and responsiveness. Planning should include designating the lead agencies in coordinating and monitoring specialized services for children and their families. Interagency plans and agreements are needed, as are clear delineation of roles and responsibilities; the idea is to not only meet psychological needs of the most immediate crisis but also to gather data to improve the knowledge available for later crises.

Finally, professionals should develop a research agenda and protocols to gain a better understanding of psychological aspects of disasters, and most important, to evaluate the effectiveness of different treatment interventions following disasters. Public and private financial support is needed to facilitate the investigations necessary for guiding future efforts and determine where intervention dollars should eventually be spent. With this effort, regional consortia of social scientists will be organized and ready to implement previously established research protocols immediately upon the occurrence of a disaster (as recommended in Vernberg, 1994).

To facilitate the systematic collection of information about the psychological needs and the effectiveness of services, there needs to be (a) a compilation of assessment and intervention protocols available for easy access, (b) a consensus protocol developed for use by researchers and clinicians enrolled in a network, (c) a national database for collection and sharing of information that uses a common protocol for analysis by a panel of investigators, and (d) a funding mechanism for the development of the protocol and maintenance of the database. To further this development, the federal Office of Human Research Protection should establish policies and recommendations to Institutional Review Boards across the country specifically dealing with common research protocols to be implemented following disasters, including approval prior to events and expeditious review after disaster strikes.

Furthermore, school districts should develop policies at local and state levels to facilitate research and interventions in the event of a disaster (as outlined by Vernberg, 1994). Policies and procedure manuals should indicate how to organize service providers who wish to intervene and provide assistance as well as those who wish to gather research data. Agreements should be established in advance to facilitate those actions. Attention should be given to the needs of children who are in special populations and for whom services are difficult to access, including rural families, children on reservations, migrant workers, the poor and those in housing projects (Joyner & Swenson, 1993). Additionally, in both research and interventions, the culture of the children and families needs to be acknowledged and considered.

In summary, the public policy issues raised above are critical for increasing our understanding of how children are affected by disasters, for identifying youth and families most at risk for adverse reactions, and for knowing when and how to intervene. Both clinicians and researchers need to consider the public policy aspects of their efforts. The issues outlined above should assist in this important process.

CONCLUSIONS

In summary, this chapter has highlighted several key issues that are important for future research and public policy pertaining to children and disasters. In the research area, efforts to develop conceptual models to predict children's disaster reactions are needed. To be maximally useful for furthering our understanding of why and how children react to disasters and how best to intervene, such conceptual models need to focus on causal risk factors that lead to children's disaster reactions, to incorporate variables that moderate linkages between predictors and outcomes, and to begin to delineate the likely processes underlying children's disaster reactions. Such efforts would yield a complex research agenda that would provide a structure and framework for the next generation of studies.

Also in the research realm, this chapter highlights the importance of further efforts to develop and evaluate disaster-related interventions. Although a number of promising treatment and prevention manuals now exist, they await further testing and evaluation. A critical need exists for empirically supported and transportable interventions that are appropriate for different phases of disaster recovery (e.g., acute vs. long-term) and that address the multiple contexts in which children function (e.g., school, family, and peer). Moreover, sensitivity to developmental and cultural issues is of paramount importance.

Finally, this chapter emphasizes the importance of public policy issues. Specific issues include using public policy to promote awareness, funding, and training of research, disaster preparedness, and postdisaster treatment programs.

In closing, we hope that the issues delineated in this chapter, as well as in the book as a whole, will serve as the springboard for the next generation of studies and interventions for children, adolescents, and families affected by disasters. Disasters can have serious and longstanding effects on children's and families' mental health and adjustment. The time has come to systematically and vigorously address the psychological and mental health needs of children affected by disasters.

REFERENCES

Aguilera, D. M., & Planchon, L. A. (1995). The American Psychological Association–California Psychological Association disaster response project: Lessons from the past, guidelines for the future. *Professional Psychology: Research and Practice, 26*, 550–557.

American Academy of Pediatrics. (2001). CHILDisaster Network. Retrieved February 15, 2002, from http://www.aap.org/disaster

American Psychiatric Association. (1994). *Diagnostic and statistical manual of mental disorders* (4th ed.). Washington, DC: Author.

American Psychological Association. (2001). Disaster response network summary information. Retrieved February 15, 2002, from http://www.apa.org/practice/drn.html

Angold, A., Costello, E. J., Farmer, E. M. Z., Burns, B. J., & Erkanli, A. (1999). Impaired but undiagnosed. *Journal of the American Academy of Child and Adolescent Psychiatry, 38*, 129–137.

Athey, J. L., O'Malley, P., Henderson, D. P., & Ball, J. W. (1997). Emergency medical services for children: Beyond lights and sirens. *Professional Psychology: Research and Practice, 28*, 464–470.

Carll, E. K. (1994). Disaster intervention with children and families: National and state initiatives. *Child, Youth, and Family Services Quarterly, 17*, 21–23.

Carlson, G. A., & Garber, J. (1986). Developmental issues in the classifications of depression in children. In M. Rutter, C. E. Izard, & P. B. Read (Eds.), *Depression in young people: Developmental and clinical perspectives* (pp. 399–434). New York: Guilford Press.

Cohen, J. A., Mannarino, A. P., Berliner, L., & Deblinger, E. (2000). Trauma-focused cognitive behavioral therapy for children and adolescents: An empirical update. *Journal of Interpersonal Violence, 15*, 1202–1223.

DeLeon, P. H. (1995). Proceedings of the American Psychological Association, Incorporated, for the Year 1994. *American Psychologist, 50*, 633–682.

Goenjian, A. K., Pynoos, R. S., Steinberg, A. M., Najarian, L. M., Asarnow, J. R., Karayan, I., Ghurabi, M., & Fairbanks, L. A. (1995). Psychiatric comorbidity in children after the 1988 earthquake in Armenia. *Journal of the American Academy of Child and Adolescent Psychiatry, 34,* 1174–1184.

Holmbeck, G. N. (1997). Toward terminological, conceptual, and statistical clarity in the study of mediators and moderators: Examples from the child-clinical and pediatric psychology literatures. *Journal of Consulting and Clinical Psychology, 65,* 599–610.

Jacobs, G. A. (1995). The development of a national plan for disaster mental health. *Professional Psychology: Research and Practice, 26,* 543–549.

Joyner, C. D., & Swenson, C. C. (1993). Community-level intervention after a disaster. In C. F. Saylor (Ed.), *Children and disasters* (pp. 211–231). New York: Plenum Press.

Kazdin, A. E. (1999). Current (lack of) status of theory in child and adolescent psychotherapy research. *Journal of Clinical Child Psychology, 28,* 533–543.

Kazdin, A. E., & Kendall, P. C. (1998). Current progress and future plans for developing effective treatments: Comments and perspectives. *Journal of Clinical Child Psychology, 27,* 217–226.

La Greca, A. M., Silverman, W. K., Vernberg, E. M., & Prinstein, M. J. (1996). Symptoms of posttraumatic stress after Hurricane Andrew: A prospective study. *Journal of Consulting and Clinical Psychology, 64,* 712–723.

La Greca, A. M., Silverman, W. K., & Wasserstein, S. B. (1998). Children's predisaster functioning as a predictor of posttraumatic stress following Hurricane Andrew. *Journal of Consulting and Clinical Psychology, 66,* 883–892.

Omer, H., & Alon, N. (1994). The continuity principle: A unified approach to disaster and trauma. *American Journal of Community Psychology, 22,* 273–287.

Ornitz, E. M., & Pynoos, R. S. (1989). Startle modulation in children with posttraumatic stress disorder. *American Journal of Psychiatry, 147,* 866–870.

Schwartz, D., & Proctor, L. J. (2000). Community violence exposure and children's social adjustment in the school peer group: The mediating roles of emotion regulation and social cognition. *Journal of Consulting and Clinical Psychology, 68,* 670–683.

Smith, P., Perrin, S., & Yule, W. (1999). Cognitive behaviour therapy for posttraumatic stress disorder. *Child Psychology and Psychiatry Review, 4,* 177–182.

U. S. Department of Health and Human Services. (n.d.). *Healthy People 2010.* Retrieved February 15, 2002, from http://www.health.gov/healthypeople/

van der Kolk, B. A. (1997). The complexity of adaptation to trauma: Self-regulation, stimulus, discrimination, and characterological development. In B.A. van der Kolk, A. C. McFarlane, & L. Weisaeth (Eds.), *Traumatic stress. The effects of overwhelming experience on mind, body, and society* (pp. 182–213). New York: Guilford Press.

Vernberg, E. M. (1994). Evaluating the effectiveness of school-based interventions after large scale disasters: An achievable goal? *Child, Youth, and Family Services Quarterly, 17,* 11–13.

Vernberg, E. M., & Varela, R. E. (2001). Posttraumatic stress disorder: A developmental perspective. In M. W. Vasey & M. R. Dadds (Eds.), *The developmental psychopathology of anxiety* (pp. 386–406). New York: Oxford University Press.

Yeast, C. (1994). APA Disaster Response Network: Psychological response to survivors of traumatic events. *Child, Youth, and Family Services Quarterly, 17,* 19–20.

INDEX

Attention problems, as risk factor, 27
Australian bushfire. *See* New South Wales bushfire
Avoidance, in PTSD, 18, 120, 159

Balkan conflict, 359
Baltimore, community violence in, 383
Bangladesh flood, 161
BASIC Ph, 370
BDI (Beck Depression Inventory), 144, 145, 227
Beck Depression Inventory (BDI) or Scale, 144, 145, 227
Behavioral contingencies, for child MVA survivors, 279–280
Behavioral functioning, and community violence, 387
Behavior Screening Questionnaire, 210
Bereavement and grief, 24, 276–277
    as addressed in intervention, 67
    and Murrah Federal Building bombings, 336, 339
Bias, of ethnocentric monoculturalism, 93
Biological reactions, 16
Biological vulnerability, acquired, 278–279
Blacks. *See* African Americans
Bombing in Oklahoma City. *See* Murrah Federal Building bombing, Oklahoma City
Bombings of embassies in East Africa, 341
Bosnia
    adolescent refugees in, 363
    children coping in, 365
    and child's vs. mother's distress, 225
    screening in, 345
Boston, community violence in, 383
Boston area blizzard and flood, 160
Brain damage, 279
Brandon (MVA case), 261–262, 277, 278, 281
Brief captivity, 316–317
Brief Symptom Inventory, 186, 189
British Child Accident Prevention Trust, 235
Buffalo Creek flood (1972), 28, 157–160, 241–243, 251–255
    design of original study on, 243–244
    design of 17-year follow-up study on, 244–246
    findings of original study on, 246–248
    findings of 17-year follow-up study on, 248–251

"Buffalo Creek Syndrome," 158
Bus accidents, 224–226
Bushfire and Me: A Story of What happened to Me and My Family, The (therapy manual), 149
Bushfires, 140. *See also* Wildfires
    family functioning and child psychopathology after, 181
    in New South Wales (1994), 140–141, 144–153, 347
California Governor's Office of Emergency Services, 170
Captivity
    brief, 316–317
    emotional, 306
    prolonged, 306–307, 316
Car crashes. *See* Motor vehicle accidents
Case conceptualization models, cultural and ethnic factors in, 91–93
Causal risk factors, 408, 409
CDI (Children's Depression Inventory), 178, 187, 191, 217, 273
Center for Mental Health Services
    research funds needed for, 418
    and terrorist attacks, 349
    web site of, 126
Ceremonies, 132
Challenger disaster, 340
Charley (MVA case), 262, 276, 277, 280
Chernobyl (Ukraine) nuclear disaster, 204, 209, 212–215
Child Behavior Checklist, 160, 187, 188, 273
Child Depression Inventory. *See* Children's Depression Inventory
Child Fernald Mental Experience (interview instrument), 40
Child Fernald Mental Experience Questionnaire, 39, 47
Child-focused disaster research. *See* Research
Child-focused interventions, 393–394
Childhood sexual abuse
    and physiological reactivity, 16
    as risk factor, 231
CHILDisaster Network, 418
Child mental health, 133
Child Post Traumatic Stress Reaction Index, 217, 312
Children, assessment of. *See* Assessment
Children, intervention for. *See* Interventions

Columbine High School shootings, 295, 296, 301
Community-based intervention, 394–395
    early, 342–344
    trauma and loss programs, 346–348
Community mental health centers (CMHCs), and South Dakota flood, 163–164
Community psychology outreach model, in Project Recovery, 166
Community studies, on disaster intervention, 130–133
Community violence, 12, 298, 381–383
    vs. acute trauma exposure, 386
    children's exposure to
        correlates of, 385–389
        mediating or moderating factors in, 389–392
        prevalence of, 383–385
        treatment for, 392–396
    mediational processes for, 412
    social policy recommendations on, 395–396
Communitywide preventive interventions, in wartime, 368–370, 375
Communitywide screening of children at risk, 344–345
Computer technology, in assessment, 46
Confronting Behavior and Support Persons Questionnaire, 41, 48
Conners' Teacher Rating Scale, 178
Conservation of resources model, 179, 182–183
    multi-level, 91
Contagion effect, in New South Wales children, 147
Continuity principle, 62, 63, 367–368, 371, 372
Continuous traumatic stress syndrome, 328
Contributing factors, 21–22
COPE Scale, modified version of, 40, 47
Coping
    anticipatory, 368
    and assessment, 38, 43
    with community violence, 389–390
    and cultural ties, 77
    and postdisaster reactions, 123
    in prolonged captivity, 306–307
    and residential fires, 180, 183, 186–187
    with wartime experiences, 364–365, 375

    in BASIC Ph program, 369–370
Coping Activities Scale, 187
Coping assistance, 131–132
Coping Efficacy questionnaire, 186
Coping material, for residential fire victims, 189–193
Coping Resources Inventory
    contact for, 47
    Hebrew version, 40
Coping styles or strategies, as risk factor, 27, 29
Coppel's Index of Social Support, 41, 47
Correlates, 408
    focus on, 22
Costs of disasters, 12–13
Counseling sessions
    and Oklahoma City bombing, 337, 349
    undue emphasis on, 416
Crime, 298
Crisis intervention, 416
    and Project Recovery, 166–167
Crisis-intervention models, 8, 253, 297, 347, 348
Crisis management, 58–59
Crisis reduction counseling, 61
Critical incident stress debriefing (CISD), 125–126, 233, 343
Croatia
    adolescent refugees in, 363
    bibliotherapy workshops in, 370
Cultural appropriateness, in Project Recovery, 165, 166
Cultural background, and children's reactions to disasters, 26–27
Culturally sensitive service delivery models, 417
Culture and cultural factors, 74–75, 78–79
    American Indians' loss of, 87
    and assessment, 414
    for child MVA survivors, 277–278
    and functional analysis for clinical practice, 91–93
    in interventions, 56
    protective and risk factors in, 77–79, 82–83
        investigation needed on, 85
    and research guidelines, 90
    and response to hostage or school-shooting situation, 313–314
    and shift in American demography, 93
Cumulative stress model, 390
Customs, as protective factor, 78–79

Dramatic play, 393
DSM–III. See Diagnostic and Statistical Manual of Mental Disorders, Third Edition
DSM–IV. See Diagnostic and Statistical Manual of Mental Disorders, Fourth Edition
DSM-based diagnoses, 92
DSM system, PTSD as excluding specific travel phobia in, 235

Early community-based intervention, 342–344
Early screening, 417
Earthquake(s), 104, 107, 108
    duration of, 109
    effects of, 110–122
        and factors in postdisaster adjustment, 122–124
        interventions following, 124–133
    Loma Prieta, 27
    studies on, 111, 118
    unpredictability of, 109
Earthquake Impact Survey, 38, 39
Earthquake Related Cognitions Questionnaire, 40, 43, 47
East Africa, bombings of U.S. embassies in, 341
Economic resources of family, 411
    and recovery, 67–68
Edinboro, Pennsylvania, shooting, 301
Education, and pattern of neglect, 28
Education Department, U.S., on school-violence procedures, 304
e-mail, for assessment, 46
Embassy bombings in East Africa, 341
EMDR (eye movement desensitization and reprocessing), 234, 282
Emergency-response activities and plans, 68–69, 419
Emotional processing, in coping assistance, 132
Emotion-focused coping strategies, 390
Emotion regulation or dysregulation, and violence exposure, 391, 412
Engaged coping, 389
Environmental contamination, 207–208
Equifinality, 22
Ethnic factors, for child MVA survivors, 277–278
Ethnicity, 74–75
    and children's reactions to disasters, 26–27

and functional analysis for clinical practice, 91–93
in Hurricane Andrew study, 80–81
in Hurricane Hugo study, 82–84
and PTSD, 84–85
    after hurricanes or earthquakes, 123
and research guidelines, 90
and SES, 76
and shift in American demography, 93
Ethnic minority research, 93
Ethnocentric monoculturalism, 277
Evaluation of Cognitive Heuristics, 40, 47
Exposure Experiences Questionnaire, An, 47
Exposure extent (duration) and intensity, as key, 25, 407
Expressive art therapies, 393
Eye movement desensitization and reprocessing (EMDR), 234, 282

False memory syndrome, 276
Families. See also Parent(s)
    and Chernobyl accident, 213–215
    and children's disaster-related reactions following Buffalo Creek disaster, 252–253
    economic resources of, 411
    and recovery, 67–68
Family, cultural, and ethnic factors, for child MVA survivors, 277–278
Family-centered approach, and American military families, 373
Family economic resources, and recovery, 67–68
Family environment, 278
Family Environment Scale, 186, 188
Family-focused interventions, 394
Family functioning, and children's psychopathology, 181
Family styles, in coping with shootings or hostage takings, 313
Family support, and children's PTSD symptoms, 331
Fears, following traumatic event or disaster, 20
Fear Survey Schedule for Children-Revised, 187, 227
Federal Emergency Management Agency (FEMA)
    and hurricanes or earthquakes, 109–110
    intervention efforts of, 65

Paradigmatic model
    of accident-related PTSD, 264–270
    for child MVA survivors, 270–271, 283
        and accident characteristics, 271–273
        and acquired biological vulnerability, 278–279
        and behavioral contingencies, 279–280
        and developmental issues, 275–277
        and family, cultural, or ethnic factors, 277–278
        and legal issues, 280–281
        and symptom assessment in children, 273–275
        in treatment, 281–283
Parent(s). *See also* Families
    and children's disaster-related reactions, 123–124, 181, 225
        after Buffalo Creek disaster, 252–253
        children's desire to protect from fire, 178
        and mass-transportation disasters, 233
        parents' neglect of children possible, 13–14
        and PTSD from violence, 330, 331
        and technological disasters, 204
        underreporting by, 13, 142–143, 161, 171, 344, 384
    and Fernald waste spill study, 217–218
    and intervention, 67, 371
    loss of, 360
    and massage for children, 127
    and Project Recovery, 168
    psychopathology in, 186
    in residential-fire study, 186, 188–189
    and TMI accident, 211, 212
Parental psychopathology or distress, as risk factor, 28–29
Parent PTSD Reaction Index, 41, 48
Pattern of neglect, 28
Pearl, Mississippi, shooting, 301
Pediatric Emotional Distress Scale, 36, 41, 48
PEF (Psychiatric Evaluation Form), 158, 243, 245, 247, 248, 249, 250
Pentagon terrorist attack, 7, 328
Perceived Benefits Scale, 40, 47
Perceived Disruption During Rebuilding Inventory, 39, 47

Perceptions of neighborhood safety, as mediating effects of community violence exposure, 390
Persian Gulf War, 359, 360
    and Kuwaiti children, 362–363
Personal (historical) continuity, 367–368
Personality, and traumatic reactions, 314
Personal Loss Scale, 39, 47
Peshtigo fire (1871), 139
Phobias, 20
    and *Jupiter* sinking survivors, 230
    travel, 235
Physiological reactivity, 16
Pilots Database Authority List, 46
Policy issues
    on community violence, 395–396
    of intervention following terrorism, 348–350
Postimpact period of intervention, study on, 111–112
Postimpact phase of children's reactions, 16–17
Postimpact phase of interventions, 56, 62
    Indicated interventions in, 58, 64–65
    selected interventions in, 58, 63–64
    universal interventions in, 58, 62–63
Posttraumatic stress (PTS)
    evaluation of symptoms of, 273
    in Hurricane Hugo study, 82, 83
    role of cognitions in, 390
    and terrorism, 329, 329–330
        in Nairobi bombing, 341
        unobservable, 344
Posttraumatic stress disorder (PTSD), 17–19, 21
    and academic functioning, 388
    and acute stress disorder, 17
    and assessment, 37
        instruments for, 48
    and attention deficit-hyperactivity disorder, 273
    and Australian bushfire, 142
    and biological/neurological changes, 278
    classical conditioning treatment for, 373
    and contributing factors, 22
    and coping style, 390
    and debriefing, 343–344
    ethnic differences in, 84–85
    and grieving process, 339
    and head injury, 279
    and intervention, 55

Stress
    of acculturation, 78
    and assessment, 35, 43
    in Chernobyl victims, 213, 214
    in children's reactions, 16
    cultural differences in, 313
    intervention programs for, 392
    from terrorism, 328
    and violent injury, 296
Stress Buffer Model, 181
Stress inoculation, 190
Stressors
    and assessment, 38
    and coping mediators, 390
    in residential-fire study, 185
Stress reactions, risk factors for, 230–232
Stress response, 180
Stress Response Questionnaire, 39, 47
Stress Scale, 39, 47
Stroop task, clinical, 273–274
Structured Clinical Interview for DSM–III–
    R, Nonpatient Version (SCID),
    245, 246, 249, 250
Structured Clinical Interview for DSM–IV,
    333
Structured Interview to Assess Types of
    Thinking About Disasters, 40, 47
Substance abuse
    among Buffalo Creek victims, 249
    among residential-fire victims, 180
Suicidality and suicide
    among Buffalo Creek survivors, 249
    and disaster-related distress, 120
    of hostage taker, 308
    rising incidence of, 305
    risk factors for, 304
Surgeon General's Report on Youth Violence,
    295, 299
Sutherland Bushfire Trauma Project
    (SBTP), 140, 153
    assessment protocol of, 152
    rationale and origin of, 141–143
    and treatment outcome research, 151
Sweat lodge, 88
Swedish children in Norwegian bus crash,
    224
Sympathy or attachment to perpetrator,
    319–320
Symptom Checklist-90-R (SCL-90-R), 245,
    249
Systematic desensitization, in residential-fire
    study, 192

Talking About Disaster: Guide (Red Cross
    brochure), 126
Teachers. See also Schools
    and behavioral diagnoses after flood,
        161
    predisaster training for, 395
    underreporting by, 13, 142–143, 344
Technological disasters, 203–205, 208–209.
    See also Mass transportation disas-
    ters; Motor vehicle accidents;
    Nuclear accidents; Toxic waste
    spills
    Buffalo Creek dam break as, 242 (see
        also Buffalo Creek flood)
    vs. community violence, 382
Teen Stress: How to Cope When Disaster
    Strikes and Things Get Tough, 168
Telephone, as support system, 369
Television
    as exposure to bombings
        of Murrah Federal Building, 336
        and PTS symptoms, 337, 339–340
    images of war on, 360
Temperament, and traumatic reactions, 314
Terrorism, 3, 296–297, 327–328, 350
    vs. community violence, 382
    effects of on children (literature re-
        view), 328–332
    intervention following, 342–348
        for Murrah Federal Building coun-
            seling, 337
        public policy implications of, 348–
            350
    need for broader understanding on
        victimhood from, 340
    Oklahoma City bombing (Murrah
        Building), 332–341 (see also Murrah
        Federal Building bombing, Okla-
        homa City)
    therapeutic intervention after, 372
    U.S. embassy bombings in East Africa,
        341
    World Trade Center attack, 7, 297,
        328, 340, 346
Theory development
    and mediational processes, 412
    and risk factors, 409
Therapeutic foster care, 318
Therapeutic interventions, 393–394
    in war situation, 370–373
Therapy manual, for New South Wales
    bushfire, 149–152

ABOUT THE EDITORS

Annette M. La Greca, PhD, received her doctorate in clinical psychology from Purdue University and is a professor of psychology and pediatrics and director of Clinical Training in the Psychology Department at the University of Miami, Coral Gables, Florida. Dr. La Greca has received grant support from the BellSouth Foundation for her work on the effects of trauma on children, including children's reactions to natural disasters and the effects of community violence on children. In addition to publishing over 150 journal articles, books, and book chapters related to children's and adolescents' emotional and physical adjustment, Dr. La Greca authored a parent–child workbook for helping children cope with the September 11, 2001 terrorist attacks. Dr. La Greca received the Distinguished Research Contribution Award from the Society of Pediatric Psychology (now APA Division 54) and served as editor of the *Journal of Pediatric Psychology*. Dr. La Greca has been the president of the Society of Pediatric Psychology and the APA Section on Clinical Child Psychology (now APA Division 53). She also chaired the APA Committee on Children, Youth, and Families. Dr. La Greca currently serves on the editorial boards of several scientific journals and is the associate editor of the *Journal of Clinical and Adolescent Psychology*.

Wendy K. Silverman, PhD, received her doctorate in clinical psychology from Case Western Reserve University and currently is a professor of psychology and director of the Child and Family Psychosocial Research Center at Florida International University in Miami, Florida. Dr. Silverman has received several grants from the National Institute of Mental Health to design and evaluate psychosocial interventions for children with anxiety disorders. She has published over 100 research articles and book chapters on childhood anxiety, including children's reactions following exposure to natural disasters and crime and violence. She also is the coauthor of three other books.

Dr. Silverman serves on the editorial boards of several scientific journals and is the editor of the *Journal of Clinical and Adolescent Psychology*.

Eric M. Vernberg, PhD, is a professor in the Clinical Child Psychology program at the University of Kansas. He earned his PhD in psychology from the University of Virginia. He directs research and intervention projects focusing on violence prevention and developmentally appropriate evidence-based treatments for children with serious emotional disorders. He has authored more than 40 scholarly papers on trauma, posttraumatic stress disorder, and other topics in clinical child psychology.

Michael C. Roberts, PhD, ABPP, graduated from Purdue University in clinical psychology with a specialization in clinical child psychology, after completing his clinical internship at Oklahoma Children's Hospital. Dr. Roberts has served as editor for the *Journal of Pediatric Psychology; Children's Health Care;* and *Children's Services: Social Policy, Research, and Practice*. Dr. Roberts has been the president of the Society of Pediatric Psychology, the APA Section on Clinical Child Psychology, and the Council of University Directors of Clinical Psychology. He chaired the APA Committee on Children, Youth, and Families. Dr. Roberts has edited or coedited the *Handbook of Clinical Child Psychology*, the *Handbook of Pediatric Psychology*, and *Beyond Appearances: A New Look at Adolescent Girls*, among other books. He is director of the Clinical Child Psychology Program at the University of Kansas. His professional and research interests include topics in services for children and families in mental and physical health care and public policy.

FOOTPRINTS ON THE MOUNTAIN

Preaching and Teaching the Sunday Readings

How beautiful upon
The mountains
Are the feet of the
One who brings
Glad tidings,
Announcing peace,
Bringing good news. (Isaiah 52:7)

ROLAND J. FALEY, T.O.R.

PAULIST PRESS
New York ◆ Mahwah, N.J.

To
Roland E. Murphy, O. Carm.
Churchman, Scholar, and Mentor

Library of Congress Cataloging-in-Publication Data

Faley, Roland J. (Roland James), 1930-
    Footprints on the mountain: preaching and teaching the Sunday readings Roland J. Faley.
        p.   cm.
    Includes bibliographical references and index
    ISBN 0-8091-3448-9 (pbk.)
    1. Lectionary preaching—Catholic Church. 2. Catholic Church—Liturgy. I. Title.
BX1756.A1F37   1994
251—dc20   93-47166
                                                                                CIP

Published by Paulist Press
997 Macarthur Boulevard
Mahwah, NJ 07430

Printed and bound in the
United States of America